Opportunity Foregone

EDUCATION IN BRAZIL

Nancy Birdsall and Richard H. Sabot
Editors

Published by the Inter-American Development Bank
Distributed by The Johns Hopkins University Press

Washington, D. C.

1996

The views and opinions expressed in this publication are those of the
authors and do not necessarily reflect the official position
of the Inter-American Development Bank.

Opportunity Foregone: Education in Brazil

© Copyright 1996 by the Inter-American Development Bank
1300 New York Avenue, N.W.
Washington, D.C. 20577

Distributed by
The Johns Hopkins University Press
2715 North Charles Street
Baltimore, Maryland 21218-4319

Library of Congress Catalog Card Number: 96-77344
ISBN: 1-886938-03-2

Acknowledgements

This volume traces its origins to the symposium "Education, Economic Growth, and Inequality in Brazil," that we held in Rio de Janeiro from March 24–27, 1991. The editors, and the authors of the chapters, owe a debt of gratitude to the symposium participants whose comments and discussions shaped and greatly enhanced the final product, especially Cândido Alberto Gomes, Eduardo Gutierrez, Carlos Langoni, Roberto Macedo, Ricardo Chaves Martins, Simon Schwartzman and Donald Winkler. Special recognition is likewise due to the many Brazilian officials with whom we worked on this endeavor, particularly in the Ministry of Education and the Applied Economics Research Institute (IPEA). We would also like to thank the Mellon Foundation, and in particular Roberto (Bert) Ifill and Neil Rudenstine, formerly of the Foundation staff; the World Bank for its generous sponsorship of this research; and the United Nations Development Programme for its support of the symposium. Our greatest debt of gratitude is to the authors of the chapters who, we believe, have considerably advanced knowledge of the economics of education in Brazil. When revising their papers they responded with time and energy to the suggestions of the commentators at the symposium. (We greatly lament the passing away of Sergio Costa Ribeiro, an invaluable colleague and contributing author in this volume, since the initial writing of his study.) We would also like to thank Barbara Rietveld and David Einhorn of the Inter-American Development Bank's Publications Section who, with great skill, oversaw the editing and publication process; and Carlos Lozada, also on the IDB staff, who was assiduous in putting the finishing touches on the manuscript. The book's shortcomings, of course, are the sole responsibility of the editors and authors.

Nancy Birdsall
Executive Vice President
Inter-American Development Bank

Richard H. Sabot
John J. Gibson Professor of Economics
Williams College

Contributors

Irma Adelman is Professor Emeritus of Agricultural Economics at the University of California at Berkeley.

Paulo de Tarso Afonso de Andre is a Senior Research Associate with the Economic Research Institute Foundation (FIPE) at the University of São Paulo.

Ricardo Barros is a Visiting Professor at the Economic Growth Center at Yale University.

Jere R. Behrman is the William R. Kenan, Jr. Professor of Economics at the University of Pennsylvania.

Nancy Birdsall is Executive Vice President of the Inter-American Development Bank.

Carlos Alberto Primo Braga is a Senior Economist in the Telecommunications and Informatics Division, Industry and Energy Department, Finance and Private Sector Development Vice-Presidency, at the World Bank.

Barbara Bruns is Division Chief for Human Resources and Poverty in the Economic Development Institute (EDI) at the World Bank.

Claudio de Moura Castro is Division Chief of the Social Programs Division in the Social Programs and Sustainable Development Department of the Inter-American Development Bank.

João Batista Gomes-Neto is Director of the Department of Statistics at the Ministry of Education in Brazil.

Sonia Dantas Pinto Guimarães is an anthropologist presently working as an education consultant throughout Latin America and the Caribbean.

Eric A. Hanushek is Professor of Economics and Political Science and Director of the W. Allen Wallis Institute of Political Economy at the University of Rochester.

Ralph W. Harbison is Division Chief of the Human Resources Sector Division, Central and Southern Europe Departments, Europe and Central Asia Region, at the World Bank.

Dean T. Jamison is Director of the Center for Pacific Rim Studies at the University of California, Los Angeles.

Estelle James is Lead Economist with the Poverty and Human Resources Division in the Policy Research Department of the World Bank.

Robert Kaplan is Chief Advisor to the Executive Vice President of the Inter-American Development Bank.

David Lam is Director of the Population Studies Center at the University of Michigan.

Laurence J. Lau is the Kwoh-Ting Li Professor of Economic Development in the Department of Economics and Co-Director of the Asia/Pacific Research Center at Stanford University.

Shucheng Liu is a doctoral candidate in the Department of Engineering-Economics Systems at Stanford University.

Alberto de Mello e Souza is an Associate Professor in the College of Education at the Federal University of Rio de Janeiro.

Mari Minowa is an Economist in the Human Capital Development Group, Mexico Country Department, Latin America and Caribbean Regional Office, at the World Bank.

Samuel Morley is a Social Policy Consultant with the Inter-American Development Bank.

João Batista Araujo e Oliveira is President of JM Associados and Director of the Instituto Brasil Século XXI.

Young-Bum Park is a Senior Fellow with the Korea Labor Institute in Seoul.

José Pastore is a Professor and Senior Researcher with the Economic Research Institute Foundation (FIPE) at the University of São Paulo.

Jean-Jacques Paul is a Professor of Economics and Researcher at the Institute for Research on Education Economics (IREDU) in Dijon, France.

David Plank is an Associate Professor in the College of Education at Michigan State University.

Lauro Ramos is currently with the Research Directorship of the Institute of Applied Economic Research (IPEA) in Brazil.

Sergio Costa Ribeiro (deceased). All those associated with this work greatly lament the passing of Sergio Costa Ribeiro, an eminent physicist who later moved into the field of education. His findings and advocacy had a lasting and profound influence on the way Brazilians think and act on matters of education.

Steven Rivkin is an Assistant Professor of Economics at Amherst College.

Donald Robbins is a Research Associate with the Harvard Institute for International Development at Harvard University and a consultant with the OECD Development Centre.

David R. Ross is an Associate Professor of Economics at Bryn Mawr College.

Richard H. Sabot is the John J. Gibson Professor of Economics at Williams College.

Christoph Schenzler is a Research Associate with the Owen Graduate School of Management at Vanderbilt University.

Ryan Schneider is a consultant with McKinsey & Company in New York; he contributed to this work while completing doctoral studies in economics at Yale University.

Nelson do Valle Silva is a Senior Researcher with the National Laboratory for Scientific Computation in Rio de Janeiro.

José Amaral Sobrinho is a consultant with the Ministry of Education in Brazil, working primarily on the Northeast Basic Education Project with the World Bank.

John Strauss is a Professor of Economics at Michigan State University.

Duncan Thomas is a Professor of Economics at the University of California, Los Angeles, and a Senior Economist with the RAND Corporation.

Stephen Vogel is an Agricultural Economist in the Rural Economy Division of the Economic Research Service, United States Department of Agriculture.

Laurence Wolff is Principal Operations Officer at the World Bank; at the time of the writing he was in the Latin America and Caribbean Regional Office at the World Bank.

Antonio Carlos da Ressurreição Xavier is a Planning Research Fellow with the Institute of Economic and Social Planning in Brasília.

Hélio Zylberstajn is a Professor of Economics at the University of São Paulo.

Foreword

Latin America has made great strides since the lost decade of the 1980s. Macroeconomic stabilization, trade liberalization, privatization and deregulation have yielded fruit: intraregional trade is booming, fiscal balances have improved, and inflation has declined. Moreover, Latin American policymakers—even in the face of political difficulties—are firmly committed to pursuing this path of market reform.

Nevertheless, the tepid economic growth in the region—an annual average growth rate of 4 percent in the 1990s—remains worrisome. To make real inroads against Latin America's chronic poverty, growth must reach at least 6 percent. Such acceleration of the rate of growth would require a second round of reforms in order to address the region's institutional and structural constraints to growth.

One important target for reform is the role of government in the provision of social services. The Inter-American Development Bank (IDB) is ready to play a strong supporting role, as evidenced by its commitment to allocate 40 percent of its loans to the social agenda: health, education, the environment, and government reform. In the education arena, our aim is not simply to expand the size of existing schooling systems. The returns on the investments we help finance will be much higher if the efficiency of the education system, as measured for example by the learning outcomes of students at a given level of costs, is increased. This cannot take place without reform of the institutions operating in the sector.

This collection of studies on education in Brazil is most welcome because it points to what needs to be done to bring about change. Brazil has made progress in increasing enrollment rates in primary and secondary schools. However, these essays document that the development of the basic education system has lagged behind that of other countries at the same level of economic development. The education system has lost its focus on enhancing cognitive and other skills of children, failing to prepare them for a modern economy. One important lesson for all of Latin America: while more resources may prove to be necessary, particularly in poor regions, there are opportunities to increase the efficiency of the system of basic education dramatically with existing levels of expenditure.

It is the IDB's hope that this book will contribute to improving understanding of the problems of the education system not only in Brazil, but in other countries in the region as well, and to providing a foundation on which educational reform strategies can be built.

Enrique V. Iglesias
President
Inter-American Development Bank

Table of Contents

SECTION IV. EDUCATIONAL POLICY ISSUES

Introduction

Brazil has the potential to join, early in the new millennium, the ranks of the world's high-income nations. It also can and must become a more just society, one in which the poor as well as the rich contribute to, and share the fruits of, economic growth. If Brazil is to realize its potential then it must markedly improve the performance of its system of education. As a nation we have made massive investments in our children, but we have not always invested wisely. As a consequence, our education system is inefficient and inequitable, and its contribution to both economic growth and social justice is much less than it could be.

Far too many Brazilian children are in primary schools of such low quality that even the brightest among them must struggle to learn. Far too many children drop out before their program of study is complete. Far too many children never attend a secondary school. Far too many school leavers enter the labor market with cognitive skills insufficient to enable them to become highly productive workers, or for Brazil to become more competitive in the increasingly knowledge-based global economy. Discouraged by poor schooling and lacking the skills to break the cycle of poverty, young women often become mothers too soon and have too many children.

Educational reform must be a high priority. We have some of the world's best primary schools and some of the world's worst. We must reduce this variance by improving low quality schools. The benefits of improving primary school quality are many: more children will complete primary school, graduate without repeating grades, emerge with higher levels of cognitive skills, and qualify for secondary school. The proportion of children who attend secondary school is much lower than in other countries at similar levels of income. We must catch up. But educational expansion should not come at the expense of the erosion of quality.

How do we finance all of these improvements? The resources that we currently commit appear to be so inefficiently allocated that significant educational reform could be accomplished without increasing public expenditure. In fact, we are willing to spend more at the central, state and municipal levels, as reflected in firm legislative commitments. That means we can make enormous progress toward a well run education system that contributes to the future prosperity of our children and our nation. That progress will ensure a sustainable commitment to making education a high priority.

The studies brought together in this volume help us to understand the constraints we face in addressing the key problems with our system of education. They help us understand the steps we must take to address them and the benefits we can reap by addressing those problems vigorously. The authors convince the reader that our success with education reform will have an important influence on the nature of the society Brazil will be in the new millennium.

Paulo Renato Souza
Minister of Education
Brazil

Overview

This book documents the poor educational performance of Brazil and considers the consequences of that performance. It examines how to raise the achievement level of Brazilian school children and increase the efficiency of the country's educational system. It offers a frank assessment of why educational performance in Brazil has lagged behind other countries and examines the barriers to educational reform. The 18 studies that comprise this book are divided into four sections.

Background and Setting

Chapter 1 discusses the economics of education in Brazil and outlines the causes of the country's poor educational performance. It then compares the Brazilian experience with that of East Asia, where large investments in education have played an important role in economic growth and reductions in poverty.

Chapter 2 details how Brazilian investments in schooling compare with other countries. Regressions of enrollment rates are estimated as a function of income and the adult male and female literacy rates (which inversely represent the relative price of school staff). Despite Brazil's relatively good situation in terms of primary schooling in 1965, the minimal increase in investments in all levels of schooling since then has left Brazil with lower enrollment rates in basic education than predicted for a country of its income level. In addition, repetition and dropout rates that are very high, given Brazil's income, mean that measured enrollment rates may overstate Brazil's performance compared to other countries.

Chapter 3 suggests the magnitude of the impact of these relatively low levels of basic education by measuring the importance of human capital (as well as of physical capital, labor and technical progress) as a source of economic growth. Data from individual Brazilian states in 1970 and 1980 are used to estimate a production function relating aggregate real output of each state to physical capital, labor, education and time. The findings suggest that one additional year of average education per person of the labor force increases real output by approximately 20 percent. There is also evidence of a threshold effect in average education at between three and four years: above that threshold there are increasing social returns to average education.

Chapter 4 analyzes the origins of Brazil's poor performance in education from a political economy point of view, emphasizing the predominance of private interests over public purposes in the formulation and implementation of educational policies. The chapter examines three mechanisms by which public resources are allocated so as to benefit particular constituencies: clientelism; public subsidies to private schools coupled with public regulation of private school fees; and "free" higher education in public universities.

Education and Earnings

This section examines the relationship between education and productivity by analyzing the effect on earnings of an individual's level of education. Using data from a single year in the 1980s, Chapter 5 focuses on the relationship between wages and schooling in the urban Brazilian labor market, taking into account other factors that also affect wages, such as parents' education, gender, age and race. The effect of education on both the wage and type of employment is neither linear nor smooth. Returns to post-primary schooling tend to be far higher than returns to primary schooling, providing empirical support for the policy recommendation that high priority be given to expansion of secondary schooling, and to improvement of quality of primary schools to insure a larger pool of potential secondary enrollees.

Chapter 6 undertakes a similar analysis, but exploits a series of data sets covering each year between 1976 and 1989. The wage-education profile in Brazil is found to be much steeper than in other countries; wage gains from university education are greater than those from primary education, contributing to large differences in wages between the skilled and unskilled and thus to high inequality of pay. Moreover, wage gains from primary education have clearly decreased since 1976, while the gains from university education have increased, contributing to the failure of income distribution in Brazil to improve.

Chapter 7 examines differences in the relationship between education and wages across industries. Large variations are found in the returns to schooling across industries in São Paulo in 1977. Inter-industry differences also exacerbate the income inequality problem. Industries with high rates of return to schooling tend to be multinational, use advanced technology, and have higher effective rates of protection. This suggests that economic policies such as protectionism exacerbate income inequality by giving the skilled and educated extra high wages.

Chapter 8 expands on the previous three chapters by considering the impact of schooling quality as well as quantity on earnings. Findings show that schooling quality affects wages in Brazil over and above the effect of schooling quantity. From a social point of view, investments in schooling quality matter, given the effects on wages.

Education and Inequality

This section examines the effect of access and returns to education on the distribution of income in Brazil and on how it has changed over time. Chapter 9 finds that a substantial proportion of the marked difference between Brazil and Korea in the inequality of pay is attributable to differences in their educational policy regime. The labor market consequences of slow educational expansion in Brazil during the 1970s and 1980s were disequalizing: increases in the demand for skilled labor offset increases in the supply of skilled labor, so that the relative wage of skilled labor did not decline. Between 1976 and 1985, the inequality of pay associated with education actually increased in Brazil, while in Korea, greater increases in the supply of educated labor resulted in reductions in inequality.

Chapter 10 analyzes social mobility in Brazil, paying special attention to the role of education in determining status. The importance of "circular mobility," based on educational background and experience, has increased since the 1970s, and thus individual variables are beginning to become more important in determining status.

Chapter 11 estimates mobility using a method based on transition matrices and the separation of new entrants into the labor market from "survivors" who remain over the entire period under investigation (1970–1980). The separation is important in understanding why inequality has widened despite increasing access to education in Brazil. Among the results, the better educated had higher mobility, regardless of the growth in their region of residence—again underlining the greater vulnerability of the poor and less educated.

The next two chapters reverse the direction of causality, examining the impact of parent income and of the distribution of income on educational attainment. Chapter 12 focuses on the "demand side" of schooling in Brazil, attempting to explain the schooling attainment of a particular cohort of Brazilian children as a response to the income and schooling of their parents. But these factors explain less than 20 percent of the 1.5 year gap in schooling attainment between São Paulo and the Northeast, suggesting that child schooling attainment will be relatively unresponsive to improvements in the socioeconomic status of households per se. Instead, direct increases in the quantity and quality of schooling are necessary to reduce the schooling gap between regions.

Chapter 13 examines, for the state of São Paulo, the influence of parental income not only on children's educational attainment, but also on the types of schools which the children attend and their performance in these schools. At the primary and secondary level, higher parent education and income is associated with choosing a private school. At the university level, the better-off students choose public institutions. Within São Paulo there are pervasive effects of social inequality on educational outcomes.

Educational Policy Issues

This section focuses on specific problems with the educational system in Brazil, starting with school quality in the Northeast. Using analyses of what determines student achievement and student promotion, and taking into account the task of improving student performance through, for example, use of more books, Chapter 14 finds that higher school quality would pay for itself by reducing repetition. Direct cost savings come from the improved flow of students through a system that has very high grade repetition.

Chapter 15 narrows this investigation of school quality by focusing on grade repetition, estimating both its determinants and educational effects. The results suggest that two factors are most important in determining repetition: student achievement, not surprisingly, and the number of grades available in the child's school (many rural schools end at fourth grade).

Chapter 16 analyzes variations in private schooling availability across regions, and examines the variables that affect the family's decision to send children to public or private school. The chapter also describes how government policies have affected access to, and quality of, private education, setting out the negative effects of the regulatory environment in Brazil on private schooling in the 1980s.

Chapter 17 examines the relative importance of family income versus school environment by studying how poor students fare in good private schools. Students in these schools are so poor that even adequate inputs and good pedagogical practices prove to be insufficient to overcome profound deficiencies in their intellectual, physical, and home background.

Higher education in Brazil is the subject of the final chapter, which focuses on the differences between public and private universities and on the importance of incorporating the type of course in any analysis. Most students at these subsidized public universities come from high-income families, especially in the courses yielding the highest income potential. Public universities have lower rates of internal efficiency, largely due to excessively high unit costs resulting from low student-teacher ratios and excess physical space. Surprisingly, these higher unit costs and higher input qualities do not appear to generate higher rates of graduation or higher salaries for graduates.

CHAPTER

1

Education in Brazil:
Playing a Bad Hand Badly

Nancy Birdsall, Barbara Bruns and Richard H. Sabot

Fundamental changes in Brazilian economic policy in the mid-1990s have dramatically slowed inflation and have set the stage for sustained growth. The country's innovative stabilization program, the *Real* Plan, has been complemented by trade liberalization, privatization of state-owned enterprises, and the beginning of fiscal reform. These gains are providing the opportunity to turn to other social and economic issues that for years had been overshadowed by the country's preoccupation with inflation.

Among the most important issues on the agenda is education. Reforming Brazil's troubled education system is both an economic and a social issue. Sustaining the country's economic growth demands a more highly-skilled and better-educated work force. And to sustain the momentum of market-oriented reforms, the benefits of growth must be perceived to be shared by the poor and rich alike. For the poor to contribute to growth and share in its benefits, education reform is essential.

Much of the discussion in this chapter explicitly compares the causes and consequences of Brazil's poor educational performance relative to that of East Asia. Although Brazil's educational performance also looks poor when compared to most of Latin America, the focus is on the Brazil-East Asia comparison because the gap in the magnitude of investments in schooling is so large, and because, more so than in Latin America, the development strategy adopted by East Asian policymakers ensured high payoffs—more rapid growth and lower inequality—to education investments.

Education Policy in Brazil

There have been important gains in education in Brazil. Indeed, enrollment in primary and secondary education expanded by 32 percent from 1970 to 1989. Nevertheless, Brazil failed to match the progress of other developing countries during this period, particularly the high-performing East Asian economies, in expanding the quantity and improving the quality of schooling. While in 1960 the coverage of basic education was much the same in Brazil as in other countries with the same per capita income, by 1990 it covered a much smaller share of its eligible population than education systems in East Asia and had greater variation in enrollment rates among regions. While international comparisons of quality are fraught with difficulties, it appears that in 1960 the quality of Brazil's system of basic education also matched that of other countries with similar incomes. However, by 1990 it had lower average quality and greater variance in quality.

Brazil's educational performance lagged in part because of a social and economic environment that discouraged educational investment. First, Brazil's unequal income distribution concentrated wealth among the elite, who resisted paying the additional taxes necessary to increase the supply and quality of subsidized education for children from poor families. Poor families had such low incomes that they had difficulty keeping their children in school and out of the workforce. They had little reason to do so when, because of the low quality of available schools, success in school was unlikely and the economic payoff to schooling was not high. Second, because Brazil adopted an inward-looking development strategy, the demand for educated labor (hence the returns to investment in education and the household demand for education) were not as high as they might have been had Brazil's economy been more open and more oriented toward exports. Third, Brazil's political system often made school systems more a source of jobs than of good public education efficiently administered for children. Finally, spending on basic education per eligible child in Brazil rose slowly during the 1970s and 1980s compared to countries in East Asia. As a share of GDP, public spending on education was as high in Brazil as elsewhere. But population growth was more rapid, and GDP grew more slowly, so absolute spending per child fell behind.

In an environment conducive neither to abundant supply nor a strong demand for basic education, poor education policy choices failed to help. While access to public primary education grew, expansion was at the expense of quality, resulting in higher repetition and dropout rates. In part due to low success rates in primary education, secondary enrollment rates lagged behind international norms. Private primary and secondary schools proliferated as many families, including the working poor, opted out of low quality public schools. But many private schools were little better than public schools, and government intervention in the private market for these schools, including via price controls, limited both their quantity and quality.

The costs to Brazil of the underperformance of its system of basic (primary and secondary) education were high. Economic growth was substantially lower and income inequality substantially higher than they would have been had the quantity and quality of basic education been closer to East Asian levels. A scarcity of educated labor helps explain both outcomes: the relatively small stock of educated labor constrained productivity growth at the same time that it sustained large earnings differentials between the educated and the uneducated. Of course, had Brazil achieved East Asian enrollment and quality levels without more labor-demanding economic policies, the growth payoff to educational investment would have been lower than in East Asia—both supply of education and demand for educated labor matter.

The lesson for Brazil: stimulating both the supply of, and demand for, high quality basic education can set the stage for a more productive labor force, faster growth and lower inequality. Policy adjustments can convert a vicious circle of low human capital investment, high inequality, and constrained growth to a virtuous circle of increased human capital investment, low inequality, and faster growth. Among the desirable policy adjustments are:

- Reinforce the shift to a more labor and skill-demanding export-oriented development strategy;
- Redirect more public resources from higher to basic education;
- Raise the quality of primary schools. As success rates in primary schools improve, expand public secondary enrollment;
- Shift from price and other regulation of private schools to evaluation and information for families;
- Modernize and professionalize the administration of basic education.

Many other developing countries have had educational policies similar to Brazil's and suffered similar adverse consequences. The policy adjustments appropriate for Brazil would benefit these countries as well.

Brazil Was Dealt a Bad Hand for Education

Conditions in Brazil in the postwar decades have not been propitious for educational advances. It is as though policymakers, in the card game of education policy, were dealt a bad hand at the start.

Skewed Distribution of Income

In some East Asian countries, "shared growth policies" led to a decline in income inequality and to rapid increases in the incomes of the poor.[1] Land reform and other policies adopted after World War II contributed to a dynamic agricultural sector, while an outward-oriented trade strategy rapidly increased the demand for labor. Income growth among the poor enabled them to make high-return investments in their children's education.

By contrast, in Brazil the unequal distribution of land and policy biases against agriculture kept more of the poor in extreme poverty and reduced their ability to afford, hence their demand for, schooling. As shown in Table 1.1, the ratio of income of the richest 20 percent of households to the poorest 20 percent was 8 in Korea in the mid-1970s, and 8.9 in Thailand, compared to 33.3 in Brazil. In Korea and Thailand, the poorest 20 percent of households had almost 6 percent of total income, compared to just 2 percent in Brazil. While Brazil and Korea had similar per capita incomes, because of more equal distribution in Korea, the absolute income of the poor was substantially higher there than in Brazil.

In East Asia, the economic and political elites adopted policies that gave the poor a greater stake in the prevailing system.[2] They saw their political and economic power as contestable—perhaps because of the proximity of the external threat of communism, and the susceptibility of the poor to alternative ideologies. In Brazil, the elites apparently saw less contestability and, therefore, less connection between their welfare and the welfare of the poor. Indifference may have been reinforced by racial and ethnic differences closely associated with income disparities.

Poverty reduces the demand for education in four ways.[3] First, the poor are less likely to know about the high returns to schooling, so that even if a family has the resources, it might not spend them on schooling. Second, for poor families, the opportunity costs of schooling may make an important contribution to household income, implying that the immediate benefits of children working may outweigh the long-term benefits of schooling. Third, the poor may not have the income to cover the direct costs (books, uniforms, transportation) of educating their children. And they are

---

[1] See Chapter 4 of World Bank (1993) for additional discussion of "shared growth."
[2] See Birdsall and Sabot (1995).
[3] See Williamson (1993) for empirical estimates of the negative impact of income inequality on enrollment rates.

not likely to have access to credit to finance schooling by borrowing.[4] Fourth, there is often a positive relationship between family income and the quality of local schools. If poor families have access only to poor quality schools, the rate of return to schooling for them may be low, irrespective of the average rate of return.

People who lack education tend to have lower incomes than those who are educated. So one generation with low demand for education for their children perpetuates both income inequality and low demand for schooling in the next generation. In aggregate it is estimated that more than half of the difference between Korea's and Brazil's secondary enrollment rates can be attributed to the difference in their initial income distribution.[5]

In East Asia, a virtuous circle: low initial inequality in the distribution of income led to high investment in human capital, which in turn helped further reduce inequality. In Brazil, by contrast, a vicious circle: high initial income inequality led to low levels of investment in human capital, particularly among the poor, which exacerbated income inequality.

Inward-looking Development Strategy

Brazil's inward-looking development strategy reinforced the country's unequal initial distribution of income because it generated little demand for moderately skilled workers, reducing the return to, and thus the demand for, schooling. By contrast, East Asia's aggressively outward-oriented development strategy provided strong incentives for the growth of manufactured exports. These industries initially generated demand for unskilled labor, but as wages rose they became increasingly skill intensive. Korea and Brazil had roughly the same shares of exports to GDP in 1960. By the mid-1980s, Korea's share of exports to GDP had increased from 9 percent to 37 percent while Brazil's remained at 8 percent. High tariffs and quotas protected the Brazilian market from international competition while an overvalued exchange rate weakened incentives to export.

Export orientation increases the demand for skilled workers—and thus the household demand for education—in two ways. First, the higher growth rate of aggregate output in an export-oriented economy increases the growth rate of the overall demand for labor. Second, an export-oriented

---

[4] See chapters by Barros and Lam, James, Braga and Andre, and Mello e Souza and Silva for measurements of the impact of parental income on children's education.
[5] See Williamson (1993).

Table 1.1. Income Distribution

Region	Country	GNP per capita growth (per annum) 1965–90 (%)	Income share of bottom 20% of households (%)	Year	Income share of highest 20% of households (%)	Ratio of top 20% to bottom 20%
ASIA	Korea	7.1	5.7	1976	45.3	8.0
	Hong Kong	6.2	5.4	1980	47.0	8.7
	Taiwan		9.5	1976	35.0	3.7
	Singapore	6.5	5.1	1982–83	48.9	9.6
	Indonesia	4.5	6.6	1976	49.4	7.4
			8.8	1987[a]	41.3	4.7
	Philippines	1.3	3.7	1970–71	53.9	14.6
			5.5	1985[b]	48.0	8.7
	Thailand	4.4	5.6	1975–76	49.8	8.9
	Malaysia	4.0	3.5	1973	56.1	16.0
			4.6	1987[c]	51.2	11.1
LATIN AMERICA	Brazil	3.3	2.0	1972	66.6	33.3
			2.4	1983	62.6	26.0
	Mexico	2.8	2.9	1977	57.7	19.9
	Peru	–0.2	1.9	1972	61.0	32.1
			4.4	1985–86[a]	51.9	11.8
	Venezuela	–1.0	3.0	1970	54.0	18.0
			4.7	1987[c]	50.6	10.8
	Costa Rica	1.4	3.3	1971	54.8	16.6
			3.3	1986[c]	54.5	16.5
	Colombia	2.3	4.0	1988[c]	53.0	13.3

Source: World Development Report, various years.
[a] Data refer to per capita expenditure.
[b] Data refer to household expenditure.
[c] Data refer to per capita income.

development strategy leads, as wage levels rise, to more skill-intensive pro-duction. In East Asia, high returns to schooling, driven by the demand for skills from the export push, kept the incentives for acquiring education strong. This led to a positive interaction between improved educational performance and faster export-oriented growth.[6]

In Brazil, the limited demand for educated workers in the protected labor market interacted with the poor quality of schooling and the high level of income inequality to weaken the household demand for education. Brazil's import-substitution strategy initially appeared to be a success, creating a temporary boom—the "Brazilian Miracle" growth years of the 1960s and 1970s—that masked the strategy's longer-term limitations. The strategy's negative effects on the accumulation of human capital were therefore protracted.[7]

One way in which export orientation boosts economic growth, and thus the demand for labor, is by lowering the risk of economic downturns associated with the accumulation of debt.[8] In 1981, Korea's debt-to-GDP ratio of 27.6 percent was actually slightly higher than Brazil's, at 26.1 percent. But the two countries' debt service ratios differed greatly: 90 percent of exports for Korea, compared with 133 percent for Brazil. Korea could service its debt and finance some of its current imports with its export earnings. Because Brazil's export earnings were not enough even to service its debt, it needed additional foreign borrowing.

Brazil's growing external imbalance was not sustainable: with higher international interest rates and rising oil costs came the recession of the early 1980s, when the growth of Brazil's economy dropped to 1 percent. This decline in output growth meant slower growth in the demand for labor. Korea's export-oriented economy responded better to the same external shocks Brazil experienced: growth declined only from 8 percent to 7.5 percent and the demand for labor remained dynamic.[9]

Besides stunting the demand for labor, Brazil's inward-looking economy used human capital less efficiently than did the East Asian economies. For human capital accumulation to pay off, those leaving the school system must find jobs where their skills are used most productively. Because Brazil did not need to compete internationally, employers and government put up less resistance to rent-seeking by workers. Organized

---

[6] See Birdsall and Sabot (1995).
[7] See Pastore and Zylberstajn (this volume).
[8] See Sachs (1985).
[9] See Sachs (1985).

demands for high wages and excessive levels of employment led to the inefficient use of human capital and ultimately became a drag on growth.[10] Labor extracted rents by raising wages to levels above the supply price, or by raising employment to levels above those justified by the derived demand for labor. To recoup, private and public firms could raise the prices they charged in their protected domestic market. Alternatively, public enterprises could hold the line on prices by receiving increased subsidies from the government, raising the tax burden. Both phenomena tended to lower rates of saving and investment and to reduce the international competitiveness of Brazil's manufacturing enterprises.[11]

With lack of dynamism in Brazil's labor market in the late 1970s and the 1980s, workers in the organized sector tended to resort to rent-seeking. In East Asia, labor was much less successful in organizing in the 1960s and 1970s. In Korea and Singapore, there had been political suppression of labor movements. More important, throughout East Asia there were regular and large increases both in real wages and in alternative employment opportunities. The dynamism of the labor market, stimulated by an export-oriented economy, reduced incentives for rent-seeking by workers.

Structure of Power

As described in Chapter 4 by Plank et al., the Brazilian government at the federal, state and local levels has not usually reflected the competition of ideologically aligned parties. It has reflected the politics of charismatic leaders who acquire power and use it in a patronage (or clientelistic) system to maintain their standing in the government. Until recently, the power structure has often been used to advance the interests of the bureaucrats making decisions and the politicians and interest groups influencing decisions.

The education system, the largest employer in Brazil and a rich source of jobs, has been hampered by the political system: teaching, administrative and maintenance appointments have been treated as political spoils. This clientelistic system perpetuates incontestable patronage, with those outside denied access to power and the benefits of economic growth.

---

[10] See Robbins and Minowa (this volume). Also see Gelb, Knight and Sabot (1991) and Birdsall, Ross and Sabot (1995).
[11] See Birdsall and Sabot (1995).

Slow Economic Growth and Rapidly Growing School-age Cohorts

Developing countries generally must choose between improving the quality and increasing the quantity of basic education.[12] East Asia's educational performance was exceptional in part because rapid increases in GDP and the slow growth of school-age cohorts (due to declining birth rates) allowed increases in educational spending per eligible child—simultaneously improving the quality and increasing the quantity of schooling—without increasing the share of national resources going to education. In addition, in East Asia a high proportion of public spending on education went to basic rather than to higher education; expansion of higher education relied more on increases in private spending, since a higher proportion of students were able to finance their education from household savings. Therefore, public spending per eligible child at the primary and secondary level was relatively high.

In Brazil, by contrast, slow economic growth and continued rapid growth of school-age cohorts, exacerbated by relatively high spending on university rather than basic education, constrained the growth of spending on basic education per eligible child. That forced Brazil to choose between improving quality and increasing quantity. Brazil directed its resources to the expansion of enrollments.[13] Because the wider pool of students gaining access to the system was generally not as well prepared as those students already enrolled, it cost more per child to maintain quality. But lacking the resources to meet these costs, the increase in quantity meant an erosion of quality. Moreover, Brazil fell further behind the international norm with regard to secondary school enrollments.

Although Brazil's public financial commitment to basic education in 1989, measured by public spending as a percentage of GDP, was not far from Korea's, public spending on basic education per eligible child was significantly different in the two countries (see Table 1.2). In Korea, public spending on basic education actually declined from 3.1 percent of GDP in 1970 to 2.7 percent in 1989, but public spending on basic education per eligible child more than quadrupled—from an estimated $95 (in 1987 dollars) to $433. In Brazil, public spending on basic education actually rose from 1.7

---

[12] See Behrman and Birdsall (1983), Behrman, Ross and Sabot (1992), and Behrman, Ross, Sabot and Tropp (1994) for discussions of this tradeoff (or lack thereof). In this volume, see chapters by Behrman, Birdsall and Kaplan, and by Hanushek et al.

[13] See James, Braga and Andre (this volume).

Table 1.2. Public Expenditure on Basic Education per Eligible Child and Some Determinants

Country	1970	1989	% Change, 1970–89
Korea			
Expenditure on basic education per eligible child	$95.3	$433.4	354.8
Public expenditure on basic education as % of GNP	3.1	2.7	−12.9
Index for absolute expenditure on basic education	100	444	
No. of children eligible for basic education (thousands)	10,074	9,848	−2.2
Brazil			
Expenditure on basic education per eligible child	$58.6	$170.8	191.5
Public expenditure on basic education as % of GNP	1.7	2.1	23.5
Index for absolute expenditure on basic education	100	316	
No. of children eligible for basic education (thousands)	32,542	35,319	8.5

Sources: UNESCO *Statistical Yearbook* for enrollment rates, number of students and expenditure by level of education; World Tables for real gross national income figures.

Notes: Absolute expenditures on basic education in real 1987 U.S. dollars used to calculate indices. Number of children eligible for basic education calculated using enrollment rates and number of students in 1st and 2nd levels: i.e. (number of enrolled students x enrollment rates) = number of those in age group eligible for basic education.

percent in 1970 to 2.1 percent of GDP in 1989, but public spending on basic education per eligible child grew much less, from about $60 to about $170 (in 1987 dollars).

Three reasons lie behind these differences:

• Korea's rapid economic growth enabled it to devote more real public resources to education without raising the share of the GDP allocated.

• In Korea, a 54 percent decrease in the birth rate between 1965 and 1980 decreased population growth to 1.1 percent between 1980 and 1990. In Brazil, the birth rate fell only 31 percent, lowering population growth to 2.2 percent. As a result, in Korea the number of children eligible for education decreased by 2.2 percent between 1970 and 1989, while in Brazil, the number of eligible children increased by 8.5 percent. So, in Korea the rate of spending per eligible child rose at roughly the rate of increase of total spending for basic education, while in Brazil the rate of spending per eligible child rose at just 61 percent of the rate of increase of total spending. This difference in demographics can be traced, in part, to the difference in the educational attainment of parents, and, in particular, of mothers. In Africa, Asia and Latin America, educated women have markedly lower fer-

Table 1.3. Size and Growth of School-age Population
(Percent)

	School-age (0–14) population as % of total population		Growth rate of primary school-age (6–11) population	
	1965	1989	1965–75	1980–85
Brazil	44	35	2.0	1.7
Hong Kong	40	22	−1.1	0.3
Korea	43	26	0.7	−0.3
Malaysia	46	37	1.9	0.2
Singapore	44	24	−1.2	−2.2
Thailand	46	34	2.9	−0.1

Sources: 0–14 population figures from World Bank data; 6–11 population figures from Lockheed and Verspoor (1991).

tility rates than uneducated women.[14] Because of earlier investments in education in Korea compared to Brazil, particularly between 1950 and 1965, women in Korea had more education by 1965, and fertility rates fell faster and farther from 1965 on than in Brazil. Fertility decline comparable to that in Korea occurred in the other countries of East Asia; by the early 1980s there was virtually no growth in school-age populations in any of the high-performing East Asian countries (see Table 1.3).

• Basic education in Korea received a steady and large share of the growing public spending on education, while Brazil increased its already large commitment to tertiary education at the expense of basic education. Between 1975 and 1989, Korea's allocation to tertiary education dropped from 12 percent of total spending on education to 8 percent, while Brazil's rose from 18 percent to 26 percent.

Education Policymakers Played a Bad Hand Badly

In 1965, Brazil's education system was superior to that of other developing countries in two respects. First, as shown in Table 1.4, Brazil, with a gross enrollment rate of 108 percent (including underaged and overaged children), had universal primary enrollment. Primary enrollment rates were

---

[14] See Summers (1992).

Table 1.4. Primary and Secondary Enrollment Rates
(Percent)

	Primary		Secondary	
Country	1965	1987	1965	1987
Brazil	108	103	16	39
High-performing East Asia				
Indonesia	72	118	12	46
Thailand	78	95	14	28
Malaysia	90	102	28	59
Korea	101	101	35	88
Singapore	105	—	45	—
Hong Kong	103	106	29	74
Developing Countries				
Low income	73	104	20	37
Middle income	92	104	26	54

Source: World Development Report (1990).

higher than in most developing countries and comparable to such East Asian countries as Korea and Malaysia. When primary enrollment rates are regressed on per capita national income for developing countries, as shown in Figure 1.1, Brazil is well above the regression line, indicating that Brazil had higher primary enrollment rates for its level of income in 1965 than predicted by cross-country comparisons.[15] Second, Brazil had a high primary enrollment rate for girls and only a small gap in educational access between boys and girls, compared with other developing countries.

Secondary school enrollment rates in Brazil, however, were not exceptional. As shown in Table 1.4, Brazil had a secondary enrollment rate of 16 percent in 1965, less than half the rate in Korea and roughly a third of the rate in Singapore. The results of cross-country regressions from 1965, displayed in Figure 1.2, show that the secondary school enrollment rate in Brazil was lower than predicted for a country at its level of income. Nevertheless, due to the exceptionally high primary enrollment rate in 1965, the expected years of schooling for a Brazilian student was above the international average.

---

[15] This analysis is described in detail in the chapter by Behrman and Schneider. The regressions control for a polynomial in average per capita income in the relevant year.

Figure 1.1. Cross-Economy Regression for Primary Enrollment Rates, 1965 and 1987

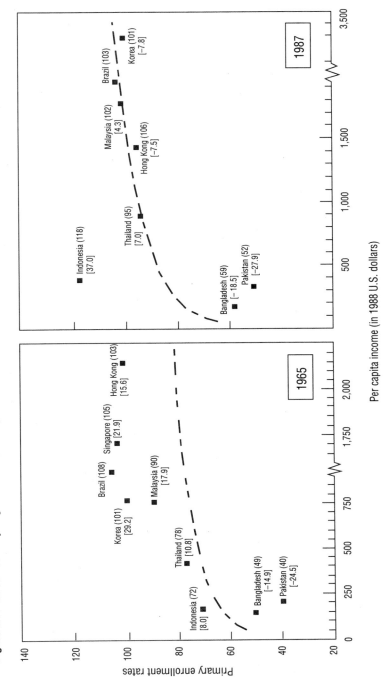

Source: Behrman and Schneider (this volume).

Note: Figures in parentheses are enrollment rates; bracketed numbers show residuals.

Figure 1.2. Cross-Economy Regression for Secondary Enrollment Rates, 1965 and 1987

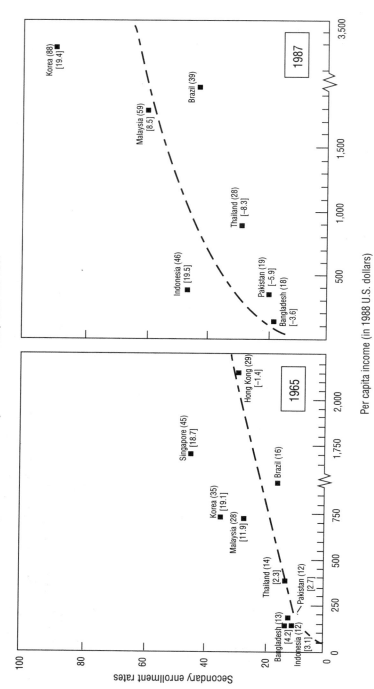

Source: Behrman and Schneider (this volume).

Note: Figures in parentheses are enrollment rates; bracketed numbers show residuals.

Table 1.5. Mean Years of Schooling of Adult Population

Country	1965	1985
Brazil	2.6	3.5
Mexico	2.8	4.1
Chile	5.0	6.0
Korea	4.4	7.8
Taiwan	3.8	7.0
Singapore	3.3	4.6
Thailand	3.2	4.9
Indonesia	1.6	3.6
Malaysia	2.8	5.0
Turkey	2.2	3.2

Source: Barro and Wha Lee (1993).
Note: Adult population = population aged 25 and over.

Over the next two decades, the expansion of Brazil's basic education system lagged behind systems in many other developing countries. As shown in the chapter by Behrman and Schneider, between 1965 and 1987 both primary and secondary enrollment rates grew more slowly in Brazil than in the representative middle-income country.[16] As a consequence, as shown in Figures 1.1 and 1.2, by 1987 Brazil's primary enrollment ratio was barely above the international average, and its secondary enrollment ratio had fallen much further below the international average.[17] A gap in the mean years of schooling of the adult population between Brazil and other countries—particularly the high-performing East Asian economies— opened between 1965 and 1985. For example, as shown in Table 1.5, in 1965 Brazil and Malaysia had similar mean years of schooling of the adult population (2.6 and 2.8, respectively). By 1985, however, the mean years of schooling had increased to 5 in Malaysia, but to just 3.5 in Brazil.[18]

Why did Brazilian education fall behind? Policymakers were dealt a bad hand—but they also played the hand badly, making policy choices that failed to help, and sometimes worsened Brazil's education situation.

---

[16] Of course, at the primary level, this was the necessary consequence of having achieved virtually universal enrollment at an early date.

[17] Moreover, the poor quality of schooling in Brazil may have resulted in an overestimation of enrollment rates. Poor quality leads to higher rates of repetition, hence to more children in school older than the usual cohort.

[18] See Psacharopoulos and Arriagada (1992) for data on similar trends for the educational composition of the labor force.

Magnitude of Public Expenditure

Brazil needed to spend *more* of its GDP to achieve the same education results as the high-performing East Asian countries. First, average GDP growth in Brazil was lower. Second, as discussed above, the size of the school-age population continued to grow in Brazil long after it started to decline in East Asia. Third, Brazil's much less equal distribution of income and education meant that the marginal student brought into the primary school system, as it expanded over the 1970s and 1980s, was poorer and had less educated parents. Hence, that student was much less prepared to learn and in need of more teaching attention and instructional materials to achieve the same outcomes as better qualified students. Fourth, the expansion of schooling since the 1960s in Brazil was increasingly to areas with lower population density and more difficult physical conditions. So, the costs of expanding schooling to these regions were higher in Brazil than in more densely populated East Asia.[19]

For Brazil to have matched other countries in the increase in enrollment rates, its investment in basic education as a share of GDP would have had to be higher. In fact, given budgetary constraints, the quantitative expansion Brazil did achieve required lowering per pupil expenditures and quality.

Allocation Among Education Levels

Public spending in Brazil favored tertiary rather than primary and secondary education. As documented in the chapter by Mello e Souza and Silva, this worked to the benefit of the wealthy, whose children could afford relatively high quality private schooling at the primary and secondary levels and were well-positioned to compete successfully for access to the highly competitive, heavily subsidized top quality public universities. Given the high returns to university education described in the chapters by Barros and Ramos and by Strauss and Thomas, a large majority of high-income families would have been willing to pay the full cost of a university education for their children. Since most of the subsidies went to children from high-income families, they did little to expand university enrollments. The low public spending at the primary and secondary levels relegated middle-

---

[19] Of course, there are remote regions in East Asia, such as Thailand's Northeast and the outer islands of Indonesia, where population density is low and the cost of providing schooling is high.

income and low-income students to poor quality public schools, making it difficult for them to do well in meritocratic testing for access to subsidized public universities.

Brazil's performance would have been better if the allocation of public spending on tertiary education had been more efficient. Although Brazil's share of education spending on higher education (about 25 percent on average) is not as high as that in some other countries, Brazil's subsidy per student in public higher education is among the largest in the world (more than $5,000 per student per year). The government has not developed lower cost, nonuniversity tertiary institutions. Rather, private universities are low in quality and excessive in cost. High unit costs make it difficult to expand public university enrollments. Brazil's higher education enrollment ratio remained constant at 12 percent of the 20–24 year old population between 1970 and 1990. About 60 percent of enrollments are private, so the 25 percent of total education spending on universities subsidizes about 4 percent of the 20–24 age group.[20]

Because most students in public higher education have the capacity to contribute to the costs of their education (44 percent of public university students come from the top income decile), a much more efficient allocation would have been to mobilize more private financing of higher education,[21] lower the budget share for higher education, and reallocate this money to primary and secondary education.[22]

Low and Declining Quality of Basic Education

In the lowest quality primary schools, generally found in Brazil's poorest districts, many teachers have themselves not completed primary school. Teachers cannot teach what they themselves do not know. As discussed in Hanushek et al., if school quality is low, children learn little and acquire few productive skills, reducing both the likelihood of progressing to the next educational level and the rate of return to schooling when competing in the

---

[20] See Paul and Wolff (this volume).

[21] It is not our contention that the gap between net private and social returns is higher for basic than for university education, though it may be. Rather, the argument that reallocating public subsidies toward basic education would increase efficiency is based on the supposition that in the absence of subsidies, liquidity constraints faced by the poor, together with capital market imperfections that preclude borrowing to finance education, will result in more foregone (high return) investment opportunities at the primary and secondary levels than at the university level.

[22] See chapters by Paul and Wolff and by Plank et al.

labor market. Parents are aware that their children are not learning much in school. Once children in low quality schools are old enough to be economically productive, parents no longer have sufficient economic incentive to keep them in school. For this reason, primary school completion rates are likely to, in part, reflect the level and trend of primary school quality.

In Brazil, the expansion of primary school coverage was associated with a dramatic decline in completion rates because the system was unable to offer adequate quality schooling to a larger and more diverse pool of students. By contrast, in East Asian countries, where quality and quantity were improved simultaneously, completion rates remained high. In Brazil, only about 36 percent of students ever complete the eight grade primary cycle.[23] Completion rates vary across regions and between urban and rural schools; in Northeast Brazil only 20 percent of students ever complete primary school and only 3 percent do so with no repetition. In the wealthier Southeast, about 50 percent complete primary school and 25 percent complete without repetition. Within a region or state, there is a difference in completion and repetition rates between the higher quality state schools and municipal schools (excluding municipal schools in the capitals, which often have characteristics similar to or better than the state schools), and between higher quality schools in urban areas and schools in rural areas.[24]

The contrast between Brazilian and Korean primary school completion rates reflects changes in the quality of their primary schools. As shown in Table 1.6, Brazil's primary completion rate of 60 percent in the 1950s was relatively high (though the 1950 figure refers to only four rather than eight grades of primary school). In Korea, the completion rate was only 36 percent.[25] Over the next three decades, Brazil's primary enrollments (for eight grades) increased to more than 100 percent in 1985, while its primary completion rate (for eight grades) dropped to 20 percent. In contrast, Korea's completion and enrollment rates rose concurrently: in the mid-1960s Korea achieved universal primary enrollment and, since then, more than 90 percent of those enrolled have completed primary education.

Similarly, high school quality is associated with low repetition rates, and low quality with high rates. Because low quality means that students do not acquire the skills necessary to pass tests and satisfy other criteria necessary to progress within the educational system, children are com-

---

[23] See chapters by Gomes-Neto and Hanushek and by Hanushek et al.
[24] See chapters by Gomes-Neto and Hanushek, Hanushek et al., and Mello e Souza and Silva.
[25] Some of this difference in completion rates is likely to be due to differences in the definition of primary school. The percentage of the eligible population then enrolled in primary school was substantially lower in Brazil (34 percent) than in Korea (69 percent).

Table 1.6. Completion Rates at Primary Level
(Percent)

Country	Year	% of population with primary education	Completion Rate
Brazil	1950	33.8	60.1
	1970	55.7	52.1
	1976	63.0	15.8
	1980	62.2	19.0
Korea	1955	68.9	36.3
	1960	40.5	91.6
	1966	52.7	96.7
Hong Kong	1960	66.1	63.8
	1971	61.9	68.0
	1981	70.3	76.2
Indonesia	1961	24.5	38.8
	1971	44.2	50.0
	1981	58.0	45.5
Malaysia	1980	64.3	66.7
Taiwan	1980	67.7	90.5
Thailand	1960	51.3	75.6
	1980	76.5	12.0

Source: Barro and Wha Lee (1993).
Notes: Primary completion rate = [(% population who have completed primary level + % who have secondary education) / (% population with primary + % with secondary education)] x 100. Population in this case is those aged 25 and over.

pelled to repeat the grade if they want to be promoted. As shown in Table 1.7, 20 percent of the pupils in Brazil in 1980 and 1988 were forced to repeat their grades, versus zero percent in both these years in Korea.[26] Ninety-nine percent of the 1987 cohort reached their final grade in Korea (without repetition), versus only 20 percent in Brazil. If a coefficient of efficiency is calculated for the first level of education,[27] Brazil ranks as the most ineffi-

---

[26] Indonesian repetition rates, however, are closer to Brazilian than to Korean rates.

[27] The coefficient of efficiency is calculated as the ratio between the theoretical number of pupil-years that it would have taken the graduates to complete the cycle of education (had there been no repetition or dropout) and the number of pupil-years actually spent by the cohort. The coefficient varies between 0 (complete inefficiency) and 1 (maximum efficiency).

Table 1.7. First Level Education: Internal Efficiency

Country	Percentage of repeaters[1]		Percentage of 1987 cohort reaching:			Coefficient of efficiency[2]	
	1980	1988	Grade 2	Grade 4	Final grade	1980	1988
Brazil	20	20	68	52	20		0.64
Costa Rica	8	11	95	88	79	.80	0.78
Venezuela	10	9	92	85	73	0.74	0.77
Mexico	10	9	91	82	72	0.74	0.77
Colombia		17	76	62	57	0.66	0.66
Thailand	8	3	87	73	59	0.78	0.74
Korea	0	0	100	99	99	0.97	1.00
Malaysia	0	0	100	99	96	0.98	0.98
Indonesia	8	10	97	89	79	0.72	0.79
Turkey		8	100	98	96		0.90

Source: World Education Report, UNESCO (1991).

[1] Total number of pupils still enrolled in same grade as the previous year, expressed as a percentage of total enrollment at first level.

[2] Coefficient of efficiency: the ratio between the theoretical number of pupil-years that it would have taken the graduates to complete the cycle of education, had there been no repetition or dropouts, and the number of pupil-years actually spent by the cohort. The coefficient varies between 0 (complete inefficiency) and 1 (maximum efficiency).

cient of the countries considered, more inefficient than the other Latin American countries in the sample. Brazil's high repetition rates are costly. On average, it is necessary to finance eight years of schooling to put a student through five years of primary school.

As the average quality of basic education declined in Brazil, the variance in school quality increased. Almost all of the decline in average quality over the past two decades is attributable to a worsening at the bottom of the quality distribution. The worst schools in Brazil operate shifts of less than four hours, lack basic sanitary facilities, have few books or other learning materials, and have teachers who have not completed primary school themselves. Meanwhile, the best Brazilian schools maintain high quality by international standards. The children of the poor tend to go to much lower quality schools than children from middle- and upper-income families.[28]

There is also an interaction between the distributions of the quantity and quality of schooling received. The quality of the education obtained by families at different incomes influences the amount of schooling their children receive. Children from high-income families obtain more schooling in part because the higher quality of their schooling enables them to qualify

---

[28] See chapters by Castro et al. and by Mello e Souza and Silva.

for entrance to the next level of education. Poor children tend to have academic disadvantages reinforced by being concentrated in low-quality schools, from which they have less likelihood of going on to higher levels of education.[29] The result is that, as discussed in the chapter by Adelman et al., intergenerational mobility is limited.

Equality of educational opportunity is one means of promoting intergenerational mobility. In Brazil inequality of educational opportunity is a severe constraint on such mobility. Where intergenerational mobility is low and levels of income inequality are high, the stage is set for the political alienation of the poor and for demagogic political leaders who offer populist policies as a panacea. Unfortunately, such policies often prove to be a constraint on growth, thereby limiting the potential for poverty alleviation. It is in the most rapidly growing countries that educational opportunities have been greatest, intergenerational mobility highest, and where poverty has declined most rapidly.[30]

Large Variance in Resources Available for Basic Education

The high variance in the quality of basic schooling in Brazil (particularly at the primary level) is the result of three factors discussed in the chapter by Plank et al.: the schooling delivery system is very decentralized; there are large variations in income per capita across regions, and between rural and urban areas within regions; and the system of educational financing is insufficiently redistributive.

Brazil has 23 states and more than 4,500 municipalities sharing the responsibility for providing primary education. The states and federal government provide secondary education. This decentralization—coupled with the large regional variations in per capita income and limited redistribution—has resulted in tremendous variance in spending per student across municipalities and even between state and municipal systems in the same municipality. In a single state in Northeast Brazil, spending per primary student in 1990 ranged from $30 to $650 in different municipal systems. In a single rural municipality, per student spending was $30 a year in municipal primary schools and $300 in state-run primary schools.[31] There is evidence from some countries that decentralization can improve the ac-

---

[29] See chapter by Mello e Souza and Silva.
[30] See World Bank (1993) and Fields (1992).
[31] See Brazilian Ministry of Education (1990).

countability of education systems and the efficiency of educational spending. But if school quality depends on local financing and if revenue-raising capacity varies markedly across localities, decentralization can also result in high variance in quality, usually to the detriment of the poor.

In Brazil, primary education is the most decentralized—nationally, about 30 percent of enrollments are municipal, 60 percent state and 10 percent private. But outside the major cities, the municipal share is much higher—up to 90 percent in the rural Northeast. The absolute level of spending is so low in some municipal schools that funding per student is inadequate to cover both the salary of a teacher with a primary school education and the costs of minimal books and physical facilities, despite the fact that wages in these areas are also low. Spending per primary student in municipal systems in the rural Northeast averages about $50 a year.[32] In these schools, there typically is no money for anything but the teacher's salary, which in the early 1990s was below the national minimum wage of $100 a month.[33]

Inefficient Use of Resources

The poorest municipal systems generally are not overstaffed to the extent that wealthier municipal systems and state systems often are. But, as discussed by Plank et al., the inefficient use of financial and human resources associated with patronage is still a serious problem. Even when the number of officials, teachers and maintenance personnel on the payroll is small, selection of these staff is often not based on merit. They often are either relatives or political supporters of the mayor. High turnover when the municipal administration changes further erodes efficiency. There also tends to be an excess of low-level and administrative personnel (cooks, watchmen, cleaning people) relative to teachers.

In many state systems in Brazil the resources available (roughly $250 per student a year) should permit a reasonable level of quality, but inefficiencies in resource use undermine quality. The main problem is overstaffing.[34] State education systems commonly employ nearly half of all state government employees (although they account for only 30 percent or less of total state spending). In many state systems (as in municipal systems), the recruitment of educational staff is driven by patronage rather than efficiency. An

---

[32] See Hanushek et al. (this volume).
[33] See Harbison and Hanushek (1993).
[34] See Paul and Wolff (this volume) for evidence of overstaffing in the university system.

indication of this is the substantial variation across states in the ratio of students to state education employees, from a low of 7:1 to a high of 19:1.

Some of the lowest (and thus most costly) student-to-staffing ratios are found in states with the worst completion and repetition rates, i.e., with the lowest quality schools. The preponderance of nonteaching personnel (sometimes a 2:1 ratio of nonteachers to teachers) is also correlated with poor completion and repetition rates.[35] If the objective is to improve student learning rather than to maximize public employment, large numbers of administrative staff in central offices—as well as some cooks, coffee servers and watchmen—could no doubt be released, freeing up resources for educational purposes.

There are two other effects of administrative inefficiency in Brazil that undermine school quality. First, too many people on the payroll puts downward pressure on average salaries and, over time, undermines the system's ability to attract and retain qualified personnel. Affecting all public school systems in Brazil, this is most apparent in states with the lowest ratios of students to staff. Second, even if average salaries are low, the pressure of the payroll tends to drive out all nonsalary spending. So, schools lack the books, materials and maintenance of physical facilities essential for learning.[36] Indeed, the lower the average skill levels of teachers, the more important these complementary inputs are for learning. In another vicious circle, however, overstaffing leads to lower teacher skills and fewer materials in the schools, and student outcomes are compromised even more.

Low-Quality Private Schools

Enrollments in private schools at all levels in Brazil have grown faster than in the public system over the past two decades.[37] Why? Families turn to private schools for one of two reasons: either they do not have access to the public system, or the private schools meet their demand for different types of education (for example, religious education or higher quality education) than the public schools provide.

At the primary and secondary levels, the tendency of relatively wealthy Brazilian households to send their children to private schools increased as the quality of public schools deteriorated. At the university level,

---

[35] See Paul and Wolff (this volume) for documentation of a similar pattern in the university system.

[36] See Castro and Fletcher (1986).

[37] See James, Braga and Andre (this volume).

working class and poor students are likely to attend private schools.[38] They may have done well enough to complete secondary school, but because of their inferior public secondary education they did not gain entrance to the heavily subsidized public university system. Children of the poor thus have to pay higher prices for a lower quality education at nonsubsidized private universities, while children from high-income families receive a high quality and high cost university education at low prices.[39]

In response to the pressure of low- and middle-income families, who were driven to the private secondary school system by the poor quality of public education, the government until recently intermittently imposed price controls on tuition for private secondary schools.[40] These controls were generally enacted during periods of high inflation, when families experiencing financial stress organized and used political pressure to ease their financial burden. As the private school system expanded, especially at the secondary level, the tuition limits drove down the quality of private schools. The net result was that the private system did not do as much as it might have (had there not been price controls and other regulations) to counteract the erosion of quality in the public school system.

High Costs of Underinvesting in Education

Brazil has paid a high price for its insufficient and inefficient investment in education. Comparisons with other developing countries show that Brazil's low human capital investment has limited increases in the productivity of the labor force. It has also limited changes in household behavior, resulting in smaller reductions in fertility rates, less healthy children, and less supplemental learning at home. The net result has been lower economic growth.

A poor education system has also meant a lost opportunity to improve Brazil's distribution of income, among the most unequal in the world.

Macroeconomic Effects of Poor Educational Investments

Cross-country comparisons have consistently shown that education endowments have a significant positive effect on the growth of output.[41] In a

---

[38] See Paul and Wolff (this volume). Note that the type of courses pursued is an important factor in the public/private decision at the university level.

[39] See Mello e Souza and Silva (this volume).

[40] See chapters by James, Braga and Andre and by Plank et al.

[41] See Barro (1991) and for a recent review of evidence, Birdsall, Ross and Sabot (1995). For evidence that this effect is relatively insensitive to changes in either specification or sample composition, see Levine and Renelt (1991).

sample of 98 countries, enrollment rates in 1966 were a key predictor of economic growth in subsequent decades. Countries with initial enrollment
rates greater than predicted, given their low initial income, were more
likely to see their incomes converge with those of high-income countries.
Likewise, within Brazil, states with higher educational endowments have
tended to grow faster. In this volume, Lau et al. show that for individual
Brazilian states in 1970 and 1980, one additional year of education per person of the labor force increases real output by 20 percent.

Cross-country growth regressions can also be used to provide a rough
measure of the growth foregone as a consequence of Brazil's low level of
investment in human capital. Compare Brazil, which in 1960 had lower enrollment rates than predicted for countries at its level of per capita income,
and Korea, which had higher than predicted enrollment rates.[42] What
would be the impact on Korea's growth path if one were to substitute Brazilian education endowments in 1960 for Korea's? The answer: Korea's
growth from 1960 to 1985 would have been 5.6 percent a year, not 6.1 percent. The reduction is slight because Brazil in 1960 was close to Korea in
primary enrollment rates, with 95 percent enrolled at the primary level in
Brazil and 94 percent in Korea. The 0.5 percentage point reduction in
growth is attributable mostly to a 16 percentage point gap in 1960 secondary enrollment rates—11 percent in Brazil, 27 percent in Korea.

What if Korea had Brazil's enrollment rates in 1970? Its growth rate
from 1980 to 1985 would have been reduced by a third. By 1970 the gap in
secondary enrollment rates had widened to 26 percentage points—26 percent in Brazil, 52 percent in Korea. If in 1970 Korea had had Brazil's enrollment rates, its growth between 1980 and 1985 would have been only 3.4
percent a year, not 5.2 percent. Because compound interest exacts a high
price on current national output from earlier reductions in the growth rate,
the 1.8 percent reduction in Korea's growth rate over 1980–85 would have
meant an 8.3 percent reduction in Korea's per capita GDP in 1985. Conversely, if Brazil had brought its enrollment rates up to those predicted for
countries at its level of GDP per capita, it would have grown faster and its
GDP per capita would be substantially higher than it is today.[43]

The effects of the suppressed demand for skills, a result of Brazil's
inward-looking development strategy and the economic stagnation of the
1980s, will continue to be felt for some years. As skill-based manufacturing
and manufactured exports expand, the demand for educated labor will in-

---

[42] See Birdsall and Sabot (1995).
[43] See Birdsall and Sabot (1995) for an explanation of how the growth rate equations took
account of differences in educational endowments in 1970 as well as in 1960.

crease. But the small pool of skilled workers will be able to demand pre-mium wages, much higher than in Korea.

Lacking skilled labor, Brazil's future may resemble Thailand's pres-ent. In sharp contrast to its East Asian neighbors, Thailand's enrollment rates, particularly at the secondary level, are substantially lower than the norm for countries at its level of income. Thailand is experiencing a success-ful export boom. The resulting extraordinary demand for labor has led to a rapid increase in wages. This, in turn, has eroded the competitiveness of labor-intensive Thai goods in world markets.

In Thailand the scarcity of skilled labor is driving up the cost of hiring educated workers even faster than the cost of unskilled labor. In Korea and Taiwan, because of the abundance of educated labor, the wages of the un-skilled rose faster than those of the skilled. Thai enterprises that have moved into the production of more skill-intensive goods are thus also faced with the problem of competitiveness in international markets.[44] Like Thai-land, Brazil will bear the burden of past underinvestment in human capital into the next century.[45]

Microeconomic Effects of Poor Educational Investments

Cross-country evidence that above average rates of investment in educa-tion are associated with more rapid economic growth is consistent with microeconomic evidence that education augments skills both in the work-place and in the home and thus improves the productivity and earnings of labor.[46] The returns to investment in education are generally competitive with the returns to investment in physical capital[47] and, because of positive

---

[44] See Birdsall and Sabot (1995).

[45] For example, in Brazil in 1985, secondary school graduates earned a roughly 89 percent pre-mium relative to the earnings of uneducated workers, while in Korea the same premium was roughly 30 percent (see Dollar, 1991 and Park, Ross and Sabot, this volume). The premium in Brazil suggests a high rate of return to secondary education in Brazil.

[46] As shown empirically in the chapters by Barros and Ramos and by Strauss and Thomas. See Becker (1964) and Schultz (1961) for the theoretical foundations of human capital analysis. Many of these empirical studies, including those in this volume, do not control for unobserved ability and motivation and family background, which may also influence productivity and earnings and be correlated with schooling.

[47] In a survey of rate of return estimates in 44 countries, Psacharopoulos (1981) found that social rates of return to education are generally competitive with returns to investment in physical capital. Returns, however, are measured by the increments to individual earnings as-sociated with increments to schooling. Since time in school is an input into the process of aug-menting skills, not an output, this approach leaves open the possibility that some other input, such as natural ability, for which schools screen but do not enhance, is actually responsible for

externalities, may increase as the stock of educated workers increases. There is evidence of a threshold effect: once a large part of Brazil's labor force has received at least seven years of education, the economic returns to education are likely to increase because the productivity of one educated worker is greater when working with other educated workers.[48]

By underinvesting in education, Brazil has foregone not only the benefits from increased productivity in the workplace but also from improved education and nutrition in the household. Enrollment rates today for girls in Brazil are higher than for boys at all levels of the educational system. But high dropout rates at the primary level and low aggregate enrollment rates at the secondary level still result in lower enrollment levels for girls in Brazil than in other middle-income countries.

Better educated women have fewer, healthier, and better educated children. Their children are healthier because mothers with higher levels of cognitive skill are able to prepare nutritious meals, take other preventive health care measures, and use medical services.[49] Their children are also better educated,[50] since educated mothers value children's education more than less educated mothers do, and because they are able to supplement classroom learning at home. In the course of daily interactions, an educated mother, at no additional cost, hones the cognitive skills that the child is developing at school. Less educated women, particularly those in the bottom half of the distribution of income, have more children, hence less time to offer each child. Moreover, less educated mothers do not have the cognitive skills to transfer that more educated women have. In sum, the low educational attainment of mothers has a long-term impact on economic growth because their children grow up less productive than they could be.[51]

Table 1.8 measures changes in what might be called the "Hothouse Effect" of mother's quality time on children, comparing Brazil and Korea. In 1965 the fertility rate was slightly higher in Brazil than in Korea (6 and 5,

---

increasing labor productivity and earnings. But there is a new generation of studies that measures the relationship between cognitive outputs of schooling and earnings, while controlling for ability and other inputs, and these studies have confirmed the human capital interpretation of the education-wage relationship. See, for example, Boissiere, Knight and Sabot (1985), Glewwe (1990), and Alderman et al. (1994).

[48] See Birdsall and Sabot (1995), Lucas (1988) and Becker, Murphy and Tamura (1990). Also see Lau et al. (this volume) for macroeconomic evidence of this threshold effect.

[49] See Thomas, Strauss and Henriques (1990, 1991).

[50] See Sathar et al. (1988). Also see Schoeni, Strauss and Thomas (1994).

[51] See Summers (1992). Also see Barro and Wha Lee (1993) for estimates, based on cross-country regressions, of the impact of fertility decline on growth.

Table 1.8. Mother's Inputs per Child, Korea and Brazil

	1965				1975				1985			
	Total Fertility Rate	Mother's education (years)	Mother's time per child	Mother's time, quality weighted, per child	Total Fertility Rate	Mother's education (years)	Mother's time per child	Mother's time, quality weighted, per child	Total Fertility Rate	Mother's education (years)	Mother's time per child	Mother's time, quality weighted, per child
Korea	5	3.2	2.6	3.9	3	4.6	4.0	6.1	2	6.6	5.2	9.8
Brazil	6	2.4	2.3	3.2	4	2.6	3.0	3.9	4	3.4	3.0	4.4

Notes: (1) Measurement used for mother's education = Average years of school for female population of age 25 and over. (2) In computing mother's time per child: only the first 12 years of a child's life were taken into account. Assumptions: a) Spacing: if TFR is < or = to 3, then 3 years apart. If TFR > 3, then 2 years apart; b) Mother's input: 100% up through age of 6; 50%, 6–12 years of age. (3) Mother's time per child: Column A: Only takes into account the effect of number of children and age; Column B: Takes into account the effects of (a) number of children, (b) age, and (c) mother's education.

respectively), and the average years of schooling of mothers was somewhat lower (2.4 and 3.2 years, respectively). By 1985 the gap in years of education of mothers had widened markedly—Korean women on average had nearly twice as many years of schooling as Brazilian women, and, partly as a consequence, the gap in the fertility rate had also widened. While Brazilian women had one-third fewer children in 1985 than in 1965, the total fertility rate in Korea had fallen even more, to half that of the rate in Brazil. The result: in 1985 mothers' time (quality weighted) per child in Korea had more than doubled since 1965 and was three times the Brazilian level.

Continuing Inequality and Low Social Mobility

Although the private and social returns to education are at least as high in Brazil as in other developing countries, the large variance in the quality of education, as well as household incomes, has kept the demand for schooling by the poor, and overall enrollment, low.[52] While the average rate of return to investment in schooling may be high, overall demand for schooling, as well as enrollment rates, will remain constrained unless the government intervenes to improve the quality of the worst-performing schools, which tend to be attended by the poor.

The large quality gap in education perpetuates Brazil's unequal income distribution. Children from poor households have much higher repetition and dropout rates than those from wealthy households; they get neither the quantity nor quality of schooling necessary to compete effectively in the labor market.[53] A consequence of underinvestment in education is not just high inequality in the distribution of current income, but the perpetuation of income inequality from one generation to the next.

The impact of human capital accumulation on the inequality of current pay is theoretically ambiguous. Educational expansion results in a change in the educational composition of the wage labor force. The growth of the educated, high-productivity part of the labor force will by itself initially tend to increase inequality. But there is a possible countervailing tendency, that is, for educational expansion to compress the educational structure of wages and thereby reduce inequality. The scarcity rents earned

---

[52] See Behrman, Birdsall and Kaplan (this volume) for evidence that the rates of return to investments in school quality are of the same or higher magnitude as those to school quantity. Assuming that expected returns influence demand for schooling, then the expected returns to low quality schooling are likely to be low, as is the demand for low quality schooling.
[53] See Mello e Souza and Silva (this volume).

by the more educated erode if the supply of such workers increases relative to demand. Whether the composition effect or the compression effect of educational expansion dominates is an empirical matter. As the chapter by Park, Ross and Sabot shows, in Korea, the compression effect dominated, and the inequality of pay declined, while in Brazil the composition effect dominated, and the inequality of pay increased.

The distribution of income is much more equal in Korea than in Brazil. A substantial portion of this equality gap stems from the difference between the two countries in educational attainment. In Korea, the proportion of high school graduates in the wage labor force rose from 32 percent in 1976 to 44 percent a decade later, and the proportion of workers with post-secondary education rose from 18 to 24 percent. By 1986 the proportion of workers with elementary school or less education had declined from 20 to only 8 percent. The wage premiums earned by educated workers in Korea also declined over the same period, consistent with the prediction that in a competitive market the returns to a factor decrease as its relative supply increases. Standardizing for other characteristics, such as employment experience, workers with a high school education in 1976 earned 47 percent more than primary school graduates. By 1986 that premium had declined to 30 percent. Similarly, the premium earned by workers with higher education declined from 97 to 66 percent. The net effect of educational expansion in Korea reduced the inequality of pay over the decade by 22 percent.

In Brazil, the story was markedly different. Between 1976 and 1985 the absolute increment to the labor force of relatively well-educated workers was so small that it required only a small increase in the demand for educated workers to offset any compression effect the increase in supply might have had on the educational structure of wages. As a result, the educational structure of wages barely changed in Brazil. For example, the wage premium for workers with higher education was 159 percent in 1976 and 151 percent in 1985, both markedly higher than in Korea. The impact of changes in the educational composition of the labor force on the inequality of pay was also substantial. By itself, the composition effect would have increased inequality by more than 8 percent.

The net effect of educational expansion in Brazil over the decade was to increase the inequality of pay by roughly 4 percent, in marked contrast to the 22 percent decline in Korea. If Brazil had adopted Korea's educational strategy—if, in other words, it had expanded primary, secondary and university education more rapidly and achieved the same average levels of schooling attainment as the Koreans—the level of inequality of pay in Brazil in the mid-1980s would have been some 17 percent lower than the inequality actually observed. This 17 percent represents more than one-quarter of the gap between Brazil and Korea in the inequality of pay. In sum, a substantial proportion of the marked difference between Brazil and Korea in inequality of pay is attributable to the difference in their educational policy regimes.[54]

A less equitable distribution of income in turn lowered the demand for schooling in Brazil relative to Korea. Another comparison illustrates by how much Korea's relatively low income inequality contributed to high enrollments, and the extent to which high inequality contributed to low enrollments in Brazil. Income inequality has been shown econometrically to be one of the determinants of differences among countries in enrollment rates. In fact, the negative relationship between inequality and enrollment rates appears to be quite large.[55] The estimated cross-country enrollment rate equation, which includes inequality as an independent variable, can be used to decompose the 27 percentage point gap between Korea and Brazil in secondary enrollment rates.

The conclusion: none of this 27 percentage point difference can be explained by Korea's higher GDP per capita. Nor did less costly teachers contribute to the explanation, because teacher pay in relation to GDP per capita was actually lower in Brazil. The larger school-age cohort in Brazil explained only a small proportion of the gap. Nearly all of the difference, then, can be explained by the greater inequality in the distribution of income in Brazil than in Korea. If income were distributed as equally in Brazil as in Korea, and other determining factors were left unchanged, Korea's secondary enrollment rate, instead of being 27 percentage points higher, would be only 6 percentage points higher.[56]

Low inequality leads to higher demand for education because the per capita income of the bottom income quintile is higher in countries with low inequality than in countries with the same average income, but higher inequality.[57] As noted above, because of budgetary constraints, poor households sometimes do not make human capital investments in their children even when the returns are high. The pressing need to use income simply to subsist precludes high-return education investment. In East Asia, the in-

---

[54] See Park, Ross and Sabot (this volume).
[55] See Williamson (1993). Barros and Lam (this volume) also show that high inequality reduces the demand for schooling within Brazil, though the effect is not as large as in the Williamson study.
[56] See Williamson (1993).
[57] See Birdsall and Sabot (1995).

comes of the poorest-income quintile are further above subsistence level than in Brazil, and fewer families live in absolute poverty. So, the ability of the poor in East Asia to invest in education has been less constrained than in Brazil.

The negative effect of high income inequality on the demand for schooling and enrollments is reinforced in Brazil by the lower density and lower average quality of schools in poor regions. For poor children, access to schools is often more difficult due to longer distances and lack of transport. This implies greater costs of attendance. And the low quality of schools makes it less likely that poor children will acquire the cognitive skills that increase productivity and pay in the labor market. These higher costs and lower payoffs reduce the rate of return to schooling for children from poor families. If the rate of return to investments in schooling is low, so too will be the demand for schooling. So both high inequality in the distribution of income, and high inequality in the distribution of quality schooling, contribute to low demand for schooling by the poor in Brazil.

From the 1950s to the early 1970s in Brazil, the economy expanded rapidly, and there were ample employment opportunities for people from lower socioeconomic backgrounds. The children of the wealthy prospered most, earning high wage premiums for their scarce skills, but children from relatively poor households also benefitted, with relatively easy access to formal sector jobs and considerable on-the-job training. During this period, as shown in the chapter by Pastore and Zylberstajn, there was much upward mobility.

In the 1980s, with Brazil's economy in stagnation, there were fewer opportunities for children from poor families to move up in the socioeconomic hierarchy relative to their parents. Most of the more attractive positions in the labor market were taken by better qualified people from high-income families. The poor, then, had less reason to invest in education. With the economy growing slowly and employment opportunities not expanding, they saw the difficulty, even with education, of competing in the labor market against children of the wealthy. Although there is always such an interaction between the rate of economic growth and the rate of return to schooling (hence, the demand for schooling), the relationship can be particularly strong for those at the bottom of the income distribution.[58] So it is likely that the economic downturn of the 1980s had a particularly adverse impact on education and incomes of the children of the poor.

---

[58] See chapters by Adelman et al. and by Pastore and Zylberstajn.

What to Do in Brazil

The shift to greater macroeconomic stability and to a more market-oriented, open and export-oriented development strategy is setting the stage for increased human capital investment in Brazil.[59] As Brazil changes its development strategy—and, as a consequence the Brazilian economy becomes more dynamic and less volatile—demand for labor and skill will increase. The returns to investment in education will increase, and as families become aware of the payoff to investments in education, so the demand for education will increase. But such a change cannot occur overnight. Educational investments have long gestation periods, and if families are to invest in the education of their children, they have to believe that in 10 to 15 years there will be a significant payoff.

The transformation in Brazil's development strategy can also improve the supply side of the education market.[60] More rapid growth means that more household and government resources will be available for education. Much of the difference between Latin America and East Asia in public spending on basic education per eligible child is accounted for by faster growth of GDP in East Asia (Table 1.2).

The quality of schooling is also likely to improve. If parents see that the payoffs to quality schooling are high, public and private resources will become available to upgrade low-quality schooling. The result can be a reduction in the variance among schools in rates of return, leading to an increase in the net output of the school system as the high dropout and repetition rates of low-quality schools decline. As discussed in the chapter by Gomes-Neto and Hanushek, when students learn more in school, they drop out and repeat less, so education systems will become much more efficient internally.

The returns to improving the quality of schooling could be very high.[61] There are two dimensions to the rates of return to investment in quality improvement. First, as shown in the chapter by Behrman, Birdsall

---

[59] See World Bank (1993) for a discussion of the role of macroeconomic stability in the "East Asian miracle." See Corbo (1991) for a discussion of the importance of sound macroeconomic management for sustained growth in Latin America. He does not, however, note that an improvement in macro-management is likely to stimulate an increase in human capital.

[60] See Barros and Lam (this volume) for evidence that increasing the supply side of education may have a far more powerful effect on enrollments than increasing demand.

[61] See Behrman and Birdsall (1983), Behrman, Ross and Sabot (1992), and Behrman et al. (1994) for evidence from a variety of countries. In this volume, see chapters by Gomes-Neto and Hanushek, and by Hanushek et al. for evidence specific to Brazil.

and Kaplan, if the quality of schooling is improved, graduates will be more productive and earn more. Second, higher quality schooling will lead to lower repetition rates, so that costs associated with repetition will be reduced. It is costly for an educational system to take seven or eight years to put a child through only four or five years of the primary school curriculum. Indeed, the analysis by Hanushek et al. indicates that the potential improvements in internal efficiency may be more than enough to pay for the costs of increasing the quality of schooling. This implies that improvements in school quality need not imply a tradeoff with the quantity provided.

As noted above, 44 percent of higher education students in federal institutions in Brazil come from the top 10 percent of the income distribution.[62] The implication is that a substantial proportion of government subsidies benefit families that can afford to pay the full costs of higher education. In principle, Brazil could direct more public resources to basic education by reducing public spending on higher education. But there is no simple way to reallocate across levels, since university funding is financed by the federal government and basic education is financed by state and local governments. And without structural changes in the way public universities are financed, reduced spending would lead to lower quality and risk a downward spiral. Efforts for structural changes in financing can include more reliance on local businesses and other private sources for universities (which need incentives to seek local funds); administrative reforms at the federal level giving universities more control over faculty hiring and salaries, and over their budgets in general; and more reliance on student fees and tuition. A system of loans and scholarships would need to ensure that the entry to the university system is not influenced by ability to pay.

Finally, Brazil's educational interests can best be served by allowing the private education system to operate relatively unhampered.[63] The government has a role to play in assessing, with standardized exams, the performance of private school students, and in ensuring minimum standards of quality and truth in advertising. But the capping of private school fees has forced false economies on private schools and eroded their quality. The government can sponsor student assessment tests and circulate comparative information on the costs and quality of private schooling—allowing parents to choose the schools they perceive to be best for their children.

---

[62] See Paul and Wolff (this volume).
[63] See James, Braga and Andre (this volume).

Brazil has created a patronage system that allows politicians and senior bureaucrats to settle political debts by giving jobs in the public administration of education to favored individuals. One consequence is that Brazil spends an unusually high percentage of its education budget on administrative expenses. The Brazilian government has the opportunity to make more funds available for basic education by reducing money allocated to administration at all levels of the education system.

The challenge for Brazil is to shift policies so as to convert a set of vicious circles into virtuous circles. Today, low levels of human capital investment mean slow economic growth and high inequality, both of which have contributed, in turn, to low levels of human capital investment. A marked increase in human capital investment would raise growth rates, lower inequality, and stimulate further investment in human capital.

Lessons from the Brazilian Experience

The comparison between Korea and Brazil offers the rest of the developing world a lesson on the advantages that stable growth and sound macroeconomic management confer on human capital accumulation. Brazil was forced into an extended period of slow growth of output and demand for skilled labor by a debt crisis, the product of its inward orientation and external imbalance. This reduced the incentive to invest in human capital. If the economy grows steadily, the incentive to accumulate human capital will increase as the demand for labor—in particular, skilled labor—increases and the risk associated with human capital investments declines. In East Asia, sustained growth over the past 30 years has generated continuous high demand for labor and skill, sending an eye-catching signal to households and to local governments: investment in human capital is a low-risk, high-return investment.

The Brazilian experience also offers a lesson on the danger of relying on excessively capital-intensive techniques of production, which can lead simultaneously to rapid, though unsustainable, growth of output and relatively stagnant demand for labor. Export orientation reduces this risk by forging a growth path that is likely to be consistent both with factor endowments and comparative advantage. A labor-demanding growth path is likely to pull up the wages of unskilled labor.[64] As wages rise, enterprises find that to remain competitive they need to shift from production pro-

---

[64] See Banerji, Campos and Sabot (1994).

cesses that demand unskilled labor into ones that demand capital and skill. When the skill-intensity of labor demand is sustained, the demand side of the economy matches the supply side of the market for educated workers, the rate of return to schooling remains high, and the output of the school system is drawn into the new skill-demanding jobs.[65]

The positive example of East Asia and the negative example of countries such as Brazil, which adopted an import-substitution industrialization strategy, suggest that one way to generate a demand-side dynamic and move to a skill-intensive growth path is to focus on manufactured exports.[66] Besides ensuring growth consistent with comparative advantage, export orientation helps ensure that labor market adjustments do not lead to rent-seeking by labor. One risk of rapid human capital accumulation is that educated school-leavers—undergoing a severe readjustment when finding themselves unemployed or in unexpectedly low-level occupations—might try to use the political process to gain jobs at wages higher than the market justifies. Squandering the benefits of human capital accumulation can be exceedingly costly. Substantial growth may be foregone when resources are diverted from savings and investment to labor subsidies.[67] Egypt, Sri Lanka and the former Soviet Union are examples of countries that successfully accumulated human capital only to find themselves in significant economic trouble because of poor use of that human capital.

In East Asia, the elite apparently saw that the advancement of the poor and working classes would legitimize and sustain their ability to remain in power. In Latin America, the elite apparently felt they could prosper even if other groups did not. A highly unequal distribution of income, a cause and a consequence of that attitude, can ultimately take a toll on growth—as it did in Brazil, where poverty constrained human capital formation and where measures to resolve fiscal problems did not garner widespread popular support until the mid-1990s.[68] In East Asia, economic opportunities for the poor led to heavy investment in human capital; unpalatable fiscal medicine was swallowed, when necessary, by all segments of the population. The East Asian elite assured gains for those near the bottom of the income distribution by adopting policies that increased the supply of, and demand for, high quality education. Educational expansion, in turn, reduced inequality and poverty.

---

[65] See Birdsall and Sabot (1995).
[66] See World Bank (1993).
[67] See Birdsall et al. (1993) and Gelb, Knight and Sabot (1991).
[68] See Birdsall, Ross and Sabot (1995).

Brazil, on the other hand, demonstrates for other developing countries the costs of severely limiting access to high quality schooling of those in the bottom quintiles of the distribution of income.

Because basic education serves the children of the poor as well as the children of the wealthy, but university education caters largely to children of the wealthy, developing countries can concentrate public resources on basic education without foregoing expansion of the university system. University education generally has a high private rate of return; families able to pay will therefore finance their children's university education themselves. Across-the-board subsidies of university education can be replaced by scholarships that target the able but needy. The substantial savings of public resources that results can be used to increase the quantity and improve the quality of basic education.

Government subsidies of primary and secondary schooling are necessary, despite high private rates of return, because social returns to these levels of education are even higher, and because of liquidity constraints in financing education that result from poverty and capital market imperfections. Even for potentially high-yield investments, poor families may not have the resources to take advantage of these opportunities. If the government does not subsidize the educational opportunities of the poor, investment in education will be less than socially optimal.

Although governments in many developing countries should increase their allocations to basic education, they should not attempt to establish a public monopoly over the provision of education. Instead, they can promote a mix of public and private schools. At the university level, greater private education will ease pressures on the government to subsidize the system inappropriately. At the primary and secondary levels, the private system can satisfy excess demand, serve as a standard of excellence, and provide a setting for educational experiments. The risk that private basic education becomes the province of the wealthy can be avoided by ensuring that public education is of high quality.

Another risk is having public schools monopolized by the children of the rich (as in Kenya at the secondary level and in Brazil at the tertiary level) because they are the highly subsidized, high-quality components of a system in which private schools offer relatively low-quality education. To avoid this, rather than erode the quality of the public system, means tested user fees may be appropriate, in combination with subsidies of private education aimed at improving school quality. The government's most important role in private education is assessing the quality of private and public education and providing parents with those assessments—and information on costs—to enable them to make intelligent choices regarding the education of their children.

Another important lesson from Brazil is not to allow the quality of the educational system to erode while trying to expand the quantity of basic education.[69] There need not be a tradeoff between improving quality and increasing quantity. By reducing student repetition rates and the associated costs, investments in quality improvement can pay for themselves. In East Asia, an impressive aspect of educational development has been the improvement of quality at the same time that quantity increased—all achieved with an overall commitment of public resources as a proportion of GDP not much larger than that made by Brazil.

Another lesson from Brazil for other developing countries is that the diversion of resources from the classroom to administration for patronage purposes subverts the aim of achieving a large high-quality system. The administrative dimension of the educational system should be kept as lean and efficient as possible. Once administration becomes bloated, vested interests develop, making it difficult to remove excess employees and reduce excess expenditures.

A final lesson from Brazil is that the household is the school's partner in educating the child. Households that cannot make adequate complementary investments in their children—perhaps because mothers are insufficiently educated—will be at a marked disadvantage, and the entire educational system will suffer. By contrast, one consequence of expanding educational opportunities for girls in East Asia was the subsequent increase in the education of mothers. Better educated mothers then served to increase the productivity of the school system. When the household augments the school, children achieve higher levels of cognitive skills with the same amount of schooling. Schooling for women thus has two payoffs. For women who take jobs, the payoff is in higher labor productivity. For educated women who continue to work in the household, the payoff is in a variety of changes in household behavior. Though some of these benefits of current investment in education may not be reaped for decades, the social returns to such investments are nevertheless high.[70]

---

[69] See Williamson (1993) for evidence of this trend in low-income countries.

[70] See Summers (1992).

REFERENCES

Alderman, H., J. Behrman, D. Ross, and R. Sabot. 1994. The Returns to Endogenous Human Capital in Pakistan's Rural Wage Labor Market. *Oxford Bulletin of Economics and Statistics.*

Banerji, A., E. Campos, and R. Sabot. 1994. The Political Economy of Pay and Employment in Developing Countries. World Bank, Washington D.C.

Barro, Robert J. 1991. Economic Growth in a Cross-Section of Countries. *Quarterly Journal of Economics* 106 (May): 407–43.

Barro, Robert J., and Jong-Wha Lee. 1993. International Comparisons of Educational Attainment. Paper presented at the conference, "How Do National Policies Affect Long-run Growth?" World Bank, February, 1993, Washington, D.C.

Becker, Gary S. 1964. *Human Capital: A Theoretical and Empirical Analysis.* Princeton: Princeton University Press.

Becker, Gary S., Kevin M. Murphy, and Robert Tamura. 1990. Human Capital, Fertility, and Economic Growth. *Journal of Political Economy* XCVIII: S12–S37.

Behrman, Jere, and Nancy Birdsall. 1983. The Quality of Schooling: Quantity Alone is Misleading. *American Economic Review* 73 (December): 928–46.

Behrman, Jere, David Ross, and Richard Sabot. 1992. Improving the Quality Versus Increasing the Quantity of Schooling for Women in Rural Pakistan. Paper presented at the 14th Annual Conference on Economic Issues, Middlebury College, April 3–4, Middlebury, VT.

Behrman, Jere, David Ross, Richard Sabot, and Matthew Tropp. 1994. Improving the Quality versus Increasing the Quantity of Schooling. Williams College, Williamstown, MA.

Birdsall, Nancy, David Ross, and Richard Sabot. 1995. Inequality and Growth Reconsidered. *World Bank Economic Review* 9(3) (September).

Birdsall, Nancy, and Richard Sabot. Virtuous Circles: Human Capital, Growth and Equity in East Asia. Williams College, Williamstown, MA. Mimeo.

Boissière, Maurice, J.B. Knight, and R.H. Sabot. 1985. Earnings, Schooling, Ability and Cognitive Skills. *American Economic Review* 75 (December): 1016–30.

Brazilian Ministry of Education. 1990. First Report of Public Primary Education Assessment System (SAEB). October, 1990.

Castro, Claudio de Moura, and Philip Fletcher. 1986. A Escola que os Brasileiros Freqüentaram em 1985. IPEA/IPLAN.

Clarke, George. 1992. *More Evidence on Income Distribution and Growth.* Working Paper 1064. World Bank, Washington, D.C.

Dollar, David. 1991. Public Policy to Promote Industrialization: The Experience of the East Asian NICs and Lessons for Thailand. In *Decision and Change in Thailand: Three Studies in Support of the Seventh Plan.* Washington, D.C.: World Bank.

Fields, Gary S. 1992. Changing Labor Market Conditions and Economic Development in Hong Kong, Korea, Singapore, and Taiwan. World Bank. Mimeo.

Gelb, Alan, John Knight, and Richard Sabot. 1991. Public Sector Employment, Rent-Seeking and Economic Growth. *Economic Journal* 101(408): 1186–99.

Glewwe, Paul. 1990. Schooling, Skills and the Returns to Education: An Econometric Exploration Using Data from Ghana. World Bank. Mimeo.

Harbison, R.W., and Eric A. Hanushek. 1993. *Educational Performance of the Poor: Lessons from Rural Northeast Brazil.* New York: Oxford University Press.

Knight, J.B., and R. Sabot. 1993. Are the Returns to Primary Schooling Really 26%? *Journal of African Economics.*

Levine, Ross, and David Renelt. 1991. *A Sensitivity Analysis of Cross-Country Growth Regressions.* Working Paper 609. World Bank, Washington, D.C.

Lucas, Robert E., Jr. 1988. On the Mechanics of Development Planning. *Journal of Monetary Economics* 22: 3–42.

Psacharopoulos, George. 1981. Returns to Education: An Updated International Comparison. *Comparative Education* 17(3): 583–604.

Psacharopoulos, George, and Ana María Arriagada. 1992. The Educational Composition of the Labour Force: An International Update. *Journal of Educational Planning and Administration* 6(2) (April): 141–59.

Sachs, Jeffrey. 1985. External Debt and Macroeconomic Performance in Latin America and East Asia. In *Brookings Papers on Economic Activity,* eds. W. Brainard and G. Perry. Washington, D.C.: The Brookings Institution.

Sathar, Zeba, Nigel Crook, Christine Callum, and Shahnaz Kazi. 1988. Women's Status and Fertility Change in Pakistan. *Population and Development Review* 14(3): 415–32.

Schoeni, Robert F., John Strauss, and Duncan Thomas. 1994. Education, Gender and Intergenerational Transmission: Evidence on Three Generations in Urban Brazil.

Schultz, T.W. 1961. Investment in Human Capital. *American Economic Review* 51(1): 1–17.

Summers, Lawrence H. 1992. *Investing in All the People.* Washington, D.C.: World Bank.

Thomas, Duncan, John Strauss, and María Helena Henriques. 1991. How Does Mother's Education Affect Child Height? *Journal of Human Resources* 26(2) (Spring): 183–211.

————. 1990. Child Survival, Height for Age and Household Characteristics in Brazil. *Journal of Development Economics* 33(2) (October): 197–234.

Williamson, J. 1993. Human Capital Deepening, Inequality and Demographic Events along the Asia-Pacific Rim. In *Human Resources in Development along the Asia-Pacific Rim,* eds. Naohiro Ogawa, Gavin W. Jones, and Jeffrey Williamson. Singapore: Oxford University Press.

World Bank. 1993. *The East Asian Miracle.* New York: Oxford University Press.

Where Does Brazil Fit? Schooling Investments in an International Perspective

2

Jere R. Behrman and Ryan Schneider

Increasing the availability of schooling is widely thought to have significant potential for increasing growth and reducing inequality in developing countries. While there may be some disagreements about just how effective schooling is for these purposes and how well empirical estimates of the impact of schooling control for factors such as ability, motivation, schooling quality and family background, there seems to be widespread agreement that the effects of schooling are substantial in many developing countries.[1]

This chapter is devoted to examining a number of dimensions of the Brazilian experience with schooling and economic outcomes. The purpose is to provide a simple, descriptive cross-country perspective regarding how Brazilian schooling investments compare with those in other developing countries, based primarily on data from the World Bank (1990), supplemented by data from UNESCO (1965, 1970). Such description is limited by the data that are available and by data measurement problems. For example, only enrollment rates and literacy rates are available to represent schooling investments and stocks of educated individuals.[2] There are no controls for grade repetition, nor for the quality of schooling.[3] Moreover, there are differences in definitions of variables such as literacy across countries. Also, only per capita GNP figures at official exchange rates are available to represent per capita income for many of the countries, so these data

---

[1] For surveys of the impact of schooling on growth and distribution, see Behrman (1990a,b,c), Colclough (1982), Eisemon (1988), Haddad et al. (1990), King (1990), King and Hill (1991), Psacharopoulos (1985, 1988), Schultz (1988, 1991), and World Bank (1980, 1981, 1990, 1991).

[2] Gross enrollment rates are used; these can be misleading, as they include students of all ages in the numerator, but only of appropriate ages in the denominator, and fail to reflect high rates of repetition associated with low quality.

[3] Some data are available on primary net enrollment rates and primary pupil-teacher ratios, but data are missing for many countries in each case (including Brazil in the second case) so we do not include them in this study. Nancy Birdsall has observed in private correspondence with us that in Brazil almost all graduates of primary school continue on to secondary school, so the

are used instead of purchasing-power-parity measures of income per capita. Even aside from the data problems, description in itself does not answer any very profound questions, nor does it provide a very firm basis for comments on causality. But it may provoke some questions about why the Brazilian experience differs, to the extent that it does, from that of other developing countries.

This chapter first looks at enrollment and illiteracy rates for Brazil in comparison with averages for all low- and middle-income countries for 1965 and 1987. This is followed by a summary of where Brazil stands with regard to total schooling enrollment rates and the implied expected years of schooling for a synthetic cohort based on cross-country regressions that control for GNP per capita and an indicator of the schooling price in the same two years. Similar relationships are then examined for males and females and the differences between them. Finally, the chapter summarizes where Brazil stands with regard to changes in these variables between 1965 and 1987 based on cross-country regressions that control for changes in real GNP per capita and in the indicator of the price of schooling during this period and for all country-specific fixed effects.

Brazilian Enrollment and Illiteracy Rates in 1965 and 1987

Table 2.1 gives primary, secondary and tertiary school enrollment rates and adult illiteracy rates for Brazil and for the averages for low- and middle-income country groups.[4]

---

low secondary schooling enrollments noted below probably in part reflect the failure of the primary schools to get students through the primary system (perhaps because of limited schooling quality), which seems to have important labor market effects in Brazil, as reported in Behrman and Birdsall (1983, 1985) and Behrman, Birdsall and Kaplan (this volume), and to affect persistence in school in Brazil as emphasized by Gomes-Neto and Hanushek (1991). Therefore, in an important sense the high Brazilian gross primary school enrollment rates may be misleading. However, similar problems exist for enrollment data for other countries used in the regressions in this study, and we do not have a basis for concluding with much confidence that they are particularly severe for Brazil. See Behrman and Rosenzweig (1992) for a discussion of problems with the cross-country data on schooling. There also are problems with the comparability of data on income, as discussed by Ahmad (1992), Heston (1992) and Srinivasan (1992).

[4] According to the World Bank (1990), Brazil in 1988 was high in the lower-middle-income country group, and was 45th from the top (or 76th from the bottom) in terms of GNP per capita in that year (out of a total of 121 countries). In terms of annual growth rates in GNP per capita for the 1965–89 period, Brazil (with 3.6 percent) tied Egypt for 14th place among the 101 countries for which such rates are given, and had the highest growth rate in the Western Hemisphere. The countries with higher reported rates were Botswana (8.6 percent), Singapore (7.2), Hong Kong (6.3), Republic of Korea (6.8), Oman (6.4), China (5.4), Lesotho (5.2), Hungary (5.1), Japan (4.3), Thailand (4), Malaysia (4), Saudi Arabia (3.8), and Cameroon (3.7).

Table 2.1. Brazilian Mean Enrollment and Literacy Rates, 1965 and 1987
(Percentage of age group enrolled in education)

| | Primary | | | | Secondary | | | | | | Tertiary | | Adult illiteracy rates in 1985 | |
| | Total | | Female | | Total | | Female | | | | Total | | | |
	1965	1987	1965	1987	1965	1987	1965	1987			1965	1987	Total	Female
Brazil	108	103	108	—	16	39	16	45			2	11	22	24
Low-income	73	104	—	95	20	37	—	29			2	—	44	58
Middle-income	92	104	86	101	26	54	22	54			6	17	26	31

Source: World Bank (1990).

Enrollment rates reflect one important component of the current investment in schooling. In 1965, Brazilian total and female primary schooling enrollment rates were over 100 percent of the numbers of individuals in the primary school age group,[5] with no gender gap. These rates were high relative to the means of 92 percent for the total and 86 percent for females for current middle-income countries. The secondary enrollment rates were 16 percent both for the total and for females, again with no gender gap. These rates were low, more so for males, relative to the means for current middle-income countries of 26 percent for the total and 22 percent for females. The total tertiary enrollment rate of 2 percent also was low relative to the 6 percent mean for current middle-income countries.

Thus, in 1965 Brazil had relatively high primary school enrollment rates and a relatively small gender gap at both the primary and the secondary levels, but relatively low post-primary enrollment rates. Therefore, Brazil seemed, more so than the average developing country, to be following the educational investment strategy of those who advocate a focus on primary schooling both for distributional reasons, and because the social returns reputedly are relatively high. Likewise, investments in males and females were relatively equal; this is consistent both with equity aims and with evidence that rates of returns (both economic and in such areas as health) tend to be as high for schooling investments in females as for males.

In 1987, Brazilian total primary schooling enrollment rates were slightly lower (presumably reflecting fewer enrollers outside of the normal primary school age range), but still over 100 percent and at about the same level as the means for all developing countries. The Brazilian total secondary school enrollment rate had increased substantially from 16 to 39 percent by 1987, but the latter level and the change both were below those for the means for middle-income countries. The Brazilian female secondary school enrollment rate had increased more than the total, from 16 to 45 percent. This implied the opening up of a gender gap favoring females at this level of schooling, a relative rarity among developing countries.[6] But despite the relatively large increase in female as compared with male Brazilian second-

---

[5] These enrollment rates are defined as, for example, the number of students in primary school relative to the population aged six to 11. If there are enough primary school students who are under six or over 11, the enrollment rate so calculated can be greater than 100 percent.

[6] Gender gaps favoring females in secondary school enrollment levels also are reported in World Bank (1990) only for Sri Lanka, the Philippines, the Dominican Republic, El Salvador, Botswana, Jamaica, Ecuador, Chile, Costa Rica, Poland, Panama, Nicaragua, Argentina, Venezuela, Trinidad and Tobago, and Romania. The magnitude of this gap is larger than in Brazil only for the Dominican Republic and Nicaragua.

ary school enrollment rates, Brazilian female secondary school enrollment rates in 1987 and their changes between 1965 and 1987 were smaller than the means for middle-income countries. Brazilian tertiary enrollment rates also increased substantially from 2 to 11 percent between 1965 and 1987, but again both the change between these years and the absolute level in the latter year were below the means for middle-income countries. Thus, by 1987, Brazil seems to have lost the relative advantage in primary schooling and not caught up with the developing country average in post-primary schooling; the investments in female schooling, however, remained relatively favorable.

Adult illiteracy rates reflect (inversely) one possibly important component of the stock of human capital. In 1985, the Brazilian total adult illiteracy rate was 22 percent, somewhat below the 26 percent mean for middle-income countries. The illiteracy rate for females was slightly higher at 24 percent, but somewhat below the 31 percent mean for middle-income countries. Thus, the relatively strong investment in basic schooling in Brazil apparently resulted in somewhat below average illiteracy by the mid-1980s, with a smaller than average gender gap in illiteracy. However illiteracy refers only to basic (probably primary) schooling, and not to the post-primary education levels at which Brazilian investments have long been below the means for middle-income countries.

Comparisons of Total Brazilian Schooling Investments with Cross-Country Experience

We now turn to comparisons of Brazilian schooling investments in 1965 and 1987 with cross-country regressions based on all countries studied in World Bank (1990) that have the necessary data. The dependent variables are the total enrollment rates for each of the three schooling levels and the expected years of schooling implied by those rates for a synthetic cohort that experiences such schooling enrollment rates.[7]

We present four cross-country regressions for each dependent variable. Each of these regressions controls for average per capita income[8] in the

---

[7] The numerators for the enrollment rates for the three schooling levels are, respectively, the number of children six to 11, 12 to 17 and 20 to 24 years old. Therefore the expected years of schooling for a synthetic cohort that faced the enrollment rates for these three schooling levels recorded for Brazil in 1987, for example, is $9.07 = 1.03*6 + 0.39*6 + 0.11*5$, given the enrollment rates for that year in Table 2.1.

[8] The distribution of income also may be important, but comparable measures of income distribution are available for relatively few countries, so we do not explore this possibility.

relevant year and the last two control for an indicator of the scarcity cost, or the price of schooling. The income and price effects can be interpreted as representing the income and price demand effects for school investments, under the presumption that such effects are transmitted in part through the political system for public schools in addition to any more direct demand effects for private schools.[9] The proxy that we use for the relative price of schooling is the adult literacy rate.[10] [11] The argument for interpreting this variable as a price variable has three components: First, the relative price of sufficiently skilled labor to staff at the school levels that most students attend, and of inputs that are complementary with schooling,[12] is inversely related to the share of the adult population that has such skills.[13] Second, the adult literacy rate is a good proxy for the relative size of the adult population with such skills.[14] Third, the literacy rate does not represent other,

---

[9] Schultz (1987, 1988) and Behrman (1987), for example, give such an interpretation. From a micro perspective, however, if schooling were purely an investment and if capital markets were perfect, income would not enter into the schooling investment decision, though interest rates would. We have not explored the possibility that interest rates enter into these relations.

[10] We actually use the literacy rates for about 1965 and 1985 because that is what is available in World Bank (1990) and in UNESCO (1965, 1970). Since adult literacy refers to a stock concept, we do not think that the slight lags between the outcomes of interest and the literacy rates have much effect on the estimates. In fact, to the extent that there is some lag in adjustment to relative scarcities, it may be preferable to use lagged values for the relative stock of literate adults.

[11] The direct measure that we would like to have is the relative price of time of adults with control for the qualifications needed to be school teachers. Such data are not readily available. Conceptually one can think of estimating such data with controls for selectivity into different occupations, but with existing data this would be an enormous task to undertake for all of the countries included in the cross-country regressions. Nancy Birdsall suggested to us that lagged secondary schooling enrollment rates might be a better proxy for the availability of teachers in Brazil than the literacy rate. To translate past enrollment rates over several decades into a measure of the stock of adults with such a level of education would be possible, but also is beyond the scope of this project (and past enrollment rates are not available for many countries before the 1960s, so assumptions would have to be made about the rates for earlier years in order to generate such a measure).

[12] For example, a child with more educated parents is likely to have a home environment that is complementary with more schooling ceteris paribus. Therefore on a more aggregated level, if adult literacy is higher, all else equal, the price of time that children spend with educated adults is likely to be less, with complementary effects on the benefits from time spent in school.

[13] In the comparison of two different situations with the same literacy rates but different demand intensities for literate labor, the relative price of literate workers is likely to be higher where the demand intensity for literate workers is greater. This means that the literacy rate is a noisy proxy for the relative price of literate adults, with the implication ceteris paribus that its coefficient is biased towards zero as a representation of the true price effect.

[14] Presumably, how good a proxy it is depends in substantial part on the levels of schooling that most students attend. That is, it probably is a better proxy for primary and lower-middle schooling than for upper secondary and tertiary schooling.

nonprice considerations.[15] Because there may be some gender segmentation in the labor markets for skilled persons, we include the literacy rates separately for adult males and females. Because the literacy rates are proxies for the relevant scarcity prices, and have some definite limitations as such, we present the regressions without them as well as with them.[16]

The four regressions that we present for each outcome are as follows: (A) only with a quadratic in real per capita GNP, with the quadratic to allow for changing marginal income effects; (B) both with a dichotomous variable for the country group (i.e., lower-middle-income, upper-middle-income, and high-income, with low-income as the reference group) into which each country falls and with a quadratic in per capita GNP to capture variations within these broad country groups; (C) same as (A) but with both the male and female adult literacy rates; and (D) same as (B) but with both male and female adult literacy rates. Since regression (A) is the simplest, we use it when we present some figures below. However, for some of the outcomes, the income effect is more consistent with the variance in the dependent variable if we include in addition the country group dichotomous variables as in (B), which suggests an added income nonlinearity beyond that captured by the quadratic in income.[17] Regressions (C) and (D), with the price proxies, are in some cases considerably more consistent with the variance in the educational investments of interest in the cross-country regressions in Tables 2.2 and 2.3.[18] For this reason we focus on alternatives (C) and (D) in

---

[15] For example, there may be cultural differences across countries that affect both the stock of literate adults and current investments in schooling of children, for which literacy may proxy in cross-country regressions. If this is the case in part, then it may be misleading to interpret the estimated impact of literacy in cross-country regressions as purely a price effect. But the regressions that include literacy rates among the right-side variables as controls still are preferred over those that do not, so that the estimated income coefficients are not biased by such cultural effects. Later in this chapter we explore the possibility that the literacy rates are representing unobserved fixed effects such as culture.

[16] Richard Sabot suggests that the literacy rate, by representing accumulative past schooling enrollments, reflects serial correlation in enrollment rates. This probably is true, but the wage for skilled labor also reflects the same phenomenon if it declines relatively with relatively more skilled labor as argued, for example, in Knight and Sabot (1990) for a particular developing country context on the basis of careful micro empirical analysis. We present estimates both with and without the literacy rates to see if the results change much if they are dropped.

[17] For example, the R^2s in Table 2.2 for primary schooling increase from 0.18 to 0.30 for 1965 and from 0.13 to 0.34 for 1987 with this addition. See also Table 2.4.

[18] For primary school enrollments, once again, the R^2s in Table 2.2, for regressions (A), (B), (C), and (D), respectively, are 0.18, 0.30, 0.48 and 0.45 for 1965 and 0.13, 0.34, 0.65 and 0.65 for 1987. For the differenced regressions over time in Table 2.4, however, the addition of the adult literacy rates does not increase so much the consistency of the estimates with the variance in the changes in the enrollment rates and in the expected years of schooling for synthetic cohorts.

Table 2.2. Cross-Country Regressions for Total Schooling Investments, 1965 and 1987

Dependent Variable		Constant	Income	Income²	Country Group			Adult Literacy Rate		R²	N	F	Residual for Brazil
					Lower-Middle	Upper-Middle	High	Male	Female				
1965 Enrollment Rates													
1. Primary	(A)	68.6 (19.2)	0.00050 (4.3)	-1.2*10-7 (2.7)						.18	96	11.9	34.8
	(B)	56.2 (12.4)	0.0032 (0.8)	-6.5*10-8 (0.7)	25.3 (3.8)	31.0 (2.1)	20.7 (0.7)			.30	96	9.2	23.7
	(C)	46.2 (6.4)	-0.00072 (0.6)	4.1*10-8 (1.1)				.82 (3.1)	-.20 (0.9)	.45	64	14.1	21.3
	(D)	41.3 (5.2)	-0.0033 (1.1)	9.9*10-8 (1.4)	11.4 (1.8)	26.1 (2.3)	27.9 (1.3)	.83 (3.2)	-.26 (1.1)	.48	64	9.4	20.1
2. Secondary	(A)	11.0 (5.9)	0.0069 (11.2)	-1.7*10-7 (7.7)						.60	94	72.9	-1.4
	(B)	8.2 (3.3)	0.0038 (1.7)	-9.9*10-8 (1.8)	9.2 (2.5)	12.4 (1.5)	25.9 (1.5)			.62	94	31.4	-4.9
	(C)	-4.7 (1.0)	0.0031 (3.9)	-6.4*108 (2.6)				.37 (2.1)	.048 (0.3)	.72	62	41.1	-8.6
	(D)	-4.4 (0.8)	-0.00097 (0.5)	2.6*10-8 (0.5)	3.0 (0.7)	7.4 (1.0)	31.3 (2.1)	.41 (2.3)	.016 (0.1)	.73	62	25.3	-8.9
3. Tertiary	(A)	1.4 (2.0)	0.0023 (6.6)	-9.1*10-8 (3.5)						.51	88	46.7	-1.5
	(B)	0.47 (0.5)	0.0041 (3.2)	-1.5*10-7 (2.9)	-0.20 (0.1)	-4.0 (1.0)	-10.7 (1.4)			.51	88	19.4	-2.0
	(C)	-2.5 (1.1)	0.0012 (2.3)	-4.3*10-8 (1.3)				.084 (1.0)	.018 (0.2)	.49	61	15.5	-3.0
	(D)	-2.4 (0.9)	0.0028 (1.8)	-1.0*10-7 (1.6)	-2.5 (1.1)	-5.8 (1.1)	-10.6 (1.1)	.086 (1.0)	.024 (0.3)	.47	61	8.9	-2.5

4. Years of School	(A)	4.7 (14.8)	0.0012 (7.8)	-6.0*10-8 (5.1)						.50	85	44.0 1.7
	(B)	3.7 (9.4)	0.0018 (3.3)	-7.7*10-8 (3.5)		-1.0 (0.6)	-3.1 (1.0)			.57	85	23.9 0.7
	(C)	2.2 (4.3)	0.00045 (3.8)	-2.5*10-8 (3.5)	1.5 (2.3)			.072 (4.0)	-.0057 (0.4)	.80	58	57.8 0.6
	(D)	1.9 (3.3)	0.00075 (2.1)	-3.7*10-8 (2.6)	-0.026 (0.1)	1.4 (1.3)	-1.6 (0.8)	.077 (4.2)	-.0085 (0.5)	.80	58	33.6 0.5

1987 Enrollment Rates

5. Primary	(A)	81.8 (23.2)	0.0059 (3.4)	-2.7*10-7 (2.8)						.13	91	7.8 10.2
	(B)	67.8 (16.8)	0.0089 (1.8)	-3.2*10-7 (1.8)	24.1 (3.7)	11.2 (0.8)	-22.4 (0.8)			.34	91	10.2 -6.0
	(C)	22.0 (2.8)	-0.0020 (1.4)	4.5*10-8 (0.6)				1.0 (4.3)	.014 (0.1)	.65	81	38.1 2.7
	(D)	21.4 (2.8)	.000086 (0.02)	-2.6*10-8 (0.2)	6.0 (1.1)	-5.2 (0.5)	-8.4 (0.3)	.97 (4.2)	.0041 (0.02)	.65	81	22.8 -2.6

6. Secondary	(A)	25.3 (9.5)	0.011 (8.5)	-3.9*10-7 (5.5)						.70	90	104.7 -7.4
	(B)	17.2 (5.6)	0.0069 (1.9)	-2.0*10-7 (1.4)	18.7 (3.8)	32.0 (3.0)	18.4 (0.8)			.77	90	60.5 -10.5
	(C)	-8.5 (1.2)	0.0063 (5.1)	-2.1*10-7 (3.3)				.48 (2.1)	.11 (0.6)	.84	80	106.0 -11.5
	(D)	-7.9 (1.2)	0.0032 (0.9)	-7.2*10-8 (0.6)	8.1 (1.8)	23.9 (2.5)	21.7 (1.0)	.51 (2.4)	-.0043 (0.02)	.85	80	68.2 -7.8

(continued)

Table 2.2. (cont.)

Dependent Variable		Constant	Income	Income^2	Country Group			Adult Literacy Rate		R^2	N	F	Residual for Brazil
					Lower-Middle	Upper-Middle	High	Male	Female				
7. Tertiary	(A)	6.1 (4.1)	0.0034 (5.9)	$-9.8*10-8$ (3.5)						.51	88	46.5	-1.7
	(B)	1.5 (0.8)	0.0016 (1.1)	$-3.5*10-8$ (0.7)	10.4 (3.7)	12.6 (2.5)	15.0 (1.4)			.57	88	24.5	-4.0
	(C)	3.3 (0.7)	0.0018 (2.9)	$-5.1*10-8$ (1.8)				-.26 (1.7)	.42 (3.5)	.65	78	37.1	-7.1
	(D)	3.0 (0.6)	0.00061 (0.4)	$-1.60*10-8$ (0.3)	5.9 (1.9)	7.5 (1.3)	13.4 (1.0)	-.26 (1.7)	.37 (3.0)	.65	78	21.9	-7.0
8. Years of school	(A)	6.6 (16.2)	0.0012 (6.3)	$-4.8*10-8$ (4.4)						.53	83	48.0	0.1
	(B)	4.8 (11.2)	0.00079 (1.7)	$-2.3*10-8$ (1.3)	3.9 (5.9)	4.4 (3.2)	2.2 (0.8)			.72	83	42.8	-1.1
	(C)	0.33 (0.4)	0.00036 (2.4)	$-1.2*10-8$ (1.6)				.095 (3.5)	.016 (0.7)	.85	73	103.7	-0.8
	(D)	0.19 (0.2)	-.000057 (0.1)	$4.0*10-9$ (0.3)	2.0 (3.8)	2.9 (2.7)	3.9 (1.5)	.099 (4.0)	-.0037 (0.2)	.87	73	73.2	-0.7

Sources: World Bank (1990) and UNESCO (1965, 1970).

Note: Enrollment rates (and therefore residuals for enrollment rates) are in percentages. Years of school (i.e., expected years of school for a synthetic cohort as defined in the text) are in years (and therefore so are the residuals for these regressions).

Table 2.3. Cross-Country Regressions for Male and Female Schooling Investments, 1965 and 1987

Dependent Variable		Constant	Income	Income²	Country Group Lower-Middle	Upper-Middle	High	Adult Literacy Rate Male	Female	R²	N	F	Residual for Brazil
1965 Enrollment Rates													
Primary													
1. Female	(A)	58.6 (14.6)	0.0065 (4.9)	-1.6×10^{-7} (3.3)						.21	94	13.7	43.4
	(B)	44.0 (8.7)	0.0054 (1.2)	-1.2×10^{-7} (1.1)	28.0 (3.7)	32.9 (1.9)	14.9 (0.4)			.33	94	10.4	31.0
	(C)	34.4 (4.7)	-0.0016 (1.4)	6.3×10^{-8} (1.7)				.67 (2.4)	.14 (0.6)	.59	62	23.1	24.5
	(D)	29.7 (3.7)	-0.0035 (1.2)	1.1×10^{-7} (1.5)	11.2 (1.7)	26.3 (2.3)	22.1 (1.0)	.63 (2.3)	.12 (0.5)	.61	62	15.0	23.4
2. Male	(A)	77.5 (21.7)	0.0041 (3.4)	-8.5×10^{-8} (2.0)						.13	94	8.2	26.8
	(B)	66.0 (14.3)	0.0021 (0.5)	-3.3×10^{-8} (0.3)	23.6 (3.5)	27.6 (1.8)	20.9 (0.7)			.23	94	6.7	16.4
	(C)	57.6 (7.2)	0.00035 (0.3)	1.5×10^{-8} (0.4)				1.0 (3.3)	-.57 (2.1)	.28	62	7.1	18.2
	(D)	53.0 (6.0)	-0.0032 (0.9)	9.4×10^{-8} (1.2)	12.3 (1.7)	27.0 (2.1)	34.9 (1.4)	.99 (3.3)	-.61 (2.2)	.30	62	4.9	16.7
3. Male-Female	(A)	18.9 (8.7)	-0.0024 (3.4)	7.4×10^{-8} (2.9)						.09	94	5.6	-16.7
	(B)	21.9 (7.4)	-0.0033 (1.2)	9.2×10^{-8} (1.4)	-4.4 (1.0)	-5.3 (0.5)	6.0 (0.3)			.09	94	2.8	-14.5
	(C)	23.2 (6.1)	0.0020 (3.3)	-4.8×10^{-8} (2.5)				.34 (2.3)	-.71 (5.4)	.62	62	26.2	-6.4
	(D)	23.2 (5.4)	0.00034 (0.2)	-1.2×10^{-8} (0.3)	1.2 (0.3)	0.73 (0.1)	12.8 (1.1)	.37 (2.5)	-.73 (5.5)	.61	62	15.1	-6.7

(continued)

Table 2.3. (cont.)

Dependent Variable		Constant	Income	Income²	Country Group			Adult Literacy Rate		R²	N	F	Residual for Brazil
					Lower-Middle	Upper-Middle	High	Male	Female				
Secondary													
4. Female	(A)	7.8 (4.1)	0.0071 (11.4)	$-1.8*10-7$ (8.1)						.61	93	73.3	1.7
	(B)	4.8 (1.9)	0.0038 (1.7)	$-1.0*10-7$ (1.9)	9.5 (2.5)	13.5 (1.6)	27.4 (1.6)			.62	93	31.8	−1.9
	(C)	−5.4 (1.2)	0.0025 (3.3)	$-5.0*10-8$ (2.2)				.12 (0.7)	.34 (2.1)	.77	61	50.7	−7.6
	(D)	−5.4 (1.1)	−0.0016 (0.8)	$4.0*10-8$ (0.9)	3.4 (0.8)	8.3 (1.1)	31.5 (2.3)	.16 (0.9)	.30 (1.9)	.78	61	31.4	−7.9
5. Male	(A)	13.8 (6.9)	0.0068 (10.3)	$-1.6*10-7$ (6.9)						.58	93	64.0	−4.1
	(B)	10.6 (3.9)	0.0040 (1.6)	$-9.7*10-8$ (1.7)	9.7 (2.4)	11.9 (1.3)	24.3 (1.4)			.59	93	27.6	−8.0
	(C)	−3.5 (0.6)	0.0038 (4.2)	$-7.8*10-8$ (2.7)				.59 (2.8)	−.21 (1.1)	.65	61	29.5	−9.6
	(D)	−3.3 (0.5)	−0.00030 (0.1)	$1.2*10-8$ (0.2)	3.1 (0.6)	6.9 (0.8)	31.2 (1.8)	.64 (3.0)	−.25 (1.3)	.66	61	18.1	−10.0
6. Male-Female	(A)	6.1 (6.0)	−0.00025 (0.8)	$1.7*10-8$ (1.4)						.01	93	1.5	−5.8
	(B)	5.8 (4.1)	0.00019 (0.1)	$6.7*10-8$ (0.2)	0.21 (0.1)	−1.6 (0.3)	−3.0 (0.3)			−.02	93	0.6	−6.2
	(C)	2.0 (0.7)	0.0013 (2.9)	$-2.7*10-8$ (2.0)				.47 (4.5)	−.55 (5.8)	.39	61	10.8	−2.0
	(D)	2.1 (0.7)	0.0013 (1.1)	$-2.8*10-8$ (1.0)	−0.29 (0.1)	−1.4 (0.3)	−0.34 (0.0)	.48 (4.4)	−.55 (5.6)	.36	61	5.9	−2.1

Years of School

7. Female												
(A)	3.9 (11.0)	0.0014 (7.7)	$-6.6*10^{-8}$ (5.1)						.50	84	43.4	2.4
(B)	2.7 (6.2)	0.0020 (3.3)	$-8.5*10^{-8}$ (3.5)						.57	84	23.5	1.4
(C)	1.4 (2.7)	0.00032 (2.7)	$-2.1*10^{-8}$ (2.9)	1.6 (2.3)	−0.90 (0.5)	−3.7 (1.0)	.049 (2.7)	.033 (2.0)	.85	57	81.2	0.9
(D)	1.0 (1.8)	0.00067 (1.9)	$-3.4*10^{-8}$ (2.4)	−0.023 (0.0)	−1.4 (1.3)	−1.9 (0.9)	.053 (2.8)	.031 (1.9)	.85	57	46.7	0.8
8. Male												
(A)	5.4 (17.4)	0.0011 (7.3)	$-5.5*10^{-8}$ (4.9)						.47	84	38.6	1.1
(B)	4.4 (11.3)	0.0017 (3.1)	$-7.2*10^{-8}$ (3.3)	1.5 (2.4)	−1.1 (0.6)	−2.8 (0.9)			.55	84	21.7	0.1
(C)	3.1 (5.3)	0.00058 (4.3)	$-2.9*10^{-8}$ (3.6)				.093 (4.4)	−.043 (2.2)	.70	57	34.0	0.4
(D)	2.8 (4.3)	0.00084 (2.1)	$-4.0*10^{-8}$ (2.5)	0.021 (0.0)	−1.4 (1.1)	−1.3 (0.6)	.098 (4.5)	−.045 (2.4)	.70	57	19.8	0.3
9. Male–Female												
(A)	1.6 (8.4)	−0.00022 (2.3)	$1.0*10^{-8}$ (1.5)						.07	84	4.1	−1.4
(B)	1.7 (6.7)	−0.00034 (1.0)	$1.3*10^{-8}$ (1.0)	−0.069 (0.2)	−0.15 (0.1)	0.93 (0.5)			.05	84	2.0	−1.3
(C)	1.8 (5.3)	0.00026 (3.5)	$-8.6*10^{-9}$ (1.9)				.044 (3.7)	−.076 (7.1)	.67	57	30.0	−0.5
(D)	1.8 (4.7)	0.00017 (0.7)	$-5.7*10^{-9}$ (0.6)	0.044 (0.1)	−0.025 (0.0)	0.59 (0.4)	.046 (3.7)	−.076 (7.0)	.66	57	16.6	−0.5

(continued)

Table 2.3. (cont.)

1987 Enrollment Rates

Primary

Dependent Variable		Constant	Income	Income²	Country Group Lower-Middle	Country Group Upper-Middle	Country Group High	Adult Literacy Rate Male	Adult Literacy Rate Female	R²	N	F	Residual for Brazil
10. Female	(A)	74.4 (18.2)	0.0073 (3.7)	$-3.3*10-7$ (3.0)						.17	87	9.8	...
	(B)	58.1 (12.6)	0.01 (2.0)	$-4.0*10-7$ (1.9)	28.3 (3.8)	12.4 (0.8)	-27.1 (0.8)			.38	87	11.6	...
	(C)	13.0 (1.6)	-0.0025 (1.7)	$5.8*10-8$ (0.8)				.76 (3.1)	.41 (2.1)	.73	77	52.6	...
	(D)	12.1 (1.5)	-0.00017 (0.0)	$-2.6*10-8$ (0.2)	7.5 (1.4)	-7.7 (0.7)	-8.4 (0.3)	.70 (2.9)	.42 (2.2)	.74	77	32.7	...
11. Male	(A)	88.8 (25.9)	0.0044 (2.6)	$-2.1*10-7$ (2.2)						.07	87	4.3	...
	(B)	76.8 (19.0)	0.0073 (1.5)	$-2.6*10-7$ (1.4)	20.7 (3.2)	8.9 (0.6)	-20.5 (0.7)			.25	87	6.7	...
	(C)	29.4 (3.6)	-0.0021 (1.4)	$5.7*10-8$ (0.7)				1.3 (5.2)	-.35 (1.8)	.54	77	23.5	...
	(D)	29.0 (3.5)	-0.00044 (0.1)	$1.3*10-9$ (0.0)	6.1 (1.1)	-3.1 (0.3)	-6.1 (0.2)	1.2 (5.0)	-.35 (1.8)	.54	77	13.8	...
12. Male-Female	(A)	14.4 (8.3)	-0.0029 (3.5)	$1.2*10-7$ (2.6)						.19	87	11.4	...
	(B)	18.7 (8.6)	-0.0039 (1.5)	$1.4*10-7$ (1.4)	-7.6 (2.2)	-3.4 (0.5)	6.6 (0.4)			.26	87	7.0	...
	(C)	16.4 (4.2)	0.00037 (0.5)	$-5.3*10-10$ (0.0)				.52 (4.5)	-.76 (8.0)	.68	77	42.5	...
	(D)	16.9 (4.3)	-0.00027 (0.1)	$2.7*10-8$ (0.3)	-1.4 (0.5)	4.5 (0.8)	2.2 (0.2)	.54 (4.6)	-.77 (8.1)	.69	77	24.9	...

Secondary

13. Female												
(A)	21.3 (7.1)	0.012 (8.2)	$-4.2*10-7$ (5.3)						.70	84	98.9	1.0
(B)	11.7 (3.5)	0.0075 (1.9)	$-2.1*10-7$ (1.4)	23.2 (4.2)	35.7 (3.0)	21.3 (0.9)			.78	84	60.3	-4.5
(C)	-6.4 (0.9)	0.0062 (5.1)	$-2.1*10-7$ (3.4)				.098 (0.4)	.52 (2.8)	.88	74	131.2	-7.7
(D)	-4.9 (0.7)	0.0025 (0.7)	$-6.0*10-8$ (0.5)	9.8 (2.1)	26.8 (2.8)	26.6 (1.2)	.086 (0.4)	.43 (2.4)	.89	74	86.2	-4.2
14. Male												
(A)	29.0 (10.7)	0.010 (7.7)	$-3.6*10-7$ (5.0)						.68	84	89.4	-15.4
(B)	20.9 (6.8)	0.0058 (1.6)	$-1.6*10-7$ (1.1)	20.0 (4.0)	33.4 (3.1)	21.0 (0.9)			.76	84	53.4	-19.3
(C)	-11.2 (1.4)	0.0060 (4.5)	$-1.9*10-7$ (2.8)				.88 (3.4)	-.28 (1.4)	.80	74	76.1	-16.4
(D)	-9.8 (1.3)	0.0036 (1.0)	$-7.8*10-8$ (0.6)	10.7 (2.1)	26.2 (2.5)	19.2 (0.8)	.86 (3.6)	-.39 (2.0)	.82	74	50.5	-14.5
15. Male-Female												
(A)	7.7 (5.7)	-0.0017 (2.7)	$6.6*10-8$ (1.8)						.16	84	9.1	-16.4
(B)	9.2 (5.2)	-0.0017 (0.8)	$5.8*10-8$ (0.7)	-3.2 (1.1)	-2.3 (0.4)	-0.30 (0.0)			.15	84	4.0	-14.8
(C)	-4.8 (1.5)	-0.00013 (0.2)	$1.9*10-8$ (0.7)				.78 (7.8)	-.80 (9.8)	.68	74	40.3	-8.8
(D)	-5.0 (1.6)	0.0011 (0.7)	$-1.9*10-8$ (0.3)	1.0 (0.4)	-0.59 (0.1)	-7.4 (0.7)	.78 (7.7)	-.82 (9.8)	.67	74	22.9	-10.2

(continued)

Table 2.3. (cont.)

Dependent Variable		Constant	Income	Income²	Country Group Lower-Middle	Country Group Upper-Middle	Country Group High	Adult Literacy Rate Male	Adult Literacy Rate Female	R²	N	F	Residual for Brazil
Years of School													
16. Female	(A)	5.9 (12.4)	0.0013 (6.0)	-5.2*10-8 (4.1)						.54	76	45.0	...
	(B)	3.9 (8.2)	0.00098 (1.8)	-2.9*10-8 (1.4)	4.5 (5.9)	4.4 (2.7)	1.9 (0.6)			.73	76	41.5	...
	(C)	-0.32 (0.4)	0.00030 (2.1)	-1.0*10-8 (1.4)				.068 (2.5)	.055 (2.5)	.89	66	134.7	...
	(D)	-0.38 (0.5)	-0.000089 (0.2)	4.8*10-9 (0.4)	2.2 (4.3)	2.5 (2.4)	3.8 (1.5)	.067 (2.8)	.040 (2.0)	.91	66	101.3	...
17. Male	(A)	7.3 (17.9)	0.0011 (5.5)	-4.0*10-8 (3.7)						.50	76	39.4	...
	(B)	5.6 (13.5)	0.00072 (1.5)	-2.0*10-8 (1.1)	3.7 (5.4)	3.7 (2.6)	1.7 (0.6)			.69	76	34.5	...
	(C)	0.53 (0.6)	0.00033 (2.1)	-1.0*10-8 (1.2)				.14 (4.6)	-.032 (1.3)	.80	66	68.0	...
	(D)	0.49 (0.6)	-.000028 (0.1)	4.3*10-9 (0.3)	2.2 (3.7)	2.7 (2.2)	3.6 (1.3)	.14 (5.0)	-.048 (2.1)	.84	66	48.9	...
18. Male-Female	(A)	1.4 (8.0)	-0.00028 (3.5)	1.1*10-8 (2.5)						.24	76	13.2	...
	(B)	1.7 (8.1)	-0.00025 (1.0)	8.8*10-9 (0.9)	-0.80 (2.3)	-0.61 (0.8)	-0.13 (0.1)			.30	76	7.4	...
	(C)	0.85 (2.3)	.000031 (0.5)	8.1*10-11 (0.0)				.071 (5.9)	-.087 (8.8)	.75	66	50.7	...
	(D)	0.86 (2.3)	.000060 (0.3)	-5.2*10-10 (0.1)	-0.034 (0.1)	0.14 (0.3)	-0.25 (0.2)	.071 (5.8)	-.088 (8.5)	.74	66	28.0	...

Sources: World Bank (1990) and UNESCO (1965, 1970).

Note: Enrollment rates (and therefore residuals for enrollment rates) are in percentages. Years of school (i.e., expected years of school for a synthetic cohort as defined in the text) are in years (and therefore so are the

discussing the regression results in these tables. We attempt, however, to note cases in which the conclusion that one draws differs importantly for one of the other alternatives. We refer to (D) or (C) as the preferred regression, depending upon whether or not the country group dichotomous variables add significantly to the consistency of the relation with the cross-country variance in a given dependent variable. In the differenced regressions in Table 2.4, however, regressions (B) usually are preferred since they are the most consistent with the variance in the dependent variables.

Table 2.2 gives the cross-country regression estimates both for 1965 and 1987 for the total enrollment rates for each of the three school levels and for the expected years of schooling for a synthetic cohort. Figures 2.1a and 2.1b plot the (A) regressions for the expected years of schooling for a synthetic cohort for both 1965 and 1987 (with the observed values indicated explicitly for Brazil, selected other Latin American countries, and Korea).

For 1965, the (C) and (D) regressions are consistent with from about half to four-fifths of the sample variances. For primary school enrollments in that year, the indicators of the country group by income have a substantial effect,[19] without an added significant impact of the quadratic in per capita income. For post-primary schooling enrollments and for the expected years of schooling, the quadratic in income represents the basic income effect, with diminishing marginal effects[20] in the (C) regressions (and with no additional significant country group effects in the (D) regressions). As indicated by the figures, although the quadratic term in income is significantly nonzero, the curvature over the range of incomes for the developing countries is not very large. For primary and secondary enrollments and for the expected years of schooling, male literacy rates have positively significant effects beyond the income effects. These signs are consistent with the interpretation of the negative price effect that is given above.

For 1987, the regressions are consistent with more (than for 1965) of the cross-country variances—from over three-fifths to over seven-eights of those variances for the (C) and (D) regressions. A comparison of regressions (C) and (D) indicates that in terms of explanatory power, the country group dichotomous variables in the (D) regression do not add anything beyond the

---

[19] We say "significant" to refer to the standard 5 percent level throughout this chapter, unless otherwise qualified.

[20] Though these effects are diminishing, they still reach maximums at very high per capita income levels (over $24,000, about $14,000, and $9,000, respectively, in comparison with an unweighted mean cross-country sample income in 1965 of $2,956, all in 1987 dollars).

quadratics in income in regressions (C). These quadratics again indicate a positive (but slightly diminishing at the margin)[21] association with income for post-primary schooling and expected years of schooling. These relations are shifted upwards relative to those for 1965, as is indicated by comparisons of the constant estimates and illustrated in Figures 2.1a and 2.1b. The male literacy rate again has significantly positive coefficient estimates for primary and secondary school enrollments and for the expected years of schooling for a synthetic cohort. In addition, the female literacy rate has significantly positive coefficient estimates for tertiary schooling.[22] If the price interpretation is correct, there are strong price effects in these demand relations.

How do Brazilian schooling investments compare with these cross-country regressions? The last column in Table 2.2 gives the estimated residuals for Brazil. In 1965, Brazil had a primary school enrollment rate that was 20.1 percent above the preferred (D) regression line, but secondary and tertiary enrollment rates that were 8.6 and 3 percent below the respective preferred (C) regression lines. The net result was expected years of schooling 0.6 years above that predicted by cross-country experience in the preferred (C) regression. In 1987, the Brazilian primary school enrollment rate was 2.7 percent above the preferred (C) regression line,[23] but secondary and tertiary enrollment rates were, respectively, 11.5 and 7.1 percent below the preferred (C) regression lines. The net result was expected years of schooling 0.8 years below the preferred (C) regression line.[24] Thus, over the two decades between these years, enrollment at each schooling level, and therefore expected schooling for a synthetic cohort in Brazil, declined relative to the cross-country regression line. For expected schooling the total effect in the preferred (C) regressions was to move from 0.6 years above to 0.8 years below the (shifting) cross-country regression line.

---

[21] And again, with the maximum effects at high per capita incomes (e.g., $15,000, $17,650, and $15,000 in comparison with an unweighted mean across countries of $4,371, all in 1987 dollars).

[22] For tertiary enrollments male literacy rates also have significantly negative coefficient estimates at the 10 percent level. These apparently reflect multicollinearity in the sense that they appear positively significant if the female literacy rates are precluded from the specification.

[23] But below the (B) and (D) alternatives with the country group controls.

[24] Though for alternative (A), Brazil is 0.1 years above the regression line.

Figure 2.1a. Cross-Country Regression for Total Expected Schooling in 1965

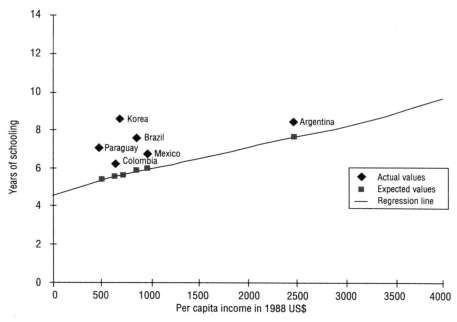

Figure 2.1b. Cross-Country Regression for Total Expected Schooling in 1987

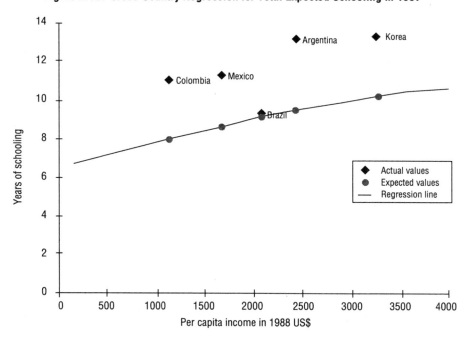

Comparisons of Male and Female Schooling Investments in Brazil with Cross-Country Experience

As noted previously, there appear to be some interesting gender patterns in Brazilian schooling investments, particularly with regard to investments in secondary schooling in 1987 that are larger for females than for males. We also considered total schooling investments relative to cross-country regressions for 1965 and 1987. Now we turn to similar considerations, but with separate relations for males and females.[25] Table 2.3 gives regression estimates similar to those in Table 2.2, but with separate relations for males versus females. In addition, this table gives estimates of the differences between male and female primary and secondary enrollment rates and the expected years of schooling for synthetic cohorts. The regression (A) lines for expected years of schooling for synthetic cohorts for 1965 and 1987 are plotted in Figures 2.2a and 2.2b for females and in Figures 2.3a and 2.3b for males.[26]

Many of the patterns in these regressions are similar to those discussed earlier in this chapter, without significant differences between the estimates for females versus males. To avoid repetition we summarize here only the results that indicate some significant difference between males and females. We again focus on the (C) or (D) regression for each outcome, depending on which is preferred, in the same sense as used earlier.

Table 2.3 shows that for 1965, regression 3(C) is consistent with over two-fifths of the variance in the difference in primary school enrollments between males and females. This regression suggests that this difference is a significant 23.2 percent for very low incomes (i.e., see constant), and then, as income increases, this gap increases at a decreasing rate and subsequently declines (but only above per capita incomes that are greater than $20,800). These estimates also imply that the gap increases signifi-

---

[25] World Bank (1990) gives data only for female enrollment rates for primary and secondary school, in addition to total enrollment rates for all three schooling levels. The estimates in this section assume that the sizes of the relevant age cohorts are the same for males as for females in order to be able to estimate male primary and secondary enrollment rates. To calculate the expected years of schooling for synthetic cohorts, it is assumed that there are no gender differences in tertiary enrollment rates. This last assumption probably results in an underestimation of the gender gap for many countries, but has a limited impact on the overall estimates because of relatively low enrollments for tertiary (as opposed to primary and secondary) schooling levels in most developing countries (including Brazil).

[26] Unfortunately, the lack of a male-female breakdown for primary schooling enrollments for Brazil in 1987 means that there is no point for Brazil on these figures for that year.

Figure 2.2a. Cross-Country Regression for Female Expected Schooling in 1965

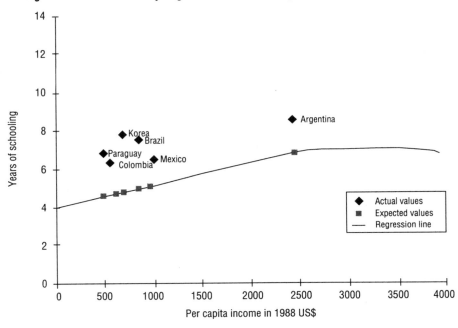

Figure 2.2b. Cross-Country Regression for Female Expected Schooling in 1987

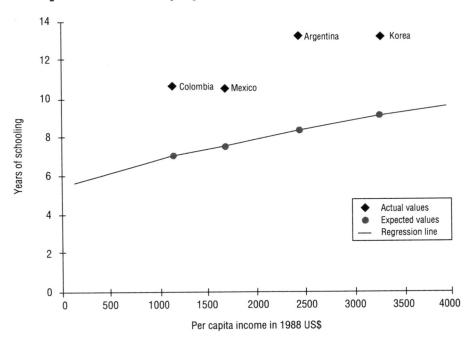

Figure 2.3a. Cross-Country Regression for Male Expected Schooling in 1965

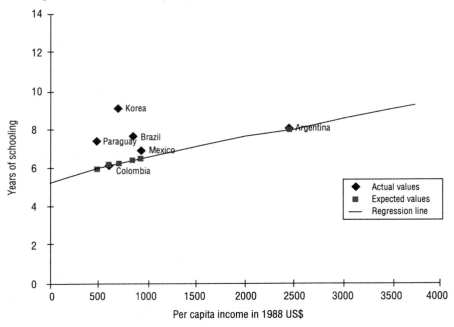

Figure 2.3b. Cross-Country Regression for Male Expected Schooling in 1987

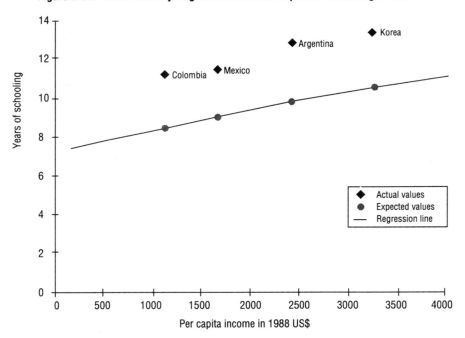

cantly with male literacy, but falls significantly (and significantly more) with female literacy.[27] This may reflect that in some countries teachers in single-sex schools are largely of the same sex as the students, so the relative scarcity value of teachers for a child depend on the stock of skilled adults of the same sex.[28] For secondary school enrollment, regression 6(C) is consistent with about two-fifths in the variance. The constant in this regression is insignificant, but again there is an initially increasing and then declining gap with income (again, with decreases only above very high per capita income levels—$24,000 in this case). Also again, male literacy rates are associated with significantly larger, and female literacy rates with significantly smaller, gender gaps in enrollment.[29] Regression 9(C) for the combined effect of gender gaps in enrollment rates in terms of the gender difference in expected years in school is consistent with two-thirds of the variance in that variable. The constant in this regression indicates that at very low income levels males have 1.8 more years of expected schooling than do females. The significant quadratic in income implies that this gap also initially increases, but at a decreasing rate, with income (above $15,000). The literacy rates again indicate a significantly positive effect of adult male literacy and a (significantly larger in absolute value) significantly negative association with adult female literacy.

For 1987, regression 12(C) is consistent with over two-thirds of the variance in the difference in primary school enrollments between males and females. This regression suggests that the difference is a significant 16.4 percent for very low incomes; this is substantially smaller than the constant in the parallel regression for 1965. In contrast to the estimates for 1965, the income effects in this regression are not significantly nonzero.[30] However, as for the estimates for 1965, these estimates imply that the gap increases significantly with male literacy but falls significantly (and significantly more) with female literacy.[31] For secondary school enrollment, the estimates are similar to those for primary school enrollment: regression 15(C) is con-

---

[27] But note the contrast with the individual estimates for males and females in regressions 1(C) and 2(C), in which only the male literacy rates have significantly positive coefficient estimates.
[28] Rural Pakistan is one such case. In this case, Alderman et al. (1991) estimate that elimination of the gender gap in the supply of primary schools (probably requiring a large expansion in the number of women teachers) would eliminate much or all of the substantial gender gap in cognitive achievement in younger cohorts.
[29] In this case the underlying regressions for females and males, 4(C) and 5(C), also indicate significant own-gender associations.
[30] Though if there only is a quadratic in income as in regression 12(A), it appears that there is a significant quadratic in income. However, regression 12(A) is consistent with less than a third as much of the cross-country variance, as is regression 12(C).
[31] But note the contrast with the individual estimates for females in regression 11(C), in which both the male and female literacy rates have significantly positive coefficient estimates.

sistent with about two-thirds of the variance, income is not significant, and the estimates imply that the gap increases significantly with male literacy but falls significantly with female literacy (though in this case without a significant difference between the absolute magnitudes of the two literacy coefficient estimates). Regression 18(C) for the combined effects of gender gaps in enrollment rates in terms of the gender difference in expected years in school is consistent with three-quarters of the variance in that variable. The constant in this regression indicates that at very low income levels males have 0.85 more years of expected schooling than do females, less than half that estimated for 1965. The quadratic in income also (as for the 1987 enrollment gap estimates) is not significant, in contrast to the results for 1967. The coefficient estimates of literacy rates again indicate a significantly positive association with adult male literacy and a significantly negative association with adult female literacy (with these two effects not differing significantly in absolute magnitudes).

How does Brazilian schooling investment compare with other countries? The last column in Table 2.3 gives the residuals for Brazil. For 1965, Brazil had female and male primary schooling enrollment rates 24.5 and 18.2 percent, respectively, above the (C) regression lines, with the male-female differential 6.4 percent below the regression line.[32] The female secondary schooling enrollment rate was 7.6 percent below the regression line and the male rate was 9.6 percent below, with the gender gap at the secondary school level 2 percent below.[33] The net result was expected years of schooling for females of 0.9 years above and for males of 0.4 years above the (C) regression lines, with the gender gap 0.5 years below the regression line. For 1987, there are no data for the gender differences in the Brazilian primary schooling enrollment rates (and none, therefore, for the expected years of schooling). For secondary school enrollment rates, Brazil was 7.7 percent below the (C) regression line for females and 16.4 percent below for males, with the net effect being 8.8 percent below the (C) regression line for the gender gap.[34]

---

[32] In this case the (A) regressions imply different magnitudes, though the same general patterns, with the respective percentages 43.4, 26.8, and 16.7. That is, control for the adult literacy rates makes Brazil appear less far above the regression line than in the regressions without such a control (particularly for females), because the prior history of relatively intense investment in basic schooling meant that there was a relatively large source of literate (skilled) labor, so the opportunity cost of adult time for primary education was relatively low.

[33] In this case, whether Brazil was above or below the regression line for females depends on whether there is control for adult literacy (for reasons parallel to those discussed in the previous note). For males and for the gender gap, the signs are the same (though the magnitudes differ) without control for adult literacy in the (A) regressions.

[34] In this case, once again, if there is not control for adult literacy, in the (A) regression Brazil is slightly above the regression line, but the signs of the residuals in the other two relations (i.e., male, and male minus female) remain the same (though the magnitudes differ some).

Comparisons of the Changes in Brazilian Schooling Investments with Cross-Country Experience

The previous two sections focused on how Brazilian schooling investments compared with the cross-country experience in 1965 and 1987. A related, but distinct, question is how did the changes in Brazilian schooling investments compare with changes in the cross-country experience. This question is of interest because of its dynamic nature and because the differenced estimates control for unobserved additive country-specific fixed effects.[35]

Table 2.4 gives such estimates. For primary school enrollment rates, estimates are consistent with from a quarter to four-fifths of the variance in the changes in enrollment rates (total, female, and male). Though the standard errors are large, the point estimates in the (B) and (D) regressions seem to indicate greater increases in primary school enrollments for countries with lower incomes in 1965 (more so for females than for males). For secondary school enrollment rates, the preferred estimates are consistent with from a third to a half of the variance, but the patterns are somewhat different than for primary school. There are increases, on the average, in the preferred (B) estimates for the total, female, and male enrollment of 12 percent for initially low-income countries; the increases are, however, significantly larger for initially lower-middle-income countries (25.4 percent) and still larger for initially upper-middle- and high-income countries (over 36 percent on the average).[36] [37] Also for the low-income countries the increases are larger for males than for females on the average, though the opposite is the case for the middle- and upper-income country groups. For tertiary school, the preferred relation (B) is consistent with 45 percent of the variance in the

---

[35] That is, these estimates, by controlling for such fixed effects, have less in the way of omitted variable bias than do the estimates in Tables 2.2 and 2.3. They may have more random measurement error due to the differencing (which would tend to lead to biases towards zero in the coefficient estimates), though Behrman (1984) shows that the control for systematic errors due to omitted variables such as for schooling quality and general educational environment that may be relatively fixed within countries over time as compared with across countries at a point in time may mean that the total bias is less for the differenced estimates.

[36] The first percentage in this sentence is from the constant in regression 4(B). The others are from the sum of the constant with the coefficients of the dichotomous variables for the initial country groups. For all of these calculations the quadratic in income (with the large standard errors for the point estimates) is ignored.

[37] For the primary school enrollment rates, the (C) and (D) regressions are more consistent with the sample variances than are the (B) regressions. However the differences are not large, the impact of the adult literacy rates are estimated with little precision, and the samples are much smaller for the (C) and (D) regressions than for the (B) regressions. Therefore we consider the (B) regressions to be preferred for the primary school enrollments as well as for the other sets of estimates.

Table 2.4. Cross-Country Regressions for Changes Between 1965 and 1987 in Total, Male and Female Schooling Investments

Dependent Variable	Constant	Income	Income²	Country Group			Adult Literacy Rate		R²	N	F	Residual for Brazil
				Lower-Middle	Upper-Middle	High	Male	Female				
1987–1965 Enrollment Rates												
Primary												
1. Total												
(A)	17.5 (9.1)	-0.0013 (2.7)	-1.3*10-7 (4.1)						.16	89	9.3	-20.9
(B)	23.9 (8.3)	-.000063 (0.1)	-5.7*10-8 (1.2)	-8.5 (2.1)	-15.7 (2.7)	-19.4 (2.6)			.23	89	6.4	-20.2
(C)	4.3 (0.9)	-.000098 (0.2)	-8.6*10-8 (2.6)				.42 (1.4)	.21 (0.7)	.31	54	7.0	-19.7
(D)	19.0 (2.7)	0.00046 (0.6)	-4.2*10-8 (0.9)	-13.3 (2.3)	-16.5 (2.3)	-21.4 (2.2)	.22 (0.8)	.23 (0.8)	.37	54	5.4	-19.1
2. Female												
(A)	20.2 (9.9)	-0.0015 (2.9)	-1.3*10-7 (3.8)						.15	83	8.6	...
(B)	24.6 (8.0)	-0.00025 (0.3)	-4.7*10-8 (0.9)	-3.5 (0.8)	-15.7 (2.6)	-18.2 (2.4)			.22	83	5.7	...
(C)	3.9 (0.9)	-0.00012 (0.2)	-7.3*10-8 (2.2)				.42 (1.4)	.35 (1.2)	.37	49	8.2	...
(D)	16.2 (2.2)	0.00042 (0.6)	-2.8*10-8 (0.6)	-8.3 (1.3)	-15.3 (2.1)	-19.0 (1.9)	.22 (0.7)	.37 (1.2)	.40	49	5.6	...
3. Male												
(A)	13.9 (6.6)	-0.00092 (1.7)	-1.3*10-7 (3.8)						.13	83	7.1	...
(B)	20.2 (6.3)	0.00017 (0.2)	-6.4*10-8 (1.2)	-9.2 (2.1)	-12.7 (2.0)	-18.0 (2.2)			.18	83	4.6	...
(C)	5.1 (1.0)	-0.00011 (0.2)	-1.0*10-7 (2.8)				.46 (1.4)	.015 (0.0)	.24	49	4.8	...
(D)	18.8 (2.4)	0.00058 (0.7)	-4.8*10-8 (0.9)	-12.4 (1.8)	-14.2 (1.7)	-22.3 (2.0)	.26 (0.8)	.026 (0.1)	.27	49	3.6	...

Secondary

4. Total												
(A)	21.7 (13.2)	0.0011 (2.5)	5.1*10-8 (1.9)						.06	86	3.7	0.0
(B)	12.0 (5.8)	-0.00050 (0.9)	-4.2*10-8 (1.2)	13.4 (4.7)	24.1 (5.7)	25.9 (4.9)			.39	86	11.8	-1.8
(C)	27.2 (6.4)	0.00029 (0.5)	1.8*10-8 (0.6)	11.7 (2.7)	21.5 (3.9)	32.1 (4.2)	-.51 (1.9)	.36 (1.4)	.33	53	1.5	-3.2
(D)	8.7 (1.6)	-0.00084 (1.4)	-7.2*10-8 (1.9)				-.22 (0.9)	.41 (1.9)	.31	53	4.3	-0.7
5. Female												
(A)	22.1 (11.1)	0.0014 (2.8)	7.4*10-8 (2.3)						.09	79	4.9	5.2
(B)	9.3 (4.1)	-0.00050 (0.9)	-3.8*10-8 (1.1)	18.2 (5.8)	34.0 (7.0)	32.1 (5.8)			.52	79	18.0	2.2
(C)	31.2 (6.4)	0.00020 (0.3)	2.0*10-8 (0.6)	17.5 (3.5)	29.6 (4.7)	38.7 (4.8)	-.88 (2.8)	.65 (2.1)	.12	46	2.6	-0.8
(D)	7.4 (1.2)	-0.00010 (1.6)	-7.6*10-8 (1.9)				-.45 (1.8)	.58 (2.4)	.47	46	6.7	1.6
6. Male												
(A)	21.6 (12.7)	0.00074 (1.8)	2.8*10-8 (1.0)						.02	79	1.7	-5.4
(B)	12.5 (5.8)	-0.00050 (0.9)	-4.6*10-8 (1.3)	12.9 (4.2)	24.2 (5.1)	21.7 (4.0)			.32	79	8.5	-7.7
(C)	24.2 (5.4)	0.00028 (0.5)	6.1*10-9 (0.2)	15.2 (3.1)	27.0 (4.4)	31.0 (4.0)	-.32 (1.1)	.30 (1.1)	-.05	46	0.5	-8.1
(D)	3.9 (0.7)	-0.00058 (1.0)	-6.4*10-8 (1.7)				.035 (0.1)	.23 (1.0)	.30	46	3.8	-6.3

(continued)

Table 2.4. (cont.)

Dependent Variable		Constant	Income	Income²	Country Group			Adult Literacy Rate		R²	N	F	Residual for Brazil
					Lower-Middle	Upper-Middle	High	Male	Female				
Tertiary													
7. Total	(A)	7.9 (7.7)	0.0019 (2.8)	-5.4*10-8 (0.7)						.24	78	13.0	-1.1
	(B)	1.6 (1.1)	0.00065 (0.8)	8.5*10-8 (0.0)	8.7 (4.5)	12.4 (5.0)	12.2 (3.3)			.45	78	13.6	-2.1
	(C)	17.1 (6.6)	-0.00052 (0.6)	8.8*10-8 (1.1)				-.31 (2.0)	.044 (0.3)	.23	51	4.9	-3.5
	(D)	8.2 (2.0)	-0.0012 (1.1)	1.1*10-7 (1.4)	10.0 (2.7)	8.7 (2.1)	12.7 (2.2)	-.31 (2.0)	.055 (0.3)	.31	51	4.2	-4.2
Years of School													
8. Total	(A)	2.6 (13.3)	0.00028 (1.8)	-3.0*10-8 (1.8)						.019	71	1.7	-1.4
	(B)	2.0 (6.9)	0.00014 (0.5)	-1.7*10-8 (0.8)	1.0 (2.5)	1.4 (2.5)	0.85 (0.8)			.099	71	2.6	-1.6
	(C)	2.9 (5.5)	.000024 (0.1)	-7.0*10-8 (0.4)				-.019 (0.6)	.024 (0.8)	-.058	44	0.4	-1.6
	(D)	1.7 (1.8)	-0.00026 (0.7)	1.1*10-8 (0.4)	1.3 (1.5)	1.6 (1.7)	2.3 (1.3)	-.011 (0.4)	.025 (0.7)	-.053	44	0.7	-1.4
9. Female	(A)	2.8 (12.5)	0.00037 (2.1)	-3.8*10-8 (2.0)						.038	63	2.2	...
	(B)	2.0 (6.4)	0.00032 (1.0)	-3.1*10-8 (1.3)	1.4 (3.3)	1.5 (2.3)	0.65 (0.6)			.18	63	3.8	...
	(C)	3.0 (4.7)	.000097 (0.4)	-1.3*10-8 (0.6)				-.038 (1.1)	.054 (1.4)	-.025	36	0.8	...
	(D)	1.1 (1.0)	-0.00017 (0.4)	3.7*10-8 (0.1)	2.2 (2.0)	2.1 (1.7)	2.9 (1.4)	-.022 (0.6)	.038 (0.9)	.010	36	1.1	...

10. Male											
(A)	2.3 (10.5)	0.00025 (1.4)	-2.5*10-8 (1.4)						.00	63	1.0 ...
(B)	1.8 (5.6)	.000068 (0.2)	-1.1*10-8 (0.4)	0.83 (1.8)	1.4 (2.0)	0.92 (0.8)			.04	63	1.5 ...
(C)	2.8 (4.3)	-.000016 (0.1)	-3.5*10-9 (0.2)				-.0057 (0.2)	.0065 (0.2)	-.10	36	0.1 ...
(D)	0.58 (0.5)	-0.00028 (0.6)	1.3*10-8 (0.4)	2.4 (2.2)	2.7 (2.2)	3.1 (1.6)	.014 (0.4)	-.011 (0.3)	-.03	36	0.9 ...

Sources: World Bank (1990) and UNESCO (1965, 1970).

Note: Enrollment rates (and therefore residuals for enrollment rates) are in percentages. Years of school (i.e., expected years of school for a synthetic cohort as defined in the text) are in years (and therefore so are the residuals for these regressions). The per capita GNP variables are in the form of differences between 1965 and 1987.

change in enrollment rates between 1965 and 1987. For this school level the average increase is relatively low and insignificant for low-income countries (1.6 percent), but significantly higher (10.3 percent) for lower-middle-income countries and still higher (above 13.8 percent) for the upper-middle- and high-income countries. The changes in enrollments at all three levels imply a gain of two years in expected years of schooling for the low- and high-income countries, and of 3.4 years for the middle-income countries (with larger point estimates for females than for males, but without significant differences). Note that in all of these sets of estimates the (C) and (D) regressions have relatively large standard errors for the adult literacy rates. This may imply that in the estimates in Tables 2.2 and 2.3, adult literacy rates basically are proxying for some unobserved variables (e.g., culture), and therefore, their effects disappear once there is control for unobserved fixed effects. If so, then the price interpretation given above is brought into question.[38] However since the samples are much smaller for the (C) and (D) estimates (since literacy rates must be available for both 1965 and 1987, in addition to the other variables for the (A) and (B) regressions), it may be that the insignificance of the literacy rates in Table 2.4 is due to the smaller (and probably selected, since the countries for which such information is not available tend to be countries with lower income in 1965) samples.

Once again, how does Brazil compare? Again, the last column gives the residuals for Brazil. For the preferred (B) regressions Brazil was 20.2 percent below the regression line for changes in primary school enrollments, 1.8 percent below for changes in secondary school enrollments, 2.1 percent below for changes in tertiary enrollments, and 1.6 years below the line for changes in expected years of schooling for a synthetic cohort. For secondary school enrollments, Brazil had a shift towards females in the gender gap relative to other country experiences, with an increase for females 2.2 percent above the regression line and one for males 7.7 percent below the regression line. Thus the two distinguishing characteristics of the Brazilian changes, relative to the cross-country changes, are small increases in schooling investment and more of a shift towards females. The first point at the primary school level may reflect in part the relatively high primary school enrollments in 1965, but it also reflects relatively smaller increments in post-primary schooling.

---

[38] But the income estimates with such controls still are likely to be the preferred ones, since one would not want to attribute to income differences across countries what are, say, cultural differences.

REFERENCES

Ahmad, Sultan. 1992. Improving Inter-Spatial and Inter-Temporal Comparability of National Accounts. Paper presented at the Conference on Data Base of Development Analysis, Yale University, 15–16 May 1992.

Alderman, Harold, Jere R. Behrman, David Ross, and Richard Sabot. 1991. The Gender Gap in Cognitive Achievement in a Poor Rural Economy. Williams College, Williamstown, MA. Mimeo.

Behrman, Jere R. 1990a. *Human Resource Led Development?* New Delhi, India: ARTEP/ILO.

_____. 1990b. *The Action of Human Resources and Poverty on One Another: What We Have Yet to Learn.* Washington, D.C.: Population and Human Resources Department, World Bank.

_____. 1990c. Women's Schooling and Nonmarket Productivity: A Survey and a Reappraisal. Prepared for the Women in Development Division of the Population and Human Resources Department of the World Bank. University of Pennsylvania, Philadelphia. Mimeo.

_____. 1987. Schooling in Developing Countries: Which Countries are the Under- and Overachievers and What Is the Schooling Impact? *Economics of Education Review* 6(2): 111–28.

_____. 1984. Sibling Deviation Estimates, Measurement Error and Biases in Estimated Returns to Schooling. University of Pennsylvania, Philadelphia. Mimeo.

Behrman, Jere R., and Nancy Birdsall. 1985. The Quality of Schooling: Reply. *American Economic Review* 75(5): 1202–05.

_____.1983. The Quality of Schooling: Quantity Alone Is Misleading. *American Economic Review* 73(5): 928–46.

Behrman, Jere R., and Mark R. Rosenzweig. 1992. The Quality of Aggregate Inter-Country, Time-Series Data on Educational Investments and Stocks, Economically Active Populations, and Employment. Paper presented at the Conference on Data Base of Development Analysis, Yale University, 15–16 May 1992.

Colclough, C. 1982. The Impact of Primary Schooling on Economic Development: A Review of the Evidence. *World Development* 10(3): 167–85.

Eisemon, Thomas Owen. 1988. The Consequences of Schooling: A Review of Research on the Outcomes of Primary Schooling in Developing Countries. Harvard University, Cambridge, MA. Mimeo.

Gomes-Neto, João Batista, and Eric A. Hanushek. 1991. Grade Repetition, Wastage, and Educational Policy. Universidade Federal do Ceará and University of Rochester. Mimeo.

Haddad, Wadi D., Martin Carnoy, Rosemary Rinaldi, and Omporn Regel. 1990. *Education and Development: Evidence for New Priorities*. Discussion Paper 95. World Bank, Washington, D.C.

Heston, Alan. 1992. A Brief Review of Some Problems in Using National Accounts Data in Level Comparisons and Growth Studies. Paper presented at the Conference on Data Base of Development Analysis, Yale University, 15–16 May 1992.

King, Elizabeth M. 1990. *Educating Girls and Women: Investing in Development*. Washington, D.C.: World Bank.

King, Elizabeth M., and M. Anne Hill, eds. 1991. *Women's Education in Developing Countries*. Washington, D.C.: World Bank.

Knight, John B., and Richard H. Sabot. 1990. *Educational Productivity and Inequality: The East African Natural Experiment*. New York: Oxford University Press.

Psacharopoulos, G. 1988. Education and Development: A Review. *The World Bank Research Observer* 3(1) (January): 99–116.

_____. 1985. Returns to Education: A Further International Update and Implications. *Journal of Human Resources* 20(4): 583–97.

Schultz, T. Paul. 1991. Returns to Women's Education. In *Women's Education in Developing Countries*, eds. E.M. King and M.A. Hill. Washington, D.C.: World Bank.

_____. 1988. Education Investments and Returns. In *Handbook of Development Economics*, vol. 1, eds. Hollis Chenery and T.N. Srinivasan. Amsterdam: North-Holland.

_____. 1987. School Expenditures and Enrollments, 1960–1980: The Effects of Income, Prices and Population Growth. In *Population Growth and Economic Development: Issues and Evidence*, eds. D. Gale Johnson and Ronald D. Lee. Madison, WI.: University of Wisconsin Press.

Srinivasan, T. N. 1992. Data Base for Development Analysis: An Overview. Paper presented at Conference on Data Base of Development Analysis, Yale University, 15–16 May 1992.

UNESCO. 1970, 1965. *Annual Yearbook.* Paris: UNESCO.

World Bank. 1991. *World Development Report.* 1991, 1990. Oxford: Oxford University Press.

_____. 1981, 1980. *World Development Report.* Washington, D.C.: World Bank.

CHAPTER 3

Education and Economic Growth: Some Cross-Sectional Evidence

Lawrence J. Lau, Dean T. Jamison, Shucheng Liu and Steven Rivkin

Physical capital, labor, human capital and technical progress are the four principal sources of economic growth of nations.[1] The rate of growth of labor is generally constrained by the rate of population growth. For industrialized countries, growth of the labor force is seldom higher than 2 percent per annum, even with international migration. For developing countries, where population growth is generally higher, annual growth of the labor force is rarely higher than 5 percent. Consequently, the rate of growth of both physical and human capital, along with technical progress, have been found to account for a major proportion of economic growth, especially for countries with high growth rates.[2]

The importance of physical and human capital and technical progress to the growth of output can be readily understood with the help of some simple arithmetic. Starting with an aggregate production function:

(1) $Y = F(K, L, ED, t)$,

where Y is the quantity of real output, K, L, and ED are the quantities of physical capital, labor and human capital, respectively, and t is an index of chronological time, the rate of growth of output can be expressed in the familiar equation of growth accounting:

$$(2) \quad \frac{d\ell nY}{dt} = \frac{\partial \ell nF}{\partial \ell nK} \cdot \frac{d\ell nK}{dt} + \frac{\partial \ell nF}{\partial \ell nL} \cdot \frac{\partial \ell nL}{dt} + \frac{\partial \ell nF}{\partial ED} \cdot \frac{dED}{dt} + \frac{\partial \ell nF}{\partial t} \cdot$$

---

[1] The terms "technical progress" and "total factor productivity" are to be understood broadly so that they include all increases in output, holding inputs constant, and in particular, all improvements in efficiency.

[2] For example, Jorgenson, Gollop and Fraumeni (1987) find that between 1948 and 1979, capital formation accounted for 46 percent of the economic growth of the United States. Growth of labor input, including human capital, accounted for 31 percent, and technical progress accounted for 24 percent.

The four terms on the right-hand side of equation (2) may be identified as the contributions of physical capital, labor, human capital and technical progress, respectively, to the growth in output.

The production elasticity of output with respect to *measured* labor input can typically be estimated as approximately 0.6 for industrialized countries and between 0.3 and 0.4 for developing countries.[3] Thus, given the rate of growth of the measured labor force, typically no higher than 2 percent per annum in industrialized countries and 5 percent in developing countries, the maximum rate of growth that can be accounted for by the growth in labor input is on the order of 1.2 percent for developed countries and 2 percent for developing countries. Any growth in output in excess of 2 percent per annum in a developing country is attributable to the growth in capital inputs, physical and human, and to technical progress. For a developing country growing at 4 percent per annum, at least half of the growth in output may be attributed to physical and human capital and technical progress. In the short and intermediate runs, physical capital is especially important for another reason—it is the only input that can be readily varied. Human capital and technical progress, because of the long gestation periods they entail, can be changed only in the longer run. Of course, at the level of the individual state, the quantity of the labor force can be much more variable than that of the country as a whole because of the possibility of inter-state migration.

Lau, Jamison and Louat (1990) estimate an aggregate production function by relating aggregate real GDP to capital stock, labor force, land and average education of the labor force based on annual data from a sample of 58 developing countries, including Brazil, for 1960–86. They find positive and statistically significant estimates for the elasticities of output with respect to average education (measured in terms of years of formal education per person of the working age population) of 0.03 for Sub-Saharan Africa, 0.10 for the Middle East and North Africa, 0.13 for East Asia, and 0.17 for Latin America. The estimated average education elasticities for South Asia are found not to be statistically significant. We note, for later reference, that since the average education of the Brazilian labor force in 1970 is approximately 3.0, the effect of one additional year of average education for the Brazilian labor force may be estimated to increase output by 0.17/3.0 = 5.5 percent, holding all other inputs constant. An increase of this magnitude is economically significant. Lau, Jamison and Louat (1990)

---

[3] See Boskin and Lau (1990) for estimates of the production elasticity of labor for industrialized countries and Lau, Jamison and Louat (1990) for developing countries. Our estimate of the production elasticity of labor for Brazil, based on cross-sectional state data, is also approximately 0.4.

also find evidence of a threshold effect of average education at approximately four years. However, it should be emphasized that what they find is a collective threshold effect that applies to the average level of education of the labor force. This should be distinguished from the threshold effect on individual education found in some microeconomic studies.

The approach of Lau, Jamison and Louat (1990) is applied to cross-sectional state data from Brazil in this study. This new approach is presented as it applies to the analysis of the relationship between output, inputs and technical progress with state-level data. By pooling data across states, it is hoped that the separate effects of economies of scale and technical progress, usually confounded by the simultaneous expansion of scale with time in the data of a single state, or for the country as a whole, can be more readily identified. (At any given point in time, production at different scales is observed. The same scale of production may be observed at different points in time.) Moreover, inter-state data typically have greater variability in the relative quantities of inputs than intra-state or country data, thus mitigating against possible multicollinearity and facilitating the identification and estimation of the aggregate production function and the effect of average education in particular.

The data and statistical model used here are discussed prior to presenting the empirical results obtained from applying the model to cross-sectional state data from Brazil for 1970 and 1980. These results are then interpreted in the light of findings from other studies and further extended.

Meta-Production Function Approach

Our approach to estimating aggregate production functions from pooled time-series and cross-section data is based on the Lau and Yotopoulos (1989) modification of the concept of the meta-production function, introduced by Hayami and Ruttan (1970, 1985), through the use of time-varying and state- and commodity-specific augmentation factors. The basic assumptions of this approach are:

- All states have access to the same technology, that is, they have the same underlying aggregate production function F(.), sometimes referred to as a meta-production function, but may operate on different parts of it. The production function, however, applies to standardized, or "efficiency-equivalent," quantities of outputs and inputs, that is:

(3) $Y^*_{it} = F(K^*_{it}, L^*_{it}, ED^*_{it})$, $i = 1,...,n$;

where Y^*_{it}, K^*_{it} and L^*_{it} are the "efficiency-equivalent" quantities of output, capital and labor, respectively, of the ith state at time t, ED^*_{it} is an "efficiency-equivalent" measure of human capital of the ith state at time t, proxied by the average number of years of education of the labor force, and n is the number of states. The assumption of a meta-production function implies that F(.) does not depend on i (but may depend on t).

• There are differences in the technical efficiencies of production and in the qualities and possibly definitions of the measured inputs across states. However, the measured outputs and inputs of the different states may be converted into standardized or "efficiency-equivalent" units of outputs and inputs. The "efficiency-equivalent" quantities of outputs and inputs of each state are not directly observable. They are, however, assumed to be linked to the measured quantities of outputs, Y_{it}'s, and inputs, Y_{it}'s, L_{it}'s, and ED_{it}'s through possibly time-varying and state- and commodity-specific augmentation factors $A_{ij}(t)$'s, i = 1,...,n; j = K,L,E. For measured output, physical capital and labor, the conversion is through the multiplication of such augmentation factors. For measured human capital, the conversion is through the addition of such augmentation factors.[4] Thus,

(4) $Y^*_{it} = A_{i0}(t)Y_{it}$;

(5) $K^*_{it} = A_{iK}(t)K_{it}$;

(6) $L^*_{it} = A_{iL}(t)L_{it}$;

(7) $ED^*_{it} = ED_{it} + A_{iE}(t)$; i = 1, ..., n.

These assumptions together imply that the aggregate production functions are the same everywhere in Brazil in terms of standardized or "efficiency-equivalent" units of outputs and inputs. Moreover, measured inputs of any state may be converted into equivalent units of measured inputs of another state. Thus, for example, one unit of capital in state A may be equivalent to two units of capital in state B; one unit of labor in state A may be equivalent to one-third of a unit of labor in state B; and the first year of average education in state A may be equivalent to the second year of average education in state B. These conversion factors may also change

---

[4] For example, m years of average education per person in the labor force in state A may be equivalent to m-2 years of "efficiency-equivalent" average education in state B. Without loss of generality, any one state may be selected as the standard. Our assumption implies that the difference in education quality between two states may, to a first approximation, be measured as a constant difference (rather than a constant multiple), uniform across all the grades.

over time. In terms of the *measured* quantities of inputs, the aggregate production functions of any two states are *not* necessarily the same. However, in terms of "efficiency-equivalent" units, these functions are, under our assumptions, identical across states. In terms of the *measured quantities of outputs*, the aggregate production function may be rewritten as:

(8) $Y_{it} = A_{i0}(t)^{-1}F(K^*_{it}, L^*_{it}, ED^*_{it})$, $i = 1, \ldots, n$;

so that the reciprocal of the output-augmentation factor $A_{i0}(t)$ has the interpretation of the possibly time-varying level of the technical efficiency of production, also referred to as output efficiency, in the ith state at time t.

There are many reasons why these commodity augmentation factors are not likely to be identical across states. Examples include differences in climate, topography, natural resources and infrastructure; in definitions and measurements; in quality; in the composition of outputs; and in the technical efficiencies of production. The commodity augmentation factors are introduced precisely to capture these differences across states. In the empirical implementation, the commodity augmentation factors for output, physical capital and labor are assumed to have the constant exponential form with respect to time. The augmentation factor for human capital is assumed to have the linear form with respect to time. Thus:

(9) $Y^*_{it} = A_{i0} \exp(c_{i0} t)Y_{it}$;

(10) $K^*_{it} = A_{iK} \exp(c_{iK} t)K_{it}$:

(11) $L^*_{it} = A_{iL} \exp(c_{iL} t)L_{it}$; and

(12) $ED^*_{it} = ED_{it} + A_{iE} + c_{iE} t$; $i = 1, \ldots, n$;

where the A_{i0}'s, A_{ij}'s, c_{i0}'s, and c_{ij}'s are constants. We shall refer to the A_{i0}'s and A_{ij}'s as *augmentation level* parameters and c_{i0}'s and c_{ij}'s as *augmentation rate* parameters. For at least one state, say the ith, the constants A_{i0}, A_{iK} and A_{iL} can be set identically at unity and the constant A_{iE} can be set identically at zero (or some other arbitrary constants), reflecting the fact that "efficiency-equivalent" outputs and inputs can be measured only relative to some standard. Econometrically, this means that the constants A_{i0}'s and A_{ij}'s cannot be uniquely identified without some normalization.

In this study, the aggregate meta-production function is specified to have the Cobb-Douglas functional form. With three inputs, physical capital labor, and human capital (average education), the production function, in terms of "efficiency-equivalent" inputs, takes the form:

(13) $\ell n\, Y_{it} = -\ell n A_{i0}(t) + \ell n\, Y_0 + a_K \ell n\, K^*_{it} + a_L \ell n\, L^*_{it} + a_E\, ED^*_{it}$.

By substituting equations (9) through (12) into equation (13), we obtain equation (14), which is written entirely in terms of observable variables:

(14) $\ell n\ Y_{it} = \ell n\ Y_0 - \ell n\ A_{i0} + a_K\ \ell n\ A_{iK} + a_L\ \ell n\ A_{iL} + a_E\ A_{iE}$
$$+ a_K\ \ell n\ K_{it} + a_L\ \ell n\ L_{it} + a_E\ ED_{it}$$
$$+ (-c_{i0} + a_K\ c_{iK} + a_L\ c_{iL} + a_E\ c_{iE})\ t,$$

which simplifies into:

(15) $\ell n\ Y_{it} = \ell n\ Y_0 + \ell n\ A^*_{i0} + a_K\ \ell n\ K_{it} + a_L\ \ell n\ L_{it} + a_E\ ED_{it} + c^*_{i0}\ t,$

where A^*_{i0} and c^*_{i0} are state-specific constants. Equation (15) is the most general specification possible under our maintained hypotheses of a single Cobb-Douglas meta-production function and commodity-augmentation representation of efficiency differences across states.

If there were a minimum of three observations per state, then it is possible to estimate the parameters of equation (15). By taking first differences of equation (15), we obtain:

(16) $\ell n\ Y_{it} - \ell n\ Y_{it-1} = c^*_{i0} + a_K\ (\ell n\ K_{it} - \ell n K_{it-1}) + a_L(\ell n\ L_{it} - \ell n\ L_{it-1}) + a_E(ED_{it} - ED_{it} - 1).$

By taking first differences of equation (16), or equivalently, second differences of equation (15), we obtain:

(17) $(\ell n\ Y_{it} - \ell n\ Y_{it-1}) - (\ell n\ Y_{it-1} - \ell n\ Y_{it-2}) = a_K\ [(\ell n\ K_{it} - \ell n\ K_{it-1}) - (\ell n\ K_{it-1} - \ell n\ K_{it-2})]$
$$+ a_L[\ell n\ L_{it} - \ell n\ L_{it-1}) - (\ell n\ L_{it-1} - \ell n\ L_{it-2})] + a_E\ [(ED_{it} - ED_{it-1}) - (ED_{it-1} - ED_{it-2})],$$

which can be used for the estimation of a_K, a_L, and a_E.

However, since only two observations per state are available, equation (17) cannot be implemented. Instead, we fall back on equation (16) and make the assumption that $c^*_{i0} = c^*_0$, that is, the rate of technical progress is the same across the states:

(18) $\ell n\ Y_{it} - \ell n\ Y_{it-1} = c^*_0 + a_K\ (\ell n\ K_{it} - \ell n\ K_{it-1}) + a_L(\ell n L_{it} - \ell n\ L_{it-1}) + a_E\ (ED_{it} - ED_{it-1}).$[5]

Equation (18) is the actual estimating equation used in this study.

---

[5] It should be remarked that the assumption of identical rates of technical progress across states is a strong assumption. However, it is not an unreasonable one given the mobility of factors and information across states. Alternatively, one can assume that the c^*_{i0}'s, which have the interpretation of the state-specific rates of technical progress, are independently and identically distributed random variables with mean c^*_0, and variance σ^2. In any case, given the available data, it is not possible to identify the individual c^*_{i0}'s.

Data

We use data from individual Brazilian states for 1970 and 1980. Data for all the variables are available for 1970, 1975 and 1980, except human capital data, which is based on national censuses and available only for 1970 and 1980. Thus we omit 1975 because comparable labor force data are not available. Acre (State 5) is omitted from the sample because of incomplete data. Mato Grosso (State 24) and Mato Grosso do Sul (State 25) are treated as a single state (25) because Mato Grosso do Sul was officially made a state only in 1979 and separate data for it for the earlier year (1970) are not available. A list of the individual Brazilian states and their code numbers is presented in the Appendix. What follows is a brief description of the variables.

(1) Real Output (Y). The aggregate real output of each state is measured as the real GDP at factor cost (plus imputed financial intermediation services) in 1970 prices.[6] The average annual rate of growth is very high— 10.66 percent. However, there is also considerable variability across the states, ranging from a low of 4.9 percent for Amapá to 17.7 percent for Rondônia.

(2) Capital (K). Capital stock data are not available for the individual Brazilian states. As a proxy, the annual quantities of industrial consumption of electricity in each state in 1970 and 1980 are used instead.[7] The rate of growth of capital is extremely rapid. The lowest average annual rate is 10 percent per annum (except for Roraima [State 3], which has an implausibly low rate of growth). The average for all states is greater than 20 percent per annum. Industrial consumption of electricity (which excludes commercial, residential and service sector consumption) is a reasonable proxy for the quantity of capital stock used in production. It has the advantage over capital stock (which is, in any case, not available) in that it already embodies a rate of utilization adjustment.

(3) Labor (L). Labor is measured as the number of persons in the economically active population irrespective of employment status.[8] It has been growing rapidly, averaging 4.7 percent for the country as a whole. The high rate of increase is partly due to the age structure of the population and partly due to the rising female labor force participation rate.

---

[6] The GDP data are taken from IBGE (1987, p. 123). The deflator used is the implicit GDP deflator published by the Central Bank of Brazil (1990, p. 28).
[7] The data are taken from IBGE (1971, 1981).
[8] IBGE (1987, p. 74).

Table 3.1. Average Years of Education of the Economically Active Population of Brazilian States, 1970 and 1980

		Male		Female		All	
Code	State	1970	1980	1970	1980	1970	1980
2	Rondônia	2.09	2.75	4.31	4.68	2.32	3.06
3	Roraima	2.62	3.48	4.77	5.91	2.94	3.98
4	Amapá	2.73	3.90	4.41	5.93	3.02	4.38
6	Amazonas	2.01	3.24	4.09	5.19	2.32	3.71
7	Pará	2.22	3.13	3.45	4.95	2.44	3.51
8	Maranhão	1.00	1.71	1.41	2.61	1.08	1.93
9	Piauí	0.92	1.66	2.01	3.55	1.10	2.08
10	Ceará	1.20	2.05	2.68	3.96	1.45	2.55
11	Rio Grande do Norte	1.36	2.36	3.31	4.64	1.64	2.93
12	Paraíba	1.13	2.01	2.56	4.09	1.36	2.50
13	Pernambuco	1.80	2.82	2.88	4.16	2.03	3.20
14	Alagoas	1.04	1.87	2.03	3.23	1.23	2.22
15	Sergipe	1.25	2.37	1.92	3.71	1.41	2.75
16	Bahia	1.40	2.23	2.19	3.59	1.56	2.57
17	Minas Gerais	2.47	3.81	4.07	5.51	2.77	4.24
18	Espírito Santo	2.47	4.04	4.40	5.79	2.79	4.46
19	Rio de Janeiro	4.98	5.93	5.49	6.66	5.11	6.16
20	São Paulo	4.04	5.22	4.81	6.06	4.23	5.48
21	Paraná	2.37	3.92	3.56	5.14	2.57	4.22
22	Santa Catarina	3.18	4.66	4.19	5.71	3.38	4.94
23	Rio Grande do Sul	3.85	4.87	4.68	6.01	4.06	5.22
24	Mato Grosso do Sul		3.59		5.16		3.93
25	Mato Grosso	2.05	3.11	3.70	5.44	2.25	3.52
26	Goiás	1.92	3.33	3.73	5.35	2.17	3.77
27	Distrito Federal	5.09	6.59	5.94	7.21	5.32	6.81
	Average	2.78	3.99	4.00	5.39	3.03	4.37

(4) Human Capital (ED). Human capital is measured as the average number of years of formal education per person of the labor force (also referred to as the economically active population) (see Table 3.1).[9] Of particular note is the large increase of 1.34 years in the average education of the labor force over the 1970s, a very significant achievement for a large developing country such as Brazil.

(5) Time (t). Time is measured in terms of decades chronologically with the year 1970 being set equal to zero, and the year 1980 being set equal to one.

---

[9] The data are taken from the national demographic censuses for 1970 and 1980. Data on labor force education for 1980 were provided by IBGE in the form of a computer printout based on data from the 1980 national census.

Table 3.2. Average Annual Growth Rates of Selected Variables of Brazilian States, 1970–80

Code	State	GDP (%) (Y)	Capital (%) (K)	Labor (%) (L)	Average Education (Year)
2	Rondônia	17.73	52.08	16.22	0.0739
3	Roraima	12.27	4.05	8.51	0.1031
4	Amapá	4.88	24.54	5.25	0.136
6	Amazonas	14.07	22.42	5.03	0.138
7	Pará	12.77	26.50	5.04	0.106
8	Maranhão	9.71	23.29	2.96	0.085
9	Piauí	9.77	23.05	3.09	0.0984
10	Ceará	10.14	14.14	3.12	0.1092
11	Rio Grande do Norte	10.77	21.16	3.72	0.1298
12	Paraíba	8.57	14.75	2.22	0.1139
13	Pernambuco	8.08	10.51	3.03	0.1175
14	Alagoas	9.23	18.45	2.38	0.0982
15	Sergipe	8.76	13.46	2.86	0.1335
16	Bahia	10.79	23.73	2.76	0.1002
17	Minas Gerais	10.60	13.41	3.14	0.1463
18	Espírito Santo	11.56	23.48	4.40	0.1675
19	Rio de Janeiro	7.85	10.60	3.92	0.1049
20	São Paulo	8.95	10.53	4.91	0.1247
21	Paraná	10.16	13.85	2.29	0.165
22	Santa Catarina	11.20	16.02	4.30	0.1558
23	Rio Grande do Sul	8.71	13.41	3.45	0.117
25	Mato Grosso	13.79	15.65	5.85	0.1507
26	Goiás	11.43	32.26	4.09	0.1597
27	Distrito Federal	13.97	40.60	9.76	0.1493
	Average	10.66	20.08	4.68	0.1243

The average annual rates of growth of real output, physical capital, labor and average education are presented in Table 3.2. Figure 3.1 presents the rates of growth of real GDP and real GDP per unit labor by state. It is apparent that GDP growth rates are all quite high, with the exception of Amapá (State 4). In addition, the rates of growth of GDP and GDP per unit labor often diverge, indicating significant inter-state movements of the labor force. For example, Rondônia (State 2) has the highest rate of growth of real GDP, but the next to lowest rate of growth of real GDP per unit labor. Figure 3.2 presents the rates of growth of capital and capital intensity (capital per unit labor). The two rates do not diverge much, suggesting that interstate capital and labor movements tend to follow each other. Roraima

Figure 3.1. Average Annual Growth of Real GDP and Real GDP per Unit Labor, Brazilian States, 1970–80

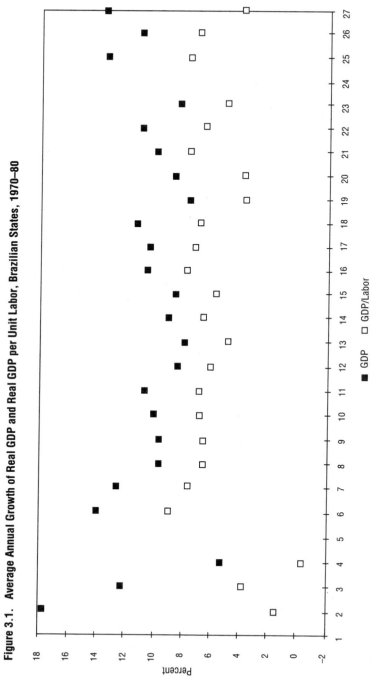

Note: Numbers on horizontal axis correspond to states (see Table 3.2).

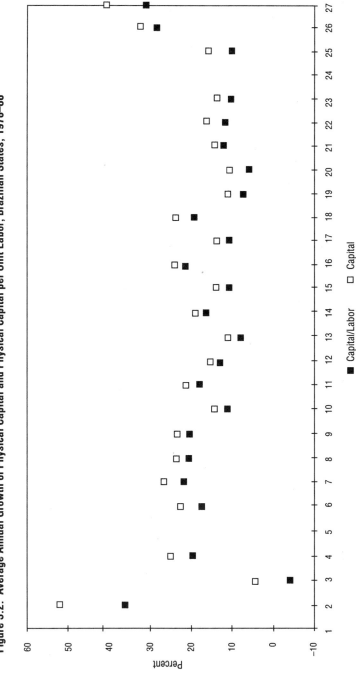

Figure 3.2. Average Annual Growth of Physical Capital and Physical Capital per Unit Labor, Brazilian States, 1970–80

■ Capital/Labor   □ Capital

Note: Numbers on horizontal axis correspond to states (see Table 3.2).

(State 3) has an implausible negative rate of growth of physical capital per unit labor.

In Figure 3.3, the rate of growth of labor productivity (real GDP per unit labor) is plotted against the rate of growth of capital intensity. With the exceptions of Roraima (State 3), Amapá (State 4), and possibly Rondônia (State 2), the growth in labor productivity appears to be positively correlated with the growth in capital intensity. In Figure 3.4, the rate of growth of labor productivity is plotted against the change in average education per person in the labor force. With the exception of Amapá (State 4), a positive relationship is discernible.

The latter half of the 1970s was a period of extraordinarily rapid growth. Average annual real GDP growth for Brazil was approximately 10 percent. It is apparent from Table 3.2 that Roraima (State 3) and Amapá (State 4) must have been outliers. Roraima had an abnormally low rate of growth of capital (industrial consumption of electricity) that was incompatible with its high rate of growth of real GDP and labor force. Amapá had an abnormally low rate of growth of real GDP given its very high rates of growth of capital and labor. Figures 3.3 and 3.4 lend further confirmation to the outlier status of both Roraima and Amapá. Consequently, both these states have been *excluded* from the sample. The estimation results for the sample including both Roraima and Amapá are not qualitatively different, but the estimated standard errors are somewhat larger. These alternative results are presented in Appendix Tables 3.1 to 3.3.

Statistical Model

We introduce stochastic disturbance terms ϵ_{it}'s into the *first-differenced* form of the natural logarithm of the aggregate production function, equation (18). We assume:

(19) $E(\epsilon_{it}) = 0$; and

(20) $V(\epsilon_{it}) = \sigma^2$; $\forall i, t$;

and the stochastic disturbance terms have identical variances and are uncorrelated across states. In the first-differenced form, our stochastic assumptions amount to saying that the influence of the stochastic disturbance term is permanent—it raises or lowers the production function permanently until further changes caused by future stochastic disturbance terms. In fact, given only two observations per state, unless the A^*_{i0}'s are assumed to be identical across states, a model without first-differencing cannot be implemented. All the standard errors presented here have been calculated

Figure 3.3. Growth of Labor Productivity and Capital Intensity

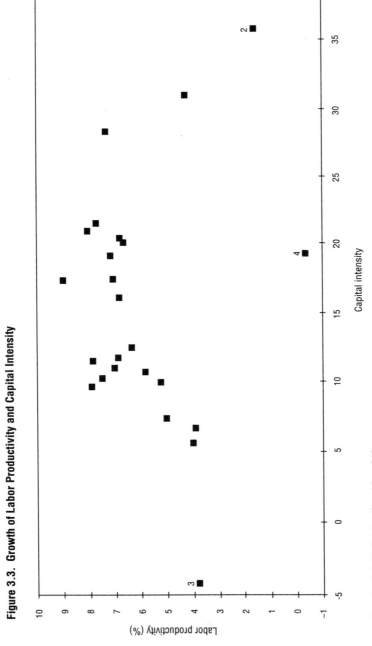

Note: Rondônia (2), Roraima (3) and Amapá (4).

Figure 3.4. Labor Productivity and Average Education of the Labor Force

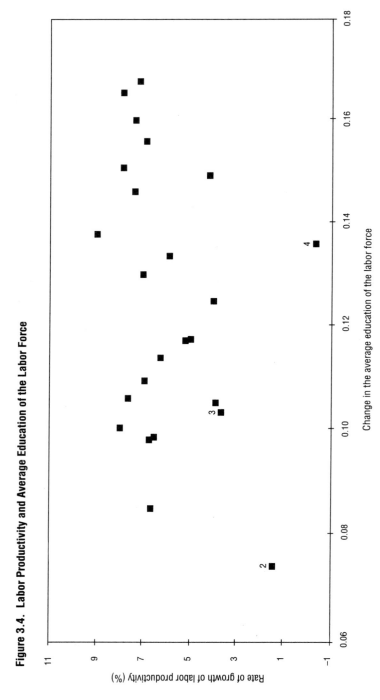

Note: Rondônia (2), Roraima (3) and Amapá (4).

on the basis of the heteroscedasticity-consistent variance-covariance matrix introduced by White (1980).

We note that the average education variable refers only to persons in the labor force and depends largely on history long past and is unlikely to be correlated with current output. Thus, the usual difficulty with respect to the "cause and effect" question is not as critical here. It is, however, not completely negligible in our state-level analysis because of the possibility of inter-state migration.

It is assumed that the right-hand side variables—the quantities of physical capital, labor and human capital—are uncorrelated with the stochastic disturbance terms. However, since individual state factors have already been taken into account in the form of the A^*_{i0}'s, the stochastic disturbance term is less likely to contain common state factors that may affect the quantities of inputs in each state. To the extent that our assumption is false, the ordinary least-squares estimator may be biased. In principle, the method of instrumental variables is an alternative. In practice, it is difficult to find state-level instrumental variables that are correlated with the inputs without being correlated with the stochastic disturbance terms. For example, while the population of a country may be regarded as more or less predetermined, the population of individual states cannot be so regarded because of the relative ease of inter-state migration. Thus, only results based on ordinary least-squares are reported in the text proper. Experimentation with the method of instrumental variables indicates that the estimates are not substantively different. The results based on the method of instrumental variables are reported in Appendix Table 3.4. The instrumental variables used are the initial (1970) levels of the natural logarithms of capital, male and female labor forces and cultivated land, and average education, along with the change in the levels of the natural logarithms of male and female labor forces and cultivated land, and fertility rate.

Empirical Results

As mentioned earlier, the 1970s was a period of extremely rapid growth in Brazil. In most states, capital, labor and average education grew rapidly. This leads to a potential identification problem—it may be difficult to isolate the effects due to each of the factors. The basic estimating equation used is equation (18).

We begin our empirical analysis by testing two hypotheses of interest. First, the hypothesis of no educational effect is tested. This hypothesis is rejected. Next, we test the hypothesis of constant returns to scale in the

Table 3.3. Tests of Hypotheses

Hypothesis	Test-Statistic	Critical value at 10% level of significance
No education effect	2.66	1.72
Constant returns to scale	5.50	1.72

Note: The values of the standard errors and variances are heteroscedasticity-consistent estimates.

Table 3.4. Estimates from First-Differenced Equation

Variable	Parameters		
Constant	0.439	0.719	
	(3.6)	(12.2)	
ℓn Capital	0.098	0.091	0.140
	(2.2)	(2.0)	(2.8)
ℓn Labor	0.412	0.397	0.409
	(3.3)	(2.8)	(2.6)
Average education	0.208		0.481
	(2.7)		(15.4)
Adjusted R^2	0.753	0.709	0.714

Note: The values of the standard errors and variances are heteroscedasticity-consistent estimates. Numbers in parentheses are t-ratios.

physical inputs, capital and labor. This hypothesis is rejected at the 10 percent level of significance. These results are presented in Table 3.3.

The estimation results from equation (18) are presented in Table 3.4. The estimated effect of average education is 0.21 and statistically significant at the 10 percent level. The estimates presented in the second and third columns of Table 3.4 show how sensitive the estimated effects of average education and technical progress are to the inclusion or exclusion of each other. Without average education, the estimated rate of technical progress increases from 4.3 percent per annum to 7.2 percent. Without technical progress, the estimated effect of education increases from 21 percent per year of additional average education to 48 percent. To isolate the effect of average education from that of technical progress, represented by the trend term, we subtract an assumed rate of technical progress of between 1 and 5 percent per annum from the rate of growth of real output before running the regression in equation (18) without the trend term. The results are presented in Table 3.5. The estimated effects of education remain positive and statistically significant, but become progressively smaller as the assumed

Table 3.5. Estimates Under Alternative Assumptions on the Rate of Technical Progress

Variable	Assumed rate of technical progress (percent per annum)				
	1%	2%	3%	4%	5%
	Parameters				
ℓn Capital	0.130	0.121	0.112	0.102	0.093
	(2.8)	(2.8)	(2.7)	(2.5)	(2.3)
ℓn Labor	0.410	0.410	0.411	0.412	0.412
	(2.8)	(3.0)	(3.1)	(3.2)	(3.2)
Average education	0.419	0.358	0.297	0.237	0.177
	(13.8)	(11.8)	(9.6)	(7.4)	(5.3)
Adjusted R^2	0.732	0.747	0.759	0.765	0.765

Note: The values of the standard errors and variances are heteroscedasticity-consistent estimates. Numbers in parentheses are t-ratios.

rate of technical progress is increased. However, even with an assumed rate of technical progress of 5 percent per annum, an increase in average education of the labor force of one year is estimated to increase output by 17.7 percent. This is a very large effect.

A 5 percent per annum rate of technical progress or growth of total factor productivity is a very high, but not implausible, rate. Traditional estimates of the rate of technical progress are on the order of 2 percent per annum. Boskin and Lau (1990) estimate the rates of technical progress for France, West Germany, Japan, the United Kingdom and the United States in the postwar period do not exceed 2 percent per annum if constant returns to scale are maintained and 4 percent otherwise. The Lau (1989) estimates of the rate of technical progress for China, Hong Kong, Singapore and Taiwan between 1952 and 1984 range from being negative (China) to 4.3 percent (Hong Kong). It is thus not unreasonable that the rate of technical progress in Brazil during the 1970s lies between 4 and 5 percent per annum. This leaves us with a large, positive and statistically significant estimate of the effect of average education on Brazilian output.[10]

The estimate of the production elasticity of labor is 0.4, which is in line with estimates obtained for developing countries elsewhere.[11] The estimate of the production elasticity of capital is 0.1, which is on the low side. However, as Table 3.4 shows, it appears to be quite robust. Moreover, Boskin and Lau (1990) obtain estimates of the production elasticities of capital for five

---

[10] Even if the outliers, Roraima and Amapá, are included in the sample, the estimated effect of average education is still a high 15 percent (see Appendix Table 3.3).

[11] See Lau, Jamison and Louat (1990).

Table 3.6. Sources of Brazilian Economic Growth, 1970–80
(Percent)

	Physical capital	Labor	Human capital	Technical progress	Total
Contribution	2.0	1.8	2.6	4.4	10.9
Percentage Distribution	19	17	24	40	100

industrialized countries of approximately 0.2. It is also possible that because of the very rapid growth in capital, the production elasticity may not
have remained constant over the whole range because of a shortage of
complementary factors.

Sources of Economic Growth

Based on the estimated parameters in column 1 of Table 3.4, we can decompose the economic growth in Brazil in the 1970s into its proximate sources.
The results of the decomposition are presented in Table 3.6. We find that
technical progress, or the growth in total factor productivity, is by far the
most important source of growth, accounting for more than 40 percent, followed by human capital, accounting for almost 25 percent. The growth in
the conventional inputs, physical capital and labor combined, accounts for
less than 40 percent of Brazilian economic growth in the 1970s.

Estimates of the Combined Contribution of Human Capital
and Technical Progress

Equation (2) may be used to obtain an alternative estimate of the growth in
output due to human capital and technical progress combined. Rewriting
equation (2) as:

$$(21) \quad \frac{\partial \ell n F}{\partial ED} \frac{dED}{dt} + \frac{\partial \ell n F}{\partial t} = \frac{d \ell n Y}{dt} - \frac{\partial \ell n F}{\partial \ell n K} \frac{d \ell n K}{dt} - \frac{\partial \ell n F}{\partial \ell n l} \frac{d \ell n L}{dt} ,$$

the combined contribution of human capital and technical progress may be
estimated once values of the production elasticities with respect to physical
capital and labor are specified, the rates of growth of physical capital and
labor being known, observed quantities. Such an exercise has been carried
out with the capital elasticity assumed to be 0.6, 0.4 and 0.2, respectively,
and the labor elasticity assumed to be 0.4. The results are presented in Table

Table 3.7. Estimates of the Combined Contribution of Human Capital and Technical Progress
(Percent)

Code	State	$\dot{Y}/Y - \dot{L}/L$	Value of capital elasticity (S_k)		
			$S_k=0.6$	$S_k=0.4$	$S_k=0.2$
2	Rondônia	1.51	−20.01	−9.60	0.82
3	Roraima	3.76	6.44	7.25	8.06
4	Amapá	−0.38	−11.95	−7.04	−2.13
6	Amazonas	9.04	−1.39	3.09	7.57
7	Pará	7.73	−5.14	0.16	5.46
8	Maranhão	6.76	−5.45	−0.79	3.87
9	Piauí	6.69	−5.29	−0.68	3.93
10	Ceará	7.02	0.41	3.24	6.07
11	Rio Grande do Norte	7.05	−3.42	0.82	5.05
12	Paraíba	6.36	−1.16	1.79	4.74
13	Pernambuco	5.06	0.56	2.67	4.77
14	Alagoas	6.86	−2.79	0.90	4.59
15	Sergipe	5.90	−0.46	2.24	4.93
16	Bahia	8.02	−4.55	0.19	4.94
17	Minas Gerais	7.46	1.30	3.98	6.66
18	Espírito Santo	7.16	−4.29	0.41	5.11
19	Rio de Janeiro	3.92	−0.08	2.04	4.16
20	São Paulo	4.04	0.67	2.78	4.88
21	Paraná	7.87	0.94	3.71	6.48
22	Santa Catarina	6.90	−0.13	3.07	6.28
23	Rio Grande do Sul	5.25	−0.72	1.96	4.64
25	Mato Grosso	7.94	2.06	5.19	8.32
26	Goiás	7.34	−9.57	−3.11	3.34
27	Distrito Federal	4.21	−14.29	−6.17	1.95
	Average	5.98	−3.26	0.75	4.77

Note: The combined contribution is computed as: $\dot{Y}/Y - S_k\ \dot{K}/K - 0.4\ \dot{L}/L$.

3.7. For a production elasticity of capital of 0.6, the estimated contributions are small and mostly negative, with an (unweighted) average of −3.3 percent per annum. The estimated contributions become higher and progressively more reasonable with lower assumed production elasticities of capital. For a production elasticity of capital of 0.2, the estimated contributions average 4.8 percent per annum, which appears reasonable given our knowledge of Brazilian economic growth during this period.

The estimated combined contributions of human capital and technical progress are plotted against the changes in average education in Figure 3.5. A positive correlation is discernible, especially for lower assumed production elasticities of capital.

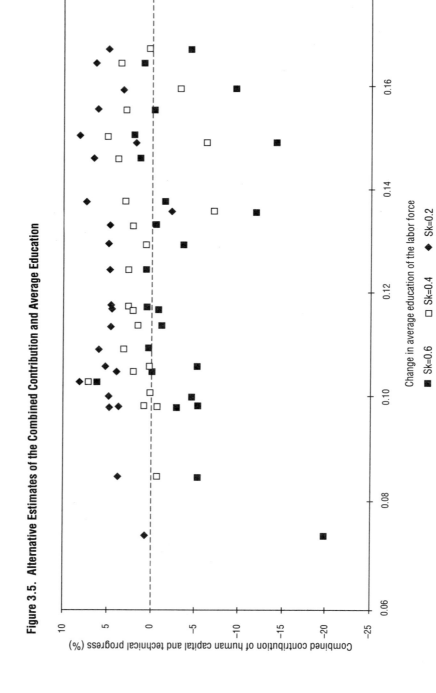

Figure 3.5. Alternative Estimates of the Combined Contribution and Average Education

Comparison with Other Studies and Further Explorations

Our estimated effect of average education on output of almost 21 percent per additional year of education is very high indeed. By comparison, based on the findings of Lau, Jamison and Louat (1990), the effect of one additional year of average education on Brazilian real output may be estimated to be approximately 5.5 percent,[12] which, it must be emphasized, is an economically significant effect. But this is a far cry from our estimate of 21 percent. Microeconomic studies of agricultural production have yielded estimated effects of education on the order of 2 percent per annum (Jamison and Lau, 1982). Studies of earnings functions have typically yielded estimated real rates of return to investment in human capital of at least 10 percent.[13] A real rate of return of 10 percent can be translated into an estimated effect of an additional year of education on output of around 4 percent under plausible assumptions.

How do we reconcile such a large estimated effect for education with those found in other studies? One way to look at our results is to ask: What proportion of the growth in Brazilian real output during the 1970s can be attributed to the increase in the average education of the labor force? The average education of the Brazilian labor force in the states in our sample increased by 1.25 years over this period. Thus, on account of the increase in average education alone, real output should have grown by 0.21 x 1.25 = 0.26, or 2.6 percent per annum. Compared with an average annual rate of growth of real output of 10.9 percent, the proportion of economic growth accounted for by the increase in education may be estimated at approximately 25 percent. This is not out of line with, say, Denison's (1967, 1979) finding that education has been responsible for between 10 and 15 percent of economic growth in the United States, especially considering that the Brazilian rate of growth has been so much higher.[14]

What are some plausible explanations for our empirical finding of such a high estimated effect for education? We first observe that such a high estimated effect probably cannot be expected to go on unchanged forever. If the effect of education were really so "high," we should be able to see it in

---

[12] Lau, Jamison and Louat (1990) report an estimated elasticity of output with respect to average total education of 0.165 for Latin America, based on a sample of 58 developing countries for 1960–86 that includes Brazil. Since the average level of education of the Brazilian labor force in 1970 is 3.03 (see Table 3.1), the effect of one additional year of average education may be estimated as 0.165/3.03 = 5.4 percent.

[13] See Psacharopoulos (1985, 1987).

[14] Recall Schultz's (1975) argument that the benefit of education is likely to be higher in a changing environment.

some other countries as well. Thus, it must be a transitory phenomenon. We examine three, not necessarily mutually exclusive, possible explanations.

   (1) A threshold effect. It is possible that between 1970 and 1980, the level of average education of the labor force in many Brazilian states finally reached the critical threshold level beyond which it would have a significant positive effect. Lau, Jamison and Louat (1990) find some evidence of a threshold level of average education between three and four years per person in the labor force. An examination of Table 3.1 indicates that a significant number of Brazilian states crossed over this threshold during the 1970s. A high measured effect between two points in time may be obtained with a threshold effect if the threshold happens to be crossed during that period. In other words, the measured effect of 21 percent per additional year applies only in the range of average education between three and four years. Over a longer period, with a much larger range of variation for average education, the *measured* effect per additional year will actually be lowered. This may account for the difference between our estimates and those obtained by Lau, Jamison and Louat (1990), which are based on data from 1960–86.

   A threshold effect may be modeled in the following way. Let a new set of human capital variables ED1, ED2, ED3, ED4 and ED5 be defined as:[15]

(22) $$ED1_{it} = \begin{cases} ED_{it} - 1, & ED_{it}\, 2 > ED1_{it} \geq 1 ; \\ 1, & ED_{it} \geq 2 ; \end{cases}$$

(23) $$ED2_{it} = \begin{cases} 0, & ED_{it} \leq 2 ; \\ ED_{it} - 2, & 3 > ED_{it} > 2 ; \\ 1, & ED_{it} \geq 3 ; \end{cases}$$

(24) $$ED3_{it} = \begin{cases} 0, & ED_{it} \leq 3 ; \\ ED_{it} - 3, & 4 > ED_{it} > 3 ; \\ 1, & ED_{it} \geq 4 ; \end{cases}$$

(25) $$ED4_{it} = \begin{cases} 0, & ED_{it} \leq 4 ; \\ ED_{it} - 4, & 5 > ED_{it} > 4 ; \\ 1, & ED_{it} \geq 5 ; \end{cases}$$

(26) $$ED5_{it} = \begin{cases} 0, & ED_{it} \leq 5 ; \\ ED_{it} - 5, & ED_{it} > 5 . \end{cases}$$

---

[15] The reader may recognize this specification of the human capital variable to be a spline. The effect of average education on output is assumed to be piecewise linear and continuous.

Table 3.8. Estimates from First-Differenced Equation with Disaggregated Average Education Variables

	Variable	Parameters
Constant	0.581	0.649
	(4.0)	(15.5)
ℓn Capital	0.061	0.090
	(1.4)	(2.4)
ℓn Labor	0.547	0.421
	(3.2)	(3.7)
ED1	0.113	
	(0.7)	
ED2	0.081	
	(0.8)	
ED3	0.251	0.208
	(2.5)	(4.0)
ED4	−0.001	
	(−0.0)	
ED5	−0.009	
	(−0.1)	
Adjusted R^2	0.821	0.832

Note: The values of the standard errors and variances are heteroscedasticity–consistent estimates. Numbers in parentheses are t–ratios.

Equation (18) may be rewritten in terms of this new set of variables as:

$$(27) \quad \ell n\, Y_{it} - \ell n\, Y_{it-1} = c^*_{i0} + a_K(\ell n K_{it} - \ell n K_{it-1}) + a_L(\ell n L_{it} - \ell n L_{it-1})$$
$$+ \sum_{j=1}^{5} a_{Ej}\, (ED_{jit} - ED_{jit-1}).$$

This specification of the human capital variables allows the slope of the average education effect per year on output to change from year to year while maintaining the continuity of the average education effect (see Figure 3.6). If there is a threshold effect of average education, we should find that the estimated coefficients a_{Ej} should initially rise and then fall with j, that is, the slope of output with respect to the number of years of education should rise somewhere between three and four years and then decline.

The results of estimating equation (27) are presented in Table 3.8. The relative magnitudes of the estimated parameters of average education are consistent with the existence of a threshold effect, or at a minimum, an interval over which the effects are convex (that is, they show increasing returns), between three and four years of average education (see Figure 3.6). The hypothesis that the marginal effect of education is independent of the level of education (that is, there is no threshold effect) can be rejected at the 10 percent

Figure 3.6. Estimated Disaggregated Effects of Education on Output

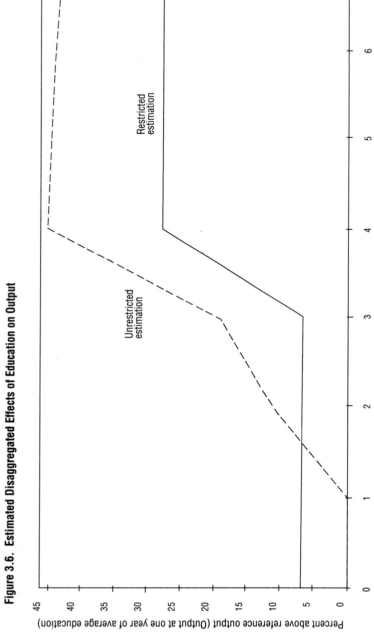

Table 3.9. Tests of Hypotheses on the Effects of Education

Hypothesis	Test–Statistic	Critical value at 10% level of significance
Identical marginal effects	21.75	7.78
Zero effects	25.91	9.24

Note: The values of the standard errors and variances are heteroscedasticity-consistent estimates.

level of significance. The hypothesis of no education effect can also be rejected. The results of the tests of these hypotheses are presented in Table 3.9.

The estimated disaggregated education effects do display the rise and fall pattern associated with the existence of a threshold, even though, with the exception of ED3, average education between three and four years, they are not statistically significantly different from zero. If the statistically insignificant effects are set equal to zero, the estimated effect of ED3 (Table 3.8) is exactly the same as the effect of the aggregated average education variable of 0.208 (see Table 3.4). One may note that the adjusted R^2 of the restricted regression (column 2, Table 3.8) is higher than that of any other regression reported in this study. The restricted as well as the unrestricted estimated effects of an additional year of education at each level of education are plotted in Figure 3.6. It shows a clearly discernible threshold. Figure 3.6 also shows how a lower estimated effect of education may be found if the observed levels of average education are more spread out on both sides of the threshold.

(2) *Capital-education complementarity.* It is also possible that physical and human capital are complements, so that the effectiveness of one is enhanced by the presence of the other.[16] If human capital turns out to be the relatively scarcer input, one would observe a high measured effect of average education. In other words, the high measured effect of average education may be due to the high rate of increase of physical capital.

Capital-education complementarity may be modeled by using a more flexible functional form such as the transcendental logarithmic production function introduced by Christensen, Jorgenson and Lau (1973). With a translog production function, equation (18) may be rewritten as:

$$(28)\ \ln Y_{it} - \ln Y_{it-1} = c^*_{i0} + a_K(\ln K_{it} - \ln K_{it-1}) + a_L(\ln L_{it} - \ln L_{it}) + a_E(ED_{it} - ED_{it-1})$$
$$+ B_{KK}((\ln K^2_{it}) - (\ln K_{it-1})^2)/2 + B_{LL}((\ln L_{it})^2 - (\ln L_{it-1})^2)/2$$
$$+ B_{EE}(ED^2_{it} - ED^2_{it-1})/2 + B_{KL}(\ln K_{it}\ln L_{it} - \ln K_{it-1}\ln L_{it-1})$$
$$+ B_{KE}(\ln K_{it}ED_{it} - \ln K_{it-1}ED_{it-1}) + B_{LE}(\ln L_{it}ED_{it} - \ln L_{it-1}ED_{it-1}) .$$

---

[16] Capital-technology complementarity has been found by Boskin and Lau (1990).

Table 3.10. Further Estimates from First-Differenced Equation

Variable	Parameters	
Constant	0.354	0.464
	(2.0)	(5.5)
ℓn Capital	−0.360	0.057
	(−1.6)	(1.4)
ℓn Labor	1.527	0.604
	(3.6)	(4.2)
Average education	0.615	0.294
	(1.8)	(3.9)
Average education*t		−0.054
		(−3.1)
$(\ell n$ Capital$)^2$	−0.005	
	(−0.2)	
$(\ell n$ Labor$)^2$	−0.246	
	(−2.0)	
(Average education)^2	−0.005	
	(−0.1)	
$(\ell n$ Capital$)^* (\ell n$ Labor$)$	−0.077	
	(1.3)	
$(\ell n$ Capital$)^*$(Average education)	−0.006	
	(−0.2)	
$(\ell n$ Labor$)^*$(Average education)	−0.048	
	(−0.8)	
Adjusted R^2	0.793	0.799

Note: The values of the standard errors and variances are heteroscedasticity-consistent estimates. Numbers in parentheses are t-ratios.

If there is capital-education complementarity, we should find:

(29) $B_{KE} > 0$.

The results of estimating equation (28) are presented in Table 3.10. The first hypothesis that we test with the transcendental logarithmic meta-production function model is that all the second-order parameters—B_{KK}, B_{LL}, B_{KL}, B_{EE}, B_{KE}, and B_{LE} are zero. This hypothesis cannot be rejected—the F-value of the null hypothesis is 1.58 against a critical value of 2.33 at the 10 percent level of significance. We conclude that the empirical evidence does not lend support to capital-education complementarity as an explanation of the high estimated effect of average education in Brazil.

(3) Education-technical progress complementarity. It has been argued by Schultz (1975) that the benefits of education may be greatest in a changing environment. The 1970s was a time of extraordinarily rapid change in Bra-

zil, with average annual rate of growth or real output exceeding 10 percent per annum. Thus, it is also reasonable to suppose that the effectiveness of education was at or near its peak. However, operationally, this hypothesis is much harder to verify independently than either the threshold hypothesis or the capital-education complementarity hypothesis. What is needed is some kind of independent measure of the degree of rapidity of change other than the rate of growth of real output itself, or of some variable closely correlated with it.

One way to construe Schultz's hypothesis, which is probably narrower than was intended, is the complementarity between technical progress or growth in total factor productivity (measuring the change holding inputs constant) and average education. The rate of technical progress is higher the higher the level of average education and vice versa.

A simple model capturing education-technical progress complementarity is given by:

(30) $\ell n Y_{it} = \ell n Y_0 + \ell n A^*_{i0} + c^*_0 t + a_K \ell n K_{it} + a_L \ell n L_{it} + a_E ED_{it} + B_{Et} ED_{it} t.$

First-differencing equation (30) yields:

$$(31)\ \ell n Y_{it} - \ell n Y_{it-1} = c^*_0 + a_K(\ell n K_{it} - \ell n K_{it-1}) + a_L(\ell n L_{it} - \ell n L_{it-1})$$
$$+ a_E(ED_{it} - ED_{it-1}) + B_{Et}(ED_{it} t - ED_{it-1}(t-1))$$
$$= c^*_0 + a_K(\ell n K_{it} - \ell n K_{it-1}) + a_L(\ell n L_{it} - \ell n L_{it-1})$$
$$+ a_E(ED_{it} - ED_{it-1}) + B_{Et}(ED_{it} - ED_{it-1})t + B_{Et} ED_{it-1}.$$

For the case $t - 1 = 0$, equation (31) simplifies into:

$$(32)\ \ell n Y_{it} - \ell n Y_{it-1} = c^*_0 + a_K(\ell n K_{it} - \ell n K_{it-1}) + a_L(\ell n L_{it} - \ell n L_{it-1}) + a^*_E(ED_{it} - ED_{it-1}) + B_{Et} ED_{it},$$

where $a^*_E = a_E + B_{Et}$. The results of estimating equation (32) are also presented in Table 3.10. Unfortunately, the estimated value of B_{Et} is negative, contrary to the prediction of the education-technical progress complementarity hypothesis. We conclude that the empirical evidence does not lend support to education-technical progress complementarity as an explanation of the high estimated effect of average education in Brazil.

Conclusions

We have applied the meta-production function approach to study the relationship in Brazil between real output and inputs, including human capital, using two cross-sections of data from individual states. We have not made explicit adjustments for the quality of capital or labor, as were done by

Denison (1962, 1967, 1979, 1985) and Jorgenson, Gollop and Fraumeni (1987). Instead, we introduce human capital, measured as the average number of years of formal education per person of the labor force, explicitly as a variable in the aggregate production function. We also introduce a time trend to capture the effect of technical progress. Any improvement in inputs not captured by the human capital variable should be reflected in technical progress.

Our results indicate that average education of the labor force has a large, positive and statistically significant effect on output. One additional year of average education is estimated to increase real output by approximately 20 percent. However, there is also evidence that this estimated effect reflects a threshold of minimum average education of somewhere between three and four years in order for education to begin to have an impact. Thus, the magnitude of the measured effect of education is likely to be transitory. It turns out to be large in this study because many Brazilian states happened to cross over the threshold during the 1970s, precisely the period covered by our sample. As the threshold is crossed, the measured marginal effect of one additional year of average education will be large. Over the longer run, the measured effect of education may be expected to decline, if the threshold really exists. However, we also believe that the effect of one additional year of average education per person in the labor force on real output is not likely to be less than 5 percent, on average, based on the results of other studies. Incidentally, a gain of approximately 20 percent over four years (assuming that the threshold occurs at four years) averages out to approximately 5 percent per year of average education, very close to the estimate based on Lau, Jamison and Louat (1990). If similar data are available for the Brazilian states for one additional year, say, 1985 or 1990, then it may be possible to improve on the precision of our estimate of the effect of average education and its threshold, if any.

The existence of a threshold suggests that there is a range of average education over which output is *convex* in average education, that is, there are increasing returns to average education, albeit only locally. There is thus some empirical support for the hypothesis of increasing returns in intangible capital such as that proposed by Romer (1986). A threshold also implies, however, that the level of investment in education required before it has any effect on output can be quite high and the gestation period may be exceedingly long, especially if a developing country starts out with a low initial level of average education. It may be decades before any effect on output can be observed. The benefits of investment in human capital, as suggested by the findings here, can also be very high and will persist for a long time because of the durability of human capital. This argues for constant, patient investments in education.

Given the threshold in the *average education* of the labor force, two additional avenues of research immediately suggest themselves. First, what is the optimal distribution of this average education? For example, is it better to have one half of the labor force with six years and the other half with two years, or for everyone to have four years? The threshold effect seems to favor, in this instance, a more egalitarian distribution, but a more detailed study is required. Second, what is the optimal mix of primary, secondary and tertiary education at the different stages of economic development? Both of these questions have direct and important policy relevance.

Finally, it should be emphasized that a threshold effect in *average* education is a genuinely macroeconomic phenomenon. It rests on "network"-type externalities not unlike that of a telephone system. The benefit of the telephone system to both the individual subscriber and the society increases with the total number of subscribers (until, of course, the telephone switches become overloaded). Similarly, the threshold on average education implies that to realize the maximum benefits of education, educated workers must have other educated workers with whom to interact. Thus, for example, it may not be as beneficial to have only a small number of highly educated workers with a resulting low level of average education of the labor force as to have a larger pool of moderately educated workers who can communicate effectively with one another. Of course, how average education will affect real output depends on the nature of the institutional environment of the economy as a whole. The macroeconomic effect of education may not be merely the sum of the microeconomic, individual effects.

REFERENCES

Boskin, M.J., and L.J. Lau. 1990. Post-War Economic Growth of the Group-of-Five Countries: A New Analysis. Technical Paper No. 217. Center for Economic Policy Research, Stanford University. Mimeo.

Bowman, M.J. 1980. Education and Economic Growth: An Overview In *Education and Income: A Background Study for World Development Report*, ed. T. King. World Bank Staff Working Paper No. 402, Washington, D.C.

Bowman, M.J. 1987. The Relevance of Education. In *Economics of Education: Research and Studies*, ed. G. Psacharopoulos. Oxford: Pergamon Press.

Central Bank of Brazil, Department of Economics. 1990. *Brasil: Programa Econômico.* Vol. 24.

Christensen, L.R., D.W. Jorgenson, and L.J. Lau. 1973. Transcendental Logarithmic Production Frontiers. *Review of Economics and Statistics* 55: 28–45.

Denison, E.F. 1985. *Trends in American Economic Growth, 1929–1982.* Washington, D.C.: Brookings Institution.

_____. 1979. *Accounting for Slower Economic Growth: The United States in the 1970s.* Washington, D.C.: Brookings Institution.

_____. 1967. *Why Growth Rates Differ: Post-War Experience in Nine Western Countries.* Washington, D.C.: Brookings Institution.

_____. 1962. United States Economic Growth. *Journal of Business* 35: 109–21.

Hayami, Y., and V.W. Ruttan. 1985. *Agricultural Development: An International Perspective.* Baltimore: Johns Hopkins University Press.

_____. 1970. Agricultural Productivity Differences Among Countries. *American Economic Review* 60: 895–911.

Hicks, N.L. 1987. Education and Economic Growth. In *Economics of Education: Research and Studies*, ed. G. Psacharopoulos. Oxford: Pergamon Press.

Instituto Brasileiro de Geografia e Estatística (IBGE). 1987. *Estatísticas Históricas do Brasil: Séries Econômicas, Demográficas e Sociais de 1550 a 1985, Séries Estatísticas Retrospectivas.* Vol. 3. Rio de Janeiro.

_____. 1981, 1971. *Anuário Estatístico do Brasil.* Rio de Janeiro.

_____. 1970. *Censo Demográfico: VIII Recenseamento Geral—1970* 1(1–24).

Jamison, D.T., and L.J. Lau. 1982. *Farmer Education and Farm Efficiency.* Baltimore: The Johns Hopkins University Press.

Jorgenson, D.W., F.M. Gollop, and B.M. Fraumeni. 1987. *Productivity and U.S. Economic Growth.* Cambridge, MA: Harvard University Press.

Kawagoe, T., Y. Hayami, and V.W. Ruttan. 1985. The Intercountry Agricultural Production Function and Productivity Differences Among Countries. *Journal of Development Economics* 19: 113–32.

Lau, L.J. 1989. A Comparative Analysis of Economic Development Experiences in Chinese Societies. In *Economic Development in Chinese Societies: Models and Experiences,* eds. Y.C. Jao, V. Mok, and L.S. Ho. Hong Kong: Hong Kong University Press.

Lau, L.J., D.T. Jamison, and F.F. Louat. 1990. *Education and Productivity in Developing Countries: An Aggregate Production Function Approach.* Working Paper WPS 612, World Bank, Washington, D.C.

Lau, L.J., and P.A. Yotopoulos. 1989. The Meta-Production Function Approach to Technological Change in World Agriculture. *Journal of Development Economics* 31: 241–69.

Lockheed, M.E., D.T. Jamison, and L.J. Lau. 1980. Farmer Education and Farm Efficiency: A Survey. *Economic Development and Cultural Change* 29: 37–76.

Psacharopoulos, G. 1987. Earnings Functions. In *Economics of Education: Research and Studies,* ed. G. Psacharopoulos. Oxford: Pergamon Press, 218–23.

_____. 1985. Returns to Education: A Further International Update and Implications. *The Journal of Human Resources* 20: 584–604.

Romer, P.M. 1986. Increasing Returns and Long-Run Growth. *Journal of Political Economy* 94: 1002–37.

Schultz, T.W. 1975. The Value of the Ability to Deal with Disequilibria. *Journal of Economic Literature* 13: 872–76.

_____. 1961. Investment in Human Capital. *American Economic Review* 51: 1–17.

White, H.J. 1980. A Heteroskedasticity-Consistent Covariance Matrix Estimator and a Direct Test for Heteroskedasticity. *Econometrica* 48: 817–38.

Appendix

Code	State	Code	State
02	Rondônia	15	Sergipe
03	Roraima	16	Bahia
04	Amapá	17	Minas Gerais
05	Acre	18	Espírito Santo
06	Amazonas	19	Rio de Janeiro
07	Pará	20	São Paulo
08	Maranhão	21	Paraná
09	Piauí	22	Santa Catarina
10	Ceará	23	Rio Grande do Sul
11	Rio Grande do Norte	24	Mato Grosso do Sul ⎫ combined as 25
12	Paraíba	25	Mato Grosso ⎭
13	Pernambuco	26	Goiás
14	Alagoas	27	Distrito Federal

Appendix Table 3.1. Tests of Hypotheses

Hypothesis	Test-Statistic	Critical value at 10% level of significance
No education effect	1.473	1.71
Constant returns to scale	7.214	1.71

Note: The values of the standard errors and variances are heteroscedasticity-consistent estimates.

Appendix Table 3.2. Estimates from First-Differenced Equation

Variable	Parameters		
Constant	0.551	0.730	
	(4.5)	(17.1)	
ℓn Capital	0.052	0.054	0.075
	(1.8)	(1.8)	(1.7)
ℓn Labor	0.515	0.486	0.616
	(6.5)	(6.8)	(4.7)
Average education	0.136		0.491
	(1.5)		(16.4)
Adjusted R^2	0.478	0.483	0.437

Note: The values of the standard errors and variances are heteroscedasticity-consistent estimates. Numbers in parentheses are t-ratios.

Appendix Table 3.3. Estimates Under Alternative Assumptions on the Rate of Technical Progress

Variable	Assumed rate of technical progress (percent per annum)				
	1	2	3	4	5
	Parameters				
ℓn Capital	0.071	0.067	0.063	0.059	0.055
	(1.8)	(1.8)	(1.9)	(1.9)	(1.9)
ℓn Labor	0.597	0.579	0.561	0.544	0.526
	(5.1)	(5.4)	(5.8)	(6.2)	(6.6)
Average education	0.426	0.363	0.300	0.238	0.177
	(14.8)	(12.8)	(10.7)	(8.3)	(6.0)
Adjusted R^2	0.454	0.469	0.483	0.494	0.501

Note: The values of the standard errors and variances are heteroscedasticity-consistent estimates. Numbers in parentheses are t-ratios.

Appendix Table 3.4. Estimation Results with Instrumental Variables

Variable	Equation 1	Equation 2	Equation 3
Constant	0.400	0.478	0.594
	(1.9)	(1.6)	(12.5)
ℓn Capital	0.103	−0.023	0.127
	(2.1)	(−0.3)	(2.7)
ℓn Labor	0.414	0.880	0.319
	(3.4)	(2.6)	(2.4)
Average education	0.223		
	(1.7)		
ED1		0.379	
		(1.0)	
ED2		0.092	
		(0.5)	
ED3		0.419	0.290
		(1.7)	(3.0)
ED4		−0.026	
		(−0.1)	
ED5		0.099	
		(0.6)	
Adjusted R^2	0.752	0.751	0.808

Note: The values of the standard errors and variances are heteroscedasticity-consistent estimates. Numbers in parentheses are t-ratios.

Why Brazil Lags Behind in Educational Development

David N. Plank, José Amaral Sobrinho and
Antonio Carlos da Ressurreição Xavier

Though one of the richest countries in Latin America, Brazil consistently lags behind its neighbors in most indicators of educational development. This chapter argues that the main reason for this lag is the predominance of private interests over public purposes in the formulation and implementation of educational policies.

We begin by examining three instances in which public resources are allocated to benefit particular constituencies: the various practices subsumed under the name of *clientelismo;* the provision of public subsidies to private schools coupled with public regulation of private school fees; and the maintenance of "free" higher education in public universities.

The second section looks at political conflicts in the educational system that focus not on the definition of policy objectives but on control of policy instruments. Three leading issues in Brazilian school politics are discussed: the distribution of resources and responsibilities between central and local authorities; the role of private schools; and the reduction of inequalities in educational attainment, especially across regions.

Finally, we discuss recent constitutional and administrative changes that offer the possibility of improvement in the educational system. Among the most important are the emergence of new organizations and administrative practices at state and municipal levels and the establishment of an actionable right to education in the 1988 Constitution.

Background

The persistent backwardness of the Brazilian educational system has been recognized and analyzed for more than six decades. Before the revolution of 1930, politicians and policymakers began to acknowledge that to join the ranks of the developed countries, Brazil would need to vastly improve its educational system (Romanelli, 1978). In their development plans and policy documents, successive governments have invariably acknowledged the country's educational problems and the threat they pose to future economic growth and social well-being. Both military and civilian regimes have called for the expansion and improvement of the school system, assigning the highest priority to the achievement of universal primary schooling and the elimination of illiteracy.

Since 1930 much has changed for the better: enrollment rates at all levels have greatly increased, universities have proliferated, and literacy rates have risen sharply. Brazil nevertheless continues to lag behind other countries in virtually all indices of educational development. The Ministry of Education (MEC) estimates that only 82 percent of children between the ages of seven and 14 are enrolled and that nearly five million children of compulsory attendance age are not in school. Only 16.5 percent of those between the ages of 15 and 19 were enrolled in secondary schools in 1989 (see Table 4.1). The literacy rate among adults is approximately 80 percent, which means that more than 17 million Brazilians cannot read and write (MEC, 1990). Far from matching the educational standards of Europe and North America, educational standards in 1990 barely exceed those of the poorest countries in the hemisphere.

The reasons for this poor performance are well known and amply documented.[1] Among them are low teacher salaries and a consequent shortage of qualified teachers, especially in rural areas; scarcity of textbooks and instructional materials; abbreviated school days; decaying and ill-equipped school buildings; administrative inefficiency; and curricular and pedagogical rigidities that perpetuate high dropout and grade repetition rates.

A variety of explanations are commonly put forward for the continuing lack of improvement in the Brazilian educational system, including scarcity of financial and human resources, as well as any number of material, institutional and political obstacles in the process of policy implemen-

---

[1] The *Pioneiros da Educação Nova* published a diagnosis of Brazil's educational problems in 1932 and recommended policies to resolve them (Romanelli, 1978, pp. 146–49). Their analyses and policy proposals have been repeated often in documents ranging from the first version of the *Lei de Diretrizes e Bases da Educação Nacional (LDB)* in 1948 to the National Development Plans promulgated by the military governments of the 1960s and 1970s to the *Educação Para Todos* manifesto published by Brazil's first post-coup civilian government in 1985 (Villalobos, 1969; Freitag, 1978; MEC, 1985). More recent examples include preliminary versions of the new LDB now under discussion in the National Congress, the education policy objectives proposed by the opposition Workers' Party, and the Collor government's *Plano de Reconstrução Nacional* (Câmara dos Deputados, 1990; *Folha de São Paulo,* 4 September 1990; Presidência da República, 1991).

Table 4.1. Enrollments in First and Second Level Education, 1980–89

	Enrollment (1st grade)	Rate(%) (7–14)	Enrollment (2nd grade)	Rate(%) (15–19)
1980	18,746,634	84.2	1,930,289	14.5
1981	18,361,803	79.8	1,967,350	14.5
1982	19,176,132	82.9	1,986,802	14.7
1983	19,767,713	85.3	1,900,500	13.9
1984	20,134,509	82.7	1,987,171	14.5
1985	19,609,311	80.9	1,998,212	14.4
1986	20,480,420	80.6	2,057,920	14.7
1987	21,163,252	81.8	2,182,866	15.5
1988	21,909,045	82.2	2,291,866*	16.0
1989	22,616,469	82.2	2,401,866*	16.5

Source: MEC (1990).
* Estimates.

tation that prevent achievement of clearly defined and universally approved educational objectives.

Explanations of this type face the monumental task of accounting for consistent policy failure in the Brazilian education system. But to attribute the persistence of Brazil's educational problems to poor policy implementation is to impute an extraordinarily low level of competence to a long line of Brazilian governments, both civilian and military. It is simply implausible to suppose that all of the laws, plans and policies put forward in the past 60 years to bring about improvements in the educational system have come to nothing for lack of leadership, money or technical skill.[2]

The argument that the ongoing problems of the educational system represent a failure to implement worthy educational policies is rooted in two closely related and equally mistaken assumptions. The first is that stated goals coincide with real goals.[3] In fact, the educational system's public objectives may be and often are significantly different from the objectives pursued by those in charge of the system. The former invariably include expanded access and improved instructional quality at all levels of the sys-

---

[2] This is even more implausible when one considers that several of Brazil's poorer and smaller neighbors have done far better in terms of progress toward these objectives.

[3] The distance between the goals that are formally stated in Brazilian education system and those that are actually pursued has been noted previously by authors such as Anísio Teixeira (1957). Earlier analyses of this disjunction focused on curriculum and administrative structure, while we focus on the distribution of resources.

tem, with particular emphasis on basic education. In contrast, the latter often include the provision of jobs and financial benefits for clients and the maximization of electoral support through the protection or advancement of special interests.

The second assumption follows from the first. It asserts that the key policy problem in the educational system is the identification of the "best" (most effective, most efficient) means for accomplishing agreed-upon system goals. In an educational system where private objectives commonly take precedence over public, however, political conflict focuses not on the definition of policy objectives but on the ostensibly technical question of the choice of policy instruments. Conflict arises not in disagreements over the merits of alternative administrative and financial arrangements but rather in a struggle for control of resources and responsibilities within the educational system.

Public Purpose and Private Interest

Debates on policy objectives in the Brazilian educational system are characterized by a remarkable degree of unanimity.[4] Political parties, candidates and public officials at all levels of government agree that the exigencies of economic progress and political democracy demand the reduction of the "social debt" owed by the government to Brazil's poorest citizens. In educational policy this has been translated into agreement that priority within the educational system should be assigned to eliminating illiteracy and ensuring universal access to basic education.[5] Despite consensus on the importance of these policy objectives, however, illiteracy in Brazil has not declined significantly in recent years. In addition, enrollment rates in basic education have barely increased, and large numbers of school-aged children remain entirely outside the educational system (MEC, 1990).

Discussions of the persistent problems of Brazilian education typically focus on identifying the causes of repeated failure to implement educational policies and achieve agreed educational objectives. Among the

---

[4] For a recent example, see the analysis of the candidates' education platforms in the 1990 gubernatorial elections in São Paulo published in *Folha de São Paulo,* 20 September 1990. The platforms are virtually identical, both in the objectives that they define and in their common failure to specify from where the resources to achieve those objectives will come. It was nevertheless notable to see education raised as an issue at all in this campaign.

[5] The obligation to eliminate illiteracy and achieve universal primary education in the 10 years following the adoption of Brazil's new Constitution (i.e., by 1998) are included among the Constitution's transitory provisions (Article 60).

commonly cited candidates for blame are the insufficiency of financial resources, the absence of political leadership, the incompetence and venality of public officials at all levels, the complexity and inefficiency of administrative structures, and the lack of timely and reliable information needed for educational planning.[6] These and similar explanations have been proposed regularly to account for the nearly uniform failure of successive policy initiatives to bring about significant and lasting improvement in the performance of the Brazilian educational system.

We will not assume the priority of publicly affirmed policy objectives and ask why worthy goals have not been attained. Rather, we assume in the analysis that follows that policy actions coincide with policy objectives, and we ask instead what policy "successes" have been achieved in the Brazilian educational system over the past six decades (Plank, 1992). The starting point is acknowledgement that the ostensible "failures" of the Brazilian educational system serve some powerful interests. The educational objectives assigned priority by these groups may depart radically from those that are universally affirmed in public debate by politicians and education officials. These actual objectives may nevertheless take precedence in decisions about the allocation of resources within the system.[7] Insofar as this is so, the advancement or protection of the interests of these groups represent policy "successes," even if they are achieved at the expense of "failure" in the achievement of other, more widely shared goals. From this point of view, the persistent backwardness of the Brazilian educational system is not attributable to problems in the implementation of policies. Instead, the situation reflects the fact that the public purposes affirmed by politicians and officials are systematically subordinated to the service of private interests.

---

[6] These are among the explanations proposed for the problems encountered in implementing the recently concluded EDURURAL Project. The same list was adduced by Castro (1989) in his analysis of the persistent problems of the basic education system. In a more recent paper, Castro and Oliveira (1991) propose a diagnosis that emphasizes the political obstacles to educational improvement. But where we argue that Brazil's educational problems can in large part be traced to resistance to change among groups that benefit from present policies, Castro and Oliveira suggest that the main hurdle for reformers is a lack of demand for expanded access and improved educational quality among the disadvantaged.

[7] Two points are worth noting in this connection. First, the most heated educational policy debates in recent years have focused on precisely those issues that place distinct private interests in conflict with the achievement of publicly-affirmed educational objectives. Second, the education policy "successes" claimed by Castro (1989)—that is, the expansion of university enrollments and the establishment of technical secondary schools—similarly advanced the interests of the relatively well-off rather than the poor.

Examples of this subordination include the many varieties of clientelistic politics that are practiced in the educational system, the provision of public subsidies to private schools and private school students, and the perpetuation of "free" higher education in public universities.

Clientelismo

Clientelismo represents the systematic subversion of public purposes in the service of private interests through the diversion of public resources to private ends. Rather than responding to the public interest through developing and implementing policies that benefit society at large, Brazilian politicians often find that their electoral prospects are best served by concluding private agreements with particular voters or groups of voters. These agreements may extend from the literal purchase of votes to the distribution of jobs and contracts to supporters, and to the provision of nominally public services to different groups on a discriminatory basis.[8] The crucial issue in Brazilian politics is therefore not what policies are to be assigned priority, but *who* is to control the instruments of power. Under these circumstances, many of the benefits of government action are captured by favored groups and individuals. Meanwhile, the interests of those with less influence (e.g., the poor, clients of opposing candidates) are systematically neglected.

Widespread reliance on special interest politics provides the clearest examples of the subordination of public purposes to private interests in the Brazilian educational system. *Clientelismo* in education comprises a variety of practices, including the provision of jobs for clients and supporters, the awarding of public contracts to political allies, and the distribution of public resources in accordance with the exigencies of electoral politics.

Providing jobs for clients is the most important and costly manifestation of *clientelismo* in the Brazilian educational system.[9] Reliance on the school system as a source of employment for political allies has a number of pernicious consequences. Administrative agencies at all levels of the educa-

---

[8] For an assessment of the market for votes in Bahia, see *A Tarde,* 23 September 1990. For the manipulation of state expenditures in São Paulo to favor some candidates and penalize others, see *Folha de São Paulo,* 23 September 1990.

[9] The literature on providing jobs for clients or *empreguismo* is extensive but not very systematic. A partial catalogue of the abuses associated with the practice is provided by Farhat (1987). With specific reference to education, an excellent review is provided by Leal (1990).

tional system are overstaffed, often with underqualified people. Each new Secretary of Education in the state of Rio de Janeiro makes approximately 4,000 political appointments; a survey in the Secretariat of Education in Ceará determined that 19 percent of all functionaries occupied their positions at the discretion of the Secretary.[10] Salaries are also provided to "ghost teachers" working outside of schools, or not working at all; Leal (1990) has estimated that 20 percent of those receiving teachers' salaries in Rio de Janeiro are in fact working elsewhere. Employment according to political rather than professional criteria results in massive turnover among school system personnel in the wake of state and local elections, as senior functionaries and school principals are replaced by the allies of the new incumbents. Similar disruptions occur at the federal level; each new Minister of Education is accompanied into office by over 300 senior administrators (Oliveira, 1984; *A Tarde,* 31 October 1987).

Perpetual turnover among system personnel virtually prevents the acquisition of professional competence among educators and rules out continuity in the execution of educational policies. Pressing educational objectives do not fall to the wayside because of problems encountered in policy implementation, Instead, serious efforts to implement policy are preempted by efforts to cultivate and expand political support through the distribution of jobs.

Examples of *clientelismo* exist throughout the educational system. For example, school construction contracts are awarded to political supporters, a practice estimated to inflate costs by as much as 40 percent (Mello e Souza, 1989). Moreover, in 1986 the rapid reallocation of federal education revenues budgeted for transfer to state governments following the election of 25 opposition governors resulted in an increase of nearly 600 percent in direct federal transfers to municipalities (CEC/IPEA, 1987; Plank, 1990). Other examples include the upsurge in educational investment that accompanies state and local elections and the decline that typically follows (Bahia, 1990), as well as periodic accounts of corruption in school feeding programs and elsewhere in the educational system (*Folha de São Paulo,* 20 and 21 April 1988; *A Tarde,* 27 August 1990). Whether legal or not, these and similar activities shift resources within the educational system toward persons and groups with political or economic ties to those in charge of the system.

---

[10] Political appointments are known as *cargos de confiança.* For Rio de Janeiro, see Leal (1990, p. 138). For Ceará, see Leite and Barreto (1983, p. 107).

Public Authorities and Private Schools

The complex relationship between public authorities and private schools provides a second set of examples of the subordination of public objectives to private interests. This relationship has two main dimensions. On the one hand, private schools receive large quantities of public money through direct and indirect transfers from federal and state governments. On the other hand, the fees that private schools charge parents are subject to regulation by public authorities. In concert, these policies serve to ensure the survival of a large number of private schools and to guarantee the "right" of parents to send their children to them. At the same time, these policies contribute to the further deterioration of the public schools, both by depriving them of potential revenues and by encouraging the flight of parents who might provide an articulate and effective voice in favor of school recuperation. As a result, the public schools are widely and accurately perceived to be schools for the poor, of no immediate concern to anyone other than those condemned to attend or work in them.

There are two distinct kinds of private schools in Brazil. High-quality, high-cost primary and secondary schools serve the children of the middle and upper classes, while low-cost schools serve poor children in areas where the public provision of schools is inadequate. Secondary schools predominate among low-cost private schools, which are found mainly in rural areas and on the urban periphery. Both kinds of schools receive public subsidies, which are essential to the survival of many low-cost schools. The regulation of school fees represents a concession to middle-class parents and has consequently had its largest effects on high-cost schools.

Public subsidies to private schools take several different forms. Private schools are exempt from the payment of both income tax and the wage tax targeted for support of primary education. These private institutions participate in a variety of agreements with federal, state and local governments in which public authorities "purchase" school places.[11] Students may receive scholarships for private school tuition from a variety of public sources at both state and federal levels, some of which are distributed through the offices of elected officials, including members of the National Congress. Under a policy known as the *Sistema de Manutenção do Ensino (SME)*, firms may withhold payment of the wage tax in order to maintain their own schools or to reim-

---

[11] Forms of purchase of school places may include the provision of space in public school buildings for private schools, the payment of public school teachers to teach in private schools, the provision of scholarships to students, and the provision of subventions to private schools that accept public school students (CEC/IPEA, 1987, pp. 14–18).

Table 4.2. Wage Tax Revenues by Agency, 1980–89
(In thousands of 1989 cruzeiros)

	IAPAS[1]	FNDE[2]	Total[3]	% FNDE
1980	874.6	169.5	1,044.1	16.2
1981	1,060.4	260.9	1,321.3	19.7
1982	1,052.8	600.6	1,653.5	36.3
1983	1,073.8	629.9	1,703.7	37.0
1984	758.7	684.7	1,443.4	47.4
1985	671.1	988.2	1,659.3	59.6
1986	1,012.9	1,352.2	2,365.1	57.2
1987	1,114.1	1,438.3	2,552.4	56.4
1988	1,087.1	1,562.0	2,649.1	59.0
1989	1,488.0	2,229.0	3,717.1	60.0

Source: FNDE (1990).

[1] The revenues collected by IAPAS (the Social Security Agency) constitute the federal (QF) and state (QE) shares of the wage tax. The percentage of the QF allocated to private schools has declined significantly in recent years, from 7 percent in 1982 to less than 2 percent in 1989. There are no data on the percentage of the QE that goes to private schools.

[2] The wage tax revenues attributed to the FNDE include both revenues collected by FNDE for the purchase of places in private schools and revenues retained by firms to maintain their own schools or reimburse the private school expenses of their employees. All of the revenues attributed to the FNDE support private rather than public schools.

[3] Row totals may differ slightly due to rounding.

burse the educational expenditures of employees or their dependents. They may also route their contributions to private schools through the *Fundo Nacional de Desenvolvimento da Educação (FNDE)* in order to provide tuition scholarships for the children of their employees (Velloso, 1987; FNDE, 1990).

In addition to providing opportunities for fraud and *clientelismo,* these policies result in the diversion of large quantities of resources from public to private schools. Since 1985, for example, more than half of all wage tax contributions have been routed through the SME rather than through the social security system (FNDE, 1990) (see Table 4.2). Direct federal expenditures on student scholarships and the purchase of school places through the FNDE, the *Fundação de Assistência ao Estudante (FAE),* the *Conselho Nacional de Serviços Sociais (CNSS)* and other agencies are also substantial (FNDE, 1990; Leal, 1990). In 1989, federal transfers to private schools amounted to 2.3 billion cruzeiros, or more than one-third of all federal expenditures on primary education. Transfers from state and local governments were also large in many states, especially in the Northeast.[12]

---

[12] In 1986, officials in the Secretariat of Education in Bahia estimated that 40 percent of all educational expenditures in the state went to support private schools. Our own more recent estimates suggest that the share going to private schools has been greatly reduced in the years since, but the amounts in question remain large.

Public authorities in Brazil have also adopted policies to protect the access of middle-class households to private education. Over the protests of private school directors, the series of economic "plans" decreed by the Sarney and Collor governments have included the regulation of private school fees, in a relatively successful effort to keep them in line with (likewise regulated) salaries.[13] The main effect of this policy has been to spare middle-class parents from the obligation of sending their children to public schools. The share of primary school children enrolled in private schools has risen substantially since 1985, with some fluctuations, while the share of secondary enrollments in private schools has declined slightly (see Table 4.3).

The role of private schools in the Brazilian educational system has been a topic of intense political controversy for four decades. A campaign to restrict the allocation of public funds to public institutions produced one of the most contentious debates in the recent Constituent Assembly (Plank, 1990), and the question has been raised again in the debate over the new *Lei de Diretrizes e Bases da Educação Nacional (LDB)*. Conflicts engendered by the regulation of private school fees have in turn been the most loudly contested educational issue in Brazil in the past five years. With respect to these conflicts, however, it is important to note that they have emerged in consequence of competition between specific private interests (e.g., between middle-class parents and the directors of private schools) and not between competing conceptions of the public interest. The majority of Brazilians who lack the economic or political resources necessary to escape from the public schools are not represented in these debates, and their interests are systematically neglected as a result.

Keeping Public Universities "Free"

A third example of the subordination of public to private interests is the perpetuation of "free" higher education in public universities. Despite the priority universally accorded to primary education and the conquest of illiteracy in political manifestos and policy documents, about 60 percent of the federal education budget continues to be devoted to the support of federal universities (Verhine, 1991; Gomes, 1988). The shares of state education budgets that go to fund state university systems are also steadily increas-

---

[13] For a discussion of the regulation of private school fees in São Paulo, see the chapter by James and Braga in this volume. The Collor government lifted controls on school fees, and there is considerable anecdotal evidence that suggests that middle-class households are returning their children to public schools.

Table 4.3. Percentage of Enrollments in Private Schools, 1960–89

	Primary	Secondary	Tertiary
1960	11.5	65.0	44.3
1970	9.0	40.1	50.5
1980	12.9	46.5	63.3
1985	12.1	33.3	59.2
1987	13.2	35.1	60.2
1989	14.5*	34.6*	61.5

Sources: IBGE, *Anuários Estatísticos,* various years; MEC (1990); and Levy (1986), Table 5.1.
*Estimates

ing. An estimated 23 percent of all public educational expenditure is allocated to higher education institutions, though these enroll only 2 percent of the students in the public education system (see Paul and Wolff in this volume).

Only about 8 percent of those in the relevant age cohort are enrolled in post-secondary education institutions, and 60 percent of these pay fees to attend private colleges (see Table 4.3). The clients of public universities are disproportionately recruited from among urban residents and members of the middle and upper classes, many if not most of whom have attended private primary and secondary schools.[14] At the Federal University of Ceará, for example, 53 percent of those enrolled in the prestigious (and expensive) faculties of Engineering, Medicine and Data Processing came from families in which the father had completed higher education, and 88 percent of those enrolled had attended private secondary schools. By way of contrast, fewer than 4 percent of all adult males in the Northeast had completed higher education in 1987, and only one-third of all Brazilian secondary students are in private schools. The disproportions were smaller but still pronounced in less prestigious faculties (e.g., Administration, Nursing) and at the State University, where more than two-thirds of students had graduated from private secondary schools (see Paul and Wolff in this volume). The failure to charge tuition in public universities thus provides a public subsidy to those least in need of it and undermines the fulfillment of other objectives, including the expansion and improvement of basic education (Saviani, 1986).

---

[14] Admission to public universities is based on successful performance on an entrance examination, which systematically favors those who have prepared for admission in relatively high-quality private schools. Those who fail to gain admission to public universities end up paying fees to attend private institutions, where the quality of facilities and instruction is commonly much lower than in public institutions.

As with the issue of public subsidies for private schools, the question of "free" public higher education has been intensely debated in recent years in the Constituent Assembly and elsewhere. The main beneficiaries of present policies are students in federal and state universities, who are relatively few but nevertheless cohesive, articulate, conscious of their own interests, and politically important. Those who pay the price to keep higher education "free" are far more numerous but almost entirely disorganized and inarticulate. Therefore, public resources for education are distributed in a way that systematically favors the privileged at the expense of those most in need of public assistance.

Summary

The need for educational reform and improvement is almost universally acknowledged in Brazil, but those who gain from present arrangements are unwilling to give up either current or prospective advantages. Though publicly affirmed goals are not achieved, this hardly represents policy "failure." In fact, the educational system is reasonably successful in serving powerful private interests, including those of politicians and their clients and middle- and upper-class households. Resources are scarce, and policy choices systematically favor those with privileged access to power. The consequences include jobs for clients; subsidies for private schools, public university students, and middle-class parents; and the continued deterioration of educational services for those from less favored constituencies.

Policy Objectives and Instruments

Political conflicts over educational objectives occur only when the interests of clearly defined and politically influential groups are directly threatened, as in the debate over "free" university education. In general, however, the most contentious educational issues have emerged elsewhere, in the struggle to control the means of policy implementation and the distribution of educational resources. Three of these policy debates have been of particular importance: the appropriate location of administrative and financial responsibility for schools, especially at the primary level; the status of regional differences in the effort to reduce educational inequalities; and the role of private schools in the educational system. These debates have animated the discussion of Brazilian educational policy for six decades, and the issues raised remain unresolved.

Administrative Decentralization

Conflicts between advocates of centralized and decentralized administration are virtually inevitable in a large and heterogeneous country, and such conflicts have a long history in Brazil. The relatively strong central authority of the Empire was displaced in 1891 by the federalism of the First Republic, under which most important administrative and political powers were delegated to the states (Souza, 1986). On the basis of an explicitly nationalist and authoritarian ideology, the Vargas dictatorship of the 1930s and 1940s established an extensive administrative apparatus that asserted central control over virtually all areas of public policy. The military regime that governed Brazil in the 1960s and 1970s further centralized administrative authority. This regime also significantly increased the share of public revenues controlled by the federal government. In contrast, the Brazilian Constitution of 1988 (similar to those of 1934 and 1946) includes a variety of measures aimed at delegating administrative and financial power to states and municipalities.

Conflict between advocates of centralization and decentralization has marked the educational system as well. A Ministry of Education, Post, and Telegraphs established by the new Republican government was disbanded shortly thereafter. In 1911 full autonomy in the establishment, maintenance and governance of schools was vested in state, local and private authorities (Romanelli, 1978). The centralization of administrative and financial authority that began under Vargas (and continued, somewhat ambivalently, under the elected governments of 1946–64) was accelerated by the military regime, but there are signs that it may be reversed under the new Constitution (Campello e Souza, 1983; Câmara dos Deputados, 1990).

Steady progress toward centralization in the educational system has been opposed at virtually every turn by advocates of decentralization and local control. The 1932 manifesto of the *Pioneiros da Educação Nova* called for flexibility, diversity and the delegation of administrative and financial control to states and municipalities (Azevedo et al., 1960). In keeping with the views of the *Pioneiros*, the Constitution of 1934 called for the states to organize their own school systems under the general guidance of the federal government, as did the democratic Constitution of 1946 and the first version of the LDB in 1948. Thus far, however, the political and administrative advantages of centralized control have proven stronger than legal mandates to decentralize power and resources.

The variety of interests at stake precludes an easy summary of the terms of the debate over the distribution of administrative resources and responsibilities, or even of the identities of the protagonists. In the debate over the LDB, for example, the proponents of decentralization included a variety of progressives, who saw the policy as an inevitable response to Brazilian diversity and a spur to political pluralism. The defenders of private education also supported the LDB because they viewed the decentralization of administrative authority as a useful protection against the regulatory power of the central government. Opponents included the architects of the economically and politically nationalist *Estado Novo*, who insisted upon central control and planning to advance the integration and development of Brazil (Villalobos, 1969; Romanelli, 1978). At present, in contrast, advocacy of decentralization tends to be associated with proponents of free markets and privatization. Progressives, instead, now tend to be skeptical of the commitment of local officials to the support of education, apprehensive about the effects of decentralization on teachers' unions and salaries, and fearful of federal government abandonment of responsibility for the education of poor children (Oliveira, 1986; Castro, 1989; Namo de Mello and Maia, 1987).

Positions on the issue often cut across organizational and geographical categories as well. State and local officials in the relatively prosperous states of the South and Southeast tend to look favorably on decentralization, which promises them greater control over local resources. Meanwhile, their counterparts in the Northeast seek first to ensure the continued flow of federal transfers (Castor and Zabot, 1989). Education officials in some states and municipalities resent the burden of compliance with the administrative procedures of the federal government, while others are adept at exploiting bureaucratic confusion in Brasília to advance local interests. The welter of competing interests involved in the debate and the complexity of the positions enunciated prevents even a clear statement of policy alternatives, far less a choice among them. The persistent failure to resolve the conflict between centralization and decentralization is not just a matter of bureaucratic detail. The indeterminate division of educational responsibilities between national, state and local governments combined with a lack of transparency in relations among the spheres of government has a variety of pernicious consequences. The most important is the maximization of administrative discretion at all levels of the educational system, which leaves the system open to the practice of *clientelismo* and responsive to the demands of special interests. Another consequence is the minimization of administrative responsibility, as it is virtually impossible to determine precisely who is responsible for ensuring Brazilian citizens' rights to education.

Table 4.4. Public Expenditures by Level of Government, 1983
(Billions of cruzeiros)

	Federal	State	Municipal
Total revenue	11,105	7,953	3,049
Percent from taxes	43	18	
Percent from transfers	19	59	

Source: World Bank (1988).

Administrative decentralization has been an objective of official educational policy in Brazil since 1971. The educational reforms adopted in that year called for shifting responsibility for primary education to municipal governments in step with the development of local administrative and financial capacity (Barretto and Arelaro, 1985). In fact, however, little decentralization has taken place. The control of tax bases remains highly centralized and unequal, and state and federal officials remain hesitant to delegate responsibility for schools to authorities at the local level (see Table 4.4).

There are signs that further decentralization may now be a prospect, however, for two main reasons. First, tax changes required by the new Constitution are projected to bring about a significant decline in the quantity of revenues controlled by the federal government, with correspondingly large gains by states and especially municipalities (Gomes, 1988). Shifts in administrative responsibility may be expected to follow the shift in resources. Second, state and local governments are increasingly assertive in their claims to control their own school systems. The emergence of organizations representing state (*Conselho de Secretários de Educação*, CONSED) and municipal (*União Nacional dos Dirigentes Municipais de Educação*, UNDIME) education officials suggests that the pressures in favor of decentralization are growing and that they now represent local aspirations as well as competing interests in national politics. The form that decentralization will ultimately take, however, is still very much in question.

Whether administrative decentralization is good or bad educational policy is not at issue here. The point is, instead, that political disagreements about the means by which the ostensible goals of the educational system are to be achieved have for 40 years almost entirely displaced efforts to actually achieve those goals. There is widespread agreement on the goals themselves but intense disagreement about how they should be achieved and about who should be entrusted with the task of achieving them.

Table 4.5. Comparative Development Indicators for Northeast Brazil and Brazil, 1989
(Percent)

	Northeast	Brazil
Literacy (10+)	64.1	81.8
Children 10-17 working	15.9	12.1
Participation in social security	29.3	50.6
Less than minimum salary earned	44.7	27.2
Piped water in residence	51.3	72.7
Infant mortality (per 1000)[*]	116.0	52.0

Sources: Veja, 21 November 1990, pp. 44–45; World Bank (1988).
[*]1985

Educational Inequalities and the Problem of the Northeast

Closely related to identifying the appropriate seat of responsibility for basic education is the problem of reducing educational inequalities and improving the quality and quantity of opportunities available to the poor. Brazilian society is marked by extreme disparities in income between social classes, urban and rural residents, and regions. The economic policies pursued by successive governments appear in many instances to have increased rather than reduced the scope of these disparities (Fishlow, 1972; World Bank, 1990). Inequalities in income are clearly reflected in other indices of social welfare, including educational access and attainment (Calsing, 1989).

Perhaps the single most striking characteristic of Brazilian society is the huge gap on virtually all indices of social and economic development between the industrialized and relatively prosperous states of the Southeast and the impoverished states of the Northeast (see Table 4.5). A major focus of the Brazilian political economy (with support from the international aid agencies) has been to reduce the chronic poverty and backwardness of the Northeastern region. In the early 1980s, the EDURURAL Project aimed to increase the quality and quantity of educational opportunities available in the region, and MEC consistently allocates the lion's share of its discretionary resources to projects in Northeastern states and municipalities. To date, however, these efforts have made relatively little difference. The Northeast remains poor and continues to lag behind the rest of Brazil in all measures of educational access and attainment. Indeed, the gap between enrollment rates in Northeastern and Southeastern states in 1980 was larger than it had been in 1940 (Plank, 1987).

The issue with respect to educational inequalities is whether they are best addressed on a regional or on another basis. It can be argued, for example, that the crucial policy problem is not so much that the Northeast lags behind other regions in educational development but that many of the people who live there lack access to schools of even minimal quality.[15] Attempts to provide additional resources in the region may or may not improve the educational opportunities of those penalized by the present system; the key issue is how new resources are distributed within the region. Simply increasing the quantity of funds transferred to the Northeast may in fact increase the advantages of the relatively privileged. This has clearly happened in the educational system: resources allocated to the region only reach the ostensible target population in a much-reduced form, having meanwhile been put to work in the service of other interests, including those of politicians and their clients (Barretto, 1983; CEC/IPEA, 1987). A report published by MEC in 1987, for example, determined that only about half of the educational resources allocated to the Northeast reached the region's classrooms. The balance is used for the support of functionaries, politicians and other interested parties, most of whom are not poor (Xavier and Marques, 1987).

There are areas of relative privilege in the Northeast, just as there are areas of brutal poverty in the Southeast. Urban municipalities in the Northeast, for example, are better off than rural municipalities in the Southeast on many indicators of social welfare (Mahar and Dillinger, 1983). Allocating resources to reduce regional inequalities without an explicit and sustained effort to direct resources to programs that benefit the poorest residents will not necessarily do much to make the distribution of income or social services more equal.

There are many in the Northeast who derive important benefits from present policies, however. Local politicians throughout the region depend on federal transfers to fund public services and nourish their political bases, and their numbers are increasing steadily with the "liberation" of new municipalities (*A Tarde*, 9 September 1990). State politicians also depend on federal transfers to fund the jobs and other benefits that sustain their clients. A change in policy that targeted resources to poor people rather than to poor states would deprive many of these people of their livelihood and of many of the political resources on which their power is based. Change is therefore resisted, despite the manifest ineffectiveness of present policies in

---

[15] The results presented by Barros and Lam in this volume suggest that inequalities in educational attainment among 14-year-olds in São Paulo and the Northeast may be due in greater measure to inequalities in the supply of schooling than to differences in household demand for education.

improving the circumstances of those to whom they are nominally directed. As in the conflict over administrative decentralization, the political dispute is rooted in the struggle to retain control of means rather than in disagreement over the ends to be accomplished.

Public and Private Schools

Conflict over the role of private schools in the Brazilian educational system is at least as old as that between advocates of centralization and decentralization.[16] Disagreement has focused on the provision of public subsidies for private schools, with the control of curriculum emerging as a subordinate issue.

Conflict over the role of private schools in the educational system succeeded the dispute between advocates of centralization and decentralization in the long controversy over the LDB and completely dominated the last five years of the debate. On one side were those who sought to ensure priority for public schools in the distribution of public resources, in accordance with the state's obligation to provide education for its citizens. Opposing them were those led by the Church who defended "freedom of choice" and called for public revenues to be distributed equally and impartially among the public and private schools to which parents chose to send their children. The advocates of free choice warned against the dangers of a state monopoly in education in the absence of public support for private schools and denied any threat to the well-being of public schools. The defenders of public education asserted the state's obligation to provide schools for all and denied any intention to restrict the independence of private schools (Villalobos, 1969; Naccaratto, 1984).

This conflict became virulent in the debate over the LDB in the 1950s and blocked approval of the law for several years.[17] With the terms of the

---

[16] In 1759, the Jesuits were expelled from Brazil in part because of a dispute with the Portuguese crown over the control of schools (Souza, 1986, pp. 25–26). In the two intervening centuries public authorities have assumed an increasing share of responsibility for education. As the educational system has expanded the percentage of children enrolled in public schools has risen steadily (see Table 4.3). Private and religious schools nevertheless continue to play an important and in many respects privileged role in the Brazilian educational system.

[17] In 1958, for example, the Archbishop of Porto Alegre asserted that "...a powerful group in the Ministry of Education and Culture in Rio de Janeiro is not only promoting secularism in education but secularism and materialism in every sphere of life." The defenders of public schools meanwhile denounced the "...ambition of the Catholic Church to achieve the greatest possible dominion over educational administration and policy" (Martins, 1976, pp. 24–26).

dispute defined so sharply and encompassing so much more than the educational issues ostensibly in question, compromise between the competing positions became extremely difficult, though a formula was eventually found.[18]

The current debate continues to revolve around the provision of public subsidies to private schools, but the focus has shifted from the question of Church influence and control in the educational system to the question of the profits of private school directors. At the heart of the debate is the inability of the public school system to provide sufficient school places of sufficient quality to serve the children of the middle class. Responsibility for the education of these children has been delegated to private schools, while the responsibility for educating lower-class children has either been left to whoever will accept it or abandoned. Although these facts are generally acknowledged, their implications remain in dispute.

Proponents of the restriction of public funds to private schools argue that profits are the primary motive of the directors of private schools and that the transfer of funds to private schools deprives the public schools of needed revenues. The defenders of private schools note the insistent demand for private education and the crucial role now filled by private schools in the Brazilian educational system.[19] They also argue that the amount of money transferred to private schools is relatively small, given the needs of the public schools, and that the schools that receive subsidies are most often those in rural areas and on the urban periphery that serve the relatively poor, rather than those that serve the elite (Mello e Souza, 1989). An end to public subsidies would therefore harm those most in need of help.

The empirical evidence on each of these points is neither complete nor conclusive, but our own research in Bahia indicates that subsidies directed to middle-class households under the SME are far larger than those

---

[18] The compromise included the requirement that religion be included as a regular subject in the curriculum of all schools and that public schools receive priority in the distribution of public funds, with subsidies to private schools permitted in cases where public educational provision was insufficient. Speaking for the defenders of the public schools, Anísio Teixeira described the LDB that was finally approved as "half a victory, but still a victory," while the leading advocate of free choice called it "the best law we could get" (Saviani, 1987, p. 98).

[19] That private schools are an essential part of the school "system" is confirmed by the recent threat of the Minister of Education to sue the owners of private schools in order to force them to keep their schools open. The closure of significant numbers of private schools would have literally catastrophic consequences for the Brazilian educational system, and for the political careers of those who allowed it to happen.

that assist the relatively poor. In 1988, the amount withheld by firms to reimburse the educational expenses of their employees was six times larger than the amount routed through FNDE for the payment of scholarships in private schools. Transfers to private schools by public agencies including FNDE, FAE, CNSS, and the State Education Secretariat, came to more than Cr$2.1 billion in 1988, an amount three times larger than the amount of wage tax revenues transferred to municipal governments by the FNDE.[20]

The resolution of the conflict between proponents of public and private schools adopted in the new Constitution (and in the new LDB being drafted) restricts transfers to private schools organized on a "nonprofit" basis, but this has not ended the debate. Some of the short-run problems that may be encountered in the implementation of this policy have been discussed by Velloso (1988). In the longer run, subsidizing private schools rather than investing in the expansion and improvement of the public schools is likely to reinforce the traditional dualism of the Brazilian educational system, at the expense of students obliged to remain in public schools.

As in the debate over the decentralization of administrative authority, the debate over public support for private schools represents a struggle over means rather than ends. There is agreement on the goals to be pursued, but disagreement about how they should be pursued—and by whom—interferes with their achievement. The policy debate has come to focus on the question of who shall provide educational services, and at whose expense, rather than on the more important question of how (or whether) a sufficient quantity of educational services shall be provided.

Summary

The sharpest and most persistent conflicts in the Brazilian educational system in the past 60 years have arisen not over the choice of policy objectives but over the choice of policy instruments. The precedence accorded to private interests over public objectives has shifted the focus of educational policy

---

[20] This accounting of transfers to private schools excludes agreements between the state government and private agencies for the provision of specific goods and services and all subventions to private schools from municipal governments. It is, therefore, an underestimate of the total amount transferred. No systematic data on state/private agency agreements or municipal subventions are available, but interviews and evidence from the *Diário Oficial* suggest that the amounts in question are large.

debate from ends to means: the question of what is to be done is posed less than the subsidiary questions of who is to do it and how. Notably, the continuing failure to define the distribution of resources and responsibilities between national, state and local officials and between public and private schools in itself serves the interests of those in charge of the system by maximizing their administrative discretion and minimizing their administrative responsibility. The debates that blocked the passage of the LDB for so many years continue unresolved, and the educational backwardness that the *Pioneiros da Educação Nova* set out to reverse in the 1930s continues as well.

Current Trends

Strategies to bring about significant and lasting improvements in the Brazilian educational system must begin with acknowledgement that the problem is neither a technical matter of policy design and implementation nor one of lack of resources. Rather, the key problem resides in the deeply rooted conflicts between competing interests in Brazilian society. These conflicts can only be resolved in the political arena, with the development of democratic institutions capable of representing and mediating divergent interests in ways consistent with the rights of Brazil's citizens. The construction of a more democratic society is by nature slow, ambiguous and ridden with conflict, and its success or failure is entirely beyond the control of planners. Moreover, the federal organization of the Brazilian government means that progress toward the establishment of democratic institutions and attendant policy reforms will occur in different ways and at different speeds in various parts of Brazil.

Existing and emerging institutional and political structures thus define the context within which competing groups pursue their interests and within which changes in educational and other policies will take place.

Democratization, Decentralization and Innovation

The political opening that began at the end of the 1970s has been accompanied by potentially important changes in administrative and political relationships within the educational system. First, educational officials at state and municipal levels have begun to abandon their traditional complaisance with respect to policy direction from the MEC and to adopt an increasingly active and critical role in the formulation and implementation of educational policies. The state secretaries have organized themselves into the CONSED while officials at the municipal level are affiliated in increasing

numbers with the UNDIME. Representatives of these organizations participate in educational policy debates at all levels and are now beginning to
define a policy agenda for state and municipal education systems on a basis
increasingly independent from the centralizing interests of the MEC.

Second, taking advantage of their newly-won autonomy in administration and policy-making, many states have undertaken significant changes in
administrative and pedagogical practice. Included among the innovations
are the extension of the school day (including the introduction of full-day
school programs in Leonel Brizola's *Centros Integrados de Educação Pública*
[CIEPs] and former President Collor's *Centros Integrados de Apoio à Criança*
[CIACs]), and the adoption of the basic cycle in the early grades.[21]

Third, freed from their exclusive dependence on the MEC, education
officials at state and municipal levels have begun to build relationships
with other institutions and specifically to enter into direct contact with
federal and state legislators. CONSED and UNDIME were important participants in educational debates during the drafting of Brazil's new Constitution, and they remain active in the current debate over a new LDB.
Educational policy debates are far more open than they were under the
military regime. With their entry into these debates, state and local officials
have further increased their administrative autonomy.

Finally, in the search for more efficient and effective procedures, three
new administrative practices have been adopted in several states: election
of school principals by parents, teachers and community members; establishment of school councils made up of teachers, students and parents; and
devolution of day-to-day financial control to the school level. Some states
(such as Minas Gerais, Espírito Santo, Mato Grosso do Sul, and Pará) have
adopted all three measures. Other states (Mato Grosso and Santa Catarina)
have adopted one, and still others (Rio Grande do Sul, Distrito Federal, and
Goiás) none.

School principals in most states are now appointed by the State Education Secretary, commonly under the guidance of local politicians. The
shift to direct elections has reduced the influence of the Secretary and
elected officials in school administration, though at the cost of enhancing
the influence of groups associated with teachers and their unions. The net
benefits of the shift have yet to be evaluated, but studies have revealed vari-

---

[21] The basic cycle integrates the first and second years of schooling, postponing promotion (or
failure) until the end of the second year. The program allows children a longer time to master
basic skills and is expected to reduce rates of repetition and dropout in the early grades.

ous problems in the relationships between elected principals and personnel in their schools. On the one hand, principals often find themselves politically isolated after their supporters' initial euphoria has dissipated. On the other hand, principals are obliged to confront the hostile opposition of those who supported other candidates.

The establishment of elected school councils is intended to provide a mechanism for consultation and for the division of responsibility between principals and those who attend or work in their schools. In principle, councils should provide a forum in which administrative decisions and school level policies are discussed and conflicts mediated. The available information suggests, however, that councils play a far more restricted role. Several states (including Minas Gerais, Paraná, and Pará) have begun to transfer funds directly to schools to cover the costs of minor repairs and other urgent expenditures. Judgments on the legality of this practice differ from state to state. In Paraná, for example, the transfer of public resources to school administrators was found to contravene state laws.

These administrative and policy innovations are emblematic of a new seriousness on the part of some state and local officials to come to terms with longstanding educational problems. None of these innovations has been an unequivocal success. However, the acknowledgement of a need for change and the willingness and capacity to experiment with new policies provide some ground for optimism with respect to eventual improvements in Brazil's educational system.[22]

Constitutional Changes

One important step in the construction of democratic institutions in Brazil was the promulgation of a new Constitution in 1988, which provided space for policy innovations such as those described above and also established new instruments for the definition and protection of the rights of citizens. Many of the important policy shifts embodied in the Constitution have yet to be fully defined in law, but the changes that they entail can already be foreseen.

---

[22] On a more pessimistic note, however, virtually all of these policy experiments have taken place in the states of the South and Southeast, where resources are more plentiful and educational problems are generally less severe. Insofar as these experiments are successful, the relative backwardness of the Northeast may increase, unless and until similar innovations are adopted in Northeastern states as well.

With respect to decentralization, the new Constitution for the first time acknowledges the autonomy of municipal education systems, which are no longer to be regarded as subordinate agencies of state governments. The concession of independence to municipalities significantly reduces the power both of the MEC and state governments, while greatly expanding the opportunity for administrative and policy innovation. At the same time, however, by introducing nearly 5,000 new actors into education policy debates, it renders the search for more efficient and equitable national policies all the more difficult.

Tax reforms, which were to have been fully implemented by 1993, assign sources of revenue previously controlled by the federal government to state and municipal authorities. In association with constitutional provisions requiring state and local governments to spend 25 percent of their revenues from taxes and transfers on education, the anticipated decentralization of resources should significantly increase the total quantity of resources available to the educational system. In addition, the corresponding reduction in the quantity of resources controlled by federal authorities may be expected to lead to further decentralization of administrative responsibility, with especially significant gains at the municipal level (Gomes, 1988).

A majority of the state constitutions that have been adopted following the approval of the federal constitution have incorporated articles directing that recent education policy experiments including the election of school principals and the establishment of school councils be institutionalized. State laws defining how these new constitutional principles are to be implemented are now being drafted.

Both federal and state constitutions include new legal guidelines to govern the budgeting process. Previously, presidents and governors developed their budgets in consultation with the heads of administrative agencies. Thereafter, budgets were submitted to the legislature for approval. Under the new constitutions, however, a budget resolution defining guidelines for public expenditure must be approved by the legislature prior to the elaboration of a budget by the executive branch. This procedure does allow for broader participation in the definition of budgetary priorities. The procedure remains flawed, however, in the opportunities that it provides for the allocation of resources for specific uses on the basis of criteria rooted in the practice of *clientelismo*.

Federal and state constitutions also require the elaboration of medium-term educational plans at national and state levels to define policy priorities for the educational system. These plans must be approved by legislators, which provides an additional opportunity for public participation in the debate over educational policies.

The new Brazilian Constitution also makes the longstanding right to education actionable for the first time by assigning legal responsibility for the provision of educational opportunities to the "relevant public authorities" (Article 208, paragraphs 1 and 2).[23] This change could prove to be the most far reaching of all, if a successful legal strategy can be devised for defining what the citizen's right to education and the government's obligation to provide it entail. The dispersion of administrative responsibility within the educational system, however, makes it difficult to determine the relevant public authorities. In addition, the general disregard for "rights" in the Brazilian legal system poses a serious obstacle to successful legal action. No citizen has yet sued to oblige the government to honor her or his right to education.

Summary

In themselves, the changes described above clearly cannot produce solutions to the problems identified earlier in this chapter. The changes do, however, mark the establishment of new opportunities for organizations and individuals to contribute to the debate over the increasingly desperate problems of the Brazilian education system. The changes also further open the way to local experimentation and innovation. Given the failure of recent Brazilian governments to assign priority to improving the basic education system, it is at the local level, in the demands of citizens and in the commitment of educators, that the search for solutions must begin.

---

[23] Speaking of previous Brazilian Constitutions, Souza (1986, p. 35) notes that "the responsibility of the State [to provide education] has always been circumscribed by philanthropic good intentions, which have served to deny legal recourse to those excluded from the educational system."

REFERENCES

A Tarde (Salvador). "Eleitores disputam tudo em troca dos seus votos," 23 September 1990.

_____. "Criação de municípios é um escândalo eleitoreiro," 9 September 1990.

_____. "Chiarelli vê uso político da merenda," 27 August 1990.

_____. "Hugo Napoleão empossado na Educação," 31 October 1987.

Azevedo, Fernando et al. 1960. Manifesto dos Pioneiros da Educação Nova, 1932. *Revista Brasileira de Estudos Pedagógicos* 34(79): 108–27.

Bahia. 1990. *Plano Decenal de Educação.* (Versão preliminar, July).

Barretto, Elba Siqueira de Sá. 1983. Novas Políticas Educacionais para Velhas Escolas Rurais: Um Estudo de Caso no Sertão do Piauí. *Cadernos de Pesquisa* 46 (August): 23–49.

Barretto, Elba Siqueira de Sá, and Lisete Regina Gomes Arelaro. 1985. A Municipalização do Ensino de 1° Grau: Tese Controvertida. *Revista da Faculdade de Educação* (Universidade de São Paulo) 11(1/2): 193–210.

Calsing, Elizeu Francisco. 1989. *Estudos de Assimetrias Educacionais no Brasil.* Brasília: Ministério da Educação e Cultura, Secretaria de Ensino Básico.

Câmara dos Deputados. 1990. Projeto de Lei no. 1.258/88.

Campello e Souza, Maria do Carmo. 1983. *Estado e Partidos Políticos no Brasil (1930 a 1964).* São Paulo: Editora Alfa-Ômega.

Castor, Belmiro Valverde Jobim, and Nircélio Zabot. 1989. Novos Papéis dos Governos na Educação Brasileira. *Revista ANDE* 8: 12–17.

Castro, Cláudio de Moura. 1989. What Is Happening in Brazilian Education. In *Social Change in Brazil, 1945–1985: The Incomplete Revolution,* eds. Edmar L. Bacha and Herbert S. Klein. Albuquerque: University of New Mexico Press.

Castro, Cláudio de Moura, and João Batista de Araújo Oliveira. 1991. Educação: Por Onde Começar? Mimeo.

Coordenação de Educação e Cultura, Instituto de Planejamento Econômico e Social—CEC/IPEA. 1987. *Relatório Anual de Acompanhamento—1987: Educação.* Brasília: IPEA.

Farhat, Emil. 1987. *O Paraíso do Vira-bosta.* São Paulo: T.A. Queiroz Editora.

Fishlow, Albert. 1972. Brazilian Size Distribution of Income. *American Economic Review* 62(2): 391–402.

Folha de São Paulo. "Quercismo em ação," 23 September 1990.

————. "Candidatos não definem recurso para educação," 20 September 1990.

————. "PT entrega projeto educacional ao governo," 4 September 1990.

————. "Desaparecem verbas federais para 5,3 milhões de merendas," 21 April 1988.

————. "Tráfico de bolsas," 20 April 1988.

Freitag, Barbara. 1978. *Estado, Escola, e Sociedade.* São Paulo: EDART Livraria Editora.

Fundo Nacional de Desenvolvimento da Educação (FNDE). 1990. *Salário-Educação: Séries Históricas.* Brasília: MEC.

Gomes, Cândido. 1988. Quatro Anos da Emenda Calmon: Qual o Seu Impacto? *Revista Brasileira de Estudos Pedagógicos* 69(162): 237–55.

Instituto Brasileiro de Geografia e Estatística (IBGE). Various years. *Anuários Estatísticos.* Rio de Janeiro: IBGE.

IPEA. Coordenação de Educação e Cultura. 1987. *Relatório Anual de Acompanhamento —1987: Educação.* Brasília: IPEA.

Leal, Maria Cristina. 1990. Os Des (mandos) do Clientelismo de Estado sobre os Recursos Públicos da Educação de 1º e 2º Graus. Doctoral dissertation, Universidade Federal do Rio de Janeiro.

Leite, Raimundo Hélio, and José de Anchieta Esmeraldo Barreto. 1983. O Comportamento Institucional da Secretaria de Educação do Ceará. *Revista Brasileira de Administração da Educação* 1 (January/June).

Levy, Daniel C. 1986. *Higher Education and the State in Latin America.* Chicago: University of Chicago Press.

Mahar, Dennis J., and William R. Dillinger. 1983. *Financing State and Local Government in Brazil.* World Bank Staff Working Paper Number 612, World Bank, Washington, D.C.

Martins, Waldemar Valle. 1976. *Liberdade de Ensino.* São Paulo: Edições Loyola.

MEC (Ministério da Educação e Cultura). 1990. *A Educação no Brasil na Década de 80.* Brasília: MEC.

_____.1985. *Educação para Todos*. Brasília: MEC.

Mello e Souza, Alberto. 1989. Considerações sobre a Distribuição dos Recursos Educacionais. *Em Aberto* 42 (April/June): 31–3.

Naccaratto, Miguel S.J. 1984. *Escola Livre e Gratuita*. São Paulo: Edições Loyola.

Namo de Mello, Guiomar, and Eny Marisa Maia. 1987. *A Municipalização do Ensino*. Brasília: CENDEC/IPEA.

Oliveira, João Batista de Araújo. 1986. Basic Education in Brazil: Municipalization, Decentralization and Debureaucratization. Emílio Odebrecht Foundation. Mimeo.

_____. 1984. Bases para Novas Diretrizes em Educação. *Educação Brasileira* 13(2): 125–51.

Plank, David N. 1992. Os Interesses Público e Privado na Educação Brasileira: Males Crônicos e Soluções Longínquas. *Revista Brasileira de Estudos Pedagógicos*.

_____. 1990. The Politics of Basic Education Reform in Brazil. *Comparative Education Review* 34(3): 538–59.

_____. 1987. The Expansion of Education: A Brazilian Case Study. *Comparative Education Review* 31(4): 361–76.

Presidência da República. 1991. *Plano de Reconstrução Nacional*. Brasília: IPEA.

Romanelli, Otaiza de Oliveira. 1978. *História da Educação no Brasil*. Petrópolis: Editora Vozes.

Saviani, Dermeval. 1987. *Educação Brasileira: Estrutura e Sistema*. Sixth edition. São Paulo: Cortez.

_____. 1986. *Ensino Público e Algumas Falas sobre Universidade*. São Paulo: Cortez.

Souza, Paulo Nathaniel Pereira. 1986. *Educação na Constituição e Outros Estudos*. São Paulo: Livraria Pioneira Editora.

Teixeira, Anísio. 1957. *Educação não É Privilégio*. Rio de Janeiro: J. Olympio Editora.

Veja. "Trancos e barrancos," 21 November 1990.

Velloso, Jacques. 1988. A Nova Lei de Diretrizes e Bases da Educação e o Financiamento do Ensino: Pontos de Partida. *Educação e Sociedade* 30 (August): 5–42.

_____. 1987. Política Educacional e Recursos para o Ensino: O Salário-Educação e a Universidade Federal. *Cadernos de Pesquisa* 61 (May): 3–29.

Verhine, Robert Evan. 1991. Higher Education in Brazil. In *International Encyclopedia of Higher Education*, ed. Philip Altbach. New York: Garland Press.

Villalobos, João Eduardo Rodrigues. 1969. *Diretrizes e Bases da Educação: Ensino e Liberdade.* São Paulo: Livraria Pioneira Editora.

World Bank. 1990. *World Development Report, 1990.* Washington, D.C.: World Bank.

_____. 1988. *Brazil: Public Spending on Social Programs.* Washington, D.C.: World Bank.

Xavier, Antonio Carlos da Ressurreição, and Antonio Emílio Sendim Marques. 1987. *Quanto Custa um Aluno nas Escolas que os Brasileiros Freqüentam?* Brasília: IPEA.

5

Wages, Schooling and Background: Investments in Men and Women in Urban Brazil

John Strauss and Duncan Thomas

There is virtually universal agreement that the correlation between wages and education is positive in a wide variety of countries.[1] The fact that there is a very large positive return to schooling in Brazil has been frequently documented, although interpretation of this correlation remains a subject of debate. In addition, the estimated returns to education in the labor market increase with the level of schooling.[2] It has been suggested this implies that as educational opportunities increase in Brazil, so will inequality. To draw this inference, however, it is necessary to understand *why* the wage-education function is convex.

We exploit the tremendous diversity within Brazil in order to draw inferences about the mechanisms underlying the relationship between schooling and labor market outcomes. There is substantial heterogeneity in the returns to education, between men and women, between those living in the Northeast and the South, between blacks and whites, between young and old, and across the distribution of education itself.

Does the positive correlation between wages and education mean that education is productive or is it just a signaling device? Answering this question requires comparing the shape of the wage-education functions for those who are self-employed with those working in the market sector (treating sector of participation as the outcomes of individual choices). Not only are there substantial returns to education in the market, where signaling may be important, but these returns persist among the self-employed, rendering it difficult to reconcile the notion that education is simply a signaling mechanism.

---

[1] See Psacharopoulos (1985) and Psacharopoulos and Woodhall (1985).
[2] See Langoni (1973, 1977), Pastore (1982), Medeiros (1982), Haller and Saraiva (1986, 1991), Lam and Levison (1991b), Lam and Schoeni (1990), Tannen (1991), and Almeida dos Reis and Barros (1991).

One type of signaling that is sometimes alleged is credentialism. This may be important at the completion of primary school grades in Brazil.[3] We estimate the wage-education functions using semi-parametric methods that place no restrictions on their shape. It turns out that the functions are certainly not linear and not even a (high order) polynomial would fit the data as well as our less restrictive estimates. For all sectors, all regions, and for both men and women, the functions are characterized by steps. The key point is that these flats and jumps occur in *different* places in the education distribution for different sub-groups. This, along with the fact the steps are observed among the self-employed, suggests rejection of the hypothesis of a sheepskin signaling effect.

The convexity of the wage-education function may be a reflection of a positive correlation between the quantity and quality of human capital investments by parents in their children. Among the dimensions of investments in quality may be sending children to better quality schools. Children who continue on to secondary and tertiary levels may go to better schools relative to the average primary schools.[4]

Alternatively, the seeming increasing returns to education may reflect selection of higher ability individuals into higher education. To what extent, then, is the estimated return to education a reflection of unobserved background characteristics (including ability)? This is an issue that has received a great deal of attention both generally and in Brazil, where social mobility is thought to be limited.[5] We include controls for parental educa-

---

[3] See Hungerford and Solon (1987) and Dougherty and Jiménez (1991).

[4] For evidence on the impact of school quality see Behrman and Birdsall (1983), Birdsall (1985) and Behrman, Birdsall and Kaplan (this volume).

[5] For a review of the literature regarding the role of unmeasured factors in estimates of return to education, see Willis (1986). In the United States, researchers have examined the robustness of estimated returns to education to information on siblings (Griliches, 1979; Behrman et al., 1980; Bound, Griliches and Hall, 1986; and Hauser and Sewell, 1986) and to information on parents (Leibowitz, 1974; Featherman and Hauser, 1978; Papanicolau and Psacharopoulos, 1979; Solon, 1989a,b; Solon et al., 1991; Willis and Rosen, 1979; Altonji, 1988; Altonji and Dunn, 1990; and Corcoran et al., 1990).

In developing countries, less attention has been paid to the role of family background in estimates of returns to education. In an early study, Carnoy (1967) found that, in Mexico, a father's occupation was strongly related to his child's wages as an adult. Behrman and Wolfe (1984) estimated household income functions for adult women in Nicaragua, using parental education as controls and found a significant positive effect of a father's schooling. Heckman and Hotz (1986) estimated male earnings functions for Panama and found positive effects for both mother's and father's schooling, with the mother's effect being larger. Using the World Bank's Living Standards Measurement Survey from Peru, Stelcner, Arriagada and Moock (1987) reported similar results for males in the market sector. Sahn and Alderman (1988) found an effect of father's predicted wages on wage outcomes in Sri Lanka. Armitage and Sabot

tion and find that while background characteristics certainly matter, they account for only a small part of the estimated return to education. Furthermore, even after controlling for background, the steps and convexity persist in the estimated wage-schooling function. This suggests that there may be self-selection among those who choose to stay at school.

In sum, the evidence supports the view that schooling is not just a credential or signal, but is probably associated with productivity enhancements that are rewarded in both the market and self-employment sectors. Returns to schooling increase with higher levels of schooling in Brazil. There is evidence, however, that a good understanding of the returns to investments in schooling needs to take account of each individual's choice of the number of years spent at school.

Data

The data for this study are drawn from the 1982 *Pesquisa Nacional por Amostra de Domicílios* (PNAD). An annual labor force survey, much like the Current Population Survey in the United States, the PNAD contains a special supplement in each year: in 1982 the focus was on education and background.[6]

Detailed information was gathered on schooling attendance and attainment for all household members over seven years of age. The richness of the survey is exploited in three dimensions that are pivotal for this study.

(1987) interacted a child's education with the parents' education and found sharply rising marginal rates of return in Kenya and to a lesser extent in Tanzania.

In Brazil, Pastore (1982) and Medeiros (1982) included indices of father's occupation in male earnings functions using the 1973 *Pesquisa Nacional por Amostra de Domicílios* (PNAD). This work has recently been updated by Pastore and Zylberstajn (this volume) with the 1982 PNAD, focusing on mobility across social classes. Haller and Saraiva (1986, 1991) and Saraiva, Pahari and Haller (1986) also used the 1982 PNAD and included father's occupational status in earnings functions for males and females, stratified by region. All these studies found positive effects of a father's occupation, which is interpreted as an indicator of the socioeconomic status of the respondent's family. However, since the father's occupation is reported only by those people who were working in the labor market at the time of the survey, interpretation of this result is somewhat ambiguous. Lam and Schoeni (1990) also used the 1982 PNAD to analyze earnings of married men. Instead of a father's occupation, they included parental schooling as well as the schooling of the spouse and parents-in-law, finding positive impacts and important interactive effects with the child's education (the marginal return rising with better family background).

[6] The PNADs are from a stratified probability sample that is nearly national in scope (except for rural areas in the north). Information was collected on some 112,000 households, accounting for over half a million individuals. Approximately 74,000 households are located in urban areas and are the subject of this study.

First, the very large sample size permits the estimation of semi-parametric wage functions that place no restrictions on the returns to education for each year of completed schooling. Second, the data is stratified in multiple dimensions to permit flexibility in the effect of education on wages across a range of socioeconomic and geographic groups. Third, the survey provides detailed information on the education of each individual's mother and father,[7] as well as the education of the spouse and the spouse's parents. These characteristics are included as indicators of family background to determine the extent to which they can explain the heterogeneity in returns to education.

In addition to estimating the determinants of total wages (measured by total income for the previous month divided by total reported hours for that month), we also distinguish wages earned in the market sector from wages in the self-employment sector, treating selection into these sectors as endogenous.[8]

Using data only from urban Brazil, three sets of log-wage functions and sectoral choice functions are estimated separately for men and women, stratified into three macro-regions which we refer to as the South, Northeast and Center-North.[9] The sample is restricted to household heads and spouses, since those are the individuals for whom information is available on the education of their mother and father. The sample is further restricted to those aged 25–60 to avoid sample selection issues that would arise using young and old household heads. The sample includes 62,087 females and 58,687 males.[10]

The distribution of completed education for the urban Northeast and South are displayed in Figure 5.1 for males and females separately. The large proportion of urban Brazilians who have no schooling is striking, although there are dramatic differences across regions. Whereas almost one-

---

[7] Occupational status of the father was only reported for those respondents active in the labor force.

[8] The PNAD collects information on primary and secondary jobs, but the job classification is only known for the primary job. For this reason, while total wage is defined as total (primary plus secondary) monthly earnings divided by total monthly hours, market wages and self-employment wages are defined using primary job information only. Less than four percent of the sample reported any secondary employment.

[9] The South: Rio de Janeiro, São Paulo, Brasília, Paraná, Santa Catarina, Rio Grande do Sul, Minas Gerais and Espírito Santo. The Northeast: Maranhão, Piauí, Ceará, Rio Grande do Norte, Paraíba, Pernambuco, Alagoas, Sergipe and Bahia. The Center-North (actually including the Center-West as well): Amazonas, Amapá, Acre, Pará, Rondônia, Roraima, Mato Grosso, Mato Grosso do Sul and Goiás.

[10] Sample means and standard deviations are reported in an earlier version of this chapter (Strauss and Thomas, 1991).

Figure 5.1. Distribution of Years of Completed Schooling by Region

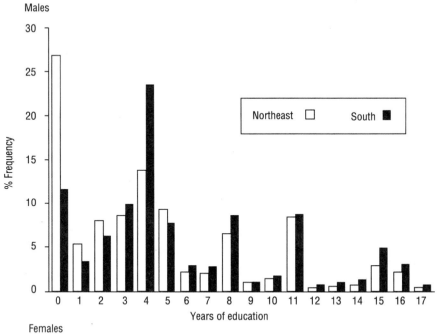

Males

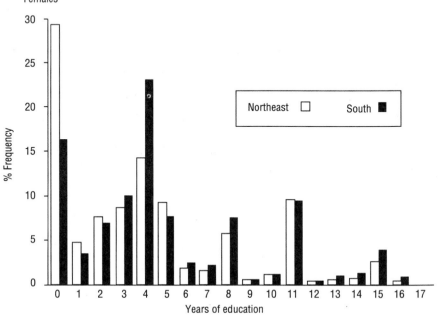

Females

third of men and women in the Northeast have no education, in the South about one-sixth of women and one-eighth of all men have not attended school. There are a series of spikes in the distribution of completed years that identify the completion of a grade or level of schooling: at four years for lower primary, eight years for upper primary, 11 years for secondary and 15 years for an undergraduate or technical degree.[11] Only 18 percent of Northeast males and 16.5 percent of females have had more than primary education (eight years of schooling). Relatively larger, but still small, proportions of people in the South have gone beyond primary school (23 percent and 20 percent for males and females, respectively). Nevertheless, because the sample size is very large, even lower frequency cells have substantial numbers of observations. For example, the fifth and ninth years of schooling turn out to be important in the South, where there are 2,856 and 368 men who have spent exactly these amounts of time at school, respectively, and in the Northeast where the corresponding cell sizes are, respectively, 1,133 and 117 men. These large cell sizes allow us to estimate effects of individual years of education with precision.

Regression Results

We estimate a series of semi-parametric wage functions in which restrictions on the shape of the relationship between wages and years of education are avoided by including a dummy variable for each of 17 years of education (see Hungerford and Solon, 1987, for a similar application using the U.S. data). In addition, the wage function regressions include age (and its square) and race of the respondent together with the education of the respondent's mother and father.[12] Separate regressions are estimated for three macro regions, and state dummies are included in each of the regressions in order to permit flexibility in the returns to education due to heterogeneity across regions in the demand for labor[13] and the quality of education.[14] Gender of the respondent is also stratified.

---

[11] Prior to the mid-1970s, lower primary level was a distinct grade, but since then, lower and upper primary school grades have been combined. The PNAD questionnaire asks which level and grade was the highest completed, distinguishing the old from the new system. We have converted these into years completed.

[12] The regressions are semi-parametric in the sense that while there are no parametric restrictions on the form of the log wage-education function, a series of additional characteristics are included in a particular parametric form.

[13] See Sedlacek and Barros (1989); Heckman and Hotz (1986); and Lam and Levison (1991b).

[14] See Behrman and Birdsall (1983, 1984); Birdsall (1985); Card and Krueger (1992); and Behrman, Birdsall and Kaplan (this volume).

Each regression includes controls for self-selection into the labor market and also into the market or self-employment sectors.[15] We estimate wage functions rather than earnings functions in order to abstract from labor force participation and labor supply decisions. This is important in terms of identifying the self-selection terms; we assume valid instruments include household nonlabor income and assets (which should affect the decision to participate but not directly affect an individual's wage).[16] In our base specification we also exclude from the wage equations existence of a spouse as well as education of the spouse and spouse's parents, while allowing these variables to influence participation decisions. We later examine the robustness of the wage equations to this identification assumption.[17]

Wage Functions: Intersectoral and Interregional Comparisons

Semi-parametric estimates of the conditional expectation of the logarithm of wages are presented in Figures 5.2 through 5.4: the slope between any two years is the marginal return to that year of education. Our discussion focuses on graphical presentation of the results; coefficient estimates and standard errors underlying these figures are reported for men and women in Appendix Table 5.1.

Figure 5.2 compares the returns to *total* wages between regions, by gender and between gender, by region. Figure 5.3 distinguishes market and self-employment wages between regions, while in Figure 5.4 market and self-employment wages are directly compared. The results are summarized in Table 5.1 in terms of average returns to schooling for each level.

Perhaps the most striking fact emerging from Figure 5.2 is that the conditional log-wage functions are neither linear nor smooth. They are convex and characterized by a series of steps; relative to the semi-parametric estimates, even a polynomial function will provide an inferior fit to the data and fail to capture these important differences in returns across the education distribution.

---

[15] Approximately 10 percent of men do not participate in the labor market in either market wage or self-employment activities. Self-selection is controlled for males as well as for females.
[16] Assets include dummy variables for characteristics of the dwelling such as type of walls, floors, sewerage, garbage disposal, roof, source of water and ownership of a water filter or refrigerator.
[17] If husbands and wives make joint labor supply decisions, then it would be inappropriate to treat a spouse's characteristics as exogenous in an earnings function, as opposed to the wage functions that we estimate.

Figure 5.2. Returns to Education: ℓn (Total Wage) by Region and Gender

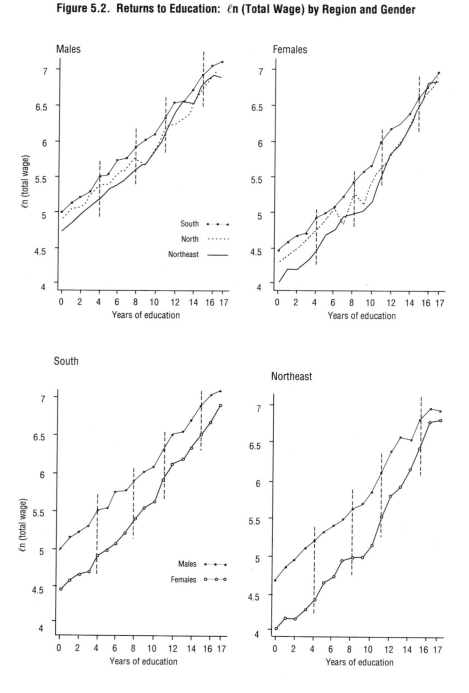

Figure 5.3. Returns to Education: ℓn (Market Wage) and ℓn (Self-employment Wage) by Region

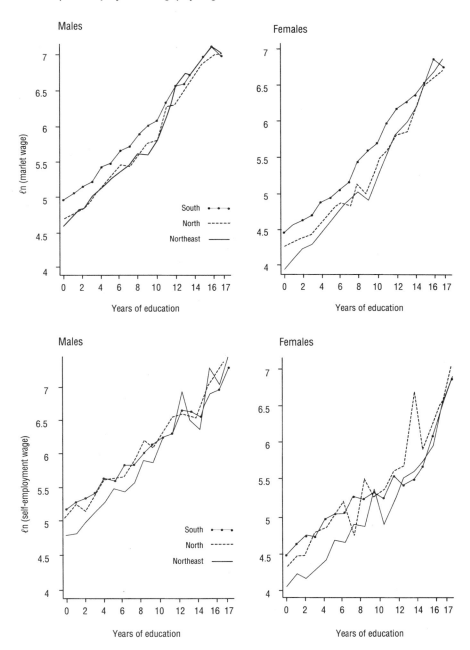

Figure 5.4. Comparison of Returns to Education in Market and Self-employment Sectors

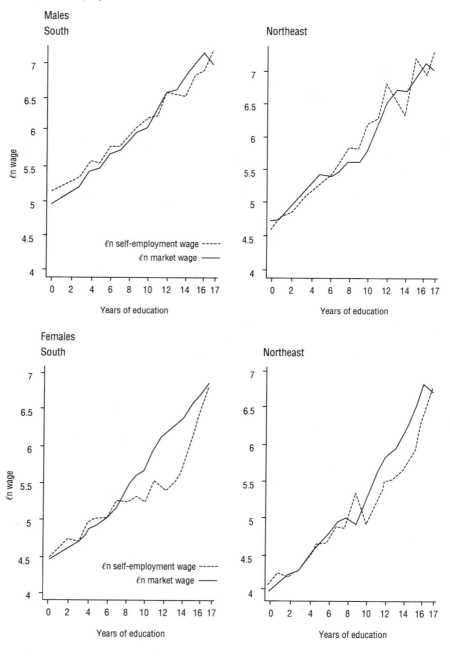

Table 5.1. Marginal Effects of Completed Education on Logarithm of Wages
(Percent)

	Men		Women	
	South	Northeast	South	Northeast
Total wage				
Primary — 1st half (1–4 yrs)	12.4	11.0	11.0	10.4
Primary — 2nd half (5–8 yrs)	10.0	10.7	12.0	13.2
Secondary (9–11 yrs)	13.3	15.1	18.1	17.1
Post-secondary (12–17 yrs)	13.1	16.1	13.6	21.0
Market wage				
Primary — 1st half (1–4 yrs)	12.0	13.2	10.0	12.1
Primary — 2nd half (5–8 yrs)	11.3	12.3	14.0	14.3
Secondary (9–11 yrs)	15.0	16.7	17.9	19.0
Post-secondary (12–17 yrs)	10.6	14.8	14.9	19.2
Self-employment wage				
Primary — 1st half (1–4 yrs)	11.0	12.4	12.0	8.8
Primary — 2nd half (5–8 yrs)	9.8	15.2	6.8	11.5
Secondary (9–11 yrs)	9.3	14.1	9.8	10.1
Post-secondary (12–17 yrs)	15.8	17.8	21.2	27.6

Notes: Estimates are mean returns to schooling within each specified level calculated from semi-parametric regressions which include a dummy for each year of completed schooling. Underlying estimates are graphed in Figures 5.2 through 5.4.

Among men in the South, the average annual return to the first four years of schooling is about 12 percent, and much of this is due to a significantly higher return to completing the first part of primary school (the fourth year) relative to the previous three years. Those who leave school the following year or one year before the end of primary school (the seventh year) gain nothing (in terms of wages) from their last year at school, and the average return to the second half of primary school is lower (10 percent). The return to secondary schooling (nine to 11 years) is higher (over 13 percent), especially for the final year. Post-secondary schooling yields a similar return (13 percent), with larger returns for the first and fourth years.[18]

Relative to the South, men are paid less in the Northeast across the entire education distribution. The return to education is smaller for primary

---

[18] The fourth year of university education (15 years total) is usually the last. Since samples are often relatively small at the top of the education distribution (over 15 years), we will pay less attention to those returns. Note, however, that in polynomial models these observations often have a very large influence on estimated returns. In our semi-parametric specification, of course, these observations do not contaminate estimated returns elsewhere in the education distribution.

schooling (about 11 percent per annum), increases to 15 percent for men who attended secondary school and to 16 percent at post-secondary levels. As in the South there is an increase in returns to higher levels of education. While the log-wage functions are convex in both regions, the convexity is greater in the Northeast so that at the top of the education distribution the differences in wages of men in the Northeast and South are small.

At the bottom of the education distribution, men in the Center-North are paid just under the levels of the South but, since returns to primary schooling are lower than in either of the other two macro-regions, men with some secondary schooling are paid about the same as men in the Northeast. Thereafter, the returns are very similar for men in the Center-North and Northeast.

Among women, the conditional log-wage function is even more convex than that for men. Average returns to the first four years of primary school are lower than for men (10 percent in the Northeast and 11 percent in the South), but returns to post-primary schooling are higher (16 percent in the South and almost 20 percent in the Northeast). In both regions, returns rise between secondary and post-secondary levels.

Returns in the Center-North are lower than in the other two regions for secondary school, but track those in the Northeast at post-secondary levels. Thus, as is the case for men, much of the interregional gap in wages at the bottom of the education distribution has disappeared at the top, and women in all regions earn about the same wage.

The lower panel of Figure 5.2 compares conditional wage functions across gender. In the South, returns to education are about the same for men and women until the last part of primary education (around six years); thereafter returns for women are, on average, about 15 percent higher than returns for men.[19] The relative patterns are similar in the Northeast, although females earn higher returns earlier (halfway through primary school); these returns drop off between seven and nine years, but then rise quite dramatically towards the end of secondary school. While the difference in the average rate is slightly higher in the Northeast (16 percent), it tends to be much higher at post-primary levels (30 percent); therefore, while the wage gap narrows with higher education in both the South and Northeast, the catch-up is greater in the poorer Northeast.

If the conditional wage functions were convex, then a quadratic would fit the data well. There is, however, evidence that an additional year at school

---

[19] The average return for eight to 17 years of schooling is 15 percent for women and 13 percent for men.

is not associated with a higher wage for every year of schooling and, in some cases, the returns to schooling are even *negative*. This is, perhaps, most noticeable for those people who complete only one year of a schooling level: that is one year more than lower primary (five years), upper primary (nine) and secondary school (12 years of schooling). While true for both men and women, this is by no means generally true across all regions. Furthermore, there are some cases where returns to education are zero for a *final* year of a particular grade (such as women in the Northeast who complete eight years of primary school). These flat regions are not simply a function of random noise in the data; as discussed below, this has important implications for interpretation of the impact of schooling on income.

Figure 5.3 is similar to Figure 5.2, except it treats market and self-employment wages separately, accounting for self-selection into each sector. The patterns for market wages and total wages are similar, but the conditional market-wage functions are less convex. Returns are higher for both men and women in the Northeast, relative to the South, particularly at post-primary levels. Thus, among men with little or no education, those in the South earn a higher wage than those in the Northeast. However, towards the top of the education distribution men in both regions earn about the same wage. The same is true for women in the two regions. There is, it seems, little incentive for the well-educated to migrate from the poorer Northeast.[20] Furthermore, relative to total wages, the gap between the market wages of men and women is narrower but still persists.

Returns to education in the self-employment sector are somewhat different. For both men and women, relative to the South, returns are higher in the Northeast for primary and secondary school, but are quite close for post-secondary education. Returns (and wages) in the Center-North track those in the South very closely. In both the Northeast and South narrowing of the gender gap does not occur until the very top of the education distribution. In the South, among those with no education who choose to work in the self-employment sector, women earn just over half a man's wage; at the top of the education distribution earnings of women are about two-thirds that of men.

Returns in the market and self-employment sectors are directly compared in Figure 5.4: broadly speaking, for the log market wage functions, there is a jump in returns at post-primary levels; for the self-employment functions this jump does not occur until post-secondary levels. Returns for

---

[20] If prices are lower in the Northeast, then there might be some incentive for people to migrate from the South to the Northeast. Since there is little evidence of migration in this direction, the higher prices of the South are presumably compensated for by better services.

both men and women are lower in the self-employment sector through the secondary level, but rise substantially and are higher for post-secondary schooling. For instance, in the Northeast, at the bottom of the education distribution, wages of men who choose to work in the self-employment sector are slightly higher than those in the market sector, but returns to education are higher in the market sector, especially for secondary school. This reverses for post-secondary levels; thus wages are very close at higher levels of education. In the two sectors, women in the Northeast earn about the same wage and return to schooling, until secondary school, beyond which point returns are higher in the market sector. Among women in the South, however, the (log) market wage function is convex through secondary school, after which it becomes linear. The self-employment wage function, on the other hand, displays near linearity through primary school, after which it becomes convex. Expected wages and returns in the two sectors are about the same for primary school, but higher in the market sector for secondary education, and then very high in the self-employment sector for post-secondary levels. At the very top of the education distribution, therefore, wages of women in the South are the same independent of their choice of sector of employment.

Wage Functions: Discussion

There are, therefore, large differences in the returns to education across regions: this is, by now, well understood.[21] Among people with little or no education, expected wages are higher in the more developed South, but higher *average* returns to schooling in the Northeast result in wages at the top of the education distribution being approximately the same in the two regions. There are also significant differences across gender, although this gap also declines with education. Little attention, however, has been paid to the differences in returns across the market and self-employment sectors and, perhaps most importantly, to how all these differences vary over the distribution of education.

Two important aspects of the nonlinearity of the conditional wage functions stand out. First, the conditional wage functions are convex and so returns to education increase with the level of education. Second, the wage functions are characterized by flat and sometimes downward sloping regions: smoothing over the differences (with parametric functional forms) misses an important dimension of the wage-education function.

---

[21] See Behrman and Birdsall (1983, 1984) and Birdsall (1985).

What might explain the increasing returns to schooling? It is possible that they reflect quality of schooling (see Behrman and Birdsall, 1983; Birdsall, 1985; and Behrman, Birdsall and Kaplan in this volume) if post primary schools are of higher quality than the average at the primary level. Higher quality second-ary schools may charge fees, which if credit constraints exist, could ration out some children. It is also possible that the structure of labor demand plays an important role. For both these reasons, we include controls for (current) state of residence of the respondent. Neither of these factors, however, can explain the fact that the curves are more convex for women than men unless school quality (and the nature of labor demand) is gender specific; furthermore, it is quite unlikely that they can explain the greater convexity in the Northeast relative to the South.

This suggests that the shape may also reflect differences in unobserved qualities of individuals who choose to continue to higher levels of educa-tion.[22] If so, the increasing returns may not reflect the potential experience of a given individual faced with the choice of whether to further his or her educa-tion. It is important to understand the underlying reasons for the convexity of the log-wage functions: if it is due to schooling quality or labor demand, then it suggests that as the level of education increases in Brazil, inequality will also increase. If, however, it is due to selectivity among those who stay at school, then as education opportunities expand, the shape of the function may change and it does *not* necessarily imply increased inequality.

What might explain the jumps and flats in the wage functions? Since the coefficients in the wage functions are estimated with precision (see Ap-pendix Table 5.1), sampling error is unlikely to be the explanation. Noting that returns tend to peak in the last year of each education level, and then decline, Saraiva et al. (1986) and Dougherty and Jiménez (1991) argue that the jumps in the wage functions reflect credentialism or sheepskin effects (al-though they admit that other factors might also matter). Among market wage earners in the South there are indeed higher returns to schooling in the last year of each schooling level (lower primary, upper primary and secondary at four, eight and 11 years, respectively) for both men and women. There are, however, also jumps in the log-wage function at six and 12 years of schooling (as well as significantly higher returns to 13 through 15 years): it is hard to see how these can be attributed to credentialism. In the Northeast, there is a jump in the market-wage function at the lower primary school (four years) for women but not for men. On the other hand there is a jump at eight years (the end of upper primary) for men but not for women. If credentialism is at work,

---

[22] See Griliches and Mason (1972) and Griliches (1977).

we would expect it to matter for both men and women and also to matter in all regions. Furthermore, there is no reason for credentials to be rewarded in the self-employed sector. Yet in the South we do see jumps in self-employment wages at four years for both men and women, at eight years for men and at 11 years for women. We also see jumps at six and 12 years for men and at seven years for women. It is very hard to see how these facts can be explained by credentialism or sheepskin effects.

Furthermore, parts of the log-wage functions are flat or downward sloping, indicating perhaps that particular years of schooling are just not very productive or even counter-productive. In the South, among men in the market wage sector, the return to education is significantly smaller at the beginning of upper primary school (fifth year) and in the 13th year (the second year of university) than in the preceding year. In the Northeast, returns *decline* in the first year of secondary school (ninth year) and third year of university education (14th year). Among self-employed men in the South, returns *decline* in the fifth, seventh, 13th and 14th years at school; among women, they decline in the third, eighth, 10th and 11th years. In the Northeast, however, returns in the self-employed sector decline in the sixth, ninth, 13th, 14th and 16th years for men and in the sixth, eighth and 10th years for women. It seems very unlikely that particular years of schooling are inherently unproductive, since this argument should apply equally to men and women as well as across regions. There exists far too much heterogeneity in the years when schooling returns decline or are negative to support the argument. Furthermore, it is very difficult to see how credentialism can explain the flats and declines.

We suspect, instead, that the jumps, flats and declines in the estimated wage functions reflect, at least in part, unobserved heterogeneity in the types of people who leave school prior to completing a level (or just after starting a new level) (Chiswick, 1973). As noted above, this may also partly explain the increasing returns to schooling over the distribution of education.[23]

---

[23] This potential education selectivity is usually ignored in wage function estimates (for exceptions, see Griliches, 1977; Griliches, Hall and Hausman, 1978; Chamberlain, 1978; and Willis and Rosen, 1979); it becomes starkly apparent when we allow flexibility in the log wage-education function. To adequately control for education selectivity requires additional data on (opportunity) costs of education, panel data (e.g., Chamberlain, 1978 and Griliches, Hall and Hausman, 1978), or the invocation of strong assumptions. Willis and Rosen (1979), for example, assume that parental characteristics affect wages only through educational attainment, so that years of completed schooling captures all human capital characteristics of the respondent. If other dimensions of human capital investment not captured by years of schooling are important, then this will not be an adequate identifying assumption. For instance, in the absence of measures of educational quality, this is unlikely to be a good assumption in Brazil. Nevertheless, attempts to treat educational attainment and current wages as jointly determined would seem a worthwhile research task.

Labor Force Participation and Self-selection in Wage Functions

The characteristics of those men and women who choose to participate in the labor force and their choice of sector (market or self-employment) is not likely to be random both in terms of observable and unobservable factors that affect wages. We account for this explicitly by modeling selection into the labor force (for total wages) and sectoral choice (the market and self-employment sectors) by the method of Lee (1983) based on estimation of a multinomial logit sectoral choice model. Education is, once again, allowed to affect each outcome without parametric restrictions.[24] Predicted probabilities from these regressions by year of education are presented in Figure 5.5.[25]

Own education is critical in allocating women between participation and nonparticipation. As women with higher education enter the labor market, they tend to go into market employment. As is true for predicting log wages, the effects of education are neither linear nor smooth. In the South, predicted market work rises from 13 percent for those with no education to only 17 percent for those with four years of education and then to 27 percent at completion of primary school. Post-primary education, however, makes a very large difference. For those who complete secondary school, predicted probabilities rise to 55 percent (with a large jump for completion of the last year) and to 84 percent for those with 15 years of schooling (an undergraduate degree). In the Northeast, predicted probabilities for market work and labor force participation increase even more dramatically among women with some secondary schooling: market work probabilities rise from 32 percent at 10 years of education to 63 percent at 11 years and then to 88 percent by the completion of an undergraduate degree (15 years).

Self-employment probabilities are fairly stable for women through primary levels of education both in the South and Northeast. Predicted probabilities fall with secondary schooling in both regions, but in the South they rise with completion of post-secondary schooling. This suggests that some better educated women enter professional types of self-employment. This rise in the probability of self-employment at the highest levels of edu-

---

[24] To reiterate, household nonlabor income, household assets, and spouse and spouse parents' characteristics serve to identify the selection effects.

[25] Covariates other than education are evaluated at sample mean values. Note that because of the non-linearity of the logit specification, this is not the same as the sample mean prediction. Multinomial logit coefficients and their asymptotic normal scores appear in Strauss and Thomas (1991).

Figure 5.5. Probability of Labor Force Participation

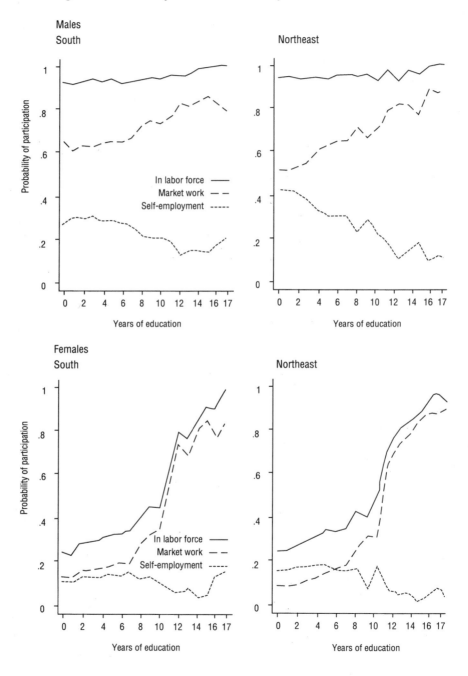

cation does not occur in the Northeast (though sample sizes in these education groups are much smaller).

For males, the relationship between employment and education is quite different. The probability of labor force participation rises only slightly with education (from 92 percent for those with no education to 99 percent for those completing 15 years in the South). The increase in the predicted probabilities of market work, though larger, is by no means as great as that for women. This is because predicted participation in market wage employment for people with very low levels of education is much higher for males; at the top of the education distribution predicted probabilities for market work are similar by gender. For example, in the South predicted probabilities of market work rise from 65 percent for men with no education to 85 percent for those who complete 15 years. In the Northeast the increase is from 51 percent to 89 percent for these two groups.

Much of the expansion of market work for men occurs at the expense of the self-employment sector. This is especially true in the Northeast, where predicted self-employment probabilities fall from 43 percent for those with no education to 23 percent at completion of primary schooling, to 18.6 percent by the end of secondary school and to just over 10 percent for those with an education of 15 years or more. In the South, probabilities of male self-employment fall with education until completion of the university level, at which point they rise. As is the case for women, this may indicate professional types of self-employment.

The existence of a spouse is associated with lower labor force participation rates among women (see Strauss and Thomas, 1991).[26] Further, higher levels of spouse education also lead to lower probabilities of female participation, consistent with a positive income effect swamping substitution effects. The effects of nonwage income are similarly negative, both for market and self-employment work, though with a decreasing marginal effect.[27] These effects all tend to be stronger for market work than for self-employment. Effects of own parents' and spouse parents' education are much weaker than the effects of a spouse's education. In the South, post-primary levels of parental education are associated with women being less likely to be in market employment than not participating at all, but more likely to be in self-employ-

---

[26] These are highly significant effects, with asymptotic t-statistics over 12.0 in all cases.

[27] For instance, in the South nonlabor income (divided by 1000) has a coefficient of –7.67 for market work versus home production, while the quadratic term is 1.41. T-statistics are over 10.0 for each. For self-employment (again contrasted with home production), the linear and quadratic coefficients are –4.14 and 0.68.

ment than not in the labor force. The spouse's mother's education has a similar effect. In the Northeast, however, both own parents' and spouse's parents' education have essentially no effect on labor force decisions of women.

For men, nonwage income also has a strong impact, leading to lower probabilities of labor force participation. As for women, the effects are somewhat stronger for market work and they are stronger in the Northeast.[28] Existence of a spouse has a very different effect on men than on women. Being married raises probabilities of work, especially market work, for men. Higher education of the spouse raises the chances of going into self-employment, although at post-primary levels of spouse education probabilities of market employment are also raised. Parental and spouse's parents' education have little effect on male participation decisions except in the South, where having a highly educated father-in-law does raise the probability of both market and self-employment work.

Having briefly discussed factors related to employment choices we are now in a position to return to a discussion of selectivity effects on log wages (these are reported in Appendix Table 5.1). Women who work in either the market or self-employment sector have, on average, significantly higher log wages than would a randomly selected woman. In the Northeast, for example, log-market wages are 30 percent higher for a woman who participates in that sector than for an average woman, holding observable characteristics constant. In the self-employment sector the differential is 27 percent. In the South the differential is only 12 percent in the market sector, but 85 percent in the self-employment sector. Controlling for own education, parents' education and the other variables in the log-wage equations, women in the South who select into the self-employment sector have a very large comparative advantage.

For men, the selection effects are quite different. Most men participate in one of the two labor sectors (although 9 percent do not participate in either). Men working in the market sector have larger log wages (conditional on observed characteristics) than the average Brazilian male in the particular region, while men in self-employment have lower log wages. Again, all these effects are significant. In the South, men in the market sector have an estimated 13 percent advantage over men with the same level of measured characteristics. In the self-employment sector there is a disadvantage of 70 percent. Similar magnitudes exist in the Northeast.

---

[28] In the Northeast, the linear and quadratic coefficients for market work are –51.24 and 83.95 (with t-statistics over 14.0) and –44.14 and 77.36 for self-employment, also being significant.

Wage Functions: Direct Background Effects

While background characteristics can affect labor force and sectoral participation choices, they may also affect log wages directly.[29] It is therefore of
interest to examine the direct effects of background on log wages. As noted,
the 1982 PNAD has information on completed education of parents of
heads of households and their spouses (if married). In our base set of specifications we use education of both parents as controls for background of the
worker.[30] Coefficient estimates appear in Appendix Table 5.1 for the three
macro-regions, separately for market and self-employment wages.

In the Northeast, we see that mother's education has significant positive effects on the log-market wages of daughters. Daughters with mothers
who have greater than primary school education enjoy a 30 percent market
wage advantage over daughters of illiterate mothers. Although this effect is
small compared to the own education effect, it is still sizeable. Mother's
education also affects the wages of sons, though by a smaller amount. In the
South, the direct influence of mother's education on daughters is only half
that in the Northeast. Sons having a mother with a second-half of primary
education have market wages 15 percent higher than those with illiterate
mothers, while the advantage to sons whose mothers have greater than primary education is over 27 percent.

Fathers' education also has a significant impact on both sons' and
daughters' log-market wages in all three regions. It has been noted that
relative to fathers' education, mothers' education has a bigger effect on labor market outcomes of children;[31] this is also true in the Center-North, the
Northeast and among sons in the South. It is not, however, universal.
Among daughters in the South, the reverse is true: the influence of fathers'
education is greater than that of the mother.

The effects of parental education on self-employment wages are
somewhat different. Fathers with post-primary education in general have a

---

[29] Years of completed schooling may be only an imperfect measure of a worker's human capital. Some investments in children, correlated with background variables, may be only partly
controlled for by education measures. Background may also be related to quality of education,
which we do not control for. In addition, self-employment wages are really a return to labor
and to fixed capital; background factors may affect resource availability, which can shift these
returns.

[30] And a dummy for those mothers and fathers whose education is not reported.

[31] Heckman and Hotz (1986) present results for earnings of men in Panama; Behrman and
Wolfe (1984) present results for schooling achievement and household income for women in
Nicaragua.

larger proportionate effect on self-employment wages than on market wages. In the Northeast, for example, self-employment wages of men whose fathers have greater than primary levels of education are 50 percent greater than sons of illiterate fathers. This may result from resources being made directly available to such enterprises. Exceptions exist for men in the South and women in the Center-North.

Wage Functions: Robustness to Background Controls

All the estimated returns to education discussed so far have included parents' education as controls for the background of the worker. While not usually included in wage or earnings functions (see Lam and Schoeni, 1990, for an exception), spouse and spouse parent characteristics may also affect wages directly. Self-employment wages include the return to self-employment capital, which is likely to be enhanced in households with better access to resources. Spouse and spouse parent characteristics may also have an effect on market wages, if, for example, there is job queuing or other forms of market segmentation. Also, given that we are not able to measure job-specific experience, returns to women are likely to depend on the degree of labor force attachment, which may be related to characteristics of both husband and possibly parents-in-law. Finally, these variables will in part pick up effects of marital sorting, together with the fact that own parents' characteristics only imperfectly measure family background.

It is of interest to compare returns to education both with and without these sorts of background controls. Many other studies, particularly using U.S. data, have demonstrated substantial declines in estimated returns. How do estimated returns in Brazil change when the spouse's education and the spouse's parents' education are added to the regressions? What happens to returns when no background variables are included? The results are presented in Figures 5.6 and 5.7.[32] The comparison for males (ignoring regional heterogeneity and sectoral choice) is discussed in the context of earnings (rather than wage) functions in Lam and Schoeni (1990).

For males, estimated returns from regressions that have controls for spouse and spouse parents' characteristics are smaller than the base set of returns (using only parents' characteristics) in all cases. The declines in

---

[32] All specifications use the same set of identifying variables for sectoral work choice, which includes all the background variables.

Figure 5.6. Returns to Education: Effect of Controlling for Background,
ℓn (Market Wage)

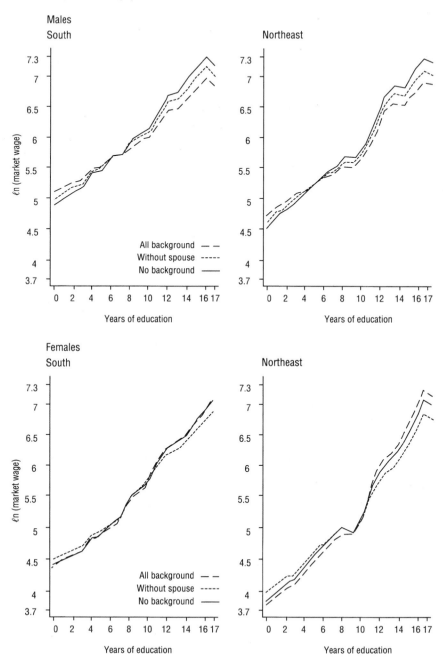

Figure 5.7. Returns to Education: Effect of Controlling for Background, ℓn (Self-employment Wage)

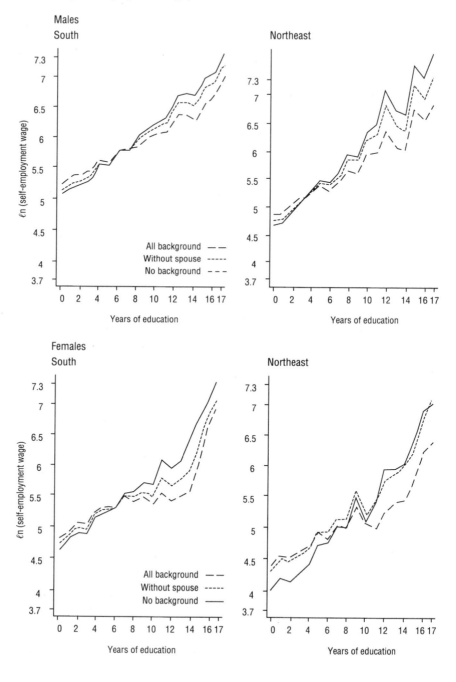

marginal returns are greater for self-employment and, in the South, at the higher end of the education distribution. For example, in the South returns to the first four years of primary school fall by 12 percent and returns to post-primary education by 21 percent when spouse and spouse parents' education are added to the log-wage equation. In the Northeast, returns to male self-employment fall 30 percent for the first four years and 19 percent for post-primary levels.[33] In the market sector male returns also fall when spouse and spouse parents' education are added to the specification, but not as much. The proportional declines are in this case greater for lower levels of education: by 18.5 percent in the South and 16.5 percent in the Northeast for the first four years.

For women, too, returns to self-employment are lowered in a highly nonlinear fashion by the addition of spouse and spouse parents' education. In both the South and Northeast returns to self-employment decline by only a very small amount for the first four years of schooling, but by 30 percent for post-primary levels.

In contrast to the other results, returns for women in the market sector are actually greater when spouse and spouse parents' characteristics are added; an anomalous and curious result especially in view of the fact that we are estimating wage rather than earnings functions. In the South, the returns are the same (at 10 percent) for the first four years, but *rise* by 18 percent for post-primary schooling. In the Northeast, the returns are slightly higher at low levels and rise from 21 percent to over 27 percent for post-primary education. Predicted female wage levels actually rise above male wages at the upper tail of the education distribution when this specification is used. This anomaly for women in the market sector apparently results from lack of robustness in the identification of who goes into the market and self-employment sectors.[34] Thus, while for men adding variables related to the spouse and spouse parents can be supported empiri-

---

[33] Returns in the South are 10 percent for early primary education with all background variables and 11 percent using only parents' education. For post-primary education the returns are 10 percent and 12 percent, respectively. In the Northeast, returns fall from 12 percent to 9 percent for the first four years and from 19 percent to 16 percent for post-primary schooling.

[34] Adding spouse and spouse parents' characteristics to the log-wage equations does not materially affect the selection effects for men, although the coefficient for self-employed workers becomes somewhat more negative. For women, however this is not the case. The magnitudes of the selection coefficients are dramatically different across the two specifications; increasing by threefold for log-market wages and fourfold for self-employment. The standard errors also increase, suggesting multicollinearity of regressors. In contrast, when no background variables are included in the log-wage equations the selection coefficients for women change, but

cally, for women this is not possible, given the resulting difficulties in identifying selection of labor force and sector participation.[35]

Removing all background characteristics raises the returns to education from the base specification (including only own parents' education) for both men and women and in both sectors. In the Northeast, male market returns rise by 11 to 12 percent when no background variables are used; the corresponding rise is greater (16 to 18 percent) for self-employment. In the South, market returns for men measure 11 percent higher throughout the education distribution, while self-employment returns increase by 8 percent for the first four years and 12 percent for post-primary levels. For women, returns to self-employment increase by 15 percent in both the South and Northeast for the first four years and by 37 percent and 24 percent, respectively, for post-primary education. Thus, again, the effects of adding background variables are nonlinear, tending to have the greatest impact at higher levels of education.

In sum, the inclusion of background characteristics has rather different effects on measured returns to education for labor market outcomes depending on own level of education, gender, region and sector of employment of workers, as well as their own levels of education. The differences also depend on exactly which set of background variables are included. In general, adding background variables reduces measured returns more for those with higher levels of education. Yet, as we have seen, the returns functions remain convex, with higher returns for the better educated, even when background controls are included. Furthermore, the inclusion of background controls does not remove the jumps, flats or even declines in the conditional wage functions; therefore, they cannot be attributed to background factors, at least to the extent we have measured them.

---

not by an order of magnitude (from .322 to .269), and the standard errors are close to the regressions based on only own parents' characteristics (around .04). Intuitively, it makes sense that the measured effect of selection should decrease as we add relevant measured characteristics to the log-wage equation. That the opposite occurs when spouse and spouse parents' characteristics are added is another indication that this specification is a poor one.

[35] Lam and Schoeni (1990) point out that the education of parents-in-law has a dramatic effect on the earnings of married men. It turns out that there also exist effects on the wages of women. However, these influences vary across gender, region and sector of employment. A father-in-law's education has positive, significant effects on market wages of males in the Northeast, but not on the market wages of females. Furthermore, the magnitude of the effects of the education of fathers-in-law on log-market wages of men is of the same magnitude as the effect of the man's *own* father, though this is not true for self-employment wages. Mothers-in-law have positive impacts on market wages of both men and women in the Northeast. For the case of self-employment wages, there are strong effects of a mother-in-law's education at higher levels on male but not female wages. There is little influence of a father-in-law's education on self-employment wages, except for a marginally significant effect at post-primary levels.

Figures 5.6 and 5.7 show the robustness of returns to education when additional background controls are used in the log-wage equations. Figure 5.8 takes a somewhat different view, using the base specification with parents' education, and stratifies the sample on the level of the father's education, thereby implicitly allowing a full set of interactions between own and father's education levels. In order to avoid small sample sizes we aggregate observations across all regions and estimate one set of regressions for the whole of Brazil. For males, lower levels of paternal education lower the level of log-market wages across the education distribution; marginal returns are not affected. For self-employment, returns to the first four years are quite similar across the different levels of father's education (*levels* are lower for children with illiterate fathers), but then returns become higher for the upper level of primary school (four to eight years) for children whose fathers have at least one year of education. At secondary levels, a distinction appears between children of fathers with four or more years of education, and with one to three years of education. Post-secondary log wages of all children grow at similar rates.

For women, log-wage levels of those whose fathers have four or more years are consistently higher, while those whose fathers are illiterate have consistently lower log wages than others. Marginal returns do not, however, seem to differ much across these groups. The same patterns tend also to be true for self-employment wages, although there is much more noise in these returns.

Wage Functions: Cohort and Race Comparisons in the Northeast

Family background clearly plays an important role in determining labor market outcomes. This role varies significantly by region, by sector of employment, by gender of the child, and by the education of the parent. We turn next to study the Northeast in more detail, reporting differences in returns and in background effects after stratifying the sample on age cohorts, in the first case, and on race in the second.

This section focuses on three age cohorts: younger (25–34 years), middle (35–44) and older (45–60). Younger age cohorts have higher levels of completed education, with a very pronounced decrease in the proportion of those with no schooling.[36]

---

[36] Among males, the proportion with no education falls from 35 percent for 45–60 year-olds to 19 percent for 25–34 year-olds. For women, the drop is even greater, from 40 percent to 19 percent. Most of the shift has been to the upper-primary, secondary and post-secondary levels (see Strauss and Thomas, 1991). Note that it is not possible to map this shift into a shift in the Brazilian educational system since many Brazilians, particularly in the older cohort, may have immigrated into the country and received their schooling elsewhere. Also, internal migration may affect the educational composition of the cohorts.

Figure 5.8. Returns to Education: Effect of Controlling for Father's Education

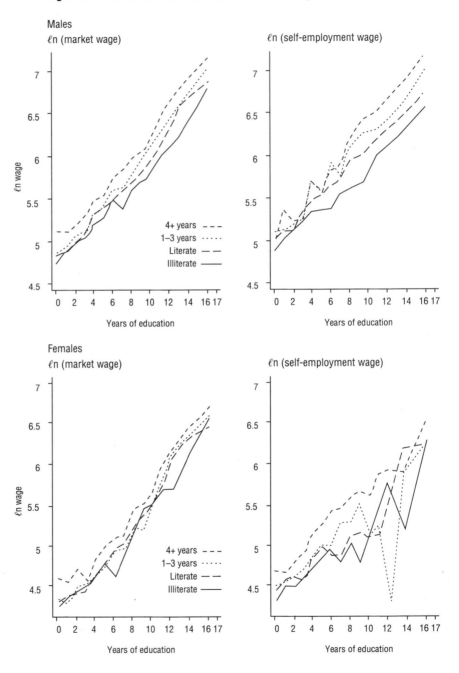

The estimated conditional wage functions are presented in Figure 5.9 for the same three age groups. Stratification by age cohort allows flexible interactions between education and age; generally returns decline with age. In the market sector, for the first half of primary school, the middle and older groups earn the same returns, which are about double those of the younger cohort. In the second half of primary school, however, the returns for the older cohort take off and as a result, the average return to the first years of schooling is a very high 15 percent for the older cohort, about 90 percent of that for the middle cohort (14 percent) and less than two-thirds that for the younger cohort (9 percent).[37]

After primary school, returns for the younger cohort increase, roughly doubling, to reach 17 percent for secondary school and 21 percent for four years of post-secondary school. Since returns for the middle cohort also increase and those for the older are slightly lower, inter-cohort differences in wage levels are narrower at the top of the education distribution than at the bottom. The patterns for women are similar, with the older cohort enjoying much higher returns to the second half of primary school, while returns for the younger and middle cohort take off during secondary school.

In the self-employment sector, the differences are less obvious. The middle cohort seems to do worst and earns lower returns than both the younger and older cohorts for the first half of primary school, although they catch up to the younger (but not older) cohorts by the beginning of secondary school.

Selection effects for women vary in a very interesting way among age cohorts. The effects are strongest for the oldest cohort; they are significant only for market wages for 35–44 year olds and are not significant at all for the younger cohort. Presumably this reflects much greater labor force participation among younger women. For men, selection effects in self-employment are stronger for the two younger cohorts, though in the market sector, selection disappears for the youngest cohort.

Returns to schooling are apparently changing dramatically over time in Brazil. As education opportunities have expanded and more children have completed primary school, economic returns to the first years of schooling have declined. Going beyond primary school, however, reaps large returns and these returns are greatest for the most recent cohorts. This increase in the nonlinearity of the log-wage education function has very

---

[37] For the older cohort, the return to the eighth year of school is negative: the average return to the first seven years is a massive 19 percent.

Figure 5.9. Returns to Education: Northeast Brazil, by Age Cohort

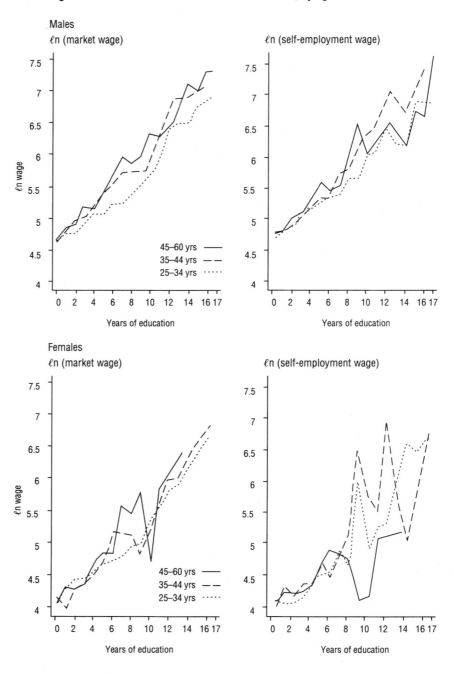

Males
ℓn (market wage)

ℓn (self-employment wage)

45–60 yrs ——
35–44 yrs — —
25–34 yrs ······

Years of education

Years of education

Females
ℓn (market wage)

ℓn (self-employment wage)

45–60 yrs ——
35–44 yrs — —
25–34 yrs ······

Years of education

Years of education

important implications for the path of income inequality in Brazil (Lam and Levison, 1991a; Almeida dos Reis and Barros, 1991).

Conditional expectations of log wages are presented in Figure 5.10 based on regressions estimated separately for blacks, mulattos and whites (including Asians). In the market sector, returns to education (and wages) are about the same for men in the three groups that have four years or less of schooling, but the returns to the second half of primary school are higher for whites and by secondary school, returns for mulattos also take off, leaving blacks behind. In the self-employment sector, returns for whites are somewhat higher after four years of education, while returns trail off for blacks at completion of secondary school; this leaves a substantial gap at post-primary levels. For women in the market sector returns are quite similar for all races through primary school, but are higher for whites and mulattos with secondary schooling. In the self-employment sector, white women are consistently better rewarded for education than either mulattos or blacks (although these estimates are quite imprecise). Differential returns by race, it appears, are greatest for men in the market sector and especially large in the upper half of the education distribution. For women, these differential returns are apparent in the market sector after primary levels, while in the self-employment sector, they persist throughout the education distribution.

For whites, selection effects are very similar to those discussed above. For mulattos, selection is significant only for males in the self-employment sector, where they are also negative, and for women in the market sector. For blacks, selection coefficients are never significant (which could be in part because of small samples).

Conclusions

We have documented numerous empirical regularities of the urban Brazilian labor market using data drawn from the 1982 PNAD. We focus on heterogeneity in outcomes: by gender, region, sector of employment, age cohort and race. Special attention is paid to nonlinearities in the conditional (log) wage function across the educational distribution. Family background factors were allowed to play a role in wage determination, both directly and through their influence on labor market participation choices.

Among the principal findings is that the influence of education on wages is large and positive and that this is invariant to inclusion of controls for parental education (though the precise magnitudes of the effects are affected). The impact of education on both participation decisions and on log

Figure 5.10. Returns to Education: Northeast Brazil by Race

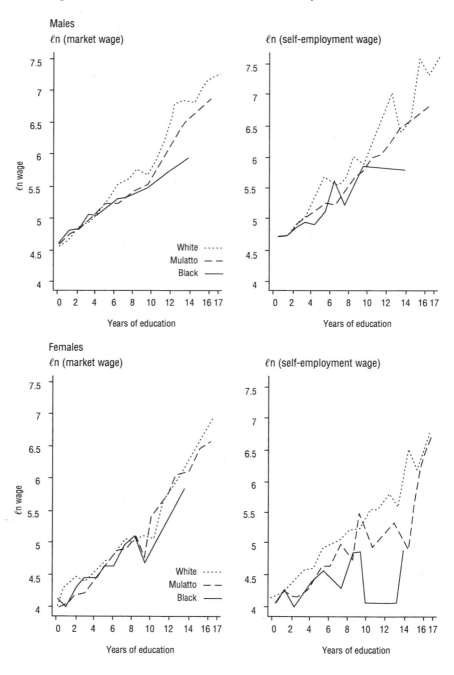

wages is neither smooth nor linear; a polynomial model will provide an inferior fit to the data. Returns to post-primary schooling tend to be much higher than returns to primary schooling or less. This is true for both market and self-employment work. The differential is greater in the Northeast than the South and, perhaps most disturbing, has been increasing over time. This suggests that educational expansion in Brazil might give rise to increasing inequality.

Particular years of schooling are associated with significantly higher returns than the year before or the year after. This often occurs at the end of a schooling level and might be construed as evidence for sheepskin or credential effects. Other years, however, are associated with no increase in expected wages or even a decline in the expected wage. Since the years in which the jumps, flats and declines in the conditional wage function occur are not uniform across gender or region, credentialism seems an unlikely explanation. Furthermore, since these patterns are observed in both the market and self-employment sectors (at different years), the evidence for credentialism is very weak.

Instead, we argue that both the convexity of the conditional wage function and the jumps, flats and declines may partly reflect different unobserved characteristics of those who complete different levels of schooling. This schooling selection problem has been prominent in the U.S. literature, but has been all but ignored in studies of developing economies. Unfortunately, either better data or strong assumptions are needed to address the problem; the assumption used in the United States (that parents' education only affects log wages through schooling decisions) is likely to be rejected in Brazil.

What causes the convexity of the conditional wage function and why are people not taking advantage of this situation by getting higher levels of schooling? Answers to both these questions may be a function of differing educational quality for different levels of schooling. Also, existing characteristics of one's family may constrain how well a child does in school as well as the quality and quantity of schooling one receives. In addition, there is also likely to be an influence on the wage structure of factors related to labor demand. Given the very serious implications of this nonlinear structure of wages for income inequality, these questions deserve more attention.

REFERENCES

Almeida dos Reis, José, and Ricardo Barros. 1991. Wage Inequality and the Distribution of Education: A Study of the Evolution of Regional Differences in Inequality in Metropolitan Brazil. *Journal of Development Economics* 36: 117–43.

Altonji, Joseph. 1988. The Effects of Family Background and Social Characteristics on Education and Labor Market Outcomes. Mimeo.

Altonji, Joseph, and Thomas Dunn. 1990. Effects of Parental Characteristics on the Returns to Education and Labor Market Experience. Mimeo.

Armitage, Jane, and Richard Sabot. 1987. Socioeconomic Background and the Returns to Schooling in Two Low-income Economies. *Economica* 54: 103–108.

Behrman, Jere, and Nancy Birdsall. 1984. Does Geographic Aggregation Cause Over Estimates of the Returns to Schooling? *Oxford Bulletin of Economics and Statistics* 46: 55–72.

———. 1983. The Quality of Schooling: Quantity Alone is Misleading. *American Economic Review* 73: 928–46.

Behrman, Jere, Z. Hrubec, Paul Taubman, and Terrence Wales. 1980. *Socioeconomic Success: A Study of the Effects of Genetic Endowments, Family Environment and Schooling.* Amsterdam: North Holland.

Behrman, Jere, and Barbara Wolfe. 1984. The Socioeconomic Impact of Schooling in a Developing Country. *Review of Economics and Statistics* 66.2: 296–303.

Birdsall, Nancy. 1985. Public Inputs and Child Schooling in Brazil. *Journal of Development Economics* 18: 67–86.

Bound, John, Zvi Griliches, and Bronwyn Hall. 1986. Wages, Schooling and IQ of Brothers and Sisters: Do Family Factors Differ? *International Economic Review* 27: 77–105.

Card, David and Alan Krueger. 1992. Does School Quality Matter? Returns to Education and the Characteristics of Public Schools in the United States. *Journal of Political Economy* 100.1:1–41.

Carnoy, Martin. 1967. Earnings and Schooling in Mexico. *Economic Development and Cultural Change* 15: 408–19.

Chamberlain, Gary. 1978. Omitted Variable Bias in Panel Data: Estimating the Returns to Schooling. *Annals de l'INSEE* 30/31: 49–82.

Chiswick, Barry R. 1973. Schooling, Screening and Income. In *Does College Matter?*, eds. Lewis C. Solomon and Paul J. Taubman. New York: Academic Press.

Corcoran, Mary, Roger Gordon, Deborah Laren, and Gary Solon. 1990. The Effects of Family Background and Community Background on Economic Status. *American Economic Review* 80: 362–66.

Dougherty, Christopher, and Emmanuel Jiménez. 1991. The Specification of Earnings Functions: Tests and Implications. *Economics of Education Review* 10: 85–98.

Featherman, David, and Robert Hauser. 1978. *Opportunity and Change.* New York: Academic Press.

Griliches, Zvi. 1979. Sibling Models and Data in Economics: Beginnings of a Survey. *Journal of Political Economy* 87: S37–S64.

_____. 1977. Estimating the Returns to Schooling: Some Econometric Problems. *Econometrica* 45: 1–22.

Griliches, Zvi, and William Mason. 1972. Education, Income and Ability. *Journal of Political Economy* 80: S74–S103.

Griliches, Zvi, Bronwyn Hall, and Jerry Hausman. 1978. Missing Data and Self-selection in Large Panels. *Annals de l'INSEE* 30/31: 137–76.

Haller, Arch, and H. Saraiva. 1991. The Income Effects of Education in a Developing Country: Brazil, 1973 and 1982. Paper presented at 1991 meetings of the Population Association of America, Washington, D.C. University of Wisconsin, Madison.

_____. 1986. Income and Education: Brazil, 1982. University of Wisconsin, Madison. Mimeo.

Hauser, Robert, and W. Sewell. 1986. Family Effects in Simple Models of Education, Occupational Status and Earnings: Findings from the Wisconsin and Kalamazoo Studies. *Journal of Labor Economics* 4: S83–S115.

Heckman, James, and Joseph Hotz. 1986. The Sources of Inequality for Males in Panama's Labor Market. *Journal of Human Resources* 21.4: 507–42.

Hungerford, Thomas, and Gary Solon. 1987. Sheepskin Effects in the Returns to Education. *Review of Economics and Statistics* 69: 175–77.

Lam, David, and Deborah Levison. 1991a. Declining Inequality in Schooling in Brazil and its Effects on Inequality in Earnings. *Journal of Development Economics* 37: 199–226.

_____. 1991b. Age, Experience and Schooling: Decomposing Earnings Inequality in the U.S. and Brazil. *Pesquisa e Planejamento Econômico.*

Lam, David and Robert Schoeni. 1990. Effects of Family Background on Earnings and Returns to Schooling: Evidence from Brazil. University of Michigan. Mimeo.

Langoni, Carlos. 1977. Income Distribution and Economic Development: The Brazilian Case. In *Frontiers of Quantitative Economics,* vol. B, ed. Michael Intriligator. Amsterdam: North Holland Press.

_____. 1973. *Distribuição de Renda e Desenvolvimento Econômico do Brasil.* Rio de Janeiro: Editora Expressão e Cultura.

Lee, Lung-Fei. 1983. Generalized Econometric Models with Selectivity. *Econometrica* 51: 507–12.

Leibowitz, Arleen. 1974. Home Investments in Children. In *Economics of the Family,* ed. T. W. Schultz. Chicago: University of Chicago Press.

Medeiros, José. 1982. Alcance e Limitações da Teoria do Capital Humano: Diferenças de Ganhos no Brasil em 1973. *Série Ensaios Econômicos* 17, Instituto de Pesquisas Econômicas, São Paulo.

Papanicolau, J., and George Psacharapoulos. 1979. Socioeconomic Background, Schooling and Monetary Rewards in the United Kingdom. *Economica* 46: 435–39.

Pastore, José. 1982. *Inequality and Social Mobility in Brazil.* Madison: University of Wisconsin Press.

Psacharopoulos, George. 1985. Returns to Education: A Further International Update and Implications. *Journal of Human Resources* 20: 583–604.

Psacharopoulos, George, and Maureen Woodhall. 1985. *Education for Development: An Analysis of Investment Choices.* Oxford: Oxford University Press.

Sahn, David, and Harold Alderman. 1988. The Effects of Human Capital on Wages, and the Determinants of Labor Supply in a Developing Country. *Journal of Development Economics* 29: 157–84.

Saraiva, H., A. Pahari, and Arch Haller. 1986. Beyond Credentialism: The Productivity of Ideology and the Ideology of Productivity. University of Wisconsin, Madison. Mimeo.

Sedlacek, Guilherme, and Ricardo Barros (eds.). 1989. *Mercado de Trabalho e Distribuição de Renda: Uma Coletânea.* Instituto de Planejamento Econômico e Social, Instituto de Pesquisas, Monografia No. 35, Rio de Janeiro.

Solon, Gary. 1989a. *Intergenerational Income Mobility in the United States.* Institute for Research on Poverty Discussion Paper No. 894–89, University of Wisconsin.

_____. 1989b. Biases in the Estimation of Intergenerational Earnings Correlations. *Review of Economics and Statistics* 71: 172–74.

Solon, Gary, Mary Corcoran, Roger Gordon, and Deborah Laren. 1991. A Longitudinal Analysis of Sibling Correlations in Economic Status. *Journal of Human Resources* 26: 509–34.

Stelcner, Morton, Ana-Maria Arriagada, and Peter Moock. 1987. *Wage Determinants and School Attainment Among Men in Peru.* Living Standards Measurement Study Working Paper No. 38, World Bank, Washington, D.C.

Strauss, John, and Duncan Thomas. 1991. *Wages, Schooling and Background: Investments in Men and Women in Urban Brazil.* Economic Growth Center Discussion Paper 649, Yale University, New Haven.

Tannen, Michael. 1991. New Estimates of the Returns to Schooling in Brazil. *Economics of Education Review* 10: 123–35.

Willis, Robert. 1986. Wage Determinants: A Survey and Reinterpretation of Human Capital Earnings Functions. In *Handbook of Labor Economics,* vol. 1, eds. Orley Ashenfelter and Richard Layard. Amsterdam: North Holland Press.

Willis, Robert, and Sherwin Rosen. 1979. Education and Self-Selection. *Journal of Political Economy* 87: S7–S36.

Appendix Table 5.1. Log-Wage Functions: Total, Market and Self-employment, Males

	Total Wage				Market Wage				Self-employment Wage			
	South		Northeast		South		Northeast		South		Northeast	
	Coeffi-cients	ΔCoeffi-cients	Coeffi-cients	ΔCoeffi-cients	Coeffi-cients	ΔCoeffi-cients	Coeffi-cients	ΔCoeffi-cients	Coeffi-cients	ΔCoeffi-cients	Coeffi-cients	ΔCoeffi-cients
Own education:												
1 yr	.137 [.022]		.129 [.030]		.107 [.025]		.172 [.039]		.100 [.050]		.020 [.062]	
2 yrs	.211 [.018]	.074 [.024]	.215 [.026]	.086 [.035]	.200 [.020]	.094 [.027]	.249 [.033]	.076 [.039]	.152 [.041]	.052 [.053]	.186 [.055]	.167 [.074]
3 yrs	.280 [.016]	.069 [.018]	.357 [.025]	.142 [.031]	.264 [.018]	.063 [.021]	.418 [.032]	.170 [.039]	.218 [.037]	.067 [.040]	.339 [.055]	.152 [.067]
4 yrs	.494 [.014]	.214 [.013]	.440 [.022]	.083 [.027]	.478 [.015]	.215 [.016]	.528 [.028]	.110 [.034]	.438 [.032]	.220 [.029]	.496 [.051]	.157 [.062]
5 yrs	.519 [.018]	.025 [.015]	.567 [.025]	.127 [.027]	.521 [.020]	.043 [.018]	.659 [.032]	.130 [.033]	.412 [.040]	-.027 [.033]	.688 [.060]	.193 [.062]
6 yrs	.727 [.024]	.208 [.024]	.646 [.046]	.079 [.048]	.711 [.027]	.190 [.028]	.799 [.056]	.140 [.057]	.647 [.055]	.236 [.054]	.632 [.109]	-.056 [.113]
7 yrs	.750 [.024]	.023 [.029]	.724 [.047]	.078 [.062]	.759 [.028]	.048 [.034]	.865 [.057]	.066 [.073]	.647 [.056]	-.001 [.066]	.779 [.116]	.147 [.150]
8 yrs	.895 [.017]	.145 [.024]	.866 [.029]	.142 [.051]	.929 [.019]	.171 [.027]	1.018 [.037]	.153 [.059]	.829 [.041]	.182 [.056]	1.102 [.079]	.323 [.126]
9 yrs	.998	.103	.929	.062	1.045	.116	.997	-.022	.948	.120	1.089	-.014

10 yrs	1.079 [.037]	.081 [.036]	1.081 [.064]	.153 [.066]	1.110 [.040]	.065 [.040]	1.197 [.076]	.200 [.078]	1.043 [.093]	.095 [.092]	1.449 [.157]	.360 [.166]
11 yrs	1.295 [.029]	.216 [.043]	1.319 [.054]	.238 [.080]	1.379 [.032]	.269 [.047]	1.521 [.063]	.324 [.093]	1.109 [.071]	.066 [.109]	1.525 [.143]	.076 [.203]
12 yrs	1.506 [.018]	.211 [.028]	1.621 [.028]	.302 [.055]	1.608 [.020]	.230 [.031]	1.919 [.038]	.398 [.063]	1.433 [.042]	.324 [.070]	2.096 [.082]	.571 [.145]
13 yrs	1.536 [.036]	.030 [.040]	1.802 [.099]	.181 [.099]	1.632 [.044]	.024 [.043]	2.123 [.110]	.204 [.107]	1.421 [.120]	-.011 [.119]	1.708 [.329]	-.388 [.323]
14 yrs	1.687	.151 [.050]	1.762 [.077]	-.040 [.122]	1.835 [.039]	.203 [.054]	2.085 [.090]	-.038 [.134]	1.360 [.096]	-.061 [.147]	1.580 [.224]	-.127 [.383]
15 yrs	1.879 [.033]	.191 [.044]	2.026 [.078]	.264 [.106]	2.015 [.037]	.180 [.048]	2.328 [.092]	.243 [.121]	1.676 [.087]	.315 [.120]	2.443 [.202]	.863 [.287]
16 yrs	2.028 [.022]	.150 [.033]	2.165 [.042]	.139 [.083]	2.167 [.024]	.152 [.036]	2.508 [.055]	.180 [.096]	1.745 [.053]	.069 [.089]	2.172 [.143]	-.271 [.223]
17 yrs	2.079 [.042]	.050 [.044]	2.135 [.092]	-.030 [.097]	2.013 [.049]	-.154 [.051]	2.411 [.108]	-.097 [.110]	2.057 [.093]	.311 [.096]	2.594 [.266]	.422 [.273]
Selection coefficient	-.048 [.027]		-.049 [.045]		.256 [.030]		.404 [.058]		-.494 [.053]		-.964 [.111]	

(Continued)

Appendix Table 5.1. (cont.)

| | Total Wage | | | | Market Wage | | | | Self-employment Wage | | | |
| | South | | Northeast | | South | | Northeast | | South | | Northeast | |
	Coefficients	ΔCoefficients	Coefficients	ΔCoefficients	Coefficients	ΔCoefficients	Coefficients	ΔCoefficients	Coefficients	ΔCoefficients	Coefficients	ΔCoefficients
Education of father:												
Literate	.037		.018		.035		.008		−.011		−.036	
	[.013]		[.020]		[.015]		[.026]		[.030]		[.045]	
1–3 yrs	.053		.080		.047		.071		.012		.081	
	[.012]		[.024]		[.014]		[.030]		[.029]		[.056]	
4–8 yrs	.113		.189		.118		.140		.073		.254	
	[.014]		[.030]		[.016]		[.030]		[.033]		[.071]	
9+ yrs	.194		.360		.188		.293		.177		.535	
	[.022]		[.046]		[.025]		[.054]		[.050]		[.118]	
Missing	.034		−.010		.049		.011		.033		.025	
	[.016]		[.027]		[.018]		[.033]		[.038]		[.063]	
Mother:												
Literate	.083		.078		.055		.030		.110		.083	
	[.013]		[.021]		[.015]		[.026]		[.030]		[.046]	
1–3 yrs	.102		.118		.073		.106		.094		.075	
	[.012]		[.024]		[.014]		[.030]		[.028]		[.057]	
4–8 yrs	.180		.186		.151		.192		.137		.118	
	[.014]		[.031]		[.016]		[.037]		[.032]		[.073]	
9+ yrs	.315		.245		.274		.146		.312		.140	
	[.024]		[.051]		[.027]		[.060]		[.056]		[.133]	

Missing	.044	.089	.032	.097	.090	.059
	[.017]	[.029]	[.019]	[.036]	[.041]	[.066]
Age	.078	.071	.084	.073	.038	-.010
	[.004]	[.006]	[.004]	[.007]	[.009]	[.016]
Age squared	-.001	-.001	-.001	-.001	-.000	.000
	[.000]	[.000]	[.000]	[.000]	[.000]	[.000]
White/Asian	.126	.103	.081	.043	.129	-.006
	[.009]	[.014]	[.011]	[.018]	[.024]	[.035]
Black	-.060	-.025	-.057	.028	-.003	.094
	[.016]	[.022]	[.017]	[.027]	[.041]	[.056]
Constant	3.009	3.144	2.873	2.897	4.665	6.018
	[.071]	[.122]	[.077]	[.144]	[.229]	[.403]
R^2	0.53	0.54	0.59	0.62	0.40	0.42
No. of obs.	33,553	11,093	24,447	7,216	9,103	3,872

Note: Estimates and [standard errors] from OLS regression with selectivity correction computed by method of Lee (1983) with multinomial logit. Standard errors corrected for estimation of regressor. State dummy variables included but suppressed from table.

Appendix Table 5.2. Log-Wage Functions: Total, Market and Self-employment, Females

| | Total Wage | | | | Market Wage | | | | Self-employment Wage | | | |
| | South | | Northeast | | South | | Northeast | | South | | Northeast | |
	Coeffi-cients	ΔCoeffi-cients	Coeffi-cients	ΔCoeffi-cients	Coeffi-cients	ΔCoeffi-cients	Coeffi-cients	ΔCoeffi-cients	Coeffi-cients	ΔCoeffi-cients	Coeffi-cients	ΔCoeffi-cients
Own education:												
1 yr	.119 [.035]		.160 [.057]		.093 [.039]		.117 [.078]		.141 [.070]		.172 [.083]	
2 yrs	.193 [.026]	.074 [.038]	.164 [.046]	.005 [.067]	.163 [.029]	.071 [.043]	.260 [.064]	.143 [.092]	.254 [.052]	.113 [.077]	.101 [.067]	−.070 [.097]
3 yrs	.229 [.023]	.036 [.027]	.269 [.043]	.104 [.055]	.228 [.026]	.065 [.031]	.308 [.056]	.048 [.075]	.233 [.047]	−.021 [.055]	.221 [.064]	.120 [.081]
4 yrs	.440 [.020]	.212 [.021]	.414 [.037]	.146 [.047]	.401 [.022]	.173 [.024]	.484 [.049]	.176 [.061]	.481 [.041]	.248 [.044]	.350 [.057]	.129 [.072]
5 yrs	.504 [.026]	.063 [.024]	.626 [.043]	.211 [.046]	.475 [.029]	.074 [.027]	.663 [.055]	.178 [.059]	.547 [.053]	.067 [.049]	.603 [.066]	.253 [.071]
6 yrs	.589 [.040]	.085 [.041]	.703 [.085]	.077 [.089]	.578 [.044]	.103 [.046]	.799 [.100]	.136 [.104]	.566 [.082]	.018 [.084]	.593 [.145]	−.010 [.149]
7 yrs	.731 [.041]	.142 [.051]	.903 [.091]	.200 [.118]	.688 [.047]	.110 [.059]	.963 [.105]	.164 [.136]	.769 [.083]	.204 [.103]	.815 [.158]	.222 [.204]
8 yrs	.920 [.027]	.189 [.042]	.942 [.053]	.039 [.097]	.960 [.029]	.273 [.048]	1.056 [.063]	.093 [.110]	.753 [.059]	−.016 [.086]	.802 [.092]	−.013 [.169]
9 yrs	1.068 [.059]	.148 [.059]	.950 [.136]	.009 [.140]	1.123 [.061]	.162 [.061]	.963 [.136]	−.093 [.140]	.838 [.139]	.085 [.140]	1.292 [.329]	.489 [.334]

10 yrs	1.136 [.049]	.068 [.072]	1.097 [.095]	.146 [.160]	1.216 [.050]	.093 [.073]	1.246 [.106]	.283 [.162]	.748 [.127]	−.091 [.178]	.836 [.174]	−.455 [.363]
11 yrs	1.462 [.026]	.326 [.048]	1.454 [.047]	.357 [.094]	1.496 [.029]	.281 [.048]	1.627 [.060]	.381 [.102]	1.048 [.073]	.301 [.129]	1.106 [.115]	.270 [.191]
12 yrs	1.648 [.059]	.185 [.056]	1.733 [.135]	.279 [.131]	1.693 [.057]	.197 [.052]	1.879 [.133]	.252 [.122]	.920 [.234]	−.128 [.231]	1.429 [.443]	.323 [.440]
13 yrs	1.707 [.052]	.059 [.070]	1.854 [.134]	.121 [.179]	1.784 [.051]	.091 [.065]	2.015 [.132]	.137 [.166]	1.006 [.167]	.086 [.276]	1.519 [.438]	.091 [.603]
14 yrs	1.862 [.041]	.155 [.056]	2.082 [.104]	.227 [.157]	1.885 [.042]	.101 [.052]	2.243 [.106]	.228 [.143]	1.168 [.185]	.161 [.233]	1.650 [.507]	.131 [.650]
15 yrs	2.050 [.033]	.188 [.037]	2.362 [.068]	.280 [.104]	2.064 [.036]	.179 [.034]	2.526 [.081]	.283 [.094]	1.583 [.102]	.415 [.188]	1.870 [.191]	.220 [.519]
16 yrs	2.212 [.047]	.162 [.041]	2.700 [.108]	.338 [.101]	2.219 [.048]	.155 [.041]	2.880 [.113]	.354 [.095]	2.006 [.111]	.423 [.133]	2.377 [.278]	.507 [.306]
17 yrs	2.425 [.082]	.213 [.084]	2.717 [0.197]	.017 [.212]	2.388 [.084]	.169 [.085]	2.779 [.186]	−.101 [.192]	2.322 [.201]	.316 [.214]	2.762 [.861]	.385 [.900]
Selection coefficient	.150 [.020]		.261 [.039]		.115 [.020]		.269 [.044]		.525 [.101]		.194 [.104]	

(Continued)

Appendix Table 5.2. (cont.)

| | Total Wage | | | | Market Wage | | | | Self-employment Wage | | | |
| | South | | Northeast | | South | | Northeast | | South | | Northeast | |
	Coefficients	ΔCoefficients	Coefficients	ΔCoefficients	Coefficients	ΔCoefficients	Coefficients	ΔCoefficients	Coefficients	ΔCoefficients	Coefficients	ΔCoefficients
Education of father:												
Literate	.033 [.020]		.021 [.034]		.025 [.022]		.011 [.043]		.061 [.041]		.031 [.053]	
1–3 yrs	.021 [.019]		−.002 [.047]		.042 [.020]		−.027 [.046]		−.008 [.040]		.026 [.061]	
4–8 yrs	.102 [.020]		.152 [.047]		.125 [.022]		.138 [.053]		.089 [.044]		.122 [.086]	
9+ yrs	.213 [.030]		.235 [.072]		.209 [.031]		.187 [.076]		.422 [.076]		.333 [.153]	
Missing	.073 [.027]		.030 [.051]		.081 [.029]		−.034 [.063]		.081 [.059]		.057 [.083]	
Mother:												
Literate	.021 [.020]		.074 [.035]		.031 [.022]		.121 [.043]		−.029 [.043]		.026 [.055]	
1–3 yrs	.059 [.018]		.180 [.039]		.031 [.020]		.195 [.046]		.097 [.039]		.173 [.065]	
4–8 yrs	.150 [.020]		.224 [.048]		.095 [.021]		.244 [.054]		.257 [.044]		.241 [.088]	
9+ yrs	.202 [.032]		.299 [.079]		.153 [.033]		.319 [.083]		.287 [.084]		.338 [.172]	

Missing	.025	.091	-.010	.142	.085	.102
	[.031]	[.058]	[.033]	[.069]	[.070]	[.097]
Age	.056	.062	.053	.045	.066	.062
	[.005]	[.011]	[.006]	[.013]	[.013]	[.020]
Age squared	-.001	-.001	-.001	-.000	-.001	-.001
	[.000]	[.000]	[.000]	[.000]	[.000]	[.000]
White/Asian	.090	.088	.103	.045	.068	.164
	[.014]	[.024]	[.015]	[.028]	[.032]	[.043]
Black	-.005	.044	.021	.066	-.070	.013
	[.022]	[.036]	[.024]	[.045]	[.049]	[.057]
Constant	2.881	2.403	2.944	2.619	1.984	2.374
	[.117]	[.240]	[.126]	[.279]	[.361]	[.498]
R^2	0.59	0.54	0.67	0.66	0.36	0.29
No. of obs.	14,770	5,246	10,254	2,871	4,515	2,373

Note. Estimates and [standard errors] from OLS regression with selectivity correction computed by method of Lee (1983) with multinomial logit. Standard errors corrected for estimation of regressor. State dummy variables included but suppressed from table.

Temporal Evolution of the Relationship between Wages and Education of Brazilian Men

Ricardo Barros and Lauro Ramos

This chapter explores the extent to which the productivity and wages of Brazilian workers can be improved through additional years of formal schooling. This is crucial to showing how educational expansion could foster economic growth in Brazil.[1] Education can "explain" up to 50 percent of the inequality of wages in Brazil, while the relationship between education and wages indicates how the labor market translates inequality in education into inequality in earnings.[2] Hence, a more accurate understanding of the relationship between education, on the one hand, and wages and productivity, on the other, is key to formulating policies aimed at increasing growth and reducing inequality, the two major long-term challenges for Brazilian society.

This study describes the changes in the wage-education relationship that have taken place in Brazil's recent past. The analysis, which uses 13 Brazilian Annual Household Surveys *(Pesquisa Nacional por Amostra de Domicílios—PNAD)* available since 1976, concentrates on the relationship from 1976 to 1989 between wages and education among Brazilian prime-age males.[3] Three wage-education relationships are estimated for each year using flexible functional forms and an increasing number of controls: the first specification includes no controls; the second controls for age; and the third includes controls for age and region of residence.

Empirical Preliminaries

The PNAD covers all urban areas and the majority of the rural areas in Brazil. The sample is based on a three-stage sampling design. With the excep-

---

[1] See Lau et al. (this volume), Langoni (1973), Almeida dos Reis and Barros (1991), Lam and Levison (1991a, b), and Ramos (1990).

[2] See Park, Ross and Sabot (this volume).

[3] There are 14 years but only 13 surveys, since in 1980 the series was interrupted to avoid overlap with the 1980 Demographic Census which, unfortunately, is incompatible with the PNADs.

tion of the first stage, the sampling scheme is self-weighted. The sampling rate varies across geographic regions and over time from 1/50 to 1/400. This sampling design generates annual samples of approximately 100,000 households (IBGE, 1981).

The unit of analysis is the individual. The universe of analysis is restricted to males between the ages of 25 and 50 years who at the time of the survey (a) were living in urban areas, (b) held at least one job, (c) worked 20 or more hours per week in all jobs,[4] and (d) were not in school.

The universe of analysis represents approximately 15 million workers in 1989—10 percent of the Brazilian population and 25 percent of the labor force. The total sample size is around 550,000 observations. It varies from 31,000 in 1986 to 57,000 in 1985 (see Appendix Tables 6.1 and 6.2).

To measure wages, W, we use labor earnings standardized by hours worked. Specifically, $W=R/H$ where R is the monthly labor gross income normally received in all jobs and H is the usual number of hours worked per week in all jobs.[5]

Education is measured by the number of years of completed schooling. Since this is not a direct question in the survey questionnaire, an algorithm is used to construct years of completed schooling from two other questions in the questionnaire. The algorithm is similar to the one used by Lam and Levison (1991a,b) and by Barros and Lam in this volume. It is described in detail in Appendix Table 6.3. Age corresponds to the individual's age at the date of the interview. For region of residence we use a categorical variable that implies a division of Brazil into 18 geographical areas. Except for a few cases where groups of states were aggregated, this division coincides with the division of Brazil into states.[6]

Temporal Evolution of the Distribution of Education

Figure 6.1 presents the distribution of workers in our universe by their number of years of schooling.[7] This frequency distribution is similar to that

---

[4] We also eliminate from the final sample all observations with incomplete information on labor income, hours worked, educational attainment, age, and region of residence. Workers who reported zero labor income were also eliminated from the final sample. Due to these criteria, close to 1 percent of the sample was eliminated (see Appendix Tables 6.1 and 6.2).

[5] Since we use log wages in our regressions, multiplying hours worked per week by a constant like 4.5 makes no difference except that it changes the estimated intercept in all regressions.

[6] These states and their respective groupings are: (a) Sergipe and Alagoas, (b) Paraíba and Rio Grande do Norte, (c) Maranhão and Piauí, (d) Pará and Amapá, (e) Amazonas, Roraima, Acre and Rondônia, (f) Mato Grosso and Mato Grosso do Sul, and (g) Goiás and Tocantins.

[7] This distribution is an average over the 13-year period covered by this study.

Figure 6.1. Distribution of the Population by the Number of Completed Years of Schooling

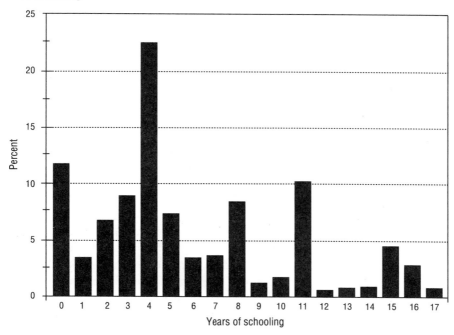

Figure 6.2. Distribution of the Population by Educational Groups

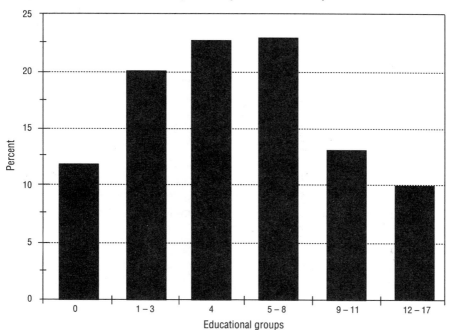

in the Lam and Levison study (1991b, Figure 5) and reveals five local peaks at zero, four, eight, 11, and 15 years of schooling. Each of the last four peaks correspond to the completion of one of the basic degrees awarded by the Brazilian educational system: lower primary (four years), upper primary (eight years), high school (11 years), and college (15 or 16 years). The number of years of schooling of 58 percent of the population is equal to one of these five local peaks. Much of this study concentrates only on this important subpopulation.

Figure 6.2 presents an aggregated version of Figure 6.1, and Figure 6.3 and Table 6.1 present the temporal evolution of this aggregated distribution. Figure 6.2 reveals that 12 percent of prime-age males in Brazilian urban labor markets still have no schooling. Also, less than one-quarter of this population has completed at least a year of high school. Finally, only about 10 percent of males aged 25–50 years in the urban labor force in Brazil have entered college.

Figure 6.4 and Table 6.2 present the cumulative distribution of the population by years of schooling for 1976 and 1989. This figure reveals that the distribution for 1989 dominates the distribution for 1976 based on the strong concept of first-order stochastic dominance. Figure 6.5 presents the temporal evolution of the mean years of schooling and its standard deviation between 1976 and 1989. This figure shows a rate of growth for mean years of schooling of approximately one additional year per decade. It also reveals a moderate increase (of approximately 0.5 years) in the standard deviation from 1977 to 1983. Figure 6.3 presents a more disaggregated view of this educational expansion from 1976 to 1989. The most impressive feature of this expansion is certainly the twofold increase in the portion of the labor force with at least one completed year of high school: whereas in 1976 only 16 percent of the population had completed at least one year of high school, by 1989 this number increased to 30 percent. The proportion of those with a college education also increased, though not as much (from 7.4 percent in 1976 to 11.8 percent in 1989). The segment of the population with no schooling decreased only slightly from 14 percent to 10 percent.[8]

As a whole, these figures reveal an undeniable improvement in the educational attainment of the Brazilian urban labor force over this 14-year period. Whether or not this progress may be considered fast enough is, however, still very questionable. Psacharopoulos (1987) considers the 1970s

---

[8] A continuing process of migration from rural to urban areas may explain part of this weak performance.

Figure 6.3. Distribution of the Population by Educational Groups, 1976–89

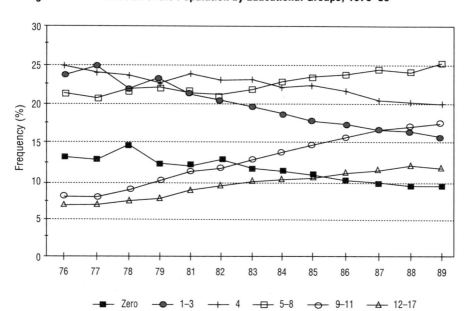

Table 6.1. Distribution of the Population by Educational Group: Temporal Evolution, 1976–89
(Percent)

Year	Educational group					
	0	1–3	4	5–8	9–11	12 – 17
1976	13.6	24.0	25.0	21.5	8.5	7.4
1977	13.3	25.0	24.5	21.1	8.5	7.6
1978	14.8	22.1	23.9	22.0	9.3	7.9
1979	12.9	23.3	22.9	22.3	10.4	8.2
1981	12.4	21.4	23.9	21.5	11.6	9.2
1982	13.1	20.8	23.1	21.2	12.1	9.7
1983	11.8	19.7	23.1	22.0	13.1	10.3
1984	11.5	18.9	22.3	22.8	13.9	10.6
1985	10.8	17.9	22.3	23.6	14.8	10.6
1986	10.3	17.4	21.7	24.0	15.4	11.2
1987	10.1	16.7	20.5	24.6	16.7	11.4
1988	9.8	16.5	20.3	24.2	17.1	12.1
1989	9.8	15.5	20.0	25.2	17.7	11.8

Figure 6.4. Cumulative Distribution of Completed Years of Schooling, 1976 and 1989

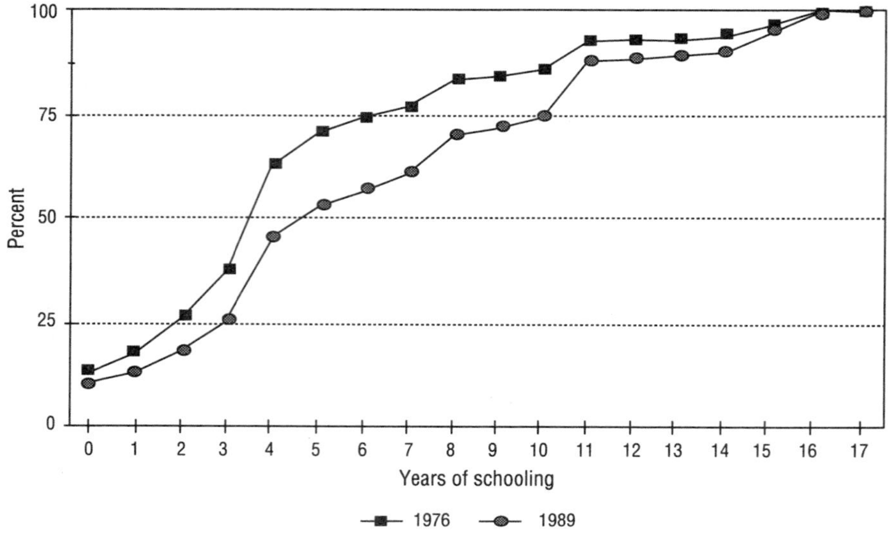

Table 6.2. Cumulative Distribution of Completed Years of Schooling, 1976 and 1989

Years of schooling	1976		1989	
	Distribution	Cumulative	Distribution	Cumulative
0	13.6	13.6	9.8	9.8
1	4.2	17.8	3.2	13.0
2	8.3	26.1	5.2	18.2
3	11.5	37.6	7.1	25.3
4	25.0	62.6	20.1	45.3
5	8.3	70.9	7.6	53.0
6	3.3	74.2	3.6	56.5
7	2.6	76.8	3.9	60.5
8	7.3	84.1	10.1	70.5
9	0.7	84.8	1.5	72.1
10	1.3	86.1	2.4	74.5
11	6.5	92.6	13.7	88.2
12	0.3	92.9	0.6	88.9
13	0.3	93.2	0.8	89.7
14	0.7	93.9	1.0	90.7
15	2.8	96.7	5.7	96.4
16	2.6	99.3	2.8	99.1
17	0.7	100.0	0.9	100.0

Figure 6.5. Mean and Standard Deviation of Years of Schooling, 1976–89

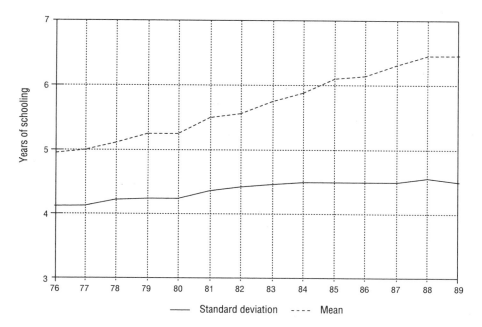

"a decade of rapid educational expansion in Brazil." Lam and Levison (1991b) claim that in the last 40 years "dramatic improvements in the distribution of schooling" have occurred in Brazil. On the other hand, Behrman (1987) estimates, based on an international cross-section, that the educational expansion in Brazil between 1960 and 1980 was far below what would be indicated by international standards.

Wage Gains from Education

Methodology

We use three models to estimate wage gains from education. These models differ with respect to the control variables they use. The first model, which uses no control variables, simply estimates the average log wage for each educational level and contrasts these averages.

The second model, which includes controls for the age of the worker, regresses log wage on age and age-squared for each education level. In other words, it allows for the regression coefficients to vary freely with the level of education of the worker. This model generates wage gains from education that vary with age. However, we only report the average gains, where the average is taken across age groups using the age distribution of our population.

The third model includes controls for age and region of residence. It regresses log wage on age and age-squared for each education level and region. Hence, this model allows the coefficients to vary freely with the level of education and region of residence of the worker. The wage gains from education estimated using this model vary with age and region of residence. As in the case of the second model, we report only the average gains, with the average being taken over age groups and regions.

Temporal Evolution: Model 1

Based on the model with no controls, Table 6.3 and Figure 6.6 report estimates of the temporal evolution of the wage gains associated with the completion of the major steps of the education ladder in Brazil, as noted earlier.[9] [10]

Inspection of the results of Model 1 reveals four important features:

(1) With the exception of lower to upper primary, wage gains associated with additional years of schooling are very large—ranging from 0.12 to more than 0.2—and are a distinguishing characteristic of Brazilian labor markets.[11] In most countries, such wage gains are relatively small, and are close to 0.10 (Psacharopoulos, 1985).

(2) The relationship between log wage and education begins concave and then becomes strongly convex after eight years of schooling. In fact, as Table 6.3 shows, the wage gains from education decrease up to the upper primary level and then sharply increase beyond that point.

(3) The wage gains at different levels of education display distinct tendencies over this period of time. At the secondary and tertiary levels, wage gains tend to increase over time, whereas at the lower levels the wage gains either remain stable (lower-primary) or even decrease (upper-primary) over the period. Consider, for example, the years 1977 and 1989: the wage

---

[9] Notice that around 60 percent of the population is included in these groups (see Table 6.2).

[10] The estimates in Table 6.3, Figure 6.6 and all other tables in this section are reported on a per schooling year basis—i.e., the wage differentials between two education levels are divided by the number of years of schooling between them. For example, the reported wage gain from zero to four years of schooling is equal to the wage differential between these two categories divided by four.

[11] See Langoni (1973), Castello Branco (1979), Velloso (1975), Senna (1976), Medeiros (1982), Almeida dos Reis and Barros (1991), Lam and Levison (1991a,b), Ramos (1990), Strauss and Thomas (this volume), Dabos and Psacharopoulos (1991), Dougherty and Jiménez (1991), and Tannen (1991).

Table 6.3. Wage Gains from Education (No Control), 1976–89

Year	Years of schooling				
	0 to 4	4 to 8	8 to 11	11 to 15	11 to 16
76	0.178	0.127	0.116	0.180	0.221
77	0.169	0.122	0.131	0.162	0.196
78	0.165	0.121	0.133	0.165	0.195
79	0.167	0.104	0.150	0.186	0.193
81	0.158	0.091	0.149	0.180	0.190
82	0.158	0.101	0.136	0.183	0.193
83	0.157	0.101	0.142	0.175	0.188
84	0.155	0.098	0.138	0.188	0.196
85	0.160	0.098	0.142	0.193	0.200
86	0.156	0.072	0.134	0.198	0.219
87	0.159	0.080	0.145	0.195	0.201
88	0.188	0.069	0.154	0.200	0.213
89	0.168	0.088	0.137	0.202	0.214
81–85	0.158	0.098	0.142	0.184	0.194

Figure 6.6. Wage Gains from Education (No Control), 1976–89

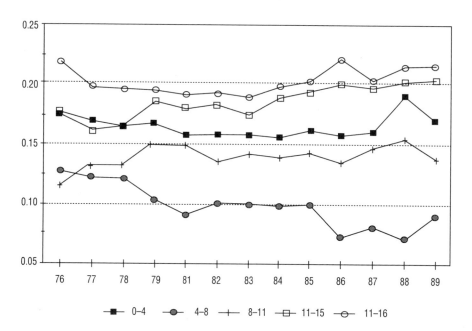

gain associated with the completion of a four-year college increased from 0.16 to 0.20 and the gain related to the completion of high school rose from 0.13 to 0.14.[12] At the same time, the wage gain associated with the completion of the upper-primary level decreased from 0.12 to 0.08. These numbers indicate a large increase in the convexity of the relationship between log wage and education over time. Since the growth pattern of the wage gains varies by education level, whether the average gain (the average being taken across education levels) actually increased or decreased over this period will greatly depend on how the gains at different education levels are weighted.

(4) There is a clear difference in the evolution of the wage gains in the different sub-periods. Wage gains at all levels of schooling in the period between 1981 and 1985 are remarkably stable, whereas in the years between 1977 and 1981 and those after 1986 they tend to widen—i.e., during these periods the relationship between log wage and education becomes increasingly convex.

Effect of Controls for Age and Region: Models 2 and 3

The results obtained using age as a control variable (Model 2) are presented in Table 6.4 and Figure 6.7. The results produced by Model 3, which controls for age and region of residence, are presented in Table 6.5 and Figure 6.8. The major effect of the introduction of controls is a slight increase in the wage gains at the primary and secondary levels and a sharp decrease in the gains at the tertiary level. Overall, the log wage-education relationship becomes flatter and much less convex, as can be seen from the average wage gains for the period from 1981 to 1985, displayed at the bottom of Tables 6.3 through 6.5. Birdsall and Behrman (1984) obtain results that are qualitatively similar but quantitatively much stronger. They use the 1970 Brazilian census to show that controls for region of origin and region of residence can reduce their estimate for the wage gain from education by almost 0.08.

Moreover, the introduction of age and region of residence as control variables serve to diminish the temporal variation. For example, if we compare the amplitude of the observed oscillations in the gains to lower primary, we see that it declines from 0.033 in Model 1 to 0.028 in Model 2 and to 0.018 in Model 3 (with the exception of 1976). Similar behavior is

---

[12] Notice that 1977 and 1978 are quite similar to, and that 1976 is very different from, all the other years in the 1970s. This is why we choose 1977, rather than 1976, as a reference for comparison.

Table 6.4. Wage Gains from Education (Control: Age), 1976–89

Year	Years of schooling				
	0 to 4	4 to 8	8 to 11	11 to 15	11 to 16
76	0.180	0.130	0.128	0.166	0.212
77	0.171	0.128	0.134	0.155	0.191
78	0.169	0.127	0.138	0.157	0.186
79	0.170	0.113	0.157	0.172	0.180
81	0.161	0.101	0.158	0.161	0.173
82	0.162	0.110	0.145	0.164	0.176
83	0.161	0.111	0.152	0.158	0.168
84	0.160	0.111	0.143	0.169	0.179
85	0.161	0.111	0.149	0.171	0.178
86	0.157	0.091	0.138	0.171	0.194
87	0.157	0.095	0.154	0.172	0.181
88	0.185	0.087	0.159	0.178	0.193
89	0.166	0.108	0.143	0.178	0.194
81–85	0.161	0.109	0.149	0.165	0.175

Figure 6.7. Wage Gains from Education (Control: Age), 1976–89

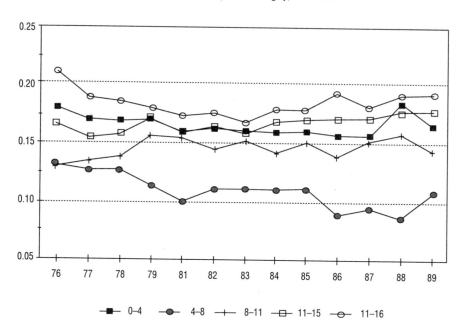

Table 6.5. Wage Gains from Education (Controls: Age and Region), 1976–89

Year	Years of schooling				
	0 to 4	4 to 8	8 to 11	11 to 15	11 to 16
76	0.133	0.143	0.138	0.165	0.153
77	0.128	0.141	0.137	0.157	0.188
78	0.131	0.137	0.144	0.150	0.184
79	0.130	0.128	0.158	0.160	0.173
81	0.127	0.111	0.159	0.158	0.177
82	0.127	0.120	0.149	0.160	0.170
83	0.128	0.123	0.153	0.155	0.168
84	0.129	0.120	0.150	0.163	0.175
85	0.127	0.121	0.155	0.166	0.173
86	0.122	0.104	0.140	0.164	0.191
87	0.114	0.109	0.159	0.168	0.177
88	0.132	0.097	0.170	0.169	0.185
89	0.115	0.113	0.157	0.170	0.184
81–85	0.127	0.119	0.151	0.160	0.173

Figure 6.8. Wage Gains from Education (Controls: Age and Region), 1976–89

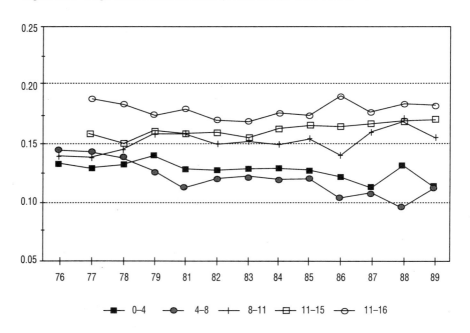

observed at the other extreme. For instance, the amplitude of the oscillations in the gains to five-years college declines from 0.031 in Model 1 to 0.026 in Model 2 and to 0.023 in Model 3.

Average Wage Gains from Education

To focus further on the temporal evolution of the wage gains from education, we compute, for each year, both the weighted and unweighted average of the first four wage gains. Table 6.5 reports the results. For the weighted average, the weights are the proportion of the overall population with no education (12 percent), with four years of schooling (22 percent), with eight years of schooling (9 percent), and with 11 years of schooling (10 percent). These averages are reported in Table 6.6 and Figure 6.9. A more commonly used alternative to this procedure is to estimate the average gain using linear regression. The average gains estimated using this procedure are reported in the last column of Table 6.6. These three results differ only to the extent that they use different weights. The weights in the regression procedure are larger for educational levels close to the mean and smaller at the extremes. The three weighting schemes are presented in Figure 6.10.

The temporal evolutions of these three averages are slightly different. The unweighted average is very stable over time. The weighted average and the one obtained by linear regression reveal some decline over time. The decline is slightly stronger when we use the weighted average than when we use the results from linear regression.

Regional Variations

Model 3 permits us not only to estimate the relationship between log wage and education controlling for region, but also to investigate how this relationship varies across regions.

Table 6.7 and Figures 6.11 to 6.14 present the average of the wage gains from education over time for six regions: the State of Rio de Janeiro (RJ), the State of São Paulo (SP), the South (SO), the East (E), the Northeast (NE), and the Frontier (FR).[13] These averages reveal some important regional disparities.

---

[13] The South is formed by the States of Paraná, Santa Catarina, and Rio Grande do Sul. The East: Espírito Santo, Minas Gerais, and the Federal District. The Northeast: Piauí, Maranhão, Ceará, Rio Grande do Norte, Paraíba, Pernambuco, Alagoas, Sergipe and Bahia. The Frontier: Goiás, Tocantins, Mato Grosso do Sul, Mato Grosso, Rondônia, Acre, Amazonas, Roraima, Pará, and Amapá.

Table 6.6. Average Wage Gains from Education, 1976–89

Year	Unwgtd.	Wgtd.	Regr.
76	—	—	0.147
77	0.141	0.140	0.143
78	0.140	0.139	0.142
79	0.144	0.140	0.144
81	0.139	0.132	0.135
82	0.139	0.134	0.138
83	0.139	0.135	0.138
84	0.140	0.135	0.139
85	0.142	0.137	0.140
86	0.133	0.126	0.132
87	0.138	0.130	0.136
88	0.142	0.131	0.138
89	0.139	0.132	0.138

Figure 6.9. Average Wage Gains from Education, 1976–89

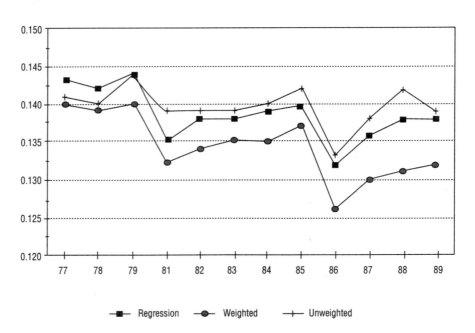

Table 6.7. Wage Gains from Education

Region	Years of schooling				
	0 to 4	4 to 8	8 to 11	11 to 15	11 to 16
RJ	0.099	0.121	0.161	0.185	0.201
SP	0.134	0.114	0.120	0.143	0.160
SO	0.133	0.132	0.167	0.136	0.158
E	0.147	0.136	0.163	0.150	0.159
NE	0.124	0.111	0.188	0.203	0.200
FR	0.118	0.104	0.152	0.155	0.162

The Northeast shows the largest gains from education at the secondary and tertiary levels, but has among the smallest gains at the primary level. A similar but smoother behavior is found for Rio de Janeiro. The opposite takes place for the East, the South and São Paulo: these regions have the smallest gains at the secondary and tertiary level, but are the ones with the largest gains at the primary level. As a consequence, the common observation that the relationship between log wage and education is steeper in the Northeast than elsewhere in Brazil must be properly qualified, since this fact is only correct at the secondary and tertiary levels.

Summary

This study investigated the temporal evolution of the wage-education relationship among Brazilian prime-age males across the period from 1976 to 1989. For each year, three wage-education relationships were estimated using flexible functional forms and an increasing number of control variables. Model 1 uses no controls; Model 2 controls for the age of the worker; and Model 3 controls for age and region of residence.

The estimated relationships reveal that in Brazil the log wage-education profile is much steeper than in other countries and convex at the secondary and tertiary levels. As a consequence, the wage gains from college are much larger than those from primary education.

Whether the wage gains from education increase or decrease over time depends on which educational level is considered. The gains from primary education clearly decrease over time, while the gains from college education increase. As a result, over the decade, there is a clear increase in convexity, mainly from 1986 to 1989.

Figure 6.10. Weights Used to Compute the Average Wage Gains From Education

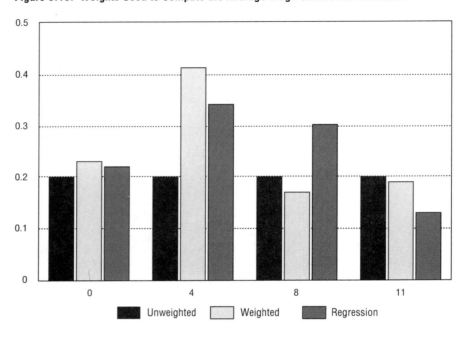

Figure 6.11. Wage Gains from Education (0 to 4 Years of Schooling)

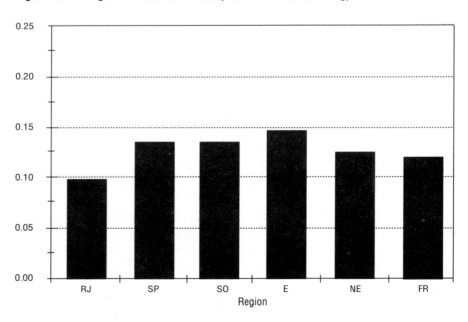

Figure 6.12. Wage Gains from Education (4 to 8 Years of Schooling)

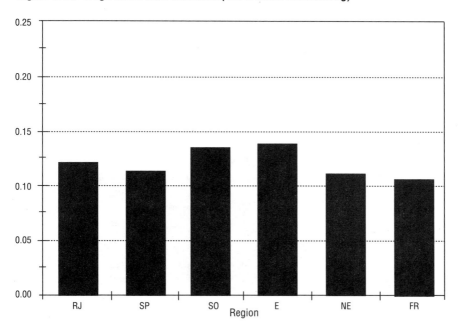

Figure 6.13. Wage Gains from Education (8 to 11 Years of Schooling)

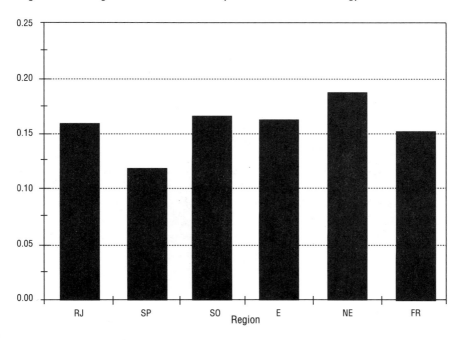

Figure 6.14. Wage Gains from Education (11 to 15 Years of Schooling)

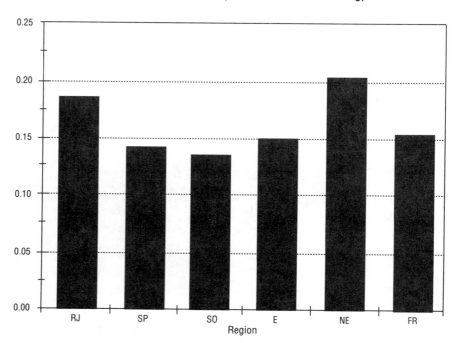

The inclusion of controls by age and region of residence tends to lower the gains from education, their variation over time, and the degree of convexity of the log wage-education relationship.

The regional analysis indicates that the Northeast region has the largest gains from education at the secondary and tertiary levels but one of the smallest at the lower levels. The opposite is true for São Paulo, implying a much more convex log wage-education relationship for the Northeast. Hence, the assertion that gains from education are larger in the Northeast than in more developed areas of Brazil (Lam and Levison, 1991b) is valid only for secondary and tertiary education. It is worth noting, however, that some studies (Psacharopoulos, 1987) find evidence that the wage-education relationship does not vary across regions, while others (Birdsall and Behrman, 1984) find larger wage gains from education in the Southeast than in the Northeast.

REFERENCES

Almeida dos Reis, J. Guilherme, and Ricardo Barros. 1991. Wage Inequality and the Distribution of Education: A Study of the Evolution of Regional Differences in Inequality in Metropolitan Brazil. *Journal of Development Economics* 36: 117–43.

Behrman, Jere. 1987. Schooling in Developing Countries: Which Countries are the Under- and Overachievers and What is the Schooling Impact? *Economics of Education Review* 6(2): 111–28.

Birdsall, Nancy, and Jere Behrman. 1984. Does Geographical Aggregation Cause Overestimates of the Returns to Schooling? *Oxford Bulletin of Economics and Statistics* 46: 55–72.

Castello Branco, R. C. 1979. *Crescimento Acelerado e o Mercado de Trabalho: A Experiência Brasileira.* Série Teses EPGE No. 1, editora da Fundação Getúlio Vargas.

Dabos, Marcelo, and George Psacharopoulos. 1991. An Analysis of the Sources of Earnings Variation Among Brazilian Males. *Economics of Education Review* 10(4): 359–77.

Dougherty, Christopher R. S., and Emmanuel Jiménez. 1991. The Specification of Earnings Functions: Tests and Implications. *Economics of Education Review* 10(2): 85–98.

IBGE. 1981. *Metodologia da Pesquisa Nacional por Amostra de Domicílios na Década de 70.* Série Relatórios Metodológicos, vol. 1.

Lam, David, and Deborah Levison. 1991a. Age, Experience, and Schooling: Decomposing Earnings Inequality in the U.S. and Brazil.

————. 1991b. Declining Inequality in Brazil and its Effects on Inequality in Earnings. *Journal of Development Economics* 37: 199–226.

Langoni, C. G. 1973. *Distribuição de Renda e Desenvolvimento Econômico do Brasil.* Rio de Janeiro: Ed. Expressão e Cultura.

Medeiros, J. A. S. 1982. Alcance e Limitações da Teoria do Capital Humano: Diferenças de Ganhos no Brasil em 1973. IPE/USP, *Ensaios Econômicos* 17. São Paulo.

Psacharopoulos, George. 1987. Earnings and Education in Brazil: Evidence from the 1980 Census. Mimeo.

————. 1985. Returns to Education: A Further International Updated Review and Implications. *Journal of Human Resources* 20(4): 583–604.

Ramos, Lauro. 1990. The Distribution of Earnings in Brazil: 1976–1986. Ph. D. dissertation, University of California - Berkeley.

Senna, J. J. 1976. Escolaridade, Experiência no Trabalho e Salários no Brasil. *Revista Brasileira de Economia* 30(2) (April/June).

Tannen, Michael B. 1991. New Estimates of the Returns to Schooling in Brazil. *Economics of Education Review* 10(2): 123–35.

Velloso, J. R. 1975. Human Capital and Market Segmentation: An Analysis of the Distribution of Earnings in Brazil 1970. Ph.D. dissertation, Stanford University.

Appendix Table 6.1. Screening Sample, 1976–89

Screening Sample	Reduction
Males	51.6
Urban Areas	25.4
Known Age	0.0
Age > 25	43.7
Age < 50	26.4
Occupied	7.6
Known Income	0.4
Positive Income	0.2
Known Hours Worked	0.2
Hours Worked > 20	0.5
Known Education	0.1
Not in School	4.2

Note: Includes eight cases where income equals 1.

Appendix Table 6.2. Sample Size by Year, 1976–89

Year	Sample Size
1976	35,332
1977	45,286
1978	49,877
1979	41,191
1981	49,067
1982	52,748
1983	52,996
1984	54,249
1985	56,978
1986	31,154
1987	32,720
1988	32,238
1989	33,459
Total	543,207

Appendix Table 6.3. Construction of the Variable "Years of Schooling"

Years of Schooling	Grade	Degree	Fraction (%)
None	—	None	11.7 (All)
One	—	Adult ed.	0.1 (79,81)
	First	Elementary	2.5 (79–89)
	First	1st grade	1.0 (All)
Two	Second	Elementary	4.6 (79–89)
	Second	1st grade	2.0 (All)
Three	Third	Elementary	6.3 (79–89)
	Third	1st grade	2.8 (All)
Four	Fourth	Elementary	14.4 (79–89)
	Fourth	1st grade	5.9 (All)
Five	First	Half 1st cycle	1.7 (All)
	Fifth	Elementary	4.5 (79–89)
	Fifth	1st grade	2.7 (All)
Six	Second	Half 1st cycle	2.2 (All)
	Sixth	1st grade	1.0 (All)
Seven	Third	Half 1st cycle	2.0 (All)
	Seventh	1st grade	1.2 (All)
Eight	Fourth	Half 1st cycle	6.1 (All)
	Eighth	1st grade	2.8 (All)
Nine	First	Half 2nd cycle	0.5 (All)
	First	2nd grade	0.7 (All)
Ten	Second	Half 2nd cycle	0.9 (All)
	Second	2nd grade	1.0 (All)
Eleven	Third	Half 2nd cycle	5.1 (All)
	Third	2nd grade	5.8 (All)
	Fourth	Half 2nd cycle	0.0 (89)
	Fourth	2nd grade	0.1 (All)
Twelve	First	Superior	0.5 (All)
Thirteen	Second	Superior	0.6 (All)
Fourteen	Third	Superior	0.9 (All)
Fifteen	Fourth	Superior	4.6 (All)
Sixteen	Fifth	Superior	2.9 (All)
Seventeen	Sixth	Superior	0.8 (All)
	—	Doc./Masters	0.1 (79–89)

7

Do Returns to Schooling Vary Across Industries?

Donald Robbins and Mari Minowa

It is widely held that the distribution of income in Brazil deteriorated during the 1960s and early 1970s and has not recuperated except for cyclical variations.[1] Evidence from many countries shows that education is an important explanatory factor of income distribution,[2] especially in less developed countries (LDCs), where the rate of return to schooling is higher and the distribution of schooling less equal.[3] The close relationship between schooling and income distribution has also been confirmed for Brazil.[4] The rate of return to schooling varies over time and place. In cross-country comparisons, Brazil has one of the highest rates of return to schooling, even among LDCs. Within Brazil, study of the deterioration of income distribution in the 1960s and 1970s has been associated with an increase in the rate of return to schooling over time. One recent study showed that there are stable differences in the rate of return to schooling across regions in Brazil.[5] However, less attention has been devoted to variation in the rate of return to schooling across industries within regions.

Explanations of the deterioration in Brazilian income distribution in the 1960s and 1970s focused largely on demand-side factors affecting the rate of return to schooling. This focus emerged because, rather than explaining the growing inequality, the predominant supply-side change —rapid growth in the college educated labor force—should have lowered the rate of return to schooling and thereby equalized income distribution.[6]

---

[1] See Bacha and Taylor (1980) and Bonelli and Sedlacek (1989).
[2] See Fields (1980).
[3] See Psacharopoulos (1985).
[4] See Fishlow (1972); Langoni (1973a,b); Velloso (1975); Senna (1976); Castello Branco (1979); Medeiros (1982); Ferreira da Silva (1987); Lam and Levison (1989); and Almeida dos Reis and Barros (1991).
[5] See Almeida dos Reis and Barros (1991).
[6] Morley (1981) argued, however, that the importance of more college graduates may have been exaggerated. He argued that the appropriate measure of the commodity supplied is not schooling but skill, consisting of schooling *and* experience, so that while the supply of college graduates had increased rapidly, the supply of skill lagged behind.

The principal demand-side theories put forth to explain the deterioration are the "Kuznets effects," "skills-differentials," "wage-squeeze," and "wage-spread" hypotheses (Bacha and Taylor, 1980). Kuznets effects hypothesizes that the deterioration in income distribution derived from the growth of the high-wage urban industrial sector. Skills-differentials (Langoni 1973a,b) hypothesizes that growth was skill-intensive; thus, with a low elasticity of substitution between labor types, this would raise the rate of return to schooling. Wage-squeeze hypothesizes that government policy, in particular minimum wages and the time structure for collective bargaining, worsened the income distribution. Wage-spread hypothesizes that some firms passed on higher profits to highly-schooled workers, while unskilled workers with little schooling in those firms received wages that were anchored to the wage floor. This is because the more highly-schooled workers belong to a stable core of laborers with whom firms may share profits. As a result, high profits and a falling wage floor widened the wage gap across workers of different schooling levels, raising the intra-firm rate of return to schooling and the overall rate of return to schooling.

Wage-Spread, Internal Labor Markets and Efficiency-Wage

The wage-spread hypothesis is closely related to the idea of the internal labor market (ILM) (Doeringer and Piore, 1971), a concept that gained popularity in the early 1970s and was widely discussed in relation to Brazil in the 1970s and early 1980s (Macedo, 1974; Morley, 1981).[7] The wage-spread hypothesis and the related ILM idea correspond closely to efficiency-wage models of the labor market; these are models where firms find it profit-maximizing to pay workers in excess of their opportunity costs (Yellen, 1984; Stigliz, 1986). Here we use efficiency-wage to also include insider-outsider and sociological models (Lindbeck and Snower, 1986).

---

[7] The ILM is an amalgam of ideas, ranging from neoclassical theory to sociological and institutional perspectives on organization and the labor market. From the neoclassical perspective, the essence of the ILM notion is that the firm finds it profit-maximizing to devise promotion and incentive schemes that are insulated from direct competition from the outside market. ILMs are largely seen as institutional responses by firms to problems of motivating workers, including eliciting worker effort when monitoring is costly, persuading experienced workers to train new hires and newly promoted workers, hindering workers with firm specific human capital from extracting rents, and preventing loss of specific human capital through worker turnover. This response features internal job ladders and a strong emphasis on seniority-based promotions that legitimize hierarchical control (Osterman, 1984). Piore (1973) argues that ILMs require large product markets, over which firms have significant control, to support specialization of occupations within the firm and to maintain the stable internal structure.

These models focus on demand-side factors affecting the structure of wages and employment. They suggest that firm characteristics are important determinants of wage structure, and that wage structure can vary across firms with different technological and product market characteristics. Knight and Sabot (1983) discuss the role of firm characteristics in the LDC context. While the wage-spread and related ILM models predict that earnings functions vary across firms, and are affected by firm characteristics, they were formulated before the analytical validity of efficiency-wage models was established in the mid-1980s. Therefore, ILM and wage-spread models do not consistently predict that workers receive rents over the spell of employment; instead, they tend to predict that in some firms workers' spot wages may deviate from the competitive wage; however, competition forces the average discounted wage over the employment spell to equalize across firms.

The efficiency-wage models that followed the internal labor market idea and the wage-spread argument go further than their predecessors in predicting that average discounted wage levels vary over industries for identical workers—i.e., that in equilibrium, workers in some industries receive long-run rents. Efficiency wages can lead to equilibrium involuntary unemployment, wage rigidity for efficiency-wage firms, and wage levels that differ across firms for identical workers. Firms may pay in excess of workers' opportunity costs for several reasons, some of which are central to the ILM idea. The goals of wage premia may be to elicit effort that is costly to monitor, minimize turnover costs, raise the quality of the applicant pool, or lower the likelihood of unionization—respectively, the "shirking," "turnover," "adverse-selection" and "union-threat" models of efficiency wages. Firms may also be willing to pay a wage premium to retain workers with firm-specific productivity when contracts cannot arbitrage away rents for specific human capital (Klein et al., 1978; Klein, 1984; Robbins, 1988) or sociological reasons (Yellen, 1984). Because the arguments leading to efficiency wages are largely related to technology and industry structure, they predict that in equilibrium identical workers earn more in some industries than in others. For example, in the shirking model of efficiency wages, firms pay wage premia because of costly monitoring, and monitoring costs are often related to the technology employed.

Testing of efficiency-wage theories has consisted largely of efforts to determine whether there are, across industries, wage premia that are not due to omitted job or worker quality or labor market disequilibrium, but are instead rents to the workers. There is substantial literature on interindustry and interfirm wage differentials supporting efficiency-wage models (Katz, 1986). Robbins (1989b) found large, statistically significant interindustry wage differentials within the manufacturing sector in São Paulo; these differentials were strongly correlated with corresponding differentials for the United States. These studies, however, have not carefully examined the possibility that these wage differentials may be systematically related to the rate of return to schooling.

While explanations of the deterioration in Brazilian income distribution in the 1960s and 1970s largely focused on demand-side factors affecting the rate of return to schooling, much of the work in this volume argues that the rate of return to schooling is high in Brazil because of a shortfall in the supply of education. Our approach, which examines demand-side factors that work to increase the average rate of return to schooling, constitutes an alternative, complementary perspective on the income distribution issue—one that can be seen as an extension of some of the earlier demand-side arguments. By our argument, efficiency-wage structures may raise the average rate of return to schooling in industry, thereby raising the average rate of return to schooling in the formal sector of the economy. Given the educational distribution, this higher rate of return to schooling would increase income inequality. This is important because if demand-side factors contribute significantly to income inequality, raising the supply of educated workers may only be partially successful at equalizing income distribution.

In exploring the relationship between schooling and income distribution in Brazil we focus on demand-side explanations of variation in returns to schooling. As in the wage-spread hypothesis, we explore the evidence of interfirm differences in the rate of return to schooling. Using data on workers from the 1977 *Relação Anual de Informações Sociais* (RAIS), a firm-reported census of workers in formal sector firms, combined with unique government survey data (CADEC) on firm characteristics, we empirically examine the possibility that the rate of return to schooling varies systematically across industries for private manufacturing firms in São Paulo. The first section looks at the relationship between the rate of return to schooling and efficiency-wage premia. It argues that traditional specifications of efficiency-wage models ignored the possibility of this relationship, and that the rate of return to schooling positively covaries with interindustry wage differentials. The data and results are then presented in two parts. The first presents tests of heterogeneity of the earnings functions across industries. The structure of the earnings functions are examined by looking at the correlations among estimated rates of return to schooling and other variables with estimated wage differentials. We then present simulations of the variance of log wages suggesting that the predominance of efficiency-wage firms can significantly raise earning inequality, and that assuming earnings functions are identical across industries leads to underestimates of the variance of log wages. In the second part, we examine the relationship between the estimated rate of return to schooling and industry characteristics.

Efficiency-Wage Models and Variation in the Rate of Return to Schooling Across Firms

Before turning to efficiency-wage models, it is useful to look at a simple derivation of the earnings function, and then briefly discuss modifications of this formulation that lead to earnings functions that vary across firms (Becker, 1964; Mincer, 1974; and Willis, 1986). Assuming that workers possess different quantities of a homogeneous human capital,[8] HC, in equilibrium, the wage for the i-th worker, W_i, will be proportional to HC_i:

(1) $W_i = A \cdot HC_i,$

where A is the rental rate of human capital. Letting human capital be an exponential function of a vector of inputs, X, such as schooling and experience, and adding a stochastic term, e_i, we may write the human capital production function as:

(2) $HC_i = \exp(X_i'\beta + e_i).$

Substituting (2) in (1) and taking the logarithm and defining $\alpha \equiv \ell n(A)$, we get the standard semi-log earnings function:

(3) $\ell n(W_i) = \alpha + X_i'\beta + e_i.$

In this formulation, the parameters of the equation, α and β, are fixed across firms in one time and place.

Some theories, however, lead to earnings functions whose parameters vary across firms. Models where firms need to encourage the accumulation of specific human capital, or elicit hard-to-monitor worker effort, may result in rising wage-tenure profiles. In competitive labor market models with seniority profiles, the intercept will drop to offset the higher returns to tenure. Writing the vector X above as $X \equiv (S,T,Z)$, where S is years of schooling, T is tenure and Z is a vector of other inputs to human capital production, this leads to the following specification:

(4) $\ell n W_i = \alpha_0 + \alpha_f + \beta_s \cdot S_i + \beta_{T,f} \cdot T_i + Z_i'\delta + e_i.$

---

[8] See Willis (1986) for a discussion of homogeneous versus heterogeneous human capital.

Because it is assumed that competition equalizes (the average present discounted value of) wages across firms, in equation (4) when $\beta_{T,f}$ is higher in a firm, the corresponding intercept, α_f, will drop to compensate. Thus, (4) will be subject to a constraint of the form $\alpha_f = g(-\beta_{T,f} \cdot T^*_i)$, where T^* is the value of tenure for the completed job spell, and $g()$ is some monotonic function. In this formulation, the earnings function varies over firms, but the rate of return to schooling, β_s, is constant across firms.[9][10]

Efficiency-wage models also lead to earnings functions that vary across firms. However, in contrast to competitive models, in efficiency-wage models average wages over the employment spell for identical workers will differ across firms. Empirical specifications of efficiency-wage models typically examined industry wage differentials, moving from firms to industries on the assumption that firms are more alike within than across industries (hereafter we will refer to industries dominated by efficiency-wage firms as "efficiency wage industries"). These interindustry wage differentials specifications assume that all parameters are constant over industries, as in equation (3), save for the intercept that varies across industries, $\alpha = \alpha_{IND}$:

(5) $\ell n W_i = \alpha_{IND} + X_i'\beta + e_i.$

This formulation implies a constant rate of return to schooling, and implies that all workers in an efficiency-wage industry, regardless of their level of human capital, earn a constant percentage mark-up over the wage they earn in a competitive firm. However, there is no a priori reason why efficiency-wage industries should treat workers with different levels of human capital in this symmetric manner, hereafter called "symmetric wage premia."

---

[9] Akerlof and Katz (1986) argue that Lazear (1981) is wrong: that a positively sloped wage-tenure profile will not completely solve the effort elicitation problem when monitoring is costly, and substitute for wage premia. The truth lies between the two studies. While, as Akerlof and Katz argue, the worker has not accumulated a bond upon hire, such profiles could reduce the wage premia paid, because from the moment of hire the worker begins to accumulate an implicit bond. This will reduce, but not eliminate, the amount of the wage premium the firms needs to pay to prevent shirking. Thus, it is possible that these tradeoffs coexist with efficiency-wage outcomes, though we would expect that as tenure profiles grow steeper and trade off with compensating decreases in the earnings function's intercept, we would expect wage differentials to decrease.

[10] While our discussion has focused on the possibility that the rate of return to schooling varies over firms, the rate of return to other variables reflecting general human capital may also vary across firms. This is because wage premia paid to a particular group within a firm would be set in some proportion to these workers' opportunity costs. Opportunity costs will be proportional to variables reflecting general human capital, and not proportional to specific human capital variables. Thus, the rate of return to general human capital variables could vary across firms.

In industries paying efficiency-wage premia, it is possible that they only offer wage premia to a subset of workers within the industry, or pay proportionately higher wage premia to this group. Hereafter, we will refer to this as "asymmetric," versus "symmetric" wage premia. We would expect an asymmetric distribution of wage premia within an industry if the factors leading to efficiency-wage premia only apply to some types of workers in the industry, or apply with different intensity across groups of workers in the industry. In particular, if in a given industry wage premia are systematically related to the workers' schooling levels, then wage premia would be asymmetric in this industry and the rate of return to schooling could deviate from the rate of return to schooling in competitive industries, as discussed more carefully below.

The foregoing discussion makes three points clear: first, that wage structure may differ across firms within competitive models; second, that by definition wage structure differs at least in the intercept between competitive and efficiency-wage models; and, third, that industries dominated by efficiency-wage firms may have asymmetric wage premia, and rates of return to schooling that differ from other industries. For these reasons, intercepts and slopes may vary across industries. To reflect the possibility of these sorts of heterogeneity of earnings functions, we adopt a specification allowing all coefficients of the earnings function to vary across industries:

(6) $\ell n W_i = \alpha_f + X_i' \beta_f + e_i.$

Structure in the Variation of the Rate of Return to Schooling Over Industries

Rates of return to schooling that vary across industries may vary systematically with interindustry wage differentials. In particular, if high-wage industries pay proportionately higher wage premia to more educated workers, then the industry-level rates of return to schooling will be positively correlated with interindustry wage differentials.[11] There are four

---

[11] If the minimum wage were to raise the wages of low productivity workers above their ex-ante competitive wage to the minimum wage, instead of disemploying them, this would flatten the wage-schooling profile and could bias the estimated correlation between the rate of return to schooling and the interindustry wage differential. However, following standard theory, we assume that a binding minimum wage truncates the distribution of employed workers, and does not lead to this bias. Furthermore, another study of this data (Robbins, 1992) finds that for the majority of workers and firms the minimum wage was non-binding for this sample.

mutually compatible reasons why this correlation may be positive. First, the "shirking" model of efficiency wages predicts that where monitoring worker effort is costly, firms may find it profitable to pay workers a wage premia, and fire workers found shirking. However, it is likely that monitoring costs rise with workers' education. Tasks performed by production workers in the modern factory are highly routinized and quantifiable; in contrast, as the education of workers rises work tends to become more diverse and outputs less tangible, harder to quantify, and hence more costly to monitor. This is reflected in management literature and practice where the measurement of blue-collar productivity has been perfected to a sophisticated science, while the measurement of white-collar productivity is, at best, highly subjective. This implies that as workers' education rises it becomes more difficult and costly to monitor workers' efforts. Consequently, more educated workers would receive wage premia to deter shirking, while less educated workers would receive smaller wage premia, or none at all. The second reason why wage premia may be asymmetric, and higher for more educated workers, is that there may be increasing returns to scale in monitoring technology. As the size of the occupational group decreases, per worker monitoring costs rise. Since the size of occupational groups tends to decrease as education rises, monitoring costs would rise with schooling level, and lead to higher wage premia for the more educated workers. The third reason for asymmetric wage premia is that wage premia may be higher for workers with supervisorial responsibilities that amplify the productivity of management personnel. Since supervisorial personnel are typically more educated, this would lead to asymmetric wage premia favoring educated workers. The fourth reason concerns incentives and specific human capital. Workers' specific human capital may lead to quasi-rents that are not contracted away upon hire (Klein, 1978, 1984; Robbins, 1988).

If general education and specific human capital are complements—as recent literature on training would suggest (Psacharopoulos, 1987)—it is probable that workers with more education accumulate more specific human capital. As a result, more educated workers receive rents, while less educated workers would not. Each of these four reasons suggests that in firms and industries where efficiency-wage rents occur, the more educated workers will receive higher wage premia than the less educated workers. Moreover, this structure to asymmetric wage premia implies that the rate of return to schooling would be higher in high-wage industries. We turn to empirical work to see whether this prediction is borne out.

Empirical work on interindustry wage differentials for the United States (Dickens and Katz, 1987) and for Brazil (Robbins, 1989a) finds that high-wage industries pay higher than average wages to workers across occupational groups (educational segments, for Brazil) within the industries. In other words, industries that paid wage premia to workers in some occupational (schooling) groups, generally paid wage premia to workers in other occupational (schooling) groups. However, these results do not show strict proportionality of log-wage premia to general human capital. Thus, these results are consistent with rates of return to schooling that differ across industries, and are correlated with interindustry wage differentials. To examine this possibility, we study the correlation between the estimated rate of return to schooling and the estimated wage differentials, which we have argued is likely to be positive.

In the next section, we will use the data and results to test the variability of the earnings functions, and then examine the structure of that variability, focusing on the relation between the rate of return to schooling and wage differentials.

Data and Results

The results are presented in three parts. We begin by testing for the heterogeneity of the earnings function across industries, then we examine the structure of that variation, in terms of the covariance of the estimated industry-level coefficients with each other and with estimated wage levels. The second part examines the relationship between the estimated rates of return to schooling to industry and average firm characteristics. The third part examines simulations of the variance of log wages under various counterfactuals.

Heterogeneity of the Earnings Function: Variation in the Rate of Return to Schooling and Its Structure

The data used to estimate earnings functions is derived from a sample of male workers in private manufacturing firms in greater São Paulo. This data, from the 1977 RAIS, is employed because of its richness and the availability of unique data on industry characteristics for this year. We obtained 77,691 observations in the final sample of male workers. Means and standard deviations of key variables are reported in Appendix Table 7.1.

In equation (6), the earnings function may vary freely across industries. We estimate this equation for two-digit industry level, focusing upon gross returns to three variables: years of schooling (S), years of experience (X), and years of tenure in the firm (T).[12] [13]

Heterogeneity of the Wage Equation

Panel A of Table 7.1 presents the averages and observed dispersions of the estimated coefficients for key variables and their interactions. The ratio of the standard deviation to the mean for the estimated parameters varies from .27 to 2.6. This ratio is highest for the coefficients on schooling and the interaction between tenure and schooling. For comparison, we also list, in panel B, similar statistics for four other variables that are not regression coefficients. For example, the first row in panel B shows that the mean of industry-level schooling means is 5.53 years, with a standard deviation of 1.29. The ratio of the standard deviation to the mean is 0.23. When this is compared to similar ratios for the estimated coefficients for schooling and schooling-squared (2.18 and 0.56, respectively), we see that the variation in schooling coefficients is large. Similar conclusions can be drawn regarding the variation in the estimated tenure and experience coefficients.

---

[12] The following variables were included as regressors in all estimated earnings functions, where the dependent variable was log (wage):

S:	years of schooling
SSQ:	years of schooling squared
X:	years of experience, proxied by age - schooling - 6
XSQ:	years of experience squared
T:	years of tenure in the firm
TSQ:	years of tenure squared
T*S:	the interaction term between tenure and schooling
X*S:	the interaction term between experience and schooling
T*X:	the interaction term between tenure and experience
NODEPS:	number of dependents
DMIG1:	equals 1 if a they are a recent migrant, in two stages, 0 otherwise
DMIG2:	equals 1 if worker is a recent migrant, in one stage, 0 otherwise
DMIG3:	equals 1 if worker is a non-recent migrant, 0 otherwise
IMIG:	equals 1 if worker is an immigrant, 0 otherwise
DCIVIL1:	equals 1 if married, 0 otherwise
LOGNOCU:	log of the number of jobs in the firm in Greater São Paulo
LOGNOBR:	log of the number of jobs in the firm throughout Brazil

[13] Preliminary results from regressions, where the data were segmented by years of schooling, suggested that estimating the earnings functions with schooling squared was superior to the specification of log (wages) as a linear function of schooling. The results of the wage equations that were quadratic in schooling closely correspond to the results from the segmented regressions that were linear in schooling. Below, we present the results from the "quadratic in schooling" specification.

Table 7.1. Variability of the Estimated Coefficients and Derivatives Across Industries
(For regression with quadratic schooling specification)

	Average	Observed dispersion (Standard deviation)	Ratio of standard deviation to average
A. Variability of coefficients on the variables:			
Schooling	0.0365	0.0796	2.18
Schooling^2	0.0084	0.0047	0.56
Tenure	0.2188	0.0589	0.27
Tenure^2	−0.0067	0.0093	1.39
Experience	0.0666	0.0244	0.37
Experience^2	−0.0010	0.0005	0.50
Tenure*schooling	−0.0010	0.0026	2.60
Experience*schooling	0.0010	0.0011	1.10
Tenure*experience	−0.0027	0.0015	0.56
B. Variability of industry means of schooling, tenure, experience and log wage:			
Schooling	5.53	1.29	0.23
Tenure	2.41	0.73	0.30
Experience	14.10	1.70	0.12
Log wage	7.67	0.38	0.05
C. Variability of estimated log wage evaluated at the mean worker characteristics:			
Estimated log wage	7.64	0.21	0.03

Table 7.2 presents estimated gross returns to schooling, tenure and experience (the derivatives of the estimated log-wage equation with respect to schooling, tenure and experience) with the means and standard deviations of these estimates at the bottom. The dispersion in estimated gross returns is large. For all three variables the ratio of largest to smallest derivative is roughly four. Another measure of dispersion is the ratio of the standard deviations to the average estimates. This ratio is roughly one-third for all three estimated derivatives. In Table 7.1, panel B, we see that the mean and standard deviation of the observed log wage are 7.67 and 0.38, respectively. Panel C of the same table reports the mean and standard deviation of the estimated log wages for industry-level earnings functions evaluated for a typical worker, using the mean characteristics of all workers in all industries. The mean and standard deviation in panel C are 7.64 and 0.21. Thus, approximately 55 percent of the variation in the

Table 7.2. Estimated Gross Returns to Schooling, Tenure and Experience
(Quadratic schooling specification)

Industry	∂lnW/∂S	∂lnW/∂T	∂lnW/∂X	R^2	Sample Size
Metallurgy	0.096	0.138	0.042	0.5319	4,946
Machinery	0.138	0.220	0.054	0.4969	4,300
Electronics	0.115	0.119	0.046	0.5799	4,212
Transport	0.130	0.129	0.043	0.5095	7,885
Wood	0.098	0.155	0.055	0.5036	790
Furniture	0.138	0.159	0.064	0.6100	639
Paper	0.161	0.102	0.049	0.5785	1,533
Rubber	0.102	0.060	0.038	0.4228	1,713
Leather	0.150	0.141	0.097	0.6705	158
Chemicals	0.103	0.174	0.055	0.5422	3,246
Pharmaceutical	0.230	0.145	0.067	0.5514	1,878
Perfumes	0.178	0.117	0.049	0.7386	643
Plastics	0.160	0.174	0.054	0.5645	2,933
Textiles	0.100	0.163	0.050	0.4757	3,654
Clothing	0.103	0.138	0.034	0.5305	1,196
Food	0.147	0.123	0.047	0.5708	4,643
Beverages	0.134	0.130	0.030	0.5511	1,499
Tobacco	0.120	0.154	0.025	0.4970	1,034
Editorial and Graphics	0.055	0.200	0.056	0.4243	2,160
Civil construction	0.119	0.140	0.034	0.2241	28,631
Mean	0.129	0.144	0.050		
Standard Deviation	0.037	0.034	0.016		

Note: All derivatives are statistically significant.

log wage across industries may be attributed to variation in the coefficients of the wage equation, rather than the variation in mean worker characteristics.

The F statistic for the test of homogeneity of earnings functions across industries is 13.2, and the null-hypothesis of homogeneity is strongly rejected. A series of stricter tests strongly supported this conclusion.[14]

---

[14] For large sample sizes, however, Leamer (1978) argues that the conventional critical values for the F test are too low, and that the value should grow with the sample size, holding the probability of Type One and Type Two errors equal. We calculated Leamer's Bayesian critical value of the F test. The resulting value is a little over 11, still rejecting the null hypothesis of homogeneity. As in the linear specification in schooling, the null-hypothesis of homogeneity

In conclusion, we find that earnings functions vary over industries. This variation differs from the common specification used in estimating interindustry wage differentials, where only the intercept term in the log-wage earnings functions varies over industries. Instead, there is wide dispersion of the estimated slope coefficients across industries. In particular, the dispersion in gross returns to schooling appears to be economically quite large and statistically significant.[15]

Structure of Variation in the Rate of Return to Schooling Across Industries

The traditional specification of the efficiency-wage earnings function assumes that if two workers with differing skill levels move from a competitive industry to an efficiency-wage industry, they would receive equal percentage increases. We have called this "symmetric" wage premia. If wage premia are symmetric over industries, then estimated interindustry wage differentials should be positively correlated with the intercepts from the estimated industry-level earnings functions. The estimated wage differentials should be uncorrelated with the estimated slope coefficients for schooling, tenure and experience, because the variance of these slope coefficients should derive from sampling error, not from structural differences in earnings functions across industries. On the other hand, we argued that the presence of efficiency-wage firms can lead to asymmetric wage premia. To explore the structure of this hypothesized asymmetry, we calculated predicted mean wages from the estimated industry level earnings functions for

---

is strongly rejected, using the conventional critical value as well as Leamer's Bayesian critical value.

The Swamy test is an alternative, more stringent, test of homogeneity related to Empirical Bayes techniques. It reflects the possibility that individual group estimates—for our case, industries—may not be drawn from truly independent populations (Swamy, 1970, 1971). The Swamy statistic compares weighted parameter estimates of the industry earnings functions to their overall mean. The weighted parameter estimates are standard-error weighted averages lying between the overall mean for all industries and the unconstrained industry level estimates, resulting in a "shrinkage" of industry parameter estimates toward the overall mean. This shrinkage necessarily leads to estimates that are less disperse than the original estimates. The Swamy test of homogeneity asks whether these less disperse parameter estimates are indeed different from their overall mean. The Swamy statistic for our data is very highly statistically significant. Therefore we strongly reject the null hypothesis of homogeneity of the earnings functions.

[15] By gross returns, we mean the measured return to schooling, without netting out the direct costs and foregone income of acquiring schooling.

observationally equivalent workers (hereafter $\hat{W}$, or "predicted wages"). We then examined the correlations of predicted wage with the estimated derivatives of the log (wage) with respect to schooling (w_s), tenure (w_T), experience (w_X), and the intercept.

We have already seen that the estimated industry-level derivatives of log wages with respect to schooling were highly statistically significant, and varied widely across industries. These, together with the correlation results, support the hypothesis of asymmetric wage premia. Instead of positively covarying with predicted wages, the correlation of the predicted wage with the intercept is negative and large (−.42). This means that industries paying generally higher wages than competitive industries (hereafter "high-wage" industries) have lower intercepts than other industries. Hence, their high wages must derive from steeper returns to some, or all, explanatory variables.

We find that for high-wage industries the only variable that receives higher rates of return is schooling. The estimated industry level derivatives of log wages with respect to schooling, tenure and experience are reported in Table 7.2. Table 7.3 reports the correlations of estimated derivatives with predicted wages. In the first column of panel A, which reports the correlations evaluated at the mean worker characteristics for the entire sample, we see that the derivative of log wage with respect to schooling is positively correlated, at 0.49, with the predicted wage. Continuing to columns two and three, we see that variation in the gross returns to experience or to tenure are not positively associated with interindustry wage premia. On the contrary, the derivative of log wage with respect to tenure is strongly negative, at −.46, and with respect to experience it is roughly zero.

In the results above, we evaluate the estimated earnings functions for the mean worker from our entire sample. To see if the structure of earnings functions varied significantly across workers, we examined the correlations between the predicted log wage and the schooling, tenure and experience derivatives evaluated for differing levels. Panel B of Table 7.3 reports the estimated derivatives of the log wage with respect to schooling, tenure and experience evaluated at mean worker characteristics for workers with two, four, eight and 13 years of schooling. The overall pattern is very close to the correlations discussed above, using the derivatives evaluated at mean characteristics for the entire sample. In panel B, we note that the correlation of estimated gross returns to schooling tends to rise with the level of schooling. The correlation is positive for all but the lowest level of schooling, and highest for average workers with eight years of schooling. Thus, in high-wage industries, unskilled workers earn wage premia, but they tend to be

Table 7.3. Correlation Between Estimated Log Wages and Estimated Returns to Schooling, Tenure and Experience
(Quadratic schooling specification)

	∂ℓnW/∂S	∂ℓnW/∂T	∂ℓnW/∂X
A. Evaluated at the mean worker characteristics for the entire sample: Estimated	0.4886	−0.4625	
			−0.0423
Log wage	(2.3759)	(−2.2132)	(−0.1796)
B. Evaluated at mean worker characteristics for workers with 2, 4, 8 and 13 years of schooling: Estimated log wage for average workers with:			
Schooling = 2	−0.1642	−0.4989	−0.2664
	(−0.7062)	(−2.4423)	(−1.1726)
Schooling = 4	0.3483	−0.4714	−0.1912
	(1.5764)	(−2.2678)	(−0.8264)
Schooling = 8	0.5687	−0.4120	0.0524
	(2.9333)	(−1.9184)	(0.2226)
Schooling = 13	0.3651	−0.1239	0.2496
	(1.6638)	(−0.5298)	(1.0936)

Note: Numbers in parentheses are t-statistics for the correlations. In calculating these correlations, industry 19 was dropped because of its very small sample size.

lower than premia earned by more educated workers; moreover, their wage premia are unrelated to their schooling. Therefore, in high-wage industries, workers with low education earn wage premia that are both proportionately lower than those of the more educated workers, and that arise from a vertical shift of the log-wage function, rather than from a higher rate of return to schooling. This result suggests that the opportunity costs of these unskilled workers in high-wage industries (and perhaps other industries) are only weakly related to schooling, since wage premia tend to be markups over opportunity costs.[16] On the other hand, workers with high education

---

[16] It is also of interest to briefly comment on the evidence for Lazear (1981). We noted earlier that the seniority wage profiles, while not solving the effort elicitation, might mitigate it. The evidence does not support this conclusion, since as wage-tenure profiles grow steeper, the intercept also rises. We find the correlation of the predicted wage with the derivative of the log

in these industries earn proportionately higher premia, which are tightly linked to the rates of return to schooling.

The main points of the above discussion are that we strongly reject the symmetry assumption, and find instead that estimated interindustry wage premia principally derive from higher rates of return to schooling, not from higher returns to other variables or higher intercepts. Alternatively, while all workers in high-wage industries tend to receive wage premia, those with higher levels of schooling receive proportionately higher wage mark-ups than those with lower levels of schooling.

Interpretation

We have already discussed four reasons why the observed wage structure might occur. Here we find that some industries not only pay higher wages, but that they pay proportionately higher wage premia to more educated workers. This wage structure supports efficiency-wage labor market models, consistent with a version of the wage-spread hypothesis that is extended to incorporate efficiency-wage labor market assumptions—the "extended wage-spread" hypothesis. The observed results do not allow a direct test of the efficiency-wage version interpretation of the wage-spread hypothesis, but lend it support. The efficiency-wage interpretation is supported by the large, statistically significant interindustry wage differentials that are strongly correlated with similar estimates for the United States. Here we have found that in addition to interindustry wage differentials being correlated with average education across industries (Dickens and Katz, 1987), the structure of high wages favors more educated workers within industries, and raises the overall rate of return to schooling, thereby increasing the inequality of the income distribution. In the next section we examine simulations of the wage distribution under alternative scenarios.

Simulated Earnings Inequality

Since we have seen that high-wage industries tend to have higher rates of return to schooling, it is plausible that the predominance of such industries

---

wage with respect to tenure, w_T, is strongly negative ($-.46$). But, in contrast to Lazear's prediction, this derivative is positively correlated with the intercept (the correlation equals .34, and the partial correlation controlling for W_S is also positive). The reason why the steeper wage-tenure profiles do not generally lead to higher interindustry wage differentials is that w_T is negatively correlated with W_S, and W_S dominates.

in the Brazilian economy may lead to greater inequality in earnings. To determine whether the presence of efficiency-wage firms can significantly raise the variance in wages, we simulated the distribution of wages differing counterfactual situations (for methodology, see Behrman, Knight and Sabot, 1983). If we interpret estimated wage differentials as efficiency-wage premia, then we would like to know by how much efficiency-wage factors raise the variance of wages in our sample. One way to gauge this is to simulate the variance in wages assuming that all workers in our sample were in low-wage industries (low rate of return to schooling), and then compare this to wages simulated under the assumption that all industries were high-wage (high rate of return to schooling) industries.

The simulation findings suggest that the shift from an economy with all low- to all high-wage industries would raise the variance of log wages dramatically. With the same population of workers as in our sample, had São Paulo industry consisted entirely of the lowest variance, low-wage industry, then the variance in estimated log wages would have been .328, compared to .784 if all workers were in the high-wage industry with the highest variance. Thus, comparing these counterfactuals suggests that efficiency-wage factors could potentially raise the variance of log wages by 71 percent. The actual variance of log wages, where we allow each industry to have a distinct earnings function and calculate predicted wages for workers in their corresponding industries, is .54, or 18 percent higher than it would be were all workers in the low-wage, low variance industry. Similarly, if all workers were in the high variance, high-wage industry, the variance of log wages (.784) would be 45 percent higher than it would be were each industry allowed to have its own distinct earnings function.

In the above calculations with industry earnings functions, we allow all parameters to vary across industries. We also simulated allowing only the schooling parameters to vary. In this case, the spread in the simulated variances from low-variance, low-wage industry to high-variance, high-wage industry is from .37 to .75, indicating that moving from all low-wage to all high-wage industries would double the variance of log wages.

Another question of interest is by how much do we underestimate the variance of log wages in São Paulo industry if we impose the same earnings function on all industries? The simulated log variance under this condition is .54. Comparing this to the simulated variance that allows full heterogeneity of earnings functions across industries (.576) suggests that we underestimate the variance of log earnings by about seven percent.

These findings indicate that an industrial structure dominated by efficiency-wage firms can significantly increase income inequality within industry. They also suggest that imposing homogeneity of industry earnings functions may negatively bias the estimated variance of log wages. It should be emphasized, however, that these are results only for Brazilian industry, and that it is likely that much greater heterogeneity of earnings functions holds across sectors, from industry to commerce, services, informal sector firms, and agriculture. Our findings also suggest that, along with the clear differences in the supply of educated workers across countries, demand-side differences in firm types and industrial composition may help explain Brazil's high rate of return to schooling, and high variance in earnings.

Relationship Between the Rate of Return to Schooling and Industry Characteristics

In the previous section, we established that wage premia are asymmetrically distributed within high-wage industries, with the more educated workers earning proportionately higher wage premia than workers with less education. We also showed that this could lead to higher earnings inequality. In this section we examine whether the estimated industry rates of return to schooling vary systematically with industry characteristics. Because the estimated rate of return to schooling, w_s, is strongly correlated with predicted wages, $\hat{W}$, it is likely that regressing w_s on the vector of industry characteristics, F, would yield similar results to previous studies that regressed $\hat{W}$ on industry characteristics (for the U.S., see Dickens and Katz, 1987; for Brazil, see Robbins, 1989b). However, the coefficients in the two regressions may diverge.

Prior studies found capital intensity, concentration, profits and size to be positively related to interindustry wage differentials (Brown and Medoff, 1989; for the United States, see Dickens and Katz, 1987). Robbins (1989a,b) found capital intensity, concentration, size and effective rate of protection to be positively related to interindustry wage differentials for Brazil. For both countries, size was more important in explaining wages within than between industries. Effective rates of protection, concentration and perhaps size are likely to raise industry rents, which along with profits would be shared with workers under rent-sharing efficiency-wage labor market theories. Capital intensity may raise monitoring costs and give workers more bargaining power under the union-threat and insider models.

The estimated industry-level derivatives of the log wage with respect to schooling were regressed on industry and industry averages of firm characteristics. The principal industry characteristics studied were the percentage of industry sales by multinational firms (MNC), the four-firm concentration ratios (CON), the percentage of industry production consumed by the top 13 percent of the income distribution (DC, for demand concentration), several measures of effective rate of protection (ERP), and dummy variables classifying industries into traditional and advanced groups related to technology. We also used industry-level averages of firm-level data from the RAIS data set and the CADEC tax records, including profits, dividends, capital, fixed assets and firm size. Profits, dividends, capital and assets were normalized to per-worker variables, while both simple arithmetic and firm-size weighted averages of firm characteristics were used. Since weighting did not substantively alter the results, and because the weighted results are more consistent with dependent variables from individual worker level regressions by industry, we only present the weighted results.

We explored various specifications, including weighted and unweighted industry average firm characteristics and varying combinations of regressors. The results are stable across these different specifications. Table 7.4 presents typical findings, where we used firm-size weighted industry averages of capital intensity and profits. The regression explains 75 percent of the variation in the industry level rate of return to schooling. This high R^2 declines to 72 percent if we drop the firm-size variable, and increases to 80 percent when we use an alternative measure for effective rate of protection. Colinearity among regressors was not a problem, with neither the signs nor significance of estimated parameters varying greatly over specifications. The estimated effects are also economically large.[17] Thus, these results appear robust and strongly statistically and economically significant. We find that fixed assets, capital intensity, percent of sales by multinationals, effective rate of protection, and more technologically advanced industries are associated with higher rates of return to schooling, while concentration, profits and demand concentration are associated with lower rates of return to schooling.[18]

As expected, these results are similar to the previous study of the correlates of interindustry wage differentials (Robbins, 1989b). However, the

---

[17] A one standard deviation change in the regressors leads to a change in the dependent variable—the derivative of log (wages) with respect to schooling—that varies from .35 to 1.25 the standard deviation of the dependent variable, with a mean effect of about 70 percent of the standard deviation of the dependent variable.

[18] We argue that industries whose long-term profits are high had transitorily low profits during the 1977 recession, and that this was responsible for the negative coefficient of profits.

Table 7.4. Explanation of Variation in Returns to Schooling

Explanatory variable	Coefficient (t-statistic)
Fixed assets (per worker)	8.34[a]
	(2.42)
Profits (per worker)	−6.13[b]
	(−3.23)
Four-firm industry concentration	−.0010
	(−3.57)
Demand concentration	−.0021
	(−3.86)
% of sales by multinationals	.0011
	(4.17)
Traditional industries A	−.0449
	(−3.46)
Traditional industries B	.0166
	(0.86)
Effective rate of protection	.0002
	(2.45)
Intercept	.2402
	(8.50)
Adjusted R-square	0.72
Number of observations	17

[a] Times 10^{-8}.
[b] Times 10^{-7}.

Notes: (1) Dependent variable is the partial derivative of log wage with respect to schooling evaluated at the mean worker characteristics. (2) "Fixed assets" and "Profits" are industry mean of firm-level variables weighted by firm sizes. (3) Traditional industries A: rubber, plastics, textiles, editorial and graphics. Traditional industries B: wood, leather, clothing, food, beverages, tobacco, civil construction. (4) Effective rate of protection is the ratio of import tax actually collected over the value of products for 1976. The rates were taken from Braga et al. (1988).

coefficient on concentration is positive when predicted wages is the dependent variable, but negative when the rate of return to schooling is the dependent variable. A possible explanation is that while concentration tends to raise rents, and thereby raise average industry wages, concentration also may engender monopsony power over more educated workers.[19]

---

[19] Two caveats are merited. First, concentration has been strongly criticized as a measure of monopoly rents and market power (Phillips, 1976). Second, Demsetz (1973) argues that observed correlations between concentration and rents is not causal; rather, size leads to rents, but since size and concentration are correlated, when not controlling for size, concentration and rents will be correlated. However, elsewhere (Robbins, 1989a) we find that interindustry wage differentials are strongly correlated with concentration even after controlling for size.

Such differential monopsony power could arise if more educated workers' skills were industry specific (i.e., transferable across firms within the industry but not to other industries) while less educated workers had more general skills.

The effect of trade protection on the pattern of wage structures is an important issue. Brazil pursued an import substitution strategy from 1945 to 1964, and then moved towards export promotion. Trade protection sharply increased between 1958 and 1963, with average tariffs doubling. After the 1964 coup, the government sharply lowered tariffs to 50 percent below their 1958 levels, although effective rates of protection remained high in absolute terms, and varied widely across two-digit industries (see Carvalho and Haddad, 1981).[20]

We use effective rate of protection measures from Braga et al. (1988). Since implicit protection measures are unavailable for 1977, we use implicit protection for 1985 (ERP85imp), which is a ratio of domestic to international prices; we also employed "true protection" for 1976 (ERP76ver), the ratio of import taxes actually collected over the value of sales in 1976. In Table 7.4 we report results with ERP76ver. The alternative specification using ERP85imp increases the R-squared and the coefficient on effective rate of protection, but does not significantly change the results for the other coefficients. The coefficient on ERP76ver is large: a change of one standard deviation in ERP76ver implies a change in the rate of return to schooling equal to 90 percent of its standard deviation. Substituting ERP85imp for ERP76ver doubles this effect, without changing other coefficients significantly. These results are especially noteworthy given that these ERP measures are quite different. ERP76ver and ERP85imp are weakly negatively correlated (–.14). Adding firm size to the regression lowers the ERP76imp coefficient to .0001, once again without changing other coefficients significantly. Thus, the regressions are quite robust. In particular, specifications using different measures of effective rate of protection yield consistently positive coefficients ranging from large to very large, without changing the other regression coefficients. These findings for effective rate of protection are similar to our previous study that regressed wage differentials on industry characteristics (see Robbins, 1989b), where the coefficient of effective rate of protection was positive and large.

We learned from this earlier study that trade protection appears to increase wage premia. Here we learn that this effect is especially pronounced for more educated workers. Through which mechanism does this occur?

---

[20] The Collor government significantly lowered effective rates of protection.

One possibility is that high effective rates of protection raise industrial concentration. However we reject that hypothesis, because industrial concentration ratios for Brazil are very highly correlated with corresponding ratios for industrialized nations (Robbins, 1989a). This suggests that industrial concentration is exogenous to wage structure and effective rate of protection, having a cause in common with industrialized countries. This common cause is most likely to be technology.

An alternative explanation reverses the direction of causality. Rather than being the cause of concentration, effective rates of protection partly result from technology and concentration. Technology (returns to scale) leads to concentration; in turn, concentration leads to rents and political power that affect the levels of effective rates of protection. The higher effective rates of protection further contribute to rents that, under efficiency-wage theories, are shared with some workers.

Conclusions

We find that industry earnings functions are heterogeneous, with large variations in the rate of return to schooling across industries. These estimated industry rates of return to schooling are strongly and positively correlated with interindustry wage differentials. This asymmetry of wage premia favors more educated workers, and may arise from monitoring costs rising with schooling, increasing returns to scale in monitoring, supervisorial responsibility rising with education, and specific human capital rising with schooling whose rents are shared with workers. This asymmetry of wage premia is likely to be accentuated by industry rents from concentration or effective rates of protection through rent-sharing. In regressions of estimated industry-level rates of return to schooling onto industry characteristics, higher effective rates of protection, fixed assets, capital intensity, percentage of sales by multinationals and more advanced technology are associated with higher rates of return. Effective rates of protection and fixed assets are associated with industry rents, and appear to magnify the asymmetric wage premia. Capital intensity may increase the cost of monitoring more educated workers, while multinationals have higher rents and are likely to adopt management policies that favor rent-sharing for the more stable and educated portion of their labor forces. Though concentration appears to cause industry rents and higher wage premia, it also appears to lower the rate of return to schooling.

These findings suggest that efficiency-wage labor market mechanisms raise the rate of return to schooling for key industries, thereby raising the average rate of return to schooling for the urban labor market. This may lead to higher inequality of income distribution (this is supported by simulations we performed), and possibly to overinvestment in secondary education in the long run. These distributional and investment consequences are nonoptimal, because efficiency-wage models principally derive from market imperfections. Two broad groups of policy options exist. The first could redirect the composition of final demand through such measures as income redistribution; this would lower the predominance of efficiency-wage firms.[21] The second group of less dramatic policy options includes acting on effective rates of protection, capital subsidies, anti-trust policy, and policy towards multinationals. Lowering effective rates of protection and subsidies to capital will tend to lower interindustry wage differentials and the average rate of return to schooling. Our results are less definitive with respect to the effect of anti-trust policy on the rate of return to schooling. Anti-trust policy lowers interindustry wage differentials and thereby the average rate of return to schooling across industries, because high-wage industries also have higher average levels of schooling. However, ceteris paribus it may raise the rate of return to schooling by lessening monopsony power over educated workers. The net effect is indeterminate. Policies affecting effective rates of protection, subsidies to capital and concentration are likely to affect the nature and degree of multinational investment, and will generally be preferred to policies aimed at directly lowering the dominance of multinational corporations that provide new technology and scarce capital to lesser developed countries.[22]

---

[21] In contrast, Bulow and Summers (1986) argue that it may be optimal to favor efficiency-wage, high value-added firms. See Sadoulet (1985) for a discussion of industry composition and income distribution.

[22] Bulow and Summers (1986) and Katz and Summers (1989) argue that wage subsidies to high-wage industries, and sometimes protection, can maximize utilitarian welfare. However, while potentially important, these are highly controversial.

REFERENCES

Akerlof, George A., and Lawrence F. Katz. 1986. *Do Deferred Wages Dominate Involuntary Unemployment as a Worker Discipline Device?* National Bureau of Economic Research Working Paper No. 2025 (September).

Almeida dos Reis, José Guilherme, and Ricardo Barros. 1991. Wage Inequality and the Distribution of Education: A Study of the Evolution of Regional Differences in Inequality in Metropolitan Brazil. *Journal of Development Economics* 36.

Bacha, Edmar L., and Lance Taylor. 1980. Brazilian Income Distribution in the 1960s: Facts, Model Results, and the Controversy. In *Models of Growth and Distribution for Brazil*, eds. Taylor et al. World Bank Research Publication.

Becker, Gary S. 1964. *Human Capital: A Theoretical and Empirical Analysis.* Princeton: Princeton University Press.

Behrman, Jere R., Knight, J.B. and R.H. Sabot. 1983. A Simulation Alternative to the Comparative R-squared Approach to Decomposing Inequality. *Oxford Bulletin of Economics and Statistics* 45(3) (August): 307–12.

Bonelli, Regis, and Guilherme L. Sedlacek. 1989. Distribuição de Renda: Evolução no Último Quarto de Século. In *Mercado de Trabalho e Distribuição de Renda: Uma Coletânea*, eds. G.L. Sedlacek and R. Barros. IPEA/INPES.

Braga, Helson C., Gilda M. C. Santiago, and Luiz Cesar M. Ferro. 1988. Proteção Efetiva no Brasil: Uma Estimativa a Partir da Comparação de Preços. April. IPEA/INPES.

Brown, Charles, and J. Medoff. 1989. Employer Size Wage Effect. *Journal of Political Economy* 97(5).

Bulow, Jeremy I., and Lawrence H. Summers. 1986. A Theory of Dual Labor Markets with Application to Industrial Policy, Discrimination, and Keynesian Unemployment. *Journal of Labor Economics* 4(3).

Carvalho, José, and Claudio L.S. Haddad. 1981. Foreign Trade Strategies and Employment in Brazil. In *Trade and Employment in Developing Countries*, vol. 1, eds. Anne O. Krueger et al.

Castello Branco, R. 1979. *Crescimento Acelerado e o Mercado de Trabalho: A Experiência Brasileira.* Rio de Janeiro: Editora da Fundação Getúlio Vargas.

da Mata, Milton. 1978. Crescimento Industrial e Absorção de Mão-de-Obra. In *Indústria: Política, Instituições e Desenvolvimento*, ed. Wilson Suzigan. Rio de Janeiro: IPEA/INPES.

Demsetz, W. 1973. Industry Structure, Market Rivalry and Public Policy. *Journal of Law and Economics* 1.

Dickens, William T., and Lawrence F. Katz. 1987. Inter-Industry Wage Differences and Industry Characteristics. In *Unemployment and the Structure of Labor Market*, eds. Kevin Lang and Jonathan Leonard. Basil Blackwell.

Doeringer, P., and M.J. Piore. 1971. *Internal Labor Market and Manpower Analysis.* Lexington, MA: D.C. Heath and Co.

Ferreira da Silva, J. 1987. Diferenciação Salarial na Indústria Brasileira. Série Teses no. 14. Editora da Fundação Getúlio Vargas, Rio de Janeiro.

Fields, Gary. 1980. *Poverty, Inequality and Development.* Cambridge: Cambridge University Press.

Fishlow, Albert. 1972. Brazilian Size Distribution of Income. *American Economic Review* 62 (2).

Katz, Lawrence. 1986. *Efficiency Wage Theories: A Partial Evaluation.* NBER Working Paper No. 1906 (April).

Katz, Lawrence, and Lawrence Summers. 1989. Industry Rents: Evidence and Implications. *Brookings Papers on Economic Activity: Microeconomics.*

Klein, Benjamin. 1984. Contract Costs and Administered Prices: An Economic Theory of Rigid Wages. *American Economic Review* 74 (2).

Klein, Benjamin, R. G. Crawford, and A. A. Alchian. 1978. Vertical Integration, Appropriable Rents, and the Competitive Contracting Process. *Journal of Law and Economics* (October).

Knight, J. B., and R. H. Sabot. 1983. The Role of the Firm in Wage Determination—An African Case Study. *Oxford Economic Papers* 35: 45–66.

Lam, David, and D. Levison. 1990. Age, Experience, and Schooling: Decomposing Earnings Inequality in the U.S. and Brazil. *Sociological Inquiry.*

————. 1989. *Declining Inequality in Schooling in Brazil and its Effects on Inequality in Earnings.* Population Studies Center Research Report No. 89–170, University of Michigan, Ann Arbor.

Langoni, C.G. 1973a. Distribuição da Renda: Resumo da Evidência. *Revista Dados* 11.

————. 1973b. *Distribuição de Renda e Desenvolvimento Econômico do Brasil.* Rio de Janeiro: Editora Expressão e Cultura.

Lazear, Edward P. 1981. Agency, Earnings Profiles, Productivity, and Hours Restrictions. *American Economic Review* (September).

Leamer, E.E. 1978. *Specification Searches: Ad Hoc Inference with Nonexperimental Data.* New York: John Wiley & Sons.

Lindbeck, Assar, and Dennis J. Snower. 1986. Wage Setting, Unemployment, and Insider-Outsider Relations. *American Economic Review* 76 (May).

Macedo, Roberto Bras Matos. 1974. Models of the Demand for Labor and the Problem of Labor Absorption in the Brazilian Manufacturing Sector. Ph.D. dissertation, Harvard University.

Medeiros, J. 1982. Alcance e Limitações da Teoria do Capital Humano: Diferenças de Ganhos no Brasil em 1973. *Ensaios Econômicos* 17. IPE/USP, São Paulo.

Mincer, Jacob. 1974. *Schooling, Experience, and Earnings.* New York: Columbia University Press.

Morley, Samuel A. 1981. The Effect of Changes in the Population on Several Measures of Income Distribution. *American Economic Review* 71.

Osterman, Paul (ed.). 1984. *Internal Labor Markets.* MIT.

Phillips, A. 1976. A Critique of Empirical Studies of Relations Between Market Power and Profitability. *Journal of Industrial Economics* 24: 241–9.

Piore, Michael J. 1973. *The Technological Foundations of Economic Dualism.* Working Paper No. 110 (May). Department of Economics, MIT.

Psacharopoulos, George. 1987. To Vocationalize or Not to Vocationalize? That Is the Curriculum Question. *International Review of Education* 33.

_____. 1985. Returns to Education: A Further International Update and Implications. *Journal of Human Resources* 20(4).

Robbins, Donald J. 1992. Worker Heterogeneity, Efficiency Wages and Minimum Wages in Developing Countries: Theory, and Evidence for Brazil. Harvard Institute For International Development. Mimeo.

_____. 1989a. Inter-Industry Wage Differentials: Evidence for Brazil and Comparison to Results for the U.S. University of California, Berkeley. Mimeo.

_____. 1989b. São Paulo, Brazil Manufacturing: The Industry and Firm Correlates of Firm Wage Differentials. Mimeo.

_____. 1988. The Brazilian Labor Market and Efficiency Wages: An Examination of the Evidence. Ph.D. dissertation, University of California, Berkeley.

Sadoulet, Elisabeth. 1985. Crescimento Desigualitário em uma Economia Sub-desenvolvida: O caso do Brasil. *Revista de Economia Política* 5(2) (April–June).

Senna, J. 1976. Escolaridade, Experiência no Trabalho e Salários no Brasil. *Revista Brasileira de Economia* 30(2).

Stiglitz, Joseph E. 1986. Theories of Wage Rigidity. In *Keynes' Economic Legacy*, eds. J.L. Butkiewicz et al. Praeger.

Swamy, P.A.V.B. 1971. *Statistical Inference in Random Coefficient Regression Models*. New York: Springer-Verlag.

_____. 1970. Efficient Inference in a Random Coefficient Regression Model. *Econometrica*.

Velloso, J. 1975. Human Capital and Market Segmentation: An Analysis of the Distribution of Earnings in Brazil. Ph.D. dissertation, Stanford University.

Willis, Robert J. 1986. Wage Determinance: A Survey and Reinterpretation of Human Capital Earnings Functions. *Handbook of Labor Economics* 1.

Yellen, Janet L. 1984. Efficiency Wage Models of Unemployment. *American Economic Review* 74.

Zaghen, P. E. M. 1980. The Determination and Distribution of Industrial Wage in Brazil. Ph.D. Dissertation, UC Berkeley, Berkeley, CA.

Appendix Table 7.1. Mean and Standard Deviation of Variables

Industry	ℓnW	S	T	X	NODEPS	DMIG1	DMIG2	DMIG3	IMIG	DCIVIL1	LOGNOCU	LOGNOBR
All	7.61 (1.09)	4.73 (3.41)	2.02 (3.75)	15.78 (8.98)	1.50 (4.86)	0.03 (0.16)	0.05 (0.22)	0.40 (0.49)	0.02 (0.15)	0.54 (0.50)	6.79 (1.77)	7.87 (1.50)
11	7.74 (1.19)	5.85 (3.62)	3.59 (6.30)	13.03 (8.11)	4.41 (17.67)	0.04 (0.20)	0.03 (0.16)	0.32 (0.47)	0.03 (0.16)	0.53 (0.50)	5.98 (1.76)	7.88 (1.53)
12	7.59 (1.24)	5.52 (3.50)	2.00 (3.02)	13.91 (8.65)	1.32 (1.80)	0.01 (0.11)	0.02 (0.16)	0.38 (0.49)	0.03 (0.17)	0.55 (0.50)	6.57 (1.28)	7.09 (1.02)
13	8.11 (1.13)	6.71 (3.80)	3.05 (3.97)	13.16 (8.48)	1.45 (1.70)	0.01 (0.12)	0.03 (0.16)	0.33 (0.47)	0.06 (0.24)	0.50 (0.50)	6.84 (1.75)	8.08 (1.31)
14	8.05 (0.96)	5.53 (3.28)	3.08 (3.60)	14.36 (8.08)	1.58 (1.80)	0.01 (0.10)	0.01 (0.10)	0.37 (0.48)	0.04 (0.19)	0.48 (0.50)	7.54 (2.96)	8.84 (1.75)
15	7.41 (0.96)	4.94 (3.25)	1.96 (3.24)	13.36 (8.41)	1.18 (1.72)	0.00 (0.06)	0.01 (0.11)	0.37 (0.48)	0.02 (0.13)	0.57 (0.49)	5.83 (1.32)	6.84 (1.09)
16	7.80 (1.02)	5.58 (3.33)	2.06 (2.84)	14.71 (9.28)	1.01 (1.52)	0.00 (0.07)	0.01 (0.09)	0.49 (0.50)	0.03 (0.17)	0.56 (0.50)	6.06 (1.18)	6.23 (0.94)
17	7.71 (1.03)	5.13 (3.56)	2.29 (3.90)	14.62 (8.65)	1.30 (1.72)	0.01 (0.10)	0.02 (0.13)	0.37 (0.48)	0.03 (0.17)	0.51 (0.50)	5.30 (1.35)	6.38 (1.10)
18	7.63 (1.05)	4.44 (3.02)	2.64 (4.46)	15.40 (8.36)	1.06 (1.66)	0.01 (0.07)	0.06 (0.24)	0.42 (0.49)	0.02 (0.14)	0.55 (0.50)	6.36 (2.00)	7.03 (1.21)
19	6.71 (1.10)	4.89 (2.87)	1.11 (1.64)	9.79 (9.68)	0.89 (1.72)	0.00 (0.00)	0.01 (0.08)	0.23 (0.42)	0.02 (0.14)	0.70 (0.46)	4.61 (1.00)	5.04 (0.41)
20	7.88 (1.36)	6.42 (4.05)	3.08 (5.08)	13.38 (8.74)	1.37 (1.78)	0.02 (0.15)	0.05 (0.22)	0.37 (0.48)	0.03 (0.17)	0.50 (0.50)	5.72 (1.38)	6.67 (1.50)
21	8.56 (1.30)	9.09 (3.86)	3.27 (4.85)	13.07 (8.53)	1.73 (1.74)	0.03 (0.17)	0.06 (0.23)	0.33 (0.47)	0.06 (0.23)	0.38 (0.48)	5.72 (2.04)	6.25 (1.90)
22	8.21 (1.27)	7.04 (4.41)	3.23 (5.11)	13.75 (9.33)	1.42 (1.67)	0.02 (0.12)	0.03 (0.17)	0.35 (0.48)	0.07 (0.25)	0.46 (0.50)	5.83 (1.77)	7.12 (1.04)

23	7.52	4.72	1.89	14.57	1.23	0.01	0.02	0.36	0.01	0.57	6.18	6.64
	(1.05)	(3.33)	(2.92)	(8.30)	(1.73)	(0.11)	(0.15)	(0.48)	(0.11)	(0.49)	(0.91)	(0.92)
24	7.34	3.88	1.70	15.24	1.02	0.00	0.02	0.53	0.02	0.62	6.77	7.12
	(0.93)	(2.67)	(3.20)	(8.74)	(1.64)	(0.06)	(0.13)	(0.50)	(0.13)	(0.48)	(1.20)	(0.94)
25	7.52	5.41	1.95	13.79	1.20	0.02	0.01	0.37	0.03	0.57	6.80	7.86
	(1.16)	(3.35)	(3.05)	(8.25)	(1.76)	(0.14)	(0.11)	(0.48)	(0.16)	(0.50)	(2.42)	(1.58)
26	7.55	4.58	2.76	16.32	1.58	0.01	0.03	0.42	0.03	0.48	6.33	7.32
	(0.96)	(3.26)	(5.14)	(9.43)	(2.07)	(0.11)	(0.18)	(0.49)	(0.16)	(0.50)	(1.65)	(1.18)
27	7.59	5.37	2.81	14.13	1.24	0.01	0.03	0.33	0.02	0.53	5.89	7.85
	(1.07)	(3.49)	(5.88)	(7.88)	(1.67)	(0.09)	(0.17)	(0.47)	(0.15)	(0.50)	(1.84)	(1.52)
28	7.52	5.18	2.33	14.35	1.22	0.03	0.05	0.14	0.00	0.54	7.54	9.28
	(0.79)	(2.65)	(5.54)	(8.79)	(1.66)	(0.16)	(0.23)	(0.35)	(0.05)	(0.50)	(1.31)	(1.42)
29	7.55	7.12	2.48	12.44	1.13	0.01	0.01	0.34	0.02	0.58	6.46	6.72
	(1.34)	(3.70)	(5.10)	(8.99)	(1.64)	(0.09)	(0.09)	(0.47)	(0.15)	(0.49)	(1.32)	(1.26)
34	7.36	3.21	0.87	18.60	1.22	0.04	0.10	0.44	0.01	0.58	7.31	8.50
	(0.93)	(2.34)	(1.44)	(8.90)	(1.94)	(0.21)	(0.29)	(0.50)	(0.08)	(0.49)	(1.22)	(1.03)

Notes: 1) See test for definition of variables. Standard deviations are in parentheses.

2) Two-digit industry codes are taken from RAIS, which uses the IBGE classification:

11: Metallurgy	12: Machinery	13: Electronics	14: Transport	15: Wood
16: Furniture	17: Paper	18: Rubber	19: Leather	20: Chemicals
21: Pharmaceuticals	22: Perfumes	23: Plastics	24: Textiles	25: Clothing
26: Food	27: Beverages	28: Tobacco	29: Editorial & Graphics	34: Civil construction

CHAPTER

The Quality of Schooling and Labor Market Outcomes

Jere R. Behrman, Nancy Birdsall and Robert Kaplan

Schooling is widely thought to be very important in determining labor productivity in developing nations, including Brazil. As a result, there are many strong advocates of increasing investment in schooling as part of the pursuit of economic growth and equity objectives. A wide range of researchers and institutions place major emphasis on formal schooling, particularly at the primary level, for the pursuit of such goals in developing countries.[1] Interest in schooling has been heightened recently by the focus on the "new economic growth theory" associated with Romer (1986), Lucas (1988), Azariadis and Drazen (1990) and others. With regard to Brazil, there has been debate about the effectiveness of schooling investments in pursuing productivity and equity objectives at least since the controversy in the early and mid-1970s about whether income distribution had deteriorated with growth in the "miracle" years. The debate extended to what should be the role of schooling investment in determining income distribution.[2]

Part of the basis for such advocacy is the association between years of schooling (or "quantity" of schooling) and wages, which is found in many cross-sectional data sets. Such an association is interpreted by some to imply substantial real rates of return to schooling investments in many developing countries. For example, largely on the basis of such associations, World Bank (1980) and Psacharopoulos (1985, 1988) claim that the average real social rate of return to primary schooling in developing countries is over 24 percent.[3]

But there are a number of possible problems in such estimates. One is that quality varies substantially across schools. If not controlled in estimates

[1] See World Bank (1980, 1981, 1990, 1991, 1993), Birdsall and Sabot (1995), Colclough (1982), Eisemon (1988), King (1990b), King and Hill (1993), Psacharopoulos (1985, 1988), Schultz (1988), Asian Development Bank (1990), Inter-American Development Bank (1993), and UNDP (1990).

[2] See, for example, Fishlow (1972), Langoni (1973), Fields (1975), Carnoy (1974), Morley (1976), Jallade (1977), Barros and Lam (this volume), and Psacharopoulos et al. (1992).

[3] In this literature, "social" refers to the incorporation of public as well as private costs, but not to the inclusion of externalities.

of labor market returns to schooling, this may cause substantial misunder-standing of schooling impact.[4] While there are have been a number of studies that investigate the impact of schooling quality on schooling achievement as measured by such indices as test scores,[5] there has been very little investiga-tion of the impact on estimated returns to schooling in terms of labor market outcomes of controlling for schooling quality. This is the case in part because most cross-sectional data sets do not have information on schooling quality to which different individuals were exposed during their school years to-gether with information on subsequent labor market outcomes.

In two earlier articles (Behrman and Birdsall, 1983, 1985), we argued that on a priori grounds the failure to control for public schooling quality in the estimates of the impact of schooling quantity on various outcomes would bias upwards the estimated return to schooling quantity, as well as provide no information about the tradeoff between investing in schooling quantity versus schooling quality. Of course, whether the bias in the estimated impact of schooling quantity outcomes is large or small is an empirical question, the investigation of which with most data sets is not possible because of the lack of information on relevant outcomes subsequent to school, such as adult wages, *and* on the quality of schooling. Therefore, we proposed an indicator of schooling quality that is available in censuses and other large data sets: the average schooling of teachers in the area in which one received primary schooling. Such a schooling quality indicator has some strengths and some weaknesses, both of which are discussed extensively in the earlier of our two studies. However, all in all, it seems a promising representation of schooling quality that circumvents the usual problem of not having information in one cross-sectional data set on both the characteristics of schools that individuals attended and on subsequent labor market outcomes.[6]

---

[4] Other possible important problems include sample selectivity, random measurement error, unobserved ability and motivation, the failure to control for externalities, and geographical biases due to failure to control for differences in prices and inputs into the production process that are complementary with labor and associated with schooling levels. For surveys and as-sessments of these biases, see Behrman (1987, 1990a,b,c), Behrman and Birdsall (1987), and Schultz (1988, 1993). In the present study, we ignore the importance of these other possible problems in order to focus on the impact of schooling quality.

[5] For example, see Alderman et al. (1992, 1993), Behrman (1993), Fuller (1986), Glewwe (1990, 1992), Glewwe and Jacoby (1991), Hanushek (1989), Hanushek, Gomes-Neto and Harbison (1992), Harbison and Hanushek (1992), Heyneman and Loxley (1983), Lockheed and Hanushek (1988), and Loxley and Heyneman (1980).

[6] There are some exceptions. For example, the Peruvian LSMS contains some retrospective information on schooling quality for current adults (King, 1990a).

We undertook estimates of the impact of incorporating schooling quality into the analysis of labor market outcomes for males age 15–35 in Brazil using data from the 1970 census. Our estimates suggest that the incorporation of schooling quality into the analysis changes understanding of the impact of schooling on such labor outcomes for the Brazilian national estimates in three major respects.[7] First, if the true specification should include the control for quality, the standard procedure without this control overestimates substantially the private returns to investing in schooling quantity. The standard procedure implies an estimated real private rate of return to investing in schooling quantity of 20.5 percent, which is about 75 percent above our preferred estimate of 11.7 percent. Thus the bias is considerable. Second, the estimated internal social rate of return to investment in schooling quality is at least as large as is the estimated social rate of return to investment in school quantity.[8] Therefore, there is at least as great social return in terms of productivity to "deepening" (in the sense of increasing quality) as to "widening" schooling (in the sense of increasing quantity of a given quality). Third, there probably is an important quality-quantity tradeoff in the allocation of resources to schooling. Concentration of resources has higher productivity returns than wider dispersion of such resources both because the social rate of return to quality is at least as great as that to quantity, as noted above, and because of positive quality-quantity interactions that are suggested by a priori theory and confirmed by the empirical estimates. This result contrasts with the suggestion of World Bank (1981) and many others that one advantage of investing in schooling in developing countries is the congruence of pursuit of equity and productivity goals. The congruence of these goals is claimed to arise since the highest returns supposedly are to expanding primary schooling, which tends to promote equity since those who otherwise would not receive primary schooling tend to be from the bottom part of the income distribution.

---

[7] We also find some important effects on regional estimates. For example, control for schooling quality reduces substantially unexplained regional differences in income, reduces urban-rural differences, and reduces almost to zero migrant-nonmigrant differences that often have been attributed to unobserved differences in individual characteristics. In the present study, however, we do not explore these regional differences because they are less central to our basic concerns.

[8] In our 1983 article, we claimed that the former is larger, but Eaton (1985) pointed out an error in our calculations that accounted for most of the difference between our estimated social rates of return to schooling quality and quantity. Therefore, in our 1985 article we amended this conclusion to read as the present text.

Thus our earlier work suggests that incorporating schooling quality into the analysis of the impact of schooling on labor market outcomes for young Brazilian adult males changes substantially our understanding of the impact of schooling investments on those outcomes.

In the present study, we further explore the impact of schooling quality on labor market outcomes for Brazilian males, using data from the 1980 census. Our exploration includes investigation of the following questions: (1) How do estimates for the same birth cohort as considered in our previous studies change with an additional decade of experience? Do the effects of schooling quality appear to strengthen over the life cycle, perhaps because individuals are better sorted into work positions for which they have comparative advantages after initial periods of searching and matching? Or, alternatively, do the effects fade because of the greater lapsed time since schooling with the concomitant greater and more recent post-schooling experiences? (2) What is the decomposition of the effects of quality versus quantity on wage rates versus those on hours worked? Are the effects similar, or are there differential effects on hours worked versus the wage rate per hour? (3) How robust are our previous conclusions to variations in the data and in variable definitions? Do they reinforce or weaken our previous emphasis on the importance of incorporating schooling quality into the analysis of the impact of schooling on labor market outcomes in Brazil?

Why Include Schooling Quality in the Analysis?

We give here a simple geometric argument for the inclusion of schooling quality in the estimation of the impact of schooling on various outcomes. This argument also suggests that school quantity and quality should enter into the relation in an interactive form, and the nature of the biases that are likely to result if schooling quality is not included.

The solid lines in Figure 8.1 give the "demand" (or the present discounted value of the marginal benefits from schooling) and the "supply" (or the present discounted value of the marginal costs of schooling) for years of schooling as presented in Becker's (1967) Woytinsky lecture.[9]

---

[9] We put "demand" and "supply" in quotation marks the first time that we use them because, although this is standard terminology, these are not demand and supply curves in the sense that such terms are used more generally in economics; i.e., these curves do not necessarily show quantity decisions by individual entities that are so small relative to the market that they cannot have a perceptible effect on market prices. We also note that this presentation assumes risk neutrality.

Figure 8.1. Demand for and Supply of Years of Schooling

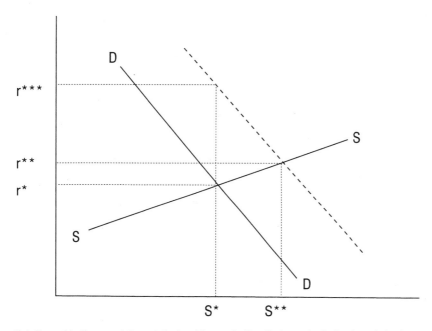

Note: Demand (or the present discounted value of the marginal benefits from schooling) and supply (or the present discounted value of the marginal cost of schooling) for years of schooling.

Underlying the demand curve is a production function for the outcome of interest in which one input is the years of schooling. For example, the wage rate that an individual receives may be produced by years in school, quality of that schooling, innate ability, motivation, and family background. This curve is downward sloping because of diminishing returns to spending time in school both due to fixed factors such as innate ability and to limited post-schooling expected lifetimes to reap whatever benefits are received from schooling. The solid line is drawn for a given set of characteristics other than time spent in school. The supply curve reflects all the costs of attending school, both monetary and in terms of the opportunity costs of time. This curve is likely to be upward sloping because of increasing costs of attending school for a longer period of time, considering the increasing opportunity cost of time with more schooling. The optimal level of schooling (S*) is where supply equals demand, so that the marginal benefit of the last unit of time spent in school just equals the marginal cost of that time (r*).

How do changes in schooling quality affect this story? Assume that schooling quality in public schools basically is determined by the government, so that the schooling quality that a particular individual faces depends upon his or her location during school ages.[10] The solid line in Figure 8.1 reflects a given level of schooling quality, as indicated above. If schooling quality were to be better, ceteris paribus, the demand curve would be higher—say, the dashed curve instead of the solid demand curve in Figure 8.1—under the assumption that better schooling quality increases the desired benefit at the margin. This has two important implications for the empirical analysis of the impact of schooling investments on outcomes, such as wage rates. First, there are interactions between quantity and the quality of schooling in the sense that the marginal return to school quantity depends on the schooling quality (and vice versa). For example, at a given quantity of school, the marginal benefits increase with higher schooling quality (e.g., to r*** instead of r* at S*). Second, schooling quality and quantity within this framework are positively correlated, with the implication that if schooling quality is not included in the specification even though, in fact, schooling quality has an impact on the outcomes of interest, the estimated impact of schooling quantity is biased upwards.[11] The positive correlation between schooling quality and quantity is illustrated by the fact that with better schooling quality, the equilibrium school quantity increases (e.g., to S** with the quality associated with the dashed demand curve in Figure 8.1).

Data

We use data from a random subsample of 5,922 males of age 25–45 (of whom 2,203 have hours worked in addition to income data so that we also can explore their average wage rate determinants) and 8,177 males age 15–35 from the one percent of households in the Public Use sample of the 1980 Brazilian census. We limit the sample to males in order to lessen selectivity problems and to make our results more comparable with those in our (and other) earlier studies. We focus on the same birth cohort considered in our

---

[10] If the school quality instead were a choice variable, schooling quality and quantity both would be chosen simultaneously so that the expected marginal benefits equaled the expected marginal costs. In such a case increased school quality would not necessarily induce more time in school in equilibrium, since marginal costs might increase more than marginal benefits.
[11] The standard expression for the omitted variable bias in a linear regression is that such bias is equal to the true coefficient of the omitted variable (in this case, schooling quality) times the correlation between the included and the omitted variable (in this case, positive by the argument in the text, though not necessarily so in the case discussed in the previous note).

earlier study: 15–35 year olds in 1970 and therefore 25–45 year olds in 1980. We also consider 15–35 year olds in 1980 in an investigation of year effects, possibly related to differing macro conditions.

The left-side variables that we use are earnings and wage rates, with the latter obtained by dividing earnings by hours worked. In our previous study, we considered only earnings. However, if hours worked is a choice variable, the wage rate is the more interesting dependent variable since it abstracts from choices about how time is used. Of course, ℓn earnings equals ℓn wage rates plus ℓn hours worked, so the difference between the estimates for ℓn earnings and ℓn wage rates gives the impact on ℓn hours worked.

The right-side variables that we use are years of schooling, post-schooling adult experience,[12] and schooling quality. As noted earlier, we use the average years of schooling of teachers in the locale in which an individual went to school as our measure of schooling quality. Our 1983 article gives an extensive discussion of the advantages and limitations of this indicator of schooling quality. In our earlier article, we defined this schooling quality variable as the average schooling of teachers at all school levels. For comparability, we use the same indicator in some of our estimates in the present study.[13]

Table 8.1 presents the means and standard deviations for the variables that we use in our estimates. For comparison, we have also included the means and standard deviations for the 15–35 year old males from our previous study, based on the 1970 census data. Years of schooling are low for Brazilian males, but with increases for more recent cohorts. The mean is about four grades for the 25–45 age group in 1980, and about an eighth higher for the 15–35 age group in the same year. Note that the 15–35 year old males in

---

[12] We define this, as in our 1983 article, as years over the age of 15 a male has been in the work force. For exploration of the sensitivity of the estimates to the use of this definition versus the more common total potential years of post-schooling experience (i.e., age minus years of school minus six, as in Mincer, 1974), see our 1985 article. In this study, we use the 1983 definition because it facilitates comparisons with the 1983 results.

[13] This measure has at least one problem that we did not recognize in our earlier article, since higher schooling levels tend to have teachers with more schooling. Thus, it confounds the impact of differences in schooling quality at identical school levels with differences in the importance of varying school levels. Therefore, we explore in this study an alternative (and probably) preferred indicator of schooling quality that is based on the schooling of only primary school teachers. For both of these indicators of schooling quality, we use the data from the 1970 census in order to keep the schooling quality measures comparable with those in our earlier studies. The results, in fact, do not change much with the choice of the schooling quality variable. In terms of consistency with the sample variance, the original measure is slightly preferred to the new one. This suggests that the new schooling quality variable tends to underrepresent urban-rural schooling quality differences (the two indicators differ primarily for urban areas, since there were very few secondary teachers in rural areas).

Table 8.1. Means and Standard Deviations for Relevant Variables
(Males by age group and data sample)

Right-hand side variables	1970 data 15–35 year olds		1980 data 25–45 year olds		1980 data 15–35 year olds	
	Mean	Standard deviation	Mean	Standard deviation	Mean	Standard deviation
ℓn earnings (Y)	4.5	1.8	8.7	1.6	8.0	2.4
Years of schooling (S)	3.0	3.5	4.1	4.3	4.6	4.0
Experience (E)	9.3	5.8	17.3	6.2	8.2	5.5
School quality (Q)	8.8	3.2	8.3	3.3	8.9	3.3
ℓn wage rate (W)			5.0	1.2	4.5	1.5
Number of observations	6,171		6,171		3,701	

1970 only had an average of three years of schooling in 1970, but by 1980, this same cohort (now aged 25–45) had an average of 4.1 years of schooling. This increase is consistent with the possibility that part of this cohort had not finished their schooling by 1970, though this seems to be a fairly large increase for an age cohort in which average schooling is relatively low.

Our measure of schooling quality increases slightly for the more recent age cohort, with about 8.3 years of schooling for teachers of the 25–45 age group, compared to about 8.9 years of schooling for teachers of the 15–35 age group. But note that for the 15–35 age group in 1970, average years of teacher schooling was 8.8, but for the same cohort in 1980 average teacher schooling was only 8.3 years. This reduction in school quality is consistent with the additional schooling noted in the previous paragraph being primarily in lower quality schools. This is not implausible given that late starting of school and grade repetition both tend to be higher in regions (and particularly in rural areas of such regions) in which schooling tends to be of lower quality.

Our measure of experience, of course, is substantially higher for the older cohort—with means of 17.3 versus 8.2 years. Their additional experience translates into the slightly higher wages for the older cohort despite their lower schooling (and assuming no systematic difference in hours and thus wage rates). The growth in experience of the cohort that was 15–35 in 1970 was eight years.[14]

---

[14] This growth in experience is less than 10 years in part because of the mean increase in years of schooling of 1.1 years discussed above, but that leaves 0.9 years that can be accounted for only by the subsample 25–45 in 1980 having on average a somewhat later birth date than the subsample that was 15–35 in 1970.

Estimates

We first consider estimates for earnings, with comparisons between the estimates for 1970 and 1980 for the same birth cohort and then for the same age group in 1980. We then turn to comparisons of estimates for wage rates versus those for earnings using the 1980 data.

Semilog Earnings Relations

In our 1983 study, we estimated four basic relations for the determination of ℓn earnings for a subsample of 15–35 year old males from the Brazilian national 1970 data. These relations are reproduced in Table 8.2. The first of these was the standard ℓn earnings relation with the right-side variables including years of schooling and a quadratic in experience. The second, in addition to the standard right-side variables, allows for the possibility that years of schooling interacts with a quadratic in schooling quality. The third includes, in addition to the standard right-side variables, an additive term for schooling quality. This can be considered to be a linear approximation to the preferred relation in which the effect of omitted variable bias on the estimated coefficient of schooling is relatively transparent from a comparison with the first relation (though there is not an interaction between school quantity and quality as in the preferred relation). The fourth relation has a quadratic expansion in school quantity and quality. An F test indicates that the fourth relation is preferred to the third. But the second and the fourth are not nested, so such a test cannot be conducted for that comparison.

At the bottom of this table are given the percentage changes in earnings given changes in years of schooling $((\delta Y/Y)/\delta S)$ and the percentage changes in earnings given changes in schooling quality $((\delta Y/Y)/\delta Q)$. The former is the real private rate of return to the time spent in schooling under Mincer's (1974) assumptions. In the second and fourth relations, these terms are not constant due to the interaction between schooling quality and quantity. Therefore at the bottom of the table, they are evaluated at the point of sample means and with one or the other one standard deviation above the means. These percentage changes are major inputs into our conclusions: quality matters, failure to control for quality results in a substantial upward bias in the estimated impact of quantity, the social rate of return to quality is at least as high as is that to quantity, and there is an implied equity-productivity tradeoff.

The first four columns of Table 8.3 present parallel estimates for the same birth cohort based on the 1980 census. Examination of the estimates in

Table 8.2. Alternative Estimates of ℓn Earnings Functions for Brazilian Males
(Ages 15–35 in 1970)[a]

Right-side variables	Relation (1)	Relation (2)	Relation (3)	Relation (4)
S	.205	−.185	.148	.047
		(2.6)	(24.6)	(1.6)
S*Q	38.1	.037		.0045
		(2.4)		(1.5)
S*Q²		−.0003		
		(0.3)		
Q			.122	−.256
			(18.6)	(4.5)
S²				.0042
				(3.4)
Q²				.022
				(6.4)
E	.303	.304	.300	.301
	(25.6)	(26.1)	(26.0)	(26.3)
E²	−.0090	−.0091	−.0091	−.0091
	(15.6)	(16.0)	(16.2)	(16.4)
ℓnY₀[b]	2.15	2.24	1.29	2.75
$\bar{R}^2$	.345	.371	.380	.389
S.E.E.	1.444	1.415	1.405	1.394
Private rate of return to S				
at $\bar{Q}$ and $\bar{S}$	20.5	11.7	14.8	11.1
at $\bar{Q} + \sigma_0$ and $\bar{S}$	20.5	21.6	14.8	12.6
at $\bar{Q}$ and $\bar{S} + \sigma_s$	20.5	11.7	14.8	14.1
Percent change in Y for change in Q: $(\delta Y/Y)/\delta Q$				
at $\bar{Q}$ and $\bar{S}$	0	9.5	12.2	14.5
at $\bar{Q} + \sigma_0$ and $\bar{S}$	0	8.9	12.2	28.6
at $\bar{Q}$ and $\bar{S} + \sigma_0$	0	20.6	12.2	16.0

[a] The absolute values of the *t*-statistics are shown in parentheses. For a more extensive discussion of the a priori bases for the specifications, see Behrman and Birdsall (1983).
[b] In columns (3) and (4), the constant estimate includes the constant in the approximations to effective schooling (i.e., r^*_0) as well as ℓn Y₀.

Table 8.3. Alternative Estimates of ℓn Earnings Functions for Brazilian Males
(Ages 25–45, 1980 data)

Right-side variables	Relation (1)	Relation (2)	Relation (3)	Relation (4)
S	0.193	0.296	0.174	0.201
	(25.2)	(5.0)	(20.3)	(7.1)
S*Q		−0.033		−0.0075
		(2.2)		(2.8)
S*Q^2		0.0020		
		(2.4)		
Q			0.051	−0.058
			(4.9)	(0.6)
S^2				0.0031
				(1.8)
Q^2				0.0084
				(1.6)
E	0.120	0.126	0.123	0.123
	(4.0)	(4.1)	(4.1)	(4.0)
E^2	−0.0024	−0.0025	−0.0024	−0.0025
	(2.9)	(3.2)	(3.0)	(3.0)
ℓnY$_0$	6.66	6.63	6.31	6.62
	(24.2)	(24.1)	(22.3)	(15.1)
Root MSE	1.433	1.431	1.426	1.424
$\bar{R}^2$	0.228	0.231	0.236	0.239
Private rate of return to S				
at $\bar{Q}$ and $\bar{S}$	19.3	16.4	17.4	16.4
at $\bar{Q} + \sigma_0$ and $\bar{S}$	19.3	18.8	17.4	14.0
at $\bar{Q}$ and $\bar{S} + \sigma_s$	19.3	16.4	17.4	19.1
Percent change in Y for change in Q: (δY/Y)				
at $\bar{Q}$ and $\bar{S}$	0.0	0.3	5.1	5.1
at $\bar{Q} + \sigma_0$ and $\bar{S}$	0.0	5.8	5.1	10.7
at $\bar{Q}$ and $\bar{S} + \sigma_0$	0.0	0.7	5.1	1.9

N = 2,203

Table 8.3, in comparison with those in Table 8.2, suggests the points described below.

First, the estimates for 1980 are consistent with less explained variation in earnings experience in 1980 than in 1970, regardless of whether the specifications include schooling quality. This result may seem surprising from the point of view of life-cycle earnings paths alone; from this perspective we would have expected the ensuing decade to have resulted in more sorting of jobs by comparative advantage as the respondents aged a decade and tended to search less and settle down into more permanent positions. However, such settling down according to comparative advantage presumably takes time precisely because some individual characteristics are not easily observed by employers. Employees also may learn more about their preferences regarding work with time (Novos, 1990). So, in fact, over time the easily observable schooling variables could become relatively less important. In addition, as more time has lapsed, there has been more exposure to individual stochastic shocks with persistent effects (e.g., chronic bad health due to injury or disease, good or bad luck due to initial job choices and contacts that are costly to change).[15]

Second, yet another possible explanation of the explained variation that is lower in Table 8.3 than in Table 8.2 is that macro conditions changed in a way so that stochastic shocks in income were more important in 1980 than in 1970, say due to differential adjustments across individual incomes to substantial macro shocks. This certainly seems plausible given the Brazilian experience. The year 1970 was during a relatively stable growth period when it is plausible that adjustment to the growth path had been considerable across the board. In contrast, 1980 was a time of substantial adjustment to the second oil shock and high international interest rates. To isolate the year effect,[16] we present estimates of the same four relations in Table 8.4 for 3,701 males who were 15–35 years old in 1980. This permits direct comparison for the same part of the life cycle (*not* for the same birth cohort) with the

---

[15] For example, an individual may have been initially employed in a firm or an industry that turned out to do worse than anticipated at the time of the initial employment decision. But the transaction costs of switching jobs and the acquisition of specific human capital limit the subsequent mobility. For evidence that initial conditions at the time of job entry condition subsequent labor market success in Brazil, see Behrman and Birdsall (1988b).

[16] However, this comparison does not enable us to identify confidently that any differences are due to adjustments to macro shocks rather than to other effects, such as secular shifts in the importance of the observed variables. Our prior is that the secular shifts have led ceteris paribus to increased, rather than reduced, importance of schooling in income determination in Brazil. If this is correct, any evidence of reduced importance of schooling in the estimates between 1970 and 1980 may well be due in substantial part to the differing macro conditions.

Table 8.4. Alternative Estimates of ℓn Earnings Functions for Brazilian Males
(Ages 15–35, 1980 data)

Right-side variables	Relation (1)	Relation (2)	Relation (3)	Relation (4)
S	0.214	0.418	0.154	0.207
	(23.3)	(5.5)	(15.0)	(5.9)
S*Q		−0.0808		−0.015
		(4.4)		(4.4)
S*Q^2		0.0054		
		(5.3)		
Q			0.144	−0.429
			(11.8)	(4.2)
S^2				0.0073
				(3.3)
Q^2				0.037
				(6.1)
E	0.337	0.348	0.351	0.347
	(15.1)	(15.7)	(16.0)	(15.8)
E^2	−0.0105	−0.0109	−0.011	−0.0106
	(9.1)	(9.56)	(9.7)	(9.5)
ℓnY$_0$	5.30	5.31	4.22	6.17
	(52.2)	(52.9)	(31.2)	(15.9)
Root MSE	2.176	2.153	2.14	2.12
$\bar{R}^2$	0.211	0.227	0.239	0.249
Private rate of return to S				
at $\bar{Q}$ and $\bar{S}$	21.4	12.2	15.4	13.8
at $\bar{Q} + \sigma_0$ and $\bar{S}$	21.4	22.8	15.4	8.7
at $\bar{Q}$ and $\bar{S} + \sigma_s$	21.4	12.2	15.4	19.7
Percent change in Y for change in Q: (δY/Y)				
at $\bar{Q}$ and $\bar{S}$	0.0	6.6	14.4	16.4
at $\bar{Q} + \sigma_0$ and $\bar{S}$	0.0	23.0	14.4	41.3
at $\bar{Q}$ and $\bar{S} + \sigma_0$	0.0	12.2	14.4	10.2

N = 3,701

estimates for 1970 in Table 8.2. This comparison suggests that there are some important year effects. The relations for 1980 systematically are somewhat less consistent with the earnings variations for the same age group compared to those for 1970. We conclude that year effects probably related to macroeconomic conditions are a large part of the explanation for the differences between the estimates for the same birth cohort in Tables 8.2 and 8.3, rather than the effects of learning and greater exposure to unanticipated persistent shock, discussed in the previous paragraph.

Third, F tests indicate that restrictions to exclude schooling quality from the third and fourth specifications are rejected in Tables 8.3 and 8.4 as well as from the second specification in Table 8.4.[17] But this result does not hold for the second specification in Table 8.3. The evidence that schooling quality is significant is specification-dependent and less robust than for the 1970 estimates in Table 8.2.

Fourth, for the 25–45 year olds, the evidence of an upward bias in the estimated impact of years of schooling in the standard estimates is less robust and less substantial for the 1980 data than for the same cohort in the 1970 data. This apparent decline in the relative importance of quality for this cohort may reflect the learning and exposure factors discussed in the first point above as well as the macro factors discussed in the second point. This shift apparently is not only due to macro conditions, however, since there is an upward bias for the 15–35 age cohort in 1980 of about the same magnitude that we found for the 15–35 age cohort in 1970.

Fifth, for comparability, we use the same schooling quality measure in Tables 8.3 and 8.4 as in Table 8.2—one based on the average schooling level of all teachers in the locale where an individual went to school. As noted, we also have experimented with an a priori preferred indicator based on the schooling of primary teachers alone. The results discussed here are quite robust to this alternative indicator of schooling quality.

Semilog Wage Rate Relations

Our original article considered only semilog earnings relations. However, one can argue that of more interest are wage rate relations if individuals differ in their hours worked, particularly if such differences in part reflect

---

[17] The F values for restricting the second, third and fourth specifications in Table 8.3 to the first specification are 4.4, 23.5, and 8.3. The parallel values for Table 8.4 are 39.5, 138.4, and 62.7. The critical F values at the one percent level are 4.6, 6.6, and 3.3.

individual choices. In such a case, the earnings relations may confound the impact of schooling on productivity (or the value of time) and that on hours worked. We now consider estimates of ℓn wage rates relations for the 25–45 age group in 1980 in Table 8.5. As noted above, since the ℓn hours worked equals the ℓn of earnings minus the ℓn of wage rates, differences between the estimates in Table 8.3 and those in Table 8.5 indicate the response of hours worked to the included variables.

We summarize the estimates in Table 8.5 and the comparison of these estimates with those in Table 8.3 with regard to three characteristics.

First, the ℓn wage rate estimates are consistent with a higher proportion of the sample variance than are the ℓn earnings estimates—as measured by the R^2s, generally over 50 percent more. Thus, systematic patterns in the response of productivity or the value of time to the included variables in these relations may be obscured in the ℓn earnings patterns by a lot of stochastic variation in the hours worked. Of course, such variations may have been particularly large in the macro conditions of 1980.[18]

Second, F tests reject the imposition of restrictions to reduce the quality-inclusive specifications to the standard specification in all three cases.[19] Therefore these results are much more robust to specification changes regarding the importance of schooling quality than is the case for the ℓn earnings estimates for the same age group.

Third, the ℓn wage rate estimates show essentially the same upward bias in the standard estimates of the private rate of return to time spent in school as the ℓn earnings estimates, and the same outcome with respect to the schooling quality-quantity interactions. The ℓn wage rates estimates suggest similar effects of schooling quality relative to school quantity at the sample means (and therefore for ℓn hours worked) as the ℓn earnings estimates. The percentage changes in earnings or in wage rates due to unit changes in school quantity and quality at the bottom of the two tables indicate that at the sample means for the fourth relation the respective quantity and quality effects are 16.4 percent and 5.1 percent for earnings, and 15.6 percent and 4.2 percent for wage rates. The impact of schooling quantity and quality is similar on productivity/value of time as on hours worked.

---

[18] Unfortunately, we are no longer able to use the 1970 data, so we cannot compare ℓn wage rate and ℓn earnings relations for that year to see if there are similar large differences in this or other respects.

[19] The respective F values are 6.7, 32.2, and 12.5, with critical F values at the one percent level of 4.6, 6.6, and 3.3.

Table 8.5. Alternative Estimates of ℓn Wages Income Functions for Brazilian Males
(Ages 25–45, 1980 data)

Right-side variables	Relation (1)	Relation (2)	Relation (3)	Relation (4)
S	0.183	0.277	0.167	0.186
	(34.3)	(6.7)	(28.1)	(9.5)
S*Q		−0.029		−0.0068
		(2.8)		(3.7)
S*Q^2		0.0018		
		(3.1)		
Q			0.042	−0.066
			(5.7)	(1.0)
S^2				0.0032
				(2.6)
Q^2				0.0082
				(2.2)
E	0.097	0.101	0.099	0.1007
	(4.6)	(4.8)	(4.7)	(4.7)
E^2	−0.0019	−0.0020	−0.0020	−0.0020
	(3.4)	(3.6)	(3.6)	(3.6)
ℓnY$_0$	3.22	3.19	2.928	3.235
	(16.8)	(16.7)	(14.9)	(10.7)
Root MSE	0.997	0.994	0.990	0.986
$\bar{R}^2$	0.356	0.360	0.365	0.370
Private rate of return to S				
at $\bar{Q}$ and $\bar{S}$	18.3	15.7	16.7	15.6
at $\bar{Q} + \sigma_0$ and $\bar{S}$	18.3	17.8	16.7	13.4
at $\bar{Q}$ and $\bar{S} + \sigma_s$	18.3	15.7	16.7	18.4
Percent change in Y for change in Q: (δY/Y)				
at $\bar{Q}$ and $\bar{S}$	0.0	0.2	4.2	4.2
at $\bar{Q} + \sigma_0$ and $\bar{S}$	0.0	5.0	4.2	9.6
at $\bar{Q}$ and $\bar{S} + \sigma_0$	0.0	0.4	4.2	1.3

N = 2,203

Conclusions

On a priori grounds, the impact of schooling quality as well as of schooling quantity would seem to be important in labor market outcomes. Moreover, the failure to control for variations in public-provided schooling quality in estimates of the impact of schooling quantity on various outcomes is likely to cause omitted variable biases that overstate the effects of years of schooling.

In our 1983 and 1985 studies, we developed such a priori reasoning, proposed a tractable empirical measure of schooling quality, and investigated the implications of schooling quality for earnings relations for Brazilian males age 15–35 in 1970. We found that quality was important in a statistical sense, that the failure to control for schooling quality biased upwards substantially the estimated private rate of return to time spent in school, that the social rate of return to investing in schooling quality was at least as high as that to investing in school quantity, and that there were definite productivity-equity tradeoffs.

In the present study, we have investigated similar phenomena for the 1980 census data, both for earnings and for wage rates. We find that there seems to have been some fading between 1970 and 1980 of the relative importance of schooling in explaining earnings variations for the 15–35 age group in 1970 (which we considered in our 1983 study), primarily, we believe, because of macro shocks. We also find, however, that life-cycle effects such as learning by employers and employees and greater exposure to persistent previously unanticipated individual events (e.g., accidents that result in permanent disabilities) seem to have important effects in mitigating the bias in estimated earnings returns to school quantity if schooling quality is not controlled; the effect of schooling quality is not robust to all specifications in our 1980 compared to 1970 estimates.

Our estimates based on wage rates rather than earnings indicate strong effects of schooling quality interacting with school quantity in 1980. The life-cycle factors that mitigate biases due to quality effects on hours worked do not do so for wage rates per hour; thus, in looking at wage rates, the preferred construct since they refer to productivity effects, it is important to control for schooling quality.

How do these results modify the conclusions in our earlier study? First, they reaffirm that schooling quality is important in Brazilian labor market outcomes. Our current results also suggest some further nuances, such as some fading of the impact of schooling quality and quantity for the 15–35 age cohort in 1970 on their 1980 earnings, probably because of the impact of macro variables and of some life-cycle factors related to hours worked. Second, they reinforce our earlier conclusion that investments in schooling quality ("deepening" schooling investments) as well as quantity ("widening" schooling investments) may be important from a social point of view. Third, they reinforce our earlier conclusion that there are likely to be substantial productivity-equity tradeoffs in schooling investments due to the productivity gains from concentrating resources in improving both the schooling quantity and quality of relatively few individuals.

REFERENCES

Alderman, Harold, Jere R. Behrman, David Ross, and Richard Sabot. 1993. Human Capital Accumulation and Productivity in Pakistan's Rural Wage Labor Market. Bryn Mawr College, Bryn Mawr, PA. Mimeo.

_____. 1992. The Gender Gap in Human Capital Accumulation in a Poor Rural Economy. Williams College, Williamstown, MA. Mimeo.

Asian Development Bank. 1990. *Human Resource Policy and Economic Development: Selected Country Studies.* Manila: Asian Development Bank.

Azariadis, Costas, and Allan Drazen. 1990. Threshold Externalities in Economic Development. *Quarterly Journal of Economics* 105(2) (May): 501–26.

Barro, R.J. 1991. Economic Growth in a Cross Section of Countries. *Quarterly Journal of Economics* 106 (May): 407–43.

Barros, Ricardo, et al. 1994. Human Resources and the Adjustment Process: Brazil. In *Human Resources and the Adjustment Process,* eds. Ricardo Paredes and Luis A. Riveros. Washington, D.C.: Inter-American Development Bank.

Becker, Gary S. 1967. *Human Capital and the Personal Distribution of Income: An Analytical Approach.* Woytinsky Lecture, University of Michigan, Ann Arbor. Republished in *Human Capital,* 2nd ed., Gary S. Becker. 1975. New York: NBER.

Behrman, Jere R. 1993. Human Resources in Latin America and the Caribbean. In *Economic and Social Progress in Latin America: 1993 Report.* Washington, D.C.: Inter-American Development Bank.

_____. 1990a. *Human Resource Led Development?* New Delhi: ARTEP/ILO.

_____. 1990b. *The Action of Human Resources and Poverty on One Another: What We Have Yet to Learn.* Washington, D.C.: Population and Human Resources Department, World Bank.

_____. 1990c. Women's Schooling and Nonmarket Productivity: A Survey and a Reappraisal. Prepared for the Women in Development Division of the Population and Human Resources Department, World Bank. Mimeo.

_____. 1987. Schooling in Developing Countries: Which Countries are the Under- and Overachievers and What is the Schooling Impact? *Economics of Education Review* 6(2): 111–28.

Behrman, Jere R., and Nancy Birdsall. 1988a. Implicit Equity-Productivity Tradeoffs in the Distribution of Public School Resources in Brazil. *European Economic Review* 32.

_____. 1988b. The Reward for Good Timing: Cohort Effects and Earnings Functions for Brazilian Males. *Review of Economics and Statistics* 70(1) (February): 129–35.

_____. 1987. Communication on Returns to Education: A Further Update and Implications. *Journal of Human Resources* 22(4) (Fall): 603–06.

_____. 1985. The Quality of Schooling: Reply. *American Economic Review* 75: 1202–05.

_____. 1983. The Quality of Schooling: Quantity Alone is Misleading. *American Economic Review* 73 (December): 928–46.

Birdsall, Nancy. 1985. Public Inputs and Child Schooling in Brazil. *Journal of Development Economics* 18(1) (May–June): 67–86.

Birdsall, Nancy, and Jere R. Behrman. 1984. Does Geographical Aggregation Cause Overestimates of the Returns to Schooling? *Oxford Bulletin of Economics and Statistics* 46: 55–72.

Birdsall, Nancy, and Richard H. Sabot. 1995. Virtuous Circles: Human Capital, Growth and Equity in East Asia. Williams College, Williamstown, MA. Mimeo.

Card, David, and Alan B. Krueger. 1992. School Quality and Black-White Relative Earnings: A Direct Assessment. *Quarterly Journal of Economics* 107(1) (February): 151–200.

Carnoy, Martin. 1974. Distribuição da Renda e Desenvolvimento Econômico: Um Comentário. *Revista de Administração de Empresas* 14(4) (July/August): 86–93.

Colclough, C. 1982. The Impact of Primary Schooling on Economic Development: A Review of the Evidence. *World Development* 10: 167–85.

Eaton, Peter J. 1985. The Quality of Schooling: Comment. *American Economic Review* 75(2) (December): 1195–201.

Eisemon, Thomas Owen. 1988. The Consequences of Schooling: A Review on Research on the Outcomes of Primary Schooling in Developing Countries. Harvard University, Cambridge, MA. Mimeo.

Fields, Gary S. 1975. A Reexamination of Brazilian Economic Development in the 1960s. Yale University, New Haven, CT. Mimeo.

Fishlow, Albert. 1972. Brazilian Size Distribution of Income. *American Economic Review* (May).

Fuller, Bruce. 1986. *Raising School Quality in Developing Countries: What Investments Boost Learning?* Washington, D.C.: World Bank.

Glewwe, Paul. 1992. *Are Rates of Return to Schooling Estimated from Wage Data Relevant Guides for Government Investments in Education? Evidence from a Developing Country.* LSMS Working Paper No. 76. World Bank, Washington, D.C.

_____. 1990. Schooling, Skills and the Returns to Education: An Econometric Exploration Using Data from Ghana. World Bank, Washington, D.C. Mimeo.

Glewwe, Paul, and Hanan Jacoby. 1991. Student Achievement and Schooling Choice: Results from Ghana. World Bank, Washington, D.C. Mimeo.

Hanushek, Eric A. 1989. The Impact of Differential Expenditures on School Performance. *Educational Researcher* (May): 45–62.

Hanushek, Eric A., João Batista Gomes-Neto, and Ralph W. Harbison. 1992. Self-financing Educational Investments: The Quality Imperative in Developing Countries. University of Rochester, NY. Mimeo.

Hanushek, Eric A., and Victor Lavy. 1992. Dropping Out of School: The Role of Opportunities and School Quality. University of Rochester, Rochester, NY. Mimeo.

Harbison, Ralph W., and Eric A. Hanushek. 1992. *Educational Performance of the Poor: Lessons from Rural Northeast Brazil.* New York: Oxford University Press for the World Bank.

Heyneman, Stephen P., and William Loxley. 1983. The Effect of Primary-School Quality on Academic Achievement Across Twenty-Nine High-and Low-Income Countries. *American Journal of Sociology* 88 (May): 1162–94.

Inter-American Development Bank. 1993. *Economic and Social Progress in Latin America: 1993 Report.* Washington, D.C.: Inter-American Development Bank.

Jallade, Jean-Pierre. 1977. Basic *Education and Income Inequality in Brazil: The Long-Term View.* Staff Working Paper No. 268. World Bank, Washington, D.C.

King, Elizabeth M. 1990a. *Does Education Pay in the Labor Market? Women's Labor Force Participation, Occupation, and Earnings in Peru.* LSMS Working Paper No. 67. World Bank, Washington, D.C.

_____. 1990b. *Educating Girls and Women: Investing in Development.* Washington, D.C.: World Bank.

King, Elizabeth M., and M. Anne Hill (eds). 1993. *Women's Education in Developing Countries: Barriers, Benefits, and Policies.* Baltimore and London: The Johns Hopkins University Press for the World Bank.

Langoni, Carlos Geraldo. 1973. *Distribuição de Renda e Desenvolvimento Econômico do Brasil.* Rio de Janeiro: Editora Expressão e Cultura.

Lockheed, Marlaine E., and Eric Hanushek. 1988. Improving Educational Efficiency in Developing Countries: What Do We Know? *Compare* 18(1): 21–38.

Loxley, William, and Stephen Heyneman. 1980. The Influence of School Resources on Learning Outcomes in El Salvador. World Bank, Washington, D.C. Mimeo.

Lucas, Robert E. 1988. On the Mechanics of Economic Development. *Journal of Monetary Economics* 21: 3–42.

Mincer, J.B. 1974. *Schooling, Experience, and Earnings.* New York: Nations Bureau for Economic Research.

Morley, Samuel A. 1976. Changes in Employment and the Distribution of Income During the Brazilian Miracle. ILO, Geneva. Mimeo.

Novos, Ian. 1990. Learning by Doing, Adverse Selection, and Firm Structure. University of Southern California, Los Angeles. Mimeo.

Psacharopoulos, G. 1988. Education and Development: A Review. *The World Bank Research Observer* 3(1) (January): 99–116.

_____. 1985. Returns to Education: A Further International Update and Implications. *Journal of Human Resources* 20: 583–97.

Psacharopoulos, George, Samuel Morley, Ariel Fiszbein, Haeduck Lee, and Bill Wood. 1992. *Poverty and Income Distribution in Latin America: The Story of the 1980s.* Washington, D.C.: World Bank.

Romer, Paul M. 1986. Increasing Returns and Long-Run Growth. *Journal of Political Economy* 94(5): 1002–36.

Schultz, T. Paul. 1993. Returns to Women's Education. In *Women's Education in Developing Countries: Barriers, Benefits, and Policies,* eds. Elizabeth M. King and M. Anne Hill. Baltimore and London: The Johns Hopkins University Press for the World Bank.

_____. 1988. Education Investments and Returns. In *Handbook of Development Economics,* eds. Hollis Chenery and T.N. Srinivasan. Amsterdam: North-Holland Publishing.

United Nations Development Programme (UNDP). 1990. *Human Development Report 1990.* New York: UNDP.

World Bank. 1980, 1981, 1990, 1991, 1993. *World Development Report, 1993.* Oxford: Oxford University Press for the World Bank.

Educational Expansion and the Inequality of Pay in Brazil and Korea

Young-Bum Park, David R. Ross and Richard H. Sabot

Educational policy in Brazil has resulted in levels of educational attainment that are lower than those achieved by other middle-income countries. For example, Brazil lies well below the line that describes the cross-country relationship between per capita income and the secondary enrollment ratio. By contrast, the Republic of Korea, which has similar per capita income, lies well above the line (Knight and Sabot, 1990). To what extent does the relatively smaller stock of human capital in Brazil contribute to greater inequality in the distribution of income? This chapter applies a method successfully used in other countries to Brazilian and Korean data in order to examine the distributional consequences of educational expansion.[1]

It long has been assumed that rapid economic growth, at least in its early phase, will be associated with high levels of inequality. Two explanations are given. First, to generate the high aggregate savings rate that is a prerequisite of rapid growth, the presumption is that income must be concentrated in the hands of the relatively rich, whose marginal propensities to save are greater than those with relatively low incomes. Second, Kuznets (1955) showed that as the labor force gradually shifts from a low-productivity, low-income sector to a high-productivity, high-income sector, aggregate inequality initially increases substantially and only later decreases.

The East Asian experience casts doubt on the tradeoff between augmenting growth and reducing inequality. Table 9.1 compares Asian and Latin American countries with respect to economic growth over the period 1960–81 and a crude measure of the distribution of income. On average, the Asian countries have grown faster and had a substantially more equal distribution of income. When the Asian countries are disaggregated into fast and slow growing groups, the distribution of income is, again, substantially more equal in the fast growing group. Brazil and Korea fit the general pat-

---

[1] See Knight and Sabot (1983) for East Africa; Mohan and Sabot (1988) for Colombia.

Table 9.1. Inequality, Education Enrollment Rates and Growth
(Percent)

Country	GNP per capita growth, per annum		Income Share of:		Ratio of top to bottom	Enrollment Rates					
						Primary		Secondary		Tertiary	
	1960–81	1965–85	Bottom 20%	Top 10%		1965	1985	1965	1985	1965	1985
ASIA											
Fast growers:											
Korea (1975)	6.9	6.8	5.7	45.3	9.95	101	95	35	94	6	32
Hong Kong (1980)	6.9	6.3	5.4	31.3	5.79	103	105	29	69	5	13
Japan (1979)	6.3	4.3	8.7	22.4	2.57	100	102	88	96	13	30
Taiwan (1975)	6.6	NA	9.5	36.0	3.68						
Unweighted average	6.7	6.0	7.3	33.5	4.59	101.3	101	48.7	85.3	8	15
Slower growers:											
Indonesia (1987)	4.1	4.3	8.8	26.5	3.01	72	118	12	39	1	7
Philippines (1985)	2.8	1.6	5.5	32.1	5.84	113	106	41	65	19	38
Thailand (1975–76)	4.6	4.0	5.6	49.8	8.89	78	97	14	30	2	20
Malaysia (1987)	4.3	4.0	4.6	34.8	7.57	90	99	28	53	2	6
Unweighted average	4.0	3.5	6.1	35.8	5.87	88.3	105	23.8	45.8	6	17.8
LATIN AMERICA											
El Salvador (1976–77)	1.5	-0.5	5.5	47.3	8.60	82	70	17	24	2	14
Peru (1985)	1.0	0.1	4.4	35.8	8.14	99	122	25	65	8	24
Costa Rica (1986)	3.0	1.4	3.3	38.8	11.76	106	101	24	41	6	23
Brazil (1983)	5.1	3.6	2.4	46.2	19.25	108	104	16	35	2	11
Mexico (1977)	3.8	2.3	2.9	57.7	19.90	92	115	17	55	4	16
Panama (1973)	3.1	2.2	2.0	61.8	30.90	102	105	34	59	7	26
Argentina (1970)	1.9	0.0	4.4	50.3	11.43	101	108	28	70	14	36
Venezuela (1987)	2.4	-0.9	4.7	34.2	7.28	94	108	27	45	7	26
Unweighted average	2.7	1.0	3.7	46.5	12.57	98	104.1	23.5	49.3	6.3	22

Source: World Development Reports.

tern. While Brazil was the fastest growing country in Latin America, its growth rate lagged behind that of Korea, where inequality is markedly lower. As the table indicates, the ratio of the income share of the top 20 percent to the bottom 20 percent is 9.95 in Korea and 19.25 in Brazil.

Differences in the stock of human capital may contribute to the explanation of this association between high growth and low inequality: educational expansion, by making human capital more abundant, has been shown to enhance economic growth and reduce inequality. As Fishlow (1972, p. 395) said in his seminal piece on Brazilian income distribution:

> "Past illiteracy and present poverty are strongly associated. But so are present poverty, future illiteracy, and probably future poverty. For this reason, the tradeoff between redistribution and growth is generally exaggerated. There are possibilities of achieving both simultaneously by improved quality of human resources."

Table 9.1 also presents primary, secondary and tertiary enrollment rates for Asia and Latin America.[2] With the exception of El Salvador, all of the countries appear to have achieved universal primary education.[3] Nor is there much difference among the fast growing Asian countries, the slow growing Asian countries and the Latin American countries at the tertiary level. There are, however, marked differences at the secondary level. In 1965 nearly half of the children in the relevant age group attended secondary school in the rapidly growing Asian economies, while in the slow growing Asian economies and in Latin America less than a quarter were in attendance. Though secondary enrollment rates increased substantially in all of the countries over the two decades, in 1985 the gap between the rapidly growing Asian economies and the others had actually widened.

A comparison of enrollment rates in Brazil and Korea corroborates the general picture, but reveals more striking differences at the secondary and tertiary levels. Between 1965 and 1985 the secondary enrollment rate increased from 16 to 35 percent in Brazil and from 35 to 94 percent in Korea. The tertiary enrollment rate was low in both countries in 1965 (2 and 6 percent for Brazil and Korea, respectively). In 1985 it rose to 32 percent in Korea but only to 11 percent in Brazil. The gaps have widened.

---

[2] Enrollment rates are total enrollments over the population in the standard age group for that level of education. Since children outside that age group sometimes are in attendance, calculated enrollment rates can exceed 100 percent.

[3] The appearance of universal primary education may be at odds with the reality. Gross enrollment rates are inflated by high repetition rates at the primary level.

Conceptual Framework

The impact of human capital accumulation on inequality is theoretically ambiguous. Educational expansion results in a change in the educational composition of the labor force. The growth of the educated, relatively high productivity portion of the labor force can have an effect on the inequality of pay similar to that described by Kuznets. Whether the change in the educational composition of the labor force raises or lowers inequality, ceteris paribus, depends on the relative sizes of the different educational categories, their relative mean wages, and their relative wage dispersions.

In a two-group model, a transfer of workers from the low to high education (and wage) group raises the variance (or log variance) until the high education group reaches a certain proportion of the total. The precise proportion depends on differences in the means and variances of the two groups.

Let μ_j be mean earnings for workers in the jth group—j = 1 (educated) or 2 (uneducated), p_j be the proportion of workers, σ_j be the variance of earnings, and σ be the variance of earnings in the population. Robinson (1976, p. 438) has shown that inequality (as measured by σ) rises to a maximum where p_1 is equal to p_1^*:

(1) $p_1^* = (\sigma_1^2 - \sigma_2^2)/2(\mu_1 - \mu_2) + \frac{1}{2}.$

This implies that p_1^* will be greater than, less than, or equal to $\frac{1}{2}$ as σ_1^2 is greater than, less than, or equal to σ_2^2. If the variance of wages of the educated group exceeds that of the uneducated ($\sigma_1^2 > \sigma_2^2$), the variance of wages in the aggregate reaches a peak after more than one-half the labor force has become educated. The condition $\sigma_1^2 > \sigma_2^2$ also implies that p_1^* is larger the smaller the difference in mean wages, that is, inequality peaks later in the process of educational expansion the lower is the premium on education. However, if the variance is higher for the uneducated group, this result is reversed.

This was the basis of Kuznets' hypothesis: the transfer of people between sectors at different income levels initially raises inequality as more people acquire high income, but eventually lowers it as fewer low-income people remain; if the expanding sector has more inequality, the peaking of aggregate inequality is delayed.

Kuznets concentrated on the "composition effect" and did not incorporate any resulting changes in the structure of wages. Indeed, he suggested that urban-rural income differentials (with which he was concerned) were likely to increase with economic development. However, with regard to educational expansion there is a tendency for the educational structure of wages to be compressed. From the competitive market prediction that the returns to a factor decrease as its relative supply increases, we expect the coefficient on education in an earnings function to decline as education expands relative to other factors. That is, we expect the premium on education to fall as supply increases relative to demand. The narrowing of the educational structure of wages should, ceteris paribus, reduce inequality. For Robinson's example, this result can be formalized by differentiation of the identity

(2) $\sigma^2 = p_1\sigma_1^2 + (1 - p_1)\sigma_2^2 + p_1(1 - p_1)(\mu_1 - \mu_2)^2$ to derive:

(3) $\partial\sigma^2/\partial p_1 = (\sigma_1^2 - \sigma_2^2) + (1-2p_1)(\mu_1-\mu_2)^2 + 2p_1(1-p_1)(\mu_1 - \mu_2)(\partial\mu_1/\partial p_1 - \partial\mu_2/\partial p_1).$

The third term captures the effect of educational expansion on the wage structure. Since we expect $\partial\mu_1/\partial p_1 < 0$ and $\partial\mu_2/\partial p_1 > 0$, this term will be negative.[4] The effect of educational expansion on inequality is therefore the net outcome of two potentially countervailing tendencies, and no a priori prediction can be made about its sign.

Whether the composition effect or the wage structure effect dominates is, therefore, an empirical matter. The compression effect of educational expansion on the wage structure was shown to outweigh the disequalizing consequences of the composition effect by Knight and Sabot (1983) in East Africa and by Mohan and Sabot (1988) in Colombia. In both settings the net effect of educational expansion was to reduce the inequality of pay markedly.

Our aim in this study, then, is to compare Brazil and Korea with respect to the influence of educational expansion on the structure of earnings and the inequality of pay. Has the markedly greater abundance in Korea than in Brazil of workers with secondary (and tertiary) education resulted in substantially more compression of the structure of wages and a greater reduction of the inequality of pay? For the 1960s, Morley (1982) found evidence of a substantially disequalizing composition effect. Can it be that in Brazil educational policy actually contributed to an increase in the inequality of pay? Because of the small initial stock of educated workers, the relatively slow pace of educational expansion and the rapid growth of demand for educated labor, the educational structure of wages in Brazil may have widened. In this case, the initial tendency for the composition effect to increase inequality would be reinforced by the increase in scarcity rents reaped by more educated workers.[5]

---

[4] If the demand for educated workers rises faster than the supply, then the wage premium to the educated will not fall and the sign of the third term will be ambiguous.

[5] Morley (1982) contends that in Brazil in the 1960s increases in the relative demand for educated workers exceeded increases in relative supply.

Methods and Data

To measure the effect of educational expansion on the inequality of pay,[6] and the relative contributions of the compression and wage structure effects, we begin by estimating a standard earnings function

(4) $Y = X\beta + \epsilon,$

where Y = the natural logarithm of individual earnings and X may be decomposed into a matrix of dummy variables representing different educational categories (E) and a matrix of other explanatory variables (Z), such as experience and controls for region, occupation, and industry, measured as deviations from the mean. The variance of Y (S_Y^2, the log variance of wages) is the sum of the variance predicted by the regression S_P^2 and the variance of the residuals S_e^2, where, if k is the number of parameters estimated,

$S_P^2 = [\beta'(X'X)\beta - Y'Y]/(N-1),$ and

$S_e^2 = [Y'Y - \beta'X'Y]/(N-k).$

The moment matrix consists of four submatrices:

$$X'X = \begin{matrix} E'E & E'Z \\ Z'E & Z'Z \end{matrix}$$

To simulate the composition effect of expanding educational attainment from some base year (B) to the comparison year (C), we replace $E_B'E_B$ with $E_C'E_C$, weighted by $(N_B/N_C)^2$ to control for the different number of observations in the two samples;[7] and adjust $Y'Y$ to reflect the change in predicted wages. To simulate the wage structure effect we replace those base year coefficients related to education with the corresponding comparison year coefficients. By combining the two effects in a single simulation and comparing the resulting measure with the level of inequality observed in the comparison year, we are able to estimate that portion of the change in inequality between the base and comparison years attributable to educational expansion.

---

[6] The simulation approach presented here follows that presented in Behrman, Knight and Sabot (1983).

[7] One has to make an assumption about how E'Z would have changed between B and C holding Z constant. Here we assume no change, i.e., we use $E_B'Z_B$. Knight and Sabot (1983) and Mohan and Sabot (1988) rebuild E'Z on the assumption that observations on Z associated with educational category j be given the comparison year sample weight. Alternatively, one could use the suitably weighted $E_C'Z_C$ matrix. The results reported below are qualitatively insensitive to this assumption.

The Korean data are taken from the Occupational Wage Survey (OWS) conducted by Korea's Ministry of Labor in 1976 and 1986. The OWS covers a stratified random sample of establishments with 10 or more regular workers. Workers in government, public education and most establishments in agriculture, forestry and fishing are excluded. The wage variable used is monthly earnings (including overtime payments) plus one-twelfth of the annual bonus.[8]

The Brazilian data come from the household survey (the *Pesquisa Nacional por Amostra de Domicílios—PNAD*) conducted by the Instituto Brasileiro de Geografia e Estatística (IBGE) in 1976 and 1985. The survey covers some 100,000 households using a stratified sample selected according to standard procedures and based on the decennial censuses. Weights were provided by the IBGE to correct for variation in sampling ratios across geographical areas. The PNAD data do not include the rural areas of the North, but are otherwise consistent with the coverage of the decennial censuses. The sample used in this study includes individuals who were 10 years old and older at the time of the survey, reported positive earnings, and were classified as employees by the IBGE.[9]

Results

Turning first to Korea, the two samples in Table 9.2 show marked increases in the educational attainment of the wage labor force, reflecting the rapid increases in post-primary enrollment ratios seen in Table 9.1. The proportion of high school graduates in the wage labor force increased from 32.2 to 43.5 percent, while the proportion of workers with post-secondary education increased at nearly the same rate, from 17.7 percent to 23.6 percent. By 1986, the proportion of workers with elementary school or less had declined from 19.6 to only 7.5 percent.

Returns to the more educated are expected to decrease if their supply increases (relative to the supply of less educated workers) faster than relative

---

[8] The parameter estimates reported below are not sensitive to the inclusion of overtime and bonuses in the dependent variable.

[9] The results reported in the text do not differ qualitatively from those estimated on broader and narrower samples of workers. The first expands the sample to include self-employed workers. The second includes only employees with signed work cards. Holding a work card is an indication of a formal employment relationship, entitling employees to a variety of government-legislated benefits (even if not followed in practice). Work card status is also associated with larger firms.

Table 9.2. Educational Composition of the Male Wage Labor Force
(Percent)

	Brazil			Korea	
	1976	1985		1976	1986
Uneducated	25.6	20.5	Elementary & Below	19.6	7.5
Primary (Lower)	45.5	40.8	Middle	30.5	25.4
Primary (Upper)	17.8	21.6	High School	32.2	43.5
Secondary	6.7	11.1	Junior College	2.6	4.8
University	4.4	6.0	University	15.1	18.8

demand. This raises the possibility that the increase in relative supply has been offset in its effect on the educational structure of wages by an increase in the skill intensity of labor demand. Table 9.3 contains a (crude) occupational composition of the labor force (in total and by level of education) for 1976 and 1986. The decline in the proportion of workers employed as laborers suggests an increase in the skill intensity of labor demand, but the change appears to be slight.[10] The table also shows substantial filtering down over time of workers with middle and higher education into lower level occupations. For example, the proportion of high school dropouts working as laborers increased from 53 to 60.5 percent. Similarly, the proportion of junior college and university dropouts in clerical, sales and service occupations rose from 35.7 to 44.8 percent. This movement into lower level occupations by the more educated, when combined with little movement among the least educated, is suggestive of a compression in the educational structure of wages, i.e., the increase in supply has exceeded the increase in demand.

To measure the extent of this compression, we estimate equation (4) for Korea, where E is a matrix of dummy variables signifying levels of educational attainment, with primary education as the base;[11] Z is a matrix of other explanatory variables comprised of experience and experience squared (Exp, Exp^2), and dummy variables controlling for region, occupation and industry. We would expect the educational structure of wages to change so that the coefficients for the top two educational categories would be lower in the equation estimated for 1986 than for 1976.

---

[10] The crude level of aggregation precludes precision in the assessment of the change in skill intensity. There may have been, for example, an increase in the skills required within the laborer category.

[11] E_{K1} = middle school; E_{K2} = high school; E_{K3} = junior college and university.

**Table 9.3. Occupational Composition of the Male Wage Labor Force
by Level of Education, Korea, 1976 and 1986**
(Percent)

	Elementary		Middle		High School		Junior Col. & University		Total	
	1976	1986	1976	1986	1976	1986	1976	1986	1976	1986
Prof. & Admin.	1.4	0.9	2.9	1.3	13.2	10.2	58.1	51.7	15.7	16.9
Clerical, Sales & Service	11.0	9.8	10.8	9.2	33.8	29.3	35.7	44.8	26.0	26.3
Laborer	87.7	89.4	86.3	89.6	53.0	60.5	6.2	3.5	61.6	56.8

**Educational Composition of the Male Wage Labor Force
by Occupation**

	Elementary		Middle		High School		Junior Col. & University	
	1976	1986	1976	1986	1976	1986	1976	1986
Prof. & Admin.	1.7	0.4	5.6	2.0	27.1	26.3	65.5	72.2
Clerical, Sales & Service	6.0	2.8	9.2	8.9	30.5	48.5	54.4	40.2
Laborer	27.9	11.8	42.7	40.1	27.7	46.3	1.8	1.5

The right hand side of Table 9.4 presents the estimated equations excluding the conditioning dummy variables. The change in the constant reflects the increase in mean nominal wages over the 10-year period. Predicted nominal wages at the sample means have risen for each education group. However, the premium earned by workers with a high school education declined by more than one-third (from .47 to .30) between 1976 and 1986. Similarly, the premium earned by workers with post-secondary education declined by more than one-fourth. As predicted, the increase in the relative supply of high school and university graduates was associated with a compression in the educational structure of wages.

The mean wages of workers with post-middle school education are in the top half of the distribution of pay; the mean wages of workers with primary education are in the bottom half. The compression of the educational structure of wages should, therefore, contribute to a reduction in

Table 9.4. Male Wage Structure, Brazil and Korea, 1976 and 1986

	Brazil			Korea	
	1976	1985		1976	1986
E_{B1}	0.488	0.449	E_{K1}	0.176	0.092
	(55.68)	(67.23)		(19.66)	(7.54)
E_{B2}	0.958	0.886	E_{K2}	0.473	0.296
	(85.70)	(110.53)		(48.19)	(23.40)
E_{B3}	1.593	1.508	E_{K3}	0.969	0.655
	(100.22)	(127.40)		(71.48)	(42.06)
Exp	0.045	0.048	Exp	0.067	0.078
	(64.97)	(83.91)		(61.90)	(69.61)
Exp^2	−0.0006	−0.0007	Exp^2	−0.001	−0.001
	(61.41)	(79.27)		(39.13)	(50.27)
Constant	1.149	7.043	Constant	10.231	11.779
$\bar{R}^2$	.546	.562	$\bar{R}^2$	.532	0.449
N	85,106	118,000		23,838	24,486
Mean ln W	1.864	8.095		11.363	12.895

Note: Dummy variables were included to control for region, occupation, industry, head of household (Brazil only); t-statistics appear in parentheses.

the inequality of pay. The right hand side of Table 9.5 and the accompanying Figure 9.1 present the results of our simulations. We estimate the inequality of pay in 1976, as proxied by the log variance of earnings, to be 0.442. Had Korea in 1976 exhibited the educational wage structure observed in 1986, the log variance of pay, at .333, would have been 25 percent lower. As predicted, the increase in the relative supply of workers with education at the high school level and beyond not only compressed the educational structure of wages, but exercised an equalizing influence on the distribution of wages. By contrast, had Korea in 1976 exhibited the educational composition of the wage labor force observed in 1986, the log variance of pay would have been, at .471, only 6.6 percent higher.

When we combine these two effects by simulating for Korea in 1976 both the educational structure of wages and the educational composition of the labor force in 1986, we find a net effect that is strongly equalizing. Had Korea in 1976 achieved the educational attainment of the labor force observed in 1986, the log variance of pay would have been, at .346, 22 percent lower. Thus, the wage structure effect (WS in the figure) dominates the composition effect (CP) to produce an equalizing combined effect (CB). In aggregate, the log variance of pay declined over the subsequent decade by a

Table 9.5. Log Variances of Pay: Intertemporal Simulations

Brazil	(1)	(2)	Korea	(1)	(2)
1976	.518	.950	1976	.235	.442
Wage structure effect	.499	.931	Wage structure effect	.126	.333
Composition effect	.596	1.027	Composition effect	.641	.471
Combined effect	.568	.991	Combined effect	.139	.346
1985	.576	1.024	1986	.152	.338

Notes: (1) Explained variance of ℓn W; (2) Explained + unexplained variance of ℓn W.

Figure 9.1. Educational Expansion and Inequality: Intertemporal Simulations

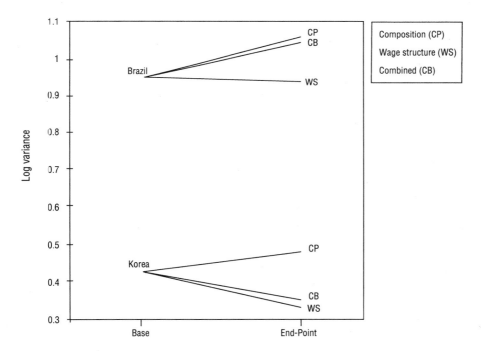

total of 24 percent to .338 in 1986. Our simulations, therefore, imply that the labor market consequences of educational expansion accounted for over 90 percent of the marked improvement in the distribution of wages that occurred over the decade.

The story in Brazil is markedly different. Table 9.2 indicates that the educational attainment of the labor force is much lower in Brazil than in

Korea. In 1985, only 17 percent of the Brazilian labor force had secondary or higher education, as compared to 67 percent of the Korean sample. Correspondingly, 61 percent of the Brazilian labor force was either uneducated or had lower primary schooling as compared to only 7 percent of the Korean sample. Between 1976 and 1985 the rise in the share of secondary and university graduates in the labor force was actually more rapid in Brazil than in Korea, but the increase was from a very small base. Hence the absolute increment to the labor force of relatively well-educated workers was quite small in Brazil. It would not take much of an increase in the skill intensity of labor demand to offset the tendency for an increase in the supply of educated labor to result in a compression in the educational structure of wages.

In Brazil, the occupational composition of the labor force did not change much between 1976 and 1985 (see the top half of Table 9.6). This contrasts with the slight shift toward more skill intensive occupations shown in Table 9.3 for Korea. Despite this, the skill intensity of labor demand appears to have increased more in Brazil because intraoccupational increases in the skill (education) intensity of labor demand were substantially greater than in Korea. In both countries, workers with secondary education filtered down from white collar to manual occupations and university graduates filtered down from professional to clerical occupations. For example, in Korea the proportion of secondary school graduates in white collar occupations declined from 47 percent to 40 percent; in Brazil the decline was from 86 percent to 78 percent.

What happened to primary school graduates is what distinguishes the two countries. In Korea in 1976, 88 percent of primary school graduates were confined to jobs as laborers whereas in that year in Brazil more than half of the workers with five to eight years of schooling were in white collar occupations. In Korea between 1976 and 1985 there was human capital deepening in lower level occupations as the more educated filtered into them. There was not, however, much increase in educational attainment in white collar occupations. By contrast, in Brazil there was a marked increase in educational attainment in high as well as low level occupations as the less educated were squeezed out of high level occupations. In professional technical and administrative occupations there was a 23 percent increase in Brazil in the proportion of workers with secondary or more education as compared to a 6 percent increase in Korea. In clerical, sales and service occupations in Korea there was only a 4.5 percent increase in the proportion with secondary or more education, whereas in Brazil there was a 52 percent increase.

In sum, there is substantial filtering down of the more educated in both Korea and Brazil. In Korea, this results in a compression of the educa-

Table 9.6. Occupational Composition of the Male Wage Labor Force by Level of Education, Brazil, 1976 and 1985
(Percent)

	Primary (Lower)		Primary (Upper)		Secondary		University		Total	
	1976	1985	1976	1985	1976	1985	1976	1985	1976	1985
Prof. & Admin.	8.0	5.3	17.3	11.8	37.8	29.6	77.5	68.8	20.9	19.1
Clerical, Sales & Service	27.5	24.7	41.3	36.6	47.9	48.5	20.6	26.5	33.6	33.2
Laborer	64.5	70.0	41.4	51.6	14.3	22.0	1.9	4.6	45.5	47.7

Educational Composition of the Male Wage Labor Force by Occupation

	Primary (Lower)		Primary (Upper)		Secondary		University	
	1976	1985	1976	1985	1976	1985	1976	1985
Prof. & Admin.	18.7	10.6	24.1	19.0	23.9	29.9	33.2	40.5
Clerical, Sales & Service	39.8	28.6	35.8	34.2	18.9	28.2	5.5	9.0
Laborer	68.9	56.5	26.5	33.5	4.2	8.9	0.4	1.1

tional structure of wages because the less educated are not filtering down. In Brazil, the less educated are filtering down as rapidly as the more educated. Hence, the wage structure is not likely to be compressed as much; i.e., we expect the increase in the skill intensity of labor demand to offset the compressive impact on the educational structure of wages of the increase in the relative supply of workers with post-primary education.

We estimate human capital earnings functions for Brazil analogous to those for Korea. Again, E is a matrix of dummy variables signifying levels of education, but in this case the uneducated and those with lower primary are the omitted category.[12] The other explanatory variables are the same as for Korea, except for the inclusion of a head-of-household dummy. The left hand side of Table 9.4 presents the estimated equations, excluding the

---

[12] E_{B1} = primary (upper); E_{B2} = secondary; E_{B3} = university.

conditioning dummy variables. A comparison of the 1976 and 1985 regressions indicates that the educational structure of wages has barely changed in Brazil despite the rapid rise in the supply of workers with secondary and university education. The growth in relative demand has been sufficient to maintain the scarcity rents earned by the educated. For example, the premium earned by university dropouts was 1.59 in 1976 and 1.51 in 1985, a decline of only five percent.[13]

Although the educational categories and the sample selection criteria are not precisely the same, a comparison of the Korea and Brazil regressions is nevertheless revealing. In 1976, the premium earned by Brazilian university dropouts relative to secondary leavers was .63 (1.59–0.96); while in Korea the premium earned by university dropouts relative to high school graduates was .50 (.97–.47). Because educational expansion compressed the educational structure of wages in Korea, but not in Brazil, over the ensuing decade, the gap in premia increased. The corresponding premia in the mid-1980s were .62 and .36.

The scarcity of educated workers, and the higher premia they earn in Brazil, suggests that the inequality of pay will be greater in Brazil than in Korea. Column (2) of Table 9.5 shows that the 1976 log variance of wages in Brazil was, at .95, more than twice the level in Korea. Moreover, our simulations indicate that, in contrast to Korea, in Brazil educational expansion resulted in no significant wage structure effect on inequality. Had Brazil in 1976 exhibited the 1985 educational wage structure, the log variance of pay, at .93, would have been only two percent lower (in contrast to the 25 percent reduction that resulted when the comparable simulation was run for Korea).

The impact of changes in educational composition, however, was substantial. Had Brazil in 1976 exhibited the educational composition of the wage labor force observed in 1985, the log variance of pay, at 1.03, would have been 8.1 percent higher. In the absence of a countervailing wage structure effect, we would expect the composition effect of educational expansion in Brazil between 1976 and 1985 to increase the inequality in pay. Indeed, when we combine the wage structure and composition effects, our simulations indicate that between 1976 and 1985 there was a small *increase* in the log variance of pay (a 4.3 percent increase to .991 in contrast to the 22 percent decline in log variance observed when the comparable simulation was run

---

[13] This aggregate wage equation may paint too gloomy a picture. Using data overlapping ours, Lam and Levison (1991) report that wage premia for the educated are lower for the youngest cohorts. Our results suggest that this trend has not yet had substantive impact on the aggregate wage distribution. We note in the concluding section evidence that any reduction in wage premia may have been temporary.

for Korea). Over this period, in aggregate, the log variance of pay in Brazil rose by 7.4 percent (in contrast to the 24 percent *drop* in log variance experienced by Korea). Thus, more than one-half of this increase in the log variance of pay can be attributed to the increase associated with educational policy.

What would the inequality of pay in Brazil have been in 1985 had educational policy resulted in educational attainment comparable to that observed in Korea in 1986? To answer this question, we conducted cross-country simulations comparable to our intertemporal simulations.[14] To simulate the composition effect of expanding educational attainment from the Brazilian 1985 level (B) to the Korean 1986 level (K), we replace $E_B'E_B$ with $E_K'E_K$, weighted by $(N_B/N_K)^2$ to control for the different number of observations in the two samples; and adjust $Y'Y$ to reflect the change in predicted wages. To simulate the wage structure effect we replace those Brazilian coefficients related to education with the corresponding Korean education coefficients. By combining the two effects in a single simulation and comparing the resulting measure with the level of inequality in Brazil for 1985, we are able to assess the impact on inequality of more rapid educational expansion in Brazil.

Table 9.7 and Figure 9.2 present the results. Holding the educational composition of the wage labor force constant, had Brazil in 1985 exhibited the educational wage structure observed in Korea in 1986, the Brazilian log variance of pay, at .75, would have been 23.3 percent lower. By contrast, had Brazil achieved the educational composition of the wage labor force observed in Korea in 1986 without any change in the educational wage structure, the log variance of pay, at 1.35, would have been 38.1 percent higher. Combining the two effects yields a decline in inequality in Brazil. According to our simulations, the net effect of Brazil having adopted the Korean educational policy regime would have been a log variance of pay of .812, some 17 percent lower than the log variance actually observed. This 17 percent difference represents over one-fourth of the gap in the log variance of pay between Brazil (at .979, from Table 9.7) and Korea (at .338, from Table 9.5).

For Brazil to move quickly to the educational composition of the wage labor force observed in Korea in 1986 is not feasible. This suggests a more realistic counterfactual: What would the inequality of pay in Brazil have been in 1985 had educational policy resulted in educational attainment comparable to that observed in Korea in 1976? The answer is provided in

---

[14] For the cross-country simulations, we recategorize the Brazilian data to correspond to the Korean educational categories and reestimate equation 4. The data do not permit us to recategorize the Korean data to correspond with the Brazilian categories.

Table 9.7. Log Variances of Pay: Cross-Country Simulations

	Korea 1986	Korea 1976
Wage structure effect	.751	.804
Composition effect	1.352	1.257
Combined effect	.812	.904
	Brazil 1985	
	.979	

Note: Explained and unexplained log variance.

Figure 9.2. Educational Expansion and Inequality: Brazil, 1985 vs. Korea, 1976 and 1986

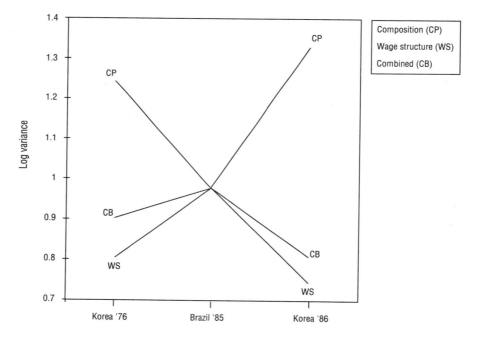

the second column of Table 9.7 and the left-hand side of Figure 9.2. As expected, because the difference in educational attainment is smaller, both the wage structure and composition effects are more muted when we substitute 1976, rather than 1986, Korean values for the 1985 Brazilian values. The net effect is still strongly equalizing. Had Brazil in 1985 achieved the level of educational attainment exhibited by Korea in 1976, the log variance of pay in Brazil would be, at .904, eight percent lower.

Table 9.8. Log Variance of Pay in Brazil Simulating the Relative Contributions of Region and Education

	Brazil 1976	Brazil 1985
Total inequality (explained + unexplained)	.949	1.024
Eliminating regional inequality	.676	.890
Eliminating educational inequality	.649	.590

These simulations focus on closing the gap in educational attainment between Korea and Brazil, while preserving all other differences. Perhaps the most obvious of these is the impact of geography on the degree of labor market integration: Brazil, which is almost a continent in size, has a population density of 17 per square kilometer, whereas Korea, with only half a small Asian peninsula, has a population density of 424. Therefore, we would expect the contribution to inequality of regional gaps in productivity and pay to be large in Brazil and small in Korea. Is the inequality of pay in Brazil attributable to education greater or smaller than the inequality of pay attributable to regional gaps? To answer this question, we reestimate a parsimonious version of our earnings functions for 1976 and 1985, deleting from the right hand side all variables other than education, experience and region. We then simulate[15] the impact on inequality, eliminating first all variance in educational attainment, and then all variance in regional location. Table 9.8 presents the results for 1976 and 1985. In both instances, we see that eliminating educational inequality reduces total inequality by more than eliminating regional inequality. This result is similar to that obtained by Fishlow (1972) using somewhat different data and methods for 1960 in Brazil.[16] Comparing our results for Brazil in 1976 with those for Brazil in 1985 further suggests that educational inequality has over time grown in importance relative to regional inequality. The direct effect of education accounted for 32 percent or (.949–.649)/.949 of the log variance of pay in 1976; 42 percent in 1985.

---

[15] In our simulations, we eliminate the direct effect by setting $E_B'E_B$ equal to zero. We cannot control for the indirect effect of education (or region) that arises through the covariance of education with the other explanatory variables. Using a parsimonious earnings function mitigates this indirect effect by attributing to education or region some of the variance that would otherwise be attributable to occupation, sector, etc.

[16] Savedoff (1990) also finds that education contributes more to inequality than regional differences.

Conclusions

A substantial proportion of the marked difference between Korea and Brazil in inequality of pay appears to be attributable to the difference in their educational policy regime. Brazil's relatively small education system has made limited progress toward more equal income distribution.[17] Fishlow reached this conclusion on the basis of his analysis of 1960 data. Our results confirm this using more recent data and go further. They suggest that because educational expansion in Brazil during the 1970s and 80s was so slow, the labor market consequences of this expansion were, perversely, disequalizing. Increases in the skill intensity of labor demand neutralized any positive impact on the educational structure of wages of increases in the supply of educated labor. Therefore, the composition effect of educational expansion dominated the usually equalizing wage structure effect. Between 1976 and 1985, inequality of pay associated with education actually increased in Brazil.

The global recession of the early 1980s affected Brazil more severely than Korea. Could the filtering down of the less educated (see Table 9.6) that contributed to our finding of stability in the educational structure of Brazilian wages be an artifact of the recession? Barros and Ramos (1991) estimated wage functions for every year between 1976 and 1989. They concluded:

> "...the estimated relationships reveal that in Brazil the wage-education profile is convex with much larger wage gains from college than from primary education. From 1976 to 1981 there is a decrease on the degree of convexity of this relationship. The period from 1981 to 1985 is a period of stability, whereas from 1985 to 1989 there is a tendency towards a widening of the differences in gains from education by educational level, i.e., in this period the wage-education relationship became increasingly convex."

This suggests that doing our analysis with more recent data would reinforce our conclusion that the inequality of pay associated with education increased.

---

[17] The results reported above refer to inequality of pay, and not to the inequality of income. While inequality of pay was less than inequality of income (Fishlow, 1972), education is likely to have influenced the inequality of nonwage components of income. This suggests that the story told here would not be much altered by shifting the focus to the inequality of income.

From the mid-1970s to the mid-1980s, continued educational expansion in Korea resulted in further reductions in the inequality of pay, implying a widening of the gap between Korea and Brazil in the inequality of pay. Brazil has dug itself into a hole. Marginal increments to the educational system have been shown to be disequalizing. For Brazil to reap the distributional benefits of educational expansion, there will have to be nonmarginal increases in the size of the education system.

REFERENCES

Ahluwalia, M.S., N. Carter, and H. Chenery. 1979. Growth and Poverty in Developing Countries. *Journal of Development Economics* 6 (September): 299–341.

Barros, R., and Ramos, L. 1991. The Temporal Evolution of the Relationship Between Wages and Education Among Brazilian Prime-Age Males: 1976–1989. Economic Growth Center, Yale University. Mimeo.

Behrman, J.R., J. Knight, and R. Sabot. 1983. A Simulation Alternative to the Comparative R2 Approach to Decomposing Inequality. *Oxford Bulletin of Economics and Statistics* 45 (August): 307–12.

Blinder, A.S. 1974. *Toward an Economic Theory of Income Distribution.* Cambridge: MIT Press.

Bourguignon, F. 1980. The Role of Education in the Urban Labour Market During the Process of Development: The Case of Colombia. Paper presented at the Sixth World Congress of the International Economic Association, Mexico City, August.

Fishlow, A. 1972. Brazilian Size Distribution of Income. *American Economic Review* 62 (May): 391–408.

Knight, J.B., and R. Sabot. 1990. *Education, Productivity, and Inequality.* New York: Oxford University Press.

_____. 1983. Educational Expansion and the Kuznets Effect. *American Economic Review* 73 (December): 1132–36.

Kuznets, S. 1955. Economic Growth and Income Inequality. *American Economic Review* 45 (March): 1–28.

Lam, D., and D. Levison. 1991. Declining Inequality in Schooling in Brazil and Its Effects on Inequality in Earnings. *Journal of Development Economics* 37:199–226.

Mohan, R., and R. Sabot. 1988. Educational Expansion and the Inequality of Pay: Colombia 1973–1978. *Oxford Bulletin of Economics and Statistics* 50: 175–82.

Morley, S.A. 1982. *Labor Markets and Inequitable Growth.* Cambridge: Cambridge University Press.

Phelps Brown, H. 1977. *The Inequality of Pay.* Oxford: Oxford University Press.

Robinson, S. 1976. A Note on the U Hypotheses Relating Income Inequality and Economic Development. *American Economic Review* 66 (June): 437–40.

Saith, A. 1984. Development and Distribution: A Critique of the Cross Country U-Hypothesis. *Journal of Development Economics* 13: 367–82.

Savedoff, William D. 1990. Os Diferenciais Regionais de Salários no Brasil: Segmentação Versus Dinamismo da Demanda. *Pesquisa e Planejamento* 20(3): 521–56.

Williamson, J. 1988. Capital Deepening Along the Asian Pacific Rim. Paper presented at the Conference on Sources of Economic Dynamism in the Asian Pacific Region: A Human Resources Approach, Tokyo, January 8–10.

World Bank. Various years. *World Development Report.* Washington, D.C.: World Bank.

10 Social Mobility: The Role of Education in Determining Status

José Pastore and Hélio Zylberstajn

Social mobility is a central concern in the sociology of development. Its proper identification helps to clarify the dynamics and flexibility of a particular social structure. Without mobility, a society tends to be stagnant, simply reproducing its social structure ceaselessly. Mobility and, specifically, vertical mobility, reflects the number of opportunities for individuals and groups to progress from one social level to another (Boudon, 1973; Amassari, 1978).

What are the repercussions of social mobility upon the individual and society? When a person moves from an occupation of low status to one of higher status, such movement tends to be accompanied not only by various economic, educational and social benefits but also by changes in values, attitudes and cultural traits. The person and her or his descendants feel these repercussions over both the short and the long run. In these cases, upward mobility functions as a mechanism of social advancement (Featherman and Hauser, 1978).

The study of vertical mobility relates the person's present social position to that of her or his own past and the past of her or his father (Havighurst, 1957). This study attempts to identify the net effect of social inheritance, individual resources and economic opportunities in determining vertical mobility. As a result, one can reach systematic comparisons of the social structures in different periods of time (Duncan, Featherman and Duncan, 1972).

In the study of social mobility, social status is a key concept (Bills, Godfrey and Haller, 1986). In sociological literature, social status is conventionally defined as the position occupied by a person in a social hierarchy of a given system of stratification. It depends on job opportunities and achieved and ascribed individual variables (Jencks, Perman and Rainwater, 1988). In modern societies, education, occupation and income are central among these achieved criteria (Haller and Saraiva, 1990), while in more traditional societies, heritage, race and religion are important ascribed criteria

(Alwin and Thorton, 1984). This is also true of industrialized societies, although the weight of the ascribed variables tend to be smaller (Bills and Haller, 1985).

This study evaluates the role of job opportunities as well as ascribed and achieved variables, paying special attention to the net effect of education in the determination of status attainment and social mobility in Brazil (Haller and Pastore, 1970). This research uses the Silva (1984) index of social status based on education, occupation, age and income (see Appendix).

By comparing data from the 1982 and 1973 household surveys *(Pesquisa Nacional por Amostra de Domicílios—PNAD)*, this study looks to answer the following questions: (1) Is the Brazilian social structure opening up or becoming more restricted as a result of social mobility? (2) Who has risen in the social structure, and why? (3) Who has descended, and why? (4) Why have some people not moved at all? (5) What is the net effect of economic and individual factors in determining these phenomena, and in particular, what is the role of education in promoting mobility?

This essay focuses on the amount and types of mobility found in Brazil over time. The two sets of data are restricted to male heads of families who are 20–62 years of age. The analysis is carried out by region and age cohort. The regional disaggregation permits identification of the impact of labor market variables at different levels of development. The age cohort analysis provides a longitudinal view of the phenomenon through time and covers the evolution of social mobility in Brazil during much of 20th century. In this respect, we re-use the 1973 study's methodology (Pastore, 1979).

The 1973 study showed that Brazil has gone through a vast process of inter and intragenerational upward mobility during the 20th century. However, most of the population climbed only a few steps on the social ladder, while a few groups climbed several steps. As a net result, the Brazilian social pyramid was "stretched" upward, which explains the coincidence of high mobility and high inequality.

Analyzing the types of mobility, the study concluded that most of the population enjoyed "structural mobility" based on labor market transformations that have taken place between their fathers' era and the beginning of their own careers and, in particular, from the shrinkage of the agricultural market and the creation of new and better jobs in the urban zones. A smaller proportion of the population enjoyed "circular mobility" based on exchanges and substitutions among existing jobs, professional experience and educational background. Thus, although structural mobility prevailed in Brazil, circular mobility, based on individual variables, was beginning to increase (Pastore, 1979).

The 1973 study assessed the effects of five variables related to this field: father's status, initial status (status at first job), age, education and migratory status (used as a dummy variable) (Stier and Grusky, 1990). At the time, Brazilian heads of families had an average of only 3.3 years of schooling. However, education was critical in determining status: each year of school in Brazil added 1.3 points to social status while age, first job and father's status added 0.5 or less, and migration subtracted slightly from it. In short, Brazilians moved upward in the social structure primarily as a result of new job opportunities and, secondarily as a result of good professional preparation. The 3.3 years of school is an extremely low mean for the amount of upward mobility that took place in the country through the 20th century.

How does the 1982 data compare? How much mobility remains, and in what direction is it going? What is the weight of structural variables and individual factors in the determination of social status? Is education becoming a more crucial determinant of social mobility?

This section presents the data regarding intergenerational mobility for 1982. Table 10.1 is a standard mobility matrix relating the status of the father (at the time the son began to work) to that of the son in 1982. It provides information on changes in the social structures and the amount and the direction of mobility.

The percentages in the totals for rows and columns represent the shifts from social class origin to social class destination. The social pyramids are very unequal; they have relatively large bases and narrow peaks. Table 10.2 provides some comparisons among father and son social structures in 1973 and 1982. They reflect the continuity of the unequal shape of the Brazilian social structure and, at the same time, a tendency toward the formation of middle class strata. In other words, the Brazilian social structure of recent times is unequal but possibly less so than in the past (Hutchinson, 1957, 1958, 1960).

The size of the middle class for the fathers cohort jumps from 26.2 percent in 1973 to 50.2 percent in 1982, and for their sons, from 48.5 percent to 66.9 percent. Between the two studies, the number of middle-class fathers practically doubled, and the lower strata were roughly cut in half: from 71.8 percent in 1973 to 37.8 percent in 1982. For the sons, the overall trend was similar though less dramatic. Notably, in the sons' social structure, the upper class increased from 3.5 percent to 4.1 percent, whereas for the fathers, it remained the same.

This evidence reveals the continuing force of upward mobility in Brazil (Morley, 1982). It does not mean, of course, that every individual moved

Table 10.1. Occupational Matrix of Intergenerational Mobility, 1982
(Percent)

Father's status	Individual status in 1982							Total for fathers
	1	2	3	4	5	6	Total	
1. Upper	32.2	27.1	22.2	11.7	5.7	1.1	100.0	2.0
2. Upper middle	14.1	30.1	27.7	19.3	7.2	1.6	100.0	5.0
3. Middle middle	4.2	9.4	37.1	24.8	16.1	8.5	100.0	41.9
4. Lower middle	4.2	13.0	20.3	44.3	16.3	1.9	100.0	13.3
5. Upper lower	3.3	10.7	19.8	38.1	24.4	2.6	100.0	7.7
6. Lower lower	0.6	3.2	23.1	28.3	21.5	23.3	100.0	31.1
Total for individuals N = 57,716	4.1	9.5	28.5	28.9	17.7	11.2	100.0	100.0

upward in relation to his father. As a matter of fact, there is an important difference revealed by the 1982 data. Table 10.3 shows that, between the two years, the proportion of downward movement increased substantially while upward movement decreased; the number of immobile people decreased from 41.6 percent in 1973 to 32.4 percent in 1982. Meanwhile, a large proportion (39.9 percent) of the mobile people continued to move upward. However, almost 30 percent of the heads of families moved downward—a new phenomenon in Brazil, since the comparable 1973 figure stood around 10 percent.

How do we reconcile this increase in downward movement with the upward stretching of the sons' social structure exhibited in Table 10.2? The two sets of data reported in Table 10.3 reveal that the proportion of upwardly mobile sons is smaller in 1982 than in 1973. Could the increase in the downward mobility be attributed entirely to the decrease of good jobs during the 1981–82 recession? Apparently not. This change seems to be a result

Table 10.2. Changes in the Brazilian Social Structure
(Percent)

Classes and social strata	Fathers' positions[1]		Sons' positions	
	1973	1982	1973	1982
Upper class	2.0	2.0	3.5	4.1
Upper stratum	2.0	2.0	3.5	4.1
Middle class	26.2	60.2	48.5	66.9
Upper middle	3.1	5.0	6.3	9.5
Middle middle	13.8	41.9	18.4	28.5
Lower middle	9.3	13.3	23.8	28.9
Lower class	71.8	37.8	48.0	28.9
Upper lower	6.9	7.7	16.0	17.7
Lower lower	64.9	30.1	32.0	11.2
Total	100.0	100.0	100.0	100.0
N =	44,307	44,307	57,716	57,716

Source: Results for 1973 come from Pastore and Haller (1982).
[1] The dates refer to the year of data gathering and not the year the person has entered the labor market.

of internal transformations in the occupational matrices. We analyze this phenomenon in more detail below.

The diagonal of the matrix in Table 10.1 reveals the amount of immobility. It shows that most of the individuals are, indeed, mobile in relation to their fathers. It shows also that the middle class comprises the largest proportion of immobile individuals: 44.3 percent are sons of mid-middle-class fathers. In all other cases, immobility is less than 40 percent.

Table 10.4, a product of the 1973 study, shows higher rates of immobility in the lower strata with a lower-lower rate of 45 percent and lower-middle rate of 46 percent. In other words, immobility in the recent past is located in higher levels of the social structure than the immobility of the past.

What does this phenomenon have to do with the relative downward trend in 1982? When one considers, for example, that the proportion of fathers of the mid-middle class jumped from 13.8 percent to 41.9 percent during the period, this implies that the individuals studied in 1982 began their mobility careers at a significantly higher level than those studied in 1973. As a consequence, these people had less space to climb and a higher probability to descend the social ladder. Moreover, to move up in the higher levels is difficult because it implies long social distances.

Table 10.3. General Patterns of Intergenerational Mobility
(Percent)

Types of mobility	1973	1982
Upward	47.1	39.9
Immobility	41.6	32.4
Downward	11.3	27.6

Table 10.4. Occupational Matrix of Intergenerational Mobility, 1973
(Percent)

Father's status	Individual status in 1973							Total for fathers
	1	2	3	4	5	6	Total	
1. Upper	29.8	22.5	27.1	12.5	5.0	3.1	100.0	2.0
2. Upper middle	15.2	28.7	28.7	15.5	6.1	5.8	100.0	3.1
3. Middle middle	8.6	14.3	36.2	18.9	10.5	11.5	100.0	13.8
4. Lower middle	3.8	8.7	21.6	46.3	14.9	4.7	100.0	9.3
5. Upper lower	3.2	7.4	20.7	35.4	23.8	9.5	100.0	6.9
6. Lower lower	1.0	2.5	13.1	21.1	17.4	44.9	100.0	64.9
Total for individuals N = 44,307	3.5	6.3	18.4	23.8	16.0	32.0	100.0	100.0

Table 10.5 shows, in fact, that, among the mobile individuals, 59.1 percent of the sons in the 1982 study moved upward whereas, in the 1973 sample, this proportion totaled 80.6 percent. Starting almost from zero, in 1973, most people had a higher chance to move up.

In terms of vertical mobility, fathers generally moved from the lower strata to the middle class. Middle-class fathers in 1982 amounted to 41.9 percent, whereas in 1973 they were 26.2 percent. Lower-class fathers de-

Table 10.5. Types of Mobility for Mobile Individuals
(Percent)

Types of mobility	1973	1982
Upward	80.6	59.1
Downward	19.4	40.9

creased from 71.8 percent in 1973 to 37.8 percent in 1982, and the upper class remained the same size (2 percent). Sons' vertical mobility occurred largely in the higher levels of the middle class and, also, in the upper class.

What was behind this accelerated vertical mobility of fathers? The 1973 study concluded that most of the social mobility in Brazil was "structural mobility" resulting from taking good advantage of new job opportunities rather than "circular mobility," in which competence, capability and competition are key factors (Hutchinson, 1958).

In order to visualize the transformation of the fathers' social structure, let us use a typical case: the individuals studied in 1973 were, on average, 40 years old; their fathers were, on average, 60 years old (disregarding whether or not they were alive in that year). Therefore, they had completed the greater part of their professional careers between ages 20 and 40, namely, between 1930–50. The fathers of the individuals studied in 1982, by the same token, had completed the greater part of their professional careers between 1940 and 1960. Labor opportunities and occupational differentiation intensified during this second period when urbanization, industrialization, trade, and public administration became dominant in Brazil. The weight of agriculture in the Brazilian labor market decreased considerably during this second period. In fact, the proportion of fathers in the lower-lower class (mainly rural occupations) decreased from 64.9 in 1973 to 30.1 percent in 1982. For the sons, the corresponding decrease was from 32 percent to 11.2 percent. During this era, the Brazilian occupational structure became more differentiated as well as more urban and industrialized.

Analysis of the middle-class strata reveals that, in addition to the growth of the mid-middle class, the upper-middle stratum enlarged substantially both for the fathers and their sons. The upper-middle class in 1982 was twice as big as in 1973. Fathers' presence in the upper-middle class also rose from 3.1 percent to 5 percent (see Table 10.2).

In 1973, most upward mobility resulted from rural-urban migration. Table 10.6 shows that 55.1 percent of those of lower-lower class origin moved up. Table 10.7 shows an even greater proportion, 67.8 percent, in

Table 10.6. Intergenerational Mobility by Social Strata, 1973
(Percent)

Types of mobility	Upper	Upper middle	Middle middle	Lower middle	Upper lower	Lower lower	Total
Upward	—	15.2	22.9	34.1	66.7	55.1	47.1
Immobility	29.8	28.7	36.2	46.3	23.8	44.9	41.6
Downward	70.2	56.1	40.9	19.6	9.5	—	11.3
Total	100.0	100.0	100.0	100.0	100.0	100.0	100.0

Table 10.7. Intergenerational Mobility by Social Strata, 1982
(Percent)

Types of mobility	Upper	Upper middle	Middle middle	Lower middle	Upper lower	Lower lower	Total
Upward	—	14.1	13.6	44.6	66.1	67.8	38.9
Immobility	23.3	24.4	44.3	37.1	30.1	32.2	32.4
Downward	76.7	61.5	42.1	18.3	3.8	—	29.6
Total	100.0	100.0	100.0	100.0	100.0	100.0	100.0

1982. By this time, most lower-class sons from rural areas were moving upward.

On the other hand, in 1973, 56.1 percent of the upper-middle class sons descended, whereas in 1982, this proportion increased to 61.5 percent. For those of upper class origin, downward movement increased from 70.2 percent in 1973 to 76.7 percent in 1982. The same pattern is observed for sons of mid-middle-class origin: their percentage of downward movement went from 40.9 percent in 1973 to 42.1 percent in 1982.

In short, intergenerational upward mobility became more difficult in 1982 as compared to 1973. Downward mobility became more prevalent.

In Table 10.8 the status change matrix indicates that in 1982, 26.1 percent of the individuals remained immobile, and 73.9 percent were in positions different from those at the beginning of their careers. Intra-generational mobility, therefore, was greater than intergenerational mobility (67.5 percent). There is one new phenomenon, however, which is

Table 10.8. Occupational Matrix of Intragenerational Mobility, 1982
(Percent)

| Beginning status | Individual status in 1982 | | | | | | | Total for fathers |
	1	2	3	4	5	6	Total	
1. Upper	60.4	16.7	9.2	6.7	6.2	0.8	100.0	1.0
2. Upper middle	26.7	48.0	14.6	6.8	3.2	0.5	100.0	1.2
3. Middle middle	15.6	25.0	37.9	13.2	7.5	0.8	100.0	8.4
4. Lower middle	5.4	12.6	15.4	54.3	11.2	1.0	100.0	10.4
5. Upper lower	4.3	13.4	23.6	34.3	22.3	2.2	100.0	27.8
6. Lower lower	0.5	3.7	31.6	25.5	19.6	19.0	100.0	51.3
Total for individuals N = 66,083	4.2	9.8	27.6	29.5	18.1	10.6	100.0	100.0

dramatically different between the two types of mobility. The upward mobility in the case of intragenerational movements was very high, 69.4 percent, and downward mobility was limited to 4.5 percent. Table 10.9 provides the comparison between the two types of mobility for 1973 and 1982. In 1973, the amount of mobility was practically identical in both cases. In 1982, however, intergenerational mobility was much greater.

Intragenerational mobility also depends upon time (Ornestein, 1976). Generally, the time involved in intragenerational mobility is less than the time involved in intergenerational mobility. However, since both surveys are based on data that asked for the father's occupation at the time when the respondent began to work, the father's status and the son's initial status refer to the same time. For example, a person who was 25 years old in 1973 and began to work at 15 entered the labor market in, approximately, 1963. His initial status refers to 1963 as well as the status of his father. In both cases, mobility covers 10 years, although in the case of the father, his career

Table 10.9. Inter and Intragenerational Mobility, 1973 and 1982
(Percent)

	1973		1982	
	Inter	Intra	Inter	Intra
Upward	47.1	54.2	39.9	69.4
Immobility	41.6	41.9	32.4	26.1
Downward	11.3	3.9	27.6	4.5

was well established in 1963 whereas the son's trajectory was just beginning. Moreover, the majority of sons were young and had a long career path to travel. This is also true for the 1982 data.

Intragenerational mobility also depends upon the point of departure (Hunter, 1988). The lower the beginning, the greater the potential space to be covered in the social ladder. In Brazil, due to early entry in the labor market, sons tend to begin in occupations of lower status; this generates some advantage for upward mobility.

To understand the meaning of upward and downward movements, therefore, the first thing to do is to examine the starting points of fathers and sons as highlighted in Table 10.10.

We have concluded so far that, in relation to 1973, Brazil in 1982 had a larger proportion of intergenerational downward movement and a larger proportion of intragenerational upward movement. In other words, in relation to their fathers, many sons descended the social ladder; in relation to the beginnings of their own careers, they ascended.

This reinforces the hypothesis that the increase of intergenerational downward movements in 1982 was due to the relatively higher position of fathers as compared to 1973. On the other hand, the sons' starting points were practically the same in both data sets: in 1973, 59.8 percent of the sons began in the lower-lower status; in 1982, the corresponding proportion was 51.3 percent. In 1973, 25 percent started in the upper-lower occupations; in 1982, this proportion was 27.8 percent. Few changes are observed in higher levels. Lower-middle-class starters amounted to 7.3 percent in 1973 and to 10.4 percent in 1982, while mid-middle starters were 6.9 percent in 1973 and 8.4 percent in 1982. The other status levels practically doubled, although the percentages remained low. In sum, many sons moved downward because their fathers were at higher positions in 1982. At the same time, most sons moved upward because they had lower starting points in 1982. Therefore, occupational opportunities seem to have remained quite open for both peri-

Table 10.10. Evolution of Social Structures 1973–82
(Percent)

Social strata	1973			1982		
	Fathers' status	Sons' start	Sons 1973	Fathers status	Sons' start	Sons 1973
Upper	2.0	0.6	3.4	2.0	1.0	4.2
Upper middle	3.1	0.7	6.5	5.0	1.2	9.8
Mid middle	13.8	6.9	18.7	41.9	8.4	27.8
Lower middle	9.3	7.3	24.7	13.3	10.4	29.5
Upper lower	6.9	25.2	16.7	7.7	27.8	18.1
Low lower	64.9	59.8	30.0	31.1	51.3	10.6
Total	100.0	100.0	100.0	100.0	100.0	100.0

ods. Notably, the shrinking of labor opportunities due to the 1981–82 recession is not reflected in the 1982 mobility data.

In light of the 1982 data, we have seen that the Brazilian population remained very mobile and, at the same time, increased its downward movement. The next paragraphs will identify the prevailing types of social mobility in 1982 and examine the balance between structural and circular mobility. Data refer to intergenerational mobility only.

In the beginning stages of the development process, structural mobility tends to prevail. Here, economic growth promotes the opening of new and more diversified occupational positions (Ganzenboom, Luijkx and Treiman, 1988; Slomczynski and Krauze, 1987). Such is the case in a range of sectors including commerce, administration and services, industry, health and education. Often, the growth of new job opportunities tends to move faster than school improvements, and significant improvisation takes place in the labor market. Structural mobility is a result of this forced filling of new job positions (Jones, 1984a,b).

Mobility tends to shift from structural to circular when society has already attained a reasonable level of development. Labor markets become more sophisticated and production is associated with higher level technology and labor productivity. Under these circumstances, professional capability, acquired through in-service training, formal education, or both, becomes a key factor for both status attainment and social mobility.

In the highly industrialized societies, more than 75 percent of total mobility is due to circular mobility and 25 percent to structural mobility. In the Brazilian case, structural mobility has been responsible for much more than 25 percent of the total: it accounted for 56.2 percent and 47.7 percent of

Table 10.11. Types of Social Mobility, 1973 and 1982
(Percent)

			In relative terms	
	1973	1982	1973	1982
Total mobility	58.5	67.5	100.0	100.0
Structural mobility	32.9	32.2	56.2	47.7
Circular mobility	25.6	35.3	43.8	52.3

total mobility in the years 1973 and 1982, respectively (see Table 10.11). The comparison between 1973 and 1982 data reveals, however, a slight shift toward circular mobility. Table 10.11 shows an increase of 8.5 percentage points in circular mobility between 1973 and 1982, suggesting an increase in the role of competence and professional capability in the determination of social status during this period. This trend may be associated with on-the-job training, education, or both. Although on-the-job training data are not available, regression analyses in the next section will detect the net effect of formal education on status attainment.

However, two considerations can be advanced at this stage. First, although higher than in 1973 (3.3), the average years of schooling remained very low in 1982 (4.4), especially considering that this sub-sample refers to heads of households. Therefore, one may suspect that the role of formal education on the aggregate social mobility rates was still modest. Second, the process of job creation due to the expansion of the economy remained vigorous during the 1960s and the 70s—the period when most of the status attainment and vertical mobility covered by the 1982 data took place. Employment reduction from the 1981–83 recession had no time to affect 1982 mobility rates.

This implies that the increase of circular mobility should be neither dramatized nor ignored. It is important to explore and to locate the main focus of this new phenomenon. In this respect, Table 10.12 reveals that circular mobility, which seems to be a very recent phenomenon, is more frequent among younger people. In fact, for the 20–30 and, particularly, the 31–40 age cohorts, most mobility is circular; this figure is smaller for the 40–50 and 51–64 cohorts.

Changes in mobility rates varied substantially by region. The Northeast achieved the greatest increase in the rate of total mobility: from 42.3 percent in 1973 to 62.8 percent in 1982, most of this downward mobility. In São Paulo and the South as well, there was an increase in downward mobil-

Table 10.12. Types of Mobility by Age Groups, 1982
(*Percent*)

	Age groups			
	(51–64)	**(41–50)**	**(31–40)**	**(20–30)**
Total mobility	62.9	68.2	69.3	67.7
Structural mobility	30.1	34.0	10.8	29.0
Circular mobility	32.8	34.2	58.5	38.7

ity. In the East, both upward and downward mobility increased, although the latter was much more pronounced. In Rio and Brasília, rates of vertical mobility and immobility did not change; however, in Brasília there was an increase in downward mobility and a decrease in upward mobility, relative to Rio. In short, downward mobility increased in all regions, with a stronger impact in the Northeast, Brasília and the South; upward mobility decreased in all regions, except the East; and immobility decreased in all regions and became stable in Rio and Brasília.

In general, between 1973 and 1982, the proportion of structural mobility decreased, while the proportion of circular mobility increased slightly. Circular mobility increased very significantly in Rio, rising from 47 percent in 1973 to 62.6 percent in 1982. Surprisingly, the next greatest increase was recorded in the Northeast, from 43.5 percent to 56.5 percent. All the other regions exhibited modest changes in the proportions of circular mobility.

Despite these changes, structural mobility continues to be the main source of social mobility in the more sophisticated labor markets and the most developed regions of São Paulo, the South and Brasília. In this respect, one may conclude that prevailing mobility types in Brazil in 1982 did not change very much compared with those of 1973. Social mobility was still dependent on the creation of new job opportunities and formal education remained poor; hence the skill demand seems to have been resolved more by improvisation than by formal training.

How might this trend manifest itself in the future? This question gains significance when taking into account the sizable downward mobility revealed by the 1982 data. As we have seen, the reverse of this tendency was due basically to the rapid upward mobility achieved by the fathers of the heads of families. This means that the space for upward mobility is decreasing in Brazil. The "easy years" for upward mobility are gone (Langoni, 1973). Rural-urban migration has been decelerated. The present respondents' fathers are in much higher positions than the respondents' fathers of two to three decades ago.

How can this picture be reversed again? We see two alternatives. The first requires a re-acceleration of economic growth and the creation of a gigantic number of good jobs in the secondary and tertiary sectors, as happened in the mid-1960s and 70s. The second requires a substantial increase in the proportion of well-trained people for the newcoming occupations.

The prospect of booming economic growth in the next five years, however, is dim, and education is deteriorating rather than improving. Brazilian heads of families—the cream of the labor market—still average only 4.4 years of school. Under these circumstances, labor productivity cannot advance much more.

In sum, if education does not improve more rapidly and if new job opportunities are not created on a large scale, the Brazilian population may experience a few decades of downward mobility, with severe social and political consequences.

Social Status Attainment

This section evaluates the role of several variables that determine social status attainment. Structural and individual variables and their effects are estimated in two ways: first, coefficients of a linear regression model, and second, path analysis coefficients. In both cases, comparisons are made with results obtained in the 1973 study.

The Linear Regression Model

The regression model includes individual variables already examined in above sections, such as father's status, initial status, education and age. Structural variables are added to account for the role of regional labor market characteristics. For each PNAD region, three labor market indicators were developed from the 1982 PNAD data: occupational differentiation, proportion of industrial employment, and the unemployment rate.

We define occupational differentiation in terms of the proportion of workers whose job title is among the 15 most common occupations. A high value in this variable indicates that the labor market of the corresponding region is not very developed, and consequently, would not be very favorable to social mobility. The proportion of industrial employment was computed by dividing industrial employment by total employment for each PNAD region. A high value in this variable indicates more favorable conditions for

Table 10.13. The 1982 Regression Model: Structural Labor Market Variables by Region
(Percent)

Region	Occupational differentiation	Proportion of industrial employment	Unemployment rate
Rio	36.3	15.6	6.4
São Paulo	38.6	26.9	4.7
East	49.5	10.4	4.4
South	52.8	13.4	2.7
Northeast	59.3	8.7	3.1
Brasília	42.1	5.4	4.2

social mobility. The unemployment rate was also computed from the 1982 PNAD data, since regional series are not available. A high regional unemployment rate indicates less favorable conditions for social mobility. The computed values for the three structural variables are reported in Table 10.13.

The regression model adopted in this study is essentially the same as that used in the 1973 study, with two modifications: in this model, the dummy variable for migration status is not included, and the three structural variables mentioned above are added.[1]

The regression model used in this study is (the symbols + or − indicate the hypothesized direction for the impact of the corresponding variable):

$$STA = CTE + A\,EDC + B\,STI + C\,IDD + D\,IDQ + E\,STP + F\,DIF +$$
$$\qquad\quad (+) \qquad (+) \qquad (+) \qquad (-) \qquad (+) \qquad (-)$$

$$G\,IND + H\,DES + (\text{Error Term})$$
$$(+) \qquad (-)$$

Where:
CTE = constant term (intercept);
EDC = household head's schooling;
STI = initial social status index of the household head;

---

[1] The variable used to indicate social status in both studies is the index developed by Silva (1973). The adjustments in occupation titles necessary to use Silva's index are indicated in the Appendix. In this study, education is measured by years of schooling. This information is not readily available in PNAD surveys; the computation used to obtain this variable is included in the Appendix. In the 1973 study, education of heads of households is in two-years-of-school groups. Comparisons between 1973–82 studies must, therefore, be made with qualifications.

IDD = household head's age;
IDQ = squared age;
STP = social status index of the father of the household head;
DIF = regional occupational differentiation;
IND = regional proportion of industrial employment;
DES = regional unemployment rate.

Mean values of the variables are presented in Table 10.14 for the 1982 data and in Table 10.15 for the 1973 data. The usual Brazilian regional differences may be realized through the examination of such variables as education (which are higher in the most developed areas such as São Paulo, Rio de Janeiro and Brasília), as well as the structural variables in Table 10.13.

Tables 10.14 and 10.15 indicate progress in average schooling (which increased from 3.3 years in 1973 to 4.4 years in 1982, a 33 percent increase), and social status (where the average index increased from 10.6 to 14.2, a 34 percent increase). The rise in fathers' social status was the largest among all the variables: the index rose from 8.1 in 1973 to 12.7 in 1982, up 57 percent.

Estimated coefficients for 1982 and corresponding results from 1973 are presented in Tables 10.16 and 10.17, respectively. Table 10.16 also presents estimated coefficients for the 1973 model with 1982 data. The variance explained by the model is relatively high, compared to other social status attainment studies. Squared-R is 0.424 for the regression with all observations and ranges from 0.312 to 0.549 in the regional and age-group regressions. Almost all coefficients are significant at very high levels of significance.

The sign for the estimated schooling coefficient is positive, and as in the 1973 study, large. Keeping all other variables constant, one additional year of schooling increases the social status index by 1.32 points, about 10 percent of the sample average's social status index.

Schooling seems to play a more important role in social status attainment in the most developed areas. Brasília has the largest estimated coefficient (1.63), followed by São Paulo (1.51) and Rio de Janeiro (1.48). The smallest coefficient is observed in the less developed area of Brazil, the Northeast (0.953). This result suggests that schooling will be increasingly important as the Brazilian labor market becomes more and more complex (Lam and Levison, 1987, 1989). Thus, regarding the impact of education on social status attainment, the results are essentially the same as those obtained in the 1973 study.

Age has the second largest impact on the social status of the head of household. Each year adds 0.448 points to the social status index (keeping

Table 10.14. Variable Mean Value by Region and Age Group, 1982

	STA	EDC	STI	IDD	IDQ	STP	DIF	IND	DES	N
Total	14.2	4.36	6.40	38.8	1630	12.7	49.7	13.3	3.94	48,678
Region										
Rio	15.1	5.85	7.72	39.6	1680	12.9	—	—	—	4,225
São Paulo	14.3	5.15	6.64	38.5	1590	11.7	—	—	—	8,204
East	15.1	4.92	6.31	38.3	1580	14.9	—	—	—	10,417
South	13.5	4.19	5.95	39.0	1640	11.1	—	—	—	7,531
Northeast	13.0	2.79	5.79	39.6	1690	11.8	—	—	—	15,422
Brasília	17.1	6.74	8.53	36.6	1440	15.6	—	—	—	2,879
Age group										
20–30	12.7	5.08	6.59	26.2	694	12.3	49.5	13.2	3.94	13,120
31–40	14.9	4.83	6.79	35.3	1250	12.8	49.5	13.3	3.95	15,583
41–50	14.6	3.85	6.15	45.2	2050	12.8	49.6	13.4	3.95	11,409
51–64	14.7	3.07	5.71	56.3	3180	13.0	50.4	13.1	3.89	8,566

Notes: STA = present status index; EDC = schooling (years); STI = initial status index; IDD = age; IDQ = squared age; STP = father's status index; DIF = occupational differentiation; IND = industrial employment; DES = unemployment rate; N = number of observations.

Table 10.15. Variable Mean Value by Region and Age Group, 1973

	STA	EDC	STI	IDD	STP	N
Total	10.6	3.3	5.9	39.6	8.1	4,418
Region						
Rio	12.5	4.4	7.5	40.1	10.4	508
São Paulo	11.5	3.9	6.3	39.8	8.2	751
East	9.9	2.9	5.3	40.0	7.6	718
South	9.4	3.2	4.9	39.5	7.2	628
Northeast	8.3	1.8	4.8	39.9	6.5	1,101
Brasília	14.4	5.3	7.9	38.2	10.9	447
Age group						
20–30	10.0	3.7	6.2	—	8.0	1,063
31–40	11.2	3.6	6.1	—	8.5	1,415
41–50	11.3	3.3	5.9	—	8.1	1,116
51–64	9.1	2.4	5.2	—	7.6	824

Notes: STA = present status index; EDC = schooling (years); STI = initial status index; IDD = age; STP = father's status index; N = number of observations.

all other variables constant). The effect varies among the regions, from 0.744 in São Paulo, to 0.220 in the Northeast. This suggests that the effect of this variable depends upon the degree of labor market development.

Table 10.16. Regression Coefficients by Region and Age Group, 1982

	CTE	EDC	STI	IDD	IDQ	STP	DIF	IND	DES	R2
Total										
82 model	−16.7	1.32	.402	.448	−.004	.129	.156	.043	.235	.424
73 model	−6.95	1.26	.408	.433	−.034	.132	—	—	—	.418
Region										
Rio	−9.53	1.48	.419	.382	−.003	.144	—	—	—	.474
São Paulo	−14.6	1.51	.410	.744	−.007	.105	—	—	—	.492
East	−9.48	1.39	.360	.540	−.005	.141	—	—	—	.391
South	−10.0	1.44	.386	.518	−.004	.160	—	—	—	.446
Northeast	−.267	.953	.375	.220	−.001	.123	—	—	—	.312
Brasília	−12.3	1.63	.469	.552	−.004	.038	—	—	—	.549
Age group										
20–30	−7.10	1.01	.451	−.32*	−.013	.126	.155	.032	.453	.383
31–40	−31.4	1.42	.405	1.36	−.017	.135	.138	.051	.06*	.460
41–50	−5.88	1.43	.381	—	−.014	.116	.140	.051	.14*	.419
51–64	−14.3	1.46	.320	.21*	−.01*	.136	.204	.03*	.356	.399

Notes: CTE = intercept; EDC = schooling (years); STI = initial status index; IDD = age; STP = father's status index; DIF = occupational differentiation; IND = industrial employment; DES = employment rate.
*Insignificant coefficients.

Table 10.17. Regression Coefficients by Region and Age Group, 1973

	CTE	EDC	STI	IDD	IDQ	STP	MIG	R2
Total	−6.25	1.45	.344	.443	−.004	.064	−.079	.427
Region								
Rio	−2.30	2.02	.058	.178	−.001	.013	−.017	.439
São Paulo	−6.06	1.36	.349	.490	−.005	.030	−.077	.359
East	−6.53	1.67	.240	.437	−.004	.164	−.559	.474
South	−13.2	1.82	.119	.708	−.007	.156	−.782	.408
Northeast	−4.38	1.27	.472	.414	−.004	.059	−.532	.375
Brasília	−11.6	1.10	.571	.320	−.003	.051	+3.72	.498

Notes: CTE = intercept; EDC = schooling (years); STI = initial status index; IDD = age; IDQ = squared age; STP = father's status index; MIG = migration status.

The effect of this variable is not significant in three of the four age groups. The only significant coefficient was observed for the 30–40 group. This suggests typical human capital behavior for social status attainment. During the early years (20–30), time seems to be used to invest in human capital (either through school or on-the-job training), and age does not affect social status attainment. Thereafter, however, returns to investment materialize: from 30 to 40, each year of age adds 1.36 points to social status; after 40, age does not contribute to social status attainment (coefficients for 41–50 and 51–64 groups are insignificant).

The coefficients for the head of household's father's social status are also all positive. The magnitude is not very large and the correlation with labor market development is negative: the lower magnitudes for this coefficient are observed in the most developed areas (São Paulo and Brasília).

The structural variables, namely, occupational differentiation, industrial employment, and the unemployment rate, do not add much to the variation explained by the model. The positive signs for two coefficients (occupational differentiation and unemployment rate) are puzzling. These results suggest that social status increases when occupational differentiation is not large and when the unemployment rate is high.

The individual variables: the regression equation estimated in this study provides evidence about the role played by attributed individual characteristics. The results show that all the achieved factors positively affect social status attainment and are positively correlated with regional labor market development. The only attributed individual characteristic included in the model—fathers' status—although also positively associated with social status attainment, is negatively correlated with regional labor market development. This suggests that, with economic development, achieved factors (education, experience, initial status) tend to play a more significant role in social status attainment (Hout, 1984).

However, this conclusion is tentative, because educational opportunities are still somewhat restricted in Brazil. Realistically, the father's social position is relevant for both education and first job status. In order to clarify the effect of the father's social status on the present social status of the household head, we estimated a path analysis model. The 1973 study, also estimated a similar model. Both sets of results are presented below.

The recursive model is depicted in Figure 10.1. Four paths are prescribed for the impact of fathers' status on present status:

    i) direct (coefficient "e");

    ii) indirect, through education (coefficient "a" x "b");

    iii) indirect, through initial status (coefficient "c" x "d");

    iv) indirect, through educational and initial status (coefficient "a" x "f" x "d").

The recursive model estimated in the 1973 study did not include the path through education and initial status. In that study, the correlation between education and initial status was considered too small, and for this

Figure 10.1. Recursive Model for Social Status Attainment

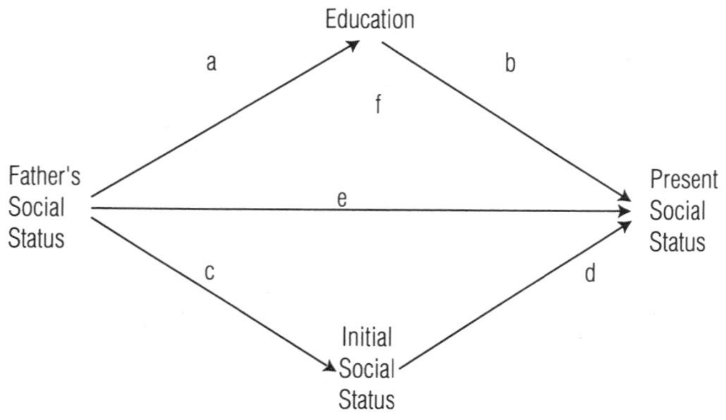

reason this path was omitted. However, since the 1982 PNAD data indicate a 0.5 correlation between those two variables, the corresponding path cannot be ignored.

Tables 10.18 and 10.19 highlight the results of both estimations. All the 1982 path coefficients are significant at very high levels of significance. Although not completely comparable, the results indicate a remarkable increase in the impact of fathers' status on present status. In the 1973 study, this total impact was 0.397; in 1982, it increased to 0.733. The largest contributor to this increase was the direct impact, which increased from 0.080 in 1973 to 0.255 in 1982.

These results indicate that fathers' status is still very important for social attainment for all regions and age groups. In fact, impacts estimated in 1982 are greater than those estimated in 1973. In addition, the comparison of direct and indirect estimated coefficients indicate that the relative effects of fathers' social status tends to be more direct in the past. In more recent periods, and in more developed regional labor markets, fathers' social status acts in a more indirect way, through education and first job status (Haller and Pastore, 1970).

The impact of education and social inheritance may vary across different levels of education. In order to clarify this, we ran the same model for four levels of household head schooling. The results (not shown here) indicate that the total impact of the father's social status on the household head's social status does not differ significantly across levels of schooling. However, the components of the total impact of the father's social status do differ across groups: the higher the educational level, the lower the direct

Table 10.18. Path Coefficients of Fathers' Social Status on Household Head's Social Status, by Region and Age Group, 1982

	Total	Direct	Indirect	Through education	Through initial status	Through initial status and education
Total	.733	.255	.478	.310	.071	.097
(%)	(100.0)	(34.8)	(65.2)	(42.3)	(9.7)	(13.2)
Region						
Rio	.724	.159	.565	.405	.051	.109
(%)	(100.0)	(22.0)	(78.0)	(55.9)	(7.0)	(15.1)
São Paulo	.721	.155	.566	.411	.059	.096
(%)	(100.0)	(21.5)	(78.5)	(57.0)	(8.2)	(13.3)
East	.754	.251	.483	.354	.043	.086
(%)	(100.0)	(35.9)	(64.1)	(46.9)	(5.7)	(11.4)
South	.733	.232	.501	.345	.069	.087
(%)	(100.0)	(31.7)	(68.3)	(47.1)	(9.4)	(11.9)
Northeast	.734	.360	.374	.156	.121	.097
(%)	(100.0)	(49.0)	(51.0)	(21.3)	(16.5)	(13.2)
Brasília	.711	.072	.639	.458	.062	.119
(%)	(100.0)	(10.1)	(89.9)	(64.4)	(8.7)	(16.7)
Age group						
20–30	.729	.204	.525	.326	.074	.125
(%)	(100.0)	(28.0)	(72.0)	(44.7)	(10.2)	(17.1)
31–40	.732	.212	.520	.365	.062	.093
(%)	(100.0)	(29.0)	(71.0)	(49.9)	(8.5)	(12.7)
41–50	.729	.260	.469	.311	.069	.089
(%)	(100.0)	(35.7)	(64.3)	(42.7)	(9.5)	(12.2)
51–64	.752	.344	.408	.249	.081	.078
(%)	(100.0)	(45.7)	(54.3)	(33.1)	(10.8)	(10.4)

impact of fathers' social status and the larger the indirect impact. In short, inheritance counts more for uneducated people.

These results seem to indicate that fathers' social status acts in two ways. For those individuals who are educated, their fathers' status provides the necessary support to continue in school. In these cases, the direct impact of fathers' social status on sons' status is small. For individuals who are not educated, the father's social status acts directly on the household head's status attainment.

This final result suggests that education does play an important role in status attainment. If education were generally available in Brazil, status

Table 10.19. Path Coefficients of Fathers' Social Status on Household Head's Social Status, by Region and Age Group, 1973

	Total	Direct	Indirect	Through education	Through initial status
Total	.397	.080	.317	.240	.077
(%)	(100.0)	(20.0)	(80.0)	(60.0)	(20.0)
Region					
Rio	.325	.002	.303	.291	.012
(%)	(100.0)	(7.0)	(93.0)	(89.5)	(3.5)
São Paulo	.330	.029	.301	.226	.075
(%)	(100.0)	(9.0)	(91.0)	(68.5)	(22.5)
East	.457	.149	.308	.252	.056
(%)	(100.0)	(32.6)	(67.4)	(55.0)	(12.4)
South	.389	.106	.283	.281	.002
(%)	(100.0)	(27.3)	(72.7)	(72.2)	(.5)
Northeast	.393	.050	.340	.236	.104
(%)	(100.0)	(13.5)	(86.5)	(60.0)	(26.5)
Brasília	.423	.005	.368	.227	.141
(%)	(100.0)	(13.0)	(87.0)	(53.8)	(33.4)
Age group					
20–30	.385	.030	.355	.216	.139
(%)	(100.0)	(7.8)	(92.2)	(56.0)	(36.0)
31–40	.382	.074	.355	.216	.139
(%)	(100.0)	(19.4)	(80.6)	(46.8)	(33.8)
41–50	.452	.066	.386	.328	.056
(%)	(100.0)	(14.6)	(85.4)	(72.8)	(12.6)
51–64	.312	−.016	.328	.285	.043
(%)	(100.0)	(−5.1)	(105.0)	(91.0)	(14.0)

attainment would certainly be facilitated by schooling. Reality reflects the opposite. For most of those people included in the 1982 sample, access to education was severely restricted. Under these circumstances, social attainment depends heavily on an individual's social background.

Conclusion

Brazil has witnessed an extended period of social mobility, with most individuals moving upward in relation to their fathers during the 1950–80 era. These four decades, however, can be divided into two periods. From 1950–70, upward mobility was intense and massive. Inequality also increased because few people managed to move long social distances, whereas the great bulk of the population moved short social distances, mainly, from lower-lower to upper-lower class or, at most, to lower-middle class. Rural-urban migration played an important role in this phenomenon (Bills and Haller, 1985).

From 1970–80, particularly between 1975 and 1980, Brazil showed a substantial amount of downward mobility. Why did the traditional upward trend begin to change? In order to answer this question, the present study explores, first, the causes of Brazilian social mobility in the remote past on the basis of the 1973 data and, second, it speculates on the role of the recession and unemployment in the recent past on the basis of the 1982 data.

The 1973 study concluded that the largest part of social mobility in Brazil, particularly during the 1950–70 period, was "structural mobility" (which results from individuals taking advantage of new job opportunities) rather than "circular mobility" (in which competence, capability and competition are the key forces), and that moving up depended on someone moving down (retiring or dying). Further, most of the heads of household studied in 1973 had fathers of low status. Agriculture remained a significant force in the Brazilian labor market during the time when their fathers entered it. These two forces—namely, the low starting point of the fathers and the plentiful labor opportunities for the sons—were responsible for the largest part of the high mobility rates.

During the 1970–80 period, upward movements between generations decreased. This was due to a combination of two new phenomena. First, the fathers' starting point was much higher in 1982 than in 1973 data. Second, labor opportunities diminished, particularly toward the very end of the decade. It seems, however, that the impact of the low starting point of the fathers is much greater than the decrease of job opportunities. In fact, the intragenerational mobility rates, including upward mobility, are much greater for 1982 than 1973. In other words, when the social status of the individual is compared to his own starting point, upward mobility is significant. In this respect, the 1982 data show that people began their careers at a very low level of status. Under these circumstances, they had enough space to move up in the social ladder.

In sum, in the 1973 and 1982 comparison, Brazil shows a larger proportion of inter-downward and intra-upward mobility. In relation to their fathers, many sons descended but, in relation to their own start, most of them ascended. This supports the hypothesis that the increase of inter-downward movements in the 1982 data was due to the higher position of fathers as compared with the 1973 data. Many sons descended because their fathers were already in higher positions when sons started working. And, most sons moved up because they had a lower starting point in their own careers. Therefore, occupational opportunities remained quite open. Both periods exhibited a large degree of structural mobility.

What can be said with regard to the trend of social mobility in recent times? We can only speculate on it. The 1981–83 recession reduced job opportunities in Brazil, particularly in the durable goods sectors. During the 1980–85 period, however, several new labor markets emerged in response to the energy crisis, including alcohol mills and a vast sugar cane complex in the interior of Minas Gerais, São Paulo and Paraná. Meanwhile, throughout the 1980s, Brazil expanded its agricultural frontier toward the west.

On the other hand, the urban population may be facing the need for better preparation to compete in the labor market and climb the social ladder. With fewer job vacancies and higher skill demand, Brazil may experience increasingly circular mobility in metropolitan regions. The first signs of this new trend are visible in the 1982 data. The younger people in practically all metropolitan regions experienced significant circular mobility.

The average level of education is gradually increasing in Brazil but it is still very low. According to the 1982 data, married male heads of families average about four years of formal schooling (not accounting for quality). In the 1973 data, this average was approximately three years. Therefore, the education level of the Brazilian labor force remains very low.

In spite of this, education affects status determination. This study examined the role of formal schooling in status determination as part of a conventional status attainment model in which inheritance and experience are included. Education was the single most powerful factor. Each additional year of schooling induces 10 percent in the status scale. Education plays an even more important role in the most developed regions of the country, particularly Brasília, São Paulo, and Rio de Janeiro.

The weight of education remains the same in the 1973–1982 comparison. However, for status attainment and mobility, schooling seems to be particularly strategic when job opportunities are tight and technology expands. This is the case in most urban areas in Brazil today and may well be the picture for the next eight to 10 years. The majority of the existing labor force in the urban areas will enjoy intragenerational mobility of short distances. The few and more educated will take advantage of long distance upward mobility. The social structure may then become still more unequal. On the other hand, long distance mobility with less education may be easier in the interior. The "easy years" for upward mobility in the urban areas have passed, and now, the new opportunities are in the interior.

REFERENCES

Alwin, Duane F., and Arland Thorton. 1984. Family Origin and Schooling Process. *American Sociological Review* 49(6): 784–802.

Amassari, Paolo. 1978. Occupational Satisfaction and Intergenerational Mobility. *International Review of Sociology* 14(3): 219–32.

Bills, David B., and Archibald O. Haller. 1985. Socioeconomic Development and Social Stratification: Reassessing the Brazilian Case. *The Journal of Developing Areas* 19(1): 59–70.

Bills, David B., Daramea Godfrey, and Archibald O. Haller. 1986. A Scale to Measure the Socioeconomic Status of Occupations in Brazil. *Rural Sociology* 50(2): 225–50.

Boudon, Raymond. 1973. *Education, Opportunity and Social Inequality*. New York: John Wiley & Sons.

Duncan, Otis D., David L. Featherman, and Beverly Duncan. 1972. *Socioeconomic Background and Achievement*. New York: Seminar Press.

Featherman, David L., and Robert M. Hauser. 1978. *Opportunity and Change*. New York: Academic Press.

Ganzenboom, Herbert B., Robert Luijkx, and Donald J. Treiman. 1988. Intergenerational Mobility in Comparative Perspective. University of California, Los Angeles. Mimeo.

Grusky, David B., and Robert M. Hauser. 1984. Comparative Social Mobility in 16 Countries. *American Sociological Review* 49(1): 19–38.

Haller, Archibald O., and José Pastore. 1970. Labor Market Segmentation, Sex, and Income in Brazil. In *Industrial Relations in the Unorganized Sector*, ed. Dorothea Gaudart. Tokyo: Japan Institute of Labor.

Haller, Archibald O., and Helcio U. Saraiva. 1990. Development and Status Inheritance. University of Wisconsin, Madison. Mimeo.

Havighurst, Robert. 1957. Educação, Mobilidade Social e Mudança Social em Quatro Sociedades. *Educação e Ciencias Sociais* 2(1): 114–219.

Hout, Michael. 1984. Status, Autonomy, and Training in Occupational Mobility. *American Journal of Sociology* 89(6): 1379–409.

Hunter, Alfred A. 1988. Formal Education and Initial Employment. *American Sociological Review* 53(5): 753–65.

Hutchinson, Bertrand (ed.). 1960. *Mobilidade e Trabalho*. Rio de Janeiro: Centro Brasileiro de Pesquisas Educacionais.

_____. 1960. Aspectos da Educação Universitária e Status Social. In *Mobilidade e Trabalho*, ed. B. Hutchinson. Op. cit.

_____. 1958. Structure and Exchange Mobility in the Assimilation of Immigrants in Brazil. *Population Studies* 12(1): 111–20.

_____. 1957. The Social Grading of Occupations in Brazil. *British Journal of Sociology* 3(8): 176–89.

Jencks, Christopher, Lauri Perman, and Lee Rainwater. 1988. What is a Good Job? A New Measure of Labor-Market Success. *American Journal of Sociology* 93(6): 1322–57.

Jones, F. L. 1984a. New and Old Mobility Ratios. *Social Forces* 45(4): 764–814.

_____. 1984b. Structural and Circulation Mobility are Alive and Well. Mimeo.

Lam, David, and Deborah Levison. 1989. Declining Inequality in Schooling in Brazil and its Effect on Inequality in Earnings. *Journal of Development Economics* 37: 199–226.

_____. 1987. Experience and Schooling: Decomposing Earnings Inequality in the U.S. and Brazil. Ann Arbor, Population Studies Center. Mimeo.

Langoni, Carlos G. 1973. *Distribuição de Renda e Desenvolvimento Econômico do Brasil*. Rio de Janeiro: Expressão e Cultura.

Morley, Samuel A. 1982. *Labor Markets and Inequitable Growth: The Case of Authoritarian Capitalism in Brazil*. New York: Cambridge University Press.

Ornestein, Michael D. 1976. *Entry into the American Labor Force*. New York: Academic Press.

Pastore, José. 1979. *Desigualdade e Mobilidade Social no Brasil*. São Paulo: T. A. Queiroz.

Pastore, José, and Archibald O. Haller. 1982. Social Mobility under Labor Market Segmentation in Brazil. In *Social Structure and Behavior*. New York: Academic Press.

Pastore, José, and Manoel Cabral. 1983. Cambios ocupacionales, movilidad e desigualdade social en Brasil. In *Movilidad ocupacional e mercados de trabajo*, ed. V. Tolman. Santiago: PREALC.

SEADE. 1989. Educação em São Paulo: Uma Análise Regional. Coleção Realidade Paulista.

Silva, Nelson do Valle. 1973 (revised 1984). Posição Social nas Ocupações. IBGE, Rio de Janeiro. Mimeo.

Slomczynski, Kazimierzu, and Tadeusz K. Krauze. 1987. Cross-National Similarity in Social Mobility Patterns. *American Sociological Review* 52(5): 598–611.

Snipp, Matthew C. 1985. Occupational Mobility and Social Class: Insights from Men's Career Mobility. *American Sociological Review* 50(4): 475–92.

Stier, Haya, and David B. Grusky. 1990. An Overlapping Persistence Model of Career Mobility. *American Sociological Review* 55(5): 736–56.

Appendix. Methodology and Data Basis

The basic source of data for this study is the *Pesquisa Nacional por Amostra de Domicílios* (the 1982 PNAD), the Brazilian annual population survey, conducted by the Instituto Brasileiro de Geografia e Estatística (IBGE). In 1982, the PNAD sample size was 131,958 households. Since the focus of this study is social mobility, a sub-file with data on heads of household was produced from the initial file. Male heads of household who are less than 20 years old and more than 64 years old were excluded. We also excluded female heads of households. Finally, we excluded all households in two regions, North and Center-West, because the samples in those regions were composed of only urban households. This same procedure was adopted in another study on mobility with a PNAD data source (Pastore, 1979). Produced from a similar data basis, results of this study can be compared with those obtained by Pastore in the 1973 study in order to search for possible changes in Brazilian social mobility patterns.

Crucial Variables

1. Occupation. Similar to the one conducted in 1973, the 1982 PNAD instrument had a supplement with questions on mobility, which provided information about individuals' occupational status at two points in time: the week the survey was conducted (variable 503) and upon obtaining a first job (variable 6,604). In addition, there was one question pertaining to the occupation of the father at the time at which the interviewed person entered the labor market (variable 6,607).

In order to allow for comparisons with the 1973 study, the same occupational classification had to be used. This required some adjustments in the 1982 list of occupations. The two classifications were basically the same, but the 1982 study was more detailed for some occupations. For those cases, occupations were regrouped in such a way that the same list of occupations was finally obtained.

2. Education. A key variable, education is measured in this study by years of schooling (variable 318). The 1982 survey for this variable aggregates those with nine to 11 years of schooling and those with 12 or more years of schooling. These two groups correspond to high school and college levels, respectively. To disaggregate the two groups, we used information on years of school and degree completed (variables 312 and 314 for those that are still in school, and variables 315 and 317 for those that are not at

Appendix Table 10.1. Transformation of Year-Degree (Variables 312, 314, 315 and 317) into Years of Schooling

Variable 314/317			Variable 312/315 (Year at school)			
(Degree)	1	2	3	4	5	6
High school	9	10	11	—	—	—
College	12	13	14	15	16	17

school anymore). We developed a conversion matrix to transform year-degree into years of schooling (Appendix Table 10.1).

3. Social status. In this study, we used the social status scale developed by Silva (1973) and used in the 1973 study. This scale is a combined computation that takes into account educational attainment (an income-education computation) and labor market experience (occupation). The procedure Silva uses to compute an individual's social status may be summarized as follows:

a) For each year of schooling, the average income of all individuals is computed;

b) For each occupation, the average of the averages of incomes (as computed in a) is computed;

c) The estimates obtained in b) are standardized and the result is a list of social status levels associated with the occupations;

d) The social status of each individual is given by the social status of his occupation.

Silva's scale is associated with each occupation in this study, according to the adjustments referred to in item 1 above. All heads of household were classified into six groups of social status: high, middle-high, middle-middle, middle-low, low-high, and low-low. This procedure allows the authors to deal with appropriate and workable mobility tables and is also adopted in Pastore's 1979 study.

In 1985, Silva updated his social status scale to reflect some of the 1982 PNAD occupations. For most of the occupations, however, the new Silva scale is the same as that of 1973. We therefore decided not to use the 1982 scale. It seemed a safer strategy to group the 1982 disaggregated occupational groups into the 1973 original groups and to use the same scale to compare mobility patterns across time. Another possible strategy might have been to build an entirely new scale for 1982. This path, however, would demand time and resources that are beyond the limits of this study.

The authors are aware, however, that a bias may be introduced because we use a social status scale built with data from the 1970 census in a study with data from a 1982 survey. It is quite possible that some occupations moved into the scale (upward or downward). If the period covered consists only of the 12 years that separate the two studies, risks would be minimized. But the study also includes the social status of the head of the household's father at the time the head of the household entered the labor market. This means that, in some cases, people's social status 30 or 40 years earlier is being defined in 1970. This is a common problem in social mobility studies. We first developed the study without taking this issue into account. At the end, however, we attempt to qualitatively evaluate the impact of this possible bias.

CHAPTER 11

Education, Mobility and Growth

Irma Adelman, Samuel Morley, Christoph Schenzler and Stephen Vogel

Until the second oil shock in 1979, Brazil enjoyed very rapid and skill-intensive growth. Despite substantial investments in education and a rapid relative increase in the supply of educated labor, educational wage differentials widened significantly in the 1960s, exacerbating other sources of rising inequality. In the 1970s the situation reversed as real income gains for the less educated rose to two to three times more than incomes of those with high school and college degrees. Yet, paradoxically, overall income inequality continued to increase. Using a slightly later time period, Park, Ross and Sabot show in this volume that this phenomenon is due to the change in the share of the more educated creating an educational Kuznets effect, which tended to increase inequality and was so large that it more than offset the decline in wage differentials.

We take a different approach to the problem here, one that distinguishes between survivors and new entrants. We define survivors as those in the labor force over the entire time period under observation. Morley (1981) showed the importance of this distinction in any investigation of the interaction between growth and inequality because upward mobility for survivors is often disguised by the relatively low starting incomes of new entrants. Here, we develop a new technique to estimate income growth for survivors and use it to show that the education differential for survivors probably widened at the same time that it narrowed for the entire population. New entrants, who were relatively well educated, started their careers in comparatively low-wage jobs. These starting points tend to disguise the amount of upward mobility enjoyed by the well educated who were already in the labor force in 1970 and who were thus in a good position to take full advantage of skill-intensive growth during the ensuing decade.

The key to the puzzle is mobility over time, because over time people can move between jobs and have expected incomes quite different from what appears to be implied by the income distribution at any point. We have reported elsewhere (Adelman et al., 1990) a technique developed for measuring income mobility using census data. We use this technique here to examine the effect of education and growth on the income of different education and income classes during the 1970s. We should note that our estimation method is a cumbersome substitute for panel data or the sort of specialized backward-looking questionnaires used by Pastore and Zylberstajn in this volume to measure mobility in 1982. These authors present a fascinating look at the mobility process. They do not, however, make a direct comparison of mobility for different education classes, relying instead on a regression analysis to determine the influence of education on status.

This study directly estimates the effect of education on mobility. Our estimates shed light on the paradoxical widening of inequality with shrinking educational differentials. The estimates will also show the powerful positive effect education had on the probability of upward mobility and will tell us something about the interaction of education, growth and mobility.

The Estimation Problem

The distribution of income at any point in time can be viewed as the result of a first order Markov process in which the probability that any individual will be in income class j at time t+1 will depend on her or his income class at time t. Formally, our interest in what happens to the income of particular groups over time could then be solved by estimating the transition matrix of the Markov process. From the reported censuses, we have the row and column sums of transition matrices, whose ijth elements are the number of people in income class j at time t and income class i at time t+1. We are looking for some way of estimating these cell entries, given our observation of the row and column sums. Since there are only 2n data points and n^2 unknowns, we need some additional data or restrictions to make progress.

Telser (1963) addressed this problem in the context of market shares for cigarettes using a time series approach. If one takes a sufficient number of observations of the distribution (in Telser's case of cigarette smokers, across brands), and if one assumes these distributions are generated by a first order Markov process, Telser showed how to derive an unbiased regression estimator of the unknown elements of the transition matrix.

Unfortunately, the time series approach is not practical for the income distribution problem in developing countries because we do not have a sufficient number of censuses. But, as an alternative, we can use regional data from the censuses themselves. If we assume either that the same first order Markov mechanism operates in each region, or that it differs across regions in a predictable way, we can proceed, as Telser did. We can use regression analysis to find the transition matrix, which minimizes the difference between the observed and the predicted regional distributions at time t+1, given the observed distributions at time t.

A similar problem has been addressed in sociology and political science. In 1953, Goodman proposed a simple regression to estimate the interior elements in a two-by-two table of individual characteristics when only the regional row and column sums of the two characteristics are known. His technique made the assumption that the interior conditional probabilities were constant across regions. Crewe and Payne (1976) applied the same general technique to get an estimate of the percentage of different occupational groups voting for the two main British political parties. The authors extended Goodman's technique by assuming that the conditional probabilities were a function of exogenous factors that vary across regions. Crewe and Payne derived a best linear unbiased estimator that simultaneously produced an estimate of the transition matrix and of the effect of the exogenous variables on the transition matrix. Their model was applied to a two-by-two case—two parties and two broad occupational classes. Our model is a simple extension of Crewe and Payne to the n-dimension case, where the n-dimensions are income classes and where we are trying to find the proportion of those in income class j in time t who move to class i at time t+1.

Let P be an nxn transition matrix whose ijth element, P_{ij}, is the proportion of workers in income class j at time t who move to class i at time t+1. Let X_i and Y_i be the observed fraction of the labor force in income class i at time t and t+1, respectively. N is the number of mutually exclusive income classes. We can then write in matrix notation:

Y = PX or,

(1) $Y_i = \sum_j P_{ij} X_j \; (i = 1,....,n)$

Equation (1) looks like a regression model where we observe the X's and the Y's and estimate the unknown transition parameters P_{ij}. Clearly, only n-1 of these equations are independent. Rather than dropping one of the equations, however, we make the equivalent restriction that the sum of each column of P_{ij}'s is equal to one. The problem with equation (1) is that we do not have enough data to estimate the P_{ij}. In our case, we have five income classes, so we are trying to estimate 25 elements of the transition matrix, but we have only five observations of the marginal totals X_i and Y_i.

We proceed by using regional observations. If the Markov process could be assumed to be the same across regions, we could increase the number of observations by taking regional observed values of the distribution. It is probably unreasonable, however, to assume that mobility is the same across regions. Instead, one would expect mobility to vary positively with many variables such as income growth and labor force structure that vary across regions. Surely, someone's chances of moving up the distribution ladder are higher in fast growing or highly industrialized regions. Following Crewe and Payne (1976), it is straightforward to modify equation (1) to take account of regional variations in the transition matrix.

We hypothesize that transition probabilities are a function of observable characteristics Z that differ across region. Thus, in the simplest form with only one variable Z:

(2) $P_{ij} = a_{ij} + b_{ij} Z$

In equation (2), Z is a variable with region-specific values. In our case, the growth rate of income was used. We also attempted to introduce education in the same manner, but it was so highly non-linear in its effects that we were forced to separately estimate the income transition matrix for each education class.

If we now substitute equation (2) into equation (1) we get:

(3) $Y_i = \sum_j (a_{ij} + b_{ij} Z) X_j \quad (i = 1,....,n)$

This is the equation system we will estimate under the two restrictions:

(4) $0 \le P_{ij} \le 1$ for all i, j.

(5) $\sum_j P_{ij} = 1$ for $j = 1,....n$

Further details about the estimation are found in the Methodology Appendix.

Data

Central to the procedure we are using here are sets of regional observations of the distribution of income by age, sex and education.[1] The goal is to obtain an estimate of the 1980 income distribution of those workers who survive from 1970—a population we label "survivors." That means that we

---

[1] We used the following 13 regions: 1. Rondônia, Acre, Amazonas, Roraima, Pará, Amapá. 2. Maranhão, Piauí. 3. Ceará. 4. Pernambuco. 5. Fernando de Noronha, Alagoas, Paraíba, Rio Grande do Norte. 6. Sergipe, Bahia. 7. Minas Gerais. 8. Rio de Janeiro, Espírito Santo, Guanabara. 9. São Paulo. 10. Paraná. 11. Santa Catarina. 12. Rio Grande do Sul. 13. Mato Grosso, Goiás, Brasília, Mato Grosso do Sul.

have to remove new entrants from the observed 1980 group in those cohorts where the labor force is larger than that of 1970. We also have to remove those who retire from the 1970 group in those cohorts where the 1970 labor force is larger than in 1980.

The problem is that we have no way of knowing which of the 1980 workers are new entrants in expanding cohorts, or which will retire in those age groups which shrank during the 1970s. We can, however, determine many of the characteristics of new entrants and retirees. For each age cohort, we first disaggregate by sex, education and region with each combination defining a cell. We then subtract the 1970 from the 1980 totals in each cell. If the difference is positive, we know there were new entrants between 1970 and 1980, with the particular characteristics of the cell. We assumed that the new entrants had the same distribution of income as the total observed for that cell in 1980. This assumption permits us to estimate the income distribution of survivors in each cell by subtracting, element by element, the vector of new entrants from the 1980 cell totals. If we then aggregate across the 130 cells (two sex, five education, and 13 regions) in each age cohort, we obtain an estimate of the 1980 income distribution of survivors. It is a vector giving the observed value of the X_i's which we will compare with the Y_i's obtained from the observed 1970 distribution.

For older age cohorts which had retirements instead of new entrants over the 1970s, we use a procedure similar to that described above to estimate the 1970 income distribution of those who would retire during the next decade. In any cell, if the 1980 number is smaller than the 1970 number, we know there were net retirements. Here, we assumed that the retirees had the same income profile in 1970 as the rest of the members of the cell, and we subtract element by element the vector of retirees from the total distribution of the population in the cell in 1970. We then aggregate across the cells as before to get a survivors' distribution for 1970. This distribution gives the vector of Y_i's which we will use in our regressions along with the X_i's obtained from the observed 1980 distribution.

Regional migration is the other complication encountered in adapting census data for income mobility estimates. Clearly, in a country such as Brazil, there is a substantial amount of interregional migration. Since we assume that mobility differs across regions, we have the choice of excluding migrants, placing them in their originating regions, or placing them in their destination regions. We chose the second of the three options because it allows us to use the observed regional distributions without making a correction for migrants similar to the one made for retirements. The disadvantage of our procedure is that for regions with substantial outmigration, the income growth that we use is not equal to that of the originating region, since some part comes from migrants to faster growing areas.[2]

The Brazilian public-use census tapes upon which this work is based are a 1 percent sample of the demographic censuses of 1970 and 1980. They contain data on earnings, age, sex, occupation, education, place of birth, current residence, time in present residence, and many other variables. We aggregated the data into the 13 regions, and we treated as migrants all those who had resided in their current region for less than 10 years. We then reassigned migrants to the region they reported as their place of birth.

We divided the 1970 population into 10 age groups: nine for five-year intervals between 15 and 60 and one over 60. We created five education groups, classifying individuals according to the last grade passed. These classifications are no education, elementary (five years or less), middle school (six to eight years), high school (nine to 12 years), and university.

Income is reported in current cruzeiros per month. We converted the 1970 data to 1980 cruzeiros using the Rio de Janeiro cost of living index. We then created the following five real income classes: no income; 0–3,599; 3,600–4,999; 5,000–11,999; and >12,000.

We set the upper limit of class two at Cr$3,599 because the 1970 minimum wage was 3,600 measured in 1980 cruzeiros. Over the subsequent decade, the minimum wage rose in real terms, reaching Cr$4,149 or $79 in 1980. This rise means that any worker holding a less than minimum wage job in 1970 would move from class two to class three by finding a minimum wage paying job in 1980. Note that the income variable that we used ostensibly includes earned income from all sources, but there is a substantial degree of underreporting, particularly of income from capital.

Education and Mobility

Before the oil shocks, Brazil was often held up as the quintessential example of inequitable growth. Between 1960 and 1980, it enjoyed one of the world's highest growth rates, with per capita income rising by 3.9 percent per year. But the benefits of this prodigious boom do not appear to have been distributed at all equally across the population. The Gini coefficient rose from .50 to .57 between 1960 and 1970 and a further 2 percent during the 1970s (Langoni, 1973; Benevides, 1985). During the 1970s, the income share of the

---

[2] An interesting question that could be explored in an extension to this work is the effect of migration on income mobility. How much do those who migrate contribute to the observed mobility patterns? Did migrants do better than those they left behind?

Table 11.4. Expected Absolute and Relative Income in 1980 for Females and Males, by 1970 Age and Education Class

Females

Income Class	15–24–1	15–24–2	15–24–3	25–39–1	25–39–2	25–39–3	40–59–1	40–59–2	40–59–3	60+ –1	60+ –2	60+ –3
						Section 4a						
0	4,044.3	3,009.2	9,674.3	4,276.4	4,650.5	7,115.4	2,307.5	4,487.9	8,895.7	13,110.2	557.9	13,990.9
0–3,600	5,845.6	4,781.6	10,130.2	3,793.7	4,328.2	7,231.6	3,270.2	4,585.8	5,418.6	2,958.5	5,065.5	5,834.4
3,600–5K	9,797.2	7,231.7	10,797.9	8,501.7	6,391.6	9,513.9	7,737.2	8,858.8	10,308.8	6,853.6	6,541.1	8,736.6
5–12K	11,543.0	9,715.6	8,645.4	7,185.4	10,982.0	11,031.2	7,663.8	9,265.32	12,369.0	6,983.8	4,312.9	12,809.8
12K Plus	7,702.0	6,645.6	16,838.5	7,361.8	7,206.6	16,167.0	9,254.1	10,084.5	12,751.2	6,086.6	7,575.4	7,205.9
						Section 4b						
0	1	0.744059	2.392082	1	1.087480	1.663876	1	1.944918	3.855124	1	0.042554	1.067176
0–3,600	1	0.817982	1.732961	1	1.140891	1.906212	1	1.402299	1.656962	1	1.712185	1.972080
3,600–5K	1	0.738139	1.102141	1	0.751802	1.119058	1	1.144962	1.332368	1	0.954403	1.274746
5–12K	1	0.841687	0.748973	1	1.528376	1.535224	1	1.208972	1.613951	1	0.617557	1.834216
12K Plus	1	0.862840	2.186250	1	0.978918	2.196066	1	1.089733	1.377897	1	1.244602	1.183895
						Section 4c						
0	1	1.0000	1.0000	1	1.0000	1.0000	1	1.0000	1.0000	1	1.0000	1.0000
0–3,600	1	1.099351	0.724457	1	1.049114	1.145645	1	0.721006	0.429807	1	40.23497	1.847941
3,600–5K	1	0.992043	0.460745	1	0.691325	0.672561	1	0.588694	0.345609	1	22.42771	1.194503
5–12K	1	1.131210	0.313105	1	1.405429	0.922679	1	0.621605	0.418650	1	14.51210	1.718755
12K Plus	1	1.159639	0.913952	1	0.900171	1.319849	1	0.560297	0.357419	1	29.24716	1.109371

Table 11.4. (cont.)

					Males							
Income Class	15–24–1	15–24–2	15–24–3	25–39–1	25–39–2	25–39–3	40–59–1	40–59–2	40–59–3	60+ –1	60+ –2	60+ –3
						Section 4a						
0	7,399.0	7,099.4	16,242.0	10,493.5	7,707.8	16,745.0	5,857.0	8,644.1	4,406.7	8,282.0	3,848.8	4,985.1
0–3,600	5,535.2	7,056.4	12,286.9	4,369.3	5,056.2	6,067.7	3,866.2	5,052.8	5,991.7	4,543.8	5,514.5	6,129.2
3,600–5K	12,979.5	10,923.5	11,867.4	8,872.7	11,028.2	14,125.1	8,467.0	8,964.2	7,350.7	9,180.1	11,245.7	9,293.7
5–12K	12,228.7	13,370.2	14,756.2	14,201.0	11,635.4	14,339.5	11,758.4	11,796.9	12,157.0	10,817.0	10,842.9	7,916.5
12K Plus	13,336.7	16,923.8	16,974.5	7,254.0	16,983.0	15,080.6	10,603.3	15,062.8	15,540.5	8,055.5	14,832.5	15,680.4
						Section 4b						
0	1	0.959508	2.195161	1	0.734530	1.595749	1	1.475857	0.752381	1	0.464718	0.601919
0–3,600	1	1.274822	2.219775	1	1.157210	1.388712	1	1.306916	1.549764	1	1.213631	1.348915
3,600–5K	1	0.841596	0.914318	1	1.242936	1.591973	1	1.058722	0.868158	1	1.225008	1.012374
5–12K	1	1.093390	1.206735	1	0.819336	1.009752	1	1.003274	1.033899	1	1.002394	0.731857
12K Plus	1	1.268964	1.272766	1	2.341191	2.078935	1	1.420576	1.465628	1	1.841288	1.946545
						Section 4c						
0	1	1.0000	1.0000	1	1.0000	1.0000	1	1.0000	1.0000	1	1.0000	1.0000
0–3,600	1	1.328621	1.011212	1	1.575441	0.870256	1	0.885529	2.059811	1	2.611540	2.241021
3,600–5K	1	0.877112	0.416515	1	1.692149	0.997633	1	0.717360	1.153880	1	2.636021	1.681909
5–12K	1	1:139532	0.549725	1	1.115455	0.632776	1	0.679790	1.374168	1	2.156991	1.215871
12K Plus	1	1.322515	0.579805	1	3.187328	1.302795	1	0.962542	1.947985	1	3.962157	3.233895

Notes: Section 4a is expected 1980 income. Section 4b is expected 1980 income relative to 1980 income for education class one. Section 4c is expected 1980 income relative to 1980 income of education class and income class one.

school and grade school graduates, there are only seven cases out of 80 where the gain of the latter exceeds that of the former.

One may ask a further question: did education confer a greater advantage to those who started at the top than at the bottom? That is, how did those with education and a good start do relative to those with education and a bad start? Section 4c of Table 11.4 addresses that question. In it, we have divided each observation in section 4b by the value in the zero income class. We learned from section 4b that education raised one's prospects of upward mobility. Here, we learn that the relative advantages of education tend to differ across gender. For females, the advantage of education for those starting in the lowest income class is so large that it dwarfs the increases in expected income further up the income pyramid. In section 4c, 17/24 of the female coefficients are less than one, implying that education confers more of an advantage to those who start at the bottom.

For males, the picture is somewhat different. Education clearly increased mobility except in the bottom income group. In the other four classes, 25/32 of the coefficients in section 4b are greater than one. This result indicates that regardless of what a man earned in 1970, his prospects were better with more education. The zero income class seems to be different. In this class, education apparently was not particularly helpful, possibly reflecting a self-selection bias. Section 4b tells us that of those in the top two education classes who had zero income in 1970, five of eight had lower income in 1980 than those who had no education. This is a surprising result, because it suggests that more education does not necessarily confer an advantage regardless of where males start their careers.

Where education helped males significantly was at the top of the 1970 income pyramid. For those lucky enough to start in the top class in 1970, education raised substantially the probability of staying in the top income class in 1980. Compare in section 4c, for example, the numbers in the bottom row with those further up the same table. Six of the eight are greater than one, and 5/8 are bigger than any of the other entries in their respective columns. This suggests that the skill requirements associated with modern economic growth made at least a high school level of education increasingly necessary for those who occupy Brazil's best paying jobs.

Altogether, the bottom portions of the table suggest quite strongly that the education differential for survivors probably widened. This contradicts the pattern we observed for the entire labor force and helps explain why the distribution became less equal even though the skill differential narrowed for the entire 1980 labor force.

Education, Mobility and Growth

What is the interaction of growth, education and mobility? This question can be directly addressed by our regression because regional income growth was used as an explanatory variable.

We found in our previous study that our growth variable generally had a positive effect on mobility (Adelman et al., 1990). Here, we can ask: did the better educated enjoy higher mobility than the less educated in the faster growing states? Does our evidence suggest a positive interaction between growth and education?

Space limitations prevent us from displaying all the growth coefficients directly. Instead, we have counted all the cases in which there is a positive growth effect. Table 11.5 indicates both the number of cases and, in parentheses, how many are significantly positive and negative. A positive growth effect means that growth raises the probability of upward mobility or lowers the probability of downward mobility. We included the bottom three terms along the main diagonal, (0,0), (1,1), (2,2), with the downward mobility cases.

Somewhat surprisingly, the table does not suggest a very strong positive growth effect. The growth coefficient is significant and has the right sign in about one-third of the regressions, but in many of these the growth coefficient's qualitative effect is small. As the reader can see from the table, for females, fast growth rates appear to lower chances of upward mobility as often as they raise them. For males, growth was far more helpful, particularly for those older than 25 in 1970. To some extent, the failure of the growth effect reflects the poorer fit of our regressions for women and people in the highest income class. Looking only at those cases where the $R^2 > .50$, which we have indicated with an asterisk in the table, a more favorable picture of the effects of growth emerges. Of these growth coefficients, 55 percent are positive and 30 percent are significant.

Turning now to the education-growth interaction, the evidence does not suggest a strong positive relationship between growth and upward mobility for the educated. Those instances where the growth coefficient is positive are not higher for the better educated except in the youngest age group. Moving across each row of the table, we do not find an increase in the number of significant positive cases. Indeed, the number falls for the three oldest male age groups and the two oldest female groups. This result indicates that upward mobility is not heavily dependent on growth, which is an unexpected and surprising result that requires further investigation.

Table 11.5. Number of Cases Where Growth Effect Is Positive

	Education Class									Total Coefficients		
	1			2			3			1	2	3
	Positive Total	Signif. Pos	Signif. Neg	Positive Total	Signif. Pos	Signif. Neg	Positive Total	Signif. Pos	Signif. Neg			
Females												
15–24	7	(6)	(4)	13*	(7)	(3)	14	(5)	(8)	17	20	22
25–39	9*	(4)	(4)	11*	(5)	(6)	15*	(7)	(3)	17	19	23
40–59	10	(6)	(5)	9	(6)	(9)	8	(4)	(7)	20	21	23
60+	9	(4)	(4)	11	(5)	(5)	10*	(1)	(4)	17	21	23
Males												
15–24	12*	(3)	(4)	11*	(6)	(3)	12	(8)	(4)	22	18	22
25–39	10*	(9)	(2)	10*	(5)	(2)	10	(6)	(6)	17	18	23
40–59	14*	(10)	(3)	9*	(7)	(4)	12	(6)	(8)	17	19	23
60+	11*	(7)	(1)	11*	(4)	(4)	13*	(5)	(3)	17	19	20

Notes: In income classes 0–3, staying in the same place is treated as downward mobility. Numbers in parentheses are number of significant positive and negative growth coefficients.
*R^2 of regression is greater than 50 percent.

Conclusions

We draw several conclusions from this work. First, the estimation procedure works quite well and provides good estimates of mobility in most cases. Our fits were good for males and for prime age females, but the fits tended to be much worse for those with high education levels or those over 60 in 1970. This result may reflect the smaller sample size in these cases.

Second, the separation of new entrants from survivors appears to be important to understanding what happened to education differentials. Whereas the reported education income differential narrowed quite sharply between 1970 and 1980, almost surely this was not true for survivors alone. Education had a strong positive effect on upward mobility at all points in the income pyramid and was particularly strong at the top. Since the educated survivors were concentrated in the upper income classes in 1970, that pattern suggests a widening of education differentials and income inequality. Finally, we could find little evidence of a positive interaction between growth, education and upward mobility. Instead, the better educated tended to have high mobility regardless of the region in which they were located.

REFERENCES

Adelman, I., S.A. Morley, C. Schenzler, and M. Warning. 1990. Measuring Income Mobility with Census Data. Vanderbilt University, Department of Economics, Nashville. Mimeo.

Adelman, I., and P. Whittle. 1980. Static and Dynamic Indices of Income Inequality. *Canadian Journal of Development Studies* 1: 27–46.

Bacha, E.L., and L. Taylor. 1978. Brazilian Income Distribution in the 60s: Facts, Model Results and the Controversy. *Journal of Development Studies* 14: 271–97.

Benevides, C.M. 1985. Income Distribution in Brazil: 1970–1980 Compared. Ph.D. dissertation, Department of Economics, Vanderbilt University, Nashville.

Bonelli, R., and G.L. Sedlacek. 1989. Distribuição de Renda: Evolução no Último Quarto de Século. In *Mercado de Trabalho e Distribuição de Renda: uma Coletânea,* eds. G.L. Sedlacek and R. Barros. Rio de Janeiro: IPEA.

Crewe, I., and C.D. Payne. 1976. Game with Nature: An Ecological Regression Model of the British Two Party Vote Ration in 1970. *British Journal of Political Science* 7: 43–81.

Fields, G. 1977. Who Benefits from Economic Development? A Re-examination of Brazilian Growth in the 1960s. *American Economic Review* 67: 570–82.

Fishlow, A. 1972. Brazilian Size Distribution of Income. *American Economic Review* 62: 391–402.

Goodman, L. 1953. Ecological Regression and the Behavior of Individuals. *American Sociological Review* 18: 663–64.

Langoni, C.G. 1973. *Distribuição de Renda e Crescimento Econômico do Brasil.* Rio de Janeiro: Expressão e Cultura.

Morley, S.A. 1981. The Effect of Changes in the Population on Several Measures of Income Distribution. *American Economic Review* 71: 285–94.

_____. 1982. *Labor Markets and Inequitable Growth: The Case of Authoritarian Capitalism in Brazil.* New York: Cambridge University Press.

Telser, L. 1963. Least Squares Estimates of Transition Probabilities. In *Measurement in Economics,* eds. C. Christ et al. Stanford: Stanford University Press.

Methodology Appendix

Available statistical packages cannot incorporate the adding up and sign restrictions expressed in equations (4) and (5). We therefore treated the problem as a non-linear programming problem. The objective function minimized is the sum of squared errors, and the constraints are given by the three equations below. This yields a non-linear programming problem with non-linear inequality constraints.

A representative equation of the constraint set is given by:

$$Y_i^r = \sum_j (a_{ij} + b_{ij} Z^r) X_i^r + e^r$$

where the r superscript indicates regional observations and e^r is the statistical error term.

In our estimation, we required that the inequality constraint hold for all values of Z in the sample and that the cross-equation constraint hold for the mean value of Z in the sample. That is:

$$0 \leq P_{ij}^r \leq 1 \text{ for all } i, j, r$$

$$\sum_i \overline{P_{ij}^r} \leq 1 \text{ for } j = 1,\ldots,n$$

$$P_{ij}^r = a_{ij} + b_{ij} Z^r \; ; \; \overline{P_{ij}^r} \text{ is the sample mean of } P_{ij}^r.$$

The above procedure yields unbiased estimates of the parameters under the usual assumptions that the distribution of the error term is iid.

Income and Educational Inequality and Children's Schooling Attainment

12

Ricardo Barros and David Lam

Education in Brazil has at least four undesirable features. First, the average educational attainment is remarkably low even when compared to other countries with similar levels of per capita income and development. Second, the inequality in education is very high. For instance, Lam and Levison (1991, 1992b) estimated a variance of years of schooling among males in Brazil that is 70 percent higher than the United States, even though mean schooling is over twice as high in the United States. A high degree of income inequality and a close link between education and income inequality are well documented features of the Brazilian economy.[1] It is clear that perhaps the most effective policy to reduce income inequality in Brazil is educational expansion, with emphasis on primary and secondary education. Such a policy would simultaneously increase the level and reduce the inequality in education, with parallel impacts on the distribution of income. A third prominent characteristic of education in Brazil is that the educational attainment of children is highly correlated with the schooling of their parents and grandparents. This is not only an indication of lack of equal opportunity, but also suggests that there are limits on the extent of social mobility in Brazil. Increasing the quantity and improving the quality of the primary and secondary public school system in Brazil seems to be an essential policy to promote equal opportunity and foster social mobility. A fourth feature is the existence of large regional disparities in children's educational attainment. As with regional differences in many socioeconomic characteristics in Brazil (Almeida dos Reis and Barros, 1991), these differences are large, temporally stable, and difficult to explain. They are likely to reflect a very unequal regional allocation of the limited Brazilian investments in education.

---

[1] See Park, Ross and Sabot in this volume for the contrasts between Brazil and Korea with regard to education and income inequality.

Improvements in educational attainment, with special emphasis on primary and secondary education, seem to be an important goal in Brazilian society. To shed some light on how this goal can be accomplished, we investigate how the schooling attainment of Brazilian children depends on the distribution of income and on the education of their parents. We have four major goals. First, we want to describe the current level of educational achievement among Brazilian children, differences in educational attainment across regions, and the patterns of educational mobility across generations. Second, we want to estimate a model that would disentangle the effect of parents' income from the effect of parents' education. Third, we want to estimate and compare the impact of changes in the mean with the impact of changes in the degree of inequality in parents' income and education. Finally, we wish to verify how much of the large regional disparities in Brazil can be explained by regional differences in the distributions of parents' income and education.

Setting and Data

Our study is based on the 1982 Brazilian Annual Household Survey (*Pesquisa Nacional por Amostra de Domicílios—PNAD*). We use this survey primarily because it includes information on the educational attainment of grandparents. As will be shown, information on grandparents' education is of particular value in trying to estimate the effect of parents' attributes on the schooling attainment of children. The entire analysis is performed separately for two important geographic areas in Brazil: the relatively poorer and less educated Brazilian Northeast and the richer and better educated state of São Paulo. The analysis is limited to urban areas. According to the 1980 Brazilian demographic census, 49 percent of the Brazilian population lives in these two geographic areas—28 percent in the state of São Paulo and 22 percent in the Northeast region.

We limit the analysis to children born in 1968. These children should have all begun their schooling in the year they turned seven, 1975, and would have turned 14 during the year of the survey.[2] We have chosen to use one "schooling cohort," and this cohort in particular, for several reasons.

---

[2] All of these children had their 14th birthday in the year of the survey, although roughly three-quarters of them would have been 14 at the time of the survey in September. We will often refer to the children in the sample as 14-year-olds for convenience, although strictly speaking, we will mean the cohort of children that turned age 14 in 1982.

Since the opportunity cost of spending time in school is strongly dependent on the age of the child, the demand for schooling will necessarily be dependent on age.[3] We know very little about the relationship between age and the value of time among Brazilian children, and have chosen to constrain the analysis to one age group in order to avoid one possible extra source of model misspecification. The fact that our data set is very large makes this choice feasible.[4]

Since we imagine the demand for schooling to be a household decision, we use the household as our unit of analysis. An observation consists of a child born in 1968, with variables reflecting the characteristics of the child's parents and grandparents. Since we are primarily interested in the effects of the characteristics of parents on schooling outcomes, we restrict our attention to children with both parents present in the household.[5] Our sample of households with at least one child born in 1968 contains 1,604 households in the Northeast and 867 households in São Paulo. When we restrict the sample to those families for which we have complete data on the schooling of both parents and all four grandparents, and the income of the

---

[3] See, for example, Psacharopoulos and Arriagada (1986) and Levison (1991) for more on the tradeoff between schooling and work in Brazil.

[4] The choice of age 14 is motivated by three facts. First, Brazil has mandatory schooling up to age 14. Since children are expected to enter the first grade when they are seven years of age, they are expected to be attending the eighth grade in the year they turn 14, in the absence of grade repetition or movements in and out of school. The eighth grade is the last grade of elementary school in the Brazilian school system, and high school is not mandatory. Second, Brazilian labor legislation states that only children age 14 or older can work without special permission. Starting at age 12, children can work under special circumstances, but employers are obliged to certify that the children they employ are currently attending school. Third, since this study relies on information from a household survey, only children currently living with their parents can be included in the analysis. The use of older age groups would lead to increasing sample selection, since the probability of children leaving home increases with age.

[5] This screening procedure leaves out of the sample all 14-year-olds whose father is not the head of the household where they were residing at the time of the survey. This eliminates about 15 percent of children in the Northeast, and about 7 percent in São Paulo. We exclude this group since the main focus of the study is the relationship between parents' attributes and their children's schooling attainment. If poorly educated or low-income parents are less likely to be in intact unions when the child is age 14, then our sample will tend to underrepresent these economically disadvantaged children. This may lead us to overstate schooling attainment of all 14-year-olds in the two regions. Even if we have a nonrandom sample of all children, we will not necessarily have any systematic bias in the estimated *effects* of parental characteristics on schooling outcomes, providing the "schooling response function" we estimate below is the same for all families, independent of their current living arrangements.

household head—the sample used for our regressions below—the sample sizes are 820 for São Paulo and 1,525 for the Northeast.[6]

Schooling Attainment of 14-Year-Olds

We use as our outcome variable the number of years of completed schooling of each child. An alternative outcome variable would be the current school attendance of each child, a measure normally expected to be a good indicator of ultimate school attainment. Current school attendance of 14-year-olds turns out to be a relatively poor measure of schooling attainment in Brazil, however. Table 12.1 demonstrates a number of important facts about the distribution of years of schooling, controlling for region and whether the child was in or out of school at the time of the survey. As expected, the distributions in the table indicate that children in school at age 14 have higher school attainment than those out of school. The distributions also show, however, that among those 14-year-olds attending school there is a surprisingly high degree of heterogeneity in schooling attainment: in São Paulo, for example, over 50 percent of 14-year-olds currently attending school had completed less than six years of schooling; in the Northeast the corresponding proportion was over 80 percent. Out of all 14-year-olds enrolled in school, only about 7 percent in the Northeast and 20 percent in São Paulo had completed the seventh grade. Our data, however, do not allow us to determine the extent to which these shortfalls result from intermittent attendance or grade repetition. As pointed out elsewhere in this volume by Gomes-Neto and Hanushek, and by Mello e Souza and Silva, grade repetition is one of the most serious problems in the Brazilian educational system, and is no doubt a major explanation for the schooling attainment shortfalls identified here.

The table provides considerable evidence that grade repetition, and not simply dropping out of school, is responsible for the low levels of schooling attainment in the Northeast. The distribution of years of schooling for 14-year-olds currently attending school in the Northeast is similar to the distribution of years of schooling of those *out of school* in São Paulo. Those currently enrolled in the Northeast have only .4 years more schooling on average than those out of school in São Paulo (3.7 versus 3.3). Because of

---

[6] Although the overall populations in these two regions are roughly similar, the average sampling proportion for the PNAD was substantially higher in the Northeast (averaging around 1/200) than in São Paulo (averaging about 1/400), making our sample almost twice as large in the Northeast.

Table 12.1. Years of Completed Schooling and Summary Statistics by Current Enrollment Status, 14-Year-Olds, State of São Paulo and Northeast Brazil, 1982

	São Paulo			Northeast		
	Out of school	In school	Total	Out of school	In school	Total
Percent completing:						
< 1 year	11.5	0.3	2.6	41.8	6.1	12.8
1 year	6.1	1.5	2.5	14.5	9.0	10.0
2 years	12.1	5.2	6.6	19.3	12.9	14.1
3 years	15.1	8.0	9.4	11.1	16.1	15.1
4 years	32.6	16.2	21.0	9.3	22.7	20.2
5 years	17.6	22.8	20.9	1.7	14.5	12.1
6 years	2.4	25.2	20.7	1.4	11.3	9.4
7 years	1.8	20.0	16.3	0.5	6.8	5.6
8 years	0.6	0.9	0.9	0.2	0.6	0.5
Mean schooling	3.27	5.13	4.75	1.46	3.67	3.25
Std. deviation	1.74	1.55	1.75	1.61	1.91	2.05
Percent < 4 years	44.9	15.0	20.9	86.8	44.0	52.1
Percent < 6 years	95.1	53.9	62.1	97.9	81.3	84.4
Weighted % in region	19.93	80.07	100.0	18.75	81.25	100.0
Sample size			820			1,525

Sources: Estimated from 1982 PNAD, using IBGE sample weights.

a very high repetition rate and large movements in and out of school in Brazil, it appears that current school attendance is a very imperfect predictor of completed years of schooling. Here we see an extreme manifestation of the problem of grade repetition. The most remarkable fact in Table 12.1 is that despite large regional disparities in school attainment—the average number of completed years of schooling in São Paulo is 1.5 years higher than the average in the Northeast—school attendance rates in the two geographic areas are almost identical. Attendance rates in both regions are around 80 percent, differing by only 1 percentage point. Based on these facts, we have chosen to use as our outcome variable the number of completed years of schooling instead of the child's current school attendance status.

The basic features of the distribution of years of schooling for 14-year-olds in São Paulo and in the Northeast can also be seen in Table 12.1. The table reveals three important facts. First, schooling achievement in both regions is very low. Children who have been continuously enrolled from age seven to 14, as mandated by law, and who have not repeated a grade, should have completed seven years of schooling. Compared to this target of seven years, there is a gap in mean schooling attainment of 14-year-olds of 2.25 years in São Paulo, and a gap of 3.75 years in the Northeast. Second, the schooling level in São Paulo is significantly higher than in the Northeast. The mean is 1.5 years higher in São Paulo, while the proportion with at least six years of schooling is 38 percent in São Paulo, compared to only 16 percent in the Northeast. Third, the Northeast, in addition to having a lower level of schooling, has more unequal distribution. The standard deviation is .3 years higher, even though the mean is 1.5 years lower. This inequality can be seen in the much higher proportions of 14-year-olds with very low schooling attainment in the Northeast. Over half of the 14-year-olds in the Northeast have less than four years of schooling, with 23 percent having completed one year or less.

Distribution of Schooling and Income for Parents

This section examines the extent to which the large regional differences in schooling outcomes documented in the previous section are a consequence of differences in the characteristics of households across regions. Household characteristics may determine child schooling attainment for a variety of reasons. As discussed by Becker (1975), higher income households may demand a greater quantity (and quality) of schooling for their children for two reasons: (1) children's schooling may be a consumption good, the demand for which increases with higher income; or (2) higher income parents face lower costs of self-financing. Better educated parents may demand more schooling for their children due to taste differences, or they may have an advantage in helping their children succeed in school. We will not be able to identify why parental education and income affect schooling attainment, but we are interested in the reduced form effect working through a variety of demand and productivity related mechanisms. Our goal is to estimate, for example, how much higher schooling attainment would be in the Northeast if parents in the Northeast had the same characteristics as parents in São Paulo.

We begin by investigating differences in the distribution of parents' characteristics in the two regions. Table 12.2 gives summary statistics for the distribution of schooling and income of the parents of 14-year-olds in São Paulo and the Northeast. The levels of educational attainment for both fathers and mothers are higher in São Paulo than in the Northeast. Fathers in São Paulo have mean schooling of 3.9 years, compared to 2.6 years for fathers in the Northeast. In São Paulo the schooling level of fathers tends to be higher than among mothers, while in the Northeast the distribution of education tends to be very similar for fathers and mothers.

Table 12.2. Schooling and Income Distribution for Parents of 14-Year-Olds, State of São Paulo and Northeast Brazil, 1982

Characteristic	São Paulo	Northeast	Difference
Father's schooling			
Mean (years)	3.92	2.57	1.35
Standard deviation (years)	3.87	3.22	0.65
Coefficient of variation	0.99	1.25	−0.27
Percent with:			
At least 1 year	79.1	57.9	21.2
At least 4 years	49.5	31.2	18.3
At least 6 years	18.7	10.8	7.9
Mother's schooling			
Mean (years)	3.35	2.62	0.73
Standard deviation (years)	3.40	2.97	0.43
Coefficient of variation	1.01	1.13	−0.12
Percent with:			
At least 1 year	73.5	62.9	10.6
At least 4 years	45.4	34.0	11.4
At least 6 years	14.1	10.9	3.2
Correlation (Mother's/father's education)	0.708	0.608	0.101
Head of household income (no. of minimum salaries)			
Mean	5.75	2.89	2.86
Standard deviation	9.06	4.01	5.05
Coefficient of variation	1.57	1.39	0.18

Source: Estimated from 1982 PNAD using IBGE sample weights.
Note: Income is number of official minimum salaries earned in previous month.

Table 12.2 also provides information on schooling inequality among parents in the two regions. Although São Paulo has a higher standard deviation of years of schooling for both mothers and fathers, this is more than accounted for by the higher means in São Paulo. The coefficient of variation of years of schooling is lower in São Paulo than in the Northeast, implying that by this measure, the distribution of parents' schooling is more equal in São Paulo than in the Northeast.

Further detail on the distribution of parental schooling in the two regions is provided in Figure 12.1, which shows the cumulative distributions for single years of schooling for mothers and fathers in the two regions. The figure shows that the most pronounced difference between São Paulo and the Northeast is the proportion with very low levels of schooling. Although the educational advantage of parents in the Southeast can be seen through-

Figure 12.1. Cumulative Distributions for Years of Completed Schooling of Fathers and Mothers of 14-Year-Olds, State of São Paulo and Northeast Brazil, 1982

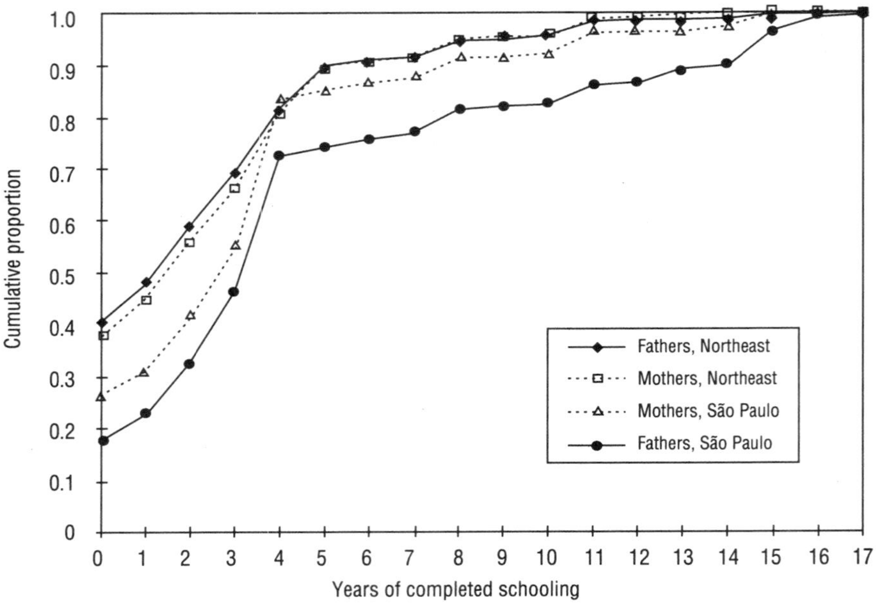

out the educational distribution, the gap diminishes somewhat at higher levels of education, especially for women. As shown in Table 12.2, very low levels of schooling in the Northeast are even more characteristic of parents than for children. Over 40 percent of fathers and 37 percent of mothers in the Northeast have less than one year of schooling, compared to 20 percent of fathers and 26 percent of mothers in São Paulo.

In comparing Tables 12.1 and 12.2, it is important to note that the completed schooling level of 14-year-olds in Brazil is already higher than the average level among both parents, indicating some improvement in educational attainment in Brazil from the last to the current generation. For example, while the mean schooling for fathers of 14-year-olds in the Southeast is slightly less than four years, the mean schooling of the 14-year-olds themselves is 4.7 years. For the Northeast, 14-year-olds have roughly .7 years more schooling than their fathers, 3.3 years compared to 2.6 years.[7]

---

[7] See Lam and Levison (1992a) for a more detailed analysis of improvements in the distribution of schooling in Brazil in recent decades.

One important determinant of intergenerational mobility in schooling is the degree of assortative mating on schooling in the marriage market. As shown in Table 12.2, there is a very high correlation in the schooling of mothers and fathers in Brazil. The correlation between husband's and wife's schooling is over .7 in São Paulo, and over .6 in the Northeast. This high correlation may play an important role, since strong positive assortative mating on schooling will tend to increase inertia in the distribution of education across generations.[8]

In addition to the schooling of parents, we are also interested in the effect of household income on the schooling attainment of children. Table 12.2 shows that the mean income of household heads is almost twice as high in São Paulo, although some fraction of this may be due to cost of living differences. Income inequality, as measured by the coefficient of variation, is high by international standards in both regions, with somewhat greater inequality in São Paulo. The degree of inequality is potentially an important determinant of the mean level of schooling attainment in each region.

Educational Intergenerational Mobility

The previous discussion demonstrates that the educational levels of children and parents are positively related across regions. Next we investigate whether this relationship also holds within each region. This hypothesis is strongly confirmed by Figures 12.2 and 12.3. These figures present the cumulative distribution of single years of schooling among 14-year-olds conditional on their father's education. With a minor exception in the case of 9–11 years for fathers in São Paulo, the figures indicate that increases in the schooling of fathers leads to unambiguous improvements in the distribution of education among children, in the sense of first order stochastic dominance. The cumulative distributions based on mother's education, not shown here, show virtually identical patterns in the two regions.

Figure 12.4 presents the mean schooling of 14-year-olds by single year of schooling of mothers and fathers in the two regions. The points are smoothed as three-year moving averages weighted by the cell sizes for each year of schooling. The figure reveals a steeper relationship between parents and children's education in the Northeast than in São Paulo, raising the hypothesis that parents' education may be a more important determinant of

---

[8] See Lam and Schoeni (1991) for an analysis of assortative mating in schooling in Brazil and its relationship to inequality in earnings.

Figure 12.2. Cumulative Distributions of Years of Completed Schooling of 14-Year-Olds by Schooling of Father, State of São Paulo, 1982

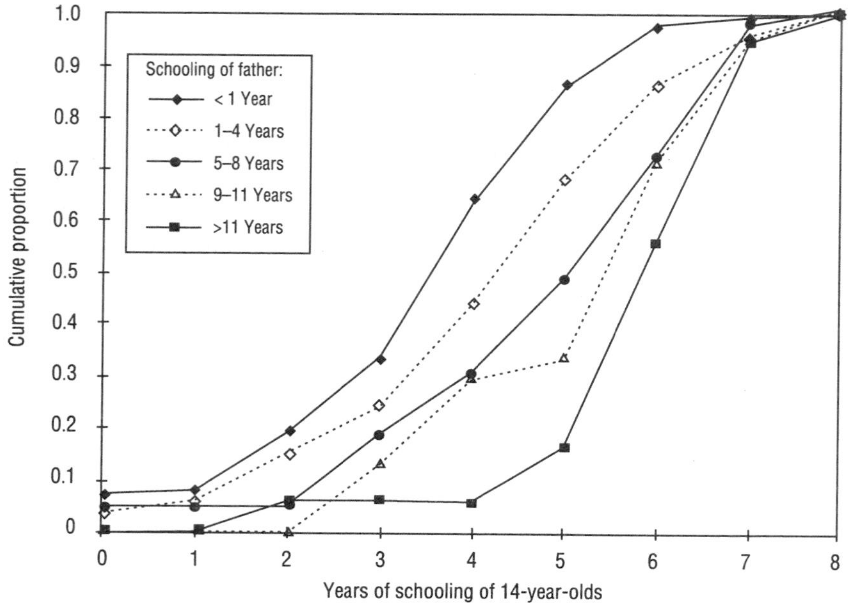

children's education in the Northeast than in São Paulo. At higher levels of parental education the mean years of schooling attainment among 14-year-olds shows little variation between the Northeast and São Paulo. There are substantially larger differences at low levels of parental schooling, however. For parents with less than four years of schooling there is roughly a one-year advantage in the schooling attainment of 14-year-olds in São Paulo compared to the Northeast.

The patterns shown in Figure 12.4 provide an important picture of the relationship between parental schooling and child schooling in São Paulo and the Northeast. Although a precise answer requires the kind of multivariate analysis we will present below, the graph provides dramatic evidence that we are unlikely to explain the large gap in schooling attainment between these two regions by differences in the characteristics of parents alone. The fact that children whose parents have less than four years of schooling (a high proportion of all children) will on average attain a full year less schooling by age 14 in the Northeast than will comparable children in São Paulo means that there is clearly more going on to explain the schooling gap between the two regions than simply the differences in the

Figure 12.3. Cumulative Distributions of Years of Completed Schooling of 14-Year-Olds by Schooling of Father, Northeast Brazil, 1982

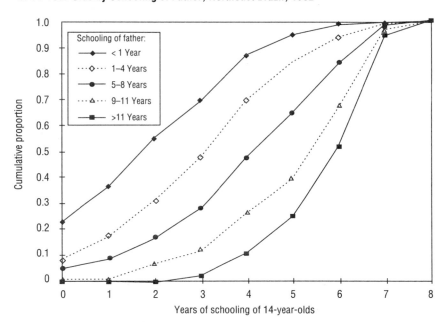

characteristics of parents. The figure suggests that even if parents in the Northeast had the higher educational attainment of parents in the Southeast, that would still leave a substantial gap in the schooling attainment of children. This question will be addressed more formally below in the context of multivariate regressions.

Since we also have data on the schooling of grandparents we can look at intergenerational mobility in education across three generations. The schooling data for grandparents are coded categorically based on the reports of adult household members about the education of their parents. Table 12.3 shows the distribution of schooling for each of the four grandparents of the 14-year-olds in the sample. It also shows the mean schooling of 14-year-olds for each category of grandparents' education.

The data for grandparents continue to show low overall levels of schooling and a substantial schooling gap between the Northeast and São Paulo. About 35 percent of fathers in São Paulo report that their fathers were illiterate, compared to 49 percent in the Northeast. The gaps between regions for grandparents' schooling are perhaps smaller than might be expected, especially for grandmothers. The proportion of mothers who report

Figure 12.4. Mean Schooling of 14-Year-Olds by Years of Completed Schooling of Parents (Three-Year Moving Averages of Single Years of Schooling of Mother and Father), State of São Paulo and Northeast Brazil, 1982

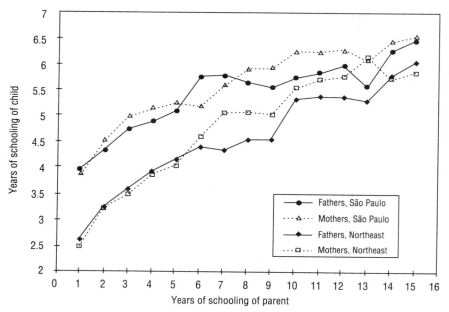

that their mothers were illiterate is 55 percent in São Paulo, compared to 57 percent in the Northeast. This small gap may reflect the fact that many of the respondents in São Paulo have migrated from the Northeast.

Table 12.3 also shows a strong positive relationship between the schooling of grandparents and the schooling of 14-year-olds. Children in both regions who have illiterate grandparents have mean schooling that is .7 to one year less than children with literate grandparents. We continue to see that simply controlling for family background is not likely to explain all of the large regional differences in child schooling attainment, however. Children in the Northeast with illiterate grandfathers have mean schooling of only 2.7 years, while children in São Paulo with illiterate grandfathers have mean schooling of 4.1 years.

The Household Education Response Function

In an earlier version of this chapter (Barros and Lam, 1991), we developed three alternative models to provide a framework for a causal interpreta-

Table 12.3. Mean Schooling of 14-Year-Olds by Grandparents' Education, State of São Paulo and Northeast Brazil, 1982

Schooling of grandparent	Father's				Mother's			
	Father		Mother		Father		Mother	
	%	S_{14}	%	S_{14}	%	S_{14}	%	S_{14}
				São Paulo				
Illiterate	34.8	4.1	51.1	4.3	32.7	4.1	55.0	4.3
Literate	16.4	5.1	12.8	5.1	20.8	5.0	13.4	5.0
1–3 Years	19.5	4.8	14.3	5.1	21.5	4.9	15.1	5.3
4 Years	14.9	5.7	11.1	5.7	16.0	5.4	11.0	5.8
5–8 Years	2.1	5.1	1.9	5.9	2.1	5.8	0.9	6.7
9–11 Years	2.1	5.2	1.8	6.3	2.1	5.8	1.7	6.5
University	1.4	6.5	0.2	7.0	1.2	5.3	0.1	5.0
				Northeast				
Illiterate	48.9	2.7	58.2	2.8	46.7	2.7	57.2	2.8
Literate	22.1	3.6	17.0	3.6	25.9	3.4	20.2	3.4
1–3 Years	11.1	4.0	8.3	4.0	12.6	3.9	11.0	4.1
4 Years	4.9	4.9	4.3	4.8	6.9	4.8	5.5	5.1
5–8 Years	0.9	5.3	0.9	5.5	1.3	5.4	1.2	5.2
9–11 Years	0.7	5.5	0.7	5.6	0.6	5.5	0.7	5.7
University	0.5	5.0	0.2	5.0	0.3	6.0	0.0	—

Source: Estimated from 1982 PNAD, using IBGE sample weights.
Notes: Columns labeled % show frequency distribution for grandparent's education. Columns labeled S_{14} give mean schooling for 14-year-olds with grandparents in that category.

tion of our empirical estimates. We briefly summarize those models here. We are interested in the "household education response function" to variations in parents' education and household economic resources. Specifically, if e_p and y are the levels of parents' education and household economic resources, respectively, then we will think of a function $f_o(e_p, y; h)$ that gives the education level of a 14-year-old child living in some household h. The derivative of f with respect to e_p indicates the response of children's education in each household to changes in parents' education, holding household economic resources constant. We are also interested in the response of children's education to changes in parents' education without holding constant the household economic resources. If $g_o(h)$ denotes the household education response function to variations in parents' education allowing economic resources to vary with parents' education, then the derivative of g with respect to e_p indicates the total response of children's education to changes in parents' education, including both "direct" effects of parental schooling on child schooling, and "indirect effects" working through increased household resources.

Let E_c denote a child's education, let E_p be a vector denoting parents' education, and let Y denote household economic resources. We assume that we can make a simple decomposition into a schooling response function shared by all households and a function that describes household level heterogeneity, so that for some household h:

$$E_c(h) = f_0(E_p(h), Y(h);h) = f_1(e_p, y) + g(h).$$

This implies that heterogeneity across households takes the form of a simple additive disturbance to the education response function. We refer to g as the household shifter and to f_1 as the population response function.

Given the joint distribution of schooling and income in the population, integrating over the f_1 function gives us the mean schooling of 14-year-olds in the population.[9] Our major goal is to estimate how household characteristics affect schooling attainment, i.e., to estimate the component f_1 of the response function. Based on this estimated f_1, we can simulate what the average education among 14-year-olds would be if we changed the distribution of schooling and income in the population.[10] For example, we want to estimate what the mean schooling attainment of 14-year-olds in the Northeast would be if parents in the Northeast had the same distribution of schooling and income as parents in São Paulo.

We consider three alternative sets of assumptions that would permit us to estimate f_1. The motivation and validity of each of these three models is directly related to how the household shifter, g, is generated. By construction, the household shifter permits the response function to differ across households. This shifter can be thought of as representing other resources available to the household, including family habits (persistence, discipline, etc.), and location decisions (proximity of good schools, for example), or unobserved resources (inherited wealth, extended family support networks) that permit otherwise equally educated and wealthy parents to have better educated children. Family habits and location decisions are forms of human capital and therefore dependent in principle on the same determinants of education and income. This joint determination is the

---

[9] Note that in this case, $E_c(h) = f_1(E_p(h), Y(h)) + g(h)$ and therefore, $\mu E_c \equiv E[E_c] = E[f_1(E_p, Y) \equiv \int f_1(e_p, y) dF_{E_p}, Y(e_p, y)$.

[10] For example, we will estimate $\mu_{E_c}^* \equiv \int f_1(e_p, y) dF_{E_p}^*, Y(E_p, y)$ for some alternative distribution F^*.

source of our fundamental identification problem. Therefore, the assumptions underlying our three models are alternative attempts to achieve identification by putting bounds on the degree of joint determination.

The Random Response Case

The first model assumes that the household shifter g is independent of household income and schooling.[11] This is the case in which unobserved household heterogeneity that affects child schooling attainment is uncorrelated with observed household characteristics such as parental education and income. In this case we can estimate f_1 by regressing children's education on parents' education and household economic resources. The implied causal interpretation of parental education in this case is that if a randomly drawn parent had received an additional year of schooling, there would have been an increase in the schooling attainment of a 14-year-old in the household by the amount implied by our estimated function f_1.

One way to justify this model is to assume that the household shifter is generated anew by each generation in a way that is independent of all past history of the household and therefore independent of parents' education and income. If we think of the household shifter as a function of family habits and location decisions, then we are assuming that parents' income and education, on the one hand, and family habits and location, on the other hand, are independently determined. Since this assumption may not be plausible we introduce two alternatives that rely on information on grandparents' education.

The Inherited Shifter Model

A common criticism of estimates of the effect of individuals' schooling on outcomes such as earnings or schooling attainment of their children is that schooling is correlated with a number of important unobserved variables. Schooling attainment, for example, may be influenced by "inherited" family background variables such as ability, taste for schooling, or access to schooling due to family connections or geographical location. One formalization of this argument is to think of an "inherited shifter" that affects child

---

[11] That is, we assume that $g \perp (E_p, Y)$, and therefore, that $E[E_c \mid E_p, Y] = f_1(E_p, Y)$.

schooling attainment and is passed on across generations. In this case we may observe high correlations between parental schooling and child schooling without any direct causal link. Increasing the schooling of a randomly drawn mother will not necessarily increase the schooling of her child if we cannot change the value of this "inherited shifter." Since we observe grandparents' education in our sample as well as parents' education, we are interested in the potential role of grandparents' education to help identify the underlying education response function f_1.

The second model, then, assumes that the household shifter is a function of grandparents' education.[12] In this model we can estimate f_1 by regressing child education on parents' and grandparents' education and household economic resources. To the extent that the grandparents' education variables control for the unobserved family background variables that are correlated with parental schooling and income, we can recover the household response function f_1.

The Noninherited Shifter Model

A quite different assumption is that the household shifter is independent of grandparents' education, implying that grandparents' education is correlated with the children's education only because it had some direct effect on the education of the parents, not because it reflects persistent household heterogeneity across generations. In other words, the shifter is not "inherited" across generations, but does represent effects of unobservable parental characteristics such as taste for schooling or locational choices. Under these assumptions grandparents' education would be a valid instrument to identify the effect of exogenous changes in parental education. In this case, an instrumental variable procedure would estimate the responses of E_c to variations in E_p and Y.

We end up estimating simple models that represent the effects of parental schooling as quadratics in father's and mother's schooling and an interaction with mother's and father's schooling. When income is included in the regression, we use a quadratic specification in the income of the

---

[12] If E_g is a vector denoting grandparents' education, then we assume the household shifter is a function of grandparents' education in the sense that $g(p) = f_2 (E_g(p), g^*(p))$ and $g^* \perp (E_p, Y)|E_p$. It follows that $\mathbf{E}[E_c|E_p, Y, E_g] = f_1 (E_p, Y) + \mathbf{E}[f_2(E_g, g^*)|E_g] = f_1(E_p, Y) + f_3(E_g)$, where $f_3(E_g) = \mathbf{E}[f_2(E_g, g^*)|E_g]$.

household head. Given our specification, children's average completed years of schooling will therefore be given by

$$\mu E_c = F(\mu(e_f), \mu(e_m), \mu(y), \sigma(e_f), \sigma(e_m) cv(y), \rho(e_f, e_m)$$
$$= \alpha_0 + \beta_0 + \alpha_1\mu(e_f) + \alpha_2\mu^2(e_f) + \alpha_2\sigma^2(e_f) + \alpha_3\mu(e_m) + \alpha_4\mu^2(e_m) + \alpha_4\sigma^2(e_m)$$
$$+ \alpha_5\rho(e_m, e_f)\sigma(e_f)\sigma(e_m) + \alpha_5\mu(e_m)\mu(e_f)$$
$$+ \beta_1\mu(y) + \beta_2\mu^2(y)(1 + cv(y)^2), \tag{1}$$

where e_f is the years of schooling of the father, e_m is the years of schooling of the mother, y is the income of the household head, $\mu(e_f) = E[e_f]$, $\mu(e_m) = E[e_m]$, $\sigma(e_f)^2 = Var[e_f]$, $\sigma(e_m)^2 = Var[e_m]$, $\mu(y) = E[y]$, and $cv(y)^2 = Var[y]/E[y]^2$. We add dummy variables for all four grandparents' schooling to estimate the "inherited shifter" model. We use these same dummy variables for grandparents' schooling as instrumental variables to estimate the "noninherited" shifter model.

Changing the Distribution of Parental Characteristics

The expression for children's average completed years of schooling in equation (1) permits us to evaluate the effect of a number of hypothetical changes in the distribution of parental characteristics. Some of these relate directly to potential policy interventions, such as increases in mean income or decreases in income inequality. Others, such as changing the mean and variance of parental schooling, do not represent feasible policy interventions in the short run, but provide insights into long-run implications of alternative schooling investment strategies. More specifically, we will be interested in evaluating how the following changes would affect the average number of completed years of schooling among 14-year-olds: the effect of increases in the average education of the mother and father, $\mu(e_f)$ and $\mu(e_m)$; the effect of increases in average income, $\mu(y)$; the effect of decreases in the inequality in education among parents, $\sigma(e_f)$ and $\sigma(e_m)$; and the effect of decreases in the degree of income inequality, $cv(y)$. Of particular interest is the relative strength of these changes. The direct impact of these hypothetical changes in the distribution of household characteristics can be evaluated by computing the following derivatives:

$$\partial F/\partial\mu(e_f) = \alpha_1 + 2\alpha_2\mu(e_f) + \alpha_5\rho(e_m, e_f)\mu(e_m),$$
$$\partial F/\partial\sigma(e_f) = 2\alpha_2\sigma(e_f) + \alpha_5\sigma(e_m).$$

For derivatives of child schooling attainment with respect to income, we will look at the derivative of completed years of child schooling with

respect to percentage changes in the mean of the household head's income, and with respect to unit changes in the coefficient of variation of the household head's income. Thus we will calculate:

$$\partial F / \partial \ln(\mu(y)) = [\beta_1 \mu(y) + 2\beta_2 \mu(y)(1 + cv(y)^2)]\mu(y)/100,$$

which can be interpreted as the effect of a 1 percent increase in the mean of the household head's income on the mean years of completed schooling of 14-year-olds. Similarly, we will calculate:

$$\partial F / \partial cv(y) = 2\beta_2 \mu^2(y) cv(y),$$

which can be interpreted as the effect of a unit change in the coefficient of variation of the household head's income on the mean years of schooling of 14-year-olds.

We can also use these derivatives to compare the relative strengths of these hypothetical interventions, and to estimate the tradeoff between changes in one variable and changes in another. For example, we can consider how much we could lower the mean schooling of fathers if we simultaneously lowered the variance in the schooling of fathers in order to keep the schooling attainment of children constant. These tradeoffs can give us useful insights into the relative impact on child schooling of a change in, for example, inequality in parental income, versus a change in mean parental income. Using the implicit function theorem, the tradeoff between the mean of fathers' schooling and the standard deviation of fathers' schooling can be expressed as:

$$[d\sigma(e_f)/d\mu(e_f)]_{d\mu(e^c)=0} = [-\partial F / \partial(e_f)]/[\partial F / \partial \sigma(e_f)]$$

$$= -[\alpha_1 + 2\alpha_2\mu(e_f) + \alpha_5\rho(e_m, e_f) \mu(e_m)]/ [2\alpha_2\sigma(e_f) + \alpha_5\sigma(e_m)]. \qquad (2)$$

Analogous expressions can be derived for the other tradeoffs we present below, all of which can be expressed as ratios of the derivatives shown above.

Empirical Results

This section presents estimates of the three alternative models, each estimated for the two regions. Table 12.4 presents regressions using only education variables. Table 12.5 adds the earnings of the household head and earnings squared to all the regressions. In all cases we estimate three alternative specifications. The first is an ordinary least squares regression using only the schooling of the mother and father. The second specification is an

Table 12.4. Response of Child's Schooling to Parents' Schooling for 14-Year-Olds, State of São Paulo and Northeast Brazil, 1982

	São Paulo			Northeast		
	OLS I	OLS II	I.V.	OLS I	OLS II	I.V.
Father's schooling (e_f)	0.1857^x	0.1529^x	0.2324	0.2685^x	0.2342^x	0.4462^x
	(0.0450)	(0.0472)	(0.3617)	(0.0352)	(0.0365)	(0.1799)
Father's schooling squared	−0.0094^y	−0.0071	−0.0870	−0.0150^x	−0.0139^x	−0.0184
	(0.0045)	(0.0045)	(0.0624)	(0.0039)	(0.0039)	(0.0259)
Mother's schooling (e_m)	0.3145^x	0.2662^x	0.9162^x	0.3676^x	0.3375^x	0.4724^z
	(0.0465)	(0.0481)	(0.3342)	(0.0384)	(0.0399)	(0.2872)
Mother's schooling squared	−0.0148^y	−0.0116^y	−0.1277^y	−0.0181^x	−0.0170^x	−0.0291
	(0.0045)	(0.0045)	(0.0560)	(0.0049)	(0.0049)	(0.0543)
Fath school*Moth school	0.0047	0.0031	0.1532^z	0.0097	0.0097	0.0028
	(0.0066)	(0.0066)	(0.0908)	(0.0064)	(0.0065)	(0.0524)
Constant	3.4844^x	3.2568^x	2.8743^x	2.0106^x	1.8654^x	1.5923^x
	(0.1083)	(0.1239)	(0.3635)	(0.0735)	(0.0829)	(0.1770)
R^2	0.2435	0.2647	0.0946	0.2897	0.3001	0.1577
F - test		1.9270^y			1.8623^y	
Sample size	820	820	820	1,525	1,525	1,525
Effect on child's schooling						
$\partial\mu(e_c)/\partial\mu(e_f)$	0.1230	0.1049	−0.0861	0.2093	0.1807	0.3570
$\partial\mu(e_c)/\partial\mu(e_m)$	0.2284	0.1973	0.4856	0.2902	0.2659	0.3249
$\partial\mu(e_c)/\partial\mu(e_f)$	−0.0571	−0.0441	−0.1531	−0.0682	−0.0610	−0.1103
$\partial\mu(e_c)/\partial\mu(e_m)$	−0.0824	−0.0824	−0.2751	−0.0762	−0.0697	−0.1637
Tradeoff:						
$d\sigma(e_f)/d\mu(e_f)$	2.1552	2.3765	−0.5624	3.0670	2.9599	3.2365
$d\sigma(e_m)/d\mu(e_m)$	2.7739	2.9608	1.7653	3.8101	3.8122	1.9843

Notes: Standard errors in parentheses. Superscripts denote significance: $x = .01$, $y = .05$, $z = .10$. Estimated from 1982 the PNAD. Effects and tradeoffs evaluated at the mean and standard deviation for the region. OLS I does not include grandparents' education. OLS II includes 12 dummy variables for categories of grandparents' education in the regression. The F-test reported is for the null hypothesis that all grandparents' education variables have coefficients equal to zero. The I.V. column reports results for the two-stage least squares regression in which grandparents' education variables are used as instruments.

ordinary least squares regression that adds the schooling of all four of the 14-year-old's grandparents as independent variables. The third specification is a two-stage least squares regression that uses the schooling of grandparents as instruments for the parents' own schooling.

According to the results in the first regression, an increase of one year of schooling of the father implies an increase in the schooling of the 14-year-old by .19 years in São Paulo, and by .27 years in the Northeast, evaluated when the father begins with zero years of schooling. Below the regression coefficients we present estimates of the derivatives of all relevant variables evaluated at the sample mean values for each region. Since the effect of parental education is concave, the derivative at mean schooling is smaller than the derivative at zero schooling. When the father has the sample mean schooling for that region, the results in the first regression show that an increase of one year of schooling of the father implies an increase in the schooling of the 14-year-old by .12 years in São Paulo, and by .21 years in the Northeast.

The concavity of the relationship between parental schooling and children's schooling also implies that a mean-preserving spread in the schooling of parents (i.e., an increase in the standard deviation of schooling that holds mean schooling constant) would decrease mean schooling of 14-year-olds. As shown in the derivatives with respect to the standard deviations of fathers' schooling, an increase of one year in the standard deviation of fathers' schooling, holding the mean constant, would imply a decrease in the mean schooling of 14-year-olds of .06 years in São Paulo and .07 in the Northeast. The effects of a one-year increase in the standard deviation of mothers' schooling are roughly similar, implying a reduction in mean schooling attainment of 14-year-olds of around .08 years in both regions.

Table 12.4 also shows the implied tradeoff between mean schooling and schooling inequality in determining the schooling of 14-year-olds. The results for the first regression for São Paulo indicate that if mean schooling of fathers were increased by one year, the standard deviation could increase by two years and the mean schooling of 14-year-olds would remain unchanged. Put another way, it would take a two-year decline in the standard deviation of fathers' schooling to have the same impact on the mean schooling of 14-year-olds as would a one-year increase in the mean schooling of fathers. Thus, relative to increasing the mean schooling of parents, reducing inequality in parental education thus appears to be a surprisingly weak instrument for improving the mean schooling of children. The analogous tradeoff for the Northeast is about three years, implying that it would take a three-year decline in the standard deviation of fathers' schooling to have the same impact on the mean schooling of 14-year-olds as would a one-year increase in the mean of fathers' schooling.

The regressions labeled OLS II include the dummy variables for the education of the four grandparents in the regression. Given the large number of dummy variables for grandparents' education, few of the individual coefficients are statistically significant. Although the coefficients for the grandparents' education variables are not included in the table, we do report the F-test for the joint significance of these variables. The grandparents' schooling variables are jointly significant at the .05 level in all regressions reported. Looking at the derivatives at the bottom of these columns, we see that the inclusion of the grandparents' education variables lowers the estimated effects of parental education somewhat. Controlling for grandparents' education, a one-year increase in the schooling of the father implies a .10-year increase in the schooling of 14-year-olds in São Paulo, and a .18-year increase in the Northeast, evaluated at the sample means. Controlling for grandparents' education, a one-year increase in the schooling of the mother implies a .19-year increase in the schooling of 14-year-olds in São Paulo, and a .27-year increase in the Northeast. The fact that the estimated effects of parental schooling decline when grandparents' education is included in the regression provides some support for the argument that parental schooling represents omitted family background variables that influence child schooling outcomes. This implies that the true effect of an exogenous increase in parental schooling is smaller than implied by conventional estimates. The effect of controlling for grandparents' schooling, a rough control for family background, is to reduce the implied effect of parental schooling by about 15 to 20 percent. This is similar to the decline in estimated returns to schooling found by Lam and Schoeni (1991) when they include similar controls for family background in earnings equations for Brazil. Although these results give support to the argument that there is a "family background bias" in conventional estimates of the effects of parental schooling on child schooling outcomes, the bias appears to be modest.

The last regression in each table is the two-stage least squares regression, using the grandparents' schooling variables as instruments. These estimates are appropriate if the correct causal model is the "noninherited shifter" model outlined above, implying that grandparents' schooling does not pick up persistent household characteristics that affect schooling and are passed on across generations. These coefficients have large standard errors, and appear relatively unstable, suggesting that using grandparents' schooling variables as instruments leads to noisy predictions of parental schooling. These results must, therefore, be interpreted with caution. Looking at the derivatives at the bottom of the columns, we see that using the grandparents' schooling variables as instruments produces higher estimates of the effects of parental schooling on the schooling attainment of 14-year-olds. Looking at the more stable estimates for the Northeast, these two-stage least squares estimates imply that a one-year increase in the schooling of fathers would increase the schooling of 14-year-olds by .36 years.

Table 12.5 adds the income of the household head and income squared to all the regressions. The specifications and samples are in all

Table 12.5. Response of Child's Schooling to Parents' Schooling and Income, 14-Year-Olds, State of São Paulo and Northeast Brazil, 1982

	São Paulo			Northeast		
	OLS I	OLS II	I.V.	OLS I	OLS II	I.V.
Father's schooling (e_f)	0.1760^x	0.1448^x	0.2261	0.2593^x	0.2309^x	0.5917^z
	(0.0449)	(0.0470)	(0.5640)	(0.0354)	(0.0367)	(0.3393)
Father's school squared	-0.0108^y	-0.0085^z	-0.0896	-0.0184^x	-0.0171^x	-0.0374
	(0.0045)	(0.0045)	(0.3896)	(0.0039)	(0.0039)	(0.0364)
Mother's schooling (e_m)	0.2955^x	0.2481^x	0.9246^z	0.3418^x	0.3180^x	0.5211
	(0.0466)	(0.0482)	(0.0684)	(0.0380)	(0.0395)	(0.4050)
Mother's schooling squared	-0.0141^x	-0.0110^y	-0.1303^y	-0.0171^x	-0.0162^x	-0.0261
	(0.0045)	(0.0045)	(0.5249)	(0.0048)	(0.0048)	(0.0645)
Fath school*Moth school	0.0034	0.0017	0.1565^z	0.0066	0.0069	-0.0215
	(0.0066)	(0.0066)	(0.0643)	(0.0063)	(0.0064)	(0.0840)
Household head income	0.0504^x	0.0504^x	0.0129	0.1593^x	0.1492^x	-0.0200
	(0.0141)	(0.0141)	(0.0961)	(0.0239)	(0.0241)	(0.6431)
Head's income squared	-0.0003^x	-0.0003^x	0.0001	-0.0023^x	-0.0021^x	0.0111
	(0.0001)	(0.0001)	(0.3675)	(0.0006)	(0.0006)	(0.0256)
Constant	3.3854^x	3.1627^x	2.8528^x	1.7791^x	1.6769^x	1.4630^x
	(0.1111)	(0.1258)	(0.0055)	(0.0795)	(0.0869)	(0.5352)
R^2	0.2553	0.2764	0.0925	0.3126	.3196	0.1186
F - test		1.9437^y			1.2813^y	
Sample size	820	820	820	1,525	1,525	1,525
Effect on child's schooling						
$\partial\mu(e_c)/\partial\mu(e_f)$	0.0992	0.0821	-0.1056	0.1744	0.1534	0.3635
$\partial\mu(e_c)/\partial\mu(e_m)$	0.2096	0.1791	0.4822	0.2620	0.2434	0.3496
$\partial\mu(e_c)/\partial\mu(e_f)$	-0.0719	-0.0597	0.1590	-0.0995	-0.0901	-0.3061
$\partial\mu(e_c)/\partial\mu(e_m)$	-0.0835	-0.0681	-0.2842	-0.0803	-0.0740	-0.2249
$\partial\mu(e_c)/\partial\mu(y)$	0.0022	0.0027	0.0008	0.0035	0.0040	0.0013
$\partial\mu(e_c)/\partial CV(y)$	-0.0296	-0.0295	0.0064	-0.0521	-0.0489	0.2560
Tradeoff:						
$d\sigma(e_f)/d\mu(e_f)$	1.3790	1.3747	-0.6643	1.7527	1.7035	1.1876
$d\sigma(e_m)/d\mu(e_m)$	2.5166	2.6316	1.6965	3.2645	3.2886	1.5540
$d\mu(e_f)/d\ln(\mu(y))$	-0.0227	-0.0331	0.0074	-0.0201	-0.0258	-0.0035
$d\mu(e_m)/d\ln(\mu(y))$	-0.0107	-0.0152	-0.0016	-0.0133	-0.0162	-0.0036
$dCV(y)/d\ln(\mu(y))$	0.0759	0.0920	-0.1220	0.0672	0.0808	-0.0049
$dCV(y)/d\sigma(ef)$	-2.4287	-2.0248	-24.6837	-1.9109	-1.8405	1.1956

Notes: Estimated from the 1982 PNAD. Standard errors in parentheses. Superscripts denote significance: $x = .01$, $y = .05$, $z = .10$. Effects and tradeoffs evaluated at the mean and standard deviation for the region. OLS I does not include grandparents' education. OLS II includes 12 dummy variables for categories of grandparents' education in the regression. The F-test reported is for the null hypothesis that all grandparents' education variables have coefficients equal to zero. The I.V. column reports results for the two-stage least squares regression in which grandparents' education variables are used as instruments.

other respects identical to the regressions in Table 12.4. Estimated effects of parental schooling in these tables refer to effects holding the income of the household head constant. In addition, we present the implied tradeoffs between mean and inequality of parental schooling and income in determining the schooling of 14-year-olds.

Comparing the derivatives implied by the first regressions in Table 12.5 with the equivalent regressions without income in Table 12.4, we see that the implied effects of parental schooling are smaller when we hold income constant. This is not surprising, given the high correlation between schooling and income in Brazil. Evaluated at the mean, a one-year increase in the schooling of the father implies a .10-year increase in the schooling of 14-year-olds in São Paulo, and a .18-year increase in the schooling of 14-year-olds in the Northeast. A one-year increase in the schooling of the mother, controlling for the schooling and income of the father, implies a .21-year increase in the schooling of 14-year-olds in São Paulo, and a .27-year increase in the schooling of 14-year-olds in the Northeast.

The direct partial effects of a household head's income are quite small. Continuing to look at the OLS estimates in the first column of Table 12.5, the derivatives $\partial\mu_c/\partial\ln(\mu_y)$ imply that a 10 percent increase in the income of the household head implies an increase of only .02 years in the completed schooling of a 14-year-old child in São Paulo, and .03 years in the Northeast, holding parental schooling constant. In other words, making a linear extrapolation using this derivative, it would take more than a 400 percent increase in the mean income of family heads to raise mean completed schooling of 14-year-olds by one full year in São Paulo. Looking across the other columns of Table 12.5, we see that this magnitude does not vary dramatically across alternative specifications.

As was the case with parental schooling in the previous regressions, the negative coefficients on the income squared term in the regressions in Table 12.5 indicate a concave relationship between the schooling of 14-year-olds and the income of the household head. This implies that a reduction in income inequality among household heads, holding all other variables including the supply of schooling constant, would imply higher mean schooling of 14-year-olds. The derivative $\partial\mu(e_c)/\partial cv(y)$ summarizes the magnitude of this effect at the means. Using the São Paulo parameters and sample statistics in Table 12.5, a decrease in the coefficient of variation of 0.1 (i.e., a reduction from the actual value of 1.57 to a value of 1.47) would increase average child schooling by .003 years. The derivative for the Northeast is larger, but still implies small effects. Even a drop in the coefficient of variation of 50 percent, from 1.5 to 1.0, would only increase mean schooling of

14-year-olds by 5/100 of a year. It is important to keep in mind that all of these hypothetical effects are based on the assumption that all other variables, including the supply of schooling, remain constant. To the extent that changes in mean income and income inequality in a region lead to changes in the supply of quasi-public goods like schooling, the effects may be very different from the simple aggregation of household-specific effects calculated here.

The final derivatives in Table 12.5 show the tradeoffs between changes in the mean and inequality of parental schooling and the mean and inequality of parental income in affecting the schooling attainment of 14-year-olds. For example, the derivative $dCV(y)/dln(\mu(y))$ shows the change in the coefficient of variation of income that would just offset a given proportional change in income. For the case of São Paulo in the first regression in Table 12.5, the increase in child schooling resulting from a 1 percent increase in the household head's income would be offset by a simultaneous increase of 0.076 in the coefficient of variation.

The tradeoff between changes in mean income and changes in mean parental schooling are especially striking. The derivative $d\mu(e_f)/dln(\mu(y))$ implies that the effect of a 1 percent increase in the mean income of household heads would be offset by a .02-year increase in the mean schooling of the father. Put another way, it would require about a 50 percent increase in mean parental income in order to have the same impact on schooling of 14-year-olds as a one-year increase in the mean education of fathers. It would take roughly a 100 percent increase in mean parental income in order to have the same impact on child schooling as a one-year increase in the mean schooling of mothers. The magnitudes for the Northeast are similar, with a 1 percent increase in parental income being equivalent to a .02-year increase in the schooling of fathers and a .013-year increase in the schooling of mothers.

The results of other regression specifications provide very similar results. While the magnitudes of the effects vary somewhat across specifications, the general pattern remains that the effects of changes in either the mean or dispersion of the household head's income on the schooling attainment of 14-year-olds is surprisingly small. If taken literally, the results imply that there would be only very modest improvements in schooling attainment in response to even very large increases in mean income or very large reductions in income inequality among household heads. A result that is very robust across specifications is that very little of the difference in the mean schooling of 14-year-olds in the two regions can be explained by differences in either mean income or inequality of income of household heads. As shown in Table 12.2, income inequality is actually lower in the Northeast than in São Paulo, implying that the effect of income inequality alone would actually lead to higher schooling attainment in the Northeast than in São Paulo. We repeat the caveat that these estimates assume that the supply of schooling is held constant. If, as seems plausible, increases in mean income or decreases in income inequality lead to increases in the supply of schooling, then those effects will be in addition to the household level effects estimated here.

Our estimate of the magnitude of the effects of parental schooling are quite similar to those of previous studies of education in Brazil. Mello e Souza (1979) presents regressions of child schooling attainment as a function of household characteristics using a family expenditure survey conducted in the city of Rio de Janeiro in 1967/68. He estimates regressions for children in narrow age groups, and includes as regressors family income, family size, dummy variables for location in the city, and the schooling of the mother. For children aged 14–15, similar to the sample we use here, Mello e Souza estimates a coefficient on mother's schooling of 0.33 (1979:133), similar to the effect we estimate for both São Paulo and the Northeast. In São Paulo, our quadratic estimate for the effect of mother's education implies that a one-year increase in mother's schooling would increase child schooling by 0.31 years when the mother has zero schooling, and by 0.23 years when the mother has the mean schooling of 2.6 years.

Birdsall (1985) uses the 1970 Brazilian census to estimate the effects of parental and household characteristics on the schooling attainment of children of different ages. Independent variables include father's and mother's schooling, both entered linearly, and the log of the father's income. Birdsall's estimates of the effects of parental education for urban Brazil are somewhat lower than ours. An increase in a mother's schooling by one year implies an increase in the schooling attainment of children aged 12–15 in urban Brazil by .11 years, controlling for the father's income, in Birdsall's estimates, compared to .21 and .26 for São Paulo and the Northeast, respectively, in our results. The effect of a one-year increase in father's schooling is .08 years in Birdsall's study, compared to .10 in São Paulo and .17 in the Northeast in our results. An important contribution of Birdsall's analysis is the use of direct measures of schooling supply and quality, including measures of the average teacher's schooling and the quantity of teachers per child in the region. Inclusion of these variables in her regressions increases the estimated effect of the mother's schooling on child schooling attainment, and has little effect on the estimated effect of the father's schooling.

The magnitude of our estimated effects of parental characteristics on child schooling attainment can be illustrated by using our regression coefficients to predict the difference in schooling attainment between São Paulo

Table 12.6. Predicted Differences in Schooling Attainment Across Regions Based on Regression Coefficients in Tables 12.4 and 12.5

Actual schooling in São Paulo	4.75	
Actual schooling in Northeast	3.25	
Actual difference	1.50	

	Predicted using São Paulo coefficients	Predicted using Northeast coefficients
Predicted difference using regressions without income	0.241	0.273
Predicted difference/Actual difference	0.161	0.183
Predicted difference using regressions with income	0.208	0.231
Predicted difference/Actual difference	0.140	0.155

and the Northeast. The predicted difference in mean schooling attainment of 14-year-olds between São Paulo and the Northeast will be given by the differences in the mean values of all of the independent variables in a given regression multiplied by the regression coefficients for each variable. We can do such a prediction in two ways, using the coefficients we estimate for São Paulo and the Northeast. Table 12.6 presents these calculations using the regressions based only on parental schooling and those that also include the household head's income.

The first two rows of the table show that the actual difference in schooling attainment between São Paulo and the Northeast is 1.5 years. The first prediction uses the regressions for the large sample that exclude the income variables. Given the differences in the means of the right-hand side variables shown in Table 12.2 and the regression coefficients for São Paulo in Table 12.4, we predict a difference in schooling attainment between the two regions of only .24 years. The predicted difference is only 16.1 percent of the actual difference, indicating that differences in the mean and variance of parental schooling explain only a small fraction of the gap in schooling attainment between the Northeast and São Paulo. When we use the regression coefficients for the Northeast we predict a slightly larger fraction of the total difference, 18.3 percent.

The final rows of the table repeat this exercise using the regressions that include the household head's income and its square. This exercise should be considered with greater caution, since it implicitly makes the strong assumption that income can be directly compared between the two regions, ignoring such problems as cost of living differences between the regions. The magnitude of the predicted difference is similar to that based on the regressions that exclude income, with this difference actually somewhat smaller when we use the regressions that include income. We explain about 15 percent of the actual difference between the Northeast and São Paulo based on these regressions.

Given the substantial differences in parental education and income between the Northeast and São Paulo, it is surprising that these differences do not appear to explain much of the large gap in schooling attainment of children between the two regions. Based on our estimates of the effects of parental schooling and income on child schooling attainment, less than 20 percent of the almost 1.5-year gap between the schooling of 14-year-olds in São Paulo and the Northeast would be eliminated if parents in the Northeast had the same characteristics as parents in São Paulo, holding the supply of schooling constant. This surprising result appears to imply that elimination of the large schooling gap between regions in Brazil will depend more on supply-side policies than on changes in the distribution of income and schooling at the household level. To the extent that parental education may be a good indicator of the household's permanent income, our results imply that even substantial increases in mean income or reductions in income inequality in the Northeast would not eliminate the gap in long-term schooling attainment, in the absence of changes in the supply of schooling.

Parental schooling and income, variables that might be considered demand-side determinants of child schooling at the household level, do not appear to be the primary cause of the schooling gap between the poor Northeast and the richer Southeast in Brazil. This may be good news from a policy perspective, since equalizing the provision of schooling between the Northeast and São Paulo may be an easier policy to implement than eliminating the large differences in socioeconomic position of parents in the two regions. Therefore, although increasing household income and reducing income inequality within and between regions in Brazil is clearly a desirable policy for many reasons, it does not appear in and of itself to be either necessary or sufficient to eliminate the gap in schooling attainment between regions. Our results suggest that it may be possible to eliminate much of this gap through policies aimed directly at the provision of schooling. As indicated elsewhere in this volume, investments in school quality in Brazil appear to have high returns in reducing grade repetition and increasing schooling attainment. Our results are entirely consistent with the view that supply-side investments in schooling quality and quantity can have large payoffs even in the absence of substantial changes in income or parental schooling at the household level. However, large increases in mean income or reductions in income inequality would be unlikely to have large effects on schooling attainment in and of themselves, in the absence of increases in schooling quantity and quality.

Conclusions

This study focused on what might be considered the "demand side" of schooling in Brazil, attempting to explain the schooling attainment of a particular cohort of Brazilian children as a response to the schooling and income of parents. Looking at the cohort of children born in 1968, all of whom should have completed seven years of schooling by the time of the 1982 PNAD survey, we find mean schooling of 4.75 years in the urban region of the state of São Paulo, and 3.25 years in the urban Northeast. A major objective was to explain this advantage of 1.5 years in the schooling attainment of 14-year-olds in São Paulo versus the Northeast. We find regional differences in the characteristics of parents that are consistent with the regional difference in child outcomes. Fathers in São Paulo have 1.3 years more schooling than fathers in the Northeast, and mothers in São Paulo have .7 years more schooling than mothers in the Northeast. The mean income of household heads in São Paulo is almost twice that of household heads in the Northeast, although income inequality among household heads is slightly lower in the Northeast. Inequality in schooling, as measured by the coefficient of variation, is higher for both fathers and mothers in the Northeast than in São Paulo.

Our regression estimates imply that a one-year increase in the schooling of the mother increases schooling of 14-year-olds by around .3 years, with slightly larger effects in the Northeast. Increases in the schooling of the father have somewhat smaller effects. The effect of parental schooling on child schooling is concave, implying that reductions in schooling inequality among parents would increase the mean schooling of 14-year-olds in the population, even if mean schooling of parents remained constant. We also estimate a concave effect of the household head's income on child schooling attainment. The effects of income appear to be quite modest, however: a 10 percent increase in the income of the household head, holding the schooling of both parents constant, would increase child schooling attainment by less than one-tenth of a year; and a reduction in the coefficient of variation of income from 1.5 to 1.0 would also increase child schooling attainment by less than one-tenth of a year.

Although differences in parental characteristics between the Northeast and São Paulo are consistent with the greater schooling attainment of 14-year-olds in São Paulo, our regression estimates suggest that only a small proportion of the gap in schooling attainment between São Paulo and the Northeast can be explained by these parental characteristics. Using our regression coefficients and differences in mean characteristics between regions to predict the difference in mean schooling attainment of 14-year-olds, we are able to explain less than 20 percent of the 1.5-year schooling gap between the Northeast and São Paulo. This suggests that child schooling attainment may be disappointingly unresponsive to improvements in the socioeconomic status of households in the absence of changes in the quantity and quality of schooling being supplied. It also suggests, however, that direct policy interventions directed at the supply side of schooling provision may be able to eliminate a large fraction of the schooling gap between regions, even while the gap in parental socioeconomic status between regions persists.

REFERENCES

Almeida dos Reis, José Guilherme, and Ricardo Barros. 1991. Wage Inequality and the Distribution of Education: A Study of the Evolution of Regional Differences in Inequality in Metropolitan Brazil. *Journal of Development Economics* 36 (July): 117–43.

Barros, Ricardo, and David Lam. 1991. Income Inequality, Inequality in Education, and the Demand for Schooling in Brazil. Paper presented at the World Bank Conference on Education, Growth and Inequality in Brazil, Rio de Janeiro, March.

Becker, Gary S. 1975. *Human Capital*. Second edition. New York: Columbia University Press.

Birdsall, Nancy. 1985. Public Inputs and Child Schooling in Brazil. *Journal of Development Economics* 18(1) (May–June): 67–86.

Lam, David, and Deborah Levison. 1992a. Declining Inequality in Schooling in Brazil and Its Effects on Inequality in Earnings. *Journal of Development Economics* 37: 199–225.

_____. 1992b. Age, Experience, and Schooling: Decomposing Earnings Inequality in the U.S. and Brazil. *Sociological Inquiry* 62(2) (Spring).

_____. 1991. Idade, Experiência, Escolaridade e Diferenciais de Renda: Estados Unidos e Brasil. *Pesquisa e Planejamento Econômico* 20(2) (August).

Lam, David, and Robert Schoeni. 1991. Effects of Family Background on Earnings and Returns to Schooling: Evidence from Brazil. Paper presented at the Annual Meeting of the American Economic Association, New Orleans.

Levison, Deborah. 1991. Children's Labor Force Activity and Schooling in Brazil. Ph.D. dissertation, Department of Economics, University of Michigan.

Mello e Souza, Alberto de. 1979. *Financiamento da Educação e Acesso à Escola no Brasil*. IPEA: Rio de Janeiro.

Psacharopoulos, George, and Ana Maria Arriagada. 1986. The Educational Composition of the Labor Force: An International Comparison. *International Labour Review* 125(5): 561–74.

13

Family Background, Quality of Education and Public and Private Schools: Effects on School Transitions

Alberto de Mello e Souza and Nelson do Valle Silva

The low average number of years of schooling in Brazil (about five years), coupled with highly unequal distribution of education, severely constrains the growth of the economy, causes high income inequality, and impedes the exercise of political rights. In the realm of education, the Brazilian system is now challenged by the need to significantly reduce the dropout and repetition rates, given that 95 percent of a cohort have access to school.

Through this study, we hope to increase the knowledge of differences between public and private schools, the factors influencing the decision to enter one or the other, and the consequent chances of promotion or dropping out. Understanding why some students progress through the education system while others repeat and drop out is important, as it helps identify the related school inputs influenced by policy decisions. There is a prevailing view that quality of education, as compared to family background variables, is more important in explaining educational achievement in underdeveloped countries (Heyneman and Loxley, 1983). However, the recent use of multilevel analysis casts doubts on this view (Riddel, 1989).

In Brazil, the paucity of data on achievement has led to the use of other more readily available dependent variables.[1] Even then, previous studies could not use school variables in their explanation. It is possible to see the strong influence of family background, especially parents' education and region, on school participation, grade attainment and the dropout decision among children aged seven to 14 (Psacharopoulos and Arriagada, 1989). Other studies show that the chances of successfully completing eight school transitions are related to variables that pertain mainly to the family background of the student. As expected, the coefficients of these variables decrease monotonically along the transitions, reflecting genuinely their smaller effects in higher transitions (Silva and Mello e Souza, 1986).

---

[1] A major exception is Harbison and Hanushek (1992).

There are clear indications that family expenditures in education have a high income-elasticity (Mello e Souza, 1979). Also, returns to quality are at least as large as those for quantity of education (Behrman and Birdsall, 1983). In updating their estimates for this volume, however, Behrman, Birdsall and Kaplan find that while the quality of education remains important, it is not as significant as previously believed. Nevertheless, there still is a trade-off between the quantity and quality of education, due to the advantages of concentrating investments in fewer individuals. It also seems that at least in some circumstances of educational deprivation, investments in quality of education can generate much higher cost savings due to increased efficiency. In the Northeast, these potential cost savings can be four times as large as the investments in quality of education. In such cases, the goals of equity and efficiency can be pursued simultaneously (Gomes-Neto and Hanushek, 1991).

The use of the public-private dichotomy usually raises two issues. First, the selection bias effect appears whenever nonschool factors are not controlled adequately in the explanation of the student's results and thus, the omitted variables may bias the effect due to the type of school. This is the case if more motivated students choose, say, private schools. Although there are procedures that may attenuate the problem, some authors deny the possibility of solving it (Murnane, 1981). In studies explaining achievement, the absence of family background or student variables should cause more problems than in this work because promotion and dropping out are also affected by school policies, which are not considered here. Second, previous studies such as those by Coleman, Hoffer and Kilgore (1982) and Jiménez, Lockheed and Wattenawaha (1988) have found that private schools are more effective than public schools in influencing achievement levels. Policy implications of such findings regarding, for example, the financing and regulation of private schools, have stirred a debate over many issues. In Brazil, the dominant issue is how to create public school conditions that encourage primary students to graduate. This concern for public education must be reflected in institutional changes that allow more resources to reach the schools and provide incentives for more effective resource use.

The data set used in this study—from the 1982 Brazilian Annual Household Survey (Pesquisa Nacional por Amostra de Domicílios—PNAD)—provides information on the student and her or his family, the quality and type (public or private) of school, and school transitions. Data limitations include the restricted use of the quality of education variables and the absence of measures describing student achievement and ability.

The student-related variables are gender, age and color. Omission of student ability and motivation probably increases the direct effect of family background. Family variables are size, income, place of residence (urban or rural), education of family head, and female-headed households. This last variable is zero if both parents are present.

The variables related to quality of education are time spent in school, availability of textbooks, frequency of homework assignments, and day or night classes. They provide insufficient information about school inputs, and still less about how they are used. Important dimensions of quality, such as the effective use of time by the student and the maintenance of an environment favorable for learning (discipline, teacher demands and stimulus) are not captured by the variables mentioned above. Absence of teachers and poor supervision, for example, are more common in public schools than in private ones. This line of reasoning reinforces the importance of how the inputs are combined compared to their availability.

We choose the state of São Paulo because both family income and public school quality impose less severe constraints on the choice of the type of schools than in most other states. First, we highlight the major objectives of the study. Second, we describe, by type of school, some characteristics of the student, his or her family, and the quality of school. Third, we present the results of a decision model regarding the choice of type of school. Finally, we comment on the results of regressions that seek to explain school entrance delay, promotion and dropout rates.

Education Outcomes and Types of Schools

The transition rates that appear in the statistics presented by the Ministry of Education (MEC) and those that are collected in the schools are quite different from those estimated through the use of PNAD and census data (Klein and Ribeiro, 1991). Particularly, the dropout rates in the first two grades of the primary level are substantially lower in the household survey. The 1982 PNAD provides better information about transition rates because it contains a specific questionnaire on education, requiring information from those who were in school in 1981 about their situation in 1982. Thus, the survey data indicate if the student was promoted and if she or he continued in school.

Information regarding transition rates by grades, in São Paulo, shows a high repetition rate in the first grade (29 percent). This figure declines to 18 percent in the second grade, and varies between 10 and 19 percent in the remaining primary grades. The schools retain more than 90 percent of the repeaters. This compares favorably with the proportion of dropouts among the students who are promoted. Thus, the majority of students who drop out (90 percent) are the ones viewed by teachers as "successful" students. The fact that the "successful" student is prone to drop out conflicts with the usual view that failure leads to dropping out. This phenomenon also occurs in the first two grades of the secondary level.

The breakdown of the data by urban and rural areas does not change the nature of the above findings. For the rural areas, the repeat rates in the first grade are the same (28 percent) and in the second grade they are higher (24 percent vs. 17 percent). For grades three to eight, the discrepancies between urban and rural repeat rates occur only in the last two grades. The proportion of dropouts among the successful students is higher for the students in rural areas, as expected, and for both areas is larger than the same proportion in relation to the students that failed.

The data can also be broken down by type of school. In this case, there are important differences in the results. First, the private school repeat rates in the first two grades are about one-third of those in public schools. For the other grades, too, repeat rates remain smaller in private schools, with the exception of grade eight. Thus, there are clear indications that either promotion standards are lower or student performance is better in the private schools. Second, the proportion of dropouts both among the students who passed and among the students who flunked is smaller in the private schools in grades one to six. Thus, the ability of private schools to retain a larger share of their students is another significant feature. For grades seven and eight, the situation is reversed. Although the reason for this reversal is not clear, it is well known that the most prestigious private schools do not retain students who are not promoted in the last four grades of the primary level. At the secondary level, the dropout rate is proportionally larger among the repeaters in private schools, with the exception of the first year.

Possible explanations for the differences in public and private schools include characteristics of the students and their family background, and variables related to quality of education and school policies. There is no direct evidence about school policies, although part of their effect is captured by the type of school.

Families, Type of School, and Quality of Education

The characteristics of the students available in the PNAD are age, sex and color. Thus, it is possible to know the proportion of students in an age group who are behind in their studies: for example, 55 percent of eight-year-olds in public schools and 16 percent in private schools lag in their studies. We also find that on average, over two-thirds of public school students are older than the norm, as compared to 36 percent of private school students. To a large extent, the explanation for this difference lies in the fact that 87 percent of private school students enter school at the proper age, compared to only half in public schools. Furthermore, whereas 8 percent of public school students were 11 years old or older when entering school, none in private schools entered at that late age.

Private schools are, relatively, chosen more by whites and orientals than by blacks and "browns." Thus, for example, whereas orientals represent 5 percent of all students in private schools and 2 percent in public ones, the corresponding proportions of "browns" are, respectively, 5 percent and 19 percent. Whites comprise 88 percent of the students in private schools and 74 percent of those in public schools.

Variables related to family background include income, size, education of the family head, and a dummy for female-headed households. Education of the head of family is much higher for students in private schools: only 39 percent of these students have families headed by individuals with no more than four years of schooling; the corresponding figure in public schools is 80 percent. Similarly, 44 percent of heads of families with children in private schools have 10 or more years of schooling, while the percentage for those with children in public school is 9 percent. The occurrence of female-headed households is somewhat greater if the child is in public school—for households of children aged seven to 14, the average percentage of households headed by females is 10 percent in public schools and 8 percent in private ones.

The demand for private education has three major components: access to school in places where the supply of public education is nonexistent; demand for schools with a specific profile (religious, teaching in other than the native language, pedagogical orientation, etc.); and demand for high quality education. Given the dismal condition of many public schools, the last factor predominates in explaining why parents are willing to pay for private education. Unfortunately, quality of education was registered in the PNAD only in 1982 and cannot be used in the regressions explaining the transition rates, which are based on information for both 1981 and 1982.

The attendance of day or night classes relates to quality of education because night classes receive over-aged students who follow a special program called *supletivo*, designed to suit their needs. In fact, this program is loosely administered and produces poor results. In the first four primary grades practically all students go to day classes. Thereafter, the proportion of students in day classes declines to 53 percent and 68 percent, respectively, in public and private schools. At the secondary level, about 40 percent of the students attend day classes in all schools.

The average period of time spent in the public schools is four hours. In private schools, this average is 13 minutes greater and presents a larger standard deviation (40 minutes vs. 22 minutes) than public schools. Thus, for most students in public schools (97 percent), the number of hours spent in school varies from three to five. The corresponding percentage for private school students is 88 percent. This may be explained by the fact that an important dimension of the services of private schools is the quantity of hours the child stays in the school; its variation influences the price of education.

The percentage of students who receive daily homework declines for the higher grades in both types of school. The proportion, however, is always higher for private schools; examples are the first grade (75 percent vs. 64 percent) and the eighth grade (45 percent vs. 27 percent). This may reflect an important difference in school policies, which interacts positively with family background. A more stimulating atmosphere at home and more frequent homework should produce higher achievement.

The availability of textbooks has proven to be one of the most effective ways to improve learning. Ninety-five percent or more students in each grade in private schools have all textbooks. In the early grades of public schools more than 10 percent of the students do not have textbooks and 5 percent do not have all textbooks. The selectivity effect reduces to 4 percent or less the proportion of students without textbooks in the last four grades.

Next, we see if the variation in the quality of education is related to family tastes and ability to invest in education, as represented by the education of the family head. We find that the proportion of both public and private school students in day classes tends to increase with education of the family head. Notably, the variation in private schools, between 57 percent and 100 percent, is much larger than in public ones (between 85 percent and 96 percent). This reflects the fact that the demand for *supletivo* from poor families is met more intensively by the private school.

Furthermore, the proportion of students receiving daily homework in public schools shows little variation (between 44 percent and 57 percent) with years of schooling of the family head. The same proportion in private schools presents a wide variation (between 31 percent and 68 percent), indicating that their services adjust to the income constraints of their clientele. A similar pattern is found in relation to the time spent daily in school. The number of minutes increases with the education of the family head for each type of school. However, the variation both among and within educational levels is higher in private schools. The homogeneity of public school policies is reflected in the smaller variation among grades (11 minutes, as compared to 32 minutes in private schools). Within educational levels, the coefficients of variation range from 9 percent to 18 percent in private schools and from 8 percent to 10 percent in public ones. Presumably, the greater adaptability of private schools is also reflected in the greater variation of their effective use of time. We thus find that, especially in private schools, quality of education is related to family background.

To determine whether quality of private school education is also related to tuition, we divided monthly tuition into 10 groups, corresponding roughly to deciles. For the lower four tuition groups, the proportion of students in day classes varies between 63 percent and 85 percent; for the other groups, the proportion varies between 84 percent and 100 percent. Furthermore, there is an inverse relationship between the proportion of those receiving a maximum of one weekly homework assignment and tuition, as it varies from 29 percent to 6 percent. The average time spent daily in school increases by more than an hour between the first and the last tuition groups. For the two highest tuition groups, the standard deviation is much higher, supporting the conclusion that higher tuition buys, among other things, more school time.

In conclusion, quality of education in private schools varies both with its price and with family background. Public schools present less variation with regard to family background, possibly because the variables used are influenced by regulations applied to them. It remains to be seen if variations in more broadly defined inputs, such as the quality of teaching and existing facilities, are not more marked.

The Choice Between Private and Public School

To study the choice between private and public school, we used a logistic response model relating a set of variables pertaining to the student and his or her family to the log odds that the student is in a private school. The model can be described by the equation:

$$\ln [\phi / (1-\phi_i)] = \beta_0 + \Sigma \beta_j X_{ij} \tag{1}$$

where ϕ_i is the probability that the ith student attends a private school, X_{ij} is the value of the jth explanatory variable for that student, and B_j is the parameter indicating the effect of these variables on the natural logarithms of the odds of being in a private school.[2]

Appendix Table 13.1 presents the results of the evaluation of equation (1) using the 1982 PNAD data. The bottom three rows of the table indicate the values of R^2, sample size N and the overall probability P (Y=1) of being in a private school. R^2 measures the proportion of reduction in error of prediction vis-à-vis the null hypothesis that all coefficients are zero (Durmouchel, 1976). The first column presents the results for the model using all the students enrolled when the data were collected, i.e., in 1982. In the next column are the results for those enrolled in the previous year, 1981. The third column restricts the sample to only those entering school in 1982. The last four columns separate those enrolled in 1982 by school cycle: those in first to fourth grade, those in fifth to eighth grade, those in secondary school and undergraduates, respectively.

The overall fit of the model (as shown by the R^2) indicates a reduction in prediction error of about 20 percent. However, the fit of the model deteriorates in higher grades: while reduction in error is as high as almost one-third of total prediction error for first to fourth graders, it is only 5.5 percent for those at college level. This phenomenon at least partially reflects the growing homogeneity of family background of students along the schooling process, given the selectivity based on cognitive performance factors related to the socioeconomic variables used in the model.

The results for those enrolled in both 1982 and 1981 are very similar. With two exceptions, all variables prove to be significant predictors of the type of school chosen. Moreover, most variables have effects in the expected direction. The strongest effect seems to be that of education of family head, with the positive sign indicating that the higher the educational level achieved by the head of the family, the higher the chances of the student being enrolled in a private school. A similar effect, although a much less strong one, can be observed for family income. These two effects imply that, other things being equal, higher socioeconomic status is associated with greater chances of private school enrollment. The second strongest effect relates to family size: bigger families lower the chances of private school

---

[2] The explanatory variables we use in the analysis of the model proposed above are the following: X_1 Family size—number of people in the family; X_2 Total Family Income—sum of income earned by family members; X_3 Place of Residence—1 if urban, O otherwise; X_4 Female Headed Household—1 if family head is a woman, O otherwise; X_5 Student's Color—1 if white, O otherwise; X_6 Student's Color—1 if brown, O otherwise; X_7 Student's Color —1 if Oriental, O otherwise; and X_8 Student's Sex—1 if girl, O otherwise.

enrollment, probably due to the decrease of the income share available for each student.

Color contrasts are also important predictors; both whites and orientals have significant coefficients. Notably, the coefficients for oriental students are particularly high, well above those for white students. The coefficient for brown, though, implies that the difference between brown and black students (the base group) is not significantly different from zero, a result that confirms observations in many previous studies of race relations in Brazil (Silva, 1981).

We did not expect the generally positive sign for female-headed households, given the notion of more fragile socioeconomic conditions among broken families. A similarly unexplained result is the significant sign for the female-male contrast. Here, we did not expect a significant difference between boys and girls in their chances of private school enrollment.

The other regressions—through secondary school—largely confirm the general results discussed above. However, the results for college enrollment actually reverse the determination observed so far, as all socioeconomic predictors and the color contrasts show negative signs. The coefficient for the effect of education of family head is particularly significant. This result strongly suggests that the better-off students are precisely those more likely to attend a public (and free) university, a perverse situation that characterizes higher education in Brazil.

Entering and Leaving the First Grade

The Brazilian Constitution makes school attendance compulsory from ages seven to 14; students during that time should complete the eight years of primary education. Clearly, reality is far from that norm, the most important reason being what happens in the first year of the student's school life.

First, many students do not enter school at age seven. As indicated before, the 1982 PNAD questionnaire included a set of questions about schooling in the previous year. Here, attention is paid to the situation of a student entering the school system in 1982. Tabulating the age of those students minus seven—the ideal age for school entrance—we find that only 54 percent were at that ideal age. Thus, on average, most students enroll in the first grade at age 7.7 instead of the prescribed seven.

Not surprisingly, the type of school correlates with the delay at entrance: while almost 87 percent of those entering first grade at private school do so at the prescribed age, the corresponding figure for public schools is only 51 percent. Even if we allow for the fact that some of the students delayed one year did in fact enter school at the correct age of seven (because the PNAD survey is taken late in the school year), we still find that the proportion of those with delay of entrance of two or more years is 16.3 percent in public schools, compared with only 2.7 percent in private schools. Thus, in average terms, students entering the first grade in private schools do so with a 0.26-year lag, while those entering public school average a delay of almost 0.81 years.

If type of school is the only variable explaining delay at entrance, it is significant, although it accounts for only 2 percent of the variance, as evaluated by an OLS regression. However, when the social background of students is included, type of school is no longer significant. All family background coefficients have the expected signs and only family income is not significant. The female variable has a negative sign, possibly because of the higher opportunity costs for boys to enter the school. All color coefficients are negative, indicating that blacks experience higher delays.[3]

When dealing with those students who make the 1981–82 transition, we are able to calculate their age/grade fitness during that school transition (Appendix Table 13.2). The dependent variable is the ideal age for the grade the student is in, minus his or her age in 1981. Therefore, the OLS regression coefficients should have signs opposite to those discussed above. The results indicate a very strong effect of education of the family head, the positive sign implying that those coming from more educated family backgrounds have significantly better age/grade fitness than those with less educated parents. The effect of family size is also very strong and opposite in sign to that of education of the family head. Also significant are the effects of female headed households (a negative one) and of all color groups.

To see whether the student successfully completed the first grade in 1981, we applied the same logistic regression model (equation 1). The results are presented in Appendix Table 13.3, and are congruent to expectations: education of family head is again the strongest predictor of promotion. Both family size and income are significantly related to grade completion and have the expected signs, indicating that children from poorer families are less likely to complete the first grade. To be female also proves to be a positive effect on completion chances, suggesting that girls are better students than boys. This is compatible with the observation that girls in the recent cohorts have more years of schooling than boys.

---

[3] When we restrict our observations to those up to 14 years of age, (to make sure that those not enrolled in regular school—that is, those in the *supletivo* track—do not interfere in the results), the only difference is the loss of significance of the color coefficients.

One unexpected result is that urban residence seems to be significant and negatively related to first grade success. This suggests that urban schools have stricter promotion criteria than rural schools, given that socio-economic differences between these two areas seem to have been properly controlled for. Finally, age/grade fitness appears to be negatively related to first grade completion. In other words, younger students are significantly less likely to be successful in their first year of schooling, when other things are held constant.

We ran separate regressions for public and private schools in order to compare interactive effects of family background and type of school. The clientele of private schools has a family income three to five times that of the public school clientele, although the coefficient of variation is about the same. The average years of schooling of the family head is 8.8 for students in private schools and 3.5 for students in public schools. Further, while the coefficients remained about the same for the public school regression, in the private school regression only family size, with a changed sign, and sex continued to be significant.

We may conclude, tentatively, that family income and education of the family head only impact public school students. Three possible explanations are suggested. First, differences in the behavior of the parents and their expectations regarding the success of the child are more pronounced in the case of public schools. Second, there are variations (related to family characteristics) both in the resources available to the public schools and in the effectiveness of their use. Third, negative attitudes of public school teachers regarding students from the poorest families significantly impacts their evaluation.

The dropout rate during or just after the first grade is about 3 percent. The last column in Appendix Table 13.3 presents the results for the logistic regression model applied to the chances of dropping out. In addition to the expected results of significant negative effects of family head education and family income on these chances, two results should be underlined. First, age/grade fitness is strongly and negatively related to the chances of dropping out, with the relatively younger students showing a higher propensity for staying in school. Second, those who completed first grade (and as we have seen, they are more likely to be older students) are actually more likely to drop out of school, ceteris paribus, than those who failed.

Therefore, the combination of this perverse causal mechanism with the fact that those students coming from poorer families enter school relatively late seems to produce a situation in which these students are subject to repeated failures up to the point that, when they finally are promoted, they also reach an age when other factors exert a decisive pull away from school. As a final remark, it should be noted that type of school is not significantly related to promotion when we control for socioeconomic family conditions.

Later Stages of Schooling

When dealing with the results for the other grades selected for analysis (fourth, eighth and 11th grades), one should keep in mind that the schooling process selects students by cognitive-academic performance, expressed in terms of promotion, which in turn is partially determined by the student's family background. This process of selectivity tends to cause both an increase in the average values of the social background variables and a decrease in the variance (relative to the mean), indicating greater homogeneity in some of those characteristics. Therefore, for instance, when we compare family size and income for students in the first and the 11th grades, we find that while family size decreases, family income increases and variance for both variables decreases. These results show that per capita family income increases almost threefold, from about Cr$15,812 in the first grade to Cr$45,277 in the 11th grade, with income level more homogeneous in the latter grade. The average years of schooling of the family head, in the same grades, increase from 3.6 to 5.8, and so does the proportion of whites (69 percent to 85 percent).

The effect of socioeconomic family background tends to decline as the schooling process continues, and actually seems to reverse itself in the end (see Appendix Table 13.4). Until eighth grade, the effects of background variables, although progressively reduced, continue in the same direction observed for the first grade: students from better-off families are more likely to be promoted and less likely to drop out; girls seem to do better than boys; and students with greater delays, as well as those who are promoted, are more likely to drop out. However, by 11th grade, the results indicate that students with more educated parents are actually less likely to be promoted to the next grade. The effect of personal characteristics seems to maintain the same direction observed before for all other schooling stages. This result indicates that those few students from worse-off families who survived up to this point are indeed better students on average than those from better-off families. An alternative explanation is that many students in secondary schools are in the *supletivo* track, with less strict requirements for promotion. However controlling for age/grade fitness does not seem to produce any substantial change in the regression coefficients. In all regressions, the coefficient of private school is not significant.

Conclusions

Based on student promotion and dropout rates among students from São Paulo using 1982 PNAD data, this study showed, first, that the two initial primary grades showed high repetition rates. Second, dropout rates were much higher among students promoted than among those not promoted. Separating the information for private and public schools, we observe that in private schools, both repetition and dropout rates are substantially lower than in public schools.

Further data analysis reveals important differences among public and private schools regarding characteristics of the student and her or his family. Thus, we find that over-aged students are more common in public schools and family income and education of the head of the family are much higher among private school students. Private schools have a somewhat larger average number of hours spent at school and a much higher coefficient of variation. In terms of the other quality variables, such as availability of textbooks and frequency of homework, private schools fare better than public schools. Overall, private schools adjust their services to the demand of their clientele, as highlighted in the relationship between education quality variables and education of the head of the family or tuition.

Initially, we estimated a decision model regarding the choice between public and private schools. For the logistic regressions including all students, family income and educational background variables and the family head coefficients have the expected sign and are highly significant. The coefficients of family size and of whites and orientals also are significant and in accordance with expectations. For the primary and secondary level regressions, family background variables maintain their importance. A reversal occurs at the university level, with the change in sign of the coefficient of those variables indicating that students with lower socioeconomic status choose private institutions.

Both the age of the child when entering school and the age/grade fitness are heavily influenced by family background variables. Promotion is explained by student characteristics (including delay of promotion), background variables, and the type of school for four grades where transitions are the most relevant: first, fourth, eighth and 11th. Dropout rates in the same grades are explained by the same group of variables, with an additional control for promotion.

The results point out the importance of family background; however, its influence declines in the higher grades, reflecting the selectivity effect. In the 11th grade, this influence is reversed, implying that the surviving students from poor families are better than the others. Dropping out is more common among older students and also among those that are promoted.

Poor students enter school late and are more prone to repeat the year; this increases their opportunity cost of staying in the school, and thus leads to their dropping out. The results of separate regressions for type of school (which explain promotion in the first grade and point out the loss of significance of family background variables in the private school regression) suggest the existence of discriminatory factors in the public schools. Overall, the evidence indicates that, to a large extent, school performance in São Paulo reflects the wide inequality existing in Brazilian society.

REFERENCES

Behrman, Jere, and Nancy Birdsall. 1983. The Quality of Schooling: Quantity Alone Is Misleading. *American Economics Review* 73(5): 926–46.

Coleman, James S., Thomas Hoffer, and Sally Kilgore. 1982. *High School Achievement:Public, Catholic and Private Schools Compared.* New York: Basic Books.

Durmouchel, W.H. 1976. On the Analogy Between Linear and Log-Linear Regression. University of Michigan, Department of Statistics. Technical Report No. 67.

Gomes-Neto, J. G., and Eric A. Hanushek. 1991. Grade Repetition, Wastage and Educational Policy. Universidade Federal de Ceará and University of Rochester. Mimeo.

Harbison, Ralph W., and Eric A Hanushek. 1992. *Educational Performance of the Poor: Lessons from Rural Northeast Brazil.* Oxford: Oxford University Press.

Heyneman, S. P., and W. A. Loxley. 1983. The Effect of Primary School Quality on Academic Achievement across Twenty-nine High- and Low-Income Countries. *American Journal of Sociology* 88(6): 1162–94.

Jiménez, Emmanuel, Lockheed, Marlaine, and Norgmuch Wattenawaha. 1988. The Relative Efficiency of Private and Public Schools: The Case of Thailand. *The World Bank Economic Review* 2(2): 139–64.

Klein, Ruben, and Sergio C. Ribeiro. 1991. O Censo Educacional e o Modelo de Fluxo: O Problema da Repetência. *Relatório de Pesquisa e Desenvolvimento* 24, Rio de Janeiro.

Mello e Souza, Alberto de. 1979. *Financiamento de Educação e Acesso à Escola no Brasil.* Rio de Janeiro: IPEA/INPES.

Murnane, Richard J. 1981. Evidence, Analysis and Unanswered Questions. *Harvard Educational Review* 51(4) (November): 483–89.

Psacharopoulos, George, and Ana Maria Arriagada. 1989. The Determinants of Early Age Human Capital Formation: Evidence from Brazil. *Economic Development and Cultural Change* 37(4) (July): 683–708.

Riddel, A.R. 1989. An Alternative Approach to the Study of School Effectiveness in Third World Countries. *Comparative Education Review* 33(4) (November): 481–97.

Silva, N.V. 1981. Cor e o Processo de Realização Sócio-Econômica. *Dados* 24(3): 391–409.

Silva, N.V., and Alberto de Mello e Souza. 1986. Um Modelo para Análise da Estratificação Educacional no Brasil. *Cadernos de Pesquisa* 58 (August): 49–57.

Appendix Table 13.1. Logistic Regressions for the Choice of School Type

Variable	Students enrolled in 1982	Students enrolled in 1981	Students admitted in 1982	Primary level: 1st to 4th	Primary level: 5th to 8th	Secondary level	University
Size of family	-0.276**	-0.254**	0.325**	-0.311**	-0.162**	-0.116**	-0.160*
Family income	0.525E-5**	0.457E-5**	0.109E-4**	0.469E-5**	0.358E-5***	0.344E-5**	-0.159E-6
Urban area	0.792**	0.927**	1.107*	1.523**	0.708*	0.718	-0.253
Female-headed household	0.327**	0.358**	1.101*	0.122	0.371*	0.007	-0.388
Education of family head	0.098**	0.109**	0.053***	0.208**	0.138**	0.054**	-0.104**
White	0.680**	0.742**	0.859	0.498	0.912*	-0.176	-4.764
Brown	-0.040	-0.214	0.509	-0.409	0.739	-0.123	—
Oriental	1.060**	0.986**	1.376**	0.564	1.146**	-0.439	-5.789
Female	0.109*	0.070	0.250	0.206**	-0.102	-0.088	0.193
Constant	-3.028**	-3.326**	-3.897**	-4.785**	-4.200**	-1.381**	8.654*
R^2(%)	20.0	19.5	28.6	31.5	16.5	6.6	5.5
N	11,524	11,159	1,586	5,936	3,623	1,394	564
P(Y=1)	0.160	0.153	0.153	0.074	0.109	0.372	0.870

* Significant at $a = 0.05$.
** Significant at $a = 0.01$

Appendix Table 13.2. Determinants of Age at School Entrance and Age-Grade Fitness

Variable	Coefficients			
	Age at school entrance			Age-grade fitness
Size of family		.097**	.098**	−.113*
Family income		−.246E-6	−.407E-6	.143E-6
Urban area		.199*	−.195*	.157
Female-headed households		.562**	.554**	−.418**
Education of family head		.062**	.065**	.108**
White		.483**	−.480**	.436**
Brown		.444**	−.441**	.310*
Oriental		.744**	−.764**	.682*
Female		.199**	−.201**	.114
Private school		.550**	.139	−.113
Constant	.812**	1.152**	1.153**	−3.389**
R²(%)	.018	.157	.158	.159
F	24.124	27.160**	24.567**	33.483

* Significant at $a = 0.05$.
** Significant at $a = 0.01$.

Appendix Table 13.3. Logistic Regression Model Estimates for Promotion and Dropping Out, First Grade

	Promotion[1]				
	Model A				
	All	Public school	Private school	Model B	Drop Out[2]
Size of family	−.062**	−.068**	.437*	−.073	.076
Family income	.203E-5**	.246E-5**	.196E-5	.207E-5**	.687E-5**
Urban residence	−.365**	.405**	1.477	−.359**	−.396
Female-headed household	.073	.066	1.358	.035	.156
Education of family head	.121**	.130**	.094	.133**	−.117**
White	.063	.082	—	.114	.517
Brown	−.240	−.224	—	−.201	.221
Female	.457**	.431**	1.560**	.468**	.010
Private school	.330	—	—	.304	—
Age/grade fitness	—	—	—	−.101**	.404**
Grade completed	—	—	—	—	.700*
Constant	.847**	.857**	−3.323*	.492	−5.270**
R²(%)	4.3	3.5	11.4	4.5	12.7
P(Y=1)	.712	.698	.894	.712	.033

* Significant at $a = 0.05$.
** Significant at $a = 0.01$.
[1] Oriental omitted due to perfect correlation with Y (all students in this group were promoted).
[2] Oriental and private school omitted due to perfect correlation with Y (all dropouts from public school).

Appendix Table 13.4. Logistic Regression Model Estimation for Promotion and Dropping Out, Fourth, Eighth and 11th Grades

Variable	4th Grade Promotion	4th Grade Dropout	8th Grade Promotion	8th Grade Dropout	11th Grade Promotion	11th Grade Dropout
Size of family	-.023	.146**	-.112	.059	.209	.062
Total family income	.205E-5*	-.523E-5**	.217E-6	-.143E-5	-.145E-7	-.207E-5**
Urban residence	.008	-1.068	.559	.275	—	1.860**
Female-headed household	-.151	-.039	-.034	-.170	-.205	.265
Education of family head	-.018	-.197	-.060	-.074**	-.159**	-.101**
White	-.134	.179	-1.134	.054	-.047	-.624
Brown	-.023	.414	-.912	.587	.212	.204
Oriental	.962	-.332	-.315	-2.616**	-1.225	-.209
Female	.552**	-.150	.482*	-.622	-.342	-.468**
Private school	-.016	-.299	.127	.131	.226	-.023
Age/grade fitness	-.039	-.425**	.037	-.455**	-.001	-.003
Grade completed	—	.754*	—	1.697**	—	-2.019**
Constant	1.951**	-3.668*	3.465**	-4.614**	1.795*	1.732
R^2(%)	1.4	18.8	2.1	16.3	7.8	9.8
P(Y=1)	.903	.118	.893	.227	.819	.582

Note: All unsuccessful students were urban residents.
* Significant at $a = 0.05$.
** Significant $a = 0.01$.

CHAPTER

14

Efficiency-Enhancing Investments in School Quality

Eric A. Hanushek, João Batista Gomes-Neto and
Ralph W. Harbison[1]

Educational research has not always been successful in providing useful guidance on policies to enhance school quality. Research has had a number of ambiguities and has been incomplete from a policy perspective, particularly regarding how resources should be employed. This chapter fills important gaps in understanding the economic and educational rationale for various decisions and, particularly, for emphasizing quality-improving policies.

This work is based on analysis of a unique data set for rural Northeast Brazil. As part of the extensive EDURURAL Project, a joint venture of the Brazilian government and the World Bank, a variety of educational improvements were tried in primary schools serving a poor population in the 1980s. Along with this educational program came a significant effort to collect data and analyze school effectiveness. The survey project provided unique longitudinal data, permitting an entirely new type of analysis relevant to school policy. While this analysis does not evaluate the EDURURAL Project itself (see Harbison and Hanushek, 1992), it does employ the data generated to investigate alternative school policies.

The fundamental question for the educational policymaker is which school inputs are most efficient in raising student achievement scores, given an available level of resources. This very simple and seemingly undisputable idea is, nonetheless, rarely the focus of policymaking. At best, education policy has been made solely on the basis of analyses of effectiveness. In this, analyses of student performance provide direct estimates of the benefits of altering different inputs into the educational process, thus allowing the inputs to be ranked on the basis of their effectiveness. This is better than having no empirical basis at all for policy determination, but it is perilous. Specifically, it does not incorporate information about the costs of

---

[1] We would like to thank Stanley Engerman, Richard Sabot and Steven Stern for helpful comments on various drafts of this chapter.

such alterations. This chapter integrates analysis of marginal educational effects with estimates of the costs of making different input adjustments.

Efficiency calculations—the appropriate basis for assessing different policies to educate a given student population—involve the joint consideration of outputs and the costs of inputs required to implement any policy. In the best of all situations, outputs can be valued in monetary terms so that costs of inputs can be compared directly to the resulting outputs—that is, cost-benefit analysis. Because output is measured in terms of academic achievement that cannot be translated into monetary terms, however, it is generally necessary to concentrate on the closely related cost-effectiveness analysis (Lockheed and Hanushek, 1988, 1994). Here, while we cannot go all of the way to a full cost-benefit analysis, we can introduce some direct measures of efficiency by putting policy determination into a dynamic context. The static calculation of cost-effectiveness of specific inputs employs the gross costs of different inputs. The net costs will differ from these because improving student academic performance also entails dynamic efficiency gains, something we can estimate.

The dynamic gains are conceptually straightforward even if seldom empirically demonstrated. When students learn more because of more or better inputs to their schooling experience, they are more likely to be promoted. This reduces the total time they spend in the system to reach any given grade level. Increasing the flow through the system implies cost savings, since fewer student-years of schooling services have to be provided on average for a student to reach the given level. These savings offset the costs of instituting the original policy change.

The cost reductions attributable to improving the student flow through schools can be quite substantial. Levels of repetition shown in the following chapter by Gomes-Neto and Hanushek imply that the average student arriving in the fourth grade in rural Northeast Brazil will already have spent 7.6 years in school, instead of the three required by steady on-time progression. This vastly understates the overall economic cost of attaining that level of schooling, since it ignores the resources expended on students who enter school but never reach the fourth grade. In fact, in rural Northeast Brazil an average of 15.2 student-years of schooling services is provided for each student who reaches the fourth grade. Repetition and dropout multiply the cost of a graduate fivefold. Since wastage is so high, even small improvements in promotion probabilities (which, of course, imply decreases in rates of repetition or dropout) can result in significant savings.

Thus, this analysis calculates the offsets to gross program costs arising from improved student flows. The result is estimates of net cost effectiveness. While this is the appropriate criterion for considering policies, we are aware of only one other attempt to consider such feedback effects (Jamison, 1978).

The results of this exercise are extraordinary. A wide range of investments made to improve educational quality can actually be thought of as making money. In other words, the savings from improved flow efficiency are often larger than the original costs of providing improved inputs in the schooling process. The finding of net cost gains through improved efficiency generally holds even when allowance is made for uncertainty in the estimates. The normally postulated tradeoff between quality and quantity of schooling appears to be quite the opposite in circumstances of severe educational deprivation: instead, there is a positive interaction wherein enhanced quality engenders increased quantity.

Quantity of Schooling

The quantitative aspects of human capital formation—access and promotion—have been the central focus of most previous development policy discussions in the educational sector. They present a number of challenges to the policymaker. For example, while governmental policy in Brazil may declare that school attendance is mandatory between the ages of seven and 14, that requirement is clearly insufficient to ensure effective human capital formation. Enforcing compulsory attendance is often impossible, particularly in rural areas where students can perform productive activities on farms. Moreover, presence in school does not guarantee that students progress through the grades or even that they learn anything while there. In fact, mandatory attendance can lead to extensive grade repetition with little gain in knowledge.

Further, the quality implications of compulsory schooling policies are potentially serious. Resources for education are constrained everywhere, particularly in those LDCs furthest from universal schooling. Expanding enrollments without commensurately expanding the resources devoted to schooling implies that other measures must be taken to reduce per pupil expenditures. The options include such steps as allowing class sizes to rise, teacher salaries (and presumably their qualifications) to fall, or availability of textbooks and other materials to decline. More perversely, if a portion of the students enrolled are disinterested and not learning, the funds used for them are effectively diverted from providing higher quality schooling for those who are appropriately prepared and motivated to take advantage of the school experience.

The budgetary tradeoffs between quantity and quality of schooling have been frequently noted (Solmon, 1986). But these discussions do not include any significant direct empirical investigation between the two.[2] The pure budgetary discussions suggest that a more or less mechanical accounting exercise will provide information about the tradeoffs. This approach, however, ignores at least two central issues. First, the linkages between quantity and quality that arise from the underlying behavior of students and teachers in the educational process are nowhere considered. Second, too much is assumed about the relationships between quality and costs.

The data generated by the EDURURAL evaluation provide a unique opportunity to address some of these gaps in policy discussions. The longitudinal structure of the data allows inferences about the relationships among school continuation, promotion and student performance. Moreover, the rich observations about families and schools permit investigation of the underlying determinants of promotion.

Student Flows and the Structure of the Data

Many students in rural Northeast Brazil never finish the first four grades, let alone attend secondary school or beyond. Students must contend with poor schools, pressing poverty, which realistically can be alleviated only by taking advantage of opportunities for immediate employment in the agricultural sector, and frequent lack of support from home. In such circumstances, students tend to progress slowly through the grades and drop out, often long before the prescribed period of compulsory attendance is completed. The consequences—low completion rates and excessive repetition in primary grades—are well known to policymakers in Brazil. What is not understood is how this situation can be improved, which in turn reflects the overall lack of knowledge about the underlying behavior of students and families.

The primary difficulty in analyzing school completion and promotion patterns has been a general lack of detailed data describing the paths of students through school and explaining the factors that influence decisions. In simplest terms, neither aggregate data nor data about a cross-section of

---

[2] A significant, if not fully satisfying, exception to this rule is the work by Behrman and Birdsall (1983) with data drawn from the 1970 Brazilian census. However, they explore the relationship between quantity and quality of schooling in the context of earnings functions and derivative rates of return, and not with respect to actual education production. See also Jamison (1978) for more direct consideration of quantity-quality issues.

students can support the kind of analyses that are required for policy purposes. These issues require longitudinal data on individual students. The EDURURAL data set, while not explicitly designed for this purpose, goes some distance toward remedying previous data inadequacies.

The EDURURAL data collection was based upon repeated sampling from the student bodies in a set of schools drawn randomly within participating (EDURURAL) and control (OTHER) municipalities. The schools were observed at three different times (1981, 1983 and 1985),[3] and during each observation a random sample of second and fourth graders was surveyed and tested. This data collection design, in which interviewers returned to the same school every two years, offered an opportunity to observe individual students repeatedly. Most important, there was a group of students—initially in the second grade—who were progressing at the expected pace so that they were in the fourth grade in the follow-up sampling. Whether or not a student was actually observed in subsequent data collection was a function of many intervening factors, including purely random sampling chances.

Using EDURURAL samples to analyze questions about the quantity of schooling depends on understanding the dynamics of the samples and utilizing the panel data on both schools and students. For analytical purposes, it is convenient to think in terms of probability models and to link the conditional probabilities of a series of basic events to their determinants. The difficulty in this analysis is that the observations of events are incomplete.

Two important linkages of the data across years can be identified. First, from the repeated sampling of the same schools, it is possible to identify whether or not a given school continues to serve its students over time. Contrasting schools that survive with those that do not offers insight into the prevalence of schools in the research area. Second, for those schools that both survive for the two-year period and have a fourth grade, it is possible to find some second grade students who are promoted to the fourth grade by the subsequent data collection. Comparing promoted students with others allows some insights into the determinants of progression in school.

The data collection scheme indicates three important points about the promotion modeling. First, the analysis is restricted to "on-time" promotions. A student still in grade two or three is treated the same as one who has dropped out; neither has progressed through school at the expected

---

[3] A special survey was conducted in one state, Ceará, for 1987. While this provides supporting information, the characteristics of the survey preclude incorporating it in this analysis (see Harbison and Hanushek, 1992).

pace. Second, some students who have progressed to the fourth grade are not identified because they have changed schools between the two survey years. Although these paths are almost certainly quite small, this measurement problem could influence subsequent analysis. Third, the sampling of students did not capture all of the fourth graders in those schools with a large (more than 10 pupils) fourth grade. Moreover, there was no explicit attempt to resurvey those tested two years earlier in the second grade. This last issue on sampling does not cause much of an analytical problem, however, because the random selection eliminates bias in the subsequent behavioral estimation. Nevertheless, the mean promotion rates observed in the sample will understate the true overall on-time promotion rates.

The aggregate patterns are illuminating. Two analytical samples were constructed by combining adjoining surveys to create longitudinal data for 1981–83 and 1983–85. For the first sample, the schools of 59 percent of the 1981 second graders (2,737 students) survive to 1983. Of these students who could potentially be matched with data for 1983, only 9 percent (249 students) are found in the fourth grade in the follow-up survey. The corresponding numbers for 1983 are 2,730 students in surviving schools and 14 percent (379) of these students found in the fourth grade in 1985. The longitudinal samples are especially important because school promotion and the development of student achievement are inherently processes that occur over time. The longitudinal information provides a unique ability to understand these processes.

One tendency that deserves mention is the propensity for schools to disappear. The sampling design called for returning to exactly the same set of schools each time, but this proved impossible because such a large number of schools disappeared. School survival is an important element of government policy, because the continuation of schooling opportunities is fundamentally determined by the level of support of schools. These issues, while very important, go beyond the scope of this chapter. They are discussed in detail in Harbison and Hanushek (1992).[4]

On-time Promotion Probabilities

Analysis of school quantity focuses on the probability that a student is promoted to the fourth grade, given that the school survives and has a fourth

---

[4] The estimated school survival models do enter into the estimation of school achievement models.

grade. Whether individual student performance is related to promotion probabilities is extremely important for policy purposes, because it offers insight into how to assess different proposals for dealing with dropout and repetition rates and their mirror image, promotion rates. Specifically, if promotion is only slightly related to actual student performance—that is, the people being left behind or dropping out are about as good academically as those being promoted—then high repetition and dropout rates indeed represent wasted resources. Direct regulatory efforts to lower this wastage and increase promotions might well be called for. On the other hand, if promotions are highly related to student quality, arbitrarily increasing promotion rates reduces wastage by continuing students with lower performance; the benefits of an external intervention program of lowering wastage would be much less.

The fundamental measuring sticks employed here are a series of specially designed tests of achievement in Portuguese and mathematics. Ultimate success of the schools is probably better defined by other measures, such as the ability of educated people to compete in the labor market, increase the productivity of their farms, participate in democratic society, and care and nurture children. These ultimate goals of schooling are, however, virtually impossible to measure at the time of schooling and can be observed only after a substantial period of time has passed. Therefore, when assessing the character and determinants of successful schooling, proxies for these true goals must be employed. This leads us to standardized tests of the subject matter contained in the school curriculum.

The Portuguese and mathematics tests employed were developed specifically for the EDURURAL Project. A team of psychometricians from the *Fundação Carlos Chagas* (FCC), a leading educational research institute in São Paulo, constructed and validated the tests. The FCC determined that existing standardized tests used in urban areas of the South would be too difficult for students in the rural Northeast. (Administration of trial tests originally developed for students in the second and fourth grade in the South indicated that they would not provide reliable discrimination among the students of the Northeast.) Tests given to students in the EDURURAL sample were developed in 1981 and marginal improvements were made in later years. The tests were criterion referenced to minimally acceptable levels of performance in second and fourth grade mathematics and Portuguese. (These performance levels were noticeably lower than what is expected in the South.) The judgments about curricular materials for each grade came from teachers, technical staff and administrators in the various educational organizations of the Northeast. The Portuguese tests cover

reading comprehension, writing, grammar and (in the fourth grade) composition; the mathematics tests cover basic numeracy items. The 1983 and
1985 tests were constructed to be parallel forms of the original 1981 test;
that is, new questions were developed to examine the same concepts and
maintain the same level of difficulty.

The analysis of promotion probabilities incorporates, in addition to the
achievement measures, a variety of factors that influence promotion or sample
observation. The full models, presented in Table 14.1, incorporate student age
and sex, parents' education, time living in the county, and state and program
indicators. Additionally, because of the random sampling of students in the
schools in each year, it is possible for an individual to be promoted on time but
not to be included in the promotion sample. To deal directly with this, the
probit models include the number of students in the schools, since the probabilities of being missed by the sampling are directly related to the number of
students in the school. The school size measure is significantly negative in the
probit models, reflecting this sampling within schools.

The promotion probability models are estimated by probit techniques.[5] For exposition, Table 14.1 converts the results of the probit estimation into estimated marginal effects on promotion probabilities evaluated at
the means for each of the variables. Estimates based on probit coefficients
that are not significantly different from zero at the 5 percent level are en-
closed in parentheses.

The table summarizes the relationship between second grade test
scores and promotion probabilities. Higher test scores consistently lead to
greater promotion probabilities; this suggests that promotion has a strong
basis in merit. Each 10 points on the Portuguese test, which has a standard
deviation of approximately 25 points, increases promotion probabilities by
about 1.5 to 2.5 percent. This implies that a student going from the 25th
percentile to the 75th percentile on the test has 5 to 9 percent higher promo-

---

[5] The complete probit models of promotion are displayed in Appendix Table 14.2 and in
Harbison and Hanushek (1992, Table C4.2), along with means and standard deviations of the
variables. The probit estimates provide a nonlinear relationship between the various explanatory
factors and the probability of survival. Because of this, the estimation of probability effects of
changing any given variable depends upon where the function is evaluated. Throughout this
chapter, probability evaluations are done at the mean values for each of the variables. Each of the
separate estimated coefficients is interpreted as the independent effect of the variable holding
constant the other variables in the estimated equation (Hanushek and Jackson, 1977). Estimates
of bivariate probit models which allow for correlations of the errors in the school survival and
promotion equations were also done, but the correlation of errors was never over 0.001. Therefore, the results reported here are based on simple probit estimates for each equation.

Table 14.1. Effects of Student Achievement on Promotion Probabilities, 1981–83 and 1983–85

Variable	1981–83	1983–85
Portuguese test	0.0014	0.0026
Mathematics test	(0.0003)	0.0009

Notes: Estimated marginal probabilities are calculated at means of variables and holding constant other factors contained in probit equations that exclude school control measures. For complete results, see Appendix Table 14.2 and Harbison and Hanushek (1992). Estimates that are not significantly different from zero at the 5 percent level are reported in parentheses.

tion probabilities. Between the 10th and 90th percentile, promotion probabilities rise by 9 to 17 percent. Since the mean observed promotion rate in the sample is only 9 percent in 1983 and 14 percent in 1985, these are significant differences due to merit.

Performance on the mathematics test does not have as strong an influence on promotion. It is statistically insignificant in the 1981–83 period and has about one-third the effect of the Portuguese test in 1983–85. (The standard deviation of the mathematics test score is approximately equal to that for the Portuguese test.) These strong results about the performance basis for promotion play a central role in estimating efficiency effects of alternative policies.

Determinants of Achievement

The EDURURAL data collection had a single purpose—to evaluate the performance of rural schools. A key element in this was to assess the impact on performance of the special inputs to schooling provided through the EDURURAL Project. Special attention focused on three categories of inputs: (i) "hardware" such as classrooms, sanitary facilities, water and electrical service, and furniture for students and teachers; (ii) "software" such as textbooks and teacher's guides, audiovisual aids, notebooks, pencils and other writing materials; and (iii) teachers who had completed specified in-service upgrading programs or pre-service academic training. Numerous challenging measurement and data collection issues were encountered: the testing of low performing primary students; the mechanics of survey collection in sparsely populated, difficult to reach areas; and the management of complicated data bases involving merging information from several levels of aggregation and disparate sources, to name but a few. The result, nevertheless, is a data set uniquely capable of supporting analysis of school performance and evaluation of programmatic interventions.

The analysis of student performance concentrates on the achievement test measures described in the previous section. The means on the Portuguese and mathematics tests for the two grade levels are displayed in Table 14.2. The statistics, based on the full test samples in each year, provide some startling evidence about the overall level of performance. The average scores for the region as a whole fall between 45 and 60 points out of a possible 100. In other words, the actual performance is not even close to the minimal standards set by the local educators who constructed the tests. The scores also show two interesting aggregate facts. First, students' performance, presumably measured on a consistent basis, showed general improvement over time only for Portuguese achievement in the second grade. The other scores do not indicate much change in the level of aggregate performance. Second, there are differences in performance across states. Scores in Ceará are consistently above those in Pernambuco and Piauí.

These aggregate scores do not, however, provide much guidance for policy. Certainly the low absolute performance levels warrant concern, but it was known before the start of the EDURURAL Project that strong remedial action was required. The key to policy changes is understanding what factors contribute to individual performance levels, and then altering those factors. The aggregate data do not provide the basis for such understanding. Therefore, we turn our attention to understanding in some detail the determinants of differences in individual student performance.

Specification of the Achievement Models

The overall framework for analysis follows a quite standard input-output specification for the educational process. The achievement of a given student at time t (A_t) is assumed to be related to current and past educational inputs from a variety of sources—the home, the school and the community. To highlight key features, we use a general conceptual model:

(1) $A_t = f(F^{(t)}, S^{(t)}, O^{(t)}, \epsilon_t),$

where $F^{(t)} =$ a vector of the student's family background and family educational inputs cumulative to time t;

$S^{(t)} =$ a vector of the student's teacher and school inputs cumulative to time t;

$O^{(t)} =$ a vector of other relevant inputs such as community factors, friends, and so forth cumulative to time t; and

$\epsilon_t =$ unmeasured factors that contribute to achievement at time t.

Table 14.2. Mean Test Performance by State, 1981, 1983 and 1985

Grade/test	Total			Pernambuco			Ceará			Piauí		
	1981	1983	1985	1981	1983	1985	1981	1983	1985	1981	1983	1985
Second grade												
Portuguese	49.0	58.7	59.5	42.9	50.0	50.7	62.8	65.8	69.6	44.7	59.6	57.0
Mathematics	45.9	51.1	49.2	42.9	46.5	42.1	57.9	57.0	56.4	38.6	49.5	47.9
Fourth grade												
Portuguese	51.5	52.2	48.4	50.0	48.7	43.4	60.5	59.0	55.5	48.5	51.6	47.0
Mathematics	48.5	48.2	50.1	49.1	44.6	44.6	59.9	55.0	55.3	40.7	47.7	50.7

Source: Harbison and Hanushek (1992).

The approach is to measure the different possible inputs into education and estimate their influence on student achievement. As described in Harbison and Hanushek (1992), this emulates the approach adopted in the Coleman Report (Coleman et al., 1966) and most follow-on studies in the United States (Hanushek, 1986) and developing countries (Fuller, 1985).

This conceptual model explicitly incorporates a stochastic, or random, error term—ϵ_t—to reflect the fact that we can never observe all of the factors affecting achievement. (Indeed, the distribution of this error term, as discussed below, has important implications for the estimation and interpretation of the effects of the other factors in the model.)

To the extent that the vector of various school factors, denoted by $S^{(t)}$ includes the pertinent instruments of policy, the relative effectiveness of possible educational strategies can be compared both to each other and, potentially, to the costs. Within the context of the EDURURAL Project, effectiveness could be ascertained in two different ways using standard regression techniques. First, in a classic experimental evaluation, it might be possible to estimate overall mean achievement differences between EDURURAL and other schools after accounting for measurable resource and family differences. Second, it would be possible to measure explicitly the specific school resources provided by the project and to include these factors in estimates of student achievement relationships. This would provide "learning weights" that can be used in assessing changes in performance induced by the specific inputs provided under the project.

The most serious drawback to these approaches is the likelihood of obtaining biased statistical estimates of the effectiveness of EDURURAL and of different school resources. The source of such bias is centered on the error term, ϵ_t, in equation 1 which includes all unmeasured influences on achievement. It is natural to expect many things to be unmeasured in the case of individual student data. The key issue is whether the collection of these factors is unrelated to the observed family, school and other influences on achievement that are measured and included in the analysis. If unrelated, standard regression analysis provides unbiased estimates of the achievement relationships. If they are systematically related, however, the parameter estimates will be biased, and their use for evaluation or policy analysis will tend to be misleading.

In a wide range of educational settings, it is difficult to accept that these error terms are uncorrelated with the measured inputs to achievement. These error terms are likely to contain a variety of unmeasured factors that are, nonetheless, systematic. First, since education is a cumulative process, the entire history of inputs is needed to characterize achievement at any point in time. This implies an enormous data collection require-ment—one that is seldom if ever accomplished. In fact, for practical rea-sons, measurements are usually limited to a single point, neglecting any variations in previous educational inputs. Second, most survey designs limit the range and character of the observed data. Even with the specially designed surveys here, for example, it is difficult to record any qualitative differences in teacher's behavior. Thus many contemporaneous factors es-cape measurement. Third, some factors nearly defy measurement. For ex-ample, most people believe that differences in innate abilities of students are important in determining achievement differences. But there is little consensus on how innate ability might be measured, and available instru-ments are not easy to administer efficiently to large numbers of children even if considered reliable. Similarly, student motivation and aspirations are important but very difficult to measure.

All these unmeasured factors are likely to be correlated with observed family and school variables. Past school situations tend to be related both to family characteristics and to contemporaneous school inputs; qualitative differences in inputs often correspond to quantity and to family choices; innate abilities, motivations and aspirations tend to be correlated with ob-served family characteristics. The risk of biased parameter estimates—and unreliable policy conclusions—is thus substantial.

One approach to dealing with this problem is to reformulate the basic achievement model to look at gains in achievement over time. If, for ex-ample, one can observe achievement at the end of an earlier time t^*, it is possible to analyze $(A_t - A_{t^*})$, or how much achievement changed between time t^* and t. Intuitively, the increase in performance in, say, a single grade would depend most upon the teacher, school and family inputs in that year. Thus, if it is possible to collect information on gains in performance, it is less risky to concentrate on just the contemporaneous values of inputs. Further, to the extent that innate abilities affect the absolute level of performance more and the growth rate of achievement less, this formulation gets around lack of measurement.[6] But this formulation, often called a value-added specification, requires repeated sampling of the same individuals.

In the actual estimation, prior achievement, A_{t^*}, is frequently included as one of the explanatory variables in the regression (instead of simply

---

[6] If two measures of prior achievement are available, it is possible to incorporate both "level" and "growth" effects directly. Boardman and Murnane (1979) develop this for the case where achievement is measured at three distinct points in time, but multiple measurements of prior achievement at a single point in time will generally suffice.

differencing it from current achievement). This has two advantages. First, it allows for differential growth in achievement based upon initial score. If, for example, high achievers are able to extract more than low achievers from subsequent instruction, the simple differencing procedure will be inappropriate. Second, the modified specification also permits measurement of achievement using yardsticks with different "units of measure" over time, that is, it allows different tests to be used in the two years.

One other aspect of analysis is highlighted by the value-added formulation. The statistical properties of the estimated regression model depend upon the distribution of the error terms, ϵ_t. When achievement in later grades is analyzed, the sample of observed children may not be representative of the entire population. Specifically, since children tend to drop out of school as time goes on, only children who have stayed in school and been promoted will be observed. Moreover, since students who perform better in school tend to be the ones who stay in school, the sample is "selected" in a specific way that relates directly to the achievement of students. This problem of "sample selection bias" has been discussed extensively in different contexts (Heckman, 1979; Maddala, 1983).

The intuition behind sample selection bias is clear. Assume that only the best students stay in school until they are observed in the sampling of schools. These are students who tend to have high unmeasured abilities, attitudes or other advantages; that is, students who have $\epsilon_t > 0$. If the statistical analyses do not take this into account, the school and family inputs are likely to be confused with high abilities of the observed students, yielding biased estimates of what would happen if, say, a set of school inputs was changed.

The most straightforward corrective procedure involves estimating the probability that an individual will appear in the sample. If this can be done, consistent estimates of the underlying achievement parameters can be obtained by including sample selection probabilities directly into the model of achievement. So it is that the probit analyses in the previous section provide the needed information for correcting the achievement models explored here.

The potential problems of sample selection are most severe when there is only a single cross-section of data on schooling. For example, if data are only available for fourth graders in a given year and many students do not make it to the fourth grade, correcting the achievement models is very difficult. One needs information about the determinants of fourth grade attendance, and this would not be directly available in the sampled data. These considerations pinpoint one of the unique and most valuable features of the sample design in the EDURURAL Project.

Finally, note that in a value-added form the potential selection problems would be further reduced. If the probability of promotion to the fourth grade was determined completely by the measured performance in the prior grade and if that prior performance was included in a value-added model, the sample selection problems would not appear. Nevertheless, because of peculiarities in the sample design for the EDURURAL research, potential biases remain even in the value-added versions, and we estimate the models in a way consistent with sample selection.[7]

Note that similar measurement errors in final achievement, A_{it}, do not cause the same problems. The error term in the equation, ϵ_t, can accommodate measurement errors as long as they are not systematically related to the explanatory factors.[8]

If there is an independent estimate of the error variance, an alternative technique is available. The classical correction procedures (Maddala, 1983) essentially use the estimated error variance to adjust the observed variance in prior achievement before the regression analysis is performed. With test scores, it is possible to use estimates of test reliability to estimate the error variance. An example of this approach in the achievement context is found in Hanushek (1986).[9]

What Makes a Difference?

We actually have two snapshots of student achievement and provide what are essentially parallel analyses of educational performance. Specifically,

---

[7] The value-added formulation does, however, introduce some of its own problems. Specifically, prior achievement is itself measured with error, because of peculiarities of the test instrument, random circumstances related to the time of measurement or test taking, and other similar factors that lower test reliability. Such test measurement errors introduce another reason for correlation of the error term in the equation, ϵ_t, with the explanatory variables and must be corrected.

[8] The severity of such problems increases with the size of the error variance relative to the variance in true prior performance. The most commonly used corrective procedure employs instrumental variables techniques.

[9] If one can find a variable that is correlated with the true prior achievement of the student but is uncorrelated with the measurement errors, the estimation can be adjusted to eliminate the problems introduced by the measurement errors. Applying instrumental variable techniques is straightforward in this case, but, when executed, has virtually no effect on any of the estimates. Therefore, no further consideration is given to the instrumental variables approach. An alternative approach when concerned about test reliability is to employ direct estimates of the variance of the measurement error (Hanushek, 1992), but this is not employed here because of concerns about how well the test reliabilities are estimated.

we can examine the achievement in both mathematics and Portuguese of fourth graders in 1983 and 1985 in a value-added framework. We concentrate here on the estimated effects of teacher and school resources. These estimates come, however, from more extensive models that incorporate the effects of families, peers in the school and classroom, state and program identification, and other environmental factors. Although the results for school resource effects are the focal point, they are *always* the marginal effects of the specific factor after allowing for variations in the other factors included in the full models. Alternative forms of these more extensive models along with the importance of the other influences on student performance are described and analyzed in Harbison and Hanushek (1992).

The following section reviews the estimation results obtained in different years and areas of performance (Portuguese and mathematics). Both for sample size reasons and completeness of the data, the results for 1983–85 should receive more weight. Most importantly, those models include direct measures of subject matter knowledge of teachers, a key descriptive element.

Physical Facilities and Learning Materials

Understanding the effects of the school facilities and materials available to students is particularly important, since they are readily adjusted through governmental policies and are thus frequently the preferred instruments of educational development programs. They are also inputs that have entered significantly into previous investigations of the educational process in LDCs. We consider two broad categories of factors: school facilities (hardware) and writing materials and textbooks (software). Table 14.3 shows how measures of these factors are related to performance.

Improved facilities are systematically beneficial to student learning.[10] The index takes on values between 0 (for a school having none of the measured facilities) and 1 (for a school with all the measured facilities). The results indicate that supplying all components of the facilities index to a school that previously had none of them could increase student achievement by 9 to 13 points. The overall picture is that quality of the physical plant is positively related to student performance.

---

[10] The components of the hardware index include the availability of specific kinds of physical plant (more than one classroom, a kitchen, sanitary facilities, storage space, offices); items of furniture (desks and chairs for pupils, table for teacher, bookcases); and water and electricity. The value of the index varies from 0 (representing the absence of all component of the index) to 1 (representing the presence of all components).

Table 14.3. Estimated Resource Parameters for Achievement Models, 1981–83 and 1983–85

	Portuguese		Mathematics	
	1981–83	1983–85	1981–83	1983–85
Hardware	11.73*	8.78*	8.32	12.40*
Software	−3.02	6.69*	−5.58	11.03*
Graded classrooms	−1.68	−3.87	4.81	−6.19*
Pupil–teacher ratio	.12	−.11	.20	−.06
Teacher education	−.33	−.13	.46	−.08
Teacher experience	.20	.06	.23	.26
LOGOS	2.00	−.22	.72	2.96
Qualificação	1.02	−2.21	2.96	−5.94*
Teacher Portuguese test	na	.17*	na	−.18*
Teacher mathematics test	na	.18*	na	.52*
Teacher salary	.02	.01	.02	.04*

na = not available.
* Coefficient significant at 95 percent level.

Research reviewed in Harbison and Hanushek (1992) has generally found that the availability of writing materials and texts is important in schooling for LDCs. The results here for software investments reinforce that view, although the results for 1981–83 are statistically insignificant (and have the wrong sign). The software index combines information about the availability of specific items supplied by the EDURURAL Project (such as chalk, notebooks, pencils, erasers and crayons) and the availability of adequate textbooks. The size of the coefficients indicate that providing a full software package improves performance by one-third to one-half standard deviations of test performance, compared to having none. Especially when combined with the strength of findings in previous studies, these appear to be strong performance results.

Table 14.3 also considers use of graded classrooms, a factor that receives elevated attention because of policy discussions in Brazil and elsewhere. The use of graded classrooms is an obviously important aspect of the organization of the school, especially where dispersed rural populations constrain school size. In rural Northeast Brazil, where class sizes are typically small, providing individual teachers for small single-grade classes rather than fewer teachers managing larger ungraded classes or multigrade classrooms has enormous economic implications. As Table 14.3 indicates, however, the use of single grade classrooms, rather than ungraded or multigrade classes, appears to affect performance generally negatively. The results for 1983–85 are especially important. The negative mathematics effect is statistically significant, and the negative Portuguese effect is almost statistically significant at the 95 percent level (t=–1.95).

The findings cast doubt upon the common presumption that moving to all graded classrooms is desirable. At the very least, the suggestion is strong that the one-room school with students at various levels taught simultaneously by one teacher is not detrimental to learning. For the context of rural Northeast Brazil, mixed-grade classrooms may in fact offer advantages. In a pedagogical environment dominated by rote memorization of material presented verbally or on the blackboard by the teacher, a student may profit from repeated hearing and seeing of the same material and from the peer teaching typical of the multigrade classroom. Another possibility is that in an environment where pupil absences are frequent because of sickness or the need for children to work, the repetition offered in a multigrade classroom saves many children from being entirely lost upon return from school after an absence.

Teachers

Though quality of teaching is an elusive concept for researchers, it has some common characteristics in the minds of the public and policymakers. These characteristics are thus often found in research. The intensity of teacher interaction with the student is typically proxied in the pupil-teacher ratio. Teacher quality is normally proxied by such variables as experience in the profession, and type and duration of both pre-employment education and in-service training. Less frequently, direct measurement of the teacher's actual cognitive mastery of the subject matter is substituted for the normal quality indicators. Finally, teacher salary is often, if rather uncritically, used as a proxy for teacher quality, on the presumption that teachers command higher pay in direct proportion to their quality.

Our data permit us to examine the validity of these presumptions about teacher quality and its measurement. Specifically we can ask three important questions. Is achievement influenced by the standard measure of quantity of teacher input to an educational process, the pupil-teacher ratio? By the standard indirect summary measure of teacher quality, teacher salary? Or by more direct indicators of teacher quality?

Pupil-Teacher Ratios

There are well-known arguments favoring altering, or more specifically reducing, class sizes. In fact, policy proposals to reduce class sizes are among the most popular throughout the world, even though they are extremely costly. As the number of students who share the time of a teacher decreases, each student potentially receives more direct attention from the teacher. To the extent individualized attention from the teacher is an important learning determinant, student achievement would be expected to benefit. On the other hand, as reviewed in Harbison and Hanushek (1992), there is little consistent evidence from past studies—in either developed or developing countries—to support policies of reduced class sizes.

The evidence from the regression analyses in Table 14.3 lends little new support to proposals for reducing class sizes. In the value-added specifications, the pupil-teacher ratio has the expected (negative) sign in the 1983–85 models but is not statistically significant. In 1981–83, however, the sign on this variable is uniformly positive, intuitively suggesting that student performance improves as class size grows. Even if we take these statistically insignificant estimates at face value, the estimated coefficients are very small, so that substantial changes in class size would be required to produce a discernible impact on achievement. For example, changing class size by 10 pupils in either direction—around sample means between 25 and 30—would alter achievement gains from second to fourth grade by at most one point, even though it would have a tremendous effect on educational costs. Again, these effects should be compared with the standard deviation of the student test scores of approximately 25 points.

Implicit Indicators of Teacher Quality

When attempting to delve into the specific teacher characteristics related to performance, researchers and policymakers typically turn to a standard list, including years of teaching experience, level of formal pre-service education, and in-service training. These factors command attention for three reasons. First, if shown to be important for student achievement, they are convenient policy instruments because they can be readily manipulated. Second, they have been the subject of frequent past policy, even in the absence of information about their importance. Third, they are frequently related closely to salary differences. While we investigate these factors, we also look at a more direct comparison. For 1985, teachers were given the same Portuguese and mathematics achievement tests as those administered to fourth grade students, which can be analyzed to determine how much the teacher contributed to the learning of the students.

Table 14.3 contains information about the relationship between teachers' pre-service educational attainment and on-the-job experience, both expressed in years, to student achievement. The estimated coefficients show that teachers with more formal education are apparently no better than those with less education. In models of both Portuguese and mathematics learning the estimated effect of teacher education is not significantly different from zero. In fact, three of the four estimates are negative, suggesting implausibly that more schooling for teachers actually lowers their performance.

The unimportance of teacher education is somewhat surprising. Within our sample, the mean schooling of teachers is between seven and eight years with a standard deviation of three years. Further, more than 20 percent of the sampled teachers themselves have *four or fewer years of schooling*. Given both the level and the variation in schooling of teachers, it seemed plausible that this would be an important indicator of quality differences among teachers. Apparently, differences in the quality of schooling of teachers are sufficiently large to obscure any possible effects of quantity differences.

None of our models suggest that teacher experience is a statistically significant determinant of Portuguese achievement of students, although the sign on the estimated coefficients suggests a positive relationship. The evidence from students' mathematics achievement is only slightly more supportive of conventional wisdom. Disregarding statistical significance, the conclusion again is that the effects are small. An additional year of experience amounts to about one-quarter of an additional point of mathematics achievement gain. This implies that an increase of one standard deviation in experience (seven years) corresponds to less than two points in added gain.

Overall, the results so far call into question the broadly held view that simply providing more educated and experienced teachers to rural schools in Northeast Brazil will by itself noticeably improve the learning performance of students.

The estimated coefficients in Table 14.3 also characterize the impact of the two in-service teacher training programs associated with the EDURURAL Project intervention. Each is specified as a dummy variable to separate teachers who are participating in the programs from those who are not at the time of our surveys.

The LOGOS Program seeks to provide teachers who have already completed the eight years of primary education with a qualification equivalent to three years of secondary school. On balance, any evidence of success of LOGOS is not very compelling; there is no consistency of results, and specifically there is no evidence that the program accomplished its objective in the late survey years when it would presumably have been having a measurable impact. On the other hand, it is admittedly early to evaluate an ongoing training program.

The evidence is even less compelling with respect to the success of the *Curso de Qualificação* program, a remedial effort to provide the equivalent of an eighth grade education to teachers who have not completed the full primary cycle. The statistically significant negative coefficients on the *Qualificação* program variable for fourth grade mathematics achievement in 1985 is disconcerting at first glance.

There is, however, a plausible alternative interpretation of the estimated negative effects of these in-service programs. In equations that include more direct measures of pre-service formal education and teacher cognitive competency, the *Qualificação* variable could simply be isolating those teachers who, precisely because of their low levels of formal educational attainment and measured subject matter mastery, are judged most in need of upgrading and are therefore encouraged to participate in the in-service *Qualificação* program. In this interpretation a negative and significant coefficient is the expected result—the right teachers have been targeted—but it does not then provide direct evidence about the efficacy of the teacher upgrade program.

Direct Measures of Teacher Quality

The survey effort also included attempts to specify and measure qualitative differences among teachers—differences that showed up in what they know or how they teach classes as opposed to how much schooling and experience they have had.

The most interesting findings on teacher quality concern the competency of the teachers themselves on the same tests of Portuguese and mathematics that were administered to the fourth grade students. (Unfortunately, administration of the achievement tests to the teachers was feasible only in 1985, so the consistency of findings across years cannot be checked.) The absolute level of teacher performance is itself interesting. As shown in Table 14.4, teachers of fourth graders did better than their students on the criterion-referenced tests of the fourth grade curriculum, but their performance was far from spectacular. Our expectation was that teachers, for whom the mean level of educational attainment is about eight years, would easily and consistently register perfect scores on tests carefully constructed to measure performance against the specific learning objectives of the fourth grade. They do not. Table 14.4 shows that the average fourth grade teacher misses one-fifth of the questions on the test of fourth grade Portuguese and still half that many on the test of fourth grade mathematics.

The estimated coefficients in Table 14.3 demonstrate the value of subject matter knowledge, as measured by teacher test scores (on fourth grade achievement tests) for student performance in 1985. The teacher's command over the mathematics subject matter he or she is expected to teach is unambiguously important in fostering student achievement in mathematics. A 10-point improvement in the mean teacher's command of her mathematics subject matter (which would still leave the mean somewhat below 100 percent) would engender a five-point increase in student achievement; this is equivalent to a 10 percent improvement over the mean score of fourth graders. The teacher's command of Portuguese is also shown to be a significant predictor of student achievement in that subject, although the size of the coefficients is less impressive than for mathematics.

The evidence on the "cross subject effects" of the teacher's command of these two subjects on student achievement in them is inconsistent. On the one hand, the teacher's knowledge of mathematics may marginally enhance student achievement in Portuguese; here there is reinforcement across subjects. On the other, there is no mechanism to explain, and it is counterintuitive to conclude, that more developed command of Portuguese by teachers is actually detrimental to mathematics achievement of students. The only reasonable explanation is that this really is a test of subject matter knowledge and not general intelligence, but we cannot investigate such ideas further given the limited data available.

Conclusions about Specific Teacher Effects

Conclusions on teacher characteristics and student achievement in rural Northeast Brazil are very similar to those found elsewhere in the world. A teacher's knowledge of the subject matter makes a noticeable difference to student learning of that subject, especially in mathematics. On balance, however, the policy instruments traditionally relied upon—class size, teacher education, in-service training and teacher experience—are not systematically and importantly related to student performance.

One simple explanation of the findings is that qualitative differences in the explicit teacher measures—say, in the quality of the teacher's schooling or the specific character of the in-service training of each teacher—along with differences in teaching skill unrelated to the measured attributes, are much more important than the readily identified dimensions employed here and elsewhere. Failure to adequately measure these deeper aspects of

Table 14.4. Mean Achievement Scores of Teachers and Students on Fourth Grade Tests, 1985
(Standard deviation in parentheses)

	Portuguese		Mathematics	
	Students	Their teachers	Students	Their teachers
1985 Fourth grade	48.5	78.3	50.1	87.3
Cross-section (1,789 students)	(18.3)	(13.8)	(23.5)	(12.6)
1985 Fourth grade	47.2	79.3	48.2	87.8
Matched sample (349 students)	(17.8)	(11.8)	(24.2)	(9.6)

Source: Harbison and Hanushek (1992).

teachers makes detection of other systematic relationships impossible. Selecting the commonly used but crude quantitative indicators of teacher characteristics is then a hit-or-miss proposition: sometimes a good teacher is found, but just as frequently one less capable.

If this is the case, education decision making must be more sophisticated. When the general levels of teacher education, training and subject knowledge are so low, policymakers cannot rely on simple traditional indicators of school "quality." Rather, when selecting teachers, policymakers should pay closest attention to what teachers can demonstrate they actually know about what they teach. This analysis has not found any performance-related selection processes to consistently identify specific teacher characteristics. This indicates that fundamental changes may be required in the teacher selection and evaluation system if there is to be a noticeable change in the performance of the school system.

Teacher Salaries

In analyzing the impact of teacher quality, salaries are a natural place to focus attention for several reasons. First, standard economic analysis suggests that, regarding hiring inputs, relative costs should be proportional to the marginal contribution of each separate input. Turned around, this implies that salary can be used as a proxy for quality—at least if schools are operating efficiently and paying teachers relative to their productivity in teaching. Second, teacher salaries are attractive policy instruments because they are easily measured and amenable to manipulation by policymakers. Third, many who bemoan the perceived low quality of the teacher force (whether in Brazil, in other LDCs, or in developed countries) also point to the relatively low pay of teachers. For example, in our rural sample, the mean teacher salary is less than 60 percent of the minimum wage.[11] Therefore, these people often turn to salary policies as a way of improving schools; by increasing salaries they would hope to attract new and better people into the teacher profession.

The estimated coefficients in Table 14.3 summarize the effects of teacher salary (measured as a percentage of the minimum wage) on student achievement.[12] These effects are estimated in two fundamental ways. First, complete models including the family and individual effects are estimated with salary as the sole descriptor of teachers. If salaries are set according to teaching productivity, this single measure will capture all of the systematic differences among teachers. Second, separate salary estimates are made for each of the three states, allowing for both differences in cost of living and differences in labor market conditions. Because the separate state estimates provide little additional information, we concentrate on the overall estimates.

In all cases, the estimated salary coefficient has the expected positive sign: as salary increases as a proportion of minimum wage, achievement is enhanced. The coefficients are, however, exceedingly small and, with the exception of 1985 mathematics performance, not significantly different from zero in the value-added models. In practical terms, the impact on achievement is very small. An increase in salary from the sample mean of about 65 percent of the minimum wage to 100 percent is associated with an achievement gain in mathematics in 1985 of fewer than 1.5 points.

These results do not lend very strong support to the idea that teacher salaries are a good measure of teacher quality. While related to teaching performance, salaries themselves apparently ignore considerable variation in teacher quality. Further, it is evident that increasing teachers' pay indiscriminately, by itself and without regard to their other characteristics, will not meaningfully enhance student achievement.

---

[11] The mean teacher salary for the reduced sample in the longitudinal value-added models is between two-thirds and three-fourths of a minimum wage, somewhat higher than the average for all teachers in our sample. This slight difference is attributable to weighting of the teachers in the analytical samples by the numbers of students they have, and to a tendency of longer established—and thus marginally higher paid—teachers to be associated with schools and students that survive over each two-year period.

[12] Note that in this section only, different estimated models are employed. Each of the other identified effects simply extracts coefficients from a common model. But here, since we replace specific measures of teacher characteristics with salary terms, separate estimates of the entire model are employed. See Harbison and Hanushek (1992, Tables C5.9–C5.12).

The situation is, of course, more complex than this simple statement. First, this conclusion is predicated on the existing institutional structure behind salaries, which tends to reward background factors such as experience or education levels, and not actual teaching performance. If this pay structure were altered, changes in pay could have a much larger impact on achievement. Second, if pay schedules were raised significantly, an entirely different group of people could be attracted into teaching. This possibility can only partially be analyzed from the current regression information.

Knowledge of the effects of various inputs on student performance is an essential component of standard policy deliberations that involve adjusting the resources available to schools. This knowledge allows prediction of the outcomes that will result from policy choices. Frequently, however, because precise empirical information is unavailable, policymakers or educators simply rely upon their guesses about the effects of different resources. Unfortunately, as we have documented, the conventional wisdom about the effectiveness of a wide variety of potential policies is simply wrong.

The previous estimates form the empirical basis for these policy and evaluation efforts. Combined in the next section with cost information, the results are used to analyze the appropriateness of many central policy ideas.

Net Cost-Effectiveness and Partial Benefit-Cost Analysis

Since improvements in student learning increase the chances that a student is promoted, any general improvements to schools will increase the flow of students through the system. Increased flow implies reduced resources to obtain a graduate of any grade and quality level, since fewer resources will be consumed by repeaters and dropouts.

To capture these effects, we calculate *partial benefit-cost ratios*, which directly compare estimated gains (in dollars) from improved student flows to the costs (in dollars) of any potential change in school inputs. It is, nonetheless, important to understand the partial nature of these calculations. Only one aspect of the benefits of an investment is considered, namely, the lessened total schooling costs arising from improving the pace of schooling. The estimates thus seriously underestimate the true total value of quality-enhancing investments in two important ways. First, they stop with the effects observed in the fourth grade, ignoring any effects later in the schooling process. Second, since the offset to costs accrues solely from the increased flow efficiency, the value of having higher achieving graduates is likewise ignored. As amply demonstrated elsewhere, both these payoffs are likely to be substantial, and policy conclusions should incorporate them.

Indeed, many educational investments are justified solely on the basis of long-run enhancements to individual skills and productivity; that is, through standard calculations of internal rates of return to investments.

The partial benefit-cost ratios can, however, provide strong policy guidance. If this ratio is greater than one, efficiency savings outweigh costs and the intervention would clearly be beneficial without even considering the spillover effects beyond fourth grade or how the achievement gains of students should be valued. A ratio between zero and one implies that net costs are lower than gross costs, but that any investment will still involve a net outlay of funds. Therefore, ascertaining whether or not a specific investment would be warranted requires added information about the parts of the analysis that are omitted: the effects on later grades and the valuation of students' higher academic achievement. Finally, a ratio of zero implies that the gross and net cost-effectiveness calculations are the same—that is, that there are no efficiency savings associated with the specific inputs. In this case, nothing is added to the information already obtained from the traditional static cost-effectiveness calculations, and any justification of investment comes solely on the basis of future productivity gains.

Calculation Methodology

The conceptual steps involved in calculating partial benefit-cost ratios are straightforward, although the actual application requires making a variety of judgments and assumptions. This section and those that follow describe the overall approach, the sources of data needed for the calculations, the results of the basic estimation, and a variety of sensitivity analyses based on alternative assumptions about key parameters of the educational process.

There are five major steps in the estimation:

(1) Calculate the expected achievement gains (in both Portuguese and mathematics) that would come from a $1 expenditure on each purchased input to be considered.

(2) Estimate how much the probability of being promoted to the next grade will increase with an added point of Portuguese or mathematics achievement.

(3) Chain the results of (1) and (2) to obtain an estimate of the increased promotion probability that accrues from a $1 investment in each input.

(4) Compare the average number of student-years required for promotion before any investment to the number after the investment, yielding the savings in student school-years that are directly attributable to the initial dollar invested.

(5) Based on the estimate of the marginal cost of a student-year of schooling, convert these time savings into dollars—that is, calculate the dollar benefits of efficiency savings flowing from the initial dollar of cost.

The previously produced analyses provide the necessary ingredients for computing partial benefit-cost analyses. Indeed, they provide more than one estimate of each of the key parameters that are inputs to such a calculation and so facilitate a check on the reliability and stability of results.

The expected achievement gains per dollar of expenditure on given inputs are simply the output of a static cost-effectiveness analysis, which combines cost and marginal effects, and are available for models of fourth grade achievement in both Portuguese and mathematics in the different years. For our purposes, we consider the different sets of parameter estimates of the achievement models for each subject to be alternative estimates of the same fundamental underlying relationships of the educational process. Similarly, the promotion probabilities associated with different achievement levels are available for 1981 and 1983.

The expected number of student-years that accumulate before a person reaches any given grade level are directly related to the promotion and dropout probabilities at each grade. If the promotion probability is low, the students will progress more slowly through the system and thus more years will be required to produce a primary school graduate. For evaluation purposes, we base our calculation on estimated transition probabilities derived from the experience in various regions of Brazil in 1982.

Finally, any savings in student years must be transformed into dollar values. Using information obtained directly from our survey data on teacher salaries and the data in Appendix Table 14.1, we obtained $29.57 as our estimate of the cost per student year of primary schools in the rural Northeast. The analogous figure from the best available Brazilian study is $31.50; for rural schools in the interior of the Center-West states, the figure calculated by the same authors is $33 (see Xavier and Marques, 1984; World Bank, 1986). Given the consistency of these three separate estimates, we have used a round figure of $30 as the cost per student year when evaluating the value of time saved.

Efficiency Returns

Table 14.5 displays both the years and dollars saved per dollar invested in six key quality-enhancing inputs to schooling. These calculations rely on promotion and dropout probabilities for low-income rural Northeast Brazil, the combination of geography and income status that most nearly ap-

Table 14.5. Estimated Flow Improvements and Partial Benefit-Cost Ratios for Selected Investments

	Saving
Student-years saved per dollar invested in:	
Software	0.1342
Hardware	0.0796
Teacher salary	0.0069
Teacher training strategies	
Four years more primary schooling	0.0113
Three years secondary education	0.0034
Dollars saved per dollar invested in:[1]	
Software	4.03
Hardware	2.39
Teacher salary	0.21
Teacher training strategies	
Four years more primary schooling	0.34
Three years secondary education	0.10

[1] Years saved valued at $30 per student-year.

proximates the areas in which our surveys were conducted (Fletcher and Ribeiro, 1989). The six inputs were selected for analysis because they are often—and were in the EDURURAL Project—the chosen instruments of public policy to improve the quality of primary schooling. The figures in Table 14.5 are the mean estimates from the alternative models of promotion and achievement. In the calculations underlying the mean benefit-cost ratios, the point estimates of all positive coefficients were employed without regard for statistical significance; all negative coefficients were treated as zero, or as having no relationship.

The results are stunning. The direct material inputs—hardware and software—produce much more than the original investment in dollars saved from increased flow efficiency. In other words, by investing in known quality-enhancing resources, it is possible to produce the same number of fourth graders, although fourth graders of higher quality, with *no* true additional costs, just savings.

Further, the magnitude of these net benefits can be breathtaking. The partial benefit-cost ratios can be greater than 2.0, signifying that twice the original cost of the investment is returned quickly in savings resulting from increased flow-efficiency brought about by investing in inputs that engender achievement gains. At least in the severely deprived environment of rural Northeast Brazil, investment in school quality is a real money machine.

We also look at teacher attributes, but place much less emphasis on these analyses. Teacher salary, as described below, cannot be interpreted as indicating what would happen with a general change in salary schedules. Instead, it says more about differentiation among individuals within the current stock of teachers. The teacher training and educational programs, while not subject to those criticisms, simply have huge uncertainties attached. There is no strong or reliable evidence about the effectiveness of these, independent of any cost considerations. None of the analysis here suggests that employing common teacher improvement strategies is likely to be very effective or efficient.

Investments in educational software—defined here as textbooks and writing materials—produce enormous benefits. These benefits exceed costs by a multiple of four, making them nearly twice as high as those accruing to investments in hardware, the next most attractive input. Hardware itself also returns a handsome premium over costs.[13] Teacher salary consistently fails to deliver in savings more than its initial cost.

While these startling results are reasonably robust across the several achievement and promotion models and data years (not shown), they could be challenged as a basis for policy determination because of uncertainties arising from three primary sources. The reliability of the findings depends centrally upon the accuracy of (1) the underlying parameter estimates of the effect of the specific inputs on Portuguese and mathematics achievement; (2) the estimated marginal effect of achievement gains on promotion probabilities; and (3) the figure used for cost per student-year of schooling. If the general conclusions were to change radically with only slight alterations in any of these, the utility of the findings for framing policy would be questionable. Therefore, we have investigated the sensitivity of these results to the underlying data on schooling.

The last of these possible challenges—erroneous evaluation of the cost per student-year—is the easiest to set aside. Three different calculation methods converged in our figure of $30, suggesting that it warrants unusual confidence.

---

[13] We did not consider the potential efficiency gains from the direct teacher training programs (e.g., LOGOS) because of the tremendous uncertainty surrounding their effectiveness.

The first two possible challenges cannot be dismissed so easily. While we attempted to ensure the best possible underlying parameter estimates, imprecision in point estimates remains. So it is important to test for the sensitivity of the results to possible bias in the achievement and promotion models that underlie the benefit cost ratios.

A series of sensitivity tests involved estimating the efficiency effects when the coefficients in the achievement and promotion models were placed at the end of 90 percent confidence bounds. While these obviously lowered the estimated effects when taken at the lower bound, the powerful efficiency effects for software and hardware investments remain. Hardware investments will still return more than their costs in efficiency gains, and software investments will return 30 percent even when calculated at the lower confidence bound (Harbison and Hanushek, 1992).

The indelible point remains that, even under these extreme estimation procedures, there is strong evidence of significant offsets to costs of investments in properly selected inputs to primary schooling. Indeed, even these very cautious estimates suggest that investments in school quality can still dramatically improve school efficiency through accelerating the flow of students.

Levels of Wastage and Potential Efficiency Gains

Another type of sensitivity of results relates to different levels of educational development and, specifically, different amounts of wastage. Are these estimates important only in the extreme conditions of the rural Northeast? What do the results say about investments outside this area?

As one might expect, the partial benefit-cost ratios are highly sensitive to the underlying transition matrices for movements from grade to grade. The benchmark, repeated in Table 14.6, is that an investment in software in low-income rural Northeast Brazil will return about $4 for each dollar it costs. But if the level of educational wastage began at that prevailing in low-income Brazil generally, the payoff would be only about $2.90 per dollar invested. While the efficiency gains are smaller, this is still a remarkable figure. If the sample areas of the rural Northeast started at the further reduced repetition and dropout levels prevailing in the most advantaged areas of the country (that is, high-income urban Southeast), the offset to investment costs, while still a considerable 52 cents per dollar of investment, would no longer exceed initial costs.

An alternative interpretation of the data of Table 14.6 puts these calculations into an overall development perspective. Suppose it is assumed that

Table 14.6. Partial Benefit-Cost Ratios for Selected Investments in Various Regions of Brazil
(Mean estimates)

Investment	Brazil		Rural Northeast		Urban Southeast	
	All	Low-income	All	Low-income	All	Low-income
Fourth grade estimates						
Software	0.81	2.86	3.12	4.02	0.60	0.52
Hardware	0.47	1.69	1.84	2.39	0.35	0.30
Teacher training strategies						
Four years more primary						
schooling	0.07	0.24	0.26	0.34	0.05	0.04

Note: Years saved valued at $30 per student year.

the underlying education production function is roughly the same in all primary schools (with variations in the quantity and quality of inputs explaining the known differences in outcomes) and that relative costs of inputs are the same throughout the country. Although it could be argued that these are strong assumptions if comparing the very worst areas with the very best, it is much more plausible when not dealing with the polar extremes. In these circumstances, the partial benefit-cost ratios broken down by geographical area are reasonable indicators of the results to be had from investments in quality-enhancing inputs outside the rural Northeast. Given these assumptions, the data demonstrate that, for most combinations of geography and income in Brazil, educational wastage remains high enough that investments in at least some, and often several, quality-enhancing inputs have partial benefit-cost ratios greater than one—that is, they pay back in monetary savings more than the cost of the investment. This conclusion, again, ignores the value of higher achieving students and cumulative effects higher up in the educational pyramid.

This analysis is, however, only suggestive. All regional flow savings were evaluated at the costs of rural Northeast schools ($30), which are obviously far less than the costs elsewhere. Other differences across regions will be similarly important, so these calculations should just be used as a starting point in a larger evaluation of educational strategies.

Consideration of Personnel and Salary Practices

The previous discussion concentrated on material inputs to the educational process, but other analyses of achievement suggest that differences in student performance related to differences among teachers are likely to dwarf those arising from material inputs.[14] Unfortunately, the methodology developed here for benefit-cost considerations cannot readily accommodate consideration of alternative teacher salary policies. The reason is simple: we do not know what the supply function for teachers with specific characteristics looks like.

The teacher salary models describe the implicit payment to existing teachers with various measured characteristics and represent the confluence of current supply and demand for teachers. They do not, however, indicate what would happen if an attempt were made to alter the schedule completely—say, by offering a sizable bounty to individuals with a deep knowledge of mathematics and Portuguese or, even more extreme, by paying teachers according to student achievement. Such policies would be designed to bring a different group of people into teaching, and we do not observe these people (who are not currently teaching) in our sample.

The previously presented calculations—based on specific, observable inputs—benefit from direct observation of data on the costs of providing the resource. Specific characteristics of teachers, such as their mode of classroom instruction or their ability to maintain classroom order, are not directly purchased. Without experience with different salary schedules, payment schemes, incentives, and the like, we cannot be sure of how much a different teacher attribute might cost. Thus, we cannot readily translate any estimates of effectiveness into the cost-effectiveness terms relevant for policy deliberations.

On the other hand, we ought not overdo this argument. First, we know that the current policies are inefficiently discriminating among teachers on the basis of unproductive characteristics. These policies clearly should not continue. Second, we know that the differences in teaching skills among teachers are extremely large, implying that there is considerable latitude in salary policies that could replicate the "money machine" effect previously described for material inputs—that is, within the fairly narrow bounds of effectiveness of school material policies, investment costs could be more than fully offset. With teachers, where the range of effectiveness is much greater, it seems plausible to expect that there are many different salary policies that could lead to self-financing results. Third, other inefficiencies, say, those arising from possible political factors in teacher hiring, also suggest considerable room for improvement. For example, regulatory procedures, such as requiring all teachers to pass subject matter examinations,

---

[14] For example, see the 1987 study of Ceará schools in Harbison and Hanushek (1992), which estimates the full differences in performance across schools.

may be appropriate if teacher hiring is too heavily based on patronage. Again, such procedures will interact with the supply of teachers, but it is plausible to presume that redirection of incentives will have desirable (efficiency-enhancing) results.

The discussion of teacher practices is simply an extension of the policy recommendations with regard to facilities. The conclusion of the previous section was that the inefficiency in the current system is so large that a variety of quality improving actions are likely to return very large dividends. With teachers, the potential for gain is larger because teachers have more leverage on student achievement, but the policy uncertainty is also larger because the determinants of teacher supply are imprecisely understood. Nevertheless, available evidence and knowledge of the current organizational structure suggest that we pursue teacher-related alternatives, both to gain immediate improvements and to produce new information on which to base future policies.

Uncertainty about the best organizational structure or reward scheme is not restricted to Brazil or to other developing countries. The United States faces similar problems with policy design (Hanushek, 1994). The answer quite broadly is developing and experimenting with alternative incentive schemes designed to reward performance and, at the same time, evaluating the results.

Conclusions

Under a wide variety of Brazilian conditions, investments in some quality-enhancing inputs to schooling cost substantially less than the savings they ultimately generate through increased flow efficiency. The results clearly are sensitive to the context in which they were developed, and, specifically, to the underlying educational parameters employed. But even substantial changes to allow for parameter uncertainty fail to erase the partial benefit-cost ratios greater than one, indicating investments in some inputs return more than their costs.

Further, the relative priority of investments in different inputs is unaltered even when the absolute payoff amounts are attenuated. Investments in texts and writing materials and in quality hardware items are essentially safe bets for returning more than they cost. The evidence is much more mixed for investments in teacher training, but even they might be money makers in some circumstances. And, there is little evidence for a simple salary policy that does not attempt to alter the current salary structure and expand the present pool of teachers.

The lower the flow efficiency of a system before an investment in quality-enhancing inputs, the greater the potential offset to the initial costs of the investment and the greater the priority that ought to be accorded to such investments. Put crudely from a national perspective, the policy prescription is to attack the worst first, because that is how the most resources are generated. These resources can then be used for further educational (or other) investments. There is a highly important positive interaction and no tradeoff at all between efficiency and equity objectives. In other words, efficiency dictates improving the quality of schools in general but beginning with the worst. Further, this conclusion does not rely on any notions of distributional effect or equity.

Finally, new light is thrown on the policy debate about automatic promotion as a device to enhance flow efficiency in primary schools, and thereby to free resources for educational investments in other children. Automatic promotion can certainly relieve clogged school systems. But it does so at some likely sacrifice of average academic achievement, or at least without necessarily enhancing student achievement. The alternate route to the same end, delineated above, generates resources for increased investment while simultaneously increasing achievement.

REFERENCES

Armitage, Jane, João Batista Gomes-Neto, Ralph W. Harbison, Donald B. Holsinger, and Raimundo H. Leite. 1986. *School Quality and Achievement in Rural Brazil.* World Bank Education and Training Series, No. EDT25. World Bank, Washington, D.C.

Behrman, Jere R., and Nancy Birdsall. 1983. The Quality of Schooling: Quantity Alone is Misleading. *American Economic Review* 73(5) (December): 928–46.

Boardman, Anthony, and Richard J. Murnane. 1979. Using Panel Data to Improve Estimates of the Determinants of Educational Achievement. *Sociology of Education* 52 (April): 113–21.

Coleman, James S., Ernest Q. Campbell, Carol J. Hobson, James McPartland, Alexander M. Mood, Frederic D. Weinfeld, and Robert L. York. 1966. *Equality of Educational Opportunity.* Washington, D.C.: U.S. Government Printing Office.

Fletcher, P.R., and Ribeiro, S.C. 1989. Modeling Education System Performance with Demographic Data: An Introduction to the PROFLUXO Model. Brasília. Mimeo.

Fuller, Bruce. 1985. *Raising School Quality in Developing Countries: What Investments Boost Learning?* World Bank Education and Training Series, No. EDT7. World Bank, Washington, D.C.

Hanushek, Eric A. 1994. *Making Schools Work: Improving Performance and Controlling Costs.* Washington, D.C.: Brookings Institution.

_____. 1992. The Trade-off Between Child Quantity and Quality. *Journal of Political Economy* 100(1) (February): 84–117.

_____. 1986. The Economics of Schooling: Production and Efficiency in Public Schools. *Journal of Economic Literature* 24(3) (September): 1141–77.

Hanushek, Eric A., and John E. Jackson. 1977. *Statistical Methods for Social Scientists.* New York: Academic Press.

Harbison, Ralph W., and Eric A. Hanushek. 1992. *Educational Performance of the Poor: Lessons from Rural Northeast Brazil.* New York: Oxford University Press.

Heckman, James S. 1979. Sample Selection Bias as a Specification Error. *Econometrica* 47: 153–61.

Jamison, Dean T. 1978. Radio Education and Student Repetition in Nicaragua. In *The Radio Mathematics Project: Nicaragua, 1976–1977*, eds. Patrick Suppes, Barbara Searle, and Jamesine Friend. Stanford: Institute for Mathematical Studies in the Social Sciences, Stanford University.

Levin, Henry M. 1975. *Cost Effectiveness.* Beverly Hills, CA: Sage.

_____. 1983. Cost Effectiveness in Evaluation Research. In *Handbook of Evaluation Research Vol. 2*, eds. Marcia Guttentag and Elmer Struening. Beverly Hills, CA: Sage.

Lockheed, Marlaine E., and Eric A. Hanushek. 1994. Concepts of Educational Efficiency and Effectiveness. In *International Encyclopedia of Education,* 2nd ed., eds. Torsten Husén and T. Neville Postlethwaite. Oxford: Pergamon.

_____. 1988. Improving Educational Efficiency in Developing Countries: What Do We Know? *Compare* 18(1): 21–38.

Maddala, G. S. 1983. *Limited-Dependent and Qualitative Variables in Econometrics.* Cambridge, MA: Cambridge University Press.

Solmon, Lewis C. 1986. The Quality of Education and Economic Growth: A Review of the Literature. In *The Quality of Education and Economic Development,* eds. Stephen P. Heyneman and Daphne Siev White. Washington, D.C.: World Bank.

World Bank. 1986. Brazil: Finance of Primary Education. World Bank Country Study. World Bank, Washington, D.C.

Xavier, A.C., and Marques. A.E. 1984. Custo Direto de Funcionamento das Escolas Públicas de Primeiro Grau na Região Centro-Oeste. Brasília: IPEA.

Appendix. Cost Estimation for Inputs Purchased by EDURURAL

Appendix Table 14.1 shows the per student economic costs of the various inputs. These are the result of somewhat tedious calculations, detailed elsewhere (Armitage et al., 1986), which use extensive information on a wide variety of inputs. Most of the basic information used in costing the inputs was obtained from the Ceará State Secretariat of Education.

The "ingredients" method is used to calculate the costs of each input (Levin, 1975, 1983). First, all the ingredients for replicating an input or program are specified in detail. For example, a remedial reading program might involve separate elements of specialized teacher time, new textbooks, and workbooks and materials. Second, an annual cost is placed upon each ingredient. The sum of these costs provides an estimated total annual cost for each intervention. Third, these costs are translated into costs per student.

Capital costs are converted into effective annual costs based on estimates of the lifetime of the capital good and an interest rate that reflects the social cost of capital. Economic lives for capital goods in this region are judgmental, and the estimates were reached after discussions with teachers and personnel from the state secretariats of education. The interest rate should reflect the productivity of the resources used in their best alternative social use. There is considerable theoretical controversy surrounding the correct social discount rates, and even larger uncertainty about the correct empirical calculation of this. Here we simply use 10 percent, a common choice in applied work.

We estimated the replication cost of each input—that is, how much it would cost to reproduce the input or program in a new setting. This cost corresponds closely to the marginal cost of an input. The costs associated with initial development or evaluation activities of the input were not included. Nor was an attempt made to allocate the overhead cost of the central administration of the education system to the various inputs. However, considerable effort was made to make sure that all the economic resources—not only the explicit direct expenditure by the state secretariats—were included. This involved, for example, estimating the opportunity costs of resources such as training facilities provided free by the local county executive (*prefeito*) and of the time spent in training by teachers.

The cost analysis required special care, because of the extremely high and volatile rates of inflation prevailing in Brazil throughout the study period. The relevant month and year were specified for the quoted price of each ingredient. These were then converted into dollar prices by dividing the Brazilian prices by the official exchange rate prevailing in the pertinent month and year to obtain a uniform basis for comparison, Movements in the exchange rate during the period were largely to maintain purchasing power parity, with very little real depreciation or appreciation.

Finally, because the achievement gains associated with each input were calculated on a per-student basis, it was necessary to calculate the costs per student of each input. This translation relied on standardized input ratios and utilization rates reflecting average current practice. While the true marginal costs of providing student inputs might differ from these average costs, depending on specific local circumstances, it is unlikely that long-run costs of major changes will differ substantially from the costs calculated here.

The calculation of the costs of teacher training and education programs also involves amortizing this training over a typical teaching career. The calculations in Appendix Table 14.2 include the two teacher training programs employed in the Northeast (LOGOS II and *Curso de Qualificação*). They also include additional formal education of teachers, calculated as providing an additional four years of primary schooling or three years of secondary schooling. These latter policies either complete primary schooling (eight years) or secondary schooling (11 years) for teachers who lack such preparation. LOGOS II was meant to provide nonformal in-service training equivalent to the former and the *Curso de Qualificação* to the latter.

As shown in Appendix Table 14.1, costs of different input packages vary dramatically. Complete software packages cost less than a quarter of complete hardware packages (on a per student basis). The teacher training programs, on an annual per student basis, are also relatively inexpensive.

Appendix Table 14.1. Annual Cost per Student of Key Educational Inputs, 1983
(In U.S. dollars)

Infrastructure inputs	
Hardware inputs	
Water	1.81
School furniture	5.45
Bookcase	0.60
Teacher table	0.33
Pupil chair	2.20
Pupil desk	2.32
School facilities	8.80
Two classrooms	2.94
Large room	2.48
Director's room	0.83
Kitchen	0.86
Toilet	1.41
Store cupboard	0.28
Total hardware	16.06
Software inputs	
Writing material	1.76
Chalk	0.03
Notebook	0.51
Pencil	0.34
Eraser	0.15
Crayons	0.73
Textbook usage (grades 2–4 package)	1.65
Total software	3.41
Alternative teacher education strategies	
In-service teacher education	
Curso de Qualificação	2.50
LOGOS II	1.84
Education within formal school system	
Four years more primary education	2.21
Three years secondary education	5.55

Source: Armitage et al. (1986).

Appendix Table 14.2. Probit Estimates of Determinants of On-time Promotion, 1981–83 and 1983–1985

	1981–83 coefficients	t-statistics	1983–85 coefficients	t-statistics
Portuguese score	0.0104	(5.6)	0.0138	(7.2)
Mathematics score	0.0020	(1.1)	0.0048	(2.9)
Female	0.2357	(3.0)	0.1949	(2.8)
Age	−0.0497	(−3.1)	−0.0920	(−6.3)
Mother's education	0.0271	(1.7)	0.0376	(2.7)
Years in county	0.0068	(3.0)	0.078	(3.8)
Piauí	0.5538	(6.6)	0.1683	(2.2)
Ceará	0.2379	(2.7)	−0.0112	(−0.1)
EDURURAL Project	−0.1473	(−2.0)	−0.0503	(−0.1)
Number of students in school	−0.0014	(−2.5)	−0.0042	(−6.5)
Constant	−1.8187	(−7.7)	−1.9209	(−5.5)
Sample size	2,737		2,730	
Mean promotion probability	0.091		0.139	
Log likelihood	−757.9		−975.6	

CHAPTER

15

The Causes and Effects of Grade Repetition[1]

João Batista Gomes-Neto and Eric A. Hanushek

Even though the problem of grade repetition is high on the policy agenda of virtually every developing country, little is known about either the causes or the educational effects of repetition. The general concern about grade repetition derives from the budgetary and social implications of having large numbers of repeaters taking up scarce positions in schools. This concern notwithstanding, fundamental disagreements about the nature of the problem have clearly inhibited the development of sensible policies.

This research, relying on unique panel data for students in Northeast Brazil, considers how the schooling system and individual students interact in determining enrollment patterns in primary schools. This investigation into underlying student and school behavior lays the groundwork for analysis of alternative policies.

Discussions of repetition are often subsumed in larger discussions of "wastage"—the combination of repetition and dropout rates.[2] This combination is unfortunate in many ways because the two phenomena are quite different in both their causes and consequences. Nevertheless, they tend to be intertwined both in the data and the policy debate. Indeed, the combination of high dropout and repetition rates has been identified as one of the main failures of the Brazilian education system, in part because the rates appear above those in other countries. A brief review of the available data and more general issues sets the stage for the analysis of grade repetition.

Reflecting the scarcity of information about the issues, disagreement arises immediately about the magnitude and form of wastage. Commonly available and cited data reveal important discrepancies even

---

[1] Reprinted with permission from the University of Chicago. This study was first published in *Economic Development and Cultural Change* 43(1) by the University of Chicago Press. ©1994 by the University of Chicago. All rights reserved.
[2] The term wastage is commonly used but clearly quite misleading unless one believes that there is no return to schooling at the levels below where students are dropping out or repeating. At best it indicates foregone opportunities associated with not completing more schooling.

among estimates of the level of aggregate wastage and its components. The Brazilian Ministry of Education (MEC), for example, estimates first grade dropout rates to be around 25 percent and repetition rates 30 percent in 1982, suggesting that dealing with dropouts (who leave the system entirely) is the first step toward fixing the Brazilian education system. On the other hand, Fletcher and Ribeiro (1989), using a statistical model, estimate the first grade dropout rate at about 2 percent and the repetition rate 55 percent, leading them to conclude that repetition is the main problem. Other researchers and even other government agencies (e.g., the *Instituto Brasileiro de Geografia e Estatística—IBGE*) also question the MEC estimates and policy conclusions.[3] Such differences show up further in more detailed investigations for specific regions of Brazil.[4] The aggregate estimates of dropout rates differ not only in level but in pattern. The estimates of the Ministry of Education, for example, suggest that dropout rates decline with grade level, while the other estimates indicate that dropout rates increase with grade level.[5] The discrepancies come from trying to infer dropout and repetition rates from aggregate age, grade and enrollment data. By not following individual students, actual observations of student behavior are missing, and the rates are subject to error-prone estimation.

Disagreements also continue about the major causes of wastage. Some concentrate on problems outside the control of the school system, while others turn to factors inside schools. A variety of problems have been identified as the main out-of-school causes for school failures, and, importantly, each is directly related to the socioeconomic status of the student.[6] High direct costs—for example, for buying uniforms, writing materials and textbooks—and sensitivity to the opportunity costs of attending school are more likely to affect children from impoverished backgrounds. Other authors also identify malnutrition, which is clearly related to social and

---

[3] For comparisons of MEC, IBGE, and PROFLUXO estimates, see Fletcher and Ribeiro (1988). Other analyses can be found in Fletcher and Castro (1986), Schiefelbein (1989) and Verhine and Melo (1988).

[4] Kafuri et al. (1985).

[5] These analyses tend to give simple comparisons of marginal probabilities and, as such, may confuse grade effects with other factors including student age.

[6] Verhine and Melo (1988), for example, suggest that factors external to schools are the primary cause of first grade dropout behavior. An alternative view concentrates on underlying political and social incentives, but these arguments go beyond our inquiry. Specifically, some authors posit that the educational system was built in such a way to maintain the status quo in Brazil's unequal order (Garcia, 1982; Oliveira, 1981; and Popovic, 1981).

economic status, as one of the causes of school failures, although the different studies are not consistent about this.[7]

The in-school explanations concentrate on specific resource constraints and the general low quality of some schools. Many researchers have pointed to problems of low quality teachers as measured by low levels of education, low salary and motivation, and poor attitudes and expectations.[8] Other analyses concentrate on specific school resources such as lack of writing materials and textbooks, insufficient material resources, and too little time in school.[9] These arguments are frequently bolstered by data on aggregate expenditures. According to the World Bank, per pupil spending across states in Brazil ranges from $24 to $227.[10]

This analysis employs data from the rural Northeast of Brazil to test the various hypotheses about the determinants and effects of grade repetition.[11] The Northeast is extreme in its deprivation and, as such, is a reasonable starting point from a policy perspective. Further, we believe that many of the basic findings are transferable to other parts of Brazil as well as to other developing countries.

Brazil's Rural Northeast

Brazil is divided politically into five regions, with the Northeast being the poorest. The Northeast encompasses 18 percent of the Brazilian land area and had about 30 percent of the Brazilian population in 1990. But it generated only 13 percent of the national product. Mean earnings in 1988 in the rural Northeast were 28 percent of the national average. While 20 percent of the population in Brazil has less than one year of schooling, this figure jumps to 39 percent in the Northeast. Moreover, in the Northeast, 39.7 percent of the population over age 15 are illiterate, compared to 21 percent for all of Brazil.

Table 15.1 compares the Fletcher and Ribeiro estimates of repetition, dropout and participation rates between Brazil and the Northeast. It also

---

[7] See Cunha (1981); Gomes-Neto et al. (1992); and Harbison and Hanushek (1992).

[8] See Armitage et al. (1986); Verhine and Melo (1988); Brandão et al. (1983); McGinn et al. (1991); and Mello (1982).

[9] See Mello (1982); Armitage et al. (1986); McGinn et al. (1991); and World Bank (1986).

[10] See World Bank (1986); Armitage et al. (1986); and Xavier and Marques (1984). The concerns about the availability of resources are heightened by the arguments of Heyneman and Loxley (1983). After comparing many educational systems, they conclude that the poorer the country, the greater the effect of the school on student performance.

[11] Dropout behavior is analyzed separately in Harbison and Hanushek (1992).

Table 15.1. Repetition, Dropout and Participation Rates in Brazil and Northeast Brazil

	Brazil	Northeast			
		Total	Urban	Rural	Rural low-income
Repetition rate (% of enrollment)					
1st grade	54	65	58	73	74
2nd grade	33	45	42	51	53
3rd grade	26	37	33	48	50
4th grade	20	32	30	44	49
Dropout rate (% of enrollment)					
1st grade	2	4	3	5	6
2nd grade	4	7	4	12	14
3rd grade	7	9	6	16	18
4th grade	18	16	11	29	30
Participation rate (% of age cohort)					
1st grade	90	79	90	68	64
2nd grade	86	71	85	55	50
3rd grade	81	63	80	42	36
4th grade	73	53	72	29	23

Source: Fletcher and Ribeiro (1988).

displays the sizable discrepancies between urban and rural areas in the Northeast. At each grade, there is more repetition in the Northeast than in the rest of Brazil, with the repetition rates in rural areas approaching double those of the country as a whole. Dropout rates rise across grades—not particularly surprising given the low overall completion levels and the increasing age of students. And, again, the rural Northeast presents a bleak picture compared to other areas.

Causes of Student Repetition

This section provides separate analyses of two components of grade repetition. First, because schools with appropriate grade levels are not necessarily available in rural areas, we study the underlying causes for a school not providing advanced grades. By comparing schools that do not provide instruction past the second grade with schools providing at least fourth grade, we obtain some insights into the determinants of schooling opportunities. We hypothesize that school and other local characteristics will be the most important factors affecting the probability that a school provides advanced grades. Second, we analyze the underlying factors affecting individual student grade repetition by comparing students retained in the second grade for two years with other students. This allows investigation of the separate effects on repetition patterns of student characteristics, family socioeconomic background, teacher and school characteristics, and community factors.

These analyses are feasible using a unique data source that permits tracking schools and students over time—a key element in any analysis of student flows. The EDURURAL data set, the basis for the micro analysis in this chapter, was constructed to permit evaluation of programs funded by a major educational loan from the World Bank to the Northeast.[12] The sampling design included primary schools in areas that received loans and aid and in areas that did not. All of the schools were found in impoverished rural areas in the states of Ceará, Pernambuco, and Piauí.

A difficulty in the sampling was that no special effort was made to follow individual students. Indeed, the EDURURAL data set was not designed to answer the two main problems treated here, i.e., what are the causes of repetition and the effects of repetition. Nevertheless, the sample design of the EDURURAL evaluation provides a unique opportunity to address these problems. The design called for repeated follow-up of sampled schools, visiting them initially in 1981 and then returning in 1983 and 1985. In each year, a random sample of students was drawn from the second and fourth graders in each school. It is possible to construct a panel, albeit limited, of students who were sampled in successive surveys. In 1983, of the 2,619 sampled students in the second grade, 506 were sampled again in 1985. From this latter group 127 students were still in second grade, forming the panel of grade repeaters employed in this and the following sections.[13]

Provision of Advanced Grades

A prerequisite for school attendance is the existence of a school with appropriate grades of instruction within a reasonable distance. School survival from year to year is not assured, as demonstrated in Harbison and

---

[12] The EDURURAL Project was a $92 million undertaking of the Brazilian government launched in 1980. It received $32 million in loans from the World Bank and involved a comprehensive set of resources supplied to specific schools. The analysis here is not, however, concerned with the specifics of the evaluation but instead merely relies upon the data generated to evaluate that project. More complete information about the EDURURAL data set can be found in Armitage et al. (1986) and Harbison and Hanushek (1992).

[13] The sample involved surveying second and fourth graders at two-year intervals. Only the 1983–85 matched sample, however, provides sufficient numbers of students repeating the second grade. The remaining 379 matched students were promoted to the fourth grade and provide the basis for estimating achievement value-added models (see Harbison and Hanushek, 1992).

Table 15.2. Factors Influencing the Probabilities that a School Ends with Second Grade, 1983–85

Variables	1983–85
School characteristics	
No. of students	−0.0014
Hardware	−0.3157
School in teacher's house	(0.1198)
Economic conditions	
Percentage selling crops	(0.0038)
Participation in emergency program	(0.0024)
Organizational/governance factors	
OME index	(0.1210)
States	
Piauí	(−0.1857)
Ceará	(−0.0353)
State—Program	
EDURURAL—Piauí	(0.0691)
EDURURAL—Ceará	0.2381
EDURURAL—Pernambuco	(−0.0671)

Source: Appendix Table 15.1.
Notes: 1) Estimated marginal probabilities are calculated at means of variables, holding constant other factors contained in probit equations that exclude school control measures; 2) Estimates not significantly different from 0 at the 5 percent level reported in parentheses.

Hanushek (1992). Additionally, given that a school has survived, it is important to know if it provides grades for further progress. A student cannot progress in a school that does not provide advanced grades. The absence of advanced grades has obvious implications for repetition patterns.

The sampling scheme of the EDURURAL Project does not allow investigation of the general question of what determines whether or not a school exists for any individual student, but it does allow tracing the history and analyzing the existence of fourth grades for those schools sampled. To do this we use a probit model to capture how school grade structure—as measured by whether or not the school provides second grade as the most advanced grade—is affected by various external factors.

Table 15.2 summarizes the results of estimates based on the school sample from the EDURURAL data base. The explanatory variables used in the models can be divided in three categories: school characteristics, local economic conditions, and governmental support. For expositional purposes, the results of the estimation are translated into estimates of marginal probabilities evaluated at the means of the separate variables. (Variable definitions and full probit models are found in the Appendix.)

Two school factors are systematically related to the terminal grade in the school. Schools serving a larger number of students and schools with better facilities and equipment ("hardware") are more likely to have a fourth grade (i.e., have a lower probability of ending at the second grade).[14] Schools with satisfactory facilities and equipment are more likely to provide complete grade structure. Further, schools located in the teacher's house—a particularly marginal type of school—are more likely to end at the second grade, but the estimated effect is not statistically significant.[15]

Local economic conditions have small and insignificant effects on the chances of having a fourth grade, although this limited estimated effect may in part reflect the rather crude measurement of local conditions. Local conditions are measured by the percentage of families that sell a portion of their crops and participate in the emergency employment program related to the severe droughts in the Northeast that limited agricultural production.

The remaining factors relate to the organization and governance of the schools. Differences in support staff were not significantly related to the school's grade structure. Specifically, beyond paying for facilities, teacher salaries and instructional equipment, governmental support for schooling typically involves both routine managerial control, inspection, pedagogical supervision and technical assistance. The *Órgão Municipal de Educação* (OME) is the specialized municipal-level government agency established to institutionalize these functions of education administration. The specific measure of OMEs is an index including both quantity and quality of staff, but variations in this had little effect on the underlying probabilities of grades beyond the second grade. Of the measures of state and program status, the only significant difference was found in the EDURURAL Project areas of Ceará, where schools were much more likely to end at the second grade. These estimates, which give comparisons to nonproject areas in Pernambuco, indicate that schools are 24 percentage points more likely to end at the second grade in Ceará areas covered by EDURURAL. The underlying reasons for these differences are, however, not known.

---

[14] The hardware index measures physical facilities in schools such as the number of classrooms, existence of a multi-purpose room, kitchen, and secretary/principal office, and desks for students.

[15] This is the marginal effect of the school's being located in the teacher's house *after* considering the quality of facilities, which typically are below average. Note, however, that there may be some definitional problems of what constitutes a fourth grade, since multigrade instruction is also common.

Influences on Student Repetition

Whether or not individual student performance is related to repetition probabilities is extremely important for policy purposes, because it offers insight into how to assess different proposals for dealing with repetition rates and their mirror image, promotion rates. Specifically, if repetition is only slightly related to actual student performance—that is, the people being left behind are about as good academically as those being promoted—then high repetition and dropout rates may indeed represent wasted resources. Direct, regulatory efforts to lower this wastage and increase promotions might well be called for. On the other hand, if repetition and dropout rates are highly related to student quality, then decreasing those rates by continuing students with lower performance yields much lower benefits.

The analysis again employs probit techniques to compare those students who repeated second grade twice with those students who followed some other path—i.e., those promoted to the fourth grade in two years, those who dropped out of school, and those who are in the third grade. Of course, the comparison group of students is not homogeneous, and policies for students who drop out are surely different from policies for repeaters. Nevertheless, this initial analysis allows us to focus directly on the issue of repetition.

Another important policy variable is whether a school provides the second grade as the most advanced grade. If a school does not have a fourth grade in 1985, it is impossible to sample a student in this grade. More importantly, the student has no place to go in that school if promotion is warranted.

The repetition model, estimated by probit techniques, is summarized in Tables 15.3 and 15.4. Again, for expositional purposes, the results of the estimation are translated into estimates of marginal probabilities evaluated at the means of the separate variables, and the estimated relationships are divided into individual factors (Table 15.3) and institutional factors (Table 15.4). The underlying probit models are found in Appendix Table 15.2.

Because of the random sampling of students in the schools in each year, it is possible for an individual to be retained but not to be included in the sample. To deal directly with this, the probit model includes the number of students in the schools, since the probabilities of being missed by the sampling are directly related to the number of students. The school size measure (not shown) is significantly negative in the probit model, reflecting this sampling within schools.

Table 15.3. Effect of Student and Family Characteristics on Repetition Probabilities, 1983–85

Characteristics	
Female student	(−0.0042)
Student's age	(−0.0015)
Portuguese test score	−0.0010
Mathematics test score	−0.0005
Father's education	(0.0002)
Mother's education	(−0.0035)

Source: Appendix Table 15.2.
Notes: 1) Estimated marginal probabilities are calculated at means of variables, holding constant other factors contained in probit equations that exclude school control measures; 2) Estimates that are not significantly different from zero at the 5 percent level are reported in parentheses.

Table 15.4. Effects of Local Economic Conditions and Governmental Supports on Repetition Probabilities, 1983–85

Characteristics	
Socioeconomic index	0.0822
OME index	−0.0418
States	
Piauí	0.0274
Ceará	0.0474

Source: Appendix Table 15.2.
Notes: 1) Estimated marginal probabilities are calculated at means of variables, holding constant other factors contained in probit equations that exclude school control measures; 2) Estimates are significantly different from zero at the 5 percent level.

Student and Family Characteristics

Student backgrounds should directly affect repetition probabilities. Students in families with better educated parents, for example, are expected to be less likely to repeat a school year compared with those whose parents have less education or are illiterate. Students with higher previous achievement are expected to be promoted with higher probability than those with lower previous achievement.

The most interesting part of the model displayed in Table 15.3 is the relationship between second grade test scores and repetition probabilities.[16]

---

[16] The Portuguese and mathematics tests employed here were developed specifically for the EDURURAL Project by a team of psychometricians from the *Fundação Carlos Chagas*. The tests, developed in 1981 and improved in later years, were criterion-referenced to minimally acceptable levels of performance in second and fourth grade mathematics and Portuguese.

The table shows that lower test scores consistently lead to greater repetition probabilities; this suggests that promotion has a basis in merit. Each 10 points on the Portuguese test, which has a standard deviation of approximately 25 points, decreases the repetition probabilities by about 1 percent. The effect of the mathematics test is half of this. Since the mean observed repetition rate in the sample is only 4 percent in 1983, these are significant differences due to merit. These results also confirm the findings of Harbison and Hanushek (1992) that achievement on the second grade test was positively related with the student on-time promotion probabilities.

Repetition probabilities are insignificantly different for girls and boys. The students' ages also have no effect on their repetition probabilities. These are both surprising, because these two variables were found to affect the student's on-time promotion probability. Mother's and father's education are also not significantly related with the repetition probabilities, although they do influence student performance and thus are implicitly important.[17]

Grades Provided by Schools

As described previously, the availability of a school with advanced grades is not assured. Our specific concern is how large a portion of repetition is related to lack of other schooling opportunities. Simply stated, a student who was in second grade in 1983 cannot be promoted in schools where second grade is the most advanced grade provided. Our probit model includes a dummy variable that equals 1 if the highest grade provided by the school is the second grade and equals 0 if the school provides grades for further progress. Not surprisingly, students in a school with second grade as its highest grade are constrained in their promotion probabilities. In fact, students placed in such schools have their repetition probabilities increased by 2.3 percentage points, which is huge compared with the mean observed repetition rate in the sample of 4 percent.[18]

The test reliability, ascertained by constructing Cronbach's Alpha coefficients, shows reliability coefficients of 0.9 or better, with the exception of the fourth grade Portuguese scores. Moreover, the test reliability tends to be stable over time and across states. For more information on the tests, see Harbison and Hanushek (1992).

[17] Verhine and Melo (1988) emphasize the importance of socioeconomic factors, which does not seem consistent with these estimates. The difference from our results may partially be explained by the restricted sample used here; all students are from poor, rural families.

[18] McGinn et al. (1991) pinpoint another characteristic of school organization—the use of multigrade instruction—as an important element of repetition. Direct analysis of this in our sample, however, did not support any different repetition patterns with the use of multigraded classes.

Economic Conditions and Governmental Support

As summarized in Table 15.4, students are more likely to repeat a year in richer areas, i.e., those with a higher socioeconomic index. We do not have a clear explanation for this except that the opportunity cost of attending school in wealthier municipalities is higher and thus students are more likely to be absent. Unfortunately, we lack direct information on absenteeism. (The alternative view is that wealthier municipalities can better afford to make investments in schooling, a hypothesis predicting the opposite sign of that observed.)

The primary organizational measure reflects the quality and quantity of personnel in the OMEs. Students in municipalities with better OMEs are less likely to be retained in the second grade. There are also distinct differences in repetition probabilities across states, as shown in Table 15.4. The repetition probabilities in Ceará are clearly the highest among the three states. A student in Ceará has a 4.7 percentage point higher chance of repeating the second grade than a student in Pernambuco (the comparison state for this analysis). Piauí also has a 2.7 percentage point higher repetition rate than Pernambuco. Again, we cannot offer any specific explanations for these differences that hold over and above any of the other factors in the model.

Summary of Repetition Factors

Grade repetition has, according to our statistical analyses, two major components. First, government provision of suitable schools with grades for student advancement is a prime factor. Other things being equal, the presence of grades beyond the second grade is an extremely strong determinant of student advancement. This suggests that government intervention to ensure appropriate schools can have a powerful effect on repetition and wastage. Firmly established schools with adequate facilities, which the government can influence directly, are required. Second, student achievement—as measured by tests of mathematics and Portuguese performance—is a key determinant of repetition. While some have suggested that repetition is based on factors other than student performance, such as local politics, the evidence points directly to the role of student performance.

Achievement Effects of Repetition

Discussions of repetition tend to neglect one important aspect of the issue: students who repeat a grade are in fact attending school, albeit in the same

Table 15.5. Achievement Scores for All Second Graders and for Grade Repeaters, 1983 and 1985

| | All second graders | | Students in second grade in both 1983 and 1985 | |
	1983	1985	1983	1985
Portuguese				
Mean	58.7	59.6	40.2	61.1
Standard deviation	23.6	25.2	25.1	22.7
N (sample size)	3,944	4,321	127	127
Mathematics				
Mean	51.2	49.2	35.7	52.4
Standard deviation	24.9	25.0	25.3	25.1
N (sample size)	3,944	4,321	127	127

grade as previously, and would be expected to learn something during the experience.[19] While this may be a very expensive way of organizing the learning process (the subject of attention below), it is nevertheless inappropriate to assume that repetition is pure waste.

A simple look at the overall achievement scores suggests that repetition does have noticeable learning effects. As shown in Table 15.5, the mean achievements of second grade repeaters in 1983 were 40.2 and 35.7 in Portuguese and mathematics, respectively. These means were more than half of a standard deviation below the means of the entire second grade sample in 1983. In 1985, however, the means of achievement in Portuguese and mathematics of the repeaters (those in the second grade in both years) were slightly above the means of the entire second grade sample.[20]

This analysis pursues two parallel lines of inquiry. First, we refine the estimates of the achievement gains from repetition just presented. Second, we explore whether differences among individual students in the achievement value of repeating grades can be explained in terms of student or school factors. The overall framework for analysis follows a quite standard

---

[19] Learning during repetition has been the subject of investigation in the United States (see Shepard and Smith, 1989, 1990). These analyses conclude that achievement after repetition is actually lowered. This somewhat surprising result may, however, reflect imperfect measurement of students' prior achievement.

[20] Note that students identified as repeaters are all children who were sampled in the second grade both in 1983 and again in 1985.

input-output specification for the educational process, but one modified to incorporate information about grade repetition.[21]

The achievement of a given student at time t (A_t) is assumed to be related to current and past educational inputs from a variety of sources—the home, the school and the community. To highlight some of the important features, we use the same conceptual model that we used in the previous chapter:

$$A_t = f(F^{(t)}, S^{(t)}, O^{(t)}, \epsilon_t),$$

where $F^{(t)}$ =   a vector of the student's family background and family educational inputs cumulative to time t;

$S^{(t)}$ =   a vector of the student's teacher and school inputs cumulative to time t;

$O^{(t)}$ =   a vector of other relevant inputs such as community factors, friends and so forth cumulative to time t; and

ϵ_t =   unmeasured factors that contribute to achievement at time t.

The approach is to measure the different possible inputs into education and to estimate their influence on student achievement. This conceptual model explicitly incorporates a stochastic, or random, error term—ϵ_t—to reflect the fact that we can never observe all of the factors affecting achievement. The estimation problem is simplified considerably if there is information on achievement at two different times; for example, at time t and at an earlier time t*. It is possible then to include the prior achievement as one of the explanatory variables in the regression and to concentrate on the specific inputs over just the period t to t'. This formulation, which is often called a value-added specification, gets around the lack of measurement of past inputs into the process and of other individual specific (but constant) factors such as ability.

Learning through Repetition—Cross-Sectional Evidence

The simple differences in means for repeating students compared to all students (Table 15.5) can potentially misstate the learning effects associated with grade repetition. When repeating students have special characteristics

---

[21] Harbison and Hanushek (1992) provide more complete information about the specific statistical models. The general framework is described in detail in Hanushek (1986).

or school circumstances that differentiate them from other students, the difference in means will misstate the separate effect of repetition.

We employ a cross-sectional analysis of achievement differences to estimate the effect of repetition on student learning. Specifically, standard models that include student, family and school factors are supplemented with information about repetition. A dummy variable that assumes one if the student is repeating a school year and zero otherwise is included to capture the independent learning effects of repetition. We estimate this model for second and fourth grades in 1983 and 1985, using the two achievement tests (Portuguese and mathematics) as dependent variables.

There are some obvious problems with this approach, and thus it should be viewed as a crude approximation of the effects of repetition. First, repetition is not exogenous but itself is affected by performance. This implies that causation runs in both directions and that the estimates of the pure learning effect of repetition are biased. Second, the repetition measure does not indicate how many years had been repeated. Instead it only indicates whether or not the student was in the same grade as the previous year. Therefore, it averages together varying amounts of repetition. Third, because of the structure of the EDURURAL data set, it is not possible to estimate the effects of repetition within a value-added context; such estimation can only be done in cross-sectional models. This heightens the chance that the estimates of the effects of repetition will be contaminated by other factors that are mismeasured.

Table 15.6 summarizes the effects of grade repetition on school achievement. It is not surprising that repetition is significant in most of the cross-section models employed here. Only for the second grade specification in 1983 for Portuguese and mathematics achievement is repetition not significant at the 5 percent level. According to the estimates, by repeating the second grade students can raise their achievements by 2.6 points in Portuguese and 4.1 points in mathematics. In the fourth grade estimates the effect on mean achievement ranges from 4.2 to 5.6 points in Portuguese and from 4.1 to 4.4 points in mathematics.

Note that these are the net relationships between achievement and repetition. If students who repeat begin at a lower level of achievement than those who do not repeat a grade, the period of repetition is more than sufficient to make up for the average starting decrement. After repeating, the students have higher test scores than those not repeating, holding constant family background and other factors.

This achievement, however, has costs. The student must have spent at least one more year in the same grade at school. Beyond the increase in op-

Table 15.6. Effect of Repeating a School Year on Achievement, 1983 and 1985
(t-statistics in parentheses)

Grade	Portuguese		Mathematics	
	1983	1985	1983	1985
Second	0.552 (0.60)	2.632 (2.81)	1.574 (1.61)	4.149 (4.41)
Fourth	4.271 (3.42)	5.562 (4.85)	4.136 (2.60)	4.385 (2.92)

Source: Appendix Table 15.4.

portunity costs, the direct costs are not negligible, even in this area where the student cost is low. Assuming that all repetition only lasts one year, the average of direct costs in raising one point in Portuguese (mathematics) through repetition in the second grade is $11.40 ($7.23) and in the fourth grade, $6.67 ($7.14). While these costs may look small in absolute terms, they are large relative to the average student cost in the rural Northeast, which is only $30.[22]

Differential Learning While Repeating Grades

From the previous analysis we can conclude that students learn when repeating. We cannot conclude anything about which factors may be most important for learning during the period of repetition. Here we consider directly whether there are systematic learning differences among the grade repeaters by estimating value-added achievement models for repeaters. We use this specification in the special matched sampled 1983/1985, where we could find 127 second grade repeaters.[23]

The results from these regressions, as shown in Table 15.7, give us little guidance about what can improve repeaters' achievement. Most of the variables used in the model are not statistically significant at the 5 percent level. The main result is that students' previous achievement is consistently related with their achievement after repetition. This, of course, is not a surprise. In short, we do not have a good explanation for what makes a difference in the achievement of repeaters.

---

[22] See Harbison and Hanushek (1992) and Xavier and Marques (1984).

[23] As described in Harbison and Hanushek (1992), revisiting sampled schools turned up a number of students sampled in two successive surveys. The models here employ the restricted sample of students in the second grade both years to understand the effects of family, community and school factors on achievement. The sample, unfortunately, is quite small, making the detection of differential effects difficult.

Table 15.7. Effect of Student and Family Characteristics on Repeaters' Achievement, 1983–85
(t-statistics in parentheses)

Variables	Portuguese		Mathematics	
Personal characteristics				
Female student	4.660	(1.23)	−9.491	(−2.28)
Age	−1.690	(−2.28)	−1.619	(−1.98)
Parents' education				
Mother's education	1.024	(1.05)	0.044	(0.04)
Father's education	−0.521	(−0.50)	1.218	(1.06)
Joint characteristics: pupil and school				
Portuguese test score, 1983	0.450	(4.18)	0.218	(1.84)
Mathematics test score, 1983	−0.002	(−0.02)	0.235	(2.29)

Source: Appendix Table 15.2, specification (1).

Beyond previous achievement, only students' ages appear to consistently affect repeaters' achievements. The effect is negative, i.e., the older students do worse than the younger ones. Mothers' and fathers' education, which was consistently significant in the general achievement model, does not appear to have any influence at all on repeaters' performance.

Although among all students, those in Ceará learned more over the period than students in Piauí and Pernambuco (Harbison and Hanushek, 1992), this does not prove true for repeaters. Repeaters in all three states perform evenly. Despite huge repetition rates, none of the states appears to have any special program for repeaters, or, if they do, such programs do not appear clearly beneficial.

Summary of Learning Effects of Repetition

The central finding from the examination of achievement is that repetition enhances a student's learning. While students who repeat are on average below average in performance before repetition, they move to above average after repetition. Therefore, repeating a grade is not pure wastage as some would suggest. On the other hand, it is a very expensive form of schooling. Among repeating students, there is, however, no information on what specific factors determine differential achievement.

This is different from evidence in the U.S., where achievement is found to decrease with repetition. The argument made is that repetition sufficiently lowers a student's self-esteem so as to negate any learning during the repeated year.

Mandatory Promotion

Mandatory promotion is sometimes suggested as a means of reducing the resources wasted by high repetition. Indeed, if promotion and its mirror image, repetition, are not highly related with the student school performance, then a mandatory promotion policy could diminish the wastage with perhaps low cost to the educational system. This, however, is not what we found in our data; promotion and repetition were strongly related with student achievement. If such a direct linkage is the case, we would expect mandatory promotion to lower the effective level of achievement associated with each grade, thus lowering overall school quality.

Nevertheless, the policy prescription cannot be decided on a priori grounds. The high repetition and dropout rates observed in the Brazilian school system, especially in primary schools, increase the cost of getting a student to any set completion level. This results simply because money is spent on people who never, or only very slowly, progress through the system. Therefore, it is worthwhile exploring this problem to try to infer what would happen if we promoted students who fail under the current system. At the very least, this allows more accurate description of the tradeoffs.

A central question is how student achievement is affected by repetition and, inferentially, by mandatory promotion. Our previous analyses gave some indication of the average effects of grade repetition. Here we pursue another logical approach, investigating in more detail the entire distribution of promotees and repeaters.

A total of 3,944 students were sampled in the second grade in 1983. Of the 506 sampled again in 1985, 127 were still in second grade while the other 379 had been promoted to the fourth grade. Table 15.5 provided the means and standard deviations of the Portuguese and mathematics achievement scores in the second grade for students who were repeating. In contrast, the students promoted on time to the fourth grade had average 1983 second grade scores of 68.6 and 56.8 for Portuguese and mathematics, respectively. Thus, they were .2 to .4 standard deviations above the mean instead of .6 to .8 standard deviations below the mean as the repeaters were. By 1985, however, the means for the repeater group are slightly above the means of all students in second grade. While close, they are still behind the group that is promoted after the two years, and it took them two additional years to catch up with the grade average.

We can also go beyond the means and look at the distribution of performance. Figures 15.1 (Portuguese) and 15.2 (mathematics) give us an idea of the distribution of the achievement of the two groups. The distributions were calculated using z-scores (standard deviations from the mean), based on the means and standard deviations for all second grade students in 1983. The distributions relate to actual second grade scores for the matched sample of students repeating second grade. Since they took the test twice (in 1983 and 1985), the gains in learning can be readily seen from the two solid lines. The dashed line indicates the score for the group of matched students who were promoted from the second grade in 1983 to the fourth grade in 1985.

These figures show clearly how grade repetition shifts the distribution of student performance. After repetition, the students are still somewhat behind the promoted students, although the distributions for mathematics become very similar. Importantly, they also show that the distributions of performance for repeaters and those promoted overlap to a significant extent. This suggests that one crude analytical approach would be to project fourth grade achievement on the basis of where each child falls in the distribution of those promoted. (For those promoted, the distribution of fourth grade scores in 1985 is known.) Such projections clearly make very strong assumptions. Significantly, they assume that the previous achievement is the only thing that influences promotion and subsequent fourth grade student achievement. Such assumptions are almost certainly false, but this approach gives us some notion of an upper bound on achievement under a mandatory promotion policy.

We estimate the achievement or, at least, a range where achievement in the fourth grade will lie if each student currently repeating the second grade were promoted. We begin by splitting the initial and final distribution into six subgroups: Z-score ≤ -2; $-2 <$ Z-score ≤ -1; $-1 <$ Z-score ≤ 0; $0 <$ Z-score ≤ 1; $1 <$ Z-score ≤ 2; and Z-score > 2. We then calculate transition probabilities based on the experiences of the promoted students. Finally, we apply these transition probabilities to the distribution of second grade scores for the repeaters. In this latter estimation we actually employ both the pre- and post-repeating score for the students. In other words, the use of the pre-repeating scores relate to a pure "mandatory promotion" policy. The post-repeating scores relate to a modified plan of a fixed number of years in each grade. Table 15.8 displays the transition probability matrices used for Portuguese and mathematics performance. These come directly from the matched sample of on-time promoted students.

Figures 15.3 (Portuguese) and 15.4 (mathematics) display the results of this estimation. The lines labeled "mandatory promotion" and "with repetition" indicate estimated fourth grade scores with mandatory promotion from second to fourth grade and with promotion after the two years of repetition

Figure 15.1. Actual Second Grade Portuguese Scores for Promotees and Repeaters Before and After Repeating Second Grade

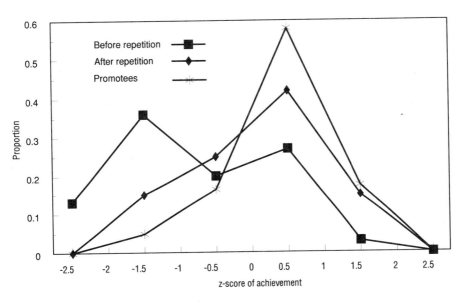

Figure 15.2. Actual Second Grade Mathematics Test Scores for Promotees and Repeaters Before and After Repeating Second Grade

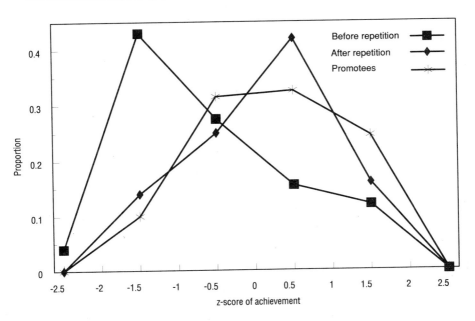

Table 15.8. Transition Probabilities: Portuguese and Mathematics Achievement, 1983–85

Initial achievement (Second grade) z-score	Follow-up achievement (Fourth grade) z-score					
	Less or equal to –2	Between –2 and –1	Between –1 and 0	Between 0 and 1	Between 1 and 2	Greater than 2
Portuguese						
Less or equal to –2	—	—	—	—	—	—
Between –2 and –1	0.25	0.50	0.25	0.00	0.00	0.00
Between –1 and 0	0.23	0.32	0.23	0.18	0.05	0.00
Between 0 and 1	0.05	0.48	0.23	0.17	0.07	0.00
Between 1 and 2	0.01	0.12	0.38	0.35	0.13	0.01
Greater than 2	0.00	0.01	0.18	0.57	0.21	0.03
Mathematics						
Less or equal to –2	—	—	—	—	—	—
Between –2 and –1	0.06	0.44	0.42	0.04	0.04	0.00
Between –1 and 0	0.03	0.32	0.38	0.16	0.11	0.00
Between 0 and 1	0.00	0.09	0.39	0.37	0.15	0.01
Between 1 and 2	0.00	0.05	0.14	0.45	0.36	0.00
Greater than 2	—	—	—	—	—	—

that are observed. These are compared to the actual fourth grade performance of the students who were promoted (line labeled "promotees").

Two key findings emerge from these estimated distributions. First, the current promotion ("promotees") group—those promoted normally by the standards of the schools—do better than the repeaters. This is not particularly surprising. Second, the mandatory promotion distribution, derived from inferring the fourth grade performance of those repeating based on their initial second grade score distribution, looks reasonably close to that obtained for delayed promotion (i.e., after repeating for two years). This is especially true for Portuguese performance, reflecting in part that mathematics performance appears to improve more than Portuguese performance through repetition.

Since the delayed promotion is very costly—the full cost of two years of schooling—mandatory promotion may be an effective alternative to the current system. This is, it must be emphasized, just a second-best policy. The best policy is to improve the quality of primary schools so that student achievement is increased directly.

One group of repeating students—those performing well on both the Portuguese and mathematics tests—are of special interest. In our sample, 14 percent of the repeating students were above the mean performance on

Figure 15.3. Actual Fourth Grade Portuguese Scores After Repetition and Mandatory Promotion Compared to Actual Scores of Promotees

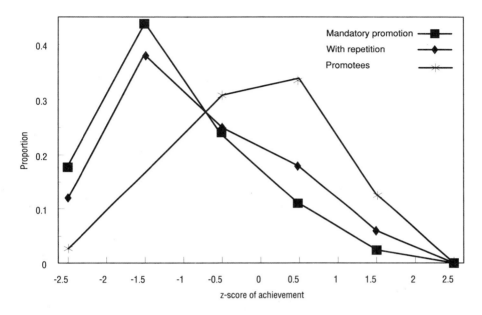

Figure 15.4. Actual Fourth Grade Mathematics Scores After Repetition and Mandatory Promotion Compared to Actual Scores of Promotees

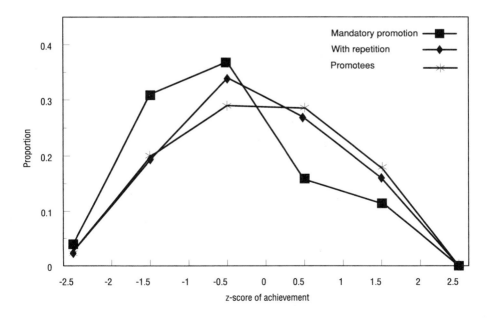

both tests when they initially took the tests. When we investigated their circumstances, however, we found that 13 of the 18 students were in schools that did not offer instruction past the second grade. This again underscores the room for alternative policies that improve quality.[24]

These findings must, of course, be highly qualified. It is quite likely that promotion involves other factors observed by the teachers but not measured by the tests that affect the learning of students. Therefore, inferring that the repeaters could acquire the third and fourth grade material at the same rate as those promoted on time is undoubtedly an overstatement.

Conclusions

It is impossible to ignore the problems of grade repetition in developing countries. The consistent pattern of students being stuck in primary grades with the concomitant demands on scarce educational resources commands the attention of policymakers in most developing countries. Yet, for its importance, there is extremely little known about either the causes or effects of repetition.

This chapter systematically investigated grade repetition in rural Northeast Brazil. Employing a unique data set that allows observation of the same students over time, it is possible to estimate the determinants of repetition. Further, the educational effects of repetition are open to analysis.

The results are straightforward. Two factors are most important in determining repetition. First, student achievement levels are very important. Low performance, and not other less educationally relevant factors, is a key element. Second, governmental policy as evidenced by supplying advanced grade levels in the schools is central. Simply put, if there is no place to go, students will stay where they are, repeating primary grades.

Repetition also has a direct impact on achievement. Repeating the second grade over a two-year period moves students from between half and one standard deviation below the mean to a position close to the mean in achievement. But this is an expensive policy, and there are quite likely to be alternative and less costly ways to improve achievement.

---

[24] The previous analysis of predicted fourth grade performance (see Figures 15.3 and 15.4) is not substantially affected by limitations on grades offered. A total of 42 students in the sample of repeating students were found in schools ending at the second grade, and these students were distributed across the performance distribution. Therefore, when we duplicated the mandatory promotion analysis with the grade-limited students eliminated, we obtained the same qualitative results.

Mandatory promotion policies would produce lower achievement in later grades (because there is learning that goes on through repetition). On the other hand, while mandatory promotion appears incongruous with a policy of improving school quality, it does seem superior to the current unguided repetition policies.

These results are based on rather small and less than perfect samples. The dearth of information about the entire process of promotion, repetition and dropping out implies that informed decision making is extremely difficult.

REFERENCES

Armitage, J., J.B. Gomes-Neto, R.W. Harbison, D.B. Holsinger, and R.H. Leite. 1986. *School Quality and Achievement in Rural Brazil*. World Bank Education and Training Series, No. EDT25. World Bank, Washington, D.C.

Brandão, Z. et al. 1983. *Evasão e Repetência no Brasil: A Escola em Questão*. Rio de Janeiro: Achiame.

Carvalho, I.M.M. 1983. Escolarização em Famílias de Classe Trabalhadora. *Cadernos do CEAS* 83 (January-February): 44–59.

Coleman, J.S., T. Hoffer, and S. Kilgore. 1982. *High School Achievement: Public, Catholic, and Private Schools Compared*. New York: Basic Books.

Coleman, J.S., E.Q. Campbell, C.J. Hobson, J. McPartland, A.M. Mood, F.D. Weinfield, and R.L. York. 1966. *Equality of Educational Opportunity*. Washington, D.C.: U.S. Government Printing Office.

Cunha, L.A. 1981. *Educação e Desenvolvimento Social no Brasil*. Rio de Janeiro: Francisco Alves.

Fletcher, P.R., and C.M. Castro. 1986. Os Mitos, as Estratégias e as Prioridades para o Ensino de 1° Grau. *Educação e Realidade* 11(1) (January–June): 35–42.

Fletcher, P.R., and S.C. Ribeiro. 1989. Modeling Education System Performance with Demographic Data: An Introduction to the PROFLUXO Model. Brasília. Mimeo.

_____. 1988. A Educação na Estatística Nacional. In *PNADs em Foco: Anos 80*, ed. D.O. Sawyer.

Fuller, B. 1985. *Raising School Quality in Developing Countries: What Investments Boost Learning?* World Bank Education and Training Series, No. EDT7. World Bank, Washington, D.C.

Garcia, R.L. 1982. A Qualidade Comprometida e o Comportamento da Qualidade. *ANDE* 1(3): 51–5.

Gatti, B.A. 1981. A Reprovação na 1ª Série do 1° Grau: Um Estudo de Caso. *Cadernos de Pesquisa* 38: 3–13.

Gomes-Neto, J.B., E.A. Hanushek, R.H. Leite, and R.C. Frota-Bezzera. 1992. *Health and Schooling: Policy Implications for Developing Countries*. Working Paper No. 306 (January), Rochester Center for Economic Research.

Hanushek, E.A. 1986. The Economics of Schooling: Production and Efficiency in Public Schools. *Journal of Economic Literature* 24(3): 1141–77.

Harbison, R.W., and E.A. Hanushek. 1992. *Educational Performance of the Poor: Lessons from Rural Northeast Brazil.* New York: Oxford University Press.

Heckman, J.S. 1979. Sample Selection Bias as a Specification Error. *Econometrica* 47: 153–61.

Heyneman, S.P., and W.A. Loxley. 1983. The Effect of Primary School Quality on Academic Achievement across Twenty-nine High- and Low-Income Countries. *The American Journal of Sociology* 88(6): 1162–94.

Jamison, D.T. 1980. Radio Education and Student Failure in Nicaragua: A Further Note. In *Radio Mathematics in Nicaragua,* eds. J. Friend, B. Searle, and P. Suppes. Stanford: Institute for Mathematical Studies in the Social Sciences, Stanford University.

Kafuri, R. et al. 1985. *Pesquisa sobre Evasão, Repetência e Fatores Condicionantes.* Goiânia: Universidade Federal de Goiás.

Lockheed, M.E., and E.A. Hanushek. 1990. Concepts of Educational Efficiency and Effectiveness. *International Encyclopedia of Education.*

_____. 1988. Improving Educational Efficiency in Developing Countries: What Do We Know? *Compare* 18(1): 21–38.

Maddala, G.S. 1983. *Limited-Dependent and Qualitative Variables in Econometrics.* Cambridge, MA: Cambridge University Press.

McGinn, N.F., M.C. Soto, S. Lopez, A. Loera, T. Cassidy, E. Schiefelbein, and F. Reimers. 1991. Asistir y aprender o repetir y desertar. Summary Report, BRIDGES.

Mello, G.N. 1982. *Magistério de 1° Grau: da Competência Técnica ao Compromisso Político.* São Paulo: Cortez.

Oliveira, R.D. 1981. Os Movimentos Sociais Reinventam a Educação. *Educação e Sociedade* 8 (January): 49–60.

Popovic, A.M. 1981. Enfrentando o Fracasso Escolar. *ANDE* 1(2): 17–22.

Schiefelbein, E. 1989. *Repetition:* The Key Issue in Latin American Primary Education. World Bank, LAC Technical Department, Human Resources Division, Washington, D.C.

Shepard, L.A., and M.L. Smith. 1990. Synthesis of Research on Grade Retention. *Educational Leadership* (May): 84–8.

————, eds. 1989. *Flunking Grades: Research and Policies on Retention.* Philadelphia: Falmer Press.

Verhine, R.E., and A.M.P. Melo. 1988. Causes of School Failure: The Case of the State of Bahia in Brazil. *Prospects* 18(4): 557–68.

Xavier, A.C., and A.E. Marques. 1984. *Custo Direto de Funcionamento das Escolas Públicas de Primeiro Grau na Região Centro-Oeste.* Brasília: IPEA.

World Bank. 1986. Brazil: Finance of Primary Education. World Bank Country Study, World Bank, Washington, D.C.

Appendix

This appendix provides variable definitions and complete statistical models that are summarized in the text.

Variable Definitions

Student Characteristics

Age	Student age (in years).
Female Student	= 1 for female student.
Pupil Works	= 1 if student works (wording of question varied slightly by year).

Family Characteristics

Mother's Education	Level of mother's formal education.
Father's Education	Level of father's formal education.
Family Size	Number of persons living in the household.

Peer Influence

Percent Families Not Farming	Proportion of families not farming (measured at school level).
Relatively Large Landholders	Proportion of families who own more than 35 percent of MÓDULO, a measure of the minimum amount of land required to support a single family according to local land characteristics. MÓDULO is developed by IBGE.
Percent Sold Crops	Percentage of families who sell crops.
Percent Female Classmates	Proportion of female classmates.
Female Classmates When Female Student	= Proportion of female classmates if the student is female; = 0 otherwise.

Joint Characteristics: Pupil and School

Homework	1 if the student does homework always.
School Lunch Every Day	1 if the school received lunch all year long.

School Lunch Some Days	1 if the school received lunch only some months a year.
Male Teacher/ Male Student	1 if the teacher and the student are both male.
Female Teacher/ Female Student	1 if the teacher and the student are both female.

School Characteristics

Graded Class	1 if it is a graded classroom.
Pupil/Teacher Ratio	Number of students divided by number of teachers in school.
Hardware Index	Index of furniture, facilities, water supply, and electricity; range=0–1.
Software Index	Index of textbook and writing material availability; range=0–1.
Teacher's House	1 if the school is in the teacher's house.
Number of Students	Sum of the number of students in kindergarten through the fourth grade.

Teacher Characteristics

Teacher Activity Index	Index of teacher classroom activities; range=0–1.
Teacher Materials Index	Index of classroom materials employed by teacher; range=0–1.
Teacher Salary	Teacher salary as a percentage of the minimum wage.
Teacher's Mathematics Test Score	Teacher's score on fourth grade mathematics test given to students.
Teacher's Portuguese Test Score	Teacher's score on fourth grade Portuguese test given to students.
Years of Teacher's Education	Level of teacher's formal education.

Years of Teacher's Experience	Years of experience as a teacher.
LOGOS II—Teacher Training	1 if teacher took LOGOS (in-service training).
Qualificação Training	1 if teacher took *Qualificação* training (in-service).

School Control

State Operated	1 if a state school.
Federally Operated	1 if a federal school.
Privately Operated	1 if a private school.

Municipal Characteristics

% Emergency	Percentage of families whose head of household works in the emergency program.
OME	Index of the quantity and quality of personnel in *Órgão Municipal de Educação;* range=0-1.
SES	Index of factors from principal components analysis of municipal economic conditions (see Armitage et al., 1986).

State—Program

EDURURAL—Pernambuco	1 if the municipality is in Pernambuco and is part of EDURURAL.
EDURURAL—Ceará	1 if the municipality is in Ceará and is part of EDURURAL.
EDURURAL—Piauí	1 if the municipality is in Piauí and is part of EDURURAL.

State

| Piauí | 1 if state is Piauí. |
| Ceará | 1 if state is Ceará. |

Appendix Table 15.1. Probit Estimates of Probability that Second Grade Is the Highest Grade in School, 1983–85

	Coefficient	t-ratio
Municipal Characteristics		
Percent selling crops	0.0123	1.55
Participation in *Emergencia*	0.0078	1.53
School Characteristics		
Number of students	−0.0044	−2.30
Hardware index	−1.0108	−2.80
Teacher's house	0.3835	1.87
OME index	0.3874	1.10
State		
Piauí	−0.5948	−1.36
Ceará	−0.1130	-0.29
Program state		
EDURURAL: Piauí	0.2212	0.63
EDURURAL: Ceará	0.7624	2.40
EDURURAL: Pernambuco	−0.2149	−0.78
Constant	−0.8279	−2.51
Sample size	489	
Mean probability	0.241	
Log likelihood	−215.59	

Appendix Table 15.2. Probit Estimates of Probability of Grade Repetition, 1983–85

	Coefficient	t-ratio
Student Characteristics		
Female student	−0.0491	−0.53
Student's age	−0.0174	−0.93
Portuguese test—1983	−0.0119	−5.06
Mathematics test—1983	−0.0056	−2.32
Parent's Education		
Father's education (years)	−0.0416	−1.43
Mother's education (years)	0.0020	0.09
School Characteristics		
Number of students	−0.0043	−3.44
School not providing advanced grades	0.2741	2.41
OME index	−0.4930	−2.24
Socioeconomic index	0.9694	4.52
State		
Piauí	0.3230	2.44
Ceará	0.5591	4.17
Constant	−0.6857	−2.29
Sample size	3,240	
Mean probability	0.039	
Log likelihood	−465.98	

Appendix Table 15.3. Fourth Grade Portuguese and Mathematics Achievement for Grade Repeaters, 1983–85

Variables	Portuguese				Mathematics			
	(1)		(2)		(1)		(2)	
State								
Ceará	1.156	(0.14)	7.038	(0.89)	9.448	(1.00)	13.265	(1.54)
Piauí	−11.886	(−1.36)	−11.745	(−1.40)	−11.474	(−1.19)	−11.248	(−1.23)
Program states								
EDURURAL: Pernambuco	−2.791	(−0.40)	−0.445	(−0.07)	3.855	(0.51)	5.457	(0.73)
EDURURAL: Ceará	3.828	(0.56)	4.997	(0.75)	4.404	(0.58)	5.364	(0.74)
EDURURAL: Piauí	9.295	(1.13)	12.373	(1.68)	11.805	(1.30)	14.598	(1.82)
Personal characteristics								
Female student	4.660	(1.23)	4.026	(1.11)	−9.491	(−2.28)	−10.009	(−2.54)
Student's age	−1.690	(−2.28)	−1.589	(−2.18)	−1.619	(−1.98)	−1.518	(−1.92)
Parents' Education								
Mother's Education	1.024	(1.05)	0.603	(0.64)	0.044	(0.04)	−0.167	(−0.16)
Father's Education	−0.521	(−0.50)	−0.596	(−0.58)	1.218	(1.06)	1.164	(1.05)
Joint characteristics: pupil and school								
Portuguese test score, 1983	0.450	(4.18)	0.442	(4.15)	0.218	(1.84)	0.211	(1.83)
Mathematics test score, 1983	−0.002	(−0.02)	−0.001	(−0.01)	0.235	(2.29)	0.243	(2.44)

(continued)

Appendix Table 15.3. *(continued)*

Variables	Portuguese		Mathematics	
	(1)	(2)	(1)	(2)
School characteristics				
Graded class	-7.216 (-1.59)	-5.761 (-1.40)	-3.576 (-0.71)	-2.271 (-0.51)
Pupil-teacher ratio	-0.047 (-0.23)	-0.119 (-0.61)	-0.210 (-0.94)	-0.258 (-1.22)
School hardware index	-3.901 (-0.43)	-3.868 (-0.43)	-0.655 (-0.07)	-1.133 (-0.12)
School software index	12.297 (1.30)	15.485 (1.69)	25.004 (2.41)	28.124 (2.82)
Teacher characteristics				
Years teacher's education	-0.017 (-0.23)		0.024 (0.03)	
Years teacher's experience	-0.278 (-0.86)		-0.170 (-0.48)	
LOGOS II—teacher training	-1.243 (-0.24)		2.238 (0.40)	
Qualificação— teacher training	4.867 (1.04)		4.979 (0.97)	
Teacher's Portuguese test score	-0.251 (-1.50)		-0.216 (-1.17)	
Teacher's mathematics test score	0.154 (1.26)		0.128 (0.95)	
Teacher's salary		0.019 (0.51)		0.013 (0.31)
Constant	65.581 (3.82)	53.842 (4.09)	47.648 (2.52)	39.297 (2.75)
Adjusted R^2	0.422	0.419	0.419	0.432
N (number of cases)	113	113	113	113
Statistic F	4.897	6.048	4.853	6.322

Appendix Table 15.4. Portuguese and Mathematics Achievement for All Second Graders, 1983 and 1985

	Portuguese		Mathematics	
	1983	1985	1983	1985
Student is repeating a grade	0.552 (0.60)	2.632 (2.81)	1.574 (1.61)	4.149 (4.41)
Student characteristics				
Female student	-0.62 (-0.02)	9.000 (2.85)	-9.816 (-3.28)	-4.489 (-1.41)
Student's age	0.375 (2.37)	0.600 (3.53)	0.878 (5.17)	1.024 (5.99)
Pupil works	-1.155 (-1.04)	-0.641 (-0.38)	0.311 (0.26)	1.810 (1.08)
Family characteristics				
Mother's education	0.599 (3.35)	0.680 (3.45)	0.533 (2.78)	0.496 (2.51)
Father's education	0.681 (3.16)	0.255 (1.14)	0.931 (4.03)	0.649 (2.87)
Family size	-0.272 (-2.06)	-0.396 (-2.88)	0.030 (0.21)	-0.120 (-0.87)
Peer influence				
Percent families not farming	3.736 (1.67)	10.269 (3.92)	-0.819 (-0.34)	1.214 (0.46)
Relatively large landholders	0.061 (3.22)	0.064 (3.00)	0.042 (2.06)	0.103 (4.82)
Percent female classmates	-4.466 (-1.46)	4.654 (1.41)	-0.551 (-0.17)	3.174 (0.96)
Female classmates when female student	5.586 (1.44)	2.116 (0.50)	1.028 (0.25)	1.800 (0.42)
Joint characteristics: pupil and school				
Homework	3.427 (4.82)	3.430 (4.67)	2.590 (3.40)	2.071 (2.80)
School lunch some day	-4.594 (-3.05)	-11.267 (-3.05)	-4.795 (-2.97)	-10.005 (-2.69)
School lunch every day	-4.958 (-3.02)	-7.945 (-2.13)	-5.863 (-3.34)	-5.565 (-1.48)
Male teacher/male student	0.503 (0.26)	8.259 (3.44)	2.285 (1.08)	5.805 (2.40)
Female teacher/female student	1.553 (0.87)	-4.122 (-2.02)	1.384 (0.73)	-1.364 (-0.67)
Percent seek 9 or more years of school		7.907 (5.04)		7.841 (4.97)
School characteristics				
Graded class	-4.174 (-4.72)	0.332 (0.39)	-2.405 (-2.54)	-1.205 (-1.41)
Pupil-teacher ratio	-0.064 (-2.19)	0.074 (2.10)	-0.038 (-1.22)	-0.008 (-0.23)
School hardware index	9.201 (5.45)	-2.243 (-1.22)	6.740 (3.72)	0.825 (0.45)
School software index	5.645 (3.12)	9.770 (4.65)	3.299 (1.70)	6.942 (3.28)

(continued)

Appendix Table 15.4. (continued)

	Portuguese				Mathematics			
	1983		1985		1983		1985	
Teacher characteristics								
Teacher's education	0.793	(5.54)	0.029	(0.20)	1.228	(8.00)	0.546	(3.68)
Teacher's experience	−0.006	(−0.10)	0.000	(0.00)	0.102	(1.62)	0.052	(0.87)
LOGOS II — teacher training	3.365	(3.11)	2.021	(1.98)	2.225	(1.92)	2.111	(2.06)
Qualificação — teacher training	−0.426	(−0.41)	0.607	(0.60)	−3.912	(−3.49)	1.494	(1.47)
Teacher activity index	5.848	(2.94)	−4.475	(−2.06)	5.315	(2.50)	0.866	(0.40)
Teacher material index	1.888	(1.09)	0.929	(0.54)	2.461	(1.33)	−0.229	(−0.13)
Teacher's Portuguese test score			−0.089	(−2.90)			−0.159	(−5.17)
Teacher's mathematics test score			0.138	(5.88)			0.123	(5.18)
State								
Piauí	11.230	(6.10)	0.298	(0.14)	−3.751	(−1.90)	−12.607	(−5.84)
Ceará	13.923	(8.87)	14.409	(7.78)	7.082	(4.21)	6.258	(3.36)
State program								
EDURURAL: Piauí	−1.973	(−1.36)	0.700	(0.42)	5.284	(3.39)	11.137	(6.71)
EDURURAL: Ceará	11.102	(7.74)	0.316	(0.23)	11.099	(7.22)	−0.697	(−0.51)
EDURURAL: Pernambuco	1.941	(1.34)	−3.866	(−2.20)	−0.981	(−0.63)	−9.139	(−5.16)
OME index	−1.323	(−0.69)	−2.306	(−1.12)	−6.620	(−3.23)	−8.987	(−4.32)
School control								
State operated	2.813	(2.20)	−0.216	(−0.15)	2.268	(1.65)	−1.919	(−1.35)
Federally operated	3.614	(0.51)	13.360	(2.51)	−3.068	(−0.40)	−3.657	(−0.68)
Privately operated	8.434	(2.33)	5.904	(1.27)	5.792	(1.49)	3.459	(0.74)
Constant	26.486	(6.66)	30.970	(5.36)	23.188	(5.44)	31.008	(5.33)
Adjusted R²	0.143		0.179		0.126		0.161	
Number of cases	3,744		3,739		3,744		3,739	
F statistics	18.887		22.470		16.358		19.807	
Mean of dependent variable	58.766		59.630		51.095		49.025	

Appendix Table 15.5. Portuguese and Mathematics Achievement for All Fourth Graders, 1983 and 1985

	Portuguese		Mathematics	
	1983	1985	1983	1985
Student is repeating a grade	4.271 (3.42)	5.562 (4.85)	4.136 (2.60)	4.385 (2.92)
Student characteristics				
Female student	10.415 (3.24)	10.745 (3.57)	-2.284 (-0.56)	-6.017 (-1.53)
Student's age	-0.583 (-2.81)	-0.962 (-5.02)	-0.768 (-2.90)	-0.798 (-3.17)
Pupil works	-5.990 (-3.70)	-6.665 (-2.90)	-3.235 (-1.57)	-5.682 (-1.89)
Family characteristics				
Mother's education	0.215 (1.00)	0.332 (1.54)	-0.044 (-0.16)	0.241 (0.85)
Father's education	-0.129 (-0.50)	-0.455 (-1.83)	0.351 (1.08)	0.049 (0.15)
Family size	-0.392 (-2.46)	-0.014 (-0.10)	-0.062 (-0.31)	0.007 (0.03)
Peer influence				
Percent families not farming	1.463 (0.62)	1.586 (0.67)	-2.157 (-0.72)	-1.810 (-0.59)
Relatively large landholders	0.042 (2.27)	-0.044 (-2.36)	0.037 (1.56)	-0.045 (-1.85)
Percent female classmates	8.592 (2.45)	5.527 (1.81)	9.911 (2.22)	3.746 (0.94)
Female classmates when female student	-7.688 (-1.77)	-5.236 (-1.32)	-12.672 (-2.29)	-0.569 (-0.11)
Percent seek 9 or more years school		7.237 (5.04)		9.168 (4.87)
Joint characteristics: pupil and school				
Homework	3.577 (3.70)	1.685 (1.91)	3.978 (3.23)	4.305 (3.72)
School lunch some day	-5.040 (-2.36)	9.666 (1.66)	-4.122 (-1.52)	11.416 (1.50)
School lunch every day	-5.907 (-2.59)	10.764 (1.84)	-3.042 (-1.05)	12.763 (1.67)
Male teacher/male student	1.364 (0.58)	2.406 (1.04)	1.937 (0.65)	5.022 (1.65)
Female teacher/female student	-1.170 (-0.57)	-3.602 (-1.92)	-0.499 (-0.19)	-2.535 (-1.03)
School characteristics				
Graded class	-0.362 (-0.30)	2.705 (2.62)	-2.417 (-1.57)	-0.461 (-0.34)
Pupil-teacher ratio	0.086 (2.40)	0.099 (2.67)	0.150 (3.29)	0.115 (2.35)
School hardware index	8.433 (3.97)	-2.046 (-0.98)	7.639 (2.82)	3.015 (1.11)
School software index	1.518 (0.72)	4.554 (2.13)	4.613 (1.71)	6.654 (2.37)

(continued)

Appendix Table 15.5. *(continued)*

	Portuguese		Mathematics	
	1983	1985	1983	1985
Teacher characteristics				
Teacher's education	0.543 (3.09)	-0.313 (-1.83)	0.816 (3.64)	-0.514 (-2.29)
Teacher's experience	0.002 (0.03)	0.041 (0.61)	0.043 (0.56)	0.240 (2.73)
LOGOS II — teacher training	0.863 (0.67)	-0.124 (-0.11)	2.192 (1.34)	-0.549 (-0.36)
Qualificação — teacher training	0.542 (0.40)	-0.662 (-0.56)	-0.046 (-0.03)	-3.129 (-2.02)
Teacher activity index	7.389 (2.70)	1.928 (0.77)	2.848 (0.82)	-5.809 (-1.78)
Teacher material index	-0.128 (-0.06)	1.073 (0.53)	0.428 (0.15)	3.378 (1.27)
Teacher's Portuguese test score		0.081 (2.06)		-0.059 (-1.15)
Teacher's mathematics test score		0.083 (1.95)		0.203 (3.64)
State				
Piauí	7.416 (3.58)	6.369 (2.79)	0.107 (0.04)	-0.777 (-0.26)
Ceará	11.825 (5.75)	13.051 (6.45)	9.383 (3.58)	7.832 (2.95)
State Program				
EDURURAL: Piauí	-3.486 (-2.03)	1.208 (0.67)	3.044 (1.39)	5.910 (2.49)
EDURURAL: Ceará	3.357 (1.63)	-0.141 (-0.09)	10.026 (3.81)	1.319 (0.63)
EDURURAL: Pernambuco	-1.223 (-0.71)	3.500 (1.92)	-1.859 (-0.85)	-1.847 (-0.77)
OME index	1.102 (0.44)	3.217 (1.40)	0.474 (0.15)	-2.586 (-0.86)
School control				
State operated	-1.448 (-0.94)	-2.726 (-1.74)	2.998 (1.53)	-4.587 (-2.24)
Federally operated	-0.246 (-0.03)	-2.929 (-0.52)	-7.366 (-0.73)	3.325 (0.45)
Privately operated	14.587 (2.98)	-0.386 (-0.10)	3.943 (0.63)	-6.621 (-1.26)
Constant	37.042 (6.98)	20.036 (2.44)	35.698 (5.28)	27.396 (2.55)
Adjusted R^2	0.131	0.161	0.131	0.120
Number of cases	1,448	1,594	1,448	1,594
F statistics	7.236	9.023	7.255	6.693
Mean of dependent variable	52.019	48.682	47.813	50.142

16

Private Education and Public Regulation

*Estelle James, Carlos Alberto Primo Braga and
Paulo de Tarso Afonso de Andre*

An important feature of the Brazilian educational system is its reliance on private institutions. The percentage of enrollments that were private in 1985 were as follows: pre-primary (36 percent), primary (12 percent), secondary (34 percent), and higher levels (58 percent). Moreover, public policies have been formulated to influence the growth and nature of the private sector. This chapter investigates the individual's choice of the public versus private sector, the determinants of private sector size across states, and the impact of government regulations over private schools at the primary and secondary levels in Brazil.[1]

Basic economic and cultural variables at the individual and community levels play a major role in shaping the size and nature of the private educational sector. Key policies adopted by the state, including provision of public education and the regulation of private education, can alter this outcome. This chapter begins with a conceptual framework that analyzes the role of the private sector in providing educational services, followed by a brief description of the private sector in the Brazilian educational system. The causes of the large differences across Brazilian states in the public-private division of responsibility are analyzed using state level variables, mainly from the 1980 census. The individual's decision to attend public or private school, or to not attend school at all, is examined for the metropolitan areas of São Paulo and Pernambuco using individual-level variables obtained from the 1982 *Pesquisa Nacional por Amostra de Domicílios—PNAD)*. Finally, we focus on the impact of government regulations on the quantity and quality of private education, based on data from schools in the state of São Paulo.

---

[1] Since the 1971 education reform, primary education is defined as comprising the first to the eighth grades, while secondary education comprises ninth, 10th, 11th, and in some cases 12th grades. Prior to 1971, primary education was four or five years, while secondary education was divided into two cycles of four and three years, respectively.

The Role of the Private Sector in Providing Educational Services

In analyzing the role of the private sector in education, we start by assuming that, through some collective choice process, each country (or state or locality) decides how much and what kind of public education to provide. Each family must then choose its preferred alternative among three options: attending no school, attending public school if available, or attending private school. The private sector thus emerges as a market response in situations where some people are dissatisfied with the amount or type of government service. Two very different patterns of private education have evolved, depending on whether they are motivated by excess demand or differentiated demand.

Excess demand for education may exist when the capacity of the public school system is less than full enrollment; that is, the option of attending a public school is not available to everyone. If the private benefits from education are high (e.g., because of labor market rewards), many people who are left out of the public schools will seek places in private schools. This was the case in many European countries in the 19th century and is also the case in many developing countries today, particularly at the secondary and higher levels.[2] The smaller the capacity of the public sector, the larger will be the excess demand for private education, ceteris paribus.

A second demand-side model views private production as a response to differentiated tastes about the kind of service to be consumed, in situations where that differentiation is not accommodated by government production. The private sector would then grow larger if people's preferences with respect to product variety are more heterogeneous and intense. We postulate that important taste differences about education stem from religious, linguistic and nationality differences that concern group identification. The greater the cultural diversity of the population and the more centralized and uniform the public educational system, the larger will be

---

[2] Examples are Kenya, where, until recently, the majority of secondary school enrollments were private, and the Philippines, where 80 percent of college enrollments are private. Among industrialized countries, Japan best fits the "excess demand" model at both the secondary and higher levels; over one-quarter of upper secondary students and three-quarters of higher education students attend private institutions, mainly because of limited space in the preferred public schools and universities. See James (1986, 1991a); and James and Benjamin (1988).

the differentiated demand for private education, coming heavily from cultural minorities.[3]

Differential preferences about quality may also lead to the development of a private alternative. In particular, a low-quality public sector may stimulate a high-quality private sector, meeting the demand of those willing and able to pay the price.[4] If we assume that educational quality has a high-income elasticity of demand and the public sector provides a quality level that just satisfies the "average" family, greater income diversity within the population implies a larger tail of upper-income people who will seek better education in the private market. (But if these upper-income people control the government, they may choose a public system that is high in quality, low in quantity and rationed to them. In that case, a large excess demand may develop.) In either case, income dispersion is predicted to lead to a large private sector, and if private schools mainly serve the upper classes they are likely to be quality-driven.

While the size and nature of the private sector in a society is thus partially determined by the source of demand, supply forces may also play a crucial role. Private schools are often established as nonprofit organizations, i.e., as organizations that cannot distribute a monetary residual. Indeed, nonprofit status is legally required for educational institutions in many countries. Even if not legally required, nonprofit organizations may have lower cost functions than for-profits or government due to donated capital or labor and tax advantages. Since research elsewhere suggests that most nonprofit entrepreneurs are motivated by ideology, particularly religious ideology, we hypothesize that private schools will be concentrated in

---

[3] The many private schools and colleges that accommodate religious or linguistic minorities (e.g., schools for Muslims, Parsees, Sikhs in India, and Chinese and Indian minorities in Malaysia) show private sector response to differentiated demand. Among Western countries, the best example of the cultural heterogeneity model is in the Netherlands, where two-thirds of the population attend privately managed schools, a response to the pervasive religious cleavage that dominated that country at the turn of the century. Switzerland, on the other hand, is an example of a country that has accommodated great linguistic differences by a highly differentiated locally controlled public school system in which the Tiebout hypothesis can operate (that is, people can move to communities that offer the kind of education they prefer), so the private sector is small. For other examples of the importance of cultural homogeneity versus heterogeneity, see James (1984, 1986 and 1987a,b).

[4] Besides Brazil, another country where differential preferences about quality seem to play an important role is the Philippines, where 25 percent and 38 percent of secondary enrollments, respectively, are in private schools, which are generally considered to be better than public secondary schools. These students, who come from predominantly upper-income families, then gain access to the scarce places at the high quality and heavily subsidized public universities. Examples from Latin America are given in Levy (1986).

areas where religious heterogeneity is high, hence many strong independent religious groups are competing for members and member loyalty
through their schools.[5]

Finally, government policies may influence the demand for and supply of private schools. As already noted, excess demand and differentiated
demand for private education depend critically upon the size and nature of
the public school system. A second important policy concerns the provision
of public subsidies to private schools, which increases the total effective demand that they face. And a third policy concerns government regulation of
private schools, which may increase their costs and hence decrease their
profitability and supply.

In sum, the relative size of private education in a society is predicted
to be a positive function of its economic and cultural heterogeneity, aug-
mented by government policies that encourage or discourage private sector
growth. (For empirical analysis of the importance of these variables in other
countries see James, 1986, 1987a,b, and 1991b,c.)

Private Education in Brazil

The private sector has traditionally played a major role in providing educational services in Brazil.[6] Since the 1960s, however, the expansion of public
schools has outpaced the growth of the private sector (see Table 16.1). The
rate of expansion in public enrollments was particularly dramatic at the
secondary level. Yet, the parallel increase in the throughput of graduates
from primary schools allowed the private sector at the secondary and
higher levels to continue to grow at a very fast pace. Overall, one could

---

[5] For example, the caste groups in Southern India and the independence movements in India
and Kenya started their own schools, with the expressed intention of inculcating their own
values and keeping their members out of the Western-dominated Christian schools. Other examples of the ideological and religious origin of private nonprofit schools are sectarian schools
in the U.S. and U.K., schools run by Catholic orders in France and Latin America, Calvinist
schools in Holland, orthodox Jewish schools in Israel, educational services provided by Mus-
lim waqfs (religious trusts) in the Middle East, and schools run by missionaries in many developing countries.
[6] The analyses developed here focus on the regular primary and secondary levels of education.
Lack of adequate data prevented the extension of the analyses to preschool and accelerated
adult education. Private provision of education, however, goes well beyond regular education
and supplementary courses. In fact, one of the most dynamic segments of the industry is composed of courses in foreign languages, computer training and intensive preparatory programs
for students taking entrance examinations for universities and colleges.

Table 16.1. Primary and Secondary Education Growth Rates in Brazil, 1950–87
(Percent)

Period/System	Primary education			Secondary education		
	Schools	Teachers	Students	Schools	Teachers	Students
1950–60						
Public	72	127	78	—	—	—
Private	86	321	212	—	—	—
Total	74	153	92	334	310	288
1960–70						
Public	60	141	96	123	339	488
Private	19	95	62	56	137	161
Total	55	130	90	77	215	276
1970–80						
Public	35	43	51	93	82	174
Private	−13	3	23	32	69	189
Total	30	35	42	56	76	181
1980–87						
Public	−4	28	14	74	38	38
Private	−10	17	18	1	−9	−14
Total	−4	26	15	36	17	14

Sources: MEC; Fogaca (1990).

characterize the 1960–80 period as an era of rapid expansion of the private educational sector despite a long-run trend of its relative diminution.

Part of the dynamism of the private sector over this period can be explained in terms of the quality-quantity tradeoff posed by expansion of the public school system. It is quite clear that rapid expansion of the public sector did improve educational access, as indicated by the increase in gross enrollment rates reported in Table 16.2. Yet, as this expansion was widely perceived to have occurred at the expense of quality, the decrease in excess demand was paralleled by an increase in the differentiated demand motive for private education at the primary and secondary levels. Simultaneously, this created a large excess demand for private higher education, which led to a growing participation of the private sector in total enrollments in higher education, from 44 percent in 1960 to 64 percent in 1980.

The 1980s brought new challenges for the Brazilian private educational system. Expansion of the public system capacity slowed as the Brazilian economy faltered, but the demand for private education also slowed

Table 16.2. Gross Enrollment Rates in Primary and Secondary Education, Selected Years

	1955	1962	1970	1975	1980	1985
Primary education (Enrollment in grades 1–8 as percentage of population age 7–14)	54.0	63.0	80.0	85.0[a]	88.0	90.0[b]
Secondary education (Enrollment in grades 9–12 as percentage of population age 15–19)	—	—	9.8	16.6	20.8	21.0

Sources: MEC; World Bank (1986).
[a] Figure for 1974.
[b] Figure for 1983.

down and fluctuated widely with economic conditions.[7] In the first half of the decade, the income effect associated with the 1981–83 recession seems to have dominated, fostering a substitution of public for private schooling. But with the temporary resumption of economic growth in the mid 1980s, this trend was reversed.

This period was also characterized by an increasingly interventionist approach at the regulatory level with respect to private education. Most private schools in Brazil (in contrast to those elsewhere) are for-profit and their owners claim that tuition controls significantly affected the profitability of the sector. They also emphasize the high instability of the rules of the game as a major deterrent to growth.

In part this trend merely reflected the general thrust of heterodox stabilization programs, which relied extensively on price controls. Beyond this, however, the 1980s witnessed the development of a new hostile attitude from the public sector toward the private educational system. Accordingly, the policy constellation faced by Brazilian private schools moved in the direction of more restrictive regulations (basically, more stringent tuition controls) and fewer facilitating policies.

For example, scholarships financed by the education salary tax for students to attend private schools fell in real value and tighter eligibility rules were adopted (Braga and Cabral, 1987); and the federal income tax allowance

---

[7] Brazilian real per capita income decreased by 0.1 percent per year on an average basis over the 1980–89 period. This negative performance was in clear contrast with the growth experience of the previous two decades, when the Brazilian economy achieved annual average growth rates in per capita income of 2.5 percent (1961–70) and 6.2 percent (1971–80) Inter-American Development Bank, 1990).

for education expenses (tuition, transportation costs, and other education-related expenses) was eliminated in the 1989 income tax reform. Despite lobbying efforts of private schools during the period of the Constituent Assembly, the 1988 Brazilian Constitution adopted a more restrictive position concerning the transfer of public resources to private schools. In the new Constitution, these transfers can only be made to private schools established as nonprofit organizations, a limitation not present in the previous Constitution (1967), although it is found in many other countries.

Despite these forces threatening its growth and stability, the private educational sector continues to play an important role in Brazil. Its relative size varies significantly across regions, but even in the poorest states its contribution is particularly important at the secondary level. In the early 1980s, for example, private schools accounted for more than 50 percent of total enrollment in secondary education in several states (e.g., Maranhão, Ceará, Alagoas, Minas Gerais, Rio de Janeiro, and Santa Catarina). Operating in a socioeconomic context characterized by highly concentrated income distribution, private enrollments are positively correlated with family income (see Table 16.3), but private schools provide educational opportunities even for the lowest income groups, underscoring their heterogeneity.[8]

Differences Across Brazilian States in the Public-Private Division of Responsibility for Education

This section explains differences across the 26 states, territories and the federal district in the proportion of private enrollments (%PVT) in 1980. Our analysis is conducted for the primary and secondary levels, pooled, with 52 observations in all. (Higher educational enrollments were omitted since they are concentrated in a smaller number of states.) We hypothesize that regional differences in %PVT are a function of differences in income, income diversity, cultural heterogeneity and public policies. More specifically,

%PVT   =   f(SEC, PCI, CULT HET, INC DIV, POL)
where:
    SEC   =   secondary dummy
    PCI   =   per capita income

---

[8] By 1983, the lowest 20 percent of households in income distribution had only 2.4 percent of total household income, while the top 20 percent accounted for 62.6 percent (World Bank, 1990).

Table 16.3. Private School Enrollments by Education Level and Income Group, 1982
(Thousands)

No. of min. sal.	Primary	Secondary	Higher
< 1	171	20	5
	(6)	(29)	(57)
1–2	324	80	21
	(7)	(35)	(58)
2–5	781	315	154
	(10)	(36)	(72)
5–10	590	326	303
	(17)	(42)	(78)
> 10	739	359	426
	(45)	(60)	(73)

Source: IBGE (1983).

Notes: The figures in parentheses report the percentage of students who are enrolled in private schools among those attending school, by education level and income groups. The numbers not in parentheses report the absolute number of students attending private schools, in thousands.

INC DIV   =   measures of income diversity, such as proportion of the population that is not "middle class"

CULT HET =   measures of cultural diversity, such as proportion of the population that is non-Catholic, foreign-born, or black

POL   =   public policies such as capacity constraints within the public sector, or subsidies to or regulations over private schools.

OLS and logit analysis were both used, and yielded very similar conclusions. OLS has the advantage that the coefficients are easier to interpret. But it has the disadvantage that the predicted value of %PVT may turn out to be >1 or <0 for some states; however, this was not a big problem since it only occurred in one state, and by a very small amount, in all regressions. Logit has the potentially greater disadvantage that the estimated parameters are sensitive to small measurement errors if %PVT is close to zero or one, which holds for several states in this study, and it assumes a smaller marginal effect at extreme values of %PVT than in the middle range, which may be a misspecification. Since both methods yielded very similar conclusions, the OLS results are presented in this chapter.[9]

---

[9] The logit results are available upon request from authors.

Construction of Variables

Per Capita Income

Ceteris paribus, we would expect per capita income (PCI) to serve as an indicator of gross demand for education as well as ability to pay for differentiated and higher quality education, both implying a positive relationship between PCI and %PVT across states. Also, high-income states are often urbanized, hence they contain heterogeneous clusters of people and offer a higher rate of return to education, which should increase %PVT. This would hold under the assumption that the public sector does not respond to the differentiated tastes or greater demand of its wealthier states, as in countries where educational decisions are centralized.

However, this assumption may not hold in Brazil, which is a federal system, with primary and secondary education largely controlled by the states. It may well be that wealthier and more urbanized states respond to popular demand by providing larger and better public schools, thereby leaving a smaller role for their private schools. Thus, until we can model public sector behavior, we cannot predict whether PCI will be positively or negatively related to %PVT.[10] In fact, by comparing the behavior of PCI in equations with and without public educational spending, we can gain some insight into the public sector response to the increased income of its inhabitants.

Income Diversity

Differentiated demand for quality of education is believed to play an important role in explaining the private sector in Brazil. We hypothesize that the more disparate the income distribution, the greater will be the share of the private sector, as those who prefer higher quality education must opt out of the public sector to get it. Also, if student peers are an input into the educational production process, high-income families will prefer to separate themselves from low-income families when the income distribution is disparate. This effect might be particularly great in recent years, as the expanding public system has enrolled more low-income students. Our main measure of income disparity is the proportion of working-age population having less than one or more than five minimum salaries (PN15) (i.e., we

---

[10] Since PCI and indices of urbanization are highly correlated, we used these as alternatives. The results for PCI, which give a better fit, are presented here.

exclude the middle-income group), and we expect this variable to have a positive effect on %PVT.

However, there are several problems with this variable. First, it does not take account of dispersion within the middle-income group. Second, the real value of a given monetary salary level varies across states. Third, in 1980 the definition of "minimum salary" differed from one state to another. The third "problem" may actually be a solution to the second "problem," if definitional differences roughly correspond to cost of living differences.

Because of these problems we also experimented with two alternative measures of dispersion in family incomes based on data from the 1982 PNAD: the Gini coefficient (calculated according to Andre, 1981) and the CV (coefficient of variation)—the ratio of standard deviation to mean, both of which give us a more generalized index of income dispersion.

Cultural Heterogeneity

Cultural (particularly religious) heterogeneity is expected to positively influence %PVT because it is a source both of differentiated demand and private nonprofit supply. In Brazil, the latter effect is expected to be weaker than in many other countries, because for-profit schools are legal and a large proportion of private schools are for-profit; hence the religious basis for educational entrepreneurship is less important, especially after the educational expansion of the last three decades. Since Brazil is predominantly a Catholic country, our main measure of religious heterogeneity is the percentage of the population in each state that is non-Catholic (PNCATH), and we expect it to have a weak positive effect.

Private schools often serve diverse ethnic or linguistic groups, and Brazil has many of these. Therefore, our second measure of cultural heterogeneity is "percent of the population that is foreign born" (FOREIGN), which is expected to have a positive effect on %PVT. The same applies to our final measure of cultural diversity, the percent of the population that is black (PBLACK).

Public Policies

While the preceding variables represent basic economic and cultural conditions that are not readily amenable to change, a variety of discretionary public policies might be expected to influence %PVT. Probably the most important policy variable is public sector capacity, which is expected to have a negative effect on %PVT in countries where excess demand is the *raison d'être* for private education. But in Brazil, at the primary and secondary levels, the public sector is supposed to accommodate everyone who wishes to attend; in this sense the system as a whole is open access and there is no overall supply constraint. At the same time, there are localized pockets of excess demand. More important, increased access is widely perceived to have been achieved at the expense of decreased spending per student, quantity at the expense of quality. We use "public spending at the primary and secondary levels, respectively" (EDSP) as the variable expected to capture these effects; it should have a negative effect on %PVT. EDSP is expressed as a proportion of GDP; we are measuring differences in the proportion of total income that is devoted to public education in different states.

One problem with EDSP is the lack of good data about public spending, particularly data that are comparable across states in an inflationary environment. A second problem is that schools often do not operate on their minimum cost functions, leaving us with an ambiguous relationship between expenditures and quality, in a value-added sense (see Hanushek, 1986). A third major problem is the endogeneity of public educational spending. For example, the "taste for education" that leads to a high %PVT may also lead to a high EDSP, so the two may appear to be positively related because of the missing "taste" variable; or, conversely, once people have decided to opt out to the private sector they may withdraw their political support for spending in the public sector, causing %PVT and EDSP to be negatively correlated but for very different reasons from those we have postulated. To deal with these endogeneity problems, we develop a model predicting EDSP and compare the OLS and 2SLS predictions of %PVT.

Besides EDSP, another public policy that has positively influenced %PVT in other countries is subsidizing private schools; but direct subsidies are not significant in Brazil. Nonprofit schools in Brazil do benefit from tax advantages, and primary schools may benefit from scholarships financed by the education salary tax, but we do not have these data broken down by state in a reliable way. Regulations of private schools, which have increased over the past decade, may indeed be important now, but probably were much less effective in 1980. Instead of including regulations in our regression we devote a later section to a more detailed analysis of how regulations, particularly price controls, have induced changes in the provision of private education over the decade.

Thus, in our regressions we explain differences across Brazilian states in the relative size of the private sector, at the primary and secondary levels, as a function of PCI, PN15, FOREIGN, PNCATH, PBLACK, and EDSP.

(Tables 16.8 and 16.9 later in this chapter will provide the basic statistics as well as the definitions of variables used.)

Results for Recursive Model of %PVT

Table 16.4 presents our results for %PVT. In equation (1) we use a simple reduced form model without EDSP. In equations (2) and (3) a recursive model is assumed, with EDSP exogenous. Equations (4) and (5) present the 2SLS version of equation (3), with EDSP endogenous, as discussed in the next section. Two different versions of EDSP are used. In equations (2) to (4), EDSP is all state spending on education (primary plus secondary plus administration) for 1980. In equation (5) we use EDSP for 1985, deflated to 1980. Data for 1985 were broken down between primary and secondary expenditures, which we use to explain %PVT primary and secondary, respectively; general administrative expenses are excluded. Our results are quite robust to all these specifications, with the exceptions noted below.

One consistently important finding is the large effect of income inequality, as proxied by PN15. A one percent decrease in the middle class increases %PVT by .8 to 1.2 percentage points, depending on specification.[11] As discussed above, there are potential problems with PN15 as a measure of inequality, so we experimented with Gini and CV as alternatives. These variables also had a significant positive effect, although not as large as that of PN15. Apparently it is the income tails that matter, more than the degree of disparity in the middle. The positive effect of PN15, together with the fact that the private sector mainly serves the upper classes, supports our hypothesis that differentiated demand for quality is the principal demand met by the private sector; upper-income groups opt out in order to separate themselves from and acquire superior education to that which is available to lower-income groups in the public schools, so the private sector is larger where these tails are larger. Income inequality, thus, is a major driving force behind the private sector in Brazil.

Cultural heterogeneity, on the other hand, plays a more limited role. For example, FOREIGN has an insignificant positive effect which becomes stronger when PCI is omitted from the equation, and the PCI effect becomes

---

[11] Note that this conclusion holds only under the assumption that PCI does not change when the middle class decreases, i.e., the increases in the "rich" and "poor" tails must exactly offset each other. In the more general case where PCI changes in a positive or negative way, this indirect effect must also be taken into account.

Table 16.4. Determinants of %PVT, 1981

	(1)	(2)	(3)	(4)	(5)
R^2	.65	.72	.72	.72	.62
C	−35.2	−4.0	−4.5	−6.1	−13.5
	(2.79)[a]	(.36)	(.39)	(.54)	(.74)
SEC	22.4	22.4	22.4	22.4	14.0
	(7.74)[a]	(8.62)[a]	(8.61)[a]	(8.61)[a]	(2.39)[b]
PCI	.13	.06	.08	.08	.12
	(2.62)[a]	(.81)	(1.65)[c]	(1.68)[c]	(2.38)[b]
PN15	1.2	.8	.8	.8	1.1
	(3.35)[a]	(2.41)[b]	(2.4)[b]	(2.47)[b]	(2.67)[a]
PNCATH	−.1	.3	−.3	−.3	−.7
	(.29)	(.55)	(.6)	(.56)	(1.18)
PBLACK	1.4	1.3	1.3	1.3	1.5
	(2.05)[b]	(1.87)[c]	(1.95)[c]	(1.97)[b]	(2.12)[b]
FOREIGN	2.5	.9	—	—	—
	(.01)	(.24)	—	—	—
EDSP80	—	−6.0	−6.1	−5.5	—
	—	(3.65)[a]	(3.87)[a]	(2.55)[a]	—
EDSP85	—	—	—	—	−7.0
	—	—	—	—	(1.64)[c]

Sources: All 1980 variables are calculated from data in the 1980 Census except %PVT, which is calculated from IBGE *1984 Statistical Yearbook*; EDSP, 1980 and GOVSP are from IBGE *1982 Statistical Yearbook*; PCI is from IBGE (1987); EDSP, 1985 is from IBGE *1987 Statistical Yearbook*; POPAGE is from the 1985 PNAD. All 1970 variables are calculated from data in the 1970 census, except %PVT, which is from IBGE *1973 Statistical Yearbook*; EDSP is from IBGE *1972 Statistical Yearbook*; PCI is from IBGE (1987).

Notes: Significance levels: a= 1 percent level; b = 5 percent level; c =10 percent level. Heteroscedasticity was present according to the Breusch-Pagan Chi-squared test and standard errors were corrected by White's (1980) method. EDSPZ was included in all equations to denote three states where EDSP was imputed. Col. 2–4 use EDSP80, primary and secondary and administrative expenses combined. Col. 5 uses EDSP85 deflated to 1980, primary and secondary separate, explaining %PVT primary and secondary, respectively. Col. 1 and 3: OLS; col. 4 and 5: 2SLS.

Definition of Variables and Data Sources

%PVT   = Percentage of students in private schools, 1970 and 1981
PN15   = Percentage of persons age 10 or more who earn less than one or more than five minimum salaries, 1980 and imputed for 1970
PNCATH = Percentage of population that were not Catholic, 1970 and 1980
FOREIGN = Percentage of state's population that was foreign born, 1980
PBLACK = Percentage of population that was black, 1980
PCI   = Per capita income, in thousands of Cr$, 1970 and 1980
EDSP   = Public educational spending at the primary and secondary levels, as a proportion of state GDP. For 1970 and 1980 EDSP combines primary, secondary and administrative spending. In some regressions 1985 spending was used, deflated to 1980, primary and secondary separately (see Tables 16.5 and 16.6).
POPAGE = Percentage of population age 7–14 and 15–19, 1985. In some regressions these two groups were aggregated and in some regressions they were applied separately to the primary and secondary levels (see Table 16.6).
GOVSP   = Noneducational public spending as a proportion of state GDP, 1980.

more significant when FOREIGN is omitted (equation 3); the multicollinearity between these variables makes it difficult to separate out their effects. PBLACK has a significant positive effect, possibly signalling an escape of whites from a heterogeneous public school system. PNCATH is never significant in Table 16.4, probably because of the predominant role played by for-profits rather than nonprofits in the Brazilian private sector.

Our final important result is the negative effect of EDSP. When public educational spending increases 1 percentage point, %PVT decreases about 6 percentage points. A higher EDSP means a larger or better public sector, which therefore diminishes the excess demand for quantity and differentiated demand for quality as a motivation for private education; it expands public enrollments and contracts private enrollments. This also means that when public educational spending increases, total educational spending does not go up by a commensurate amount, since some potential private spending is crowded out.

Closely related is the positive effect of PCI, which is greater when EDSP is omitted from the equation. This suggests that, as per capita income increases, the public sector does not respond by spending a higher proportion of GDP on education; instead, the demand for private education grows.

Overall, we are able to explain about two-thirds of the variance in percentage of enrollments that are private at the primary and secondary levels across Brazilian states on the basis of these social and economic characteristics of the region, particularly its income inequality and key policy choices about public spending.

Determination of EDSP and Simultaneous Determination of %PVT

As discussed above, these results may be biased because EDSP may be endogenous, determined simultaneously with %PVT. Therefore, in this section and in Table 16.5 we explore the determination of EDSP. (For a discussion of the collective choice process that determines EDSP, see James, 1991c.)

We assume that EDSP = f(SEC, PCI, POPAGE, GOVSP, %PVT) where:

POPAGE = proportion of the population that is primary (7–14) or secondary (15–19) school age;
GOVSP = noneducational public spending as a proportion of GDP; and the other variables are as defined earlier.

SEC may have a positive effect because of technological factors that make secondary education more costly to produce than primary, or negative if people have a lower effective demand for secondary than for primary

Table 16.5. Determinants of EDSP

	(1)	(2)	(3)	(4)
R^2	.51	.51	.51	.5
C	−.1	−.1	−1.1	−1.3
	(.14)	(.18)	(.82)	(.94)
SEC	—	—	1.7	1.7
	—	—	(1.08)	(1.04)
PCI	0	0	(.12)	(.02)
	(1.44)	(1.46)		
POPAGE	0	0	.1	.1
	(.01)	(.03)	(1.21)	(1.19)
POPAGESEC	—	—	−.2	−.2
	—	—	(1.64)^c	(1.69)^c
GOVSP	.2	.2	.1	.1
	(10.3)^a	(9.05)^a	(2.12)^b	(2.65)^a
PVT	—	0	—	0
	—	(.18)	—	(.39)

Notes: EDSPZ was included in all equations to denote three states where GOVSP and EDSP were imputed. Col. 1 and 2 are for EDSP, 1980, primary, secondary and general administrative expenses combined. Col. 3 and 4 are for EDSP, 1985, deflated to 1980, primary and secondary separately. POPAGE is proportion of population age 7–19 in col. 1 and 2. In col. 3 and 4 POPAGE is 7–14 at the primary level, 15–19 at the secondary level. Col. 1 and 3: OLS; col. 2 and 4: 2SLS.

education (e.g., some families who attend primary school plan to drop out of secondary school, but the converse cannot be true). PCI is expected to have a positive effect if the income elasticity of demand for public educational spending exceeds one, and a negative effect otherwise. POPAGE is a proxy for effective demand; this is expected to raise EDSP at the primary level but not necessarily at the secondary level, since a decision to have many children involves a quantity-quality tradeoff, that is, to invest a little in each of many children rather than a lot in each of a small number of children.[12] GOVSP captures the fact that some states use public rather than private delivery of services because of its redistributive function; EDSP may be high in these states for the same reason.

Indeed, in Table 16.5 POPAGE has no effect in equations (1) and (2), where primary and secondary spending are combined, but in equations (3) and (4), where these two are separated, the positive effect at the primary level is cancelled out by the negative effect at the secondary level, consistent

---

[12] See Rubinfeld (1977) for evidence that families with school-age children are more likely to vote for larger school budgets in the U.S. See James (1991c) for evidence from a cross-section of 50 countries that POPAGE has a positive effect at the primary but not secondary level.

with our expectations; the age distribution of the population helps to explain the educational spending decisions of different states. This is consistent with observations in other countries (James, 1991c).

But by far the most significant variable in all the equations is GOVSP. Apparently, state governments that spend more in general also spend more on education, ceteris paribus. On the other hand, consistent with our earlier surmise, PCI has no effect on EDSP.

Equations (4) and (5) in Table 16.4 and equations (2) and (4) in Table 16.5 present the 2SLS results with POPAGE, POPAGESEC and GOVSP omitted from the PVT equation, and PN15, PNCATH and PBLACK omitted from the EDSP equation, for purposes of identification. Our results are virtually unchanged. Income, income inequality and EDSP remain the main determinants of %PVT in columns (4) and (5) of Table 16.4, while GOVSP and POPAGESEC play a key role in Table 16.5, and %PVT is never close to significance as a determinant of EDSP. Thus it appears that EDSP influences %PVT but not vice versa; and the recursive OLS model of %PVT does not lead one astray.

%PVT in 1970

We wanted to investigate whether the principal demand factor for the private sector has changed through time. For this purpose, we secured data from 1970. A number of factors make these data noncomparable with 1980, including the fact that some states have disappeared and others have been created, the educational system was restructured, the income distribution was reported in terms of cruzeiros, the equivalent of PN15 was imputed, EDSP was not disaggregated between primary and secondary, data on race was not collected, and a huge rate of inflation, which may have varied across states, made it impossible to calculate real income and expenditure charges. In view of these problems, we simply ran equation (3) from Table 16.4 separately for 1970, using the available data.

In 1970, the Brazilian educational system was divided into three parts: primary grades (1–5), medium grades, first cycle (6–9) and medium, medium second cycle (10–12). Since medium functioned as secondary in 1970, it is treated as secondary in column one of Table 16.6. However, to make it more comparable with the 1980 structure, medium first cycle is aggregated with primary in column two. The results indicate that PNCATH was somewhat more important and PN15 somewhat less important in 1970, more like the situation in other countries, but EDSP remains a major determinant of interstate differences in private sector size.

Table 16.6. Determinants of %PVT, 1970

	PVT1	PVT2
R^2	.66	.58
C	2.7	8.7
	(.2)	(.62)
SEC	29.9	24.5
	(9.35)[a]	(7.56)[a]
PCI	2.2	3.2
	(.58)	(1.13)
PN15	.7	.6
	(1.66)[c]	(1.34)
PNCATH	.5	1.1
	(.87)	(1.73)[c]
EDSP	−6.3	−8.6
	(2.43)[b]	(3.77)[a]

Notes: Significance levels: a = 1 percent level; b = 5 percent level; c = 10 percent level. Heteroscedasticity was present and was corrected by White's method. Col 1: medium grade, first cycle was counted as part of secondary. Col 2: medium grade, first cycle was counted as part of primary.

Family Choice About (Private) School Attendance

In this section the individual family, rather than the state as a whole, is the unit of analysis. The family's schooling decision is viewed as a two-stage process: first, a decision is made about whether to attend or evade school, and second, for those attending, a decision is made about whether to use a public or a private school.[13] We divide the schooling experience into three levels—elementary, junior high and senior high; the first two levels are four years in duration and the third level is three to four years long. We use data from the 1982 PNAD, which includes questions about attendance at public

---

[13] The schooling decision might have been conceptualized as a ternary choice model whereby the "child" decides on whether to evade school or to attend a private or public school at every school level. Given that our models are logits, thus derived under the Choice Axiom (choice odds are invariant to the choice set), it is well-known that they exhibit a sort of stochastic "independence of irrelevant alternatives." The choice model for any proper subset of the original set of alternatives is also logit and independent of the preferences for the excluded alternatives (see Luce, 1959; McFadden, 1974). This implies that the model for the choice between private and public schools, the main topic of this chapter, is the same whether we state it under a binary or a ternary alternative model. This would not have been true had we adopted a Thurstonian viewpoint (Thurstone, 1927) and postulated an underlying multinormal probability distribution instead of a logistic distribution.

versus private school for nine metropolitan regions in Brazil. This chapter analyzes the cases of São Paulo and Pernambuco.

We hypothesize that the child's decision about school attendance is a function of background variables such as family income (FAMINC) and size (FAMSZ), parental education (FAED and MOED), child's gender (a dummy taking the value of 1 if male), and race (oriental, black or mixed, with white as the omitted category). We also include, in some regressions, grandparents' education (FAFAED, FAMOED, MOFAED, MOMOED), to test for long-term intergenerational effects.

Table 16.7 presents results about school attendance at the primary, junior high and senior high school levels, respectively. Table 16.8 presents results about the public-private school choice. For example, the first column in Table 16.7 includes all those aged 7–14 who have not yet completed primary school; we use logit to estimate the probability that a child falling into this category will be attending school versus dropping out. The first column in Table 16.8 estimates, for the group in school, the probability that such a child will be attending private rather than public school. The second column in Table 16.7 includes all those aged 11–17 who completed primary but have not yet finished junior high school, and estimates the probability that these children will still be in school; Table 16.8 estimates for the group still in school, the probability that they will be in private school. The third columns in Tables 16.7 and 16.8 do the same for the 15 to 20-year-old age group and senior high school.

The large decrease in the number of observations as we move from columns one to two and two to three in Table 16.7 stems from the exclusion from higher schooling levels of those who did not complete lower levels. For example a 13-year-old who drops out of primary school is included in column one, but when that child reaches the age of 15, he or she is excluded from columns one and two, since the child is no longer in the primary school age category and, since he or she has not graduated from primary school, is not in the eligible category for junior high school either. This dropout due to noncompletion is especially great when moving from the primary to the secondary level in Pernambuco. But the small disparity in observations between Tables 16.7 and 16.8 is surprising at first glance, since it suggests that most people in the relevant age range who have not completed the appropriate school level report themselves as still attending school (e.g., of the 7–14 year olds who have not completed primary school, about 85 percent still appear to be in school in São Paulo, and 75 percent in Pernambuco). This appears to be inconsistent with official reports about the high dropout rate prior to primary school completion in Brazil. One pos-

Table 16.7. School Attendance Decision[1]

	São Paulo			Pernambuco		
	Primary	Jr. High	Sr. High	Primary	Jr. High	Sr. High
$-2 \lg L (0)$[2]	8,134.78	4,781.33	1,631.67	6,419.93	1,965.77	636.31
$-2 \lg L$ gain	3,930.68	2,213.12	928.28	1,820.81	1,162.55	399.09
CONST	1.35	1.26	2.61	1.36	1.63	3.12
	(8.53)[a]	(6.43)[a]	(6.63)[a]	(9.27)[a]	(4.24)[a]	(4.43)[a]
FAMING	6.1	0.92	−0.1	4.02	1.88	1.49
	(6.40)[a]	(4.91)	(0.17)	(3.42)[a]	(1.00)	(0.65)
FAED	1.11	1.8	0.46	0.55	1.06	−0.75
	(5.19)[a]	(6.93)[a]	(1.26)	(2.96)[a]	(2.62)[a]	(1.34)
MOED	1.76	2.08	0.84	2.56	1.5	2.14
	(7.33)[a]	(7.14)[a]	(1.79)[c]	(11.99)[a]	(3.57)[a]	(2.71)[a]
FAMSZ	−1.15	−1.05	−1.36	−0.92	−0.06	−0.93
	(6.00)[a]	(4.22)[a]	(2.56)[b]	(6.24)[a]	(0.14)	(1.31)
MALE	−0.16	−0.24	−0.15	−0.21	−0.61	−0.83
	(2.00)[b]	(2.42)[b]	(0.74)	(2.95)[a]	(3.17)[a]	(2.30)[b]
YELLOW	−0.06	0.67	−0.82	9.52	ns	ns
	(0.10)	(1.11)	(1.97)[b]	(0.00)	—	—
MIXED	−0.01	−0.02	0.02	−0.23	0.08	−0.51
	(0.10)	(0.17)	(0.00)	(2.62)[a]	(0.39)	(1.33)
BLACK	−0.1	−0.00	−0.93	−0.07	−0.48	−1.52
	(0.62)	(0.00)	(2.09)[b]	(0.40)	(1.26)	(2.29)[b]
N	5,868	3,449	1,177	4,631	1,418	459

Source: 1982 PNAD.
Notes: a = significant at 1 percent level; b = significant at 5 percent level; c = significant at 10 percent level. ns = no oriental students at junior or high school level in Pernambuco.
[1] For each variable, the first row gives bi, the marginal effect on $\ell n [(PR/(I-PR)]$ and the second row gives the t statistic. The marginal effect of each variable on PR, the probability of attending school, varies through the sample space so this transformation requires specification of the characteristics of the individual or group in question.
[2] $-2 \lg L (0) = -2$ [log of the maximum of the sample likelihood function] with all coefficients restricted to 0 (pure change model); $-2 \lg L$ gain $= -2 \lg L(0) - [2 \lg L(B)]$ where the second term is the log of the maximum of the sample likelihood function for the coefficient vector shown in the table.

sible explanation is that there is an overreporting of school attendance in PNAD, which may bias downward the magnitude and significance of our coefficients. Another possible explanation is that the official statistics on dropout rates are incorrect. A third explanation, supported by our data, is that dropout rates are quite low until age 12 but rise dramatically thereafter; the 15 to 25 percent figures are an average of these two disparate groups.

Table 16.8. Choice of Private School[1]

	São Paulo			Pernambuco		
	Primary	Jr. High	Sr. High	Primary	Jr. High	Sr. High
$-2 \lg L (0)^2$	7,027.13	4,060.46	1,476.40	4,886.69	1,784.16	584.63
$-2 \lg L$ gain	5,365.95	2,624.66	239.42	2,228.99	913.92	177.85
CONST	−2.97	−2.81	−0.72	−1.9	−3.07	−1.92
	(9.04)[a]	(8.52)[a]	(2.43)[b]	(8.90)[a]	(7.69)[a]	(3.62)[a]
FAMING	3.89	4.28	2.84	7.53	7.47	5.8
	(7.30)[a]	(7.75)[a]	(5.43)[a]	(8.03)[a]	(6.86)[a]	(3.77)[a]
FAED	1.67	0.68	0.44	0.92	0.92	1.35
	(8.54)[a]	(3.39)[a]	(2.01)[b]	(5.31)[a]	(3.43)[a]	(3.43)[a]
MOED	0.78	1.09	0.52	1.11	1.68	0.99
	(3.52)[a]	(4.72)[a]	(1.99)[b]	(5.73)[a]	(5.36)[a]	(2.20)[b]
FAMSZ	−2.72	−2.24	−1.87	−1.24	−0.5	−0.75
	(5.12)[a]	(4.29)[a]	(3.90)[a]	(5.27)[a]	(1.20)	(1.26)
MALE	−0.19	0.05	−0.01	0.13	0.5	−0.09
	(1.44)	(0.35)	(0.00)	(1.30)	(2.83)[a]	(0.35)
YELLOW	−0.14	0.09	−0.44	12.87	ns	ns
	(0.37)	(0.24)	(1.07)	(0.00)	—	—
MIXED	−1.11	−0.15	0.23	−0.2	−0.69	−0.49
	(3.29)[a]	(0.52)	(0.82)	(1.81)[c]	(3.87)[a]	(1.94)[c]
BLACK	−1.06	−0.06	−0.13	0.27	−2.02	0.27
	(1.48)	(0.10)	(0.22)	(1.24)	(1.97)[b]	(0.39)
N	5,069	2,929	1,065	3,525	1,287	421

Source: 1982 PNAD.

Notes: a = significant at 1 percent level; b = significant at 5 percent level; c = significant at 10 percent level. ns = no oriental students at junior or high school level in Pernambuco.

[1] For each variable, the first row gives bi, the marginal effect on ℓn [(PR/(I−PR)] and the second row gives the t statistic. The marginal effect of each variable on PR, the probability of attending school, varies through the sample space so this transformation requires specification of the characteristics of the individual or group in question.

[2] $-2 \lg L (0) = -2$ [log of the maximum of the sample likelihood function] with all coefficients restricted to 0 (pure change model); $-2 \lg L$ gain = $-2 \lg L(0) - [2 \lg L(B)]$ where the second term is the log of the maximum of the sample likelihood function for the coefficient vector shown in the table.

Results

Results using the individual family as the unit of analysis are consistent with those using the state as the unit of analysis. Our predictive ability is quite high, as shown by the gain in the log of the maximum of the sample likelihood function. Not surprisingly, family income and parental education have the most consistently strong and significant effects: a low

FAMINC, FAED and MOED increase the probability that a child will drop out of school, with the MOED effect stronger than FAED in most cases. (However, family income has little or no effect on continuation to junior high and high school levels: the disproportionate dropout rate of low-income children is concentrated at the primary level.) At the same time, a high family income and parental education increase the probability of attending private school. The tendency of low-income students to drop out of (public) school and high-income students to attend private school is consistent with our earlier finding that a community with a small middle class will have a high %PVT, all other things remaining constant.

Large family size has a negative effect on (private) school attendance, a choice of quantity over quality of children, but this effect is much weaker in Pernambuco. The effect of race on school decisions is inconclusive; in some cases whites seem more likely than other groups to attend school, especially private school. Similarly, the effect of gender is ambiguous. For example, males are more likely than females to attend primary school in São Paulo, but among those who complete primary school, females are more likely to attend junior high. Gender does not seem to affect private school choice in any consistent way.

We evaluated the grandparent effect as four separate variables and also measured their combined effect. Data on grandparents were missing for a large number of observations, reducing the feasible sample size when they were included. We ran our "restricted sample" with and without the grandparent education variables and found that while as a group they usually did not affect the decision to drop out of school, they did have a small positive effect on the decision to attend private school. The sign and significance of the other variables was largely unaffected by the sample size and the inclusion or exclusion of grandparents. Therefore, in the interest of parsimony, in the text we present our tables for the full sample without grandparents.[14]

Impact of Regulation on the Private Sector: São Paulo in the 1980s

This section considers how public policies, particularly policies regarding tuition, can influence the quantity and quality of the private sector. We start with a set of theoretical predictions about the impact of price controls, and follow with an examination of the behavior of a group of schools in São Paulo.

---

[14] The tables for the restricted sample with and without grandparents, and the test for grandparental effects are available on request from the authors.

Impact of Price Controls on Private Schools: Theory

Suppose that the private school sector is initially in long-run equilibrium with revenue per teacher (RT) equal to costs per teacher and similarly for revenue (and cost) per student (RS). One can express these equalities as follows:

$$RT = P(ACS)(TL)(1-S) = W + TTR + r\,K/L + MR \tag{1}$$
$$RS = P(1-S)(SL) = \frac{[W + TTR + r\,K/L + MR]\,(SL)}{(ACS)(TL)} \tag{2}$$

where:

RT	=	revenue per teacher per year
RS	=	revenue per student per year
P	=	tuition rate per student per class
ACS	=	average class size
TL	=	number of classes per year taught by the average teacher
SL	=	number of classes per year attended by the average student
S	=	proportion of students who are on scholarship
W	=	basic wage per year of teacher with minimal training
TTR	=	average teacher training costs per year (above minimal levels) that are covered by the school directly or via a wage premium
r K/L	=	cost of borrowed capital and ancillary supplies per teacher per year
MR	=	minimum necessary return on equity, entrepreneurship and risk-taking, per teacher, per year.

Assuming perfect information, tuition and quality adjust to where the benefits of marginal improvement just equal their marginal costs. In equilibrium, variety may be found to satisfy diverse tastes and incomes. If there is no X-inefficiency, W, TTR, rK/L, ACS and TL may be used as proxies for quality. However, if schools are not operating on minimum cost curves, these variables may also indicate inefficiency (Hanushek, 1986).

Now, let us assume that price controls are imposed and the tuition ceiling falls below the zero-profit competitive market equilibrium value. To eliminate losses as P falls, this requires corresponding cuts in costs per teacher (W + TTR + r K/L) or an increase in tuition-paying students per teacher [(ACS)(TL)(1–S)]. Put another way, if efficiency does not increase, either scholarships, teacher salaries or school quality must fall (see equations 1 and 2). And if enough savings are not achieved, the school closes, diminishing quantity supplied by the education industry.

Under binding price controls, fewer schools will enter the education industry and those that do enter will tend to be of high quality and expensive, in a regulatory environment where starting prices are not controlled but price increases are. While existing high quality schools can reduce their quality levels and still find a clientele, those schools at the bottom of the quality spectrum may fail to find sufficient consumers when they downgrade quality (because they fall below the minimum acceptable quality levels) and may go out of business. Thus the entry of high tuition, high quality schools and the closure of low quality, low tuition schools may restore the previous equilibrium in the long run, given a stable regulatory environment and constant underlying supply and demand conditions.

In the short run, much of the brunt of price controls will probably be borne by teachers, either by increasing their workload (ACS and TL) or decreasing their salaries (W and TTR), particularly if the supply of teachers is inelastic. As the elasticity increases over the longer run, this should diminish the ability of the education industry to attract and retain teachers, particularly high quality teachers with alternative opportunities. Schools may also try to economize on teaching costs by hiring more part-time teachers, a common cost-cutting method of private schools.

In many countries there is political tension between consumers, who want to keep prices low, and teachers, who want to keep wages high, which may require higher prices. In our empirical investigation we try to determine how this tradeoff was resolved in the Brazilian case and how much of the costs of price controls were passed on to teachers.

In an environment in which differentiated demand for quality plays a major role in explaining the performance of the private sector, one may expect that some consumers will conspire with their schools to subvert the system—e.g., by accepting a system of "voluntary" contributions or ancillary fees for the use of laboratories, computers and other facilities. This would be the case, in particular, at schools attended by children from high-income households that are more likely to have a high effective demand for quality. Thus, quality differences between education received by high- and low-income households will be exacerbated.

Finally, we anticipate that over time the regulated schools will endeavor to "capture" the regulatory body and thereby mitigate the effects of the price controls. In sum, if binding price controls are imposed, we would expect the following:

- The profit rate will fall;
- Fewer new schools will enter;

- Most of the new schools will be high quality, high tuition schools;
- Some old schools, particularly the low quality schools, will close;
- Less building maintenance and expansion will take place;
- Average class size will increase;
- The student-faculty and student-staff ratio will grow;
- Fewer full-time teachers will be hired and teaching loads will increase;
- More part-time teachers will be hired to economize on teaching costs;
- Real teacher salaries will fall;
- Less supplies, equipment and books will be purchased by the school and more of these costs will be shifted to parents;
- Fees will be imposed for the use of laboratories, computers, etc.
- Schools will engage in more discussions with parents about their high and rising costs and the need to increase tuition in order to maintain quality;
- "Voluntary" contributions from parents will increase, especially in the high quality schools serving high-income families;
- More vigorous efforts will be made to seek contributions from other sources, especially in the religious nonprofit schools;
- Over time, the regulated private schools will seek to "capture" the regulators.

Public Regulation of Private Schools in São Paulo

In Brazil, the array of regulations controlling the functioning of private schools is extensive. The public sector does not play a very active role either in providing information to schools about how to produce high quality, or in helping consumers evaluate school quality, two functions that might be justified on market failure grounds. Instead, detailed regulations govern the operations of private schools.

The area that has almost monopolized the attention of regulatory authorities over the last few years is the question of price controls. Brazilian regulations concerning private tuition can be traced back to Decree-Law No. 532 of April 16, 1969, which bestowed the power to control the prices of private schools to the Federal Education Council (*Conselho Federal de Educação—CFE*), each State Education Council (*Conselho Estadual de Educação—CEE*), and the Federal District Education Council (*Conselho de Educação do Distrito Federal*). The state councils and their Commissions for Educational Prices (*Comissão de Encargos Educacionais—CEnE*) are the main agents in the regulatory process. Over the years, tuition control rules have varied across states. In general terms, however, they tend to converge under the guidance of the CFE.

Originally, tuition controls were rationalized as an instrument to constrain pricing behavior that led to abnormal profits. This rationale reflected the belief that schools had a certain amount of market power stemming from limited supply in a given geographic area, consumer immobility and lack of information. Of course, it also implicitly assumed that the regulatory authorities were better positioned than market forces to evaluate and govern the sector.

The recourse to price controls in Brazil since 1986 has become a much more generalized component of heterodox stabilization attempts implemented by the Sarney and Collor administrations. In other words, since the Cruzado Plan the control of school tuition has reflected not only the regulatory activities of the councils, based on their understanding of the economics of the industry, but also the impact of macroeconomic programs based on generalized price freezes. After every heterodox shock, the educational councils have been put in the uncomfortable position of implementing policies designed outside the boundaries of the educational sector, without taking into account eventual disruptive implications for the educational system. It is no surprise that the "noise" generated by price controls applied to schools increased significantly in the second half of the 1980s.

The main elements of regulation during the 1980s were:

- Growing reliance on price controls;
- Continuous changes in the rules of the game. Guimarães (1990), for instance, points out that approximately 240 different regulations concerning school tuitions were introduced in Brazil between 1986 and 1990;
- Initial compliance by the industry, followed by periods of noncompliance at an accelerating rate, as indicated by many complaints about "illegal" price increases;
- Numerous conflicts between the schools, their consumers and the regulators, that raise the administrative, transaction, and uncertainty costs of the education industry.

The Impact of Tuition Controls in São Paulo [15]

This section examines the impact of price controls over private education. Although the available evidence does not permit statistical testing, we believe a picture emerges that is roughly consistent with our hypotheses.

---

[15] For a more detailed account of the development of regulations in São Paulo, see Campino, Braga and Cyrillo (1986) and Braga and Cyrillo (1988).

We first sought to obtain data on school revenues, not easy since private schools are reluctant to provide this information, and because the high rate of inflation during much of this period further limits the "memory" of the sector. We were able, however, to establish a proxy for the relative prices of private schools in the city of São Paulo, using information contained in the Consumer Price Index from the *Fundação Instituto de Pesquisas Econômicas* (CPI-FIPE).

The CPI-FIPE provides an indicator of the cost of living for families with an income between two and six minimum wages in the city of São Paulo. One of the items explicitly considered in the index is "educational expense." Tuition accounts for 84 percent (since 1984) of the weight of this item in the construction of the index. Approximately 46 schools (serving the relevant income class) provide monthly information about their prices to FIPE. Table 16.9 presents this information for the period 1974–90 in the format of an index showing relative movements in tuition and the CPI-FIPE.

Our index of the relative price of education moved up and down inconclusively during the 1970s, but the relative weight of tuition clearly decreased in the mid-1980s. Of course, we cannot attribute these changes solely to regulation, since we have not controlled for other variables affecting price, such as changes in per capita income, income inequality, factor costs and public educational spending. These other variables, however, would seem to have offsetting effects on price, a priori.[16] On balance, the evidence is consistent with the proposition that price controls were not binding prior to 1982 but began to affect the evolution of tuition thereafter.[17] Through most of the heterodox era, real tuition was maintained at a much lower level than that which prevailed previously.

However, this trend was reversed toward the end of 1989. By 1990, tuition returned to relative levels similar to those prevailing in the 1970s and by 1991 it far surpassed these levels. A closer look at month-by-month changes during 1989–91 reveals that each price shock provided a brief period of stability followed by a period of rising tuition rates, so that by late 1991 the index was more than treble its value in early 1989 and higher than

[16] For example, the decline in real income per capita cited in footnote seven would tend to dampen the demand for and price of private education, but rising factor prices discussed below would tend to increase the price. The expansion in public school capacity, but the perceived decline in quality, would have similar offsetting effects.

[17] For further details on the regulatory environment prior to 1982, see Braga and Cyrillo (1988).

Table 16.9. The Relative Price of Education in the City of São Paulo, 1974–90

A. Monthly Average, 1974–90

1974	1975	1976	1977	1978	1979	1980	1981	1982	1983	1984	1985	1986	1987	1988	1989	1990	1991[a]
1.57	1.68	1.72	1.95	1.84	1.65	1.53	1.53	1.79	1.56	1.32	1.38	1.09	1.29	1.35	1.11	1.65	2.65

B. Monthly Changes, 1989–91

	Jan	Feb	Mar	Apr	May	Jun	Jul	Aug	Sept	Oct	Nov	Dec	Avg
1989	0.92[b]	0.93	0.88	0.82	0.99	0.98	1.09	1.29	1.26	1.26	1.37	1.56	1.11
1990	1.56	1.53	1.99[b]	1.69	1.57	1.41	1.45	1.51	1.59	1.68	1.83	2.04	1.65
1991	2.43[b]	2.48	2.52	2.38	2.79	2.79	2.99	2.89	2.80	2.64	2.49	na	2.65

Source: FIPE.

Note: The index reflects the behavior of tuitions of nonelite schools in the city of São Paulo deflated by the CPI-FIPE. In 1984 the weight of the item tuitions in the CPI-FIPE was changed from 1.71845 to 1.1443, reflecting the results of a new household survey for families with income between two and six minimum wages.

[a] January–November, 1991.

[b] Price shocks (i.e., imposition of strong price controls throughout the economy) occurred in January 1989, March 1990, and January 1991 (as well as February 1986 and June 1987). This would have affected both the numerator and denominator of our index, but possibly with different time lags and to different extents.

at any previous time. Apparently, the regulatory authorities had not been able (or anxious) to effectively enforce price controls.

This reversal during the last two years is consistent with theories predicting that price controls will not be effective in the long run and that regulated groups will eventually "capture" the regulatory agency. The number of CEE-SP (State of Education Council of São Paulo) members linked to the private schools has increased over time according to information provided by knowledgeable observers, possibly in response to the lobbying efforts of the industry against the more effective controls of the 1980s.

The reversal may also be a response to supply changes, described below. If the ratio between price and costs has fallen, we would expect a decrease in the quantity of school places offered or, at least, in the rate of entry to the industry. Thus, information about entry and exit provides us with indirect evidence about the changing profitability of private schools, due in part to price controls. According to data provided in Table 16.10, net entry (new schools minus schools closed) was still positive but declining over the 1985–90 period in São Paulo. However, most of the openings and closures were at the pre-primary levels. If we exclude schools that were purely pre-primary or pre-primary combined with primary, we observe a net entry rate that has dwindled almost to zero. For the country as a whole, the number of private primary schools and private secondary students actually declined. This may be contrasted with 1950–70, when private primary education grew rapidly, and 1960–80, when private secondary education greatly expanded. Although many other factors besides government regulations were undoubtedly involved in this process, the evidence is consistent with the hypothesis that the uncertainty, transactions costs and price constraints imposed by the government dampened the growth of the private sector in the 1980s. This in turn may have contributed to the price resurgence at the end of the decade.

Have price controls affected elite and nonelite schools in different ways? In order to address this question we worked with two sets of schools offering primary or secondary education in São Paulo. The first set had approximately 40 nonelite schools—a subset of the FIPE sample—which basically provide services to the modal family-income range (two to six minimum salaries). The second set consists of approximately 40 schools that belong to an association of elite, high tuition schools (entitled "O Grupo").

We expected that the elite schools would be better positioned to evade price controls, because their clientele would place a higher value on quality and would be willing to pay for it. Information concerning the tuition of

Table 16.10. Entry and Exit in the Education Industry, City of São Paulo, 1985–90

Year	Preprimary	Preprimary and Primary	Preprimary, Primary and Secondary	Primary and/or Secondary	Total
		A. New Schools			
1985	32	9	0	13	56
1986	5	9	0	13	28
1987	8	11	0	12	31
1988	6	12	1	10	29
1989	2	12	3	9	28
1990	3	6	1	8	20
		B. Closed Schools			
1985	6	3	0	5	14
1986	4	0	0	7	11
1987	11	1	0	3	15
1988	8	3	0	5	16
1989	12	5	0	9	26
1990	7	4	0	7	18

Sources: CEE-SP; Secretaria de Educação-SP.
Notes: The schools considered are those under the *Divisões Regionais de Ensino da Capital* (DRECAP 1, 2 and 3). Figures may not exactly add to total because of missing information.

these schools was provided by the CEE for December 1988, July 1989, and March 1990 and is presented in Table 16.11 for primary and secondary education. On the average, elite schools did raise their tuition (at both levels) faster than nonelite schools between December 1988 and July 1989, as expected. But between July 1989 and March 1990, nonelite schools readjusted their tuition much more than elite schools; the net effect was to narrow rather than widen their relative tuition rates.[18] It should be emphasized, however, that the low quality of the data limits our capacity to derive any firm conclusions here.

---

[18] One explanation for this reversal is that nonelite schools followed more closely the instructions of the employers' association *(Sindicato dos Estabelecimentos de Ensino do Estado de São Paulo —SIEESP).* Amid the chaos brought by the rapidly rising inflation of this period, the SIEESP tried to recoup its prior losses by advocating indexed contracts for tuitions, defying the prevailing regulatory norms in the latter part of 1989. Schools that adopted these contracts were able to increase their tuitions at a faster pace than other schools. The elite schools that belong to "O Grupo" seem to have lagged behind in this process—according to some observers because of their adversarial relationship with the SIEESP.

Table 16.11. Tuitions for a Sample of Schools in the City of São Paulo

	Number of observations	Mean	Standard deviation	Rate of growth		Number of observations	Mean	Standard deviation	Rate of growth
			A. Primary						
December 1988	48	22.18	9.12	—		46	71.14	29.16	—
July 1989	48	84.31	34.34	280.12		46	335.66	362.19	371.83
March 1990	48	2,947.73	1,058.04	3,396.30		46	7,438.40	2,047.10	2,116.05
			B. Secondary						
December 1988	55	25.70	10.46	—		15	67.88	12.66	—
July 1989	57	102.11	38.96	297.32		15	281.61	55.73	314.86
March 1990	59	3,400.90	1,326.69	3,230.62		15	7,846.90	2,044.90	2,686.44

Source: CEE-SP.

Notes: Tuitions (in cruzeiros) as informed by the schools to the CEE-SP in the first semester of 1990. Nonelite schools belong to the sample utilized to estimate the CPI-FIPE. Elite schools belong to the association entitled "O Grupo." The rate of growth reflects the nominal growth of the average tuition in the period considered.

Table 16.12. Indices of Tuition Paying Students per Teacher, Elite Private Schools in the City of São Paulo, 1987–90

| Year | Primary | | Secondary |
	1–4	5–8	
1987	100.00	100.00	100.00
1988	102.82	103.79	98.34
1989	106.10	101.64	101.21
1990	102.82	99.34	101.56

Source: Questionnaire applied to private schools.

Notes: Indices are based on (ACS) (TL) (1–S) (see text for explanation). Indices reflect observations for seven schools for grades one to four, eight schools for grades five to eight, and four schools for secondary education.

We also expected that new entrants to the industry would be high-tuition schools, while most of the closing units would be nonelite schools. The data available in the CEE-SP did not allow us to pursue this line of analysis with respect to schools leaving the industry. In the case of new schools, however, the 46 observations obtained for new primary courses in 1988 and 1989 had a higher average price than that prevailing for our sample of nonelite schools in the same years. But we cannot ascertain whether this difference is statistically significant.

In order to assess the impact of tuition controls on other aspects of school performance, we applied a questionnaire to a subgroup of elite schools. Of the 23 schools contacted, 11 partially answered the questionnaire;[19] these were the elite schools with superior accounting and administrative practices.

For these schools, the index of tuition-paying students per teacher, [(ACS) (TL) (1–S)], over the 1987–90 period is reported in Table 16.12. We expected to find an upward trend in this index over these years, reflecting efforts to adjust to price controls via productivity increases, quality decreases, or reduced scholarships. The results obtained, however, are inconsistent with this hypothesis; we see little change in the index. In part, this can be explained by the simple fact that schools do not have, at least in the short run, complete control over the relevant variables. The number of scholarships, for instance, cannot be diminished substantially given legal determinations that bind school behavior (mandatory scholarships for sons

---

[19] A Brazilian consulting company (XYZ Consultoria) that specializes in providing administrative guidance to private schools helped us choose the schools in the sample and applied the questionnaire.

Table 16.13. Real Wage Indices for a Sample of Elite Schools, City of São Paulo

Period	Wage/Tuitions[1]				1–4 Wage/ CPI-FIPE[2]	Public School Wage/CPI-FIPE[3]
	Pre-Primary	1–4	5–8	Secondary		
June 87	100.00	100.00	100.00	100.00	100.00	100.00
June 88	91.49	103.23	103.03	94.63	135.47	52.28
June 89	98.18	107.43	107.90	106.02	174.64	101.53
Mar 90	80.77	85.85	88.90	82.99	156.78	65.31
June 90	82.82	88.35	89.01	79.19	111.92	63.29
Oct 90	73.89	80.85	81.71	88.35	149.14	93.28

Sources: Questionnaire applied to private schools and APEOESP.
[1]Indices reflect observations for eight schools for preprimary, nine schools for grades one to four, 10 schools for grades five to eight, and six schools for secondary courses.
[2]Wages of professors teaching grades one to four of primary school deflated by the CPI-FIPE.
[3]Wages of professors in public schools in São Paulo deflated by the CPI-FIPE.

and daughters of school personnel). The alternative of increasing ACS is constrained by the physical layout of the schools; many private schools operate in buildings whose room size cannot easily be expanded. And the reliance on a higher TL cannot be significantly pursued if labor relations between school owners and teachers are conflictive. Also, the clientele of these elite schools may have been willing to increase prices informally (through contributions, lab fees, etc.) rather than face decreases in quality.

Looking for evidence of other cost adjustments, we calculated the ratio of wages to tuition between June 1987 and October 1990 for the elite schools that answered our questionnaire (see Table 16.13). Consistent with the terms of trade data for a broader group of schools given in Table 16.9, it appears that the mark-up of price over wages decreased until 1989 but increased thereafter. This corresponds to the fact that wages rose faster than the CPI-FIPE until 1989 but slower thereafter. The private schools have apparently been able to economize on labor costs in recent years. This may have been a delayed response to effective price controls in the earlier period, or it may simply be a response to a weak labor market, as real wages of public school teachers also declined sharply.

The position of the teachers is actually worse than reflected in Table 16.13 due to the timing of wage payments and tuition revenues in a period where prices were increasing over 10 percent per month. The CPI-FIPE is calculated as of the beginning of the month and tuition is usually received at the beginning of the month, but wages for month t are paid at the beginning of month t + 1; in effect, workers are required to make a loan to the schools, and this becomes an important source of profits in a period of double-digit and accelerating monthly inflation. Since the acceleration was faster than anticipated, the implicit interest rate included in the wage rate was probably less than the actual inflation rate, implying a negative real interest rate. According to industry sources, this time spread between receipt of tuition and payment of wages was one of the main reasons why schools have been able to stay afloat despite the price controls. These points support the proposition that, in recent years, the teachers have borne much of the brunt of the deteriorating financial condition of the schools. If price constraints can be passed back to the workers, this may mitigate quantity and quality declines in the short run.

Summing up, the Brazilian experience with tuition controls provides a cautionary tale for those who advocate government regulation of private schools. First of all, effective regulation is very difficult to achieve. When it is *not* achieved, the credibility of the government is badly damaged; when it *is* achieved, it adds high transaction and uncertainty costs to the education industry, and some of the consequences may be different from those intended. While we have not been able to establish conclusively the effect of controls on quantity, quality or wages, it appears that relative tuition prices moved downward but then reasserted themselves, the growth of private schools and enrollments came to a halt, and the real wages of teachers declined by the end of the 1980s, together with the increasing regulatory efforts over this period.

Conclusion

This chapter started by discussing the family variables that influence the student's decision about school attendance and the public-private choice, as well as the state-level variables that influence variations in the relative size of the private sector across regions. We found that family income and income dispersion within the community play a major role in these equations. Consistent with our hypothesis that private primary and secondary education in Brazil is driven by a differentiated demand for quality, high-income families are more likely to use private schools and the private sector will be larger in states where families are polarized into high- and low-income groups, rather than falling into a large middle class. This suggests that educational achievement and the quality of education received by diverse income groups will be similarly polarized in these communities.

While family income and income distribution within the community thus determine who goes to school, who chooses private school, and why equilibrium levels of public versus private education differ across states, it appears that government policies can strongly influence the quantity and probably the quality of private education. If public educational spending increases faster than GDP, excess demand and differentiated demand for private education decrease; thus, educational spending is a potent control mechanism.

We also investigated the effects of the regulatory environment, which became increasingly hostile to private education during the 1980s. In particular, price controls were imposed, tightened, and seem to have become binding by the mid-1980s. These policies are found in many other countries as well, a political response to the numerous families, especially working class families, who use private schools and do not see a link between the price schools charge, the available places, and the quality offered.[20]

Unfortunately, we were not able to measure whether changes in school quality or efficiency stemmed from the price controls. We did, however, observe that real wages of teachers dropped, tuition rose slower than the CPI (until 1989), and the growth of the private sector came to a virtual halt. This halt may have been responsible for the rapid rise in tuition as price controls ceased to be effective in recent years. The long-run effects on educational access and quality remain to be seen.

---

[20] The case of the Philippines is another good example (see James, 1991a).

REFERENCES

Andre, Paulo. 1981. An Exact Estimator of the Gini Coefficient for Stratified Random Samples. University of Illinois, Urbana-Champaign. Mimeo.

Braga, Carlos A.P., and Manuel C. Cabral. 1987. O Salário-Educação e o Financiamento do Ensino de 1º Grau no Estado de São Paulo. Research report. FIPE, São Paulo.

Braga, Carlos A.P., and Denise C. Cyrillo. 1988. Educação: Uma Análise do Custo/ Aluno da Rede Privada. In *Brasil 1980: Os Desafios da Crise Econômica*, eds. C.A. Rocca et al. São Paulo: IPE/USP.

Campino, Antonin. C., Carlos A. Primo Braga, and Denise C. Cyrillo. 1986. Critérios para o Reajuste de Anuidades Escolares no Estado de São Paulo. Research report, FIPE, São Paulo.

Fogaca, Azuete. 1990. Educação. In *A Política Social em Tempo de Crise: Articulação Institucional e Descentralização*, vol. 4, eds. Caudio L. Salm and L.C. Eichenberg Silva. Brasília: MPAS/CEPAL.

Guimarães, O. 1990. *Você É o Dono da Escola*. Curitiba: Posigraf.

Hanushek, Eric. 1986. The Economics of Schooling: Production and Efficiency in Public Schools. *Journal of Economic Literature* 24: 1141–77.

Inter-American Development Bank (IDB). 1990. Economic and Social Progress in Latin America. Washington, D.C.: Inter-American Development Bank.

Instituto Brasileiro de Geografia e Estatística (IBGE). Various years. *Anuário Estatístico do Brasil*. Rio de Janeiro: IBGE.

_____. 1987. *Estatísticas Históricas do Brasil: Séries Econômicas, Demográficas e Sociais de 1950 a 1985*. Vol. 3. Rio de Janeiro: IBGE.

James, Estelle. 1991a. Private Higher Education: The Philippines as a Prototype. *Higher Education* 21: 198–206.

_____. 1991b. Public Policies Toward Private Education. *International Journal of Educational Research* 15: 359–76.

_____. 1991c. Why do Different Countries Choose a Different Public-Private Mix of Educational Services? Mimeo.

_____. 1987a. *The Political Economy of Private Education in Developed and Developing Countries*. World Bank Discussion Paper EDT81. World Bank, Washington, D.C.

_____. 1987b. The Public/Private Division of Responsibility for Education: An International Comparison. *Economics of Education Review* 6: 1–14.

_____. 1986. The Private Nonprofit Provision of Education: A Theoretical Model and Application to Japan. *Journal of Comparative Economics* 10 (September): 255–76.

_____. 1984. Benefits and Costs of Privatized Public Services: Lessons from the Dutch Educational System. *Comparative Education Review* 28: 255–76.

James, Estelle, and Gail Benjamin. 1988. *Public Policy and Private Education in Japan.* London: Macmillan.

Levy, Daniel. 1986. *Higher Education and the State in Latin America.* Chicago: University of Chicago Press.

Luce, Robert. 1959. *Individual Choice Behavior: A Theoretical Analysis.* New York: Wiley.

McFadden, Daniel. 1974. Conditional Logit Analysis of Qualitative Choice Behavior. In *Frontiers of Econometrics,* ed. P. Zarembka. New York: Academic Press.

Rubinfeld, Daniel L. 1977. Voting in a Local School Election: A Micro Analysis. *Review of Economics and Statistics* 59: 30–42.

Thurstone, L. 1927. A Law of Comparative Judgement. *Psychological Review* 34: 273–86.

White, Halbert. 1980. A Heteroscedasticity-Consistent Covariance Matrix Estimator and a Direct Test for Heteroscedasticity. *American Economic Review* 48(4): 817–38.

World Bank. 1990. *World Development Report.* New York: Oxford University Press.

_____. 1986. *Brazil: Finance of Primary Education.* Washington, D.C.: World Bank.

17 Dealing With Poor Students

Claudio de Moura Castro, Sonia Dantas Pinto Guimarães,
João Batista Araujo e Oliveira and Sergio Costa Ribeiro

One usually finds well equipped, private schools for the rich, contrasting with ill equipped and understaffed public schools for the poor. Exceptions only confirm the rule. These same exceptions, however, also suggest improvements in the public school system that could lead to better education for poor students.

The literature on school effects and effectiveness warrants the two major hypotheses examined in this chapter. First, in developing countries, school effects are larger than in developed ones and may be very large indeed, as suggested, among others, by Heyneman and Loxley (1983). Second, individual school inputs, such as teacher qualifications and textbooks, can make a noticeable difference in learning outcomes (see Birdsall, Behrman and Kaplan in this volume; Farrell and Heyneman, 1989; and Lockheed and Hanushek, 1988).

The private schools examined here, exceptional as they are, offer a unique experimental design to test these hypotheses. These schools are sponsored by large corporations working in heavy construction, mining and other industrial sectors in remote areas of Brazil and abroad. The schools will be referred to as corporation-sponsored (CS) schools. These schools cater to corporation workers' children, thus mixing in the same classrooms the children of higher level staff (about 10 to 20 percent) with those of the lowest paid workers.

CS schools are run by a major private educational organization, the *Sistema Pitágoras de Ensino*. Pitágoras has two lines of work. First, it runs its own elite schools, primarily located in major Brazilian cities, and catering to upper middle-class students. Second, it runs CS schools under contract. At the time of this writing, Pitágoras was running 13 such schools, with a total student population of 20,000 scattered over seven states in Brazil and two other countries. Pitágoras claims that it attempts to keep comparable quality standards between its two lines of work.

Though treated here as private schools, it is difficult to define CS schools as such, given that some of the sponsoring firms are public enterprises and that the schools do not select highly qualified students. This chapter compares some unusual private schools for the poor—the CS schools—with the public schools that workers' children in extremely poor and remote Brazilian towns would normally attend. Three major questions are addressed: Do these private schools make any difference for the poor? Are the gains worth the cost? Are current findings derived from educational production function models appropriate to explain the results?

Sampling and Methodology

This study looked for circumstances that revealed a scarce commodity: good schools for the poor. This search led to schools where workers' and bosses' children were educated together. Such semi-experimental studies are not concerned with representative sampling. On the contrary, the sample was based on the opposite criterion to reveal aspects that would be impossible to detect in other schools.

A major criterion for choosing the schools within the CS network was the availability of state and municipal public schools in the same area, with which CS schools could be compared. To these were added the two elite schools run by Pitágoras at its own headquarters; these schools will serve as a standard of quality.

The public schools were selected on the basis of proximity to the CS schools and to the location where most workers lived. In other words, we tried to select the schools where workers would have sent their children if the CS school were not available. In each case we selected one state and one municipal school, ending up with six public schools.

The public schools can be divided into state and municipal schools. The state schools meet the standards of a minimally decent school in a poor country, with most of the essential ingredients necessary for basic operations. One of these state schools, however, was clearly much better equipped and managed than the others. The municipal schools hardly qualified as schools. Management and administrative resources and teaching conditions were never adequate or consistent. In addition, these schools operate (at least nominally) in three shifts, but in some instances the number of students enrolled in each shift is greater than the number of school desks. School hours hover around 17 hours per week, but this figure is much lower for the evening shifts.

The two elite schools are representative of well-endowed middle- and upper-class private, urban schools. They are fully equipped and staffed, offering courses from K-12, operating five hours a day, 25 hours per week. Contrasting with all the other schools in the sample, including the CS schools, virtually all students come from fee-paying, middle- and upper-class families, and most teachers have higher education degrees, including those teaching lower grades.

The CS schools present more variety. Since this variety is important in interpreting the data, some comments are warranted about each school. The schools share a number of characteristics: a central orientation from Pitágoras, embodied by the school principal, who is always an experienced member of the Pitágoras staff; adequate and often good or even excellent physical conditions; sufficient if not abundant equipment and instructional materials; libraries with at least 600 books, and a relatively intensive record of book lending; and teaching staff generally selected by Pitágoras on the basis of experience and meritocratic criteria. But the differences among CS schools are even more important for our analytical purposes than the similarities.

The school in Tucuruí has been in operation since 1973, but Pitágoras took over its management in 1986. The school was a large operation up until the mid-eighties, with 4,672 students enrolled in 14 different school units within the hydroelectric power plant that was being built. Some of these schools kept students separated according to the living quarters of their parents, and hence, segregated by socioeconomic status. At the time of the data collection, there were only two school units (with 2,398 students) where all socioeconomic origins mixed in the various classrooms. Moreover, as the power plant construction was coming to a close, the organizational climate was very tense, and there was a constant outflow of students, as their parents were laid off or transferred to other construction sites.

In the CS school in Niquelândia the situation was quite different. The school was opened in 1983, but Pitágoras took over its management at the beginning of 1990, the year of the data collection. Most staff belonged to the school operated under previous management, and therefore, the experience accumulated by Pitágoras with handling heterogeneous classes of students was still far from being implemented.

The school in Teofilândia was set up by Pitágoras in 1989 under a contract with a public mining corporation. The school enrolled 532 students by the end of 1990, and was the school most similar to the elite schools of Pitágoras. In an open exam to select teachers, for example, only five out of 200 local candidates were accepted. Students are classified by levels of competence, rather than by age or previously attained grade. As a result, classes are slightly more homogenous from an achievement perspective.

The sample thus totals 11 schools—three CS, two elite, three state, and three municipal schools. Within each school, we randomly selected a variable number of students from different classes in grades one and three for tests and interviews. Overall, we collected socioeconomic data from 600 student questionnaires; administered 1,200 tests to these same students; and conducted 40 interviews with teachers, principals, local educational authorities, and staff members of the sponsoring firms.

Three sets of data were collected: student achievement, costs and management, each of which is described below.

Students in first and third grades took achievement tests in Portuguese and mathematics. These tests were developed by the *Fundação Carlos Chagas*. The tests' main feature is that they correspond to the curricula effectively used by average Brazilian public urban schools, rather than what is laid out in the official programs. Test questions were prepared by public school teachers and validated with a large sampling of such schools. However, the sampling mechanism does not allow us to say that these schools are really representative of the population of Brazilian public schools (Vianna, 1989). What can be said is that most of the students in the Carlos Chagas sample live in middle-sized and large cities. The students are typical neither of the few leading public schools nor of the rural schools such as those typical of our sample.

We chose grades one and three for two major reasons. First, standardized tests and comparative results were readily available from the *Fundação Carlos Chagas*. Second, since many Brazilian students do not go beyond these grades, our comparisons are not biased by selective dropping out. As well, these tests were administered by the research team within a space of three weeks starting in late October 1990 in order to reduce the differences in the total amount of teaching students received. Additional questionnaires applied to the tested students provided data on socioeconomic background and other individual and family characteristics.

Cost data were collected using a modified version of the questionnaires previously used in the studies by *Estudios Conjuntos de Integración Económica Latinoamericana* (ECIEL) (Castro and Frigotto, 1980). The responses to the more than 50 questions were obtained in the field by one of the authors and allowed us to map out the usual factors of education production and their related costs.

The questionnaire included a built-in redundancy to check the accuracy of the answers and to compensate for lack of information from some sources. The data on the questionnaires were completed through interviews with the principals and local authorities, as well as through in loco parentis observation. In the case of two of the CS schools and the two elite Pitágoras schools, we also collected data directly from their respective financial departments.

This questionnaire estimated the costs of school inputs, such as buildings and facilities, equipment, supplies and instructional materials; the costs of maintenance, operations and personnel; and the costs associated with school lunches, transportation and school uniforms. Additional details on cost data collection and methodology are presented in the Appendix.

In addition to the questionnaires and direct observations mentioned above, several other questionnaires were also adapted from the ECIEL studies to query principals, first and third grade teachers, administrators and other managers of the corporations sponsoring the CS schools. Whenever possible, we conducted additional interviews with local educational authorities. These interviews highlighted the functions and activities of administrators and managers and their influence on the schools' day-to-day operations.

How Schools and Costs Differ

To a great extent, the administrative and management practices observed are congruent with the basic characteristics of the schools found in the sample. The public schools in the sample share the common characteristics of Brazilian public schools. Teachers earn relatively low salaries, schools are physically decrepit, and facilities and equipment are inadequate. School administrators lack autonomy, and principals describe themselves as powerless to make decisions concerning administrative, financial or pedagogic matters. The municipal schools are always worse than the public ones.

Each CS school is run under unique contractual arrangements between the sponsoring firm and Pitágoras. Overall, all material and human resources coming into these schools are far better than those of the public schools. CS schools are closer to the typical Brazilian private school catering to upper middle-class families. Teacher salaries are significantly higher than those of public school colleagues, and principals are well paid and enjoy considerable autonomy.

CS schools are perceived as different from the local public schools by the respective communities. They are well built, well maintained, and adequately staffed. One of the schools allows enrollment of fee-paying students not associated with the mining enterprise, but the other schools are restricted to the workers' children. As a result, students have to leave these schools when their parents quit their jobs with the firm, thus creating major problems for the students. Principals in the public schools report the shock experienced by CS students returning to public schools and encountering the dramatic contrast in resource levels.

Indeed, CS management practices differ significantly from those of public schools. The salaries of principals are a good indicator. In the CS schools, the salaries of the principals are much higher than those of teachers, probably revealing a focus on management. Moreover, principals' autonomy and authority are radically different and reveal much more than monetary values.

In the public schools there is virtually nothing to be managed. Books come (or do not come) from the *Fundação de Assistência ao Educando* (FAE) of the Ministry of Education based on criteria that change every year or with each new Minister of Education. The state or the municipality hires teachers, and the principal has no authority in these matters. There is virtually no parental participation, in large part because there are no channels for expression or for the exercise of community power over the school. The most important function of principals seems to be managing the battalion of janitors jammed on the payroll of what are generally decrepit schools. Notably, we could not observe any relation between the number of these employees and the appearance of the school.

In the CS schools, by contrast, the principal is accountable to the sponsoring corporation and to Pitágoras; the latter, in turn, receives pressure from the employees to provide a decent school. Principals report that this pressure comes particularly from the more highly qualified workers, for whom a good school is part of their contractual arrangements. In order to respond to this pressure, the principals have to rely on well qualified technical staff. In addition, instructional materials are considered an integral part of the basic inputs—not an uncertain gift from the central education authorities.

In short, the appearance, inputs and patterns of management of the CS schools are comparable to those of the typical private elite schools. Thus, it is not surprising that CS school costs differ dramatically from those of the public schools with which they were compared.

As is the case in most cost studies, we are primarily interested in comparisons. Given the nature of the data available, the limitations associated with data gathering, and the corrections and adjustments that had to be made, the actual absolute figures must be analyzed cautiously. Relative values are less risky and more instructive, since the biases tend to cancel out one another. Table 17.1 presents the cost data for each school.

Table 17.1. Summary of Costs for Pitágoras, State and Municipal Schools
(In 1990 U.S. dollars)

	Pitágoras B. Horizonte	%	Pitágoras Teofilândia	%	Pitágoras Niquelândia	%	Pitágoras Tucuruí	%	State Teofilândia	%	Municipal Teofilândia	%	Municipal Niquelândia	%	State Niquelândia	%	State Tucuruí	%	Municipal Tucuruí	%
Number of students	3,707.00		532.00		554.00		2,398.00		512.00		828.00		846.00		1,258.00		1,775.00		902.00	
CAPITAL COSTS																				
Building cost	3,990,214.00		572,644.00		596,325.00		2,581,207.00		165,324.00		267,361.00		273,190.00		406,208.00		569,918.00		291,255.00	
Equipment cost	62,385.00	.3	20,811.00	1	21,828.00	1	82,593.00	1	7,192.00	1	10,926.00	1	7,624.00	.6	12,359.00	0	13,450.00	1	9,605.00	
Maintenance	1,956.00								648.00						540.00					
10% building + equip.	405,259.90		59,345.00		61,815.30		266,380.00		17,251.60		27,828.70		28,081.40		41,856.70		58,336.80		30,086.00	
Total serv. capital	405,259.90		61,301.50		61,815.30		266,380.00		17,899.60		27,828.70		28,081.40		41,856.70		58,876.80		30,086.00	
Total/student	109.32	19	115.23	18	111.58	19	111.08	24	34.96	29	33.61	17	33.19	24	33.27	16	33.17	37	33.35	37
LABOR COSTS																				
Teaching	77,605.00		10,954.00		8,598.00		34,524.00		2,670.00		7,183.00		4,000.00		10,938.00		4,892.00		3,024.00	
Technical	13,923.00		5,659.00		2,811.00		8,362.00						263.00		3,247.00					
Administrative	26,426.00		3,643.00		7,048.00		10,789.00		911.00		4,010.00		2,712.00		2,987.00		2,724.00		941.00	
Total year	1,415,448.00		243,072.00		221,460.00		644,100.00		42,972.00		134,316.00		77,220.00		206,064.00		91,392.00		47,580.00	
Total/student	381.83	68	456.90	70	399.75	69	268.60	58	83.93	70	162.22	82	91.28	66	163.80	77	51.49	58	52.75	59
STUDENT SUPPLIES																				
Indiv. supplies/year	73.00		83.00		67.00		80.00		1.60		1.60		13.00		15.00		4.70		3.00	
Sundry							6.00						1.30		2.00				1.00	
Total	73.00	13	83.00	13	67.00	11	86.00	18	1.60	1	1.60	1	14.30	10	17.00	8	4.70	5	4.00	4
TOTAL LABOR COSTS	381.83		456.90		399.75		268.60		83.93		162.22		91.28		163.80		51.49		52.75	
TOTAL SCHOOL COSTS (=LABOR+CAPITAL)	491.15		572.13		511.33		379.68		118.89		195.83		124.47		197.08		84.66		86.10	
TOTAL SOCIAL COSTS (=LAB+CAP+STUDENT)	564.15	100	655.13	100	578.33	100	465.68	100	120.49	100	197.43	100	138.77	100	214.08	100	89.36	100	90.10	100
Teachers/Personnel	0.68		0.54		0.47		0.64		0.75		0.64		0.62		0.64		0.64		0.76	
Technical/Personnel	0.12		0.28		0.15		0.16		0.00		0.00		0.04		0.19		0.00		0.00	
Admin./Personnel	0.22		0.18		0.38		0.20		0.25		0.36		0.34		0.17		0.36		0.24	

Table 17.2. Direct and Total Costs Per Student
(In U.S. dollars)

	Direct Costs	Total Costs
Public schools	102	136
CS schools	376	488

Table 17.2 summarizes the annual costs per student in each type of school. Direct costs include personnel and instructional materials. Total costs also include capital costs. These cost differences between schools are very large.

Figure 17.1 illustrates the breakdown of the three major categories of costs: personnel, capital and instructional materials. Not only does the total amount of resources in the two types of schools vary significantly, but the patterns of resource allocation also differ. As expected, personnel represents the majority of the costs: 59.5 percent in the public schools, and 66.5 percent in the CS schools.

Notably, these two systems spend their money differently. Although the percentage spent on teacher salaries is comparable (65 percent in the public schools versus 58 percent in the CS schools), teachers are better paid in CS schools because 58 percent of a larger per capita cost represents much higher salaries. Another difference lies in the availability of technical personnel, who represent 18 percent in the CS schools and 7 percent in the public schools. This may, however, reflect an incorrect classification, since public schools sometimes classify as technical some staff members who are in fact administrative. Three of the six public schools spend nothing on technical personnel, and this is closer to the reality of public schools. The major difference, however, is on administrative expenditures: public schools average 28 percent and CS schools around 20 percent. In the CS schools, the major administrative budget item is the salary of the principals and administrative assistants. In the public schools, this same budget item pays for the salaries of cleaners, janitors, security guards, and other similar personnel.

Not surprisingly, we find that teachers receive low salaries and that public school teachers are paid even less than their colleagues in the private sector. Figure 17.2 shows the average salary for a typical 20 hour per week contract for a certified secondary school teacher at the various types of schools. The average CS school teacher salary is almost four times greater than the lowest pay in public schools and at least three times greater than the average pay in public schools.

Figure 17.1. Breakdown of Major Costs for CS vs. Public Schools
(Percent)

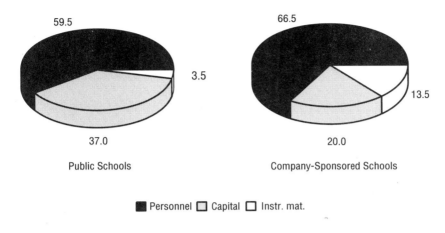

Public Schools

Company-Sponsored Schools

■ Personnel □ Capital □ Instr. mat.

These differences tend to be significantly reduced, however, when corrected for effective teaching hours. We computed all the costs of the hours available in the teaching contracts in each school and divided by the total number of effective teaching hours reported as being offered by each school. The actual teaching cost of one hour of instruction is $2.30 in the public system and roughly double, $4.90, in the CS schools. This difference is much less than that indicated by the comparison of absolute salaries and suggests possible inefficiencies. In fact, on average, public school teachers teach little more than 10 hours per week, though they are paid to teach 20. Moreover, our data overestimate the actual number of hours taught in the public schools, since most schools do not actually offer all reported classes. Thus, the actual salary differences between public and CS schools per hour effectively worked by teachers is less than double.

The expenditures related to equipment shown in Figure 17.1 include classroom and office furniture, audio-visual and other educational materials, shelves and books in the library, and miscellaneous items such as stoves, refrigerators and fans. There are marked differences between how these two school systems allocate and use such resources.

In the public schools, classroom furniture alone represented 65 percent of all equipment expenditures. Yet, in at least two schools we visited, these items were insufficient or in poor shape. Virtually no resources are allocated for administrative supplies or educational materials. No public

Figure 17.2. Weekly Teacher Remuneration in Public vs. Private Schools
(In U.S. dollars)

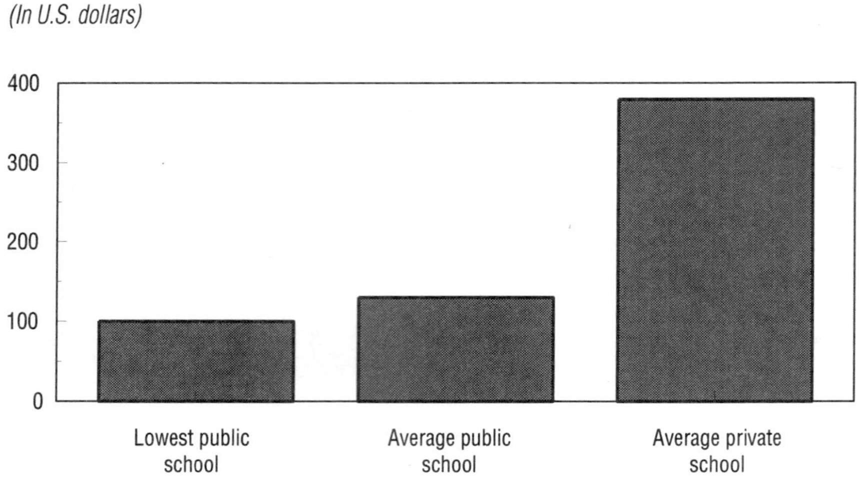

Note: Months of data collection may be affected by inflation, depending on how close or how far from salary adjustments. All figures as of August 1990. Salary for a typical 20-hour per week contract for a certified secondary school teacher.

school had a library. Virtually all schools had stoves and some, refrigerators, which are essential items to support the school lunch program. By contrast, the CS schools offered a large variety of educational equipment, particularly related to instruction. Each CS school had a library with at least 500 books and a monthly record of at least 600 individual requests.

Expenditures on instructional items such as textbooks and notebooks vary dramatically between systems. In the case of the public schools, we encountered two complications in collecting the data. Two of the six schools provided lists of materials to be acquired by students, including books and school supplies such as notebooks or scissors. In these two cases, purchase costs were computed, regardless of item availability. For the public schools, the costs of books provided by the FAE were not computed, since books do not regularly arrive at the schools. No public school in the sample received books in 1990, and none of these schools had books available for each third grader. By contrast, in the CS schools, books and materials are required and available; when they are not bought directly by the parents or through the school, they are provided by the PTA.

Figure 17.3 illustrates the differences in the allocation of resources for instructional materials between these two systems. In absolute terms, these expenditures are always less than $6.50 in the public schools, and in most

Figure 17.3. Annual Expenditures per Student on Instructional Materials in Public vs. CS Schools

(In U.S. dollars)

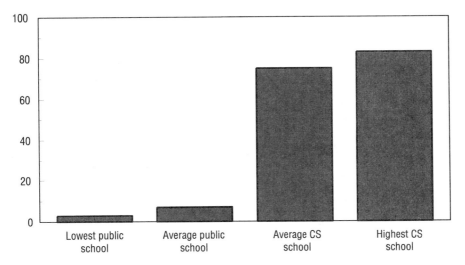

cases, they are close to zero. On average, instructional materials represent 13.5 percent of the total costs of private schools. The difference between the CS and the public school expenditures can be as large as 52 times.

Overall, these data show two important differences between these two types of schools. First, the levels of expenditures differ remarkably. The costs of the CS schools are closer to those of elite private schools and much higher than those of public schools. Second, the level and quality of the inputs in these two systems, as well as the way in which they are allocated, are also different. Public schools spend less on personnel than the CS schools. Moreover, much of the small public school personnel budget pays nonteachers. Public schools also spend virtually nothing on instructional materials. CS schools spend more on personnel, teachers and instructional materials. In addition, these schools ensure that all students acquire or receive the necessary tools for learning.

CS schools are better managed and funded than public schools. Resource allocation is more consistent, as reflected in the balanced mix of inputs used. Technical assistance and quality control by the Pitágoras group ensures that standards typical of private elite schools are met. Students from working class backgrounds are mixed with students from higher socioeconomic status (SES). It would be only natural, then, to expect that CS students would outperform their colleagues in the public schools.

Table 17.3. Achievement Scores for CS, State and Municipal Schools

	1st. Grade Port	1st. Grade Math	3rd. Grade Port	3rd. Grade Math
Pitágoras				
Elite 1	27.0	25.7	20.8	21.6
Elite 2	27.6	23.9	20.8	22.1
Niquelândia	21.6	10.0	13.9	10.6
Teofilândia	20.6	17.5	15.4	13.1
Tucuruí 1	23.1	18.5	—	—
Tucuruí 2	—	—	18.6	14.9
State				
Niquelândia	20.9	12.6	13.2	11.4
Teofilândia	—	13.5	10.6	10.1
Tucuruí	10.1	13.8	14.8	10.5
Municipal				
Niquelândia	11.6	10.8	10.4	8.4
Teofilândia	—	13.3	10.2	6.4
Tucuruí	13.6	13.3	10.5	4.9
Mean Sample	19.54	15.72	14.58	12.18
Mean CS	21.73	15.35	15.97	12.89
Mean Elite[1]	27.28	24.80	21.41	21.85
Mean Public[2]	14.03	12.88	11.61	8.60
Mean C. Chagas[3]	20.42	22.42	18.54	20.45

[1]Mean elite includes the two Pitágoras schools at headquarters.
[2]Mean public includes municipal and state schools.
[3]The Carlos Chagas sample is explained in the text. It was based on a sample of public schools in 20 large cities.

Since the major purpose of this research was to identify school effects on poor students, the family and educational background of each student had to be carefully controlled. Particular attention was devoted to the preparation of a questionnaire to identify the SES of families through questions that could be understood by first and third grade students.

Table 17.3 presents the Portuguese and mathematics test results. Means are displayed for each school. In the first row, all schools in the sample are displayed, with an additional breakdown for the two CS schools from Tucuruí. This breakdown was necessary because one of the schools held the first grade and the other school began at the second grade. At the bottom of Table 17.3, the means are presented for the CS schools, the elite schools, and the public schools.

The mean for the group of 20 public schools studied by the *Fundação Carlos Chagas* using the same tests are also presented (Vianna, 1989). This group does not represent a random sample of Brazilian schools, since schools were chosen by the respective secretariats of education and represent the best public schools from highly urbanized areas in different parts of the country. First, we compare the data of the overall sample with those of the *Fundação Carlos Chagas*. Then, we compare the data of CS schools with those of public and elite schools.

Compared with the averages of the Carlos Chagas sample, two facts become immediately obvious. First, the elite schools perform consistently better, and in some cases (first grade Portuguese) much better than those of the Carlos Chagas sample (27.28 vs. 20.42). Second, the scores of the Carlos Chagas sample are consistently superior to those of the CS and the public schools. The only exception is the Portuguese scores of first graders from CS schools (21.78 vs. 20.42). In other words, the Carlos Chagas sample performs in between the level of the elite private schools and the level of the entire group of schools from our poor localities.

Overall, the differences between averages are fairly high. As seen in the box-plots in Figures 17.4 and 17.5, we found practically no overlap between the three distributions of means. In other words, there are practically no groups in our sample obtaining scores which reach the mean of the Carlos Chagas sample. When we examined the Carlos Chagas sample broken down by towns (not shown in Figures 17.4 and 17.5), we did not find any case in which the mean of this sample is as low as that of our sample.

These comparisons confirm the previous observations that the Carlos Chagas sample is probably representative of the higher end of the metropolitan public school distribution. It also suggests that in our own sample (except for the elite schools) we might be dealing with a population that falls far below an average definition of poor. Unfortunately, our SES indicators cannot be compared with those of the Carlos Chagas sample, since the latter did not include such controls. Our own analysis and field observations suggest, however, that the populations in our sample are indeed below the level of the average Brazilian poor.

When the scores for the students within our sample are compared, Table 17.3 suggests that the results of CS school students are better than those of public school students. The differences between CS schools and the public schools are much larger—significantly large in most cases. The differences between these means may be statistically significant. However, this would not take into account the differences in socioeconomic background within the groups, particularly within the CS schools. Inferring that CS schools are better on the basis of these average values alone would certainly mask the central issue under discussion, namely, the effects of CS schools on the poorer students. To deal with this question, we must compare the results of students who fall within similar SES categories.

The need for this analysis is straightforward. Here, we are attempting to identify a second-order effect, since the SES of the students in our sample—as is the case in any country—is responsible for the greater part of the variance. Thus, we attempted to desegregate the sample in order to better control the SES of our clientele. Had we pooled the schools by city, we would have drawn incorrect conclusions. As seen in Figures 17.4 and 17.5, schools within each city are markedly different as far as their respective students are concerned. Therefore, we need to examine the differential impact of schools for the types of students to which schools cater.

Given the large data base, conventional analysis of variance would require a large number of tables—difficult both to visualize and interpret. At the same time, the number of observations within each school (our unit of analysis) was fairly small in some cases, thus precluding a more sophisticated statistical analysis. For this reason we opted for box plots used in statistical analyses of data of this nature, which seem particularly relevant to highlight the questions under investigation in this study. If there is a significant overlap in the distribution of SES and a small overlap in the distribution of scores, then other factors—such as schools—can explain such differences. Opposite distributions could lead to a similar conclusion: if there is a strong overlap in the distribution of scores and a limited one in the SES distribution, school effects could explain student results, pushing up the scores of those from lower SES or pushing down those from higher SES.

Figures 17.4 and 17.5 display the simplified box plots for each school and grade sampled with the distribution of scores. Figure 17.4 presents the data for the first grade and Figure 17.5 for the third grade. Each figure combines achievement and SES scores for a given grade (first or third) and discipline (Portuguese or math). To construct the SES scale, we combined the scale of ownership of consumer durables, characteristics of the dwelling, and occupational status of the father.

Thus constructed, these figures allow a visual inspection of the data. The horizontal line shows the full range of scores observed. For example, for first grade Portuguese (Figure 17.4), scores of the 24 students from the CS school at Niquelândia range from 18 to 28 points. The length of the boxes displays the range of 25 percent of scores above and below the median. The median of each distribution of scores is shown as a vertical bar drawn within each box. Thus, in the same example, the CS student median in Niquelândia is around 21 points.

Figure 17.4. Achievement Scores and SES, First Grade

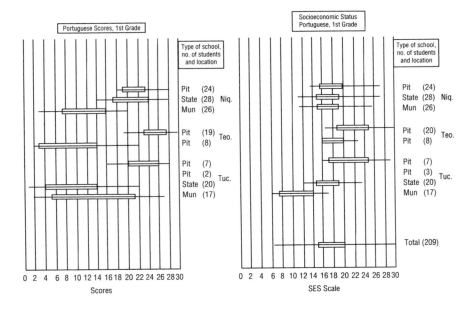

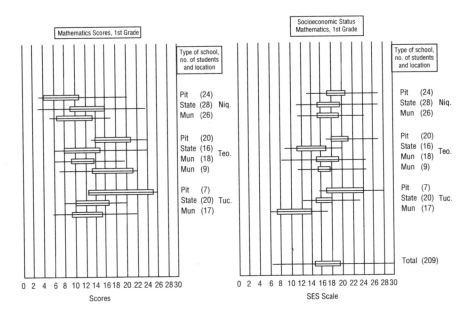

Figure 17.5. Achievement Scores and SES, Third Grade

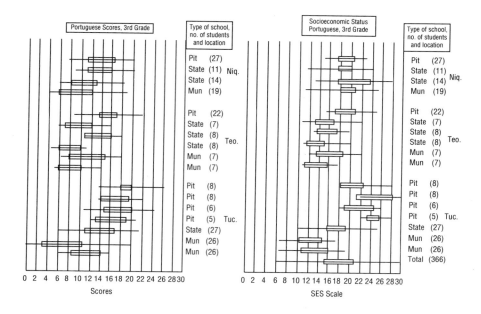

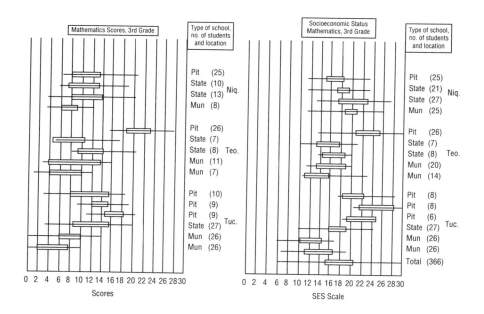

Table 17.4. Scores According to SES

SES Level		Probability of significance			
		1st grd. Port	1st grd. Math	3rd grd. Port	3rd grd. Math
Lower	Pit/State	0.001	n/s	0.02	n/s
Higher	Pit/State	0.027	n/s	0.01	0.0001
	Niquelândia	n/s	n/s	n/s	n/s
Lower	Teofilândia	—	n/s	0.00003	0.007
	Tucuruí	0.008	n/s	0.003	n/s
	Niquelândia	n/s	n/s	n/s	n/s
Higher	Teofilândia	—	n/s	n/s	0.001
	Tucuruí	0.004	n/s	0.02	0.002

n/s = not significant

Reading these figures is straightforward. The most interesting observations come from comparing the parts that indicate distribution of scores in a discipline (left-hand side of Figure 17.4) with those that indicate distribution of SES (right-hand side). For example, when comparing the results of Niquelândia in first grade Portuguese, students from the municipal schools belong to roughly the same SES as students from the other schools (compare means and the range of the distribution in the upper left hand figure), but the scores are markedly lower; there is virtually no overlap in the distribution of scores. In first grade math, CS school students coming from lower SES than those from other schools perform at about the same level.

Upon visual inspection, it becomes obvious that in the majority of cases the performance box typically moves in the same direction as the SES box. This is not surprising. But, if true, it also means that CS schools do not make much difference for the poorest students. Yet, upon closer inspection it becomes possible to detect subtler results.

Table 17.4 shows the significance of these comparisons in conventional Analysis of Variance (ANOVA) tests. For each comparison, groups have been broken down into lower and higher SES (but higher SES does not mean "high," as these are both very poor groups).

The municipal schools consistently yielded significantly lower results in all analyses and were thus eliminated completely from the data presented in Table 17.4. By doing so, we eliminated the benefit of the doubt, which could be used to explain the clearly better results of the CS schools vis-à-vis the average of public schools, and even more so in relation to the municipal schools. Indeed, this is a central epistemological issue raised by this study. The municipal schools mentioned here can barely be defined as schools, given the lack of essential elements. In the same vein, applying an incremental view to these schools—that adding isolated inputs such as better trained teachers or a few dollars' worth of school supplies would make a significant difference—is incompatible with our view of the goals of the schooling process. Rather, we focused on comparing two sets of schools that, in different ways, behave organically—one with minimal resources, the other with all the basic resources generally considered necessary to operate a "good" school.

The upper half of Table 17.4 compares the combined results of students from lower and higher SES in CS and state schools, independent of school location. Five out of the eight comparisons are favorable to CS school students, as indicated by the probabilities of significance presented in each row. The bottom half of Table 17.4 compares CS students in each city with those of the state school in the same city. In at least eight of 22 comparisons, CS results were statistically significant, both for lower and higher SES students.

Taken as a whole, these results are not very impressive. However, the data seem to indicate that CS schools might be performing a useful function. Overall, the differences are always in the expected directions, even when they are not statistically significant. But the data from Tucuruí are particularly important. Pitágoras has been operating this school for six years (as opposed to one or two years at the other schools). In five of eight comparisons illustrated in Table 17.4, the students from CS schools performed significantly better.

Yet, the absolute achievements of all schools in our sample are rather low, and the relative achievements of CS schools are also well below what could be expected, particularly if one takes into consideration the higher unit costs. Why are these differences so small?

Conclusions

The results presented above are intriguing in that they seem to challenge the existing literature on school effects in developing countries. The quality and cost of the inputs available in the CS schools would lead one to expect a much better student performance.

From the pool of schools operated by Pitágoras, we selected all those for which natural control groups (public schools) could be found. It is possible that these three schools might not be representative of the overall CS system. One school has been under Pitágoras management for one year, another for two years, and the third, where Pitágoras has been operating for over five years, was in the process of phasing out and thus was in turmoil. Would these reasons be enough to dismiss the expectations set out in the literature? After all, these are schools with significantly more inputs than the others, clearly outstanding in their respective communities, and deliberately striving to achieve. Why are the differences so small?

Another explanation might lie in the social composition of the clientele. Our data suggest that students in these remote areas live under extremely poor conditions and are much more isolated than the average poor Brazilian. This might help to explain the limited effect of a richer school environment on the very poor. This limitation could be attributed to the inadequacy of the teaching methods and inputs or to the insufficiency of resources to overcome other, more basic deficiencies.

Concerning the hypothesis of the inadequacy of teaching methods, one should consider the fact that the longer Pitágoras is in place, the better the academic results tend to be. In other words, it seems that the school learns as time passes, and this process leads to an improvement in the performance of the students. It takes time for schools to learn how to deal with different types of students and how to adapt to different clienteles and environments. In other words, applying the same model of the elite schools—or any other universal set of prescriptions including curricula, programs and textbooks—would not directly lead to success, particularly for the poorest students. Sound educational principles, however, may be effective when adapted to the local circumstances of each school. This task requires sound management and some external pressure and accountability. And this takes time.

Another hypothesis suggested by our municipal school data and based on our own judgment is that to operate with a minimum of coherence, schools require a minimum threshold, both in terms of acceptable achievement and required inputs. Schools without a minimum level of inputs—typical of the municipal schools in our sample—can hardly be classified as schools. Applying conventional production function analysis in which achievement scores are the dependent variable misses the mark on what it takes to make an effective school. The cost-effectiveness of isolated inputs to improve schoolwide test results by a few points should be contrasted with the total ineffectiveness of school systems that fail to provide even a minimally desirable level of instruction. These are schools that consistently fail students and that reinforce a sense of inadequacy. From a broader perspective, it does not matter whether such failures accompany slightly higher achievement scores, even if these marginal improvements can be reached in cost-effective ways. The conclusions or recommendations of any such analyses may be profoundly misleading—one of the major shortcomings of certain types of work based on production function models.

Perhaps these models could have been applied to compare the state with the CS schools, but we chose not to do so due to the high heterogeneity of the sample of schools. Pooling all schools together would require the use of dummies for each school to highlight critical differences. Unfortunately, the complex pattern of different schools would require too many dummies, considering the relatively small number of total observations available. This situation would lead to a confusing and possibly misleading interpretation of the multiple regression data.

Overall, our data challenge but do not entirely contradict the existing evidence on school effects. Students from CS schools came out somewhat better, and in some cases, significantly better than public school students. Even though differences in means are below the expectation, they indicate that the direction is correct, and that these schools produce students who read better and have a higher command of mathematics. This is certainly not a trivial result. What the data challenge, however, is the mechanical or automatic effect of isolated inputs, or even a certain combination of inputs. It is not realistic to provide a school with one or more inputs—such as textbooks or highly trained teachers—and expect miraculous results. Interactions might occur between approaches, inputs and clienteles, which can make schooling more or less effective depending on its relevance to the circumstances.

Even though our data do not allow us to conclude that CS schools are more efficient than public ones, the data do raise some interesting questions about resource allocation. The pattern of expenditures in the CS schools seems to make more sense, as more inputs are devoted to academic matters. In the absence of better guidelines for an ideal input mix and for the threshold necessary for independent variables to have any significant effect, CS schools appear to be headed in the right direction. Whether the costs justify the differences in learning outcomes is open to judgment. But it is very likely that significant improvements can only be achieved and sustained when certain minimum input levels are met.

Yet, the central question raised by this study remains unanswered: what makes a school good for the poor? Our study was not particularly well designed to respond to this question. To a large extent, this reflects our simplistic view, based on the literature on school effects, about what constitutes a good school. In the absence of a full analysis, we share our thoughts on this matter below, based on our observations, interviews and analyses.

All the CS schools in the sample match our conventional image of a good school. CS schools have the basic elements that well-functioning schools are supposed to have, namely a curriculum, adequate staffing, local leadership and management, external standards and evaluation criteria. External control exists in various forms. Both Pitágoras and the sponsoring firms have created a permanent mechanism of checks and balances to ensure high quality. Notably, this argument does not apply to private schools in general.

Private schools typically respond to parents' perceptions and expectations, and these vary enormously between the sophisticated middle and upper classes. In contrast to these schools, and those of the schools in our sample, CS schools suffer a different kind of immediate pressure coming from the few higher-level staff from the sponsoring firms who have no option, and want to make sure that the school they have for their children performs adequately. This might represent an even stronger pressure over these schools, and certainly much more than what could be brought to bear by less informed parents of poor students in remote areas alone.

Some may argue that CS schools are responding to such pressures by accommodating the needs of the better students—demonstrated by the higher averages of the school as a whole, but not of the poorer students. The argument, however, does not stand up. First, at least some CS schools tend to improve the performance of poorer students. Second, there is nothing in the way these schools and classrooms are managed that would indicate any such preference. What happens in CS schools takes place everywhere in the world: better students benefit more than others from improvements made by schools.

The pedagogy of failure and the threat of repetition, which may be effective for middle- and upper-class students, may not act as a powerful inducement for poorer students to work harder. After all, these students are always expected to fail, and indeed, they do fail too often in the public schools (Klein and Ribeiro, 1991). Schools such as the one in Teofilândia are attempting to reverse this situation. Rather than flunking poor students or threatening them with failure, these schools are using placement testing and grouping procedures to provide students with the kind of education they need to succeed. Preliminary results show that differences among students in low- and high-performance groups tend to decrease with time. For example, only 30 percent of students in the low-performance first grade are considered by their teachers to perform above average as opposed to 66 percent of students in the high-performance first grade. However, 44 percent of the students in the low-performance fourth grade are considered above the average, as compared to 53 percent in the high-performance fourth grade. Even though these indicators are not very reliable, they suggest that adequate grouping increases the chances of success for lower performers. What the results strongly indicate, however, is a major difference in CS schools' expectations. All students are expected to succeed, and each school is there to ensure that they do.

In our sample, the CS schools are consistently serious and well managed, while the public schools vary widely in their approach. One of the state schools offers a decent education and in some cases approaches the quality of inputs of the private system. By contrast, another state school in the sample is quite deficient, and the entire sample of municipal schools offers deplorable instruction.

In short, what seems to make a difference for the poor is a school that attempts to conform itself to conventionally held quality standards, but which is able to adapt its expectations to the realities of the student population. The worst public schools in the sample operate in the domain of fiction: the government pretends it is paying teachers, teachers pretend they are teaching, and students pretend they are learning. And no one evaluates results. Marginal improvements made in these schools by boosting one or more variable in isolation are probably the worst use of public resources. Even when isolated analyses of unit costs and learning gains look promising, such observations are totally inadequate in reflecting the complexity of the phenomenon at hand.

Schools working to become reputable, as in the case of CS schools, seem to present a more promising approach. These schools are clean and orderly. They have a program of studies, and a principal who ensures that the program is delivered. They have reasonably well-selected and well-paid teachers and a support staff. Teachers are expected to facilitate their students' success. And teachers expect that their students will succeed. Libraries exist and are frequently used by students and teachers. Textbooks and minimally adequate materials are always available and on time. And finally, parents and sponsors care about results, achievement, costs and quality control.

In principle, it does not matter whether such schools are public or private. There are no inherent reasons why private schools must be good and public ones bad. But there is also nothing inevitable about it. Apparently, there is a minimum threshold of inputs below which no socially or educationally relevant outcomes can be expected. Beyond this minimum, there is nothing that is automatic or that can be guaranteed by pre-cooked formulae about the best input mix.

REFERENCES

Castro, Claudio C., and Gandencio Frigotto. 1980. *La educación en América Latina: Un estudio comparativo de costos y eficiencia.* Washington, D.C.: ECIEL/OAS.

Farrell, J.P., and S.P. Heyneman. 1989. *Textbooks in the Developing World. Economic and Educational Choices.* Washington, D.C.: EDI Seminar Series.

Heyneman, Steve, and William Loxley. 1983. The Effect of Primary-School Quality on Academic Achievement Across Twenty-nine High and Low-income Countries. *The American Journal of Sociology* 88(6): 1162–94.

Klein, Ruben, and Sergio C. Ribeiro. 1991. O Censo Educacional e o Modelo de Fluxo: O Problema da Repetência. *Relatório de Pesquisa e Desenvolvimento* 24, Rio de Janeiro.

Lockheed, Marlaine, and Erik A. Hanushek. 1988. Improving Educational Efficiency in Developing Countries: What Do We Know? *Compare* 18(1): 21–38.

Vianna, Eraldo M. 1989. Avaliação do Rendimento de Escolas de 1° Grau da Rede Pública: Um Estudo em 20 Cidades. *Educação e Seleção* 19: 33–98.

Appendix. Cost Methodology

We collected capital costs in a peculiar way. The majority of cost studies consider only recurrent costs, obtained through balance sheets or financial statements. Obviously, the schools have to pay their bills and need this kind of information. In a discussion about resource utilization, however, this is not enough. It is essential to include the alternative uses of the resources (opportunity costs) mobilized in the construction of buildings or in the acquisition of equipment. To make a complex discussion simple, we used shadow prices as indicators of capital costs. This is the rental cost of similar facilities, which was added to the operational costs. To the shadow price, we also added a capital cost of 10 percent a.a. (including depreciation and maintenance).

Costs reflected in accounting documents are defined by administrative and legal norms. In a cost study, definitions derive from the purpose of the research. In this case, we wanted to compare different schools in order to understand why some function better than others, or why some are more expensive. But costs also reflect accidental factors that, if included, could hide phenomena of a more general nature. For example, one of the schools examined received as a donation an entire library with over 20,000 volumes. Adding the value of these books to the costs of the school would be a distortion.

By the same token, very large or underutilized schools would be excessively expensive, and their costs would not necessarily help explain differences in performance. In the case of large samples, the law of large numbers would cancel out these accidental factors, and corrections would be recommended. But this was not the situation in our limited and differentiated sample.

What we did, in practice, was to estimate the average area of a school (square meters per student) for the public and private schools. We then multiplied these averages by the average cost of construction (which does not vary significantly between the two cases). Ten percent of these costs were added to correspond to the capital costs, as described above. Costs of land can also be distorted in many ways. There is no reason to compute the total cost of a lot when a mayor decides to build a school on a 20,000 square meter lot. For simplicity sake, we increased the costs of construction by 35 percent to cover land costs.

In addition, the costs of sophisticated pedagogic equipment have been included, since they reflect the intention of providing a different type of teaching environment. Furniture and equipment are also important inputs for the operation of schools. These items were exhaustively listed, and their costs estimated by one or more qualified person in each place. Costing these components did not present major difficulties, and they represent very little in the total costs.

In principle, we intended to include operational costs (water, electricity, telephone, etc.). Unfortunately, we could not obtain reliable information on such costs. We decided to ignore what little information was available because such costs have been observed in this and similar studies to have a minimal impact on total costs (between 1 and 5 percent).

Personnel costs are the most important data in any study of this kind. In this case, the data were sufficiently reliable. Personnel costs were obtained from payroll information. Inflation was dealt with by using the value of the official dollar on the 15th day of the payroll month. Obviously, the dollar is not a perfect deflator, and salary adjustments make quantum leaps. We had no way to account for these two limitations. We also decided to exclude indirect costs associated with personnel. In the case of private firms—within which our private schools are included—social security and benefits can represent 50 percent or more of payroll. Even though such costs are not comparable in the public schools, there are still some social security benefits covered at higher levels of administration. Thus, we decided to exclude these costs in both systems.

The cost of instructional materials used by students was based on the actual cost of the list prepared by the schools, regardless of whether these materials were bought by the students, provided by the schools, or not bought at all. This method overestimates the costs in the public schools, where most students did not buy or did not have the books and materials listed. In the private schools, the listed materials are either bought by the school and deducted from the payroll, provided by the PTA, or bought directly by the students.

18

The Economics
of Higher Education

Jean-Jacques Paul and Laurence Wolff

Higher education in Latin America is considered by many to be in a state of crisis. In Brazil this is certainly the case. In the press and in meetings and discussions throughout Brazil there is a growing debate on how higher education should change to meet the challenges of the 21st century.

This debate is important to Brazil. Worldwide economic success is increasingly based on an ability to incorporate new technologies into industrial processes rather than on the simple exploitation of natural resources. This requires, among other things, a sophisticated labor force at technical and managerial levels as well as on the factory floor. Brazil's large public expenditures do not seem to be providing an adequate return to society in terms of meeting this goal.

Much of the debate in Brazil focuses on the most efficient role of the state in supporting and overseeing higher education. Brazil's public institutions are widely considered to be excessively costly, poorly managed and inefficient. Unit costs are among the highest in the developing world. Free tuition for public institutions results in subsidizing higher-income students while loans for poorer students attending private institutions are inadequate. In spite of being highly selective, public institutions seem to be inefficient in terms of ensuring that students complete their course work on time. Like most other countries, Brazil is finding itself forced, not only for financial but also for equity and efficiency reasons, to consider how to increase private sector financing of higher education, both by establishing tuition charges in public institutions and by supporting the growth of private education.

A major problem in the debate is a lack of data and information on the issues under discussion. This chapter helps to provide such information by answering the following questions:

• To what extent do Brazilian public institutions that specialize in high-cost science and technology and other programs differ from private institutions that primarily offer lower-cost, market oriented programs?

- What is the internal efficiency of the various types of Brazilian institutions of higher education in terms of percentages of entering students who graduate and number of years to produce a graduate?
- What are the comparable unit costs of public and private institutions and what is the explanation for these differences?
- What is the socioeconomic background of students attending the various types of higher education institutions?
- What kinds of jobs do graduates of various types of higher education institutions get?

It should be emphasized that this study provides only partial answers to all of the above questions, since it is based mainly on secondary analysis of existing data on all institutions and on detailed surveys of individual institutions. With this caveat, it is hoped that the conclusions will put our understanding of higher education in Brazil on a firmer factual basis, and provide some guidelines for other Latin American countries as well.

Description and History of the System

Higher education enrollment in Brazil has grown over the past 30 years from less than 100,000 in 1960 to nearly 1.6 million in 1989. The overall gross enrollment ratio is now 12 percent. Growth was particularly rapid from 1965–80. Figure 18.1 summarizes the growth of public and private institutions.

Currently, federal institutions, most of which are universities, account for 22 percent of enrollments (see Table 18.1). State institutions enroll an additional 13 percent, with the vast majority in São Paulo and Paraná. Municipal institutions, also mainly in the Southeast and South, enroll 5 percent of students. The proportion of private education has grown from 44 percent in 1965 to 60 percent in 1989. Private institutions are generally divided between secular institutions (44 percent) and those with religious, mostly Catholic affiliation (16 percent). Higher education is further divided between universities, which account for 51 percent of enrollment, and free standing faculties or schools, or groups of schools, with 49 percent of enrollment.

Higher education in Brazil is diverse in terms of institutional mission, costs and quality. Two state universities (in São Paulo) have high quality undergraduate programs and enroll one-quarter of all Brazil's graduate students. About 12 federal institutions and two private Catholic universities offer undergraduate programs reported to be of relatively good quality. Private higher education can be divided into three types: (i) higher quality Catholic institutions; (ii) other private universities, both religious and secu-

Figure 18.1. Evolution of Enrollment in Higher Education in Brazil

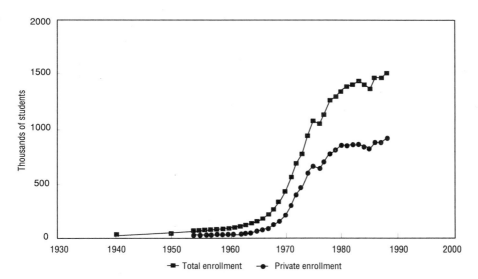

lar; and (iii) a large number of "isolated faculties," run essentially as businesses, and offering low-cost education, usually through night classes.

Brazil's current model of a small but higher quality public system is similar to that of Japan, Indonesia, Chile and Colombia. Brazil's enrollment ratio of 12 percent is somewhat lower than that of neighboring Latin American countries such as Chile, Argentina and Venezuela, where enrollments range up to 25 percent of the higher education age population. This is to a great extent the result of weaknesses at the lower levels of education, with a relatively small percentage of children in Brazil completing primary and secondary education.

Diversity of Course Offerings

It has been hypothesized that public institutions would have greater enrollment in higher cost and more traditional courses of study, especially in science, engineering and the arts, since they have larger and more stable sources of financing. Private institutions would be more likely to have enrollments in lower cost areas such as law and social sciences, as well as in courses more closely tied to the evolving labor market, such as data processing. As can be seen in Table 18.2, federal institutions do have higher percentages of enrollment (above their overall 22 percent) in the more costly areas of agronomy, pharmaceutics, veterinary science, medicine, engineering, physics, chemis-

Table 18.1. Enrollment by Governing Authority and Institutional Type

	1960	1975	1985	1989	% of total
Federal	34,986	248,849	344,617	340,203	22
Universities		236,595	330,178	323,675	21
Nonuniversities		12,254	14,439	16,529	1
State	16,062	107,111	160,067	211,946	13
Universities		58,196	117,692	154,386	10
Nonuniversities		48,915	42,375	57,560	3
Municipal	867	54,265	83,342	75,434	5
Universities		4,143	15,414	21,663	2
Nonuniversities		50,122	67,928	53,771	3
Private	41,287	662,323	817,309	943,276	60
Universities		166,996	242,974	363,512	23
Nonuniversities		495,327	574,335	579,765	37
Aggregate total	93,202	1,072,548	1,405,335	1,570,860	100

Source: Ministry of Education (MEC).
Note: Figures for 1960 and 1975 do not include graduate enrollment, which is estimated at less than 2 percent.

try, geology and nursing. Federal institutions also predominate in the traditional areas of library science, music and statistics. In comparison, private institutions predominate in administration, accountancy, pedagogy, general science, law and social studies, all of which are traditionally considered lower cost courses of study, as well as data processing, architecture, psychology and social communications. However, private institutions also enroll significant numbers of students in the traditional high-cost areas. For example, 42 percent of all enrollments in medicine and 50 percent of all enrollments in engineering are in private institutions.

To further study this question a factor analysis of 10 types of institutions and 43 courses of study was undertaken. The institutions defined were federal and state universities and faculties; municipal institutions; religious universities and faculties; and secular universities, "federations of faculties" and faculties. The results show one major and one minor axis. The first axis opposes the federal and state universities to other institutions, mainly the secular private faculties and groups of faculties. It explains 53 percent of the variance of distribution and shows that the federal and state institutions mainly cover agronomy, pharmaceutics, veterinary science, medicine, engineering, chemistry and geology, while the other institutions cover the less expensive areas of administration, accounting, pedagogy, general science, law and social studies. The second axis, which explains 17 percent of the variance, opposes private universities to state and municipal institutions. In this case the public institutions appear to be more involved in the preparation of

Table 18.2. Predominating Course of Study by Main Type of Institution

Course	Federal Institutions	State & Municipal Institutions	Private Institutions
Accounting			X
Administration			X
Agronomy	X	X	
Architecture	X		
Art	X		
Biology	X	X	
Data Processing			X
Dentistry	X	X	
Home Economics	X		
Economics			X
Engineering	X		
Geography	X	X	
Geology	X	X	
History	X	X	
Law			X
Library Science	X		
Literature		X	
Mathematics	X	X	
Medicine	X		
Music	X	X	
Nursing	X	X	
Nutrition	X		
Pedagogy			X
Pharmacy	X	X	
Philosophy	X	X	
Physics	X	X	
Physiotherapy			X
Psychology			X
Chemistry	X	X	
Science		X	X
Sociology			X
Social Science	X		
Social Studies			X
Sports		X	
Statistics	X	X	
Teacher Training		X	X
Tourism			X
Industry	X		X
Veterinary Medicine	X	X	

Source: Ministry of Education (MEC).

Note: Percentage of total enrolled in each particular course of study is greater than the average for the type of institution. For example, enrollment in federal institutions is 22 percent of total and enrollment in, say, agronomy in federal institutions is greater than 22 percent of all students enrolled in agronomy courses in all institutions.

teachers, including the liberal arts subjects of history, science, literature and geography. In comparison, the private universities are more heavily involved in data processing, architecture, psychology and social communications. Law is covered equally by these two types of institutions.

State and municipal institutions appear to have some of the character-istics of both federal and private institutions. At the same time, there are significant differences among the private institutions. For example, the pri-vate faculties are more linked to the liberal arts teaching careers, while the private universities focus more on data processing, psychology and social communication. The religious institutions predominate in philosophy.

Table 18.2, the factor analysis, and the raw data clearly show that the various types of institutions do specialize as hypothesized. A further corrobo-ration of this can be obtained by examining graduate enrollment. More than 50 percent of total graduate enrollment is in federal institutions. An addi-tional 35 percent is in two São Paulo state institutions, the University of São Paulo (USP) and the State University of Campinas (UNICAMP). Only about 20 percent of all graduate enrollment is in private institutions, mainly the Catholic University of Rio de Janeiro (PUC-Rio) in science and engineering and the Catholic University of São Paulo (PUC-São Paulo) in social science. But it is important to note that, while there is a relative specialization, there is no monopoly: the same course of study is supplied by more than one type of institution and vice versa. This result signifies that the student, once he se-lects his field of study, can choose between various types of institutions.

Internal Efficiency

Internal efficiency in higher education can be measured in two ways—per-centage of entering students who graduate, and the number of years to pro-duce a graduate. For both of these measures, available data must be interpreted and estimated. The concept underlying this study is that of the educational production function, as presented by Hanushek (1986). The ob-jective is to identify two parameters of this function: the completion rate and the numbers of years to produce a graduate. Output is considered in later sections of this chapter, at a micro level, through the earnings of the graduates.

Completion Rates

To measure the percentage of entrants who graduate, the usual approach is to get a ratio of entering students five years earlier to graduates in the current year. These data were not available. It was therefore necessary to use entering and completion data for the same year (1988). As enrollment in higher education has been relatively static in the 1980s, this approach does not bias the results significantly. The raw data is based on 3,007 observations of enrollment by institutions and course of study made available by the Ministry of Education (MEC). Based on the data used, the overall completion rate for the entire higher education system is estimated at about 50 percent.

There are several hypotheses to be tested. The first is that students attending institutions that charge tuition (e.g., private institutions) are more likely to complete their courses rapidly. The second is that more selective institutions will have better flow rates, since students would be more academically able and therefore less likely to drop out than those in the less selective institutions. This data was available, and institutions were divided between those that accepted more or less than one-third of their applicants. A third hypothesis would be that courses of study with expected higher earnings would retain students better, and they would complete their courses more rapidly. To test this hypothesis, published estimates on average earnings for four main courses of study (in the *Guia do Estudante*, a commercially prepared guide for entering students) were used. It was assumed that literature and humanities have low earnings and selection criteria, while engineering and medicine have high earnings and selection criteria, so the latter therefore should have higher internal productivity. Other hypotheses are that institutions with large enrollments have lower productivity, that night schools have lower productivity, and that older institutions and programs have higher productivity.

Data on all the above, along with the MEC observations of enrollments by course of study and institutions, were entered into a regression equation, the results of which are summarized in Table 18.3. The dependent variable in the equation is Log (PROD/1-PROD), where PROD is the estimation of the completion rate. This variable was estimated by an ordinary least squares regression.

With regard to administrative status and selectivity, it appears that institutional selectivity has a strong effect on completion rates within each type of institution. This effect ranges from 9.5 percent in federal institutions to nearly 20 percent in secular private institutions. However, administrative status appears to have little or no effect on completion rates, with the exception that freestanding faculties have slightly better completion rates (2.6 percent).

With regard to field of study, health has the best completion rates, confirming the hypothesis that courses of study with high selectivity and future pay are likely to retain students. However, agrarian sciences also retain

Table 18.3. Productivity Equation

Variable/Modality	Parameter	Marginal effect (%)
Administrative status and initial selectivity		
Federal and R≤3	Omitted	
Federal and R>3	0.380***	9.5
State and R≤3	−0.162	
State and R>3	0.550***	13.8
Municipal and R≤3	0.012	
Municipal and R>3	0.639***	16.0
Secular priv. and R≤3	0.144	
Secular priv. and R>3	0.795***	19.9
Religious priv. and R≤3	0.108	
Religious priv. and R>3	0.612***	15.3
Kind of organization		
University	Omitted	
Federation of faculties	0.009	
Independent faculties	0.105***	2.6
Field		
Exact sciences	−0.237***	−5.9
Biological sciences	0.144	
Engineering	−0.150	
Health	0.851***	21.3
Agrarian sciences	0.602***	15.1
Social sciences	−0.011	
Humanities	0.182*	4.6
Literature	Omitted	
Shift		
Day	Omitted	
Night	−0.101	
Number of admissions		
Adm.≤50	0.137*	3.4
50<Adm.≤80	0.142**	3.6
80<Adm.≤130	0.146**	3.7
Adm.>130	Omitted	
Date of creation		
Before 1971	0.225***	5.6
1971 and after	Omitted	
Intercept	−0.649***	
R^2		0.1279***
N		3,007
Average productivity	0.502	

Note: Level of significance: *10 percent; **5 percent; ***1 percent.

students, while engineering, which would be expected to have a high completion rate, does not do any better than literature and social sciences. This may be a result of excessively high academic demands set by the teaching staff, with the result that students change from engineering into less demanding courses. Such a result should be examined in more depth, bearing in mind the long-term needs of the country for engineering manpower.

The equation reveals no difference between day and night courses. It shows some minor increases in completion rates of courses enrolling less than 130 students, as well as some minor increases in completion ratios for courses established before 1971.

Years to Produce a Graduate

Using available data from MEC it is possible to estimate the number of years to produce a graduate. This estimate requires an assumption that dropouts on average complete half the course. While this assumption has been proven correct in studies of three universities in Ceará, it needs to be empirically tested elsewhere. Assuming that this is the case, we can draw the following equations for total enrollment (ENR), new enrollees (ADM), dropouts (DROP), graduates (GRAD), and the time to produce a graduate (TIME):

$$ENR = GRAD \times TIME + DROP \times TIME/2$$
$$\text{with } DROP = ADM - GRAD$$
$$\text{it follows that, } TIME = ENR/(GRAD + DROP/2)$$

As can be seen in Table 18.4, the average number of years to produce a graduate is 4.5. Federal universities take the longest period of time (6.1 years), while freestanding state, municipal and private faculties take the shortest period of time—about four years. However, the length of courses of study range from medicine (six years) to engineering (five years), to a number of three-year courses, especially in teaching. To try to break down these differences, we use another regression equation similar to that for completion rates.

The equation in Table 18.5 shows that even when entering the course of study, type of institution is most important. The exception is health, which has the longest period of study, and humanities (teaching), which has the shortest. Productivity is lowest in federal institutions and highest in municipal and private institutions.

In short, federal institutions have the lowest internal productivity, while private institutions have the highest. This is in accordance with human capital theory that assumes students paying for their studies will be moti-

Table 18.4. Time to Produce a Graduate

Type of institution	Years
Federal universities	6.1
Federal faculties	5.1
State universities	5.0
State faculties	4.1
Municipal universities	4.1
Municipal faculties	3.7
Secular universities	4.4
Federations of secular faculties	4.0
Secular faculties	4.0
Religious universities	4.8
Federations of religious faculties	4.3
Religious faculties	3.8
Mean	4.5

vated to complete them more rapidly. On the other hand, it may be that private institutions, not wishing to discourage their fee paying students, have lower standards. From this point of view, it is important to examine performance in the labor market of the graduates of the different types of institutions.

Costs of Higher Education

There is currently a great deal of debate over the costs of higher education in Brazil. It is alleged that public higher education is excessively costly. Reliable data on costs are difficult to estimate, and it is all but impossible to break down costs by the traditional categories of teaching, research, student services and administration. Furthermore, the high rate of inflation and fluctuating exchange rates in Brazil mean that international comparisons can be very misleading, especially when the exchange rate from one month to another can vary by as much as 30 percent.

Costs of Private Higher Education

A previously unused source of information for the costs of private higher education is the data gathered by the *Caixa Econômica Federal* (CEF) on tuition charges in private institutions. These data are relatively reliable because the CEF manages the student loan scheme and pays tuition directly to private institutions; therefore the figure should be a fairly good estimate of

Table 18.5. Production Time Equation

Variable/Modality	Parameter
Administrative status and initial selectivity	
Federal and R≤3	Omitted
Federal and R>3	−0.365**
State and R≤3	−1.973***
State and R>3	−1.141***
Municipal and R≤3	−2.547***
Municipal and R>3	−1.225***
Secular priv. and R≤3	−2.214***
Secular priv. and R>3	−1.199***
Religious priv. and R≤3	−2.128***
Religious priv. and R>3	−1.331***
Kind of organization	
University	Omitted
Federation of faculties	−0.654***
Independent faculties	−0.184***
Field	
Exact sciences	−0.146
Biological sciences	−0.583*
Engineering	0.131
Health	−0.347**
Agrarian sciences	−0.041
Social sciences	0.171
Humanities	−0.374***
Literature	Omitted
Number of admissions	−0.001***
Date of creation	−0.012***
Intercept	−0.649***
R^2	0.2391***
N	3,015
Average time	4.51

Note: Level of significance: *10 percent; **5 percent; ***1 percent.

costs in those private institutions that receive relatively little from other sources such as investments, government subsidies, and private contributions. With the exception of a few of the larger Catholic institutions, these additional sources of income are minimal. The year of the data is the second

Table 18.6. Annual Fees per Institution and Course of Study
(In 1989 U.S. dollars)

	Administration	Science	Health	Humanities
Municipal universities	1,930	1,952	2,652	1,452
Municipal faculties	1,225	1,331	1,613	592
Secular universities	1,781	2,324	3,233	1,717
Fed. secular faculties	1,744	2,174	2,166	1,781
Ind. secular faculties	1,413	2,148	3,106	1,253
Religious universities	1,745	2,387	3,528	1,842
Fed. religious faculties	1,253	1,633	2,566	1,530
Ind. religious faculties	750	1,496	2,143	1,055

Source: Caixa Econômica Federal.

semester of 1989. The fees are translated into U.S. dollars on the basis of the exchange rate of July 1989, when the fees were supposed to be paid.

Table 18.6 summarizes the results of the data for eight types of private institutions[1] in accordance with the breakdowns described previously. The results are also broken down by four categories of courses of study: social science and administration, science and engineering, health, and humanities and teaching.

As can be expected, tuition is highest in the health sciences, where it ranges from $1,500 to $3,500, followed by science and engineering ($1,500 to $2,400). Tuition is lowest in the social sciences and humanities ($600 to $1,800). In general, the municipal institutions and the religious faculties have the lowest fees, while the private universities have the highest.

A model was built to examine these differences in greater detail. The independent variable is the logarithm of the annual fees. The explanatory variables are the course of study and the type of institution. One hypothesis to be tested was that institutions in poorer parts of the country might charge lower tuition. Therefore the state's per capita income was built into the model.

The results of the model in Table 18.7 show, first, that per capita income by state has a significant effect on fees. As can be expected, health sciences are 52 percent more expensive than humanities, followed by science, 31 percent more expensive, and social science, 6 percent. Municipal faculties are the least expensive, followed by religious faculties. Secular and religious universities are the most expensive. This is more than likely a result of the higher quality offered by these institutions.

---

[1] It should be noted that municipal institutions are permitted to charge fees and most of them are private in all but name.

Table 18.7. Equation of Logarithm of Annual Fees

	Coefficient	Elasticity (%)
Per capita income[1]	0.0078***	0.78
Administration[2]	0.0610**	6.09
Science[2]	0.3173***	30.60
Health[2]	0.6088***	52.73
Municipal universities[3]	−0.1599**	−15.85
Municipal faculties[3]	−0.6564***	−55.42
Fed. secular faculties[3]	−0.0676*	−6.75
Ind. secular faculties[3]	−0.2032***	−20.03
Religious universities[3]	0.1311***	13.03
Fed. religious universities[3]	−0.1135***	−11.30
Ind. religious universities[3]	0.3834***	−36.33
Intercept	6.5881***	
R^2	0.3964***	
N		1,802

Source: Computed according to Kennedy's (1981) formula.
Note: Level of significance: *10 percent; **5 percent; ***1 percent.
[1] In U.S. dollars.
[2] Compared with humanities.
[3] Compared with secular universities.

Costs of Public Education: International Comparisons

Unit costs in federal institutions in 1988 are estimated at $7,930 per student (Paul and Wolyneck, 1990). This estimate is based on official statistics on enrollment and the Ministry of Education budget, using official exchange rates prorated on a monthly basis during 1988. Gaetani and Schwartzman (1991) argue that unit costs in some institutions would be reduced by an additional 25 percent if the costs of university hospitals (about 10 percent in many institutions) and of payments to retired teachers (estimated at 15 percent for some institutions) were discounted from the overall budget. They further argue that these unit costs would be about 40 percent lower if the parallel rather than the official exchange rate were used, which would put the federal institutions in a more favorable light in international comparisons. However, retirement costs may be considered a part of wages. In addition, most developing countries have a fluctuating gap between the official and parallel exchange rates, and the cost of retirees as well as hospitals are often included in international estimates.

Because the main determinant of costs in higher education worldwide is teaching, which normally accounts for 70 percent of costs, the use of student-teacher ratios, which are not subject to problems of exchange rates cor-

Table 18.8. Higher Education: Student-Teacher Ratios in Selected Countries

Country	Total faculty	Student enrollment	S/T ratio	Year
Argentina	41,804	707,016	16.9	1986
Chile	11,603	132,254	11.4	1984
Colombia	37,557	331,150	8.8	1987
Japan	195,276	1,965,023	10.1	1986
Korea	33,340	1,040,166	31.2	1990
Malaysia	4,717	47,946	10.2	1987
Spain	48,360	900,417	18.6	1986
UK	31,432	360,800	11.5	1986
Brazil[1]				
Federal	25,497	224,665	8.8	1988
State	14,658	130,481	8.9	1988
Private	10,989	323,766	29.5	1988
United States				
Public 4-yr. inst.	319,000	5,544,000	17.4	1989
Private 4-yr. inst.	218,000	2,631,000	12.1	1989

Sources: UNESCO *Statistical Yearbook* (several years); and MEC (1988).
Note: Figures for some countries are aggregate (private plus public).
[1] Faculty figures are in FTE.

rections and are relatively stable over time, provide a somewhat better way of doing cross-country comparisons. Full-time equivalent (FTE) student-teacher ratios in Brazil's federal institutions average 8.8:1. As can be seen in Table 18.8, with the exception of Colombia, Brazil's student-teacher ratio in federal institutions is the lowest among the countries compared.

Table 18.9 provides unit cost estimates for selected developed and developing countries, and it compares them with estimates for Brazil of unit costs based on the official and the parallel exchange rates. Even making the exchange rate adjustment suggested by Gaetani and Schwartzman, Brazil's unit costs in federal institutions are equal to about half of those in the United States, Japan and Australia, and are significantly higher than those of its Latin American neighbors. This is quite striking considering that faculty salaries average no less than $20,000 per year.

Another element of importance is the ratio of students to nonteaching personnel. While no international comparisons are available, the current student-to-nonteaching staff ratio in Brazilian federal institutions is 3.9:1 (it was 5.1:1 in 1980). In short, despite the usual caution attached to international comparisons, Brazil's federal system is undoubtedly one of the most expensive systems in the world, especially considering Brazil's salary levels. The main determinant of these high costs is the large numbers of teaching and nonteaching staff compared to students.

Table 18.9. Unit Cost in Public Institutions
(In U.S. dollars)

Country	Unit Cost	Year
Japan	5,968	1985
UK		
Universities	12,950	1986
Polytechnics	6,160	1986
United States	8,724	1984
Philippines	3,492	1985
Spain	906	1985
Australia	6,126	1987
Brazil—using official exchange rate	7,930	1988
Brazil—using parallel exchange rate	4,760	1988
Venezuela	1,625	1989
Chile	1,030	1990

Sources: OECD (1989); James (1989); Paul and Wolyneck (1990).

Comparisons within Brazil

Table 18.10 provides estimates of FTE student-teacher ratios for federal, state, and private universities. The overall student-teacher ratio in federal institutions is 8.8:1, compared to 10:1 in state universities and 29:1 in private universities. A review of the data on an institution-by-institution basis shows the following:

- Federal institutions vary greatly in student-teacher ratios, from about 4:1 to about 12:1. A few small specialized institutions in agriculture and medicine have around 4:1 ratios.
- In terms of student-teacher ratio, there are no economies of scale among the 23 universities. In fact several of the largest institutions, such as the Federal Universities of Pernambuco and Paraíba, have student-teacher ratios of less than 7:1, and the largest institution, the Federal University of Rio, has a ratio of 8:1.
- The highest student-teacher ratios in federal institutions appear among the youngest institutions. While this may in part be a result of a lack of graduate education, it may also be a result of an inadequate ability to lobby MEC to authorize new positions.
- Among state-run institutions, USP, the largest and best higher education institution in Brazil, has a student-teacher ratio of 10:1. UNICAMP, with the highest percentage of enrollment at the graduate level (31 percent), has a ratio of 7:1, as does the State University of São Paulo (UNESP). Most other state institutions have ratios of 10:1 or above.

Table 18.10 . Student-Teacher Ratios in Brazilian Universities, 1988

Type of institution	Faculty			Students			Student/Teacher ratio	
	Part-time	Full-time	Total faculty	FTE[1]	Undergraduate	Graduate	Head-count	FTE
Federal	9,616	32,202	48,818	37,010	305,030	16,075	8	9
State	5,806	11,753	17,559	14,656	127,197	3,284	7	9
Municipal	765	54	819	437	17,178		21	39
Private: Catholic	2,480	266	2,746	1,506	41,236	180	15	27
Private: Other religious	1,217	192	1,409	801	23,453	144	17	29
Private: Secular	7,261	898	8,159	4,529	158,280	271	19	35
Total for private universities	13,732	2,046	15,778	8,912	270,891	2,775	17	30

Source: MEC (1988).
[1] Assuming that one full-time appointment equals two part-time ones.

• Graduate education, which requires lower student-teacher ratios than undergraduate education, affects the ratio at UNICAMP, where nearly one-third of enrollment is at the graduate level, and USP, where a quarter of enrollment is at the graduate level. Among federal institutions, the federal universities of Rio (18 percent) and Minas (9 percent) have the largest portions of enrollment in graduate education.

A review of unit costs in 1988 for 36 federal universities confirms the variations noted in the student-teacher ratios. The highest unit costs are in the Federal University of Viçosa ($13,600), which is a specialized agricultural institution. The three universities in Rio also have among the highest unit costs ($9,000–$12,600). The lowest unit costs are in institutions in the North and Northeast with little graduate education ($5,400–$9,000).

Paul and Wolyneck (1990) estimated that unit costs in federal institutions are 60 percent higher than the unit costs of the University of São Paulo, in spite of both its quality and the fact that 25 percent of USP's enrollment is in graduate education. However, Gaetani and Schwartzman (1991) argue that more than 9,000 students in USP reported as full-time graduate students are in fact not engaged in full-time study or research. After eliminating these students and taking out funds for retirees, they argue that the difference is only about 13 percent. However, Paul and Wolyneck note that there are also significant numbers of "ghost" students in federal institutions. The conclusion, even after accepting Gaetani and Schwartzman's revisions, is that, despite the quality of USP, it does not appear to be particularly cost efficient, yet nevertheless has lower unit costs than the major federal institutions with which it is compared.

From 1983–89, the number of teachers in federal universities increased from 43,000 to 44,500, while the number of students declined from 340,000 to 318,000. Thus the nominal student-teacher ratio decreased from 7.9:1 to 7.1:1. From 1980–89 the number of nonteaching staff increased strikingly from 65,000 to 92,000.

Institutional case studies undertaken by Vahl (1991) break down expenditures in 1989 by budgeting categories, faculties and departments for two federal universities, Minas Gerais (UFMG) and Santa Catarina (UFSC). Table 18.11 summarizes the information on these institutions as well as four other private institutions, the Catholic universities of Minas Gerais and Paraná, and the two "community-based" universities of Ijuí and Blumenau. The average unit cost of the two federal universities studied is $9,400 per student. The nominal student-teacher ratio is 7:1. Full-time teachers are required to teach 8–14 hours per week and are expected to prepare classes

Table 18.11. Comparison of Federal and Private Universities: Quality Efficiency Measures and Cost, 1989

Efficiency measure	Federal[1]	Private[2]
Square meters per student	28	6
Number of chairs per student	1.6	0.8
Occupancy rate of chairs (%)	32	66
Yearly subsidy per student per meal (US$)	31	0
Number of library books per student	23	15
Ratio of students to administrative staff	3.8	18.7
Percent of students in graduate programs	9	2
Percent of students in daytime courses	81	51
Percent of students in high-cost courses	48	36
Percent of classes with less than 10 students	23	0.4
Percent of classes with more than 40 students	10	47
Students per teachers	7	16.3
Students per teacher FTE	6.9	30.1
Percent of total faculty full-time	82	16
Percent of total faculty part-time	18	19
Percent of total faculty hired on hourly basis	0	65
Percent of faculty with graduate degrees	55	16
Books and chapters written per year as a ratio per faculty	18	0.03
Cost per student in US$	9,378	986

[1] Based on case studies by Vahl (1990) of two federal universities (UFMG and UFSC).
[2] Based on case studies by Vahl of PUC-MG, PUC-PR, UNIJUI, and FURB.

and undertake research during the rest of the time (compared to 24 hours in the private institutions). The top salary for a full professor is around $2,300 per month in the federal institutions (compared to $1,600 per month in the private universities surveyed). The number of nonteaching staff in the two federal institutions is equivalent to about 25 percent of student enrollment (compared to 5 percent of enrollment in the private institutions). The average salary of the nonteaching staff is roughly $1,000 per month in the two federal institutions (compared to $300 in the private institutions).

Vahl sought to break down costs by program of study. Since universities do not keep systematic records of this sort, only rough estimates covering teaching costs (but not maintenance and materials) are possible. The average cost breakdowns in UFMG and UFSC are as follows: science and technology, $9,447; biomedical sciences, $11,985 (e.g., medicine, $11,844, dentistry, $13,059, and nursing, $11,755); and humanities and social sciences, $6,854 (e.g., law, $6,681, mathematics, $7,290, and pedagogy, $9,863). The cost differential between science and law is about 1.5:1, compared with a U.S. differential ranging from 2 to as much as 5:1. Federal universities rarely use the combination of very large lectures accompanied by smaller classes common to the United States.

Another element of interest is space utilization. The two federal universities surveyed, UFMG and UFSC, provide 28 square meters per student, compared to six square meters in the four private universities surveyed. The former has an average of 1.6 seats for every student enrolled in the system compared to 0.8 in the private institutions. Assuming that classes can take place eight hours in a day (a reasonable expectation, with classes running from 8–12 a.m. and 2–6 p.m.), and students attend about four classes of one hour per day, on average seats in the two federal institutions are utilized about 30 percent of the time, compared to 66 percent utilization in the comparable private institutions. Based on this analysis, the physical facilities in the two federal universities surveyed are adequate to serve about twice the number of students currently being served without initiating any night classes. Put differently, if the cost per square meter of construction and furnishing is about $400, then the government has invested about $190 million in excess physical facilities in the two universities studied. While it is difficult to generalize to all federal universities, if all federal institutions were in fact similarly over-built, then the total excess capital investment would be on the order of more than $1.6 billion. Since private institutions normally put aside capital funds or pay mortgages for construction and refurbishing, the costs of the physical facilities in the public sector should be annualized and added to the recurrent cost to get an economic cost per student comparable to the private institutions. Assuming a 30-year life of physical facilities, a 10 percent discount rate, and a cost of physical facilities per student of $11,400, the unit costs per student in the two federal institutions surveyed should be increased by $1,200 or an additional 15 percent.

In part, the higher unit costs of federal institutions are a result of higher quality staff, many of whom undertake research, as well as of programs in science and engineering, and graduate programs. The two federal institutions surveyed undertake research and extension and have many programs in higher-cost areas such as medicine and engineering. In particular, teachers in the two federal institutions surveyed reportedly produced 1,034 books, chapters of books and articles in 1989, which is an average of .18 per faculty member. Almost 10 percent of the students at the two federal universities surveyed are at the graduate level. Forty-eight percent of the enrollment is in high-cost courses, defined as science, engineering, agriculture and medicine, compared to 36 percent in the four private universities surveyed. Furthermore, in 1989, the federal universities provided for 421 specialized training and extension courses, compared to about 176 in the private universities. Finally, around half of the federal

Table 18.12. Costs and Quality in Two Federal and Two Private Universities, 1988

	UFMG	UFSC	PUC–Rio	PUC–SP
Percent graduate students	11	10	17	15
Percent staff with doctorate	20	18	30	15
FTE student-teacher ratios	8:1	8:1	10:1	16:1
Student-nonteaching staff ratios	3:1	4:1	11:1	14:1
Unit costs in US$	9,179	7,852	4,535	2,089

Sources: Student-teacher ratios from Table 18.10. Unit costs from Table 18.11. Other data from Vahl (1991) and Tramontim and Braga (1989, 1990).

university faculty have advanced degrees (doctorate or master's). These figures all represent higher quality input and more research output than the vast majority of private universities in Brazil.

PUC-Rio and PUC-SP are the two private institutions acknowledged to be among the highest quality in Brazil, with high percentages of graduate students, and with input and output quality measures similar to UFMG and UFSC. Table 18.12 shows that unit costs in the two federal universities are twice as high as PUC-Rio and about four times as high as PUC-SP, which have equally high quality staff and major graduate programs. It should be noted that PUC-SP focuses on the social sciences and has very little enrollment in medical or hard sciences. Therefore its unit costs should be compared with estimated unit costs of over $6,000 for the two federal universities in humanities and the social sciences (Vahl, 1991). PUC-Rio's enrollment profile is similar to the two federal institutions surveyed, since it has a very strong science and engineering program (but no medical school), much of it supported by grants from FINEP (the Agency for Financing of Studies and Projects). These qualifications notwithstanding, these two best private institutions offer programs similar to those of the best two federal institutions, but at less than half the cost. This appears to be mainly a result of higher student-staff ratios as well as a much leaner administration.

It should be noted that UFMG and UFSC are among the oldest and best federal institutions. In contrast, the Federal Universities of Ouro Preto, Mato Grosso, Juiz de Fora and Espírito Santo have negligible graduate enrollment and are reported to undertake little or no research, but have FTE student-teacher ratios of 9:1 or less and unit costs ranging from $6,500 to $9,000.

Socioeconomic Background of Students

A recent study of parental income of students attending federal institutions (Gomes, 1990) found that parents of 44 percent of students earned 11 or

Table 18.13. Parental Income of Federal University Students by Region, 1989 Sample Data

Parental income (Minimum salaries per month)	Percentages						Total Students
	North	Northeast	Southeast	South	Center-West	Brazil	
Up to 3	13	35	14	30	9	18	620
4–10	10	32	19	27	12	37	1,282
11–20	7	25	23	29	15	20	700
21–30	5	23	28	27	17	11	389
31–50	7	17	30	28	18	8	284
Over 50	4	18	23	39	16	5	182
Percent of total students	9	28	21	29	13	100	
Total students in sample	304	968	728	991	466	3,457	3,457

Source: Gomes (1990).
Note: One minimum salary = $55 at time of data collection.

more minimum salaries. This compares with an estimated 10 percent in the general population. As can be seen in Table 18.13, students in the South and Southeast had much higher parental income than those in the North and Northeast—a result of the higher incomes in these regions.

It has been hypothesized that the students from the highest socioeconomic background attend federal universities, while the poorer students attend private institutions. Studies by Paul of three universities—in Fortaleza, Ceará and of a private institution in São Paulo—suggest a more complicated pattern.

Socioeconomic Status (SES) in Ceará

The study in Ceará examined the three federal, state and private universities in Fortaleza. It should be noted that, throughout Brazil, private institutions are very diverse. Overall, higher education enrollment ratios in Ceará are 5.1 percent, compared to 11.1 percent in São Paulo. The vast majority (90 percent) of students in São Paulo attend private institutions, compared to only 33 percent in Ceará. In the Northeast, enrollment in private education is relatively low, since most children drop out of primary education. Therefore the comparison of private education in Ceará should not be considered comparable to that of, say, Rio and São Paulo.

The three institutions in Fortaleza are roughly comparable in size. The federal university has a student body of 13,000; the student bodies at the private and state universities are, respectively, 12,000 and 10,000. Unit teaching costs are estimated at $4,100 in the federal university, $2,500 in the state university, and $1,600 in the private one. The differences in unit costs are due in part to the different types of courses offered, with the federal institutions offering more of the higher cost science and engineering specialties. Courses in social science, teacher training and nursing are offered by all three institutions; law and engineering are offered by the federal and private institutions; and medicine and dentistry are reported to be of high quality in the federal institutions. The state university focuses on teacher training, and the private university has high enrollments in ancillary health services such as occupational and physical therapy. According to a survey of students, the main reason for selecting the federal institution was its reputation; for the state institutions, availability of night courses; and for private institutions, rejection by the state or federal university.

Table 18.14 shows the federal and private institutions have a similar socioeconomic profile, while students in the state institutions have a distinctly lower socioeconomic status. Students in the federal university are more likely to be 18 or younger at entrance. Fully 85 percent of the private university students attended private schools. The corresponding proportions for federal and state university students are 80 and 68 percent, respectively. This is a striking ratio, considering that only 35 percent of all secondary school enrollment in Ceará is in private institutions. It suggests that the public secondary institutions are mainly serving students of lower socioeconomic origin and weaker academic ability. It is furthermore interesting to note that about half of the students in the three institutions are working. This figure is slightly lower (43 percent) for the federal university. In short, the students of a higher SES attend both the federal and private universities, with the higher quality students attending the federal university. The state university serves students of lower SES.

When the data is broken down by course of study, a more complex pattern emerges. Crossing students' characteristics by course of study and institutions shows that socioeconomic background, gender and courses of study are closely related. Of the 10 courses with students with the highest socioeconomic background, five are in federal institutions: civil engineering, data processing, medicine, dentistry and administration. Three courses are in state institutions: administration, data processing and veterinary medicine. Two courses are in the private university: data processing and administration. Among the 10 courses that score lowest on socioeconomic status of students are three federal university courses (geography, nursing and literature); five state courses (literature, pedagogy [night], geography [night and day], and science [night]); and two courses in the private university (geology and literature [night]). Clearly, then, certain courses attract students of higher or lower socioeconomic status, irrespective of whether

Table 18.14. Personal Characteristics by Institution
(Percentage of total)

	Federal	State	Private
Father's occupation: high or high-middle	46.6	35.3	51.7
Father's educational level: higher	33.6	19.5	30.7
Age at admission: 18 years and less	38.1	20.1	26.3
Public secondary education	20.4	32.3	15.9
Did not attend *cursinho*	59.7	43.2	45.6

they attend public or private institutions. In the more prestigious courses of study, students are generally younger and male, and are more likely to have attended private secondary schools, but not *cursinhos*, which are privately run courses to prepare students for the university entrance examination. The least prestigious courses in any institutions are those associated with teacher training, where most of the students are female. It is probable that the *cursinhos* are designed specifically to help students attending the lower quality public secondary schools.

The study also shows that students attend classes 19 hours per week in the federal and state institutions and 16 hours in the private university. They study 16 hours per week in the federal institution, 13 in the state, and 14 in private. However, when the data are broken down by course of study, the most prestigious require nearly four hours additional study time per week than the least prestigious, and students work fewer hours per week. Students' expenditures per month are mainly for books (70 percent of total expenditures). However, when broken down by course of study, humanities students spend about $15 per month compared to the more prestigious majors for which expenditures are above $24 per month. Overall, students also spend $26.60 on clothing, $18.67 on entertainment, and $8.40 on travel per month.

SES in a Private University in São Paulo

As noted above, the situation in Ceará is very different from that in the Southeast, since higher education in the Northeast serves a small elite. To determine whether the situation in Ceará is similar to that elsewhere, we gathered information on the private University of Mogi das Cruzes located in the city of the same name in the state of São Paulo. This university enrolls 17,000 students, and offers courses in engineering, medicine, law, administration, economics, accounting and various liberal arts fields for prospec-

Table 18.15. Characterization of Students at the University of Mogi das Cruzes
(Percent)

	Proportion of new admissions	= <18	Father's higher education	Public secondary	No *cursinho*
Engineering (day)	7.8	30.4	30.4	49.6	53.5
Engineering (night)	18.0	20.5	23.7	68.9	67.3
Biomedical science (day)	15.4	24.8	34.2	39.9	25.6
Biomedical science (night)	8.8	11.4	12.2	62.8	69.5
Law (day)	2.8	24.3	35.7	43.7	56.3
Law-Adm-Eco-Acc. (night)	27.1	15.5	16.0	59.0	68.6
Teacher training	20.1	14.8	13.1	61.6	72.6
Total	100.0	18.7	20.9	57.5	61.1

tive secondary school teachers. Table 18.15 summarizes the background of students in the seven courses of study at the university.

As can be seen, the same pattern occurs in this institution as in Ceará. Engineering, biomedical science (day), and law (day) are more likely to have younger students, students whose fathers have higher education degrees, and those who attended private secondary schools. On the opposite extreme are night courses and teacher training courses. Compared to Ceará, the students in this institution on average are likely to be older, to have attended public secondary schools, and to have fathers with lower levels of education. Furthermore, in Ceará, students in the more prestigious courses of study were less likely to have attended the *cursinho*, while they are more likely to have done so in São Paulo.

In summary, the socioeconomic status of higher education students in Brazil appears to vary greatly by subject of study. Private institutions are heterogenous and offer a variety of courses to students with different socioeconomic backgrounds. The most prestigious courses of study, especially medicine and engineering, are more likely to attract students from the upper classes. The main difference is that all students prefer the federal institutions because of the free tuition and a perception of higher quality and reputation. If well-to-do students are not accepted into prestigious courses in federal institutions, then they attend the same courses in private institutions. Students of lower socioeconomic status are likely to attend the less prestigious courses in either the public or private institutions. Women are concentrated in the lower prestige courses of teaching and nursing; however, they also predominate in dentistry and administration.

Figure 18.2. Education and Income in Brazil

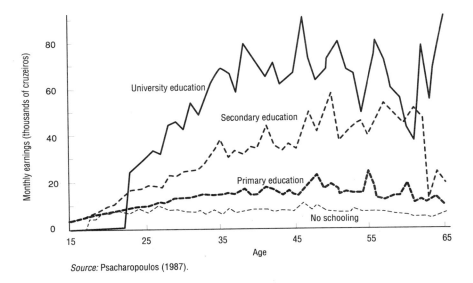

Source: Psacharopoulos (1987).

It should be noted that only a small elite attend any higher education institution in the Northeast. In the South, where twice as high a percentage of the cohort attend higher education institutions, the vast majority of which are private, the difference between public and private institutions may be significant even among the lower prestige courses.

The Labor Market for Graduates

Studying the labor market for graduates provides a way to evaluate the quality of the output of higher education institutions. Private institutions are more technically efficient in producing graduates, in that they have better internal productivity and lower unit costs. But it is important to check whether the shorter time to produce a graduate and the lower costs in the private institutions do not result in lower quality of the output. Few studies have tried to relate the characteristics of the college and subsequent earnings. One effort was by James et al. (1989), conducted in the United States. This study shows that the effect of the institution is small, while curriculum choice is important.

Overall, the effect of education on earnings is very important, as can be seen in Figure 18.2. Paul and Ribeiro, in collaboration with researchers from the Federal University of Ceará, undertook a tracer study of graduates from the three institutions in Ceará to relate the earnings of higher education graduates by institutions and subject of study. The researchers drew a random sample of 5,500 of 12,944 graduates from 1984 to 1986. After two mailings, 2,140 (39 percent) responded to the questionnaire. The questionnaire was then sent to a second random sample of 100 graduates, half of whom did not respond; the other half had moved and did not receive the questionnaire. On locating the latter 50 graduates the researchers found that they had the same characteristics (with the exception of mobility) as those who answered the original questionnaire. Based on this sample, it can be safely concluded that the respondents were good representatives of the universe.

Three parameters were studied: 1) whether graduates were working; 2) what type of occupation they were in; and 3) what their income was. Table 18.16 presents the estimated employment situation of the universe of students (based on a weighted average of the sample).

There is low unemployment among graduates of all three institutions. This is contrary to popular opinion in Brazil. However, it should be noted that 50 percent of these graduates were already working while they were attending school. In terms of high, middle, and low prestige jobs,[2] the breakdown of graduates of federal and private institutions is roughly similar, while the state university has more graduates at lower-level jobs. The low results of the state institutions appear to be mainly a result of its large primary and secondary teacher training programs.

We built a regression model to determine the effects of courses of study, institutions, and other attributes on earnings. The model covers the entire population and includes 11 groupings of majors, as well as date of graduation, age, type of institutions, gender, and father's level of education. The results (see Table 18.17) show that dentistry/medicine have the highest earnings, followed by data processing, accounting, administration/ economy/law, engineering, chemistry/statistics, home economics/librarian, ancillary medical services, nutrition/social services, agronomy, and teacher training. As expected, those who graduate later earn less than those who graduate earlier. Females earn strikingly less than males (–60.8 percent), even after taking their major into account. As expected, graduates with better educated fathers earn more. After accounting for majors, graduates of the federal university earn 6.5 percent more than graduates from the state university, but there is no difference with the private university.

---

[2] High: executives, engineers, professional, professors; middle: secondary teachers, mid-level staff; low: primary teachers, low-level staff.

Table 18.16. Labor Market for Graduates in Ceará
(Percent)

Employment and Unemployment by Institution

	Federal	State	Private	Total
Employed	95.9	95.6	94.6	95.4
Unemployed	4.1	4.2	5.4	4.6
Total	100.0	100.0	100.0	100.0
	(4,545)	(3,506)	(4,414)	(12,465)

Job Level by Institution

	Federal	State	Private	Total
High-level jobs	50.8	29.4	50.8	44.8
Middle-level jobs	28.1	36.0	28.2	30.3
Low-level jobs	21.1	34.6	21.0	24.8
Total	100.0	100.0	100.0	100.0
	(4,598)	(3,492)	(4,364)	(12,454)

Graduates by Categories of Courses of Study

	Federal	State	Private	Total
Administration/ Accountancy/ Economics	11.3	16.4	31.5	19.8
Teacher training	19.9	54.8	7.8	25.5
Nursing	2.7	5.5	5.7	4.5
Others	66.2	23.3	55.0	50.2
Total	100.0	100.0	100.0	100.0
	(4,786)	(3,643)	(4,515)	(12,944)

To focus more closely on the importance of type of institution, we constructed a second model (see Table 18.18), which includes only the majors offered by all three universities. No clear trends emerge from this analysis. Graduates in teacher training from the private university earn less than the graduates of the other universities. Graduates in administration/accountancy/economics from the state university do better than others. Graduates in law from the private university have much higher earnings than those from the state or federal universities, but this may in part be because many were already working before graduating.

Overall, the results of the tracer study in Ceará provide a number of surprising results. In the first place, the earnings differences between

Table 18.17. Global Earnings (logarithm) Models

Variable	Coefficient	Std. Error	Elasticity[1]
Intercept	6.594	0.063	
Accounting/Administration/Economics/Law[2]	0.103***	0.031	10.8%
Teacher training[2]	−0.733***	0.036	−107.9%
Dental/Medical/Veterinary[2]	0.525***	0.044	68.8%
Ancillary medical services[2]	−0.283***	0.038	−32.7%
Domestic economics/Librarian[2]	−0.217***	0.081	−23.8%
Social communication/Psychology[2]	0.012	0.066	
Statistics/Chemistry/Industrial chemistry[2]	−0.214***	0.071	−23.7%
Nutrition/Social services[2]	−0.333***	0.058	−39.3%
Agronomy[2]	0.334***	0.060	−39.3%
Data processing[2]	0.348***	0.080	41.2%
Working at graduation[3]	0.277***	0.021	31.9%
Graduate in 1985[4]	−0.074***	0.022	7.7%
Graduate in 1986[4]	−0.257***	0.022	29.2%
Age	0.003*	0.002	0.3%
Federal[5]	0.064***	0.025	6.5%
Private[5]	0.031	0.026	
Females[6]	−0.475***	0.018	60.8%
Father with secondary or sup.[7]	0.132***	0.018	14.1%
R^2			0.132***
N			7,281

Note: Significance level: ***1 percent; **5 percent; *10 percent.
[1] The elasticity is computed according to the formula $ê=exp(ê-1/2V(ê))-1$, with e equal to the value of the regression coefficient and V equal to its variance.
[2] Compared with engineering.
[3] Compared with people not working at graduation.
[4] Compared with graduate in 1984.
[5] Compared with state university.
[6] Compared with males.
[7] Compared with father with educational level lower than secondary.

graduates from different institutions are due more to differences in course of study rather than to the institution. Teacher training is particularly poorly remunerated. The quality element in the federal university is at best of relatively minor importance. Higher education in Ceará, though very selective, does not equalize market opportunities in the labor market. Gender and social origin have a very important effect on earnings.

Conclusions

This study has relied on a combination of original data and opportunistic analysis of existing data to try to shed some light on the economics of

Table 18.18. Elasticities for the Models by Major
(Percent)

Regressor	Adm/ Acc/Eco	Teaching	Nursing	Eng.	Law
Working at graduation[1]	19.7	35.5	34.9		263.5
Graduate in 1985[2]		12.0	−28.2	−10.8	−53.8
Graduate in 1986[2]	−21.3		−1.47	−38.2	−105.6
Age					1.2
Federal[3]	−9.1	8.4			
Private[3]	−10.3	−12.5			36.1
Female[4]	−44.1	−93.9		−19.2	−50.0
Father with sec. or sup.[5]	14.5		29.2	13.5	127.1
R^2	0.0932	0.1701	0.3000	0.0804	0.5447
N	1,583	1,845	357	598	832

Note: Variables significant at least at 10 percent level.
[1] Compared with people not working at graduation.
[2] Compared with graduates in 1984.
[3] Compared with state university.
[4] Compared with males.
[5] Compared with father with educational level lower than secondary.

higher education in Brazil. The conclusions must be considered tentative, pending further corroboration of results in other studies. Since we know very little about these questions, an important conclusion in itself is that much additional research is needed to help insure informed policy decisions. The more important conclusions are summarized below.

As expected, public institutions tend to focus on higher cost areas such as medicine and engineering. The internal efficiency of private institutions is higher than most public institutions. This is more than likely a result of the fact that private institutions charge tuition. The socioeconomic background of students entering higher education is much higher than that of the population as a whole. The higher SES students, as well as males, enter the more prestigious courses of study in public and private institutions. Contrary to popular belief, the SES of students *within* individual public and private institutions varies greatly and depends more on the type of course offered than on whether the institution is public or private.

In the Northeast (Ceará), public institutions do not appear to be significantly superior to private institutions in terms of quality of training, as measured by income after graduation and type of student attending. Rather, the main difference appears to be in course of study. Each university offers a range of courses of study and the students with the best scores on the university entrance examinations enter the more prestigious courses. Students overwhelmingly prefer the public institutions, which are free. However, students who choose a high prestige course of study, but are unable to enter a public institution, will go to a private institution offering a similar course of study. Overall, upper-class students, who are more likely to have attended private secondary schools, attend the most prestigious courses of study in both public and private institutions. Holding constant the course of study, the students receive similar earnings, regardless of which type of institution they attended.

It should be noted that only a small elite attend any higher education institution in the Northeast. In the South, where twice as high a percentage of the cohort attend higher education institutions, the vast majority of which are private, the difference between public and private universities may be significant even among the lower-prestige courses.

The federal institutions have higher input quality, as measured by percentages of teachers with advanced degrees, library holdings, student-teacher ratios, and costs per student. However, it is difficult to explain the high costs of public institutions solely by higher quality instruction, and much of these high costs are due to inefficient use of resources. For example, physical space in federal institutions, as measured by square meters per students, appears to be far higher than needed as compared to international norms as well as to Brazilian private institutions. Also, student-staff ratios in federal institutions are far lower than in comparable private institutions and are well below averages in countries of similar or higher income levels.

REFERENCES

Gaetani, F., and J. Schwartzman. 1991. *Indicadores de Produtividade nas Universidades Federais.* Documento 1/91. NUPES/USP, São Paulo.

Gomes, M. 1990. Personal Background of the Brazilian University Student. Doctoral dissertation.

Hanushek, E. 1986. The Economics of Schooling. *Journal of Economic Literature* 24(3) (September): 1141–77.

James, E. 1989. Differences Between Public and Private Higher Education: An International Perspective. Mimeo.

_____. 1979. Product Mix and Cost Disaggregation: A Reinterpretation of the Economics of Higher Education. *Journal of Human Resources* 12(2).

James, E., N. Alsalam, J. Conaty, and To Duc-Le. 1989. College Quality and Future Earnings: Where Should You Send Your Child to College? *American Economic Review* 79(2) (May): 247–52.

Kennedy, P. 1981. Estimation with Correctly Interpreted Dummy Variables in Semi-Logarithmic Equations. *American Economic Review* 71(4).

MEC (Brazilian Ministry of Education). 1988. *Sinopse do Ensino Superior.*

OECD. 1989. *Evolution des Modes de Financement de l'Enseignement Supérieur.* OECD Monographs on Higher Education. Paris, OECD.

Paul, J.J., and E. Wolyneck. 1990. *O Custo do Ensino Superior nas Instituições Federais.* Documento 11/90. NUPES/USP, São Paulo.

Paul, J.J., and Z.D. Ribeiro. 1990. As Condições de Vida e de Trabalho dos Alunos do Ensino Superior Brasileiro: O Caso das Universidades de Fortaleza. *Educação Brasileira* 13(26) (January/July): 71–127.

_____. 1991. O Mercado de Trabalho para os Egressos do Ensino Superior de Fortaleza. Mimeo.

Psacharopoulos, G. 1987. Education and Development: A Review. *Research Observer* 3(1). World Bank, Washington, D.C.

Tramontim, R. and R. Braga. 1990. Ensino Superior: Perspectivas para a Década de 90. IPEA, Brasília. Mimeo.

_____. 1989. As Universidades Comunitárias: Um Modelo Alternativo. IPEA/ IPLAN/CEC, São Paulo.

UNESCO. 1989, 1990, 1991. *Statistical Yearbook.*

Vahl, T.R. 1991. Universidades Públicas e Privadas: Síntese Comparativa de Alguns Indicadores de Universidades Comunitárias e Universidades Federais. Mimeo.

Subject Index

Author Index